Lecture Notes in Artificial Intelligence   10498

Subseries of Lecture Notes in Computer Science

More information about this series at http://www.springer.com/series/1244

Jonas Beskow · Christopher Peters
Ginevra Castellano · Carol O'Sullivan
Iolanda Leite · Stefan Kopp (Eds.)

Intelligent
Virtual Agents

17th International Conference, IVA 2017
Stockholm, Sweden, August 27–30, 2017
Proceedings

 Springer

Editors

Jonas Beskow
KTH Royal Institute of Technology
Stockholm
Sweden

Christopher Peters
KTH Royal Institute of Technology
Stockholm
Sweden

Ginevra Castellano
Uppsala University
Uppsala
Sweden

Carol O'Sullivan
Trinity College
Dublin
Ireland

Iolanda Leite
KTH Royal Institute of Technology
Stockholm
Sweden

Stefan Kopp
University of Bielefeld
Bielefeld
Germany

ISSN 0302-9743   ISSN 1611-3349   (electronic)
Lecture Notes in Artificial Intelligence
ISBN 978-3-319-67400-1   ISBN 978-3-319-67401-8   (eBook)
DOI 10.1007/978-3-319-67401-8

Library of Congress Control Number: 2017952717

LNCS Sublibrary: SL7 – Artificial Intelligence

Printed on acid-free paper

This Springer imprint is published by Springer Nature
The registered company is Springer International Publishing AG
The registered company address is: Gewerbestrasse 11, 6330 Cham, Switzerland

Preface

This volume presents the proceedings of the 17th International Conference on Intelligent Virtual Agents (IVA 2017). The annual IVA conference represents the main interdisciplinary scientific forum for presenting research on modeling, developing, and evaluating intelligent virtual agents (IVAs) with a focus on communicative abilities and social behavior. IVAs are intelligent digital interactive characters that can communicate with humans and other agents using natural human modalities such as facial expressions, speech, gestures, and movement. They are capable of real-time perception, cognition, emotion, and action that allow them to participate in dynamic social environments. In addition to exploring theoretical issues, the conference showcases working applications. Constructing and studying IVAs requires knowledge, theories, methods, and tools from a wide range of fields such as computer science, psychology, cognitive science, communication, linguistics, interactive media, human–computer interaction, and artificial intelligence.

The IVA conference was started in 1998 as a Workshop on Intelligent Virtual Environments at the European Conference on Artificial Intelligence in Brighton, UK, and was followed by a similar one in 1999 in Salford, Manchester, UK. Subsequently, dedicated stand-alone IVA conferences took place in Madrid, Spain, in 2001; Irsee, Germany, in 2003; and on Kos, Greece, in 2005. In 2006 IVA became a full-fledged annual international event, first held in Marina del Rey, California, followed by Paris in 2007, Tokyo in 2008, Amsterdam in 2009, Philadelphia in 2010, Reykjavik in 2011, Santa Cruz, California in 2012, Edinburgh in 2013, Boston in 2014, Delft in 2015, and Los Angeles in 2016.

IVA 2017 was held in Stockholm, Sweden, at the Swedish National Museum of Science and Technology (Tekniska Museet) and KTH Royal Institute of Technology (Kungliga Tekniska Högskolan).

IVA 2017's special topic was "Situated Intelligent Agents", that is, agents that have awareness of and/or make use of their environment (physical or virtual). The theme addresses the synergies between agents with different embodiments, from embodied virtual characters to social robots. Advances in both domains require the development of computational capabilities that allow robots and virtual characters to engage in those direct, unstructured, and dynamically evolving social interactions that characterize humans. We particularly welcomed contributions that addressed the cross-fertilization of state-of-the-art insights and methods from the domains of embodied virtual characters, computer games, social robotics, and social sciences in order to support the development of skills necessary to enable the vision of designing better machines capable of achieving better action, better awareness, and better interaction to engage in intuitive, lifelike, sustained encounters with individuals and groups.

The interdisciplinary character of IVA 2017 and its special topic are underlined by the conference's three renowned keynote speakers:

- Bilge Mutlu, University of Wisconsin–Madison, USA
- Petra Wagner, Bielefeld University, Germany
- Iain Matthews, Oculus Research, USA

IVA 2017 received 78 submissions. Out of the 50 long paper submissions, only 13 were accepted for the long papers track. Furthermore, there were 17 short papers selected for the single-track paper session, while 22 poster papers and 9 interactive demos were on display.

This year's IVA also included three workshops that took place before the main conference:

- "Interaction with Agents and Robots: Different Embodiments, Common Challenges", organized by Mathieu Chollet, Ayan Ghosh, Hagen Lehmann, and Yukiko Nakano
- "Workshop on Conversational Interruptions in Human-Agent Interactions (CIHAI)", organized by Angelo Cafaro, Eduardo Coutinho, Patrick Gebhard, and Blaise Portard
- "Persuasive Embodied Agents for Behavior Change", organized by Femke Beute, Robbert Jan Beun, Timothy Bickmore, Tibor Bosse, Willem-Paul Brinkman, Joost Broekens, Franziska Burger, John-Jules Ch. Meyer, Mark Neerincx, Rifca Peters, Albert "Skip" Rizzo, Roelof de Vries, and Khiet Truong

We would like to express thanks to the rest of the conference's Organizing Committee, listed herein. We would also like to thank the Senior Program Committee and the Program Committee for helping shape this excellent conference program and for their time, effort, and constructive feedback to the authors. Additionally, we want to thank our keynote speakers for sharing their outstanding work and insights with the community. Further, we would like to thank our sponsors, including Springer, Disney Research, and Furhat Robotics, and the organizers of IVA 2016 and the IVA Steering Committee.

August 2017   Jonas Beskow
                                                                 Christopher Peters
                                                               Ginevra Castellano
                                                                  Carol O'Sullivan
                                                                     Iolanda Leite
                                                                      Stefan Kopp

Organization

Conference Chairs

Jonas Beskow   KTH Royal Institute of Technology
Christopher Peters   KTH Royal Institute of Technology
Ginevra Castellano   Uppsala University

Program Chairs

Carol O'Sullivan   Trinity College Dublin
Iolanda Leite   KTH Royal Institute of Technology
Stefan Kopp   University of Bielefeld

Workshop Chairs

Candace Sidner   Worcester Polytechnic Institute
Björn Thuresson   KTH Royal Institute of Technology

Sponsorship Chair

André Pereira   Furhat Robotics

Posters and Demo Chair

Catharine Oertel   KTH Royal Institute of Technology

Gala Chair

Jens Edlund   KTH Royal Institute of Technology

Publication Chairs

Maurizio Mancini   Università degli Studi di Genova
Giovanna Varni   Université Pierre et Marie Curie

Publicity Chair

Maike Paetzel   Uppsala University

Webmaster

Fangkai Yang   KTH Royal Institute of Technology

Senior Program Committee

Elisabeth André	University of Augsburg
Ruth Aylett	Heriot-Watt University
Timothy Bickmore	Northeastern University
Joost Broekens	Delft University of Technology
Dirk Heylen	University of Twente
Jill Lehman	Disney Research Pittsburgh
James Lester	North Carolina State University
Stacy Marsella	Northeastern University
Yukiko Nakano	Seikei University
Michael Neff	UC Davis
Ana Paiva	INESC-ID and University of Lisbon
Catherine Pelachaud	CNRS - ISIR, Université Pierre et Marie Curie
Laurel Riek	UC San Diego
Stefan Scherer	University of Southern California
Gabriel Skantze	KTH Royal Institute of Technology
Hannes Vilhjálmsson	Reykjavík University
Michael Young	University of Utah

Program Committee

Sean Andrist	Microsoft Research
Kirsten Bergmann	Bielefeld University
Elisabetta Bevacqua	Lab-STICC, Ecole Nationale d'Ingénieurs de Brest (ENIB)
Johan Boye	KTH Royal Institute of Technology
Hendrik Buschmeier	Bielefeld University
Ronald Böck	Otto von Guericke University Magdeburg
Angelo Cafaro	CNRS-ISIR Université Pierre et Marie Curie
Liz Carter	Disney Research
Mathieu Chollet	USC Institute for Creative Technologies
Luísa Coheur	INESC-ID and Instituto Superior Técnico, Technical University of Lisbon
Iwan de Kok	Bielefeld University
Etienne de Sevin	University of Bordeaux
Joao Dias	INESC-ID and Instituto Superior Técnico, Technical University of Lisbon
Damien Dupr	Queen's University Belfast
Kevin El Haddad	UMONS
Benjamin Files	US Army Research Laboratory
Samantha Finkelstein	Carnegie Mellon University
Farina Freigang	Bielefeld University
Patrick Gebhard	DFKI GmbH
David Gerritsen	Carnegie Mellon University
Emer Gilmartin	Trinity College Dublin

Elena Corina Grigore	Yale University
Jacqueline Hemminghaus	AG SCS, CITEC, Bielefeld University
Laura Hoffmann	Bielefeld University
W. Lewis Johnson	Alelo Inc.
Patrik Jonell	KTH Royal Institute of Technology
Markus Kächele	University of Ulm
James Kennedy	Disney Research
Peter Khooshabeh	US Army Research Laboratory
Dimosthenis Kontogiorgos	KTH Royal Institute of Technology
Kangsoo Kim	University of Central Florida
Mei Yii Lim	Heriot-Watt University
Benjamin Lok	University of Florida
José David Lopes	KTH Royal Institute of Technology
Samuel Mascarenhas	INESC-ID and Instituto Superior Técnico, Technical University of Lisbon
Maryam Moosaei	University of Notre Dame
Radoslaw Niewiadomski	University of Genoa
Aline Normoyle	University of Pennsylvania
Magalie Ochs	LSIS
Jean-Marc Odobez	IDIAP
Catharine Oertel	KTH Royal Institute of Technology
Andrew Olney	University of Memphis
Slim Ouni	LORIA - Université de Lorraine
Alexandros Papangelis	Toshiba Research Europe
Florian Pecune	CNRS - LTCI
Andre Pereira	Furhat Robotics
Eli Pincus	USC Institute for Creative Technologies
Ronald Poppe	Utrecht University
Aditi Ramachandran	Yale University
Tiago Ribeiro	INESC-ID and Instituto Superior Técnico, Technical University of Lisbon
Lazlo Ring	Northeastern University
Justus Robertson	North Carolina State University
Astrid Rosenthal-Von der Pütten	University of Duisburg-Essen
Nicolas Sabouret	LIMSI-CNRS
Najmeh Sadoughi	University of Texas at Dallas
Samira Sheikhi	University of Chicago
Malte Schilling	ICSI Berkeley
Ari Shapiro	USC Institute for Creative Technologies
Mei Si	Rensselaer Polytechnic Institute
Kalin Stefanov	KTH Royal Institute of Technology
Stefan Sutterlin	Oslo University Hospital, Norway
Reid Swanson	Independent
Ha Trinh	Northeastern University
Daniel Ullman	Brown University

Volkan Ustun   USC Institute for Creative Technologies
Leo Wanner   ICREA and University Pompeu Fabra
Fangkai Yang   KTH Royal Institute of Technology

Sponsors

Springer

Disney Research

Furhat Robotics

Contents

Contents

Contents

Pedagogical Agents to Support Embodied, Discovery-based Learning

Ahsan Abdullah[1] ✉, Mohammad Adil[1], Leah Rosenbaum[2], Miranda Clemmons[2], Mansi Shah[2], Dor Abrahamson[2], and Michael Neff

[1] University of California, Davis**
aabdullah@ucdavis.edu, madil@ucdavis.edu, mpneff@ucdavis.edu
[2] University of California, Berkeley
leahr@berkeley.edu, mclemmons@berkeley.edu, emansishah@berkeley.edu, dor@berkeley.edu

Abstract. This paper presents a pedagogical agent designed to support students in an embodied, discovery-based learning environment. Discovery-based learning guides students through a set of activities designed to foster particular insights. In this case, the animated agent explains how to use the Mathematical Imagery Trainer for Proportionality, provides performance feedback, leads students to have different experiences and provides remedial instruction when required. It is a challenging task for agent technology as the amount of concrete feedback from the learner is very limited, here restricted to the location of two markers on the screen. A Dynamic Decision Network is used to automatically determine agent behavior, based on a deep understanding of the tutorial protocol. A pilot evaluation showed that all participants developed movement schemes supporting proto-proportional reasoning. They were able to provide verbal proto-proportional expressions for one of the taught strategies, but not the other.

Keywords: pedagogical agents, discovery-based learning, dynamic decision networks

1   Introduction

Discovery-based learning is an educational activity paradigm whereby students are led through well-specified experiences that are designed to foster particular insights relevant to curricular objectives. It differs from many of the applications in which pedagogical agents have traditionally been used, in that the knowledge desired for the student is never explicitly stated in the experience. Rather, the child discovers it on her or his own. Testing also differs, as the goal is a deeper conceptual understanding, not easily measured by right or wrong answers. Although discovery-based learning has been a major approach in reform-oriented pedagogy for over a century in classrooms, only recently has begun to be incorporated into interactive technology. The broadest objective of the current paper

---

** The first two authors made equal contributions to technical aspects of the research.

© Springer International Publishing AG 2017
J. Beskow et al. (Eds.): IVA 2017, LNAI 10498, pp. 1-14, 2017.
DOI 10.1007/978-3-319-67401-8_1

is to highlight an approach, along with challenges and responses, for building autonomous pedagogical agents for discovery-based interactive learning.

This work explores the application of pedagogical agents to the experiential goal of discovery-based learning. In particular, we add a pedagogical agent to an embodied math learning environment, MITp, designed to teach children proportion. MITp is described in detail in Sec. 2. The basic idea is that a child is encouraged to move two markers on a screen with her fingers. As she does this, the screen changes color. If the height of the two markers is in a particular ratio, say 1:2, the screen will go green, and as the ratio varies away from this it will go to yellow, and then red. The child is never told anything about ratios or proportion or how to make the screen green. Rather she is guided to discover different ways to create a green screen, and by doing so, begins to build an understanding of proportion. This system has been used extensively in learning research with a human tutor guiding students. In this work, we seek to understand what is required to make an animated pedagogical agent effective in this tutoring role.

MITp is an embodied learning experience where the child learns through performing physical movements. Embodied pedagogical agents are particularly useful in this setting because of the engagement they engender and, most importantly, because they can enact virtual actions and gestures they wish the learner to perform.

This type of learning application creates unique computational challenges. Chief among them, it is very difficult to measure the student's progress when it is not possible to ask

Fig. 1: A child listens to the pedagogical agent explain concepts within the MITp learning environment.

questions with right or wrong answers that are easy for a computer to grade. Our design process employed a deep analysis of the process used by human tutors, including reviewing many hours of video recorded interactions. We identified the key stages in the tutorial process, the types of actions tutors took and when they took them. From this analysis, we identified the following activity types the agent must engage in: *instructing* the child what to do; *valorizing* success; *waiting* so the child can explore on her own; *providing remedial training* when the child is blocked and *advancing* the child through the tutorial process.

While the human tutor sits beside the learner, we placed our animated agent on the other side of the screen from the child, with access to the same touch surface as the learner (Figure 1). Dubbed *Maria*, our agent can execute a sequence of action blocks. Each block consists of any subset of spoken audio, facial animation, lip syncing and body animation, including arm and finger gestures. There are well over 100 actions that the agent can perform. We use Dynamic Decision Networks to decide when the agent should perform an action block and which action to perform.

We have conducted a pilot evaluation of the system. It showed that students were able to effectively explore the screen to find greens and enact a particular search strategy taught by the system. Students provided proto-mathematical descriptions of one solution strategy, although not the other. The results demonstrate good progress and also illuminate potential directions for future work.

2 MITp Learning Environment and Tutorial Protocol

Fig. 2: The MITp environment. The screen is green when the hands' heights match a pre-programmed ratio.

The current study builds upon an earlier educational-research effort to design and evaluate embodied-interaction technology for mathematics instruction. Specifically, the pedagogical agent described herein was integrated into an existing activity design architecture called the Mathematical Imagery Trainer for Proportionality (MITp) [1, 2, 17], which we now present.

Proportional reasoning is important yet difficult for many students. It involves understanding multiplicative part-whole relations between rational quantities; a change in one quantity is always accompanied by a change in the other, and these changes are related by a constant multiplier [6, 26, 31].

Our MITp approach to support students in developing multiplicative understanding of proportions draws on embodiment theory, which views the mind as extending dynamically through the body into the natural-cultural ecology. Thus human reasoning emerges through, and is expressed as, situated sensorimotor interactions [3, 25]. Educational researchers informed by these theories have created technologies to foster content learning through embodied interaction (e.g., [5, 11]).

The MITp system (Figure 2) poses the physical challenge of moving two hands on a touch screen to make it green, a result which occurs when the ratio of hand heights matches the pre-programmed ratio of 1:2. Through this process, students can develop pre-symbolic mathematical understanding by engaging in this embodied activity and building particular movement schemes related to proportions. By introducing specific tools into the environment, here a grid and numbers, students are given progressively more mathematical tools with which to express those strategies.

The MITp system has been extensively tested for its educational effectiveness. Using qualitative analyses, the researchers demonstrated the variety of manipulation strategies students developed as their means of accomplishing the task objective of moving their hands while keeping the screen green [17]. Moreover, it was shown that students engaged in deep mathematical reflection as they were guided to compare across the strategies [2]. The studies have presented empirical data of students shifting from naive manipulation to mathematical reasoning as they engage the frames of reference introduced into the problem space and the tutor's critical role in facilitating this shift [1].

2.1 Interview Protocol

Maria is programmed to lead students through a series of activities on the MITp touchscreen, each supporting the development of particular movement strategies deemed relevant to proportional reasoning. Broadly, the two main phases are exploration, targeting the strategy "Higher-Bigger," and "a-per-b." In "Higher-Bigger," participants meet Maria on a screen with a red background, which is later overlaid with a grid. Participants are instructed to move the cursors up and down to make the screen green. At each green, Maria valorizes their work and asks them to make another green, either higher, lower, or elsewhere. Other than moving the cursors up and down, participants receive little guidance on particular movement strategies. With time, the grid is overlaid on the screen. The goal of this stage is for students to notice that when they make a green higher on the screen, the gap between their hands is bigger ("Higher-Bigger"). Next, in the "a-per-b" phase, participants are given instructions to start at the bottom of the screen, move their left hand up one grid unit, and then place their right hand to make green. Finally, the grid is supplemented with numerals. Participants are periodically asked to reflect on their rule for making green. Though Maria does not (yet) recognize speech, these reflections promote verbal description through which the developers can assess the participants' proto-proportional understanding. Participants took about 20 minutes on average to complete the task.

While participants interact with Maria, the presiding human interviewers try to minimize human-to-human interaction, albeit occasionally they respond to participant queries, confusion, or frustration.

3 Related Work on Pedagogical Agents

Our work finds its roots in previous work on Pedagogical agents and Intelligent Tutoring Systems. Intelligent tutoring systems are computer softwares designed to simulate a human tutor. Pedagogical agents aid the process by adding a human-like character to the learning process. Research over the past few decades [21] has validated the positive impact of having an embodied presence in virtual learning environment. They have been a success primarily because they add emotional and non-verbal feedback to the learning environment [22]. More expressive pedagogical agents tend to improve the learning experience [15].

Intelligent tutoring systems (ITS) have been developed for a wide range of topics. Cognitive Tutors [24] have been adapted to teach students mathematical and other scientific concepts like genetics. The Andes Physics tutor [36] focuses on helping students in introductory Physics courses at college level. Writing Pal [33] and iStart [19] help students in developing writing and reading strategies respectively. Decision theoretic tutoring systems have also been very successful and range from generic frameworks like DT Tutor [29] to domain specific systems such as Leibniz [13]. The feedback and learning mechanism behind all these activities revolves around the tutor provided instructions or some sort of rule specification, followed by student responses, given as either text or multiple choice selections, to posed challenge questions. Our discovery based learning methodology differs fundamentally as the system never describes how to achieve the desired goal, and the student response has to be gauged in real-time based solely on the touch screen coordinates. There are not questions that can be used to directly gauge progress.

Pedagogical agents can interact with the student in various roles, such as interactive demonstrators, virtual teammates and teachers. Steve [20] is an early example of a demonstration based pedagogical agent to train people to operate ship engines. INOTS [7] teaches communication and leadership skills to naval officers. The agent is questioned about a case by officers during training, and their performance is evaluated by rest of the class watching this interaction. AutoTutor [14] is a modern system used to teach concepts in Science and Mathematics. The student agent works with the human student to solve the problems in different ways. Adele [34] and Herman the Bug [27] are two classic pedagogical agents designed to teach medicine and botanical anatomy respectively. Decision Networks have also previously been used in the development of adaptive pedagogical agents such as [8] and [32] and for narrative planning [28]. These decision theoretic agents work on concrete feedback from the user in form of biological signals or responses to questions. In fact, all the above mentioned agents use the standard teach and test framework in order to gauge student's performance, allowing them to focus on specific concepts in the learning that the student is struggling with. Our pedagogical agent operates in a quite different, discovery-based learning paradigm. Some previous pedagogical agents have also targeted more open-ended learning environments. For example, a system designed for children with ASD allows children to interact with the system by telling stories, control the agent by selecting pre-defined responses or author new responses to create new stories [35]. Related work has sought to use agents not as instructors, but as virtual peers [23, 12].

4 System

4.1 System Overview and Architecture

An overview of our MITp autonomous agent system architecture is shown in Figure 3. It consists of a control system and Unity3D front end. Students interact with our agent using a touch screen. The screen is virtually divided into left and right halves around the agent, designating two large tracks where the learner can move the markers. Maria is standing in the middle as shown in Figure 1 and can reach most of the screen. The Unity client sends the system state consisting of the two touch locations to the control system, which then instructs the agent to perform particular actions by specifying Action IDs.

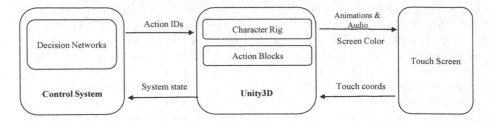

Fig. 3: System Architecture

The control system employs dynamic decision networks [10] to model the behavior of our pedagogical agent. The decision networks are updated based on the evidence received from Unity and history maintained throughout the interaction. They may decide to do nothing or have the agent perform one of many pre-designed actions, depending on what appears most efficacious in the current context. Triggered actions are sent to Unity as action block IDs. Each action block consists of an audio file, a facial animation and a body animation. Our database contains 115 different action blocks.

Generating meaningfully labelled data for learning agent behavior is a challenge in a discovery-based setting. At this point, we do not make assumptions about student's learning during interaction and instead rely on a robust tutorial process which can adapt and provide remedial instruction if the student is struggling. Modeling student's learning on the fly requires mapping from patterns of finger movement to their mental state, which remains future work. Due to these issues, learning based techniques such as [18] are not a good fit for the current problem. DDNs allow us to leverage our strong understanding of the tutorial process by pre-encoding it into system parameters.

4.2 Decision Networks

Decision networks find their roots in *Bayesian Networks* [30], which are graphical models consisting of chance nodes representing a set of random variables. Random variables are events that could possibly occur in the given world. Chance nodes, drawn as ovals in the graph, can take any type of discrete value, such as a boolean or an integer. These values are generally finite and mutually exclusive. Arcs between these nodes capture conditional dependencies. Cycles are not allowed. Given the conditional probabilities, prior and evidence, inferences can be made about any random variable in the network.

Decision networks [16] extend Bayesian Networks by using Bayesian inference to determine a decision that maximizes expected utility. Decision networks add decision and utility nodes, represented by a rectangle and diamond respectively. Decision nodes represent all choices the system can make while the utility node captures our preferences under different factors impacting the decision. This concept can be further extended to *Dynamic Decision Networks* (DDNs)

[10]. DDNs consist of time varying attributes where there are conditional dependencies between nodes at different time steps. Decisions made in previous time steps can impact the probability distribution or state of the network in future steps. DDNs provide a useful way of modeling evolving beliefs about the world and changing user preferences.

4.3 Building Decision Networks for Experiential Learning

Discovery-based learning is challenging compared to other learning settings because the pedagogical agent must make decisions with very impoverished information as there is no continuous stream of concrete verbal or q&a based feedback that the agent can use to assess the student's understanding. For example, in our case, we only have student's touch coordinates on the screen as input. Our agent guides the learner through the discovery process using this input and a deep understanding of the tutorial process, encoded in the DDNs. Per the tutorial analysis, the agent must *instruct, valorize, wait, provide remedial training* and *advance* the child to the next stage. To decide if the agent should *wait*, the child must have a notion of the passage of time, which can be combined with the child's activity pattern to determine if allowing time for exploration is appropriate. *Remedial* actions are triggered when the child is not executing desired movement patterns after repeated instructions and ample trial time. An example remedial strategy involves the agent displaying a marked location for the child's one hand and then encouraging them to find green by only moving the other hand. Based on their performance, the agent may ask students to repeat activities to deepen their learning.

The learning experience progresses through multiple activities tied to particular interaction strategies: "Higher-Bigger" exploration without and with the grid, "*a*-per-*b*" without and with numbers, and an optional "speed" activity. All the activities are modeled using dynamic decision networks. Space limitations preclude discussion of each, but we will explain our approach using the "Higher-Bigger" task as an exemplar.

Exploring "Higher-Bigger" is the introductory activity students go through, as outlined in Sec. 2. The activity guides the student to find greens at several locations on the screen, with the goal of having the child realize that the separation between her hands is larger for greens higher on the screen than greens that are lower. Figure 4 and 5 show the decision network which governs the behavior of our pedagogical agent for this activity at two different points during an interaction.

The decision network is updated multiple times each second to ensure real time responses. The network encodes our agent's belief about the state of tutorial process and student's interaction at each time step. Factors impacting the agent's decision for the network shown in Fig. 4 and 5 are:
Goal : Models agent's temporally evolving expectations for the student. During this activity the student is first expected to find a couple of greens anywhere on

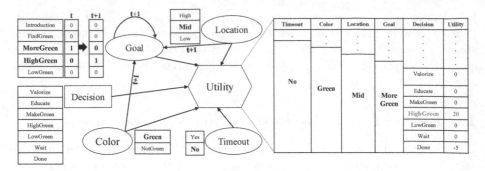

Fig. 4: Decision Network for the exploration task at time step t. This figure shows an example query and update mechanism of our decision network. The arcs labeled t+1 indicate that the state of Goal node at time $t+1$ depends on the state of Location, Color and Goal at time t. At time t, the agent's goal is for the student to find *MoreGreen* on screen. The student finds green somewhere in the middle of the screen, and the evidence for nodes Location, Color and Timeout (bold words) is set. We now query the network to give us a decision with maximum utility given the circumstances represented by the network state. As shown in green, the agent decides to guide the student to the new task of finding green in the upper portion of the screen.

the screen, followed by greens in specific portions of the screen. Possible node states are shown in the network above.

Timeout : Models the time elapsed since important events. It includes time since the last agent action, time since last touch by the student, time since the last green and time since last achieved goal. These factors, both individually and in combination, are critical in behavioral modeling when the student is struggling in finding patterns on the screen.

Location : Captures the portion of the screen that the student is currently exploring, discretized into {*High, Medium, Low, NA*}.

Screen Color : Models the current screen background color as a binary node that can be either be green or non-green.

Decision : Decision node that contains all the high level decisions the agent can take. For this activity, the agent can choose to instruct the student about the current task, valorize them, prompt them to explore different areas for green, provide location specifications for finding a green or stay quiet to give the student time to think and explore.

At each time step, the network is updated with available evidence and provides a decision with maximum expected utility. Directed arcs in the network above show conditional dependencies. Those labeled as 't+1' show temporal dependencies, such that the state of node *Goal* at time t+1 depends on the goal, screen color and finger touch coordinates of the user at time t.

5   Evaluation

This section describes our first explorative experimental evaluation, methods, results and discusses implications for future pedagogical agent technology.

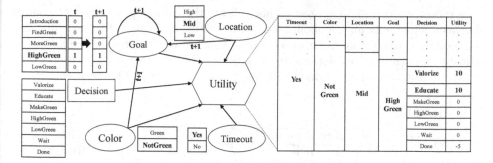

Fig. 5: At this point, the child is either actively exploring, but failing to satisfy the goal, or has stopped interacting with the system. The agent queries the network for the optimal decision to make after setting evidence for Timeout, screen Color and current exploration Location on the screen (bold words). The decision network suggests Valorization and Educating the child about the task as actions of equal and optimal utility (shown in blue). We choose either action randomly. Remedial activities override the decision network and are triggered if there have been multiple continuous timeouts and student hasn't been able to achieve a goal for an extended time.

5.1 Experiment Description

The agent followed the protocol outlined in Sec. 2.1.

Participants included 10 children (5 male, 5 female) aged 9 - 12 years old.

Data Gathering: As participants worked with Maria, three sets of data were collected simultaneously. One researcher used an objective-observation instrument, detailed below, to note the occurrence and frequency of key participant movements and expressions. A second researcher took qualitative field notes of the participant's interaction with Maria. Finally, the interview session was video and audio recorded. The qualitative field notes and video records were used to verify key moments indicated in the observation instruments.

Note that these data sources are consistent with qualitative methods. As this system represents a new genre of agent-facilitated, discovery-based learning, we first seek to understand the types of interactions and insights that emerge as children work with the system. Such qualitative work is not consistent with statistical analyses or pre/post comparison, which pre-suppose which ideas will emerge as salient for participants and considers only those insights that can be quantitatively evaluated. With a qualitative understanding in hand, later work can focus the system on insights deemed most mathematically productive, at which stage a quantitative evaluation would be appropriate. This progression is well established within grounded theory [9] and design based research [4].

Observation Instrument: A one-sheet observation instrument was used during each interview to code, in real time, when each participant exhibited particular benchmark movements and expressions. These movements and expressions were determined in consultation with researchers familiar with analogous, human-run interviews. For example, a participant expression of "the higher I go on the screen, the bigger the distance must be between my hands to make green" is a proto-proportional expression that reflects the changing additive difference between numerator and denominator. Additionally, a movement scheme of raising the right hand 2 units for every 1 unit increase in the left hand reflects the constant multiplicative relationship between equivalent ratio (e.g., 4:8 and 5:10). These two strategies are termed "Higher-Bigger" and "a-per-b," respectively.

5.2 Results

Subject	Greens by Screen Region			"a-per-b"	"Higher-Bigger"	"a-per-b"	Other Insights
	Low	Middle	High				
1	14	4	5	1	0	1	1
2	12	7	7	8	0	1	3
3	6	9	3	4	0	2	2
4	10	16	7	1	0	0	5
5	11	4	6	7	0	2	1
6	11	15	7	9	0	0	4
7	9	11	5	4	0	2	2
8	7	5	5	5	0	1	3
9	8	15	8	5	0	2	2
10	2	7	10	4	0	0	3

Table 1: Frequency of greens, by region, and "a-per-b" performance.   Table 2: Participant expressions by category.

The observation instrument was designed to measure study participants' physical movements and/or verbal and gestural utterances that would imply they are engaging in "the higher, the bigger" or "a-per-b" strategies as their means of solving the bimanual manipulation problem. Performance of a particular movement pattern suggests that the participant is enacting a perceptuomotor strategy that could result in conceptual learning. Verbal description of those movements in proto-mathematical terms indicates further progress along that learning pathway per our instructional design.

As indicated in Table 1, all participants produced green low down, in the middle, and high up on the screen. Interestingly, no participant described the changing distance between their hands at these various regions (Table 2). Additionally, all participants performed the "a-per-b" strategy (Table 1 indicates the number of times this was observed), and 7 participants verbally described it, such as "for every 1 my left goes, my right goes 2." Notably, all participants developed other insights into the system's functioning, which fell into 1 of 4 categories: observational ("Generally, my right hand has to be on top"), feedback-based ("If you see the red screen flash [to green], move back to where you were"), memorization ("4 and 7 or 8 will make green. 6 and 11 or 12 will make green. 2 and 3 makes green."), and procedural ("Keep one hand in one spot and move your other hand around").

Unanticipated was that researchers were obliged to interact with participants on average twice per interview. In 7 of the 10 interviews, this interaction involved researchers restating the "a-per-b" instructions with similar phrasing to Maria's.

5.3 Discussion

We are encouraged by the widely adopted movement strategies, both for making green in all regions of the screen and in adopting the *"a-per-b"* strategy. Instructed by Maria, and largely independent of human intervention, all participants developed movement schemes supporting proto-proportional reasoning.

This work surfaced a gap, however, between participants' performed movements and their descriptions thereof. Participants adeptly made green in all regions of the screen and performed the *"a-per-b"* strategy, yet they did not develop proto-mathematical descriptions of "Higher-Bigger," only of *"a-per-b."* Comparing the conditions of *"a-per-b"* work with the conditions for "Higher-Bigger" work suggests sources of this disparity. In the *"a-per-b"* phase, participants received verbal instructions for the target movement strategy as well as a visual grid and numerals. The verbal instructions highlighted discrete, alternative hand movements (laying the "_-per-_" foundation) while the grid and numerals drew attention to unit quantities (supporting specifically *"1-per-2"*). In contrast, instructions for the "Higher-Bigger" phase did not explicitly mention the distance between participants' hands. Additionally, students were not instructed to follow a particular green progression, for example making green low down, in the middle, and up high, that would facilitate noticing a growing distance. Future efforts should focus on understanding how to embed in the pedagogical agent's models and actions the nuances of human-tutor actions that have led students to attend to the interval between their hands.

Patterns in researcher intervention suggest another area for design iteration. Researchers consistently interacted with participants by repeating the *"a-per-b"* instructions after participants worked unsuccessfully for 3 or more minutes. During this time, participants developed a host of less effective movement patterns - alternating left and right but moving each 1 unit or raising the left hand to the top of the screen then raising the right hand. Though Maria repeated fragments of her original instruction, the timing and particular fragment selected often did not correct the participant's movement. And while researchers tried to mimic Maria's exact instructional language, their choice of *when* to give those instructions and *which words to emphasize* gave more information than Maria is programmed to do. Further work is required to analyze these researcher interventions and convert their decisions into procedures for the autonomous agent.

Overall, we find this work to tentatively support the added value of a virtual agent in discovery-based learning environments. The agent provides feedback on student work and suggests corrective or novel movement strategies that would likely not arise in agent-free work. In particular, the agent draws the student's attention to multiple parametric regions of the problem space, such as particular spatial locations on the monitor, that had not occurred to the student in their free exploration, and the agent suggests new spatial-temporal interaction schemes, such as introducing a sequential bimanual manipulation regime where the student was trying only simultaneous actions. The agent also provides encouragement, validating the students' efforts and encouraging them to explore in new ways. As none of the participants noticed the "Higher-Bigger" relationship, this first prototype was somewhat less successful than human tutors. However, this is not surprising. Human tutors perceive a wider range of student behaviors (posture, oral expressions, facial expressions) contemporaneous with their on-screen actions, giving more information upon which to determine the pacing and content of guidance. Additionally, human tutors enjoy the full range of their gestural and verbal vocabularies in responding to and guiding participants. Consequently, we did not expect that the virtual agent would perform to the same benchmark as human tutors. Nevertheless, we see the results of this work as a success, then, in that all participants performed, and almost all expressed, the proportional "a-per-b" relationship under the virtual agent's guidance.

6   Conclusion

The MITp system presents a very challenging application for pedagogical agents as they must determine appropriate actions based on very little feedback from the learner, in this case, only the location of two markers on the screen. Such constraints are typical of discovery-based learning, where the asking of concrete questions is limited, and the learner is given freedom to explore. The system performed quite well on the task, leading to appropriate movement patterns in all cases and desired verbal expressions for one of the two movement strategies taught. This suggests that the potential for pedagogical agents in discovery-based learning is high and that DDNs represent an effective control strategy.

The system was effective due to a very thorough understanding of the tutoring protocol that was then encoded in the DDNs. In our case, this was based on an analysis of human-led tutoring of the same task. Two significant shortcomings were noted in the study, students failed to verbally explain the "Higher-Bigger" pattern and some amount of human intervention was required, generally when students failed to progress later in the last task. Both of these suggest the need to further refine the protocol encoded in the DDNs. Future work should consider using verbal input from the learners.

Acknowledgements

Financial support for this work was provided by the National Science Foundation through grants IIS 1320029 and IIS 1321042. We gratefully acknowledge Huaguang (Chad) Song, Arman Kapbasov, Rhea Feng, Austin Berbereia, Quan Pham, Gregory Moore and Jessica Sheu for helping develop character content and Alyse Schneider, Virginia Flood and Seth Corrigan for valuable analysis and for providing voice and motion data. Finally, we thank the many children and their parents who participated in our IRB-approved studies.

References

1. Abrahamson, D., Gutiérrez, J., Charoenying, T., Negrete, A., Bumbacher, E.: Fostering hooks and shifts: Tutorial tactics for guided mathematical discovery. Technology, Knowledge and Learning 17(1-2), 61–86 (2012)

2. Abrahamson, D., Lee, R.G., Negrete, A.G., Gutiérrez, J.F.: Coordinating visualizations of polysemous action: Values added for grounding proportion. ZDM 46(1), 79–93 (2014)
3. Anderson, M.L., Richardson, M.J., Chemero, A.: Eroding the boundaries of cognition: Implications of embodiment. Topics in Cognitive Science 4(4), 717–730 (2012)
4. Anderson, T., Shattuck, J.: Design-based research: A decade of progress in education research? Educational researcher 41(1), 16–25 (2012)
5. Antle, A.N.: Research opportunities: Embodied child–computer interaction. International Journal of Child-Computer Interaction 1(1), 30–36 (2013)
6. Boyer, T.W., Levine, S.C.: Prompting children to reason proportionally: Processing discrete units as continuous amounts. Developmental psychology 51(5), 615 (2015)
7. Campbell, J., Core, M., Artstein, R., Armstrong, L., Hartholt, A., Wilson, C., Georgila, K., Morbini, F., Haynes, E., Gomboc, D., et al.: Developing inots to support interpersonal skills practice. In: Aerospace Conference, 2011 IEEE. pp. 1–14. IEEE (2011)
8. Conati, C.: Probabilistic assessment of user's emotions in educational games. Applied Artificial Intelligence 16(7-8), 555–575 (2002)
9. Creswell, J.W.: Qualitative inquiry and research design: Choosing among five approaches. Sage Publications (2012)
10. Dean, T., Kanazawa, K.: A model for reasoning about persistence and causation. Computational intelligence 5(2), 142–150 (1989)
11. Duijzer, C.A., Shayan, S., Bakker, A., Van der Schaaf, M.F., Abrahamson, D.: Touchscreen tablets: Coordinating action and perception for mathematical cognition. Frontiers in Psychology 8 (2017)
12. Finkelstein, S., Yarzebinski, E., Vaughn, C., Ogan, A., Cassell, J.: The effects of culturally congruent educational technologies on student achievement. In: International Conference on Artificial Intelligence in Education. pp. 493–502. Springer (2013)
13. Gluz, J.C., Cabral, T., Baggio, P., Livi, P.: Helping students of introductory calculus classes: the leibniz pedagogical agent
14. Graesser, A.C., Lu, S., Jackson, G.T., Mitchell, H.H., Ventura, M., Olney, A., Louwerse, M.M.: Autotutor: A tutor with dialogue in natural language. Behavior Research Methods 36(2), 180–192 (2004)
15. Hasegawa, D., Shirakawa, S., Shioiri, N., Hanawa, T., Sakuta, H., Ohara, K.: The Effect of Metaphoric Gestures on Schematic Understanding of Instruction Performed by a Pedagogical Conversational Agent, pp. 361–371. Springer International Publishing, Cham (2015)
16. Howard, R.A.: Readings on the principles and applications of decision analysis, vol. 1. Strategic Decisions Group (1983)
17. Howison, M., Trninic, D., Reinholz, D., Abrahamson, D.: The mathematical imagery trainer: From embodied interaction to conceptual learning. In: Proceedings of the SIGCHI Conference on Human Factors in Computing Systems. pp. 1989–1998. ACM (2011)
18. Jaakkola, T., Singh, S.P., Jordan, M.I.: Reinforcement learning algorithm for partially observable markov decision problems. In: Advances in neural information processing systems. pp. 345–352 (1995)
19. Jackson, G.T., Boonthum, C., McNAMARA, D.S.: istart-me: Situating extended learning within a game-based environment. In: Proceedings of the workshop on intelligent educational games at the 14th annual conference on artificial intelligence in education. pp. 59–68. AIED Brighton. UK (2009)

20. Johnson, W.L., Rickel, J.: Steve: An animated pedagogical agent for procedural training in virtual environments. SIGART Bull. 8(1-4), 16–21 (Dec 1997)
21. Johnson, W.L., Lester, J.C.: Face-to-face interaction with pedagogical agents, twenty years later. International Journal of Artificial Intelligence in Education 26(1), 25–36 (2016)
22. Johnson, W.L., Rickel, J.W., Lester, J.C.: Animated pedagogical agents: Face-to-face interaction in interactive learning environments. International Journal of Artificial intelligence in education 11(1), 47–78 (2000)
23. Kim, Y., Baylor, A.L.: A social-cognitive framework for pedagogical agents as learning companions. Educational Technology Research and Development 54(6), 569–596 (2006)
24. Koedinger, K.R., Corbett, A., et al.: Cognitive tutors: Technology bringing learning sciences to the classroom (2006)
25. Lakoff, G., Núñez, R.E.: Where mathematics comes from: How the embodied mind brings mathematics into being. Basic books (2000)
26. Lamon, S.J.: Rational numbers and proportional reasoning: Toward a theoretical framework for research. Second handbook of research on mathematics teaching and learning 1, 629–667 (2007)
27. Lester, J.C., Stone, B.A., Stelling, G.D.: Lifelike pedagogical agents for mixed-initiative problem solving in constructivist learning environments. User modeling and user-adapted interaction 9(1), 1–44 (1999)
28. Mott, B.W., Lester, J.C.: U-director: a decision-theoretic narrative planning architecture for storytelling environments. In: Proceedings of the fifth international joint conference on Autonomous agents and multiagent systems. pp. 977–984. ACM (2006)
29. Murray, R.C., VanLehn, K.: Dt tutor: A decision-theoreticdynamic approach for optimal selection of tutorial actions. In: International Conference on Intelligent Tutoring Systems. pp. 153–162. Springer (2000)
30. Pearl, J.: Probabilistic reasoning in intelligent systems (1988)
31. Piaget, J., Inhelder, B.: The psychology of the child, vol. 5001. Basic books (1969)
32. Prendinger, H., Ishizuka, M.: The empathic companion: A character-based interface that addresses users'affective states. Applied Artificial Intelligence 19(3-4), 267–285 (2005)
33. Roscoe, R.D., McNamara, D.S.: Writing pal: Feasibility of an intelligent writing strategy tutor in the high school classroom. Journal of Educational Psychology 105(4), 1010 (2013)
34. Shaw, E., Ganeshan, R., Johnson, W.L., Millar, D.: Building a case for agent-assisted learning as a catalyst for curriculum reform in medical education. In: Proceedings of the International Conference on Artificial Intelligence in Education. pp. 509–516 (1999)
35. Tartaro, A., Cassell, J.: Authorable virtual peers for autism spectrum disorders. In: Proceedings of the Combined workshop on Language-Enabled Educational Technology and Development and Evaluation for Robust Spoken Dialogue Systems at the 17th European Conference on Artificial Intellegence (2006)
36. Vanlehn, K., Lynch, C., Schulze, K., Shapiro, J., Shelby, R., Taylor, Treacy, Weinstein, A., Wintersgill, M.: The andes physics tutoring system: Lessons learned. International Journal of Artificial Intelligence in Education 15(3), 147–204 (2005)

WalkNet: A Neural-Network-Based Interactive Walking Controller

Omid Alemi ✉ and Philippe Pasquier

School of Interactive Arts + Technology
Simon Fraser University, Surrey, BC, Canada
{oalemi, pasquier}@sfu.ca

Abstract. We present WalkNet, an interactive agent walking movement controller based on neural networks. WalkNet supports controlling the agents walking movements with high-level factors that are semantically meaningful, providing an interface between the agent and its movements in such a way that the characteristics of the movements can be directly determined by the internal state of the agent. The controlling factors are defined across the dimensions of planning, affect expression, and personal movement signature. WalkNet employs Factored, Conditional Restricted Boltzmann Machines to learn and generate movements. We train the model on a corpus of motion capture data that contains movements from multiple human subjects, multiple affect expressions, and multiple walking trajectories. The generation process is real-time and is not memory intensive. WalkNet can be used both in interactive scenarios in which it is controlled by a human user and in scenarios in which it is driven by another AI component.

Keywords: agent movement · machine learning · movement animation · affective agents

1 Introduction

Data-driven movement animation manipulation and generation techniques use recorded motion capture data to preserve the realism of their output while providing some level of control and manipulation. This makes them more suitable for generating affect-expressive movements, compared to the physics-based approaches to modelling and generating movement animation. Data-driven techniques bring the possibility of augmenting a corpus of motion capture data so that human animators have more assets at their disposal. Furthermore, one can use movement generation models in interactive scenarios, where a human user or an algorithm controls the behaviour of the animated agent in real-time.

With the increasing demand for content for nonlinear media such as video games, a movement controller that supports generating movements in real-time based on the given descriptions has applications in AI-based agent animation, interactive agent control, as well as crowd simulation.

© Springer International Publishing AG 2017   15
J. Beskow et al. (Eds.): IVA 2017, LNAI 10498, pp. 15-24 , 2017.
DOI 10.1007/978-3-319-67401-8_2

Data-driven methods allow for manipulation of the motion capture data, either by concatenating, blending, or learning and then generating data. Concatenation methods repeat and reuse the movements in a motion capture corpus by rearranging them, making longer streams of movements from shorter segments. In blending, the representations of two or more motion capture segments are combined to create a new segment that exhibits characteristics from the blended segments. Compared to other techniques, machine learning models are better at generalizing over the variations in the data and generating movements that do not exist in their training corpus. Some of the machine learning techniques also provide mechanisms for controlling and manipulating what is being generated, making them suitable for controlling virtual agents.

The body of the research on machine-learning-based movement generation has some challenges. Controlling the movements of an agent requires a description of the movement to be generated, and a machine learning model that is capable of mapping those descriptions to movement, in real-time. In this regard, the majority of the works suffer from one or more of the following: (1) they do not support controlling the generated movements (e.g., [3]), (2) they only support controlling a single factor (e.g., [1]), (3) the controlling factor is often not clearly defined with respect to an agent's internal state(e.g., [13]), or (4) the generation process is computationally and/or memory intensive (e.g., [14]).

In order to overcome the above limitations, we present WalkNet, a walking movement controller for animated virtual agents. At its core, WalkNet uses a neural network to learn and generate its movements based on a set of given controlling factors. The factors are chosen to work directly with the internal state of the agent, corresponding to the planning, expression, and personal movement signature dimensions of movement. In future, we intent to extend the model to support controlling the functional dimension as well. The agent can plan its walking movements based on any given trajectory. The affective state is modelled by the valence and arousal dimensions of affect. Furthermore, the movement generation model is capable of exhibiting distinctive personal movement signatures (styles). This allows for using the same model for a group of agents that each portray a different character. The main contributions of our approach are summarized below:

- Walknet provides control over multiple dimensions of movement in a single model.
- Learned over a limited sample of affective states (i.e., only high, neutral, and low points) and only two human subjects, WalkNet learns a generalized space of affect and movement signature.
- The generation process is real-time. Unlike graph and tree based structures, there is no need for search or optimization to generate desired movements.

2   Background and Related Work

Controlling Movement Generation In data-driven movement-generation approaches, different techniques, and the combinations of them are used to control and manipulate the characteristics and qualities of motion capture data. These include organizing the data using specialized data structures, such as motion graphs [8,5], as well as blending and interpolating multiple segments. Regarding the machine learning models, there are multiple ways that they support controlling the generation: 1) Train a separate model for each point in the factor space. Each model is trained only on the data that correspond to that particular point, thus only imitating the same factor value. To control the generation, one has to switch between the models. 2) Using a parametric probability distribution, in which the parameters of the distribution are a function of the controlling factors [6], allows for controlling the statistical characteristics of the generated data. 3) By designing the machine learning model in a way that provides a mechanism for a factor variable to control the characteristics of the generated movements. In particular, Factored Conditional Restricted Boltzmann Machine (FCRBM) uses a context variable (Figure 3.b) that controls the behaviour of the network through gated connection between the observations and the hidden variables [12].

Machine Learning Methods for Movement Generation Machine learning models that are used for learning and generating motion capture data range from dimensionality reduction (DR) techniques (e.g., [10]), to the Gaussian Process Latent Variable Models (GPLVMs) (e.g., [14]), Hidden Markov Models (HMMs) (e.g., [2]), temporal variations of the Restricted Boltzmann Machines (e.g., [12,1]), Recurrent Neural Networks (e.g, [3]), and Convolutional Autoencoders combined with Feed-Forward Networks (e.g., [7]).

DR techniques do not handle the temporality of the motion capture data. Furthermore, the dimensionality-reduction-based techniques rely on preprocessing steps such as sequence alignments and fixed-length representation of the data. The main limitation of the GPLVMs is that they demand heavy computational and memory resources, which makes them unsuitable for real-time generation. HMMs overcome the limitations of the two aforementioned families of models but provide a limited expressive power regarding capturing the variations in the data. Neural networks provide a better expressive power than HMMs. Convolutional Autoencoders have shown promising results in generating motion capture data and offline controlling [7]. Factored Conditional RBM (FCRBM), with its special architecture that is designed to support controlling the properties of the generated data, has shown to be able to generate movements in real-time, and learn a generalized space of the movement variations [12,1].

Affect-Expressive Movement Generation Taubert et al. [11] combine a Gaussian process latent variable model (GP-LVM) with a standard HMM that learns the dynamics of the handshakes, encoded by the emotion information. Samadani et al. [10] use functional principal component analysis (FPCA) to generate hand movements. Alemi et al. [1] train an FCRBM to control the valence and arousal dimensions of walking movements.

Our Approach We build WalkNet on top of the previous work by the same authors [1], extending the affect-expression control with the walking planning

Fig. 1. The affect model described by valence and arousal dimensions with the 9 zones recorded in the training data. The mapping to the categorical emotion labels are based on Plutchik and Conte [9]. H: high, N: neutral, L: low, V: valence, and A: arousal.

and personal movement signature. Our work differs with graph-like structures as it does not require to build an explicit and fixed data-structure, does not require search and optimization for generating movement, and does not require storing the movement data for generation. It also differs from the work of Crnkovic-Friis and Crnkovic-Friis [3] as it provides a mechanism to control the generated data. It allows for real-time and iterative generation compared to the work of Holden et al. [7].

3   Training Data

For training the model, we use a set of motion capture data that provides movements with variations in walking direction (planning), the valence and arousal levels (expression), and the personal movement signature. As we could not find a publicly available motion capture database that provides movements with such variations, we recorded our own set of training data. The complete data set is publicly accessible in the MoDa database[1].

The training data includes the movements of two professional actors and dancers (one female, one male). Each subject walks following a curved figure-8-shaped path. The turning variations in this pattern allow the machine learning model to learn a generalized space of turning directions. To capture a space of affect-expression, each subject performs each movement with nine different expressions along the valence and arousal dimensions [9], shown in Figure 1.

---
[1] http://moda.movingstories.ca/projects/29-affective-motion-graph

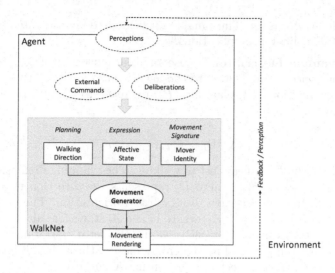

Fig. 2. The WalkNet controller, embedded in an agent model.

Using the dimensional representation of affect over the categorical systems allows for interpolation and extrapolation of the affect states, as well as transitions. Each valence and arousal combination is repeated four times to capture enough motor variabilities.

The original motion capture data consists of a skeleton with 30 joints, resulting in 93 dimensions including the root position, with their rotations represented in Euler angles. The data is captured at 120 frames-per-second. We use exponential maps [4] to represent joint angles to avoid loss of degrees-of-freedom and discontinuities. We replace the skeleton root orientation and translation by the delta values of the translational velocity of the root along the floor plane, as well as its rotational velocity along the axis perpendicular to the floor plane. We remove the dimensions of the data that are constant or zero and downsample the data to 30 frames-per-seconds. The final data set used for the training consist of 18 motion capture segments (2 subjects × 9 affective states), containing 37,562 frames in total, with 52-dimensional frames.

4   The Walking Controller

System Overview As shown in Figure 2, at the core of the WalkNet, the movement generator, a Factored, Conditional Restricted Boltzmann Machine (FCRBM), generates a continuous stream of movement. The movement stream is modulated by a set of controlling factors, determined from the internal state of the agent or through external commands. From an agency perspective, we organize these factors into different dimensions, mainly the *function*, the *planning*, the *expression*, and factors that together make the *personal movement signature* of the agent. WalkNet does not make any assumptions on how the agent movement descriptor is set. Thus, making it flexible to be integrated into various agent models for different applications.

Agent Movement Descriptor We use an agent movement descriptor AMD to formalize the contributing factors to the agent's movements at time t along the dimensions of function (F), planning (P), expression (E), and personal movement signature (S):

$$\text{AMD}_t = \langle F_t, P_t, E_t, S_t \rangle$$

In WalkNet, the F is always set to walking. The planning dimension of walking is defined by $P_t = \langle D_t \rangle$ where D_t represents the direction that the agent intends to walk towards, relative to its current orientation. The expression dimension is defined by $E_t = \langle V_t, A_t \rangle$ where V_t and A_t stand for valance and arousal levels at time t respectively. Currently, we use the actor/performer's identity as a proxy to model the personal movement signature, through a weighted combination of a K-dimensional vector, representing K subjects:

$$S_t = \{I_t^1, I_t^2, .., I_t^K \mid \sum_k^K I_t^k = 1\}$$

We recognize that this is a simple way of capturing movement signature. In the future, we plan on learning a representation that captures the personal movement signature.

Training Data Annotation Here we describe how we annotate our data to capture different states of the factors in the agent movement descriptor.

As we have two human subjects in our training data, we use a 2-dimensional label with a one-hot encoding scheme for the movement signature.

We use the valence and arousal representation of affect to annotate the expression of affect. Each movement segment in the training data is labeled with low, neutral, and high for both their valence and arousal levels. After experimenting with different ranges, we use the values of 1, 2, and 3 to represent low, neutral, and high levels in the annotations. Although the training labels are discrete, the valence and arousal values are continuous in nature, and for the generation, one can specify any real value within the range of $[0, 4]$, as the FCRBM is able to interpolate or extrapolate between those discrete states.

For annotating the heading direction, we determine the labels using a method that is inspired from Kover et al. [8]. For the label at frame t, considering the projection of the traveled path of the skeleton root on the ground floor, we select two points on the path, one at a very close distance to the current location, and another one at a slightly further location from the current location (Figure 3.a). We calculate the angle between the two lines that result from connecting the two chosen points and use this angle as a measure of the heading direction. After scaling the angle to have a value between -1 and +1, directions towards the right of the subject are associated with positive numbers, and directions towards the left of the subject are associated with negative numbers.

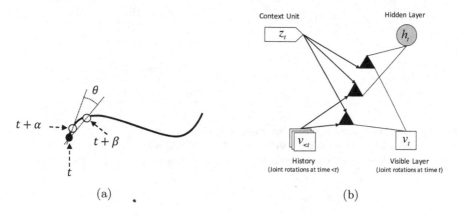

Fig. 3. (a): Calculating the direction of the subject in the training data. (b): FCRBM's architecture with valence and arousal labels modulating the interactions between the past visible, current visible, and current hidden units.

Initial experiments showed that using only a one-dimensional label vector for modelling the direction parameter causes poor results when asking the model to generate movement for the values that are around the center of the continuum. The problem arises from the fact that the model associates high values with one end of the spectrum and low values with the other end of the spectrum, while semantically, there is no difference between each end. This issue is overcome by using a two-dimensional vector $D = [L, R]$ to annotate the two polarities of the direction. The two dimensions of this vector complement each other, following the relationship $R = 1 - L$ in a normalized case. Therefore, the direction is encoded as two labels, one for right and one for left.

As a result, each frame t of the training segment s is annotated with a 6-dimensional label of the form:

$$L_t^s = \langle I^{s^1}, I^{s^2}, V^s, A^s, R_t, L_t \rangle$$

Note that as the identity of the subject and the valence and arousal levels are fixed for each training segment, only R_t and L_t values are changed between each frame of the same segment.

Movement Generator We use an FCRBM to generate the movements of the agent. As shown in Figure 3.b, FCRBM learns the autoregressive, as well as the nonlinear temporal patterns in a time-series. Every weight in FCRBM is modulated by the value of its context unit, making it possible to change the energy landscape of the model by changing the value of the context unit, and effectively controlling the model's prediction. In WalkNet, the FCRBM learns to predict the next motion capture frame, given a recent history of the motion capture frames, as well as the movement descriptors fed to its context unit Z. This results in a predictive function in the form of:

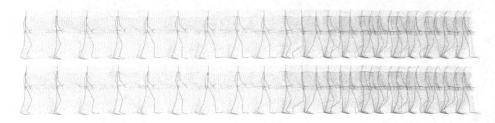

Fig. 4. WalkNet's output. Top: making a transition from a high valence and high arousal affective state to a low valence and low arousal state. Bottom: making a transition from a low valence and high arousal affective state to a high valence and low arousal state.

$$M_t = f(M_{<t}, Z_t), Z_t = \langle I_t^1, I_t^2, V_t, A_t, R_t, L_t \rangle$$

By iteratively calling this function and feeding it with the generated frames from the previous cycles, we can continuously generate movements that are modulated by the given descriptors.

5   Results

In this section, we demonstrate the capabilities of WalkNet in generating realistic motion capture data. We use an FCRBM with 150 hidden units and 400 factors, trained for 3000 epochs. The model takes 12 past motion capture frames as input and predicts the next frame, modulated by a vector of 6 dimensions (Z).

Affect Expression By specifying different values for the valence and arousal levels in the agent movement descriptors, WalkNet can generate a variety of affect expressions, even for those values that do not exist in the training data. This allows for generating walking movements for any point in a range of $[0, 4]$. With this, one can not only generate walking movements for high, neutral, and low levels of valence and arousal but also make transitions from one state to another (Figure 4).

In a previous work by the same authors [1], a study was conducted to validate the expressiveness of the movements. The analysis shows that independent human observers can successfully identify different levels of arousal. However, they can only correctly identify the low valence levels, and often confused the neural and high valence levels. The analysis reached the same results for the recorded movements of human actors as well. We believe that due to the lack of facial expression, recognition of valence through movements, as represented by a stick figure, is often challenging for humans.

Movement Signature WalkNet can generate signatures that are interpolations between the two actors. The difference in the generated movement signatures are demonstrated in the accompanied video[2].

---

[2] https://youtu.be/3JBfGF4tsmA

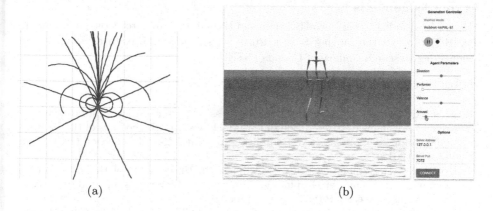

(a)   (b)

Fig. 5. (a) The projection of the agent's movements on the ground floor plane, making turns with different angles. (b) The interactive controller.

Navigation As the results are demonstrated in Figure 5.a, different values for the direction factor generates movements along curves with different curvatures.

Interactive Control WalkNet through a graphical user interface (GUI) developed for this purpose. The GUI allows the user to choose the parameters of the model, while the agent's movements are rendered in 3D in real-time. A snapshot of the GUI is shown in Figure 5.b. A video of the GUI is also provided[2].

Generating each frame takes 0.0063 seconds on a MacBook Pro with an Intel(R) Core(TM) i7-4850HQ CPU at 2.30GHz. Thus, at 30 frames-per-second, it takes 0.1890 of a second to generate the movements for each second.

6   Conclusion and Future Work

This paper introduces WalkNet, a walking movement controller. It can generate realistically-looking walking movements in real-time, while modulating them using an agent movement descriptor that specifies the expression of affect through the movement, the walking direction, and the personal movement signature of the agent.

WalkNet is designed with integration into agent models in mind. It does not make any assumption on how the movement descriptor is specified, making it possible to be used in interactive scenarios, in which a user directly controls the agent's movements, or in scripted or AI-driven applications. For example, given a target path to follow, by observing the traveled path, the agent can continuously correct its course to stay on the target path.

In future, we plan to perform more formal and quantitative evaluation of the model. Furthermore, we intend to use more human subjects in the training data. Another future direction is to extend the model to include more than one type of movement (function). For example, allowing the agent to switch from walking to standing to sitting while performing hand gestures.

Acknowledgements

This work is funded by the Social Sciences and Humanities Research Council of Canada (SSHRC) through the Moving Stories Project, as well as the Natural Sciences and Engineering Research Council of Canada (NSERC).

References

1. Alemi, O., Li, W., Pasquier, P.: Affect-Expressive Movement Generation with Factored Conditional Restricted Boltzmann Machines. In: Proceedings of the International Conference on Affective Computing and Intelligent Interaction (ACII). pp. 442–448 (2015)
2. Brand, M., Hertzmann, A.: Style Machines. In: Proceedings of the 27th Annual Conference on Computer Graphics and Interactive Techniques. pp. 183–192. ACM Press/Addison-Wesley Publishing Co. (2000)
3. Crnkovic-Friis, L., Crnkovic-Friis, L.: Generative Choreography using Deep Learning. In: Proceedings of the 7th International Conference on Computational Creativity (2016)
4. Grassia, F.S.: Practical Parameterization of Rotations Using the Exponential Map. Journal of Graphics Tools 3(3), 29–48 (1998)
5. Heck, R., Gleicher, M.: Parametric Motion Graphs. In: Proceedings of the 29th Representation Learning Workshop. International Conference on Machine Learning. pp. 129–136. ACM Press (2007)
6. Herzog, D., Krueger, V., Grest, D.: Parametric Hidden Markov Models for Recognition and Synthesis of Movements. In: Proceedings of the British Machine Vision Conference. pp. 163–172 (2008)
7. Holden, D., Saito, J., Komura, T.: A Deep Learning Framework for Character Motion Synthesis and Editing. ACM Transactions on Graphics (TOG) 35(4), 138–11 (2016)
8. Kovar, L., Gleicher, M., Pighin, F.: Motion Graphs. In: SIGGRAPH '02: Proceedings of the 29th Annual Conference on Computer Graphics and Interactive Techniques. pp. 473–482. ACM Press (2002)
9. Plutchik, R., Conte, H.R.: Circumplex Models of Personality and Emotions. American Psychological Association (1997)
10. Samadani, A.A., Kubica, E., Gorbet, R., Kulić, D.: Perception and Generation of Affective Hand Movements. International Journal of Social Robotics 5(1), 35–51 (2013)
11. Taubert, N., Endres, D., Christensen, A., Giese, M.A.: Shaking Hands in Latent Space - Modeling Emotional Interactions with Gaussian Process Latent Variable Models. In: Advances in Artificial Intelligence, 34th Annual German Conference on AI. pp. 330–334. Springer (2011)
12. Taylor, G.W., Hinton, G.E.: Factored Conditional Restricted Boltzmann Machines for Modeling Motion Style. In: Proceedings of the 26th Annual International Conference on Machine Learning (2009)
13. Tilmanne, J., d'Alessandro, N., Astrinaki, M., Ravet, T.: Exploration of a Stylistic Motion Space Through Realtime Synthesis. In: Proceedings of the 9th International Conference on Computer Vision Theory and Applications. pp. 1–7 (2014)
14. Wang, J.M., Fleet, D.J., Hertzmann, A.: Multifactor Gaussian Process Models for Style-Content Separation. In: Proceedings of the 24th International Conference on Machine Learning. pp. 975–982. ACM Press (2007)

A Virtual Poster Presenter using Mixed Reality

Vanya Avramova ✉, Fangkai Yang, Chengjie Li,
Christopher Peters, and Gabriel Skantze

KTH, Stockholm, Sweden
`avramova,fangkai,chengjie,chpeters,skantze@kth.se`

Abstract. In this demo, we will showcase a platform we are currently developing for experimenting with situated interaction using mixed reality. The user will wear a Microsoft HoloLens and be able to interact with a virtual character presenting a poster. We argue that a poster presentation scenario is a good test bed for studying phenomena such as multi-party interaction, speaker role, engagement and disengagement, information delivery, and user attention monitoring.

1 Introduction

Interacting with a virtual character on a 2D display is very different from a physical robot or another human being. When viewed on a display, the animated agent does not share the same space as the observer. This makes it very hard to engage in *situated interaction* with the agent, where the shared space is of importance. For example, the agent cannot have exclusive mutual gaze with one of the observers: it will either appear to look at nobody, or at everyone in the room, the so-called Mona Lisa effect [2]. Also, it becomes hard to reach joint attention to objects in the shared environment. This is why situated interaction so far has been explored mostly in human-robot interaction scenarios, where these problems are avoided [2]. However, physical robot platforms are typically very expensive to build, alter and maintain. A consequence is that most researchers use the same platforms, which limits the exploration of possible designs, and by extension the possibilities for various forms of interactions. Some platforms provide flexibility in appearance, such as the Furhat robot head [1], where an animated face is back-projected on a mask, allowing for different animations to be displayed. Such flexibility makes it possible to study how the robot's appearance affect the interaction, including phenomena like the uncanny valley [4]. However, most robots still have very limited flexibility when it comes to the rest of the body, which can have important communicative functions (such as posture and pointing gestures).

We are currently developing a platform which will allow for situated interaction with virtual agents, and thereby provide a possibility to experiment with the effects of agent appearance on the interaction. The idea is to use Mixed Reality (MR), a technology that facilitates the overlay of computer graphics constructs onto the real world. Unlike Virtual Reality (VR), the graphics does not completely replace the environment. This is important for social interaction,

J. Beskow et al. (Eds.): IVA 2017, LNAI 10498, pp. 25–28, 2017.
DOI 10.1007/978-3-319-67401-8_3

Fig. 1. The virtual presenter in mixed reality, as seen from the user's perspective.

since it allows the user to directly perceive her own body in a natural way. Also, physical objects (such as a table or objects under discussion) can be mixed with virtual objects, or augmented with virtual artifacts. Using this platform, we will investigate interactional phenomena that are specific to situated interaction, for example the impact of multimodal behaviour (speech, facial expression, full-body motions, conversational formations) and embodiment on turn-taking and joint attention.

A virtual agent in mixed reality can of course have important applications, such as virtual museum guides, tutors, pets, companions, etc. But the platform could also be used for the development of virtual replicas of robots, and test them out in interaction with humans, before they are manufactured, greatly reducing the development costs and increasing the room for experimentation.

In this "meta" demo, we will showcase the current status of the platform by allowing the user to interact with a virtual character which is presenting a poster that shows the current status of the platform, as illustrated in Figure 1. We think that a poster presentation scenario is a good test bed for studying phenomena such as multi-party interaction, speaker roles, engagement and disengagement, information delivery, and user attention monitoring (cf. [3]).

2   Platform

The platform involves four major components: The IrisTK multi-modal dialogue framework (www.iristk.net), a full-body animation controller [6], Unity3D, and the Microsoft HoloLens. An overview of the architecture is shown in Figure 2.

IrisTK has previously been used in several studies on human-robot inter-action, and is especially targeted towards multi-modal, situated interaction [5]. IrisTK provides a set of modules for receiving sensory data from the users and the environment (e.g., speech recognition, body locations, item locations), and merges these into a 3D model of the physical situation (i.e., the status of agents

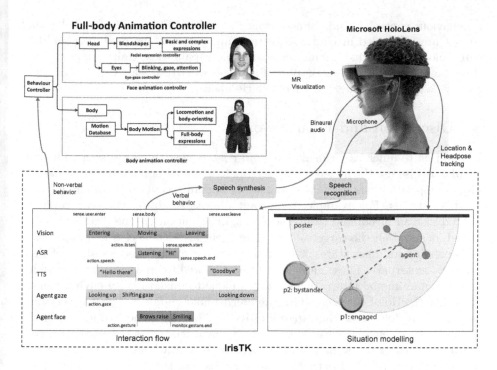

Fig. 2. Platform architecture.

and objects). This situation model can then be used to make higher-level inferences about when users enter and leave the interaction space of the robot, the conversational roles of the users, and where the agents' attention is targeted. When applied to human-robot interaction scenarios, IrisTK typically uses a sensor like Microsoft Kinect to track users and receive audio from the user. In this setting, we instead use the input and output modalities provided by the Microsoft HoloLens. The HoloLens scans the room in order to be able to track the users position and head pose, and contains gyro and accelerometer sensors. This allows it to position virtual agents and objects in the 3D environment and render them on the see-through display. The HoloLens can also give binaural audio to the user, effectively simulating the auditory experience of different locations of the virtual agent.

The full-body animation controller is part of a character behaviour toolkit supporting and enabling the development of expressive social interaction behaviours for small groups of virtual characters [6] . It supports parameterised control of their facial expressions, gaze, body gestures and posture using the face and body animation controller (see Figure 2), as well as locomotion, body orientation and free standing formations using a formation controller. Coordinated multimodal behaviours (facial expressions animated via blendshapes, gaze motions and full-body motion-captured animations) are controlled through a behaviour controller and defined using hierarchical FSMs. The controller and toolkit are embedded in Unity 3D, a real-time game engine providing sophisticated modern rendering, animation and audio capabilities. Unity supports real-time interaction through its support of a variety of virtual reality and augmented reality devices, including the Microsoft HoloLens.

3 Discussion and Future work

In addition to quick experimentation and control over the agent's embodiment, we plan to also use the mixed reality setting to explore unorthodox but situationally appropriate interaction cues, and study human acceptance and adaptability to these signals. For example, important objects in the setting can be highlighted instead of pointed to by the agent, or attention can be drawn by using sound localized on the target object. The agent also has access to unique ways of expressing its inner state, or its understanding of the affective state of their human counterpart. These methods will be explored to enable a platform which provides multimodal interactive settings unique to mixed reality environments.

While the HoloLens is capable of rendering holographic imagery at very high resolution, it does so at the expense of its field of view. The boundaries of the visible view screen are relatively small, and may often truncate holographic content as the wearer turns their head. This presents a drawback for the interaction, as the view cuts off objects that the wearer feels that they should be able to see, especially on the vertical view axis. We have to consider carefully the scale and placement of holograms in the interaction settings, so that the immersiveness of the experience is minimally affected.

References

1. Al Moubayed, S., Skantze, G., Beskow, J.: The furhat back-projected humanoid head-lip reading, gaze and multi-party interaction. International Journal of Humanoid Robotics 10(1) (2013)
2. Al Moubayed, S., Skantze, G.: Turn-taking Control Using Gaze in Multiparty Human-Computer Dialogue: Effects of 2D and 3D Displays. Proceedings of the International Conference on Audio-Visual Speech Processing 2011 pp. 99–102 (2011)
3. Eichner, T., Prendinger, H., André, E., Ishizuka, M.: Attentive Presentation Agents. In: Intelligent Virtual Agents, pp. 283–295. Springer Berlin Heidelberg, Berlin, Heidelberg (2007)
4. Paetzel, M., Peters, C., Nyström, I., Castellano, G.: Congruency matters - How ambiguous gender cues increase a robot's uncanniness. In: International Conference on Social Robotics. vol. 9979 LNAI, pp. 402–412 (2016)
5. Skantze, G., Moubayed, S.: IrisTK: A statechart-based toolkit for multi-party face-to-face interaction. In: ICMI'12 - Proceedings of the ACM International Conference on Multimodal Interaction (2012)
6. Yang, F., Li, C., Palmberg, R., der Heide, E.V., Peters, C.: Expressive Virtual Characters for Social Demonstration Games. In: 9th International Conference on Virtual Worlds and Games for Serious Applications (VS-Games) (submitted)

Multiparty Interactions for Coordination in a Mixed Human-Agent Teamwork

Mukesh Barange ✉, Julien Saunier, and Alexandre Pauchet

Normandie Univ, INSA Rouen Normandie, LITIS, 76000 Rouen, France
{surname.lastname}@insa-rouen.fr

Abstract. Virtual environments for human learning enable one or more users to interact with virtual agents in order to perform their tasks. This collaboration necessitates that the members of the team share a set of beliefs and reason about resources, plans and actions to be implemented. This article introduces a new multiparty coordination model allowing several virtual and human agents to dialogue and reason about the tasks that the user must learn. The proposed model relies on a shared plan based approach to represent the beliefs of the team members. The management of the multiparty aspect makes it possible to differentiate the behaviors to be produced according to the type of receiver of a communication: recipient or listener. Finally, in the context of learning a procedural activity, a study examines the effect of our multiparty model on a learner. Results show that the use of proactive pedagogical agents with multiparty competencies boosts the construction of common beliefs.

Keywords: Virtual agents; virtual environment; human-agent interaction; teamwork; collaboration; multiparty interaction protocol.

1 Introduction

Virtual Learning Environments (VLE) have been defined as a range of systems that comprise features like a designed information space, a social space being a "place", and participants that are active and present actors [7]. In the context of human-agent teamwork, VLE allow one or more users to interact with embodied agents in virtual reality (VR) in order to learn a task. These tasks can be procedural, technical, functional or non-functional, performed individually or in a team. The collaboration between team members necessitates to share a set of common beliefs and to reason about the plans, actions and resources [23]. This sharing is difficult to implement in completely-software systems; it also faces problems when including humans in the team. In the context of a mixed team, using dialogues in natural language facilitates the interaction with the user.

This article proposes an original model of multiparty team coordination, allowing several virtual agents and a user to dialogue and reason about the tasks that the user has to learn. This model relies on a shared mental model to construct the states of the beliefs of team members, similarly to [2], and focuses on an explicit representation of the multiparty information sharing protocols in

© Springer International Publishing AG 2017
J. Beskow et al. (Eds.): IVA 2017, LNAI 10498, pp. 29–42, 2017.
DOI 10.1007/978-3-319-67401-8_4

the learning situations. In particular, we detail how multiparty conversations are used to establish and maintain the coordination between the team members. The multiparty aspect makes it possible to differentiate the behaviors to be produced according to the type of receiver of a communication: recipient or listener. To validate the contribution of this model, an experimental study within the framework of a VLE was carried out.

This article is organized as follows: section 2 proposes a state of art on coordination models and on multiparty communications. Section 3 describes our model of coordination for mixed teams, while in section 4 this model is applied in the context of multiparty protocols. Section 5 presents the results of an experiment that compares reactive and proactive behaviors of agents having multiparty communication and coordination capabilities in the context of VLE. Finally, Section 6 concludes the article.

2   Multiparty Coordination and Communications

Coordination, the mechanism by which several entities can take into account each others' activities to carry out tasks, is a fundamental problem in multiagent systems (MAS). Traditionally, coordination is managed either using implicit subsymbolic models or using a semantic approach based firstly on language acts, secondly on updating mental states to maintain the shared knowledge and to reason locally, and finally on the interaction with the other agents [4].

Numerous works have attempted to formalize the notion of teamwork to integrate natural coordination mechanisms. According to the joint intention theory [6], team members must share a common intention to achieve a joint goal. However, this theory does not guarantee that team members follow the same action plan to reach the joint goal, as the shared plan theory requires that team members at least know how to perform actions [10]. It also does not guarantee that team members engage towards the group to achieve the joint goal. [9,25] proposed collaborative problem solving based on collective mental attitudes.

Several models of human-agent teamwork have been proposed. Collagen [19] and its extension DiamondHelp [18] are constructed on the discourse theory to enable human-agent collaboration to solve problems such as route planning. The methodology of Coactive modeling [12] helps system developers to identify the interdependence relations between different collective activities and therefore design systems that provide coordination and teamwork. The team coordination modeled with Brahms+KAoS [22] is governed by teamwork policies where communication is managed by notification protocols. These work do not address what kinds of communication decision interdependency exist in a team and how this interdependency impacts a single agent's communication decision.

In a mixed human-agent team, the virtual agents must adapt to the variability in behaviors of the human team members [12]: humans can modify the activity context and, unlike virtual agents, they do not necessarily follow coordination protocols between team members. Authors in [12] address the necessity to identify different ways that human and agent can assist each others to achieve collective goals. Moreover, one of the characteristics of human teams is that the members proactively provide information to other team members by anticipating their needs [13]. Zhang et al.,[26] addressed the issues of concurrency of communication dealing with dynamically changing information and of decision interdependency in multiagent teamwork. Their approach only considers one-to-one model *i.e.* one provider and one needer. In this case, agents consider interaction with their counterpart agents and make decisions. However, in the context of a mixed human-agent teamwork, the agents must not only inform the team members (human and virtual) of what has been done, but also assist the user about the actions to be performed.

From the point of view of the mode of information exchange, a difference between MAS and human teams resides, in the second case, in natural broadcast information sharing. For example, [8] emphasizes how overhearing improves efficiency. Indeed, information such as "already in conversation" can be inferred only by observing that an exchange is occurring, without knowing the message content. A typology of the communication participants is given in [20]: (a) speaker (emitter), known or unknown to the participants; (b) addressee (recipient), actively participating in the dialogue; (c) auditor, expected and known by the emitter, but passive in the dialogue; (d) destination group, not necessarily known *a priori*; (e) overhearer (listener), active receiver (authorized by system rules); (f) indiscreet receiver (receiver not permitted by system rules). In mixed communications, three roles can be distinguished: the sender, the recipient(s) (considered as a destination group) and the listener(s). Kumar *et al.* [14] studied the properties of group communications in human societies and their application to MAS. In particular, communications must support unexpected actors, messages can be sent to a group whose members are unknown from the emitter and the listeners can be unaware of the other receivers. Kamali *et al.* have proposed a new semantics for certain dialogue acts in the context of group communications, in order to support communications extended to a set of listeners [13]. In this work, the authors observe that considering communications between several agents as a unit and not as a multiplicity of one-to-one communications improves the inference capabilities of the agents.

Virtual environments define intrinsically the modalities of information exchange. For example, the Mission Rehearsal Exercise [24] is designed to simulate military missions. The authors focus on multi-modal interaction: messages, signals, gestures, *etc.* The application requires to simulate, among other things, overhearing. Overhearing is necessary from a VR perspective, because many human social behaviors in interactive context can only be described through this process. On the other hand, in this work some problems such as understanding spoken words in a multiparty context [3], and more generally the problems inherent to natural language (not considered in this article), and finally how the agents apprehend multiparty and role detection (addressee, auditor, etc.) remain to be handled.

Thus, a common coordination model is needed to unify the theories guided by mental attitudes (belief, desire and intention) [6,10,25] and a multiparty interaction mechanism. The aim is to ensure effective collaboration among team members by establishing joint and mutual beliefs in mixed man-agent teamwork.

3   Coordination Model for Mixed Human-Agent Teams

In the context of a mixed human-agent teamwork, we propose a coordination model based on the joint intention theory [6], the shared plan theory [10] and collaborative problem solving [25] to define how collective decisions affect the team members' intentions. The common point of these approaches is the shared mental model, *i.e.*, a hypothetical construct that represents the global state of the team perceived by each team member. Coordination mechanisms can be deduced from the goal commitments considering the shared knowledge.

3.1   Collective Mental Attitudes

This section describes modal operators on mental attitudes concerning a group G, a formula φ and a time t. Mutual-Belief(G, φ, t), means that, at t the group G has a mutual belief that φ holds. The operator Group-Bel(G, φ, t) means that, at t, every member of G believes that φ holds. Group-Des(G, φ, t) specifies that every agent of G has a desire to attain φ. The semantics of Group-Goal(G, φ, t) indicates that the agent knows that all team members want to achieve a goal φ at a time or another. Similarly, Group-Int(G, φ, t) describes that every agent of G has an intention to attain φ. A joint desire Joint-Des(G, φ, t) conveys the fact that two or more agents can be motivationally connected by the same state of the world that each of them wishes to bring about. A joint goal Joint-Goal(G, φ, t) points to a state of the world that two or more agents consider both achievable and as a possible candidate for being moved up to joint intention-status. A joint intention Joint-Int(G, φ, t) conveys the idea that: (a) two or more agents are individually committed to achieve a particular state of the world; and (b) each of them intends the others to be individually committed to achieve that state. The detailed semantics of these operators can be found in [6,9].

3.2   Model of Collective Commitment

Our proposition of coordination model in a human-agent team specifies multiparty interaction protocols within the team. Team members can have several goals to achieve collectively. They need to collectively choose a common goal as the shared team goal. All members can actively participate in this decision making.

Once the goal is collectively chosen, all team members have a belief $Group-Goal(G, \varphi, t)$ that group G has a goal φ, and they also believe that the other members have the same belief. As the agents collectively decide to achieve φ, they build φ as a persistent goal ($PGOAL$) which is an individual commitment to achieve φ. $PGOAL$ can be defined as follows [6]:

$$\begin{aligned} &\text{PGOAL}(A_i,\ \varphi,\ q)\ \equiv\ \text{Bel}(A_i,\ \neg\varphi)\ \wedge\ \text{Goal}(\ A_i,\ \diamond\varphi)\ \wedge \\ &\quad \text{Know}(A_i,\ [\text{Until}\ [\text{Bel}\ (A_i,\ \varphi)\ \vee\ \text{Bel}(A_i,\ \odot\neg\varphi)\ \vee\ \text{Bel}(A_i,\ \neg q)]\ \text{Goal}(\ A_i,\ \diamond\varphi)]) \end{aligned}$$

A_i believes that φ is false and has the goal that φ becomes true ($\text{Goal}(A_i,\ \diamond\varphi)$). Moreover, A_i knows that before abandoning that goal, it must believe that either φ is true, φ will never be true ($\text{Bel}(A_i,\ \odot\neg\varphi)$), or q, an escape-clause, is false.

If any of the team members discovers that the goal has been achieved or is no more achievable, it drops its intention to achieve the goal. However, other team members could continue to waste their effort for a goal that is already achieved or no more achievable. Hence, for efficient coordination, each member should not only be committed towards the group goal, but also should be able to communicate the status of the team goal if necessary. To mutually bind team members together, we now define the *joint persistent goal*.

Joint Persistent Goal (JPG_1). The joint persistent goal JPG has been defined in [15] to bind persistent goal and intention to work together to achieve individual goals. We redefine the JPG as the JPG_1 by moving from individual to collective goal. We consider that the agent has a persistent goal φ and is individually committed towards the group to achieve this goal. An agent can drop the goal when it discovers that the goal has been achieved, or is impossible to achieve, or the escape-clause q is not valid. Upon that, the agent constructs a $PGOAL$ to reach mutual belief about φ or q. Formally, JPG_1 is defined as:

$$\begin{aligned} &\text{JPG}_1(A_i,\ G,\ \varphi,\ q,\ t_i)\ \equiv \\ &\quad \text{Mutual-Belief}(G,\ \neg\varphi,\ t_i)\ \wedge\ \text{PGOAL}(A_i,\ \varphi,\ q)\ \wedge \\ &\quad \text{Mutual-Belief}(G,\ \text{Joint-Goal}(G,\varphi,\ t_i),\ t_i)\ \wedge \\ &\quad (\text{Until}\ [\text{Mutual-Belief}(G,\varphi,t_i)\ \vee\ \text{Mutual-Belief}(G,\odot\neg\varphi,t_i)]\ \text{WMG}(A_i,G,\varphi,q,t_i)) \end{aligned}$$

where Weak Mutual Goal (WMG) :

$$\text{WMG}(A_i,\ G,\ \varphi,\ q,\ t_i)\ \equiv\ \text{Mutual-Belief}(G,\ \text{PWAG}(A_i,\ G,\ \varphi,\ q,\ t_i),\ t_i))$$

where Persistent Weak Achievement Goal (PWAG) :

$$\begin{aligned} \text{PWAG}(A_i,\ G,\ \varphi,\ q,\ t_i)\ \equiv\ &[\text{Bel}(A_i,\varphi)\ \wedge\ \text{PGOAL}(A_i,\ \text{Mutual-Belief}(G,\ \varphi,\ t_i),\ q)]\ \vee \\ &[\text{Bel}(A_i,\ \odot\neg\varphi)\ \wedge\ \text{PGOAL}(A_i,\ \text{Mutual-Belief}(G,\ \odot\neg\varphi,\ t_i),\ q)]\ \vee \\ &[\text{Bel}(A_i,\ \neg q)\ \wedge\ \text{PGOAL}(G,\ \text{Mutual-Belief}(G,\ \neg q,\ t_i),\ \neg q)] \end{aligned}$$

When an agent has JPG_1, it must work towards the achievement of the goal until there is a mutual belief regarding the status of the goal φ. Therefore, the agent can rely on other team members to know the status of the goal.

When the team has the joint intention to achieve a common goal, there is a gap between the common intention and the realization of the team activity because of the uncertainty about the commitment of each member. A joint intention can be dropped if a group member leaves the group for any reason.

Joint Commitment. The joint commitment is a motivational attitude that provides the necessary elements to link the joint intention and the realization of the team activity. Joint commitment includes the *role* [5] and the *social dependency* ($\text{S-Dependency}(A_i,G,\varphi)$) [16] of the team members. In a group, each agent takes the relevant role in the plan ($\text{Influence}(A_i,G,r_i)$). Along with the sequence of actions to be performed by team members, the shared plan also provides information about different collaborative situations that include (a) interdependencies of team members on action sequence, (b) resource dependencies, and (c) anticipating the information needs. Thus, additional conditions must be associated with the joint intention to achieve a persistent joint intention in order to ensure the team commitment for acting collaboratively.

There exists a joint commitment in G to achieve the shared goal φ at a time t_i, if and only if (a) the team members mutually believe that φ will be true, (b) G has the ability to achieve the goal φ collectively, (c) G has the joint intention to achieve φ, (d) there exists a shared plan (P_φ) collectively chosen by the team to achieve φ $(\text{Prefer}(A_i, \varphi, P_\varphi))$, (e) each role r_i to be performed in the shared plan P_φ $(r_i \in Roles(P_\varphi))$ has been adopted by team members, and the team members are socially dependent on the team, (f) every team member has a joint persistent goal JPG_1, and in that case, it is mutually known by the team, and (g) the joint intention to achieve φ continues to hold until φ is true, or there exist at least one team member who has dropped the intention, and this is mutually known by the team.

Joint-Commitment$(G, \varphi, q, t_i) \equiv$
  Joint-Ability$(G, \varphi, t_i) \wedge ([\forall A_i \in G \mid (\text{JPG}_1(A_i, G, \varphi, q, t_i) \wedge$
    Mutual-Belief$(G, \text{JPG}_1(A_i, G, \varphi, q, t_i), t_i)) \wedge \forall A_i \in G \ \text{Prefer}(A_i, \varphi, P_\varphi) \wedge$
    $\forall r_i \in \text{Roles}(P_\varphi) \mid (\exists A_i \in G \mid \text{Mutual-Belief}(G, \text{Influence}(A_i, G, r_i), t_i)) \ ] \wedge$
    [Joint-Int$(G, \varphi, t_i)]) \wedge \forall A_i \in G \mid \text{S-Dependency}(A_i, G, \varphi) \wedge \text{PWAI}(G, \varphi, t_i)$

where Persistent Weak Achievable Intention (PWAI) is defined as:

PWAI$(G, \varphi, t_i) \equiv$ Mutual-Belief$(G, \neg\varphi, t_i) \wedge$
  (Until $[\exists A_i \in G \mid \neg\text{Influence}(A_i, G, r_i) \wedge \text{Mutual-Belief}(G, \neg\text{Influence}(A_i, G, r_i), t_i)]$
    Joint-Int$(G, \varphi, t_i))$

JPG_1 is used as a conditional clause. Therefore, due to the persistent nature of JPG_1, team members communicate with each other to establish a mutual belief about the status of the goal. The JPG_1 condition in the joint commitment provides the flexibility to deal with intentions that are generated by joint goals or by other sources such as dialogue. We can now define the individual commitment for a single agent as a special case of joint commitment.

Commitment$(A_i, \varphi, \Theta, t_i) \equiv$
  $\exists G, A_i \in G \mid \text{Singleton}(G, A_i) \Rightarrow$ Joint-Commitment$(G, \varphi, \Theta, t_i)$

Team members not only need to cooperate during the phase of team construction, but also need to maintain the cooperation during the realization of a shared plan. Team members have action dependencies with each others and they need to synchronize their actions during the execution of a shared plan. After the plan deliberation and decision-making, each agent updates its individual intention to perform an action α under the motivational condition Θ.

Intention-to (Int.To). An agent A_i intends at time t_i to perform an action α under the constraint Θ when 1) A_i commits to do α, and 2) A_i believes that it will be able to perform α, which is the basic level action, or if α is a complex action then A_i elaborates the plan to achieve α at time t_i:

(a) Multiparty Interaction: listen

(b) Group coordination

Fig. 1: EAST project, Wind Turbine Environment

Int.To(A_i, α, t_i, Θ) $\equiv$
  Commitment(A_i, α, Θ, t_i) $\wedge$
  [(basic.level(α) $\wedge$ Exec(A_i, α, t_i, Θ)) $\vee$
  ($\neg$basic.level(α) $\wedge$ Able(A_i, α) $\wedge$ Elaborate-Individual(A_i, Plan(A_i, α), t_i, Θ))]

The operator *Elaborate-Individual* refers to the process of extending A_i's plan to perform action α at time t_i as defined in [10].

Following the shared plan theory, we can describe the following intentional attitudes in terms of commitments: Intention-That (*Int.Th*), Potential-Intention-To (*Pot.Int.To*) and Potential-Intention-That (*Pot.Int.Th*). The mental attitudes *Int.To* and *Pot.Int.To* are used for actions, whereas *Int.Th* and *Pot.Int.Th* are used for propositions. Int.Th(A_i, p, t_p, Θ) represents that the agent A_i intends that the proposition p holds at time t_p. While *Int.To* is applied to individual actions, *Int.Th* can be used to initiate team activities. *Int.To* is used to represent goals to which agents are fully committed, while *Pot.Int.To*($A_i, \alpha, t_\alpha, \Theta_\alpha$) refers to possible goals to which agents are not fully committed. In the same way, Pot.Int.Th(A_i, p, t_p, Θ_p) represents potential intention that p holds at time t_p under the constraint Θ_p. The agent needs to deliberate before it can be applied as a full flagged intention.

4 Multiparty Protocols

This section illustrates how our coordination model allows flexible protocols in a multiparty context. To evaluate our model, we consider a case study derived from the EAST (Scientific and Technical Learning Environments) project [21]. In a VLE, a user, the learner, and two virtual agents must coordinate to perform a maintenance protocol in a wind turbine. In this scenario, team members must successively introduce themselves, discover their task, check the weather, remove obstacles, choose appropriate tools and access the wind turbine (6 sub-tasks). For example, figure 1a shows a multiparty interaction, while figure 1b illustrates a task in which the two virtual agents and the learner must coordinate to move a trunk to clear the entrance of the wind turbine. In these contexts, virtual agents

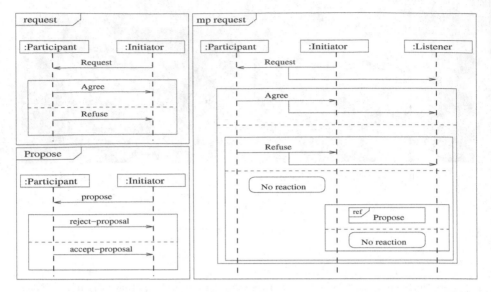

Fig. 2: Classic *request* and *propose* protocols *versus multiparty request* protocol.

interact with the user and with each other. They can also provide pedagogical information on tasks or about the environment. To do this, they possess a semantic description of these elements in a UML model from MASCARET [5].

4.1 Multiparty Dialogues

Two situations can be distinguished in a multiparty context.

The first, that we call *listen*, is that of a classic communication between a sender and a receiver, but during which one or more hearers also perceive the exchanged information. In this case, the listener can form beliefs 1) on the transmitted information, *e.g.,* when a task has been performed, 2) on the issuer of the information, *e.g.,* that she has performed the task, and 3) on the receiver, *e.g.,* that the receiver has the information that the task is finished. For example, in figure 1a, the user asks a question to an agent while the other agent listens.

The second situation, that we call *group*, corresponds to the simultaneous transmission of a message for several recipients. In this case, all the recipients form the same beliefs. For example, in figure 1b, the user can ask the team to start moving a trunk. Semantically, the difference with the situation of *listen* concerns the commitments involved in the message.

4.2 Multiparty Request

The dyadic *request* protocol (figure 2) allows an agent to request information or to perform a task for another agent. It consists in the sending a request by the initiating agent and the receiver responds with an *accept*, a *refuse* or no reply.

The multiparty request protocol (*Mp Request*) is an extension of dyadic request protocol. In addition to the two fully intended participants, one or more listening agents are likely to receive *request* messages and their responses (or non-responses). The agent that receives the *request* message decides whether the message is addressed to it, whether it is a listener, or whether the message is addressed to the group. In the case where the participant refuses the request or if the participant does not respond, listeners have the opportunity to initiate a *propose* protocol with the initiator or to perform the task themselves. Semantically, this corresponds to the addition of a *Pot.Int.To* belief on reception of the initial *request* message, and the intention can be aborted if the task has been executed or otherwise, can be transformed into *Int-To*.

In the classic protocol, after a failure (because of a *refuse* or *failure*) the initiator must contact other agents with new *request* protocols, each of these protocols having a process cost. With the *Mp Request*, in the case where a listener agent can satisfy the request, it can spontaneously start a *propose* protocol to satisfy the failed request of the initiator. It is therefore an opportunistic behavior, since the listener agent bases its action on a message it was not meant to receive. In this protocol, roles can be taken indifferently by an agent or a user.

However, receiving a *request* addressed to the group differs from receiving a simple act of *request* in the sense that the agent creates a *Pot.Int.Th* instead of a *Pot.Int.To*. One can note that the *Pot.Int.Th* provides weak semantics and thus more flexibility. In mixed human-agent teams, agents must provide an opportunity for the user to engage in a conversation and any team member can satisfy the speaker's need. Thus, each addressee evaluates the constraints Θ_α for *Pot.Int.Th* before constructing any intention (*Int-To*) to perform α.

The difference between the *listen* and the *group* is the cardinality of the first message. In the case of *listen*, the message is initially intended for a single agent and concerns only one action. However, with *group*, this is a collective request (*e.g.*, a task to be carried out by three members) that can relate to a plan.

Finally, similarly to *Mp Request*, we introduce a *Mp Inform* to improve the belief construction in an opportunistic manner. It enables the agents to infer shared beliefs from inform messages. In particular, it allows agents to improve their shared beliefs with those of other team members.

4.3 Reactive and Proactive Behaviors

The agents can act according to two modalities: reactive or proactive. In reactive mode, they update their beliefs during multiparty dialogues but do not take opportunistic initiatives to provide information or to perform tasks that are not directly requested. In proactive mode, the agents implement the multiparty protocols described above, and also exhibit behaviors anticipating the information needs of other team members. They construct beliefs about the members' needs when they do not perform expected tasks or when they explicitly show the need for additional information. These information needs may be linked to:

Action execution: thanks to the shared plan approach, the agent can inform about the next task to perform, elicit the resources necessary for its execution and explain (to a human team member) how to perform the action;

Collective decision: the agent can propose certain resources, *e.g.,* during a collective task where each agent must choose some position, share resources, communicate a goal to build a joint goal, or propose a choice of plan;
Goal: thanks to persistence of collective commitment, the agent can inform about the status of the current activity, *i.e.,* the performed or waiting tasks.

All these behaviors allow team members to maintain a common understanding of the state of tasks and actions to be performed within the team and to provide pedagogical assistance to the user when the user needs it.

5   Experimental Evaluation

To evaluate the effects of the construction of shared knowledge in VLE, we have considered two experimental conditions. These conditions are based on reactive and proactive nature of agent behaviors. In both conditions, autonomous virtual agents can work as equivalent team members with a user in a collective activity. In the first condition, the agents exhibit only reactive behaviors during interaction initialized by the user. In the second condition, the agents exhibit proactive behaviors and thus can proactively support the effective coordination during the task. We consider two aspects of evaluation which include the interaction: (1) between two members (*e.g.,* a user and an agent), and (2) between three members (*e.g.,* a user and two agents). We have thus defined two hypotheses:

- **Hypothesis 1:** the construction of shared knowledge is faster with proactive agents than with reactive agents.
- **Hypothesis 2:** users need to make less effort to build shared knowledge with proactive agents than with reactive agents.

5.1   Method

Participants. Since the VE's goal is to train students to a procedural task, a call was made through which 16 students from an engineering school in France were recruited (11 men and 5 women, aged between 19 and 23 - mean=20.41 years, SD=1.37). The native French language was imposed as a controlled condition.

Data Collection. In order to evaluate the impact of the behavior of an agent, several measures were used: execution duration of actions, total time required by the user to perform a task, number of consultations for actions, number of errors during an action, and the dialogue interaction between team members.

Procedure. The evaluation process involves three steps. In the first step, participants were informed on the general context of the activity to interact with virtual agents who are members of the team and about the general course of interactions, but no description of the procedure was given to participants. The scenario used in this experiment has been described in section 4. In the second step, participants are invited to perform an experiment. In each experiment, three team members (an avatar controlled by the learner and two autonomous

Table 1: Experimental Conditions

Condition	Characteristics of the scenario
C1: Reactive	The two virtual agents have reactive behaviors.
C2: Proactive + Reactive (Mixed)	Sebastien exhibits both the reactive and proactive behaviors, and Pierre only has reactive behaviors.

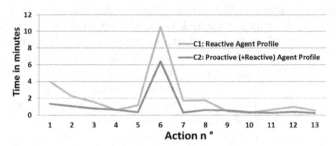

Fig. 3: Execution time of actions required by the user

agents *Sebastien* and *Pierre* endowed with the communication and coordination capabilities are located in the workshop of a wind turbine company. Each participant is asked to perform one of the two experimental conditions (see table 1).

In condition C2, since all agents have the same information on the environment and on the task, one or more agents with proactive behavior would not change the content of information proactively given to the user.

5.2   Results

Construction of Shared Knowledge. Figure 3 shows the execution times of actions required by users in both experiments. Applying a Student test, we obtain $t = 2.952$ and $p = 0.012$. The result is significant at $p < 0.05$ and the time required by the user to perform the actions is much higher in the reactive case (in C1, execution time = 26.57 min, in C2 execution time = 13.05 min). One of the reasons is that in both scenarios, the user does not know the sequence of actions in advance. Therefore, in the experimental condition C1, the user takes more time to know what to do and how to do it. Since agents are reactive in C1, they only provide information if the user requests them. However, in C2, with the agent being proactive, through our proposed coordination model, the agent can proactively inform the user about their actions, resources and the status of the shared team task. Thus, the total time required for the construction of shared knowledge about the task and its realization is less in C2 than in C1. These results support the hypothesis that the construction of shared knowledge is faster with proactive agents than with only reactive agents.

Engagement of the Learner. We also analyzed the 16 traces of dialogues between users and agents. The number of conversations initiated by the user was higher (maximum 28, average 20) in C1 where both agents are reactive (mean of conversational interactions in C1 is 46.18, with $SD = 11.077$), than in C2 (maximum 12, average 9) where one of the agents is proactive (mean of conversational interactions in C2 is 36.75, with $SD = 3.85$). The number of information consultations is less in the case of a proactive agent in comparison with the condition with only reactive agents. One way ANOVA test has been performed to analyze the variance on the number of utterances initiated by users in both conditions. The f-ratio value is 78.06452 and the p-value is < 0.00001. The result is significant at $p < 0.05$. This result supports the second hypothesis that the users need to make less effort, in terms of initiating interactions, to build shared knowledge with proactive agents than with reactive agents. The reason is that proactive pedagogical agents provide information by anticipating the information needs of the user and reduces the efforts of the the user to ask for this information. On the contrary, with only reactive agents, the user must take initiatives to request information or pedagogical assistance.

We also observed that the users were more prone to interact with Sebastian in both experimental conditions (73% of the user initiated dialogue interactions with Sebastien). The users seem more comfortable talking to Sebastien because 1) in both conditions, it is Sebastien who introduces the members of the team and 2) Sebastien is the proactive agent in C2 thus, it leaves the impression of providing information during the learning activity.

6   Discussion

The proposed model of teamwork coordination differs with related works in several aspects. For example, Cohen and Levesque [6] defines *joint commitment* simply in terms of escape conditions without any account of the nature of relationships between group members. Therefore, their notion fails to explain why a group of agents should be committed to acting in a collaborative way [16]. However, in our definition of *joint commitment*, this shortcoming is handled by binding team members together through the notion of shared plan. That is, they make collective decision for the choice of the shared plan and adopt the appropriate goals. Sharing the same plan allows team members to identify the situations when they need to cooperate with each others. Furthermore, compared to the collaboration model for agent-agent teamwork of [9], our model establishes and maintains coordination in a mixed human-agent team. Thanks to the concepts of *Pot.Int.To* and *Pot.Int.That* derived from joint commitment, multiparty protocols provide the flexibility to manage the behavior of humans in a mixed team. An important difference with the multiparty protocols for MAS defined in [20], is that the sender agent does not explicitly define the recipients and listeners of a message, which is not desirable in a mixed team.

Several issues remain. The participants mentioned that the movement of the head during the conversation was not realistic. The reason is that we manage the turn-taking through time-outs threshold, which could be improved according to the user and the turn-taking repartition. It will be interesting to integrate more dynamic and continuous turn-taking behavior, such as that presented in [11], to provide a more natural interaction. Another important remark is concerned with the limited natural language capabilities and the limited vocabulary for the agent. It would be interesting to integrate the dialogue modelling approach based on the data with the semantic modelling based approach. For example, the statistical approach based on dialogue corpus proposed in [1] can be used to find the most frequent dialogue patterns. These patterns can then be used to construct dialogue models in combination with the semantic modelling of VE [5] to provide more flexible and adaptable dialogue management capabilities. Furthermore, endowing emotion expression capabilities to the virtual agents [17] would enable us us to integrate an affective component in VLEs.

7 Conclusion

This article has presented a new model of multiparty coordination allowing several virtual agents and a user to dialogue and reason about tasks. This model focuses on an explicit representation of the multiparty information sharing protocol. The management of the multiparty aspect makes it possible to differentiate the behaviors to be produced according to the type of receiver of a communication: recipient or listener. A multiparty *request* protocol is explicitly explained in both situations for a mixed human-agent team. Finally, a study illustrates the effect of reactive and proactive behaviors on a learner in the context of learning a procedural activity. The results show that the use of proactive agents speeds the building of common beliefs, and that users need less effort to construct shared knowledge with proactive agents. An important reason is that the proposed coordination model allows agents to proactively provide user with her information need. This model takes advantage of the joint intention theory and the shared plan theory to establish and maintain coordination using collective mental attitudes.

Acknowledgements

This work was supported by the NARECA project (ANR-13-CORD-0015).

References

1. Ales, Z., Pauchet, A., Knippel, A.: Extraction de motifs dialogiques bidimensionnels. Revue d'intelligence artificielle 29(6), 655–684 (2015)
2. Barange, M.: Task-Oriented Communicative Capabilities of Agents in Collaborative Virtual Environments for Training. Thesis, UBO, Brest, France (2015)
3. Bohus, D., Horvitz, E.: Multiparty turn taking in situated dialog: Study, lessons, and directions. In: SIGDIAL. pp. 98–109 (2011)
4. Cao, Y., Yu, W., Ren, W., Chen, G.: An overview of recent progress in the study of distributed multi-agent coordination. Transactions on Industrial informatics 9(1), 427–438 (2013)
5. Chevaillier, P., Trinh, T.H., Barange, M., Devillers, F., Soler, J., De Loor, P., Querrec, R.: Semantic modelling of virtual environments using MASCARET. In: SEARIS. Singapore (2011)

6. Cohen, P.R., Levesque, H.J.: Confirmations and joint action. In: IJCAI. pp. 951–957 (1991)
7. Dillenbourg, P., Schneider, D., Synteta, P.: Virtual learning environments. In: 3rd Hellenic Conference" Information & Communication Technologies in Education". pp. 3–18. Kastaniotis Editions, Greece (2002)
8. Dugdale, J., Pavard, J., Soubie, B.: A pragmatic development of a computer simulation of an emergency call center. In: COOP. pp. 241–256 (2000)
9. Dunin-Keplicz, B., Verbrugge, R.: A logical view on teamwork. In: Games, Actions and Social Software, LNCS, vol. 7010, pp. 184–212. Springer (2012)
10. Grosz, B.J., Kraus, S.: Collaborative plans for complex group action. Artificial Intelligence 86(2), 269 – 357 (1996)
11. Jégou, M., Lefebvre, L., Chevaillier, P.: A continuous model for the management of turn-taking in user-agent spoken interactions based on the variations of prosodic signals. In: Intelligent Virtual Agents - 15th International Conference, IVA 2015, Delft, The Netherlands, August 26-28, 2015, Proceedings. pp. 389–398 (2015)
12. Johnson, M., Bradshaw, J.M., Feltovich, P.J., Jonker, C.M., Van Riemsdijk, M.B., Sierhuis, M.: Coactive design: Designing support for interdependence in joint activity. Journal of Human-Robot Interaction 3(1), 43–69 (2014)
13. Kamali, K., Fan, X., Yen, J.: Formal semantics for multiparty proactive communication in agent teams. In: Advances in Agent Communication. LNAI (2006)
14. Kumar, S., Huber, M.J., McGee, D., Cohen, P.R., Levesque, H.J.: Semantics of agent communication languages for group interaction. In: AAAI. pp. 42–47 (2000)
15. Levesque, H.J., Cohen, P.R., Nunes, J.H.T.: On acting together. In: AAAI. pp. 94–99 (1990)
16. Panzarasa, P., Jennings, N.R., Norman, T.J.: Formalizing collaborative decision-making and practical reasoning in multi-agent systems. Journal of Logic and Computation 12(1), 55–117 (2002)
17. Pelachaud, C.: Modelling multimodal expression of emotion in a virtual agent. Philosophical Transactions of the Royal Society of London B: Biological Sciences 364(1535), 3539–3548 (2009)
18. Rich, C., Sidner, C.L.: Diamondhelp: A generic collaborative task guidance system. AI Magazine 28(2), 33 (2007)
19. Rich, C., Sidner, C.L., Lesh, N.: Collagen: applying collaborative discourse theory to human-computer interaction. AI Mag. 22(4), 15–25 (2001)
20. Saunier, J., Balbo, F., Pinson, S.: A formal model of communication and context awareness in multiagent systems. Journal of Logic, Language and Information 23(2), 219–247 (2014)
21. Saunier, J., Barange, M., Blandin, B., Querrec, R.: A methodology for the design of pedagogically adaptable learning environments. The International Journal of Virtual Reality IJVR-16 01, 15–21 (2016)
22. Sierhuis, M., Bradshaw, J.M., Acquisti, A., Hoof, R.V., Jeffers, R., Uszok, A.: Human-agent teamwork and adjustable autonomy in practice. In: I-SAIRAS (2003)
23. Tambe, M.: Towards flexible teamwork. Journal of artificial intelligence research 7, 83–124 (1997)
24. Traum, D., Rickel, J.: Embodied agents for multi-party dialogue in immersive virtual worlds. In: AAMAS. pp. 766–773. ACM Press (2002)
25. Wooldridge, M., Jennings, N.R.: The cooperative problem-solving process. J. of Logic and Computation 9(4), 563–592 (1999)
26. Zhang, Y., Ioerger, T.R., Volz, R.A.: Decision-theoretic proactive communication in multiagent teamwork. In: Systems, Man and Cybernetics, 2005 IEEE International Conference on. vol. 4, pp. 3903–3908. IEEE (2005)

A Dynamic Speech Breathing System for Virtual Characters

Ulysses Bernardet[1] ✉, Sin-hwa Kang[2], Andrew Feng[2], Steve DiPaola[1], and
Ari Shapiro[2]

[1] School of Interactive Arts and Technology, Simon Fraser University, Vancouver,
Canada
{ubernard,sdipaola}@sfu.ca

[2] University of Southern California, Institute for Creative Technologies, Los Angeles,
California
{kang,feng,shapiro}@ict.usc.edu

Abstract. Human speech production requires the dynamic regulation
of air through the vocal system. While virtual character systems commonly are capable of speech output, they rarely take breathing during
speaking – speech breathing – into account. We believe that integrating
dynamic speech breathing systems in virtual characters can significantly
contribute to augmenting their realism. Here, we present a novel control
architecture aimed at generating speech breathing in virtual characters.
This architecture is informed by behavioral, linguistic and anatomical
knowledge of human speech breathing. Based on textual input and controlled by a set of low- and high-level parameters, the system produces
dynamic signals in real-time that control the virtual character's anatomy
(thorax, abdomen, head, nostrils, and mouth) and sound production
(speech and breathing). The system is implemented in Python, offers a
graphical user interface for easy parameter control, and simultaneously
controls the visual and auditory aspects of speech breathing through the
integration of the character animation system SmartBody [16] and the
audio synthesis platform SuperCollider [12]. Beyond contributing to realism, the presented system allows for a flexible generation of a wide
range of speech breathing behaviors that can convey information about
the speaker such as mood, age, and health.

Keywords: Speech breathing, speaking, breathing, virtual character,
animation

1   Introduction

In animals, breathing is vital for blood oxygenation and centrally involved in
vocalization. What about virtual characters? Does the perceivable presence or
absence of this behavior that is so vital in biological systems play a role in how
they are perceived? Is breathing movement, frequency, sound etc. effective at
conveying state and trait related information? These are some of the questions
that motivate the research into breathing in virtual characters presented here.

© Springer International Publishing AG 2017
J. Beskow et al. (Eds.): IVA 2017, LNAI 10498, pp. 43-52, 2017.
DOI 10.1007/978-3-319-67401-8_5

Breathing is a complex behavior that can be studied both, on its own, and in relation to other behaviors and factors such as emotion and health. In the work we present here, we focus our interest on the dynamic interplay between speaking and breathing, on what is called "speech breathing". From a functional perspective, the respiratory system needs to provide the correct pressure drive to the voice box [10]. Consequently, breathing is implicated in many aspects of speech production [20] such as voice quality, voice onset time, and loudness.

1.1 Related work

Breathing in virtual human characters As [18] point out, the more realistic virtual characters are becoming overall, the more important it is that the models are realistic at the detail level. Though the importance of including the animation of physiological necessities such as breathing has been recognized [14], few virtual character systems actually take breathing into account. In their interactive poker game system, [6] include tidal breathing – inhalation and exhalation during restful breathing – of the virtual characters as a means of expressing the character's mood. Models of tidal breathing that strive to be anatomically accurate include those developed by [18,21]. Recent models are usually based on motion data captured from participants [15,17]. Modeling work on breathing in conjunction with speaking is sparse, and the work of [9] on the development of infant speech production one of the few published works.

Physiology of (speech) breathing A number of experimental studies have investigated the relationship between the two processes of breathing and speaking. Empirical research has shown that the respiratory apparatus is sensitive to the demands of an upcoming vocal task, and that kinematic adjustments take place depending on where speech was initiated within the respiratory cycle [13]. The two distinct parts of the speech breathing process are the filling of the lungs referred to as "inhalation" or "inspiration", and the outflow of air – exhalation or expiration – that drives the voice box. Figure 1 shows the key parameters relating to the dynamics and interplay between breathing and speaking. Inspiration normally takes places at construct boundaries such as at the end of a sentence [7,8,19]. The key parameter pertaining to expiration is the utterance length, i.e. the number of syllables or words produced on one speech breath. In speech breathing one cycle of inspiration and expiration is referred to as "breath group" (Figure 1). In their study [19] found that 'breath group' lengths during both, reading and spontaneous speech tasks, had a duration of 3.84 seconds with a rather large standard deviation of 2.05 seconds. While relatively stable within a single participant, larger differences, ranging from 0.3 to 12.6 seconds, were found between participants.

In this paper, we present our work on a dynamic speech breathing model. The system consists of several tightly synchronized processes for inspiration and expiration animation, inspiration sound, audible speech, and facial animations (lip synch, mouth open, and nostril fare). All behavior is generated in real-time

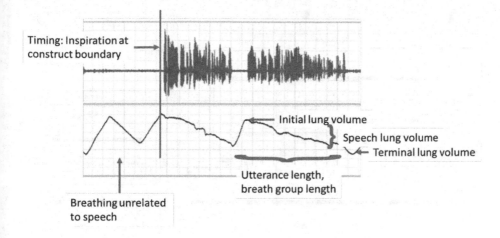

Fig. 1: Dynamics of speech breathing

and controllable via a set of low- and high-level parameters. Our goal is to provide a dynamic and tunable speech breathing system that contributes to augmenting the realism of computer generated virtual humanoid characters.

2 Dynamic speech breathing system

2.1 System overview

The open input to the system is the text, while tunable inputs are parameters controlling the speech and the breathing processes. At the output side, generated by the *control model*, the system produces dynamic control signals for shapes (thorax, abdomen, head, nostrils, and mouth) and sounds (speech and breathing).

2.2 Control model

At the core of the speech breathing control model stands the oscillation between two fundamental processes: inspiration and expiration (Figure 2).

Inspiration process Physiologically, the function of inspiration is filling the lungs with air. In our model, inspiration comprises four independent, parallel processes: Triggering of facial animations (mouth and nostrils), inspiration animation (thorax, abdomen, neck), playback of inspiration sounds (see implementation section for details), and speech preparation. $length_{inspiration}$ is only the tunable parameter for the inspiration process. It is an independent parameter, because, based on what is know about physiological processes, the length of the inspiration is mostly independent of both, the length of the utterance and the lung volume. The inspiration animation consists of breathing-induced shape changes to

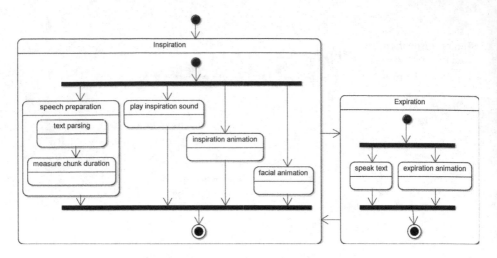

Fig. 2: State diagram of the dynamic breathing model

the chest and stomach, as well as a pitch rotation of the head along the coronal axis. All three of these changes are driven by a linear function LF with a slope defined as $\frac{volume_{lung}}{length_{inspiration}}$. The variable $volume_{lung}$ in turn, is a function of the length of the upcoming speech output (for details see "speech preparation process" below). Maximal volumetric and angular changes are set through the parameters $volume_{thorax}$, $volume_{abdomen}$, and $amplitude_{neck\ motion}$, respectively. Additionally, the model controls the change to two other shapes: The flaring of the nostrils, and the opening of the mouth. The maximal amplitudes for these are set by, $amplitude_{nostril\ flare}$, and $amplitude_{mouth\ open}$, respectively.

The system can produce two different inspiration sounds; breathing through the mouth and breathing through the nose. The Loudness of these two sound types is controlled by the parameters $amplitude_{sound\ mouth}$, and $amplitude_{sound\ nose}$, respectively. For clarity, we use the term "loudness" when referring to sound amplitude, and "volume" when referring to volumetric entities such as lungs.

Parallel to these processes, which produce perceivable output, runs the speech preparation process. Speech preparation comprises two steps. In a first step, the input text is parsed to extract the text chunk that will be spoken. The following steps define the text parsing algorithm (also see Figure 3):

- Step through text until number of syllables specified by the $length_{utterance}$ parameter is reached
- Map the position back onto the original text
- Search text forward and backward for the position of "pause markers" period (".") and underscore ("_")
- If the position of both pause markers (in number of characters) is larger than the parameter $urgency_{limit}$, define pause at word boundary
- Otherwise, define pause at position of pause marker, with priorities "." > "_"

– Identify text chunk for utterance and set remaining text as new input text

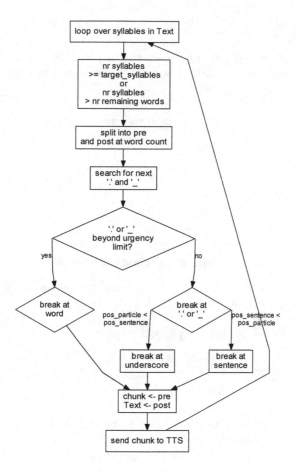

Fig. 3: Flow chart of the text parsing process

Note that we introduce the concept of "pause markers" to be able to have a more fine-grain control of the speech breathing process. The $urgency_{limit}$ parameter effectively defines how much flexibility the model has in terms of deciding when to insert inspiration into the text stream (see detailed explanation below).

The second step of the speech preparation process is the measurement of the upcoming speech output length (in seconds). This is done in an empirical fashion by sending the text to the text-to-speech system (TTS) and measuring the length of the generated audio bitstream. This approach is necessary because the actual length of the spoken text depends on the speech parameters, e.g. rate, as well as on the specifics of the text-to-speech system, e.g. the voice used.

Expiration process Two parallel processes make up the expiration phase: The generation of the stream of spoken output by the TTS and the expiration animation. The two parameters directly controlling the speech production are $prosody_{rate}$ and $prosody_{loudness}$. As for inspiration, a linear function controls thorax, abdomen, and neck. However, in the expiration case, the slope of the function is defined as $\frac{volume_{lung}}{length_{speech}}$.

The output of the oscillation between the inspiration and expiration process, as well as the speech and breathing sounds is illustrated in Figure 4.

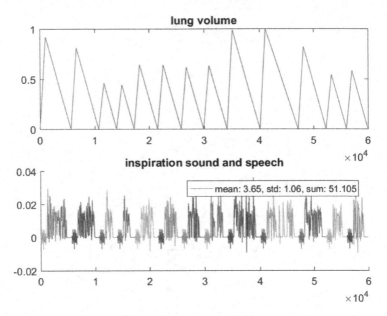

Fig. 4: Time course of the model behavior and outputs. The top saw-tooth function is used to control the thorax and abdomen shapes, as well as the pitch angle of the head. The lower panel shows the speech and breathing sound output of the model.

Abstract control Tuning individual low-level parameters is not desirable in most applications; rather, we would like to have a more abstract control model with a limited set of parameters. Additionally, the abstract control model ensures that low-level parameters are in a sensible causal relationship. While we subsequently lay out the parameters of the model, Equation 1 shows the qualitative model. Two parameters are related "breathing style": *ThoraxVsAbdomen* defines how much the character is chest or stomach breathing, while *MouthVsNose* controls inspiration through mouth vs. nose. The overall capacity of the lung is defined by $capacity_{lung}$; The parameter $amplitude_{breathing\ sound}$ controls the overall loudness of the inspiration sound, while $opening_{inspiration\ channels}$ the "inspiration channels" are opened. Low-level parameters that remain independent are $speaking_{loudness}$, $prosody_{rate}$, $length_{inspiration}$, and $amplitude_{neck\ motion}$.

$$
\begin{aligned}
amplitude_{sound\ nose} &= MouthVsNose * amplitude_{breathing\ sound}\\
amplitude_{sound\ mouth} &= (1 - MouthVsNose) * amplitude_{breathing\ sound}\\
amplitude_{nostril\ flare} &= MouthVsNose * opening_{inspiration\ channels}\\
amplitude_{mouth\ open} &= (1 - MouthVsNose) * opening_{inspiration\ channels}\\
volume_{abdomen} &= \frac{ThoraxVsAbdomen * capacity_{lung}}{100}\\
volume_{thorax} &= \frac{(1 - ThoraxVsAbdomen) * capacity_{lung}}{100}\\
length_{utterance} &= \sqrt{\frac{capacity_{lung}}{speaking_{loudness}}} * norm_{syllables}\\
length_{inspiration} &= \frac{capacity_{lung}}{100}\\
urgency_{limit} &= length_{utterance} * 2
\end{aligned}
\tag{1}
$$

2.3 Implementation

Breathing sounds The nose and mouth breathing sounds were recorded from one of the authors using a Rode NT1-A microphone, iRig PRE preamplifier, and Audacity software [1]. Post recording, the sound files were normalized and lengthen to five seconds by applying a Paulstretch filter using Audacity. During run-time, the sounds are played back using the audio synthesis and algorithmic composition platform SuperCollider [12]. The amplitude and length of the play back are controlled by applying a trapezoid envelope function to each of the waveforms (nose and mouth sound).

Real-time control architecture The core controller of the system is implemented in the Python programming language. The control commands for the sound playback are sent to SuperCollider via the Open Sound Control (OSC, [2]). Concurrently, the controller, via the 'm+m' middleware software [5], sends messages to the SmartBody virtual character system, where the character animation and rendering take place [16]. Thorax, abdomen, as well as facial animations, are implemented using blendshapes, while the head and mouth are controlled at the level of joint-angles. From within SmartBody, control signals are sent to the text-to-speech system (Microsoft TTS with the "Adam" voice from CereProc [3]. To facilitate parameter tuning and control, we developed a Graphical User Interface that was designed using Pygubu [4] and is based on Python's Tkinter module.

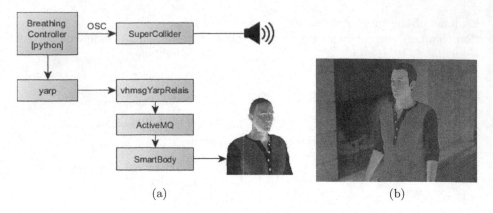

(a)   (b)

Fig. 5: (a) Software architecture of the speech breathing control system (b) Screen capture of the virtual character controlled and rendered using the Smart-Body system [16]

3   Discussion and Conclusion

We present a real-time control system for speech breathing in virtual characters, that is based on empirical knowledge about human speech behavior and physiology. The system receives input text and produces dynamic signals that control the virtual character's anatomy (thorax, abdomen, head, nostrils, and mouth) and sound production (speech and breathing). At the core of the speech breathing control model stands the oscillation between inspiration and expiration. The independent control of the physiologically grounded speech parameters allows the system to produce in real-time a wide range of speech breathing behaviors. In its present form, the control system offers the ability to produce physiologically grounded parameters of speech, e.g. utterance length function of speaking loudness and lung capacity.

The biggest limitation of the control system at this moment is the delicacy of the timing. A system intrinsic fragility stems from measuring the utterance length during the inspiration phase; if this measurement takes longer than the inspiration, the subsequent temporal coordination is compromised. An extrinsic source of potential desynchronization is the lag of speech onset in the Text-To-Speech system. A second limitation is that the TTS does not allow for variations in pitch. Especially pitch declination over an utterance, which might be related to subglottal pressure, and hence breathing [11] might be important for realism.

Next steps in the development of the system include the empirical investigation of the effect speech breathing has on factors such as realism and relatability. At the technical level, future steps include the improvement of the breathing animation to a state of the art implementation as presented e.g. in [17]. At the conceptual level, the system will be extended to include the control of speech breathing parameters with the goal of generating the expression of abstract constructs such as personality and emotion. For example, fast pace and shallow breathing may lead to the perception of anxiety, while long and deep breathing may lead to the perception of calmness.

Acknowledgements

This work was supported by Institute for Information & Communications Technology Promotion (IITP) grant (No. R0184-15-1030, MR Avatar World Service and Platform Development using Structured Light Sensor) funded by the Korea government (MSIP).

References

1. http://www.audacity.audio/
2. http://opensoundcontrol.org/
3. http://www.cereproc.com/
4. https://github.com/alejandroautalan/pygubu
5. Bernardet, U., Schiphorst, T., Adhia, D., Jaffe, N., Wang, J., Nixon, M., Alemi, O., Phillips, J., DiPaola, S., Pasquier, P.: m+m: A Novel Middleware for Distributed, Movement Based Interactive Multimedia Systems. In: Proceedings of the 3rd International Symposium on Movement and Computing - MOCO '16. pp. 1–21. ACM Press, New York, New York, USA (2016), http://dl.acm.org/citation.cfm?doid=2948910.2948942
6. Gebhard, P., Schröder, M., Charfuelan, M., Endres, C., Kipp, M., Pammi, S., Rumpler, M., Türk, O.: IDEAS4Games: Building expressive virtual characters for computer games. In: Lecture Notes in Computer Science. vol. 5208 LNAI, pp. 426–440 (2008)
7. Henderson, A., Goldman-Eisler, F., Skarbek, A.: Temporal Patterns of Cognitive Activity and Breath Control in Speech. Language and Speech 8(4), 236–242 (1965)
8. Hixon, T.J., Goldman, M.D., Mead, J.: Kinematics of the Chest Wall during Speech Production: Volume Displacements of the Rib Cage, Abdomen, and Lung. Journal of Speech Language and Hearing Research 16(1), 78 (3 1973), http://jslhr.pubs.asha.org/article.aspx?doi=10.1044/jshr.1601.78
9. Howard, I.S., Messum, P.: Modeling Motor Pattern Generation in the Development of Infant Speech Production. 8th International Seminar on Speech Production pp. 165–168 (2008)
10. Huber, J.E., Stathopoulos, E.T.: Speech Breathing Across the Life Span and in Disease. The Handbook of Speech Production pp. 11–33 (2015), http://dx.doi.org/10.1002/9781118584156.ch2
11. Ladd, D.R.: Declination: a review and some hypotheses. Phonology 1(1), 53–74 (1984)
12. McCartney, J.: Rethinking the Computer Music Language: SuperCollider. Computer Music Journal 26(4), 61–68 (12 2002), http://www.mitpressjournals.org/doi/10.1162/014892602320991383
13. McFarland, D.H., Smith, A.: Effects of vocal task and respiratory phase on prephonatory chest wall movements. Journal of speech and hearing research 35(5), 971–82 (10 1992), http://www.ncbi.nlm.nih.gov/pubmed/1447931
14. Rickel, J., Information, U.S.C., André, E., Badler, N., Cassell, J.: Creating Interactive Virtual Humans: Some Assembly Required. IEEE Intelligent Systems (2002)

15. Sanders, B., Dilorenzo, P., Zordan, V., Bakal, D.: Toward Anatomical Simulation for Breath Training in Mind/Body Medicine. In: Magnenat-Thalmann, N., Zhang, J.J., Feng, D.D. (eds.) Recent Advances in the 3D Physiological Human. Springer (2009), http://graphics.cs.ucr.edu/papers/sanders:2008:TAS.pdf
16. Shapiro, A.: Building a character animation system. In: Motion in Games. pp. 98–109 (2011)
17. Tsoli, A., Mahmood, N., Black, M.J.: Breathing life into shape. ACM Transactions on Graphics 33(4), 1–11 (7 2014)
18. Veltkamp, R.C., Piest, B.: A Physiological Torso Model for Realistic Breathing Simulation. In: Proceeding 3DPH'09 Proceedings of the 2009 international conference on Modelling the Physiological Human. pp. 84–94 (2009)
19. Winkworth, A.L., Davis, P.J., Adams, R.D., Ellis, E.: Breathing patterns during spontaneous speech. Journal of speech and hearing research 38(1), 124–144 (2 1995), http://www.ncbi.nlm.nih.gov/pubmed/7731204
20. Włodarczak, M., Heldner, M., Edlund, J.: Breathing in Conversation : An Unwritten History (2015)
21. Zordan, V.B., Celly, B., Chiu, B., DiLorenzo, P.C.: Breathe easy. In: Proceedings of the 2004 ACM SIGGRAPH/Eurographics symposium on Computer animation - SCA '04. p. 29. ACM Press, New York, New York, USA (2004)

To Plan or Not to Plan: Lessons Learned from Building Large Scale Social Simulations

Anton Bogdanovych ✉ and Tomas Trescak

MARCS Institute for Brain, Behaviour and Development,
School of Computing, Engineering and Mathematics,
Western Sydney University, NSW, Australia
a.bogdanovych@westernsydney.edu.au; t.trescak@westernsydney.edu.au

Abstract. Building large scale social simulations in virtual environments requires having a large number of virtual agents. Often we need to simulate hundreds or even thousands of individuals in order to have a realistic and believable simulation. One of the obvious desires of the developers of such simulations is to have a high degree of automation in regards to agent behaviour. The key techniques to provide this automation are: crowd simulation, planning and utility based approaches. Crowd simulation algorithms are appropriate for simulating simple pedestrian movement or for showing group activities, which do not require complex object use, but are not suitable for simulating complex everyday life, where agents need to eat, sleep, work, etc. Planning and utility based approaches remain the most suitable for this situation. In our research we are interested in developing advanced history and cultural heritage simulations and have tried to utilise planning and utility based methods (the most popular one of which is used in the game "The Sims"). Here we examine pros and cons of each of the two techniques and illustrate the key lessons that we have learned with a case study focused on developing a simulation of everyday life in ancient Mesopotamia 5000 B.C.

1 Introduction

Using Virtual Reality for reconstructing sites of high historical or cultural significance and showing how these sites were enacted in the past is becoming more and more popular. 3D modelling helps to visualise historical buildings and artefacts that at present only remain in the form of significantly damaged architectural structures or museum exhibits scattered around the world. Populating the reconstructed 3D environments with virtual agents helps to illustrate how these buildings and objects were used by people and to highlight the key technological or cultural aspects of the simulated society.

Supplying such Virtual Reality simulations with virtual agents that are capable of convincing and historically or culturally authentic behaviour beyond simple crowd simulation algorithms is difficult and costly. Virtual agents must be able to play different social roles, adhere to social norms, actively use surrounding objects, interact with other agents and even engage into interactions with humans. Modern video games are a good illustration in regards to the potential of having such simulations, but the cost of developing video games is very

© Springer International Publishing AG 2017
J. Beskow et al. (Eds.): IVA 2017, LNAI 10498, pp. 53–62, 2017.
DOI 10.1007/978-3-319-67401-8_6

high. For example, the estimated cost of developing Crysis 3, one of the popular modern video games, is $66 Million [5]. Such a level of spending is not feasible when it comes to research simulations.

In this paper we discuss different techniques that could help to make agent-based historical, cultural and other kinds of virtual simulations (which we call "social simulations") more affordable by automating the process of populating a virtual environment with a large number of virtual agents. One of the key research questions that arises with building such social simulations is how to supply virtual agents with goals and plans for achieving these goals in a believable and culturally/historically authentic manner? In regards to supplying agents with complex goals, which can consistently lead to believable behaviour in a social simulation, one of the key approaches is to develop some sort of a computational simulation of agent needs (similar to Maslow's pyramid of needs [8]) and generate goals in response to a particular need requiring satisfaction. Each need can be seen as a reservoir that is replenished (satisfied) after performing the relevant action (e.g. sleeping to reduce fatigue) and depleted in response to other actions (e.g. walking will increase fatigue).

As for developing plans (sequences of actions that lead to satisfying these generated goals), there are two popular approaches that game developers and academics use: AI Planning [7] and utility based methods, the most popular one of which is used in the game "The Sims" [1]. In our work we have developed a computational simulation of needs and have applied both utility based methods and AI planning for making our agents satisfy those. The key objective of this paper is to share the lessons learned form applying these techniques and explain what are the pros and cons of both when applied to building social simulations.

The remainder of the paper is structured as follows. In order to facilitate a reader's understanding of the discussed techniques we first present an example scenario related to building a social simulation in Section 2. In Section 3 we explain how a utility based approach similar to the one used in The Sims can be used for social simulations. Section 4 explains the use of AI planning for need satisfaction. Section 5 outlines the results of our comparative study and analyses the pros and cons of each of the needs satisfaction methods. Finally, Section 6 provides a summary of lessons learned and concluding remarks.

2   Example Scenario: Ancient Mesopotamia 5000 B.C.

To illustrate the issues involved in building social simulations and discuss how it is possible to automate agent behaviour in those, we suggest to consider the simulation of everyday life in ancient Mesopotamia around 5000 B.C.[1] shown in Figure 1. For this simulation we have reconstructed 3 small ancient settlements using the settlement maps produced by the archeologists from [3].

Based on the knowledge obtained from history experts we could design the following simplified scenario portraying a day of an average citizen: an average

---

[1] Accompanying video is available at: https://youtu.be/5yEF2A7LEL0

Fig. 1. Social Simulation Example: Everyday Life in Ancient Mesopotamia 5000 B.C.

agent in our simulation should start its day at around 6AM in the morning. Soon after waking up the agent would eat breakfast by preparing the food from storage or obtaining food through work. The agent would eat 4 times a day with intervals between meals being close to 6 hours. In-between meals the agent would work to satisfy immediate hunger or comfort. There is hardly any recreation time. If there is, the agents should explore the city or chat with each other.

The type of work an agent must perform depends on the social role this agent plays in the simulation. For simplicity, consider a scenario where each of the agents plays one of the following 4 social roles: Fisher, Baker, Potter and Shepherd. Figure 2 outlines the key tasks that these agents must perform at work: milking sheep, making pots, baking bread and fishing.

The first step of building the simulation involved modelling the buildings and the settlement layout based on the results of archaeological excavations and information provided by subject matter experts. The next step was to manually design the appearance of the base population of 2 agents. Treating the appearance of the agents from the base population as genetic code allows to automatically generate a desired number n of the simulation inhabitants following the approach in [11]. Given that each of these agents must play one of the aforementioned 4 roles we can either equally allocate the generated agents into the given 4 roles ($n/4$ - shepherds, $n/4$ - potters, $n/4$ - bakers and $n/4$ - fishers) or come up with a way of specifying the role distribution in the simulated society (e.g. 20% shepherds, 20% potters, 30% bakers and 30% fishers).

The key question this paper tackles is: once an agent has been created and has been assigned with a particular role how can we make this agent automatically generate goals and plans, so that it simulates believable behaviour consistent with the aforementioned scenario?

Fig. 2. The Four Agent Roles: Shepherd, Potter, Baker, Fisher

3 Utility Based Method: Replicating the AI of The Sims

One of the most popular video games that simulates agent behaviour through modelling needs is "The Sims". Due to its commercial nature it was difficult for us to obtain a detailed explanation of the process agents in The Sims game use to address their needs, as most of such information is considered a trade secret by game developers and they are often not interested in sharing it with the public. In our exploration we had to rely on conference presentations, blogs, videos and white papers. The most comprehensive formal explanation is available in [1].

The essence of the approach taken by The Sims is that every agent is supplied with a set of needs. These needs do not decay uniformly, but their decay rate is determined by functions similar to those shown in the Figure 3. Each of the needs is represented by a value from the $[-100 \cdots + 100]$ interval, where $+100$ means that the need is 100% satisfied and -100 means that the need is 100% suppressed. The values for each need decrease over time as per Figure 3 and can be increased through interactions with objects that can satisfy them.

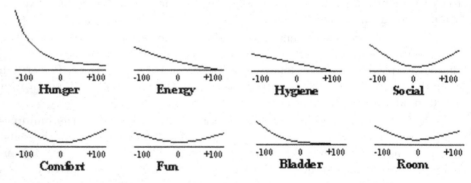

Fig. 3. Need Decay and Happiness Weights in The Sims [1]

There are no explicit goals that the agents have to generate and then pursue. Instead, the agents are driven by their desire to improve their mood. The mood of an agent is simply a sum of all the numeric values for agent needs as: $Mood = Hunger + Energy + Comfort + Social + Bladder + Room + Fun + Hygiene$.

Most of the "intelligence" in this game is stored in the objects rather than in the agents. Every time an agent finishes performing some action in response to an attempt to improve its mood it recomputes the current mood and then acts based on the information communicated by the surrounding objects. Some of the objects are capable of modifying the agent mood, so such objects continuously broadcast the details of how they can address each of the agent needs. An example that is relevant to our scenario from Section 2 is shown in Figure 4.

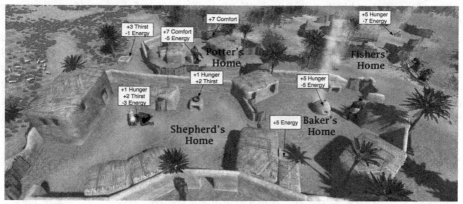

Fig. 4. The Overview of the Agent Architecture

To decide which action to perform next, an agent would compute the potential mood value using the information about the possible need changes broadcasted by every object and would then choose to interact with the object that provides the highest value of the resulting mood. Once the agent approaches an object and communicates that it wants to interact with it, the object would send a recipe (in our case a finite state machine) that prescribes what the agent must do to update its mood in accordance with the broadcasted values.

To avoid inter-agent conflicts in our implementation each agent owns a particular set of objects and only the owner can can interact with those. In our scenario from Figure 4, for example, all the objects located in the Shepherd's Home are owned by the shepherd agent and cannot be used by othes. There are also shared objects, which have no owner and can be used by any agent. An example of a shared object is the pot in the Potter's Home. This pot can be used by any agent and would increase the comfort of this agent by +7, but the supplied finite state machine would request from the agent using it to create another shared object of type food and leave it in exchange for the pot. Once an agent commits to interact with an object it can no longer stop the interaction and it is no longer possible by other agents to interact with this object.

Concerning the scenario from Figure 4, if an agent plays the role of a shepherd it can satisfy its hunger (+1) and thirst (+2) by interacting with a sheep. Once it approaches the closest sheep it must follow the actions expressed in the finite state machine that it supplies. This would involve approaching a pot, carrying the pot to the sheep, playing the milking animation, playing the drinking animation and then returning the pot to its original place. This would result in the decay of energy (-3). Alternatively, if there is milk available in storage this agent could choose to interact with the corresponding pot that would satisfy the agent's hunger (+1) and thirst (+2) with no energy decay. All agents can satisfy their thirst (+3) by using the shared object "well", but they will loose some energy (-3). A baker agent could satisfy its hunger (+5) by interacting with a stove. This would involve collecting the wheat in the field, preparing the dough, putting it in the stove and then eating the bread. Fishers could satisfy hunger (+5) through a fire place. This object would make them collect their fishing gear, walk to the boat, board it, play the fishing animation, return back with the fish, cook it on the fire and then eat it. Potters can not directly satisfy their hunger, but could only satisfy it if they have stored food in their possession. They can obtain stored food through trade with agents of other 3 roles. These agents would require pots from the pot maker to address their comfort (+7) and would trade the food they produce for pots. The comfort need is addressed by all agents through having food in storage. The energy need is satisfied through sitting down or sleeping. The social need is addressed by talking with the closest agent.

4 AI Planning in Social Simulations

An alternative approach to the utility based needs satisfaction is to make agents generate a goal (e.g. make the value of hunger greater than +50) every time a given need reaches a critical value (e.g. hunger = 0) and then dynamically build a plan that can satisfy this goal using AI planning [7]. The key idea behind planning is to annotate every action an agent is capable of performing with pre-conditions (in our simulation this is the state the agent must have in order to perform this action) and post-conditions (how the state of the agent would change if a particular action is performed). Once the actions are annotated, an agent can dynamically obtain a sequence of actions that leads to satisfying the generated goal by performing a search through the action space.

The key traditional benefit of using planning in video games is that the resulting agent behaviour appears diverse and dynamic, because agents can easily integrate rapid changes in the environment (e.g someone taking away an object that is necessary for completing a task) and find an alternative if such alternative exists. Additionally, game developers are no longer required to manually design plans (e.g. finite state machines embedded in the game objects) to specify how particular objects are to be enacted. Instead, the agents are capable of dynamically building such plans. But those benefits come at a cost of reduced performance, as every time an agent must make a decision it has to conduct an exhaustive search for a plan instead of simply executing a finite state machine.

To illustrate the benefits of planning for social simulations Figure 5 shows a simplified example where an agent with the role "Potter" and whose current state includes "HasWater" constructs its plan from the list of the following actions:

- FindWater (**pre-condition** = "NoWater", **post-condition** = "HaveWater")
- Work (**pre-condition** = "HaveClay", **post-condition** = "HavePot")
- MakeClay (**pre-conditon** = "WaterInClay, **post-condition** = "HaveClay")
- AddWater (**pre-condition** = "HaveWater, **post-condition** = "WaterInClay")
- Trade (**pre-conditon** = "HavePot", **post-condition** = "HaveFood")

Through analysing pre-conditions and post-conditions of each of these actions the agent is able to search for a plan that leads to obtaining food through trade and involves creating a pot and then exchanging it for food. The resulting plan is: AddWater→MakeClay→Work→Trade→HaveFood. This search starts with

| HaveWater | AddWater | MakeClay | Work | Trade |

Fig. 5. PotMaker Planning Example: AddWater → MakeClay → Work → Trade.

the agent generating a goal "HaveFood". It can then find "Trade" as an action that has this goal state as a post-condition. This backwards search continues until the agents finds a sequence of actions that leads from its current state "HaveWater" to the goal state "HaveFood". If at some stage the water pot is removed from the agent's home its state is updated to "NoWater" and the pre-condtion "HaveWater" of the "AddWater" action will not be satisfied, so the plan for the "HaveFood" goal would need to start from the "FindWater" action.

Due to performance issues in the vast majority of the games where AI planning is used the actual number of agents that do planning is very small [2]. In social simulations we need hundreds of agents, so this is a problem, but, many agents in social simulations would have very similar goals and would frequently need to repeat similar routines, so there is potential for plan reuse.

There are different ways one can do planning, but the most popular approach used by the gaming community is the goal-oriented action planning (or GOAP) [9]. We have modified the classical GOAP implementation to fit our purposes (e.g. to include dynamic heuristics, allow for cycles in plans, work with real numbers instead of binary predicates, etc.), but even those optimisations did not help to reach real-time performance. Moreover, complex agent behaviour was difficult to structure using the classical form expected by GOAP. As a result, we have considered the use of Hierarchic Task Networks (HTN) [6]. In our prior work we have used Electronic Institutions [4], the structure of which adheres to HTN, as the way of expressing norms in social simulation, so we were able to combine GOAP and HTN via Electronic Institutions. While an average plan generation using classical STRIPS (for 22 actions) was around four minutes, with Electronic Institutions we brought it down to 100 milliseconds. Further details of integrating Electronic Institutions into our simulations are beyond the scope of this paper, but curious readers would find further details in [10]. What is important for this paper is that through integrating Electronic Institutions we were able to reach real time performance when planning with many agents.

5 Experiments

We have conducted a series of experiments using the scenario described in section 2 with the aim to understand the key visual and statistical differences between AI planning and The Sims approach. These experiments where performed on an Alienware 7 laptop computer with the screen resolution of 1027x768.

Low performance is one of the key reasons for the limited use of planning in video games. An acceptable performance measure widely used in games development is frame-rate (how many frames per second (FPS) can be shown during game play). The higher is the frame-rate the more fluent is the game experience. It is often considered unacceptable to have the frame-rate lower than 30 FPS.

The frame-rate is dependent on many factors: a number of visible actors, a number of polygons that must be rendered at a given moment, etc. These parameters are very specific to each particular game. So, it is difficult to have a comparison that is beneficial to wider audiences if we were to only do experiments with our particular game. Therefore, we have conducted most of our experiments in a simple 2D environment where agents are represented as circles and objects they interact with represented as cubes. In this way we can eliminate game specific performance issues that are not related to planning.

Figure 6 shows a graph that represents the relationship between the frame-rate (vertical axis) and the number of agents (horizontal axis) in the Sims implementation. As can be seen from this graph, we were able to work with over 4000 agents in a 2D simulation and still have the comfortable frame-rate of 30 FPS. We have also measured the frame-rate in the 3D gaming environment outlined in Figure 1. There we had around 350 agents visible to the player at the frame-rate of 30 FPS. Having 400 agents reduced the frame-rate to 25 FPS.

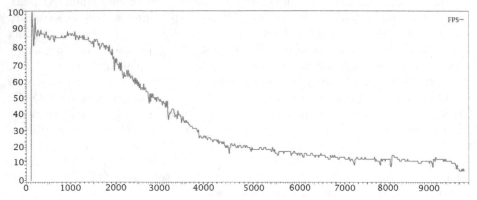

Fig. 6. Agents Controlled by a Sims like Model: Framerate vs Agent Number

Figure 7 shows the results we were able to achieve in the 2D simulation using AI Planning. Here we were only able to generate 105 agents and have the frame-rate about 30 FPS and then it would start to sharply decline. In the 3D simulation we could only have 50 agents that use planning at 30 FPS.

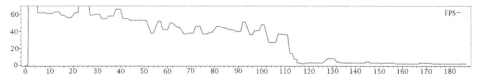

Fig. 7. Agents Controlled by a Classical Planner: Framerate vs Agent Number

These results were not very encouraging, so we have decided to modify the planning mechanism of our agents by supplying global plan memory (cache). This memory is used to routinely store the details about the current state of the planning agent, its goal, role and the generated plan. Before generating a new plan we were then checking whether there is a record in memory that contains the plan for an agent with the same role, goal and state. If such record exists then we would execute the recorded plan instead of searching for a new plan.

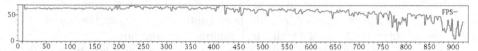

Fig. 8. Agents Controlled by a Planner with Memory: Framerate vs Agent Number

Figure 8 shows the results of using planning with memory within our 2D simulation. Unlike video games, social simulations are quite repetitive, so using plan memory resulted in significant performance improvements. We were able to achieve the performance of 30 FPS while having 770 agents present in the 2D simulation and close to 200 agents present in the 3D simulation at 30 FPS.

6   Discussion and Conclusion

We have compared two different approaches to automating agent behaviour in large scale social simulations. Both approaches relied on first building a computational model of needs and then having these needs controlling the actions the agent would choose to perform. The first approach to need satisfaction that we tested was the utility based method from The Sims game. The benefit of this method is that it is relatively simple to implement and the resulting performance is very high, potentially allowing to have thousands of agents in a simulation. But the key drawbacks of this approach are the following: the behaviour of the agents appears scripted, it is very difficult to come up with correct values for need changes that should occur when an agent interacts with an object that could satisfy them (e.g. Hunger +5 and Energy -7 offered by the fisher's fire place). If it is required to portray limited resources in the environment then The Sims implementation could be associated with believability issues, as lack of resources might lead to agents not being able to complete their plans and all resources that they use could be irreversibly lost as the fact of agents obtaining those cannot be reflected in their state. The Sims approach also has scalability problems. When adding new objects these numbers must be recomputed across the board, new finite state machines must be designed to support utilising this new object and some of the existing state machines might have to be modified if the use of this object is required in the corresponding plans. Another significant issue was supporting agent interactions with one another. The Sims approach is useful when agents act in isolation, but if they have to conduct complex tasks together it is difficult to have them synchronised without breaking believability.

The use of planning allowed to achieve more believable and emergent behaviour and solve the aforementioned synchronisation issues. It was also much easier to design the system and modify it by adding new objects. But the use of planning was associated with a significant performance loss. Through various kinds of optimisation (integrating Electronic Institutions and plan memory) we were able to achieve having 770 agents in the 2D simulation running at 30 FPS and close to 200 agents running in our particular 3D simulation at 30 FPS. There is a lot of room to optimise our 3D simulation and with improved hardware we could, of course, generate more agents. We could also overcome the agent number limitation by using classical gaming strategies like hiding agents when they are not in the line of sight or by only performing planning for the agents that the user is currently looking at and use a simpler technique.

Our concluding suggestion would be to certainly focus on planning and work on strategies to optimise it if your goal is to build a research simulation that is similar to the scenario described in this paper, where low frame rates are not very critical and where you can potentially use a powerful super computer for running the simulation. But if you are building a commercial game that needs hundreds or thousands of agents running on a personal computer then performance problems associated with planning would outweigh the believability benefits and it is better for you to follow The Sims approach to needs satisfaction. Finally, for simulations with a high degree of agent interaction (e.g. trading, working together) planning is a better choice due to increased believability and reduced design complexity.

References

1. AI Game Programmers Guild, http://gameai.com/wiki/index.php?title=The_Sims: The Sims (2011)
2. Champandard, A.J.: In-Depth Study of Planning in Top AAA Games. AiGameDev.com (February 28) (2014)
3. Crüsemann, N., van Ess, M., Hilgert, M., Salje, B.: Uruk. 5000 Jahre Megacity (2013)
4. Esteva, M.: Electronic Institutions: From Specification to Development. Ph.D. thesis, Institut d'Investigació en Intelligència Artificial (IIIA), Spain (2003)
5. Gauder, J.: Crysis 3 cost $66 million to make, can next gen sustain such budgets? GameChup Video Games News at http://www.gamechup.com/crysis-3-cost-66-million-to-make-can-next-gen-sustain-such-budgets/ (2013)
6. Ghallab, M., Nau, D., Traverso, P.: Automated Planning: Theory and Practice. Morgan Kaufmann Series in Artificial Intelligence, Elsevier (2004), https://books.google.com.au/books?id=eCj3cKC_3ikC
7. Hendler, J.A., Tate, A., Drummond, M.: AI planning: Systems and techniques. AI magazine 11(2), 61 (1990)
8. Maslow, A.H.: A theory of human motivation. Psychological review 50(4), 370–396 (1943)
9. Orkin, J.: Applying goal oriented action planning in games. In: AI Game Programming Wisdom 2, pp. 217–229. Charles River Media (2002), http://web.media.mit.edu/~jorkin/GOAP_draft_AIWisdom2_2003.pdf
10. Trescak, T., Bogdanovych, A., Simoff, S.: Populating virtual cities with diverse physiology driven crowds of intelligent agents. In: Proceedings of the Social Simulation Conference (SSC 2014). pp. 275–286 (2014)
11. Trescak, T., Bogdanovych, A., Simoff, S., Rodriguez, I.: Generating diverse ethnic groups with genetic algorithms. In: Proceedings of the 18th ACM symposium on Virtual reality software and technology. pp. 1–8. VRST '12, ACM, New York, NY, USA (2012), http://doi.acm.org/10.1145/2407336.2407338

Giving Emotional Contagion Ability to Virtual Agents in Crowds

Amyr Borges Fortes Neto[1] ✉, Catherine Pelachaud[2], and Soraia Raupp Musse[1]

[1] Pontifical Catholic University of Rio Grande do Sul (PUCRS), Porto Alegre, RS,
Brazil,
`soraia.musse@pucrs.br amyrneto@gmail.com`,
WWW home page: `http://www.inf.pucrs.br/vhlab`
[2] Institut des Systmes Intelligents et de Robotique UPMC - CNRS, Paris, France,
`catherine.pelachaud@isir.upmc.fr`

Abstract. Recent advances in crowd simulation models attempt to recreate realistic human behaviour by introducing psychological phenomena in virtual agents. In this direction, psychology studies on personality traits, emotions and emotional contagion attempt to cope with emerging behaviours such as panic spreading and fight picking. This work depicts a way to introduce a model of emotional contagion in the scope of crowd simulation. Challenges regarding the applicability of an emotional contagion model considering great number (hundreds or thousands) of agents are depicted. Results shows that the dynamics of space and time creates emergent behaviour in crowd agents that are tuned with emotional contagion phenomena and crowd behaviour as described by literature.

1 Introduction

Models of crowd simulation have been used for applications in films and video games, architecture, security and contingency plans. Films and video games usually present crowds for visual effects, generating great number of actors for epic war tales or cheering crowd background. Applications for architecture and contingency plans are usually meant to measure the security of a building project in terms of evacuation routes, corridor and stairway width, doors and passages that might result in bottlenecks. But, whatever the application is, it is always desirable to have the most realistic simulation possible, to obtain reliable results that support serious decision making.

In the pursuit of more realistic observable behaviour in virtual crowd agents, recent works on the field have incorporated psychological theory in their models. Personality traits models such as the OCEAN, also known as Big-Five [1], and Eysenck's PEN [2] has been incorporated in virtual crowds [3] [4] [5] to create heterogeneity of agent's behaviours in the crowds. Since personality can influence emotional characteristics in people, later work [6] incorporated emotion models, such as the OCC, and also emotional contagion models to allow emotions to spread in crowds.

© Springer International Publishing AG 2017
J. Beskow et al. (Eds.): IVA 2017, LNAI 10498, pp. 63–72, 2017.
DOI 10.1007/978-3-319-67401-8_7

Following the tendency of modelling characteristics of human psychology, such as personality traits, emotions and emotional contagion, and being aware that emotions can influence decision making process, the objective of this work is to incorporate a model designed to cope with emotional contagion in crowd simulation context.

2   Related Work

The pioneering work in crowd simulation is Reynolds' flocks, herds and schools [7]. Based on a particle approach, all agents have attraction (velocity matching) and repulsion forces (collision avoidance), combined with a goal force (flock centering). Other works proposed different steering methods such as Helbing's empirical Social Force Model [8], Musse and Thallman [9] approach based on group hierarchy and the HiDAC model of Pelechano [10] which aims to controlling individual agents in high density crowds. Researchers on crowd simulation have integrated models derived from psychology studies, such as OCEAN [3] and Eysenck's PEN [5]. The objective is to promote heterogeneity of agents by adjusting steering parameters according to individual personality traits. Later, emotions and emotional contagion models are introduced [6] [4], allowing agents to change behaviour and respond to other agents' actions as the simulation evolves. Durupinar [6], applies a contagion model derived form spreading of diseases proposed by Doods & Watts [11].

The work proposed by Tsai et al. [12] performs a comparison of Bosse [13] model with Durupinar model [14] (which used the same contagion model as in Durupinar [6]) and shows slightly better performance of the first over the later, according to the metrics and scenarios tested by Tsai et al. The authors suggests that the primary cause of the statistically significantly worse performance found with the epidemiological/social contagion model of Durupinar [14] is in the mechanism of contagion itself, which is probabilistic and uses a binary representation of the effect, which means that the contagion will either take place, or not, depending on a given probability threshold. The opposite would be a contagion that occurs in a constant gradual manner, depending on contagion strength and emotional levels apprised, as in in the work of Bosse et. al [13]. The main difference of this work with the work of Durupinar [6] is the emotional contagion model adopted.

In our work we use BioCrowds [22], a collision free navigation method for agents animation. In addition, we proposed to use the model proposed by Bosse et. al [24]. The goal if this method is to cope with contagion of one unspecified emotion in agents of a group. The variables involved in this model are listed in Table 1 and must be in the range $[0, 1]$.

Mathematically, Bosse and colleagues defines the emotion of an agent as a value q in the range $[0, 1]$, that represents the intensity of an unspecified emotion in a given instant. Suppose A is an agent in group G, being G defined as the set $G = \{A_1, A_2, ..., A_{N-1}\}$, the dynamic of A's emotion level is given by the

Table 1: Variables to be considered on the emotional contagion process

Variable	Purpose
q_j	Represents instantaneous emotion level of agent j.
ε_S	Represents the S agents expressiveness.
δ_R	Represents R agents emotional susceptibility.
α_{SR}	Represents the influence S has over R, notice that α_{RS} can be different from α_{SR}.
η_j	Bias to determine the models tendency to amplify or absorb emotions on agent j.
β_j	Bias tendency to amplify emotions upward or downward on agent j.
NI	Negative Impact of the amplification model.
PI	Positive Impact of the amplification model.

variation dq/dt occurred by contagion of emotions of other group members over agent A and computed by Equation 1.

$$dq_A/dt = \gamma_A \left[\eta_A \left(\beta_A PI + (1 - \beta_A) NI \right) + (1 - \eta_A) q_A^* - q_A \right]. \tag{1}$$

The resulting dq_A/dt is then clamped in the range $[0, 1]$. The channel strength γ_A is computed as in Equation 2:

$$\gamma_A = \sum_{S \in G \setminus \{A\}} \gamma_{SA}. \tag{2}$$

And γ_{SA} is the strength of emotional contagion from a sender agent S over agent A (the receiver of emotional contagion) and computed as $\gamma_{SA} = \varepsilon_S \alpha_{SA} \delta_A$. The overall group's emotional influence over agent A denoted by q_A^* is an weighted average of other agents' emotional state, and can be computed by:

$$q_A^* = \sum_{S \in G \setminus \{A\}} \omega_{SA} q_S. \tag{3}$$

And the weights ω_{SA} are proportional to the contagion channel, and are computed by:

$$\omega_{SA} = \frac{\varepsilon_S \alpha_{SA}}{\sum_{C \in G \setminus \{A\}} \varepsilon_C \alpha_{CA}}. \tag{4}$$

The amplification model, identified by the terms PI and NI in Equation 1, is designed to cope with emotional spirals [16][17], and is computed respectively as in equations: $PI = 1 - (1 - q_A^*)(1 - q_A)$ and $NI = q_A^* q_A$.

This summaries the formulation on Bosses work. The results published by the authors [24] confirm the ability of the model in simulating desired emotional behaviours, such as spirals. For such reasons, it was adopted to continue in the crowd simulation scenario.

3   Methodology of Proposed Model

The main challenge of adapting the model of Bosse et. al. [13] into BioCrowds
[22] is that the original Bosse model copes with one group of agents. In crowds,
there are several groups, as well as individuals not belonging to any group. And
they all must be able to promote and suffer emotional contagion. Another challenge is to benefit from both models: navigation and emotional contagion. The
model of emotion contagion carries emotion information and also promotes the
ability for agents to spread this information to other agents. The model of crowd
simulation carries spatio-temporal information, since agents are instantiated in a
virtual environment, and navigate in this environment as a function of time. The
variables used in this model are summarized in Table 2. To benefit from variation

Table 2: Variables of the extended model

Variable	Purpose
$q_{A_n}(t)$	is the instantaneous emotional level of agent A_n in time frame t.
ε_{A_n}	is the expressiveness of the agent A_n. It strengthen the contagion channel when A_n is the sender of emotion.
δ_{A_n}	Is the susceptibility of agent A_n. It strengthen the contagion channel when A_n is the receiver of emotion.
η_{A_n}	Is the bias that controls the amplification model and the absorption model in agent A_n, according to Equation
β_{A_n}	Bias the positive impact (PI) and negative impact (NI) in the amplification model in A_n defined in Equation 11.
og_{A_n}	determines the attenuation in the emotion contagion channel promoted by that fact that A_n does not belong to the same group as the sender.
$\boldsymbol{x}_{A_n}(t)$	determines the position of agent A_n in instant t.
$\boldsymbol{g}_{A_n}$	Denote the direction pointing to agent's A_n goal.

of agents' positions, we propose the strength of contagion to be impacted with
distance, since it might be harder to identify people's facial, gestural and vocal
expressions with increasing distance. To accomplish this feature, we propose to
replace the relationship (or attachment) measure between agents, denoted by
α_{A_i,A_j}, for a function of the distance between agents $\{A_i, A_j\} \in C$, resulting in
a new α_{A_i,A_j} which is not constant. As a result, the attachment between agents
(α) vary in time, as agents move. The variation of contagion strength is one
characteristic that differs this model from Bosse's model.

$$\alpha_{A_j A_i} = \begin{cases} min(1, 1/d) & d \leq p_{A_i} \\ 0 & d > p_{A_i} \end{cases}, \tag{5}$$

where d is the Euclidean distance between agents A_i and A_j. In order to profit
from the group information already present in crowds, we propose a measure of

outer group affinity, denoted by og_{A_n}. It measures the affinity of agent A_n to catch emotions from agents that does not belong to his/her group. So, α_{A_i,A_j}, considering group information, can be rewritten as in Equation 6.

$$\alpha'_{A_j A_i} = og_{A_i}\alpha_{A_j A_i}. \tag{6}$$

To cope with inter-group emotional contagion (since intra-group contagion is already contemplated by Bosse's model) we explore a property of the original model when the interaction is *dyadic*, i.e., interaction between exactly two agents. In this case, C equals the set $C = \{A_i, A_j\}$ with only two agents A_i and A_j. The contagion strength channel for agent A_i can be written as in Equation 7.

$$\gamma_R = \gamma_{A_i} = \sum_{A_j} \gamma_{A_j A_i}, \text{ when } A_i = R \text{ and } A_j = S. \tag{7}$$

And since A_j is the only agent in the sum, this results in Equation 8.

$$\gamma_{A_i} = \gamma_{A_j A_i} = \varepsilon_{A_j}\alpha'_{A_j A_i}\delta_{A_i}. \tag{8}$$

Also, the weights to compute q^*, denoted by ω_{SA} in Equation 3, for the dyadic particular case can be written as in Equation 9.

$$\omega_{SA} = \frac{\varepsilon_S \alpha_{SA}}{\sum_{C \in G \setminus \{A\}} \varepsilon_C \alpha_{CA}} = \omega_{A_j A_i} = \frac{\varepsilon_{A_j}\alpha'_{A_j A_i}}{\sum_{A_j} \varepsilon_{A_j}\alpha'_{A_j A_i}} = \frac{\varepsilon_{A_j}\alpha_{A_j A_i}}{\varepsilon_{A_j}\alpha_{A_j A_i}} = 1, \tag{9}$$

And the total influence of the group over agent A_i is given by q_{A_j} as in Equation 10.

$$q^*_{A_i} = \sum_{S \in G \setminus \{A_i\}} \omega_{SA_i} q_S = \sum_{A_j} \omega_{A_j A_i} q_{A_j} = q_{A_j}, \tag{10}$$

because all weights $\omega_{A_j A_i} = 1$ in the case of two agents in the group. The variation of emotional level dq/dt can now be computed by Equation 11.

$$dq_{A_i}/dt = \gamma_{A_i}\left[\eta_{A_i}\left(\beta_{A_i}PI + (1 - \beta_{A_i})NI\right) + (1 - \eta_{A_i})q_{A_j} - q_{A_i}\right], \tag{11}$$

where η_{A_i} and β_{A_i} are both parameters of agent A_i, $\gamma_{A_j A_i}$ is given by Equation 8, q_{A_i} and q_{A_j} are the current emotional level for agents A_i and A_j respectively. Also, the Positive Impact PI and the Negative Impact NI are computed by Equations 12 and 13 respectively, replacing $q^*_{A_i}$ for q_{A_j}, according to Equation 10.

$$PI = 1 - (1 - q_{A_j})(1 - q_{A_i}). \tag{12}$$

$$NI = q_{A_j}q_{A_i}. \tag{13}$$

The model must be able to manage more than one emotion, which we now denote as $e_m \in \{e_0, e_1, ..., e_{M-1}\}$, describing a scenario with M emotions. We can define one emotion profile, denoted by $E^{e_m}_{A_n}$ as in Equation 14.

$$E^{e_m}_{A_n} = <q^{e_m}_{A_n}, \varepsilon^{e_m}_{A_n}, \delta^{e_m}_{A_n}, \eta^{e_m}_{A_n}, \beta^{e_m}_{A_n}, og^{e_m}_{A_n}, g^{e_m}_{A_n}>. \tag{14}$$

And the set of all emotion profiles in a scenario, denoted by E_{A_n} for agent A_n, can be written as follows: $E_{A_n} = \{E_{A_n}^{e_0}, E_{A_n}^{e_1}, ..., E_{A_n}^{e_{M-1}}\}$. Allowing us to define agent $A_n =< E_{A_n}, x_{A_n}, p_{A_n}, g_{A_n} >$. Finally, the current emotional state of agent A_n, denoted by ψ_{A_n}, can be defined as $\psi_{A_n} = e_m \implies q_{A_n}^{e_m} = max(q_{A_n}^{e_0}, q_{A_n}^{e_1}, ..., q_{A_n}^{e_{M-1}})$.

The emotional state ψ_{A_n} is the label of the emotion denoted by e_m which has higher emotional level $q_{A_n}^{e_m}$ than any other emotion in Ψ. So, the emotion that the agent actually responds to is the one pointed by ψ_{A_n} and evaluated each simulation iteration.

Notice that the parameter g_{A_n} seems redundant with the parameters $g_{A_n}^{e_m}$ contained within each $E_{A_n}^{e_m} \in E_{A_n}$ (see Equation 14), but that is on purpose. The objective with apparent redundancy is to allow the agent to overwrite its original goal with the goal defined by its current emotional state ψ_{A_n}. This way, agents can change goals as they change emotional state. Also, goals associated to emotions are optional. If one particular emotion profile $E_{A_n}^{e_k}$ does not have a goal defined, whenever $\psi_{A_n} = e_k$ the original agent's goal g_{A_n} is used. The new variables used in the model for contagion in crowds are summarized in Table 2.

4 Simulations and Results

In all tested scenarios, there is always one agent A_0 generating emotional energy by means of upward spiral. To accomplish this, parameter $\eta_{A_0} = 0.5$ and $\beta_{A_0} = 1$. The objective is to observe how the emotional energy of A_0 will spread through the crowd. Also, it was decided that $\varepsilon_{A_i} = 0.5$ and $\delta_{A_i} = 0.5$ for all agents $A_i \in C$ where $i = [0..N - 1]$. This choice makes both expressiveness and susceptibility of agents active, but not so strong, and not so weak. Finally, a control emotion is defined in all scenarios. Since this emotion is meant as control, it does not spread ($\varepsilon = 0$ and $\delta = 0$), and is set to $q_{initial} = 0.8$ working as a threshold. The emotion A_0 creates energy is represented in RED, and the emotion used as control is represented in $BLUE$.

4.1 Standing Agents

Figure 1 shows the last simulation frame for standing crowd (agents not moving) with 50, 80 and 110 agents in scenarios with same dimensions. This way, agent density increases case-by-case. It is possible to notice that, as the number of agents increases, also more agents of the crowd change their initial status $BLUE$ to RED. This is because in low densities, agents' get isolated from each other, since the contagion is limited to the proxemics space (circles in the figure). Also, it is possible to observe that emotions converge to a monotonicity in concordance with Hatfield et. al findings [15].

4.2 Counterflow scenario

We propose varying the expressiveness (ε) and the susceptibility (δ) of the agents in group G by four manners: i) $\varepsilon_k = 0.1$ and $\delta_k = 0.9$, ii) $\varepsilon_k = 0.1$ and $\delta_k = 0.1$,

Fig. 1: Standing Agents experiment with 50, 80 and 110 agents in the crowd. In Figure 1(a) one can observe that no agents suffer contagion, because there is no agent inside A_0 interaction space. In Figure 1(b), some agents suffer contagion, but are isolated from the rest of the crowd as the circles representing interaction spaces shows. In Figure 1(c) only agent A_{45} does not suffer contagion because he/she is isolated from the rest of the crowd.

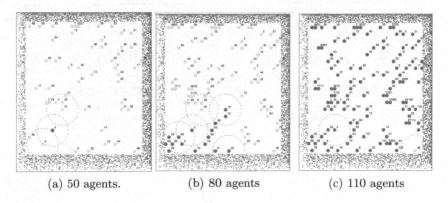

| (a) 50 agents. | (b) 80 agents | (c) 110 agents |

iii) $\varepsilon_k = 0.9$ and $\delta_k = 0.9$, and iv) $\varepsilon_k = 0.9$ and $\delta_k = 0.1$. And for every case, we want to measure the speed in which the emotion spreads in the crowd, by comparing the curves of emotions of some agents in the crowd.

In Figure 2 it is possible to observe curves of instantaneous emotional levels for the four proposed emotional profiles. In Figure 2(a), the emotion profile with agents shy (low expressiveness) and susceptible (high susceptibility) tends to achieve emotional equilibrium above threshold, meaning that the group tends to follow the influence of A_0, which is expected due to the fact that the susceptibility is set high. But Figures 2(b) and 2(c) suggests that susceptibility does not handle alone the impact of A_0 over the group and vice-versa. Actually, in both cases where group expressiveness is high the resistance of the group in changing emotional status rises. Supposedly, since group agent's expressiveness is high, giving agents have more strength to influence each other and A_0. This makes a sort of resistance (or inertia) of a group to be impacted with different emotion due to stronger contagion channel from one member of the group towards others. Other tests performed but not presented here also suggests that increasing the number of agents in the group the resistance to contagion also increases.

4.3   Same direction scenario

Finally, emotions are known to drive actions. Furthermore, emotion monotonicity is known to strengthen group bonds if they are positive emotions (such as joy) increasing feelings of acceptance in group members[20][21]. Knowing this, with the objective of measuring behavioural responses to emotions, we propose a scenario with agent A_0 generating RED energy ($\eta_{A_0} = 0.5$ and $\beta_{A_0} = 1$) , plus 110 agents (with $\eta_{A_k} = 0$) in a virtual environment of measures 17×20, and

Fig. 2: Counterflow experiment with 5 agents in G, varying emotion contagion profile in agents of group G.

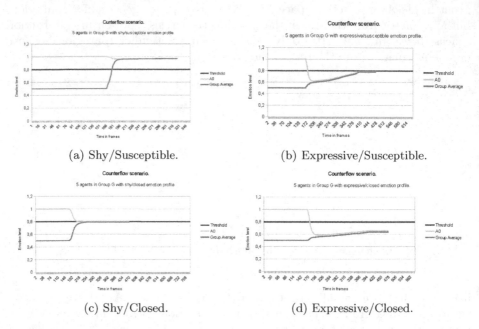

(a) Shy/Susceptible.   (b) Expressive/Susceptible.

(c) Shy/Closed.   (d) Expressive/Closed.

with two exits. In Figure 3 some frames of this scenario simulation are pictured. Figure 3(a) pictures the first frame of the simulation. There it is possible to observe agent A_0 in red in the bottom entrance of the scenario, with current goal pointing to the top exit since their emotional state is RED. The remaining agents have emotional state $\psi_{A_k} = BLUE$, indicated by their colour. No goals are associated to emotional state $BLUE$, so they remain with a goal to its current position by default. In Figure 3(c), the last frame of the simulation is pictured. Notice that many of the agents that turned RED were never inside agent's A_0 interaction space, but instead had suffered contagion indirectly from other agents, resulting in contagion beyond dyads[18].

In this experiment, it was possible to observe the emergence of a group leader. Although the scenario is configured with 111 individuals (110 plus A_0) with no group predefined, as agents interact and converge emotionally, they also approach each other as they converge to common objective.

5   Final Considerations

This work presented an emotional contagion model adapted for crowd simulation context. This gave origin to a new Bosse-Biocrowds extension which benefit from both models. To implement those features, the parameters had to be integrated into a new set of parameters, keeping information about agent movement and goal (BioCrowds) along with information related to agents' emotional profiles

Fig. 3: Agents walking in the same direction.

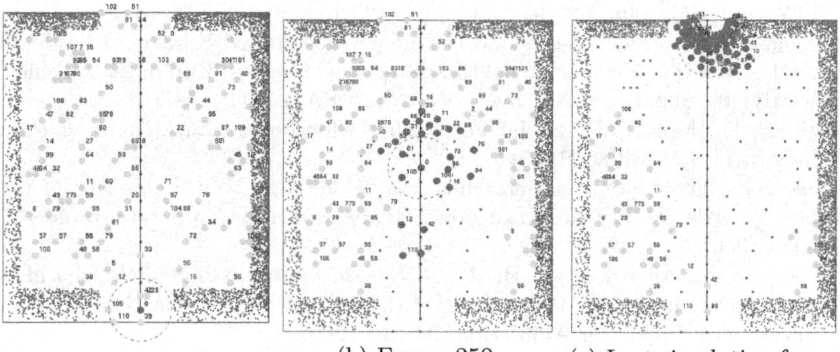

(a) First simulation frame   (b) Frame 250.   (c) Last simulation frame

(parameters derived from Bosse's model). We measured the impact of density of agents over contagion. It was observed that, due to a limitation in contagion distance imposed by our parameter setting, some groups of agents are isolated, and thus they do not suffer contagion from the leader agent. Furthermore, by associating goals with emotions, it was possible to observe agents changing their goals as they changed emotional state. As a result, agents that suffer emotional state changing due to contagion tend to converge to the same goal, getting physically close to each other. All this emergent behaviours are result of the emotional energy generated by one single agent, the position and trajectories of remaining agents in the crowd, and the time window agents keep inside each other interaction space. Results are in tune with theories by Le Bon [19] and Hatfield & Cacioppo [15].

Acknowledgements
The authors wanted to ackowledge The Brazilian Agencies CNPq and CAPES.

References

1. Goldberg, L.R.: An Alternative "Description of Personality": The Big-Five Factor Structure. Journal of Personality and Social Psychology. 59(6), 1216–1229 (1990)
2. Eysenck, H.J., Eysenck, M.W.: Personality and Individual Differences: A Natural Science Approach. Plenum Press. New York, NY (1985)
3. Durupinar, F., Allbeck J., Pelechano , N., Badler, N.: Creating Crowd Variation with the OCEAN Personality Model. Proceedings of the 7th International Joint Conference on Autonomous Agents and Multiagent Systems(AAMAS 08). Padgham, Parkes, Müller and Parsons. 1217–1220 (2008)
4. Lhommet, M., Lourdeaux D., Barthès, J.P.: Never Alone in the Crowd: A Microscopic Crowd Model Based on Emotional Contagion. 2011 IEEE/WIC/ACM International Conferences on Web Intelligence and Intelligent Agent Technology. 2, 89–92 (2011)
5. Guy, S.J., Kim, S., Lin, M.C., Manocha, D.: Simulating Heterogeneous Crowd Behavior Using Personality Trait Theory. Eurographics / ACM SIGGRAPH Symposium on Computer Animation, 43–52 (2011)

6. Durupinar F., Gdkbay, U., Aman, A., Badler N.I.: Psychological Parameters for Crowd Simulation: From Audiences to Mobs. IEEE Transactions on Visualization and Computer Graphics. 22(9), 2145–2159 (2016)
7. Reynolds, C.W.: Flocks, herds and schools: A distributed behavioral model. SIG-GRAPH '87: Proceedings of the 14th annual conference on Computer graphics and interactive techniques. ACM, New York, NY, USA. 25–34 (1987)
8. Helbing , D., Molnar, P.: Social Force Model for Pedestrian Dynamics. Physical Review E. 51, 4282–4286 (1995)
9. Musse, S.R., Thalmann, D.: Hierarchical Model for Real Time Simulation of Virtual Human Crowds. IEEE Transactions on Visualization and Computer Graphics. 7(2), 152–164 (2001)
10. Pelechano, N., Allbeck, J.M., Badler, N.I.: Controlling Individual Agents in High-density Crowd Simulation. Proceedings of the 2007 ACM SIGGRAPH/Eurographics Symposium on Computer Animation. 99–108 (2007)
11. Dodds, P.S., Watts, D.J.: A generalized model of social and biological contagion. 232(4), 587–604 (2005)
12. Tsai, J., Bowring, E., Marsella, S., Tambe, M.: Emotional Contagion with Virtual Characters. Proceedings of the 11th International Conference on Autonomous Agents and Multiagent Systems. 3, 1193–1194 (2012)
13. Bosse, T., Duell, R., Memon, Z., Treur, J., van der Wal, C.N.: A Multi-agent Model for Emotion Contagion Spirals Integrated within a Supporting Ambient Agent Model. Principles of Practice in Multi-Agent Systems. 5925, 48–67 (2009)
14. Durupınar, F.: From audiences to mobs: Crowd simulation with psychological factors. Bilkent University (2010)
15. Hatfield, E., Cacioppo, J.T., Rapson, R.L.: Emotional Contagion. Cambridge University Press, New York (1994)
16. Fredrickson, B.L., Joiner, T.: Positive emotions trigger upward spirals toward emotional well-being. Psychological science. 13(2), 172–175 (2002)
17. Poggi, I.: Enthusiasm and Its Contagion: Nature and Function. Affective Computing and Intelligent Interaction: Second International Conference. 410–421 (2007)
18. Dezecache, G., Conty, L., Chadwick, M., Philip, L., Soussignan, R., Sperber, D., Grèzes, J.: Evidence for unintentional emotional contagion beyond dyads. 8(6), e67371 (2013)
19. Bon, G.L.: The Crowd: A Study of the Popular Mind. Criminology series, Macmillan (1896)
20. Cosmides, L., Tooby, J.: Evolutionary psychology and the emotions. Handbook of emotions. 2, 91–115 (2000)
21. Spoor, J.R., Kelly, J.R.: The Evolutionary Significance of Affect in Groups: Communication and Group Bonding. 7(4), 398–412 (2004)
22. Bicho, A.L.: Da modelagem de plantas dinmica de multides: um modelo de animao comportamental bio-inspirado. University of Campinas - UNICAMP. Campinas (2009)
23. Hall, E.T.: The Hidden Dimension. A Doubleday anchor book. Anchor Books (1990)
24. Bosse, T., Duell, R., Memon, Z., Treur, J., van der Wal, C.N.: Agent-Based Modeling of Emotion Contagion in Groups. Cognitive Computation. 7(1), 111–136 (2015)

Selecting and Expressing Communicative Functions in a SAIBA-Compliant Agent Framework

Angelo Cafaro ✉², Merijn Bruijnes ✉¹, Jelte van Waterschoot¹, Catherine Pelachaud², Mariët Theune¹, and Dirk Heylen¹

¹ Human Media Interaction, University of Twente, The Netherlands
[m.bruijnes, d.k.j.heylen, m.theune,
j.b.vanwaterschoot]@utwente.nl
² CNRS-ISIR, Pierre and Marie Curie University, France
[cafaro, pelachaud]@isir.upmc.fr

Abstract. In SAIBA-compliant agent systems, the Function Markup Language (FML) is used to describe the agent's communicative functions that are transformed into utterances accompanied with appropriate non-verbal behaviours. In the context of the ARIA Framework, we propose a template-based approach, grounded in the DIT++ taxonomy, as an interface between the dialogue manager (DM) and the non-verbal behaviour generation (NVBG) components of this framework. Our approach enhances our current FML-APML implementation of FML with the capability of receiving on-the-fly generated natural language and socio-emotional parameters (e.g. emotional stance) for transforming the agent's intents in believable verbal and non-verbal behaviours in an adaptive manner.

Keywords: Dialogue management, communicative function, FML, multimodal behaviour, SAIBA

1 Introduction

Generating natural multimodal behaviour for an embodied conversational agent requires producing utterances accompanied with appropriate non-verbal behaviours and the capability to 'colour' these behaviours to adapt to the social situation [2, 15]. In a SAIBA system [7], an *Intent Planner* produces intents composed of communicative functions (and the topic) that are translated into expressive multimodal behaviours by a *Behaviour Planner*. This is typically the joint task of a Dialogue Manager (DM) on the one hand (intent planner) and a non-verbal behaviour generation (NVBG) system on the other (behaviour planner). The challenge is to dynamically create behaviour that is believable and fits the social situation.

An author can manually craft a dialogue scenario to control the display of a believable agent's social behaviour. However, this is a rigid approach that requires authoring of each utterance and, even when several variants for each utterance exist, it is likely there will be not enough variability to accommodate all social situations. In a more dynamic approach, it is difficult to retain control of the results, which might lead to unbelievable generated content. It is hard to automatically generate (non)verbal behaviour supporting, for instance, emphasis on words. For easy authoring, while escaping rigidity of pre-scripted files, we propose re-usable scripts, templates, that offer flexibility in the way their content is delivered [17].

In this paper, we propose a SAIBA-compliant interface between a DM and an NVBG system that allows the DM to dynamically instantiate the communicative functions that are sent to the NVBG. We follow a template-based approach that builds on the DIT++ taxonomy of communicative functions [3]. DIT++ supports dynamic variability of produced content, both verbal and non-verbal behaviour, while ensuring a certain degree of control over the resulting behaviours. The main challenge in this approach is defining templates that have appropriate placeholders where the system can enter or modify variables to create appropriate behaviour. Additional challenges are the automatic selection of these templates and setting the value of the variables.

The contribution of this paper is threefold: (1) We propose an enhancement to FML through the definition of FML Templates that serve as an interface between a DM and a SAIBA-compliant NVBG platform. (2) We describe the mechanism adopted by the DM to fill the placeholders provided in the FML templates. (3) We provide insights into the benefits of using a template-based FML representation within the SAIBA framework.

2 Related Work

The work presented in this paper is part of the *Artificial Retrieval of Information Assistants – Virtual Agents with Linguistic Understanding, Social skills, and Personalised Aspects* (ARIA-VALUSPA) project[3] in which we create agents that are capable of holding multimodal social interactions in challenging and unexpected situations. The demo scenario is Alice in Wonderland where the agent portrays Alice. In this paper, we describe the interface between the DM and the NVBG system of the ARIA-VALUSPA framework depicted in Figure 1 and described in Section 3.1. We have grounded our work in two standards, respectively, for describing communicative functions (DIT++) and for representing them (FML-APML).

The **Dynamic Interpretation Theory** (DIT++) taxonomy, an ISO standard [3], is a comprehensive, application-independent system for classification and analysis of dialogue with information about the communicative acts that are performed by dialogue segments (a turn can be a dialogue segment). DIT++ has been used before in the design of a DM module [6]. The **FML-APML** is an evolution of the Affective Presentation Markup Language (APML) [13] and is used by the NVBG system component in the ARIA framework described in Section 3.1. The original FML-APML tags encoded the communicative intentions of an agent following the categorization of Poggi [16]. Contrary to the representation proposed by Cafaro et al. [4], the set of tags in the FML-APML supports features regarding the timing and importance of communicative functions. The timing is specified with attributes inspired by the BML recommendations [7] and makes possible absolute or relative timings of functions with symbolic labels for referencing. Emotional states can be described and these tags also give the possibility to specify an *intensity* (from 0 to 1).

---

[3] https://aria-agent.eu

The dialogue management component in our work extends Flipper [11], a DM based on the principles from the TrindiKit DM as an information state based DM [8]. Other DM systems have been proposed lately. Rich and Sidner proposed DISCO [17], a task-based DM based on collaborative discourse theory. In addition to offering content-wise placeholders such as DISCO, our approach also supports a parametric instantiation of accompanying communicative functions (e.g. emotion and level of emphasis). Morbini et al. have created FLoReS [14], a DM that facilitates the creation of structured dialogues with the use of domain experts. We use a similar approach with forward-looking goals in the form of communicative functions, though our approach differs from FLoRes in the agent's intent generation, where we update our information state in real-time with topics of interest and emotional state of the user and insert these in behavioural templates. OpenDial is a toolkit for developing spoken dialogue systems created by Lison [10]. His main contribution was adding the possibility to learn probabilities for the responsive behaviour of the agent, even with small amounts of data, and still make it easy to author the dialogue models. The authoring of dialogues is similar to that of dialogues created with our DM Component with high-level templates, with placeholder and mapping between utterances and intents. The Virtual Human Toolkit uses question answering algorithms to select the agent's response. However, they do not utilize an information state, or an agent mental state, to alter the responses of the agent [9]. Finally, Mairesse and Walker developed PERSONAGE [12], a parametrizable NLG tool that produced text outputs varying along the extraversion personality dimension of the Big 5 [5]. In PERSONAGE a broader set of parameters is employed compared to our system, however the authors' focus is language generation whereas we propose a richer output that includes instances of speech acts (i.e. language) but is also supported by a variety of socio-emotional communicative functions later transformed into multimodal behaviour.

3 An FML-Template based Dialogue Manager

3.1 The ARIA Framework

The ARIA framework has an architecture composed of three major blocks of modules: Input, Agent Core and Output, as shown in Figure 1. Each block itself consists of a number of modules. The Input block is mainly responsible for collecting and processing audio-visual data about the user. The Social Signal Interpretation framework (SSI) [18] in the input block gathers multimodal audio-visual user data and interprets, for instance, the user's emotional state in terms of valence and arousal, and the text uttered by the user. This data is then fed to the Agent Core which analyses it to decide on the agent's response behaviour. The main component of the Agent Core is the Dialogue Manager (DM), which is an evolution of Flipper [11]. Based on the input from SSI, the Core block produces FML-APML scripts that serve as input for the Output generation block. In the Output block, the NVBG component is responsible for rendering the agent, displaying animated behaviour and playing synthesized speech using the CereVoice Engine text-to-speech (TTS) tool developed by CereProc [1]. The three blocks use ActiveMQ as a message broker for communication.

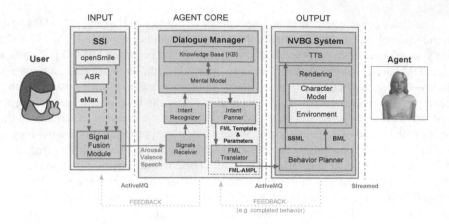

Fig. 1. Overview of the ARIA Framework architecture.

This paper focuses on the interface between the Agent Core and the Output gener-ation block, also highlighted in Figure 1 by the dashed red square. More specifically, we describe the working mechanism of our DM (Section 3.2) and the mechanism that allows it to interface with the NVBG component (Sections 3.3 and 3.4)[4].

3.2 FML-Templates

The DM decides when the agent needs to communicate with the user and what to say. Expressing this intent is done via the FML Translator, which communicates with the NVBG component in order to generate, in real-time, the appropriate verbal and non-verbal behaviour. The DM provides the FML Translator two types of information: (1) an FML Template, and (2) a set of parameters that depend on the selected template. These parameters are retrieved from the information state to add variability in the behaviour specified in the FML template. In this section we describe the set of FML Templates that we have created, the available parameters in these templates, the process to choose a template and the values for its parameters and the final transformation to FML-APML.

FML Templates are based on the DIT++ taxonomy and are categorized accordingly. The DIT++ taxonomy describes dialogue segments in terms of communicative func-tions. When the agent receives user input the communicative function of this input can be used to formulate an appropriate response. A dialogue segment can have multiple functions. We split up such segments into smaller units so that only one communicative function remains per unit. For example, assuming that the user asks a question (e.g. a DIT++ *set question*) as interpreted by the Intent Recognizer which is part of the Agent Core (see Fig. 1), an agent's response can indicate that it understands there was a ques-tion (i.e. *positive feedback* function) and, at the same time, can be a reply to the question (computed by the Intent Planner as an *inform* function as a response). For each of the

---

[4] The code is provided at: https://github.com/ARIA-VALUSPA/ARIA-System. Additionally, an example scenario is provided at: https://github.com/ARIA-VALUSPA/ARIA-System/wiki/Documentation.

relevant communicative functions contained within DIT++, we created an FML Template with a subset of parameters (described in the following section). An overview of the DIT++ communicative functions in our FML Templates is shown in Table 1.

In addition to the existing DIT++ communicative functions *answer, agreement,* and *disagreement* (subfunctions of *inform*), we need additional *inform* functions in order to fine-tune the way the agent provides information. DIT++ supports adding more specific communicative functions [3], so we introduce two more inform subfunctions, *elaborate* and *explain*, which are used to give more examples and an explanation of a topic.

Table 1. An overview of our FML-Templates categorized according to DIT++ taxonomy.

Class	Goal	Sub-classes
Information Transfer	Obtain or provide information	Question: set I choice I prop I check Inform: agreement I disagreement I answer I elaborate I explain
Feedback	Provide or elicit information about the processing of the previous utterance(s)	Auto: positive I negative Allo: positive I negative Elicitation
Interaction	Structure the dialogue (e.g. turn or topic management)	Contact: check I indication Time: stalling I pausing Turn: take I accept I grab I keep I assign I release Topic: introduction I preclosing I announceShift
Social Obligations	Social policies during the dialogue	Salutation: initial I return Introduction: initial I return Gratitude: initial I return Apology: initial I return Valediction: initial I return

FML Template Parameters. The DM can modify parameters in FML Templates to 'colour' the agent's behaviour. The parameters are in the form of XML elements and their attributes as shown in Table 2. The **Element** column indicates the name of an element as it appears in the FML Template. The three last elements enhance FML-APML with additional constructs supporting placeholders for adding variability as described in

Table 2. The parameters of our FML Templates are elements and changeable attribute values.

Element	Attribute
emotion	type, intensity, importance
emphasis	level, importance
certainty	type, intensity, importance
voice	type
var	type
alternative	type, name
alt-option	ref

this section. The **Attribute** column indicates an element's attribute that has a selectable or changeable value (i.e. by the DM). The attribute *type* of a **<var>** element can be: *sentence*, *topic*, *user*, or *agent*. The *type* for **<certainty>** can be *none*, *uncertain*, or *certain*. The **<alternative>** elements have a *type* attribute that can be: *static*, *dynamic*, or *selectable*. The *name* attribute is a string used to link multiple selectable alternative tags by name. The **<alt-option>** elements can be children of selectable alternatives and their *ref* attribute is used for choosing a specific one. When multiple selectable alternatives have the same name (i.e. they are linked), the given alt-option is selected in all linked selectable alternatives whereas the other alt-options are discarded (see the example in the next section for more details). The attributes *intensity*, *importance*, and *level* are float values ([0..1]).

Standard FML-APML tags. The **<emotion>** tag has a *type*, *intensity* and *importance* attribute. This tag sets the emotion the agent should express and it can be combined with other communicative functions. The **<emphasis>** tag, if it is present in a template, emphasizes verbally and non-verbally a defined part of the agent's speech. The **<certainty>** tag allows the DM to specify whether a communicative function should be expressed (via non-verbal behaviours) with certitude or incertitude. The **<voice>** tag has originally been defined within the CereVoice Engine to synthesize speech with different emotional stances. It is now included in FML-APML and its attribute, named type, can have four possible values supported by the CereVoice Engine (angry, happy, calm, sad).

Additional tags. Our FML Templates contain additional tags augmenting FML-APML. We defined these additional tags on top of the standard FML-APML ones to overcome the limit of using pre-scripted FML-APML instances and to support more variability in dialogue and behaviour generation phases. We created tags that are placeholders for words and full sentences, and tags that are constructs for adding variability to the pre-defined result (i.e. the FML script that is sent to the NVBG system).

A **<var>** is a placeholder for constituents. For instance a sentence, a topic, or the name of the user or agent. One example use is self-referencing of the agent: "Hello, I am **<var type="agent">**".

An **<alternative>** is a placeholder that supports alternative texts or FML-c blocks of elements that can be selected. Three alternative types exist: *static*, *selectable* and *dynamic*. A **static** alternative contains a list of child tags that include FML content. When present, one of the alt-option children is randomly selected with a uniform distribution. A static alternative allows the DM to fully delegate the generation of the FML to the FML Translator. However, changes or additions to this construct need to be scripted *before runtime*. An example of a static alternative tag is shown in listing 1.1.

```
<alternative id="alt1" type="static">
  <alt-option>For <tm id="tm1"/>instance:</alt-option>
  <alt-option>For <tm id="tm1"/>example:</alt-option>
</alternative>
```

Listing 1.1. Example of a static alternative.

With a **selectable** alternative it is possible to conditionally select one of the alt-options that are available via the *ref* attribute, as opposed to randomly selecting one of them. The Agent Core has full control over the resulting FML-APML sent to the NVBG by choosing which alternative should be produced. Multiple chunks of selectable alternatives can be linked together if they have the same *name* attribute. The result is that the selected alt-option (via *ref*) is also selected for the other linked selectable alternatives. In the following example, giving Bob as input value for the user name (i.e. var) the "named" alt-option of the *positive-feedback* selectable alternative yields to "Yes Bob" when chosen. The emphasis tag belonging to the named alt-option in the second alternative (i.e. alt2) is also selected as it belongs to a linked alternative, see listing 1.2.

A **dynamic** alternative receives as input a list of semicolon separated items (e.g. words) of which one is randomly selected with a uniform distribution probability. This allows the DM to change the possible variations *at runtime*, but it has the disadvantage of requiring the DM to provide actual text content. For example, the dynamic alternative tag shown below could take from the DM a list of items such as: *"bike; car; foot"* (see listing 1.3).

```
<speech id="s1">
<alternative id="alt1" name="positive-feedback" type="selectable">
 <alt-option ref="named">Yes <tm id="tm0"/><var id="var1" type="user"/><tm id="tm1
      "/></alt-option>
 <alt-option ref="no-named">Yes</alt-option>
</alternative>
</speech>
<alternative id="alt2" name="positive-feedback" type="selectable">
 <alt-option ref="named"><emphasis id="emp1" start="s1:tm0" level="strong" end="
      s1:tm1" importance="1"/></alt-option>
 <alt-option ref="no-named"></alt-option>
</alternative>
```

Listing 1.2. Example of a selectable alternative.

```
<tm id="tm0"/>
 <alternative id="alt1" type="dynamic"/>.
<tm id="tm1"/>
```

Listing 1.3. Example of a dynamic-alternative.

Finally, **<var>** and **<alternative>** tags can be **nested**. It is possible to create nested structures by including within any type of alternative: **<var>** elements or other **<alternative>** types (n.b. within one level of recursion though).

3.3 Dialogue Management as FML Template Selection

Selecting and modifying FML Templates is described as a pipeline. After a new utterance has been detected by SSI, the Intent Recognizer computes the user's communicative functions. More specifically, an NLP component extracts keywords (based on nouns/verbs/adjectives) to determine the topic of the user's utterance and the communicative functions according to DIT++. The result of this computation is also stored in the agent's mental model. Next, the Intent Planner in the Agent Core has internal precondition rules that are activated when matching with the user's communicative function and topic of interest. Each FML Template is coupled to a unique set of preconditions and once those are activated, the corresponding FML Template is chosen.

Depending on the Template, the Intent Planner needs to select the appropriate values for the available parameters. Those are retrieved from the agent's mental state. The agent's utterances are currently stored in an internal database and are constrained to the Alice in Wonderland scenario. Additionally, the agent's utterance can be augmented with an emotional expression (e.g. a frown or a raise in pitch when angry). Our DM supports both a static way of defining the agent's emotion (e.g. always happy, sad) or a more dynamic way (e.g. mirroring the user's emotion, or taking the output of computational models of emotions).

Once all parameters have been retrieved, the FML Translator takes the FML Template and the required parameters as input and generates a full FML-APML script that is compliant with the SAIBA behaviour planner within the NVBG system.

3.4 FML Translator

The job of the FML Translator is to transform a given FML template and its input parameters into an FML-APML script that is processable by the NVBG system for generating synthesized speech and accompanying non-verbal behaviour. The FML Translator algorithm takes the following steps to accomplish this transformation task:

1. Find *selectable* <**alternative**> elements and replace them with the selected alternative-item's content.
2. Find *dynamic* <**alternative**> elements, randomly choose an alternative from the list of items given in input and replace it.
3. Find *static* <**alternative**> elements, randomly choose an alternative's content and discard the others in the final FML-APML script.
4. Find <**var**> elements and replace those according to the given DM input.
5. Find <**voice**> tags (for CereVoice) and replace the emotion attribute OR remove the voice brackets if input is not given.
6. Find and replace values for FML attributes (e.g. emotion *type* and *intensity*).

Behaviour Generation. The NVBG system is a SAIBA-compliant platform that expects to receive communicative functions from an intent planner represented in FML. The FML-APML implementation of FML is currently used. FML-APML input is transformed to BML (i.e. behaviour) according to a *Multimodal Behaviour Lexicon* and probabilistic rules. The *lexicon* can be seen as a dictionary in which an entry is a communicative function (described with category and type). For each entry (i.e. function), a set of behaviours (involving facial expressions, gaze, gestures, etc...) to accomplish the function is proposed along with several alternatives that are named *behaviour sets*. Each behaviour set comes with a probability determining the likelihood of being chosen among the others in the entry. A basic lexicon can have a discrete uniform distribution associated to each behaviour set, for example, each alternative has an equal probability of being chosen with respect to the other alternatives in the same entry. As a result, any given set of communicative functions represented in FML-APML can be accomplished in different ways.

4   Conclusions and Future Work

We have created an interface that offers variability content-wise, but also at a functional level thanks to the possibility of choosing, for example, the emotional expression and emphasis. In general, basing the templates on a taxonomy of communicative functions provides a solid background for the DM to work with. The templates do not only deal with generated natural language, but also include a standard representation of communicative functions which makes transforming the given input into multimodal generated verbal and non-verbal behaviour a simpler task for the NVBG system. In our ARIA Framework, the agent combines basic NLP, social signal detection, and communicative functions planning to optimally structure the dialogue with the user. The system is modular and can be extended (e.g. with emotion and natural language generation engines) to achieve more flexibility and variability.

We have proposed a mixed approach of control over audio-visual results of generated multimodal behaviour while still leaving room for variability. It should be remarked that the more dynamically content has to be generated (e.g. using dynamic alternatives) the more intelligent the decision-making of the DM needs to be. For instance, automatically filling a dynamic alternative list with appropriate verbal content requires natural language understanding: the agent needs to respond appropriately to the content of the user's utterance. Static alternatives offer the advantage of yielding more controlled results by reducing the burden of decision-making in the DM and delegating it to the transformation phase (i.e. FML Translator). However, variability can only be obtained with costly off-line authoring. Finally, selectable alternatives represent a compromise between the two. It allows an author to prepare what can be said while offering the DM the capability to select appropriate behaviour.

Authoring of a dialogue scenario is one of the main efforts when developing an agent in most frameworks. By utilizing FML Templates, the author can reuse dialogue features that occur often. In addition, as a dialogue scenario grows over time, the pool from which to pick a template to reuse becomes larger.

Some limitations need to be addressed in future work. First, a sentence provided as input clause is not divided in smaller segments of information. The DM should be able to point to parts of a sentence with more accuracy. This would allow the agent to refer to specific information from a segment of a sentence it has said. This is relevant, for example, when the agent is interrupted and needs to determine whether the information contained in a segment was understood. We plan to overcome this issue by adding a step to the transformation process that takes into account the presence of special markers within a sentence indicating specific portions to emphasize, and make more precise the generated emphasis behaviour. Finally, authoring of templates, attributes, and values can become complex with large dialogue scenarios. A GUI editor would benefit our approach and the other SAIBA-compliant agent systems, and would make authoring considerably easier. Developments towards such an editor are under way.

Acknowledgements

This work is supported by the European project H2020 ARIA-VALUSPA. We are grateful to Alexandru Ghitulescu for his help in developing the FML Translator.

References

1. Aylett, M., Pidcock, C.: The CereVoice Characterful Speech Synthesiser SDK. In: Pelachaud, C., Martin, J.C., André, E., Chollet, G., Karpouzis, K., Pelé, D. (eds.) Intelligent Virtual Agents, LNCS, vol. 4722, pp. 413–414. Springer (2007)
2. Bruijnes, M.: Believable suspect agents: response and interpersonal style selection for an artificial suspect. Ph.D. thesis, University of Twente (2016), sIKS dissertation no. 2016-39
3. Bunt, H., Alexandersson, J., Choe, J.W., Fang, A.C., Hasida, K., Petukhova, V., Popescu-Belis, A., Traum, D.R.: Iso 24617-2: A semantically-based standard for dialogue annotation. In: LREC. pp. 430–437 (2012)
4. Cafaro, A., Vilhjálmsson, H., Bickmore, T., Heylen, D., Pelachaud, C.: Representing Communicative Functions in SAIBA with a Unified Function Markup Language. In: Bickmore, T., Marsella, S., Sidner, C. (eds.) Intelligent Virtual Agents, Lecture Notes in Computer Science, vol. 8637, pp. 81–94. Springer International Publishing (2014)
5. Goldberg, L.R.: An alternative "description of personality": the big-five factor structure. Journal of Personality and Social Psychology 59(6), 1216–1229 (1990)
6. Keizer, S., Bunt, H., Petukhova, V.: Multidimensional dialogue management. In: van den Bosch, A., Bouma, G. (eds.) Interactive Multi-modal Question-Answering, pp. 57–86. Springer (2011)
7. Kopp, S., Krenn, B., Marsella, S., Marshall, A.N., Pelachaud, C., Pirker, H., Thórisson, K.R., Vilhjálmsson, H.H.: Towards a common framework for multimodal generation: The behavior markup language. In: Proceedings of the 6th international conference on Intelligent Virtual Agents. pp. 205–217. IVA'06, Springer-Verlag, Berlin, Heidelberg (2006)
8. Larsson, S., Traum, D.R.: Information state and dialogue management in the TRINDI Dialogue Move Engine Toolkit. Natural Language Engineering 6(3&4), 323–340 (2000)
9. Leuski, A., Traum, D.: NPCEditor: Creating Virtual Human Dialogue Using Information Retrieval Techniques. AI Magazine 32(2), 42–56 (Jul 2011)
10. Lison, P.: Structured probabilistic modelling for dialogue management. Ph.D. thesis, University of Oslo (2013)
11. ter Maat, M., Heylen, D.: Flipper: An Information State Component for Spoken Dialogue Systems. In: International Workshop on Intelligent Virtual Agents. pp. 470–472 (2011)
12. Mairesse, F., Walker, M.: PERSONAGE: Personality Generation for Dialogue. In: Proceedings of the 45th Annual Meeting of the Association of Computational Linguistics. vol. 45, pp. 496–503. Association for Computational Linguistics (2007)
13. Mancini, M., Pelachaud, C.: The FML-APML language. In: Why Conversational Agents do what they do. Workshop on Functional Representations for Generating Conversational Agents Behavior at AAMAS (2008)
14. Morbini, F., DeVault, D., Sagae, K., Gerten, J., Nazarian, A., Traum, D.: FLoReS: A Forward Looking, Reward Seeking, Dialogue Manager. In: Natural Interaction with Robots, Knowbots and Smartphones, pp. 313–325. Springer (2014)
15. Ochs, M., Sabouret, N., Corruble, V.: Simulation of the dynamics of nonplayer characters' emotions and social relations in games. IEEE Transactions on Computational Intelligence and AI in Games 1(4), 281–297 (2009)
16. Poggi, I.: Mind, hands, face and body: A goal and belief view of multimodal communication. Weidler Buchverlag Berlin (2007)
17. Rich, C., Sidner, C.L.: Using Collaborative Discourse Theory to Partially Automate Dialogue Tree Authoring. In: Proceedings of the 12th International Conference on IVAs. pp. 327–340. Springer-Verlag, Berlin, Heidelberg (2012)
18. Wagner, J., Lingenfelser, F., Baur, T., Damian, I., Kistler, F., André, E.: The social signal interpretation (SSI) framework: multimodal signal processing and recognition in real-time. In: Proceedings of the 21st ACM International Conference on Multimedia. pp. 831–834 (2013)

Racing Heart and Sweaty Palms

What Influences Users' Self-Assessments and Physiological Signals When Interacting With Virtual Audiences?

Mathieu Chollet ✉, Talie Massachi, and Stefan Scherer

Institute for Creative Technologies, University of Southern California, 12015
Waterfront Drive, Playa Vista, CA, USA
{mchollet, tmassachi, scherer}@ict.usc.edu

Abstract. In psychotherapy, virtual audiences have been shown to promote successful outcomes when used to help treating public speaking anxiety. Additionally, early experiments have shown its potential to help improve public speaking ability. However, it is still unclear to what extent certain factors, such as audience non-verbal behaviors, impact users when interacting with a virtual audience. In this paper, we design an experimental study to investigate users' self-assessments and physiological states when interacting with a virtual audience. Our results showed that virtual audience behaviors did not influence participants self-assessments or physiological responses, which were instead predominantly determined by participants' prior anxiety levels.

Keywords: Virtual Audience, Public Speaking, Physiological State

1   Introduction

Interactive systems that use virtual agents are becoming increasingly common as tools to train social skills or mitigate social phobias. Virtual audiences, collections of virtual agents situated in a virtual environment that simulate a public speaking situation, are an instance of such interactive systems that have been proposed for treating public speaking anxiety and for improving public speaking ability. Clinical trials have shown that virtual audiences can be beneficial for treating public speaking anxiety as part of a larger psychotherapy treatment [9, 8]. In a previous study, we investigated whether they could also be beneficial in improving public speaking skills; we found that interactive virtual audiences led to positive training outcomes while simultaneously receiving high ratings of engagement [3].

Early experiments have shown that virtual audiences displaying different behaviors can affect the level of anxiety participants experience [7]. However, it is only recently that the perception of virtual audience behaviors was systematically investigated [5, 2], and it is still unclear exactly what affects a user's self-efficacy and psychological state when interacting with virtual audiences, in particular to what extent those are influenced by virtual audience behaviors. In this paper, we present an experiment where we exposed participants to virtual

J. Beskow et al. (Eds.): IVA 2017, LNAI 10498, pp. 83–86, 2017.
DOI 10.1007/978-3-319-67401-8_9

audiences varying their behavior through the course of the participants' presentations. We investigated the impact of audience behaviors and users' prior levels of public speaking anxiety on their self-assessments and physiological signals.

2   Experimental Study

We recruited 28 participants (14F, 14M) from a pool of students and interns working at our institute during the summer 2016. These participants performed public speaking presentations in front of a large LCD screen showing a life-size audience. Before the experiment, they filled out a demographics questionnaire and the Personal Report of Confidence as a Speaker (PRCS) [6]. The participants were recorded through a variety of sensors: a webcam (centered on their face for monitoring facial expressions), a Microsoft Kinect and a microphone. Additionally, an Empatica E4 wristband[1] was used in order to capture participants' electrodermal activity (EDA) and heart rate (HR).

The participants' task was to realize 4 impromptu presentations. Before each presentation, the participant was given a list of controversial topics (*e.g.* "The two-party system makes the USA ungovernable"), accompanied by suggestions of figures and talking points related to the topics. After selecting one topic, the participant was given 5 minutes to prepare notes and was then instructed to make a 5 minutes presentation about this topic in front of a virtual audience. We used the Cicero virtual audience system, which can express various levels of audience arousal and valence through audience non-verbal behavior [2]. During each of those presentations, the virtual audience was configured to behave following a fixed set of four valence trajectories. The set of trajectories constituted the experimental condition, and was randomly chosen within a set of 6 conditions. For instance, in the $HNHL$ condition, the audience started in a high valence state, gradually changed its behavior to display a neutral valence after 45 seconds (HN), then back to positive (NH), and finally ended in a low valence state (HL). Each of the trajectories lasted for 45 seconds. Between each trajectory, a 5-second pop-up appeared on the screen, asking the participant to give a self-rating of their performance with a hands gesture (holding out the number of fingers corresponding to their self-rating on a 5-scale). After the first 3 minutes, the audience then picked trajectories randomly, and continued behaving until the participant was finished.

3   Results

In this section, we describe the statistical analyses we conducted on the collected data to explore four research hypotheses.

H1a: self-assessments are affected by audience behavior - For this analysis, we group participants' self-assessments based on which audience trajectory they follow (*e.g.* HL is group 1, NL is group 2, *etc*). For all 6 trajectory

---

[1] https://www.empatica.com/e4-wristband

types, mean scores were in the $[3.46, 3.74]$ interval with standard deviations in the $[0.89, 1.03]$. There were no statistically significant differences between group means as determined by one-way analysis of variance (ANOVA) comparing the effect of the audience trajectory type on self-assessment scores ($F(5, 408) = 1.40$, $p = 0.22$). This result indicates that the audience behavior did not seem to alter the participants' self-assessments, therefore we reject **H1a**.

H1b: self-assessments are affected by anxiety - We conduct additional analyses to try to identify whether participants' public speaking anxiety levels, obtained by using their answers to the PRCS questionnaire, influenced their self-assessments. From the PRCS questionnaires, we extract one anxiety value ($prcs \in [0, 1]$) per participant, and we group participants into 3 groups depending on their public speaking anxiety levels: low-anxiety group ($prcs <= 0.33$, self-assessments: $Mean = 3.93$, $SD = 0.83$), mid-anxiety group ($0.33 < prcs <= 0.66$, $Mean = 3.42$, $SD = 0.85$) and high anxiety group ($0.66 < prcs <= 1$, $Mean = 2.78$, $SD = 0.89$). An ANOVA showed that the effect of prior anxiety on self-assessments was significant ($F(2, 411) = 48.07, p < 0.001$). Post-hoc t-tests showed a significant difference between the three different group pairs: **H1b** is confirmed (Low and Mid: $t(349) = 5.7, p < 0.001$. Low and High: $t(288) = 9.5, p < 0.001$. Mid and High: $t(218) = 5.0, p < 0.001$).

H2a: participants' physiological states are affected by audience behavior - We realize correlation analyses between physiological features and the audience behavior trajectory. We assign an integer ($\in \{-2, -1, +1, +2\}$) to the audience trajectories according to the valence change they correspond to; for instance, the trajectory HL corresponds to a strong negative change and is assigned -2. We computed a number of physiological features, such as the mean and standard deviations of the raw EDA and HR signals, as well features extracted from these with specialized software [1, 4], such as features of the phasic component of the skin conductance response, and heart rate variability features. We did not find any significant correlations between the audience trajectory valence integers and any of the physiological measures we collected. All the correlation coefficients were found to be inferior to 0.05, with $p > 0.3$. Thus, **H2a** is rejected.

H2b: participants' physiological states are affected by public speaking anxiety - We conduct further correlation analyses to determine whether participants' self-reported public speaking anxiety was related to variations in users' physiological signals. We found significant negative correlations between anxiety scores and questionnaire answers and physiological features. The more anxious participants felt a lower arousal while interacting with the audience than less anxious participants, confirming **H2b**. Additionally, we found significant negative correlations between HRV and anxiety scores, e.g. for $RMSSD$ (Root Mean Square of the Successive Differences), a common measure of HRV: $\rho = -0.27, p = 0.000$. This is unsurprising, as HRV is related to stronger emotional regulation capabilities, which presumably would lead to lower apprehensions about public speaking and perhaps higher enthusiasm to participate in a public speaking situation.

4 Conclusion

The results of our study show that our virtual audience stimuli were unable to have a significant impact on the participants, both on the level of their self-assessments, and physiological signals. Instead, we found that the prior level of public speaking anxiety had a strong effect on the self-assessments of speakers, validating. On the physiological level, while the audience's behaviors did not affect the participants, we found that the participants that displayed higher self-assessments were significantly more aroused. Both those results indicate that most of the variation in user experience when interacting with our virtual audience stimuli were determined by participants' public speaking anxiety levels. It is unsurprising that more confident participants could be more likely to attribute higher scores to their presentations. Finally, we observed that more anxious participants experienced less physiological arousal. An interpretation of this result could be that they were more withdrawn from the interaction compared to confident subjects who would perhaps engage more enthusiastically with the system.

References

1. Benedek, M., Kaernbach, C.: A continuous measure of phasic electrodermal activity. Journal of neuroscience methods 190(1), 80–91 (2010)
2. Chollet, M., Chandrashekhar, N., Shapiro, A., Morency, L.P., Scherer, S.: Manipulating the perception of virtual audiences using crowdsourced behaviors. In: International Conference on Intelligent Virtual Agents. pp. 164–174. Springer (2016)
3. Chollet, M., Wortwein, T., Morency, L.P., Shapiro, A., Scherer, S.: Exploring Feedback Strategies to Improve Public Speaking: An Interactive Virtual Audience Framework. In: Proceedings of UbiComp 2015. ACM, Osaka, Japan (2015)
4. Geisler, F.C., Vennewald, N., Kubiak, T., Weber, H.: The impact of heart rate variability on subjective well-being is mediated by emotion regulation. Personality and Individual Differences 49(7), 723–728 (2010)
5. Kang, N., Brinkman, W.P., van Riemsdijk, M.B., Neerincx, M.: The design of virtual audiences: Noticeable and recognizable behavioral styles. Computers in Human Behavior 55, 680–694 (2016)
6. Paul, G.: Insight vs. Desensitization in Psychotherapy: An Experiment in Anxiety Reduction. Stanford University Press (1966)
7. Pertaub, D.P., Slater, M., Barker, C.: An experiment on public speaking anxiety in response to three different types of virtual audience. Presence: Teleoperators and virtual environments 11(1), 68–78 (Feb 2002)
8. Price, M., Anderson, P.L.: Outcome expectancy as a predictor of treatment response in cognitive behavioral therapy for public speaking fears within social anxiety disorder. Psychotherapy 49(2), 173 (2012)
9. Safir, M.P., Wallach, H.S., Bar-Zvi, M.: Virtual reality cognitive-behavior therapy for public speaking anxiety: one-year follow-up. Behavior modification p. 0145445511429999 (2011)

Effects of Social Priming on Social Presence with Intelligent Virtual Agents

Salam Daher ✉[1], Kangsoo Kim[1] Myungho Lee[1], Ryan Schubert[2],
Gerd Bruder[1], Jeremy Bailenson[3], and Greg Welch[1]

[1] University of Central Florida, Orlando FL 32816, USA,
salam@knights.ucf.edu
[2] University of North Carolina, Chapel Hill, NC 27599, USA,
[3] Stanford University, Stanford, CA 94305, USA

Abstract. This paper explores whether witnessing an Intelligent Virtual Agent (IVA) in what appears to be a socially engaging discussion with a Confederate Virtual Agent (CVA) prior to a direct interaction, can prime a person to feel and behave more socially engaged with the IVA in a subsequent interaction. To explore this social priming phenomenon, we conducted an experiment in which participants in a control group had no priming while those in an experimental group were briefly exposed to an engaging social interaction between an IVA and a nearby CVA (i.e. a virtual actor). The participants primed by exposure to the brief CVA-IVA interaction reported being significantly more excited and alert, perceiving the IVA as more responsive, and showed significantly higher measures of Co-Presence, Attentional Allocation, and Message Understanding dimensions of social presence for the IVA, compared to those who were not primed.

Keywords: Virtual Agent, Virtual Human, Social Priming, Social Presence, Co-Presence

1 Introduction

An intelligent virtual agent (IVA) can provide a flexible and versatile means to communicate verbal and spatial information with real humans. IVAs can be especially valuable when the presence of an actual human is not safe or feasible, such as in medical emergencies or military training. An IVA can be embedded not only in immersive virtual environments but also in the real world via augmented reality technologies to share the physical space with real humans [20]. For IVAs, it is desirable to facilitate a high sense of presence, co-presence, and social presence in order to elicit behavior in real humans that matches what can be observed between humans in the real world [9]. Lombard and Ditton define *presence* as the sense of non-mediation, which means that one can perceive presence via a technological medium if one can be oblivious to the existence of the medium [21]. There are many interpretations of the terms *social presence* and *co-presence*, e.g., see [7]. Goffman et al. indicate that *co-presence* exists when

© Springer International Publishing AG 2017
J. Beskow et al. (Eds.): IVA 2017, LNAI 10498, pp. 87–100, 2017.
DOI 10.1007/978-3-319-67401-8_10

people sensed that they were able to perceive others and that others were able to actively perceive them [12]. Blascovich et al. define *social presence* both as a "psychological state in which the individual perceives himself or herself as existing within an *interpersonal* environment" (emphasis added) and "the degree to which one believes that he or she is in the presence of, and interacting with, other veritable human beings." [5, 6]. Harms and Biocca illustrated co-presence as one of several dimensions that make up social presence, and they evaluated the validity of their social presence measures with questionnaires [13]. While there is no universal agreement on the definitions of these terms, for the purpose of this paper we consider *social presence* to be one's sense of being socially connected with the other, and *co-presence* to be one's sense of the other person's presence.

Most previous research on interaction with IVAs focused on the perceived behavioral realism *while* directly interacting with the IVA. However, we believe that the observed behaviors *prior to* such direct interaction will have an important influence on the initial and perhaps lasting impression of the IVA. For example, there is evidence from psychology that perceptions of intelligence and disposition can be influenced by observations of a person's behavior prior to an interaction and an individual's apparent mood can be "contagious"—transferred to another person via implicit nonverbal behaviors [3, 8, 32].

In this paper, we explore the question of whether social presence can also be contagious. We use the word "Confederate" to indicate that the person is intentionally part of the experiment even though the participants may *not* think of that person as part of the experiment. Specifically, we used a *confederate virtual agent* or CVA. We present an experiment in which we test whether perceiving a socially engaging interpersonal discussion between an IVA and a CVA—i.e., exhibiting apparent social presence—can subsequently lead to the participant feeling increased excitement, alertness, and social presence with respect to the IVA.

This paper is structured as follows: Section 2 provides background information on IVAs, behavioral models, priming, and presence. Section 3 describes our experiment in which we analyze effects of an initial interaction between an IVA and a CVA on the subsequent perception of social presence with the IVA. Section 4 presents the results, which are discussed in Section 5. Section 6 concisely summarizes our experiment, the results, and presents our conclusions.

2   Background

While IVAs can be used as a replacement for real humans in certain situations, people usually do not treat an IVA exactly as they would treat a real human. For instance, in studies where medical students interacted with either an IVA or a real human pretending to have the same symptoms, participants appeared less engaged, sincere, and interested, and had a poorer attitude towards the IVA [30]. In an experiment with a computer graphics representation of an IVA, its advice was more rarely sought out compared to a physically present robot [25]. Often people treat IVAs as mere pixels instead of replacements for humans, even when compared to robots that occupy a physical space. One explanation for this phenomenon is the low sense of presence, social presence, and co-presence induced by the IVA. In this paper we aim to increase the sense of social presence by exposing participants to a "social priming" *before* the interaction with the IVA.

Bailenson et al. studied participants' sense of co-presence in a multi-user shared immersive virtual environment while manipulating the non-verbal behavior of their virtual self-representations. The participants reported a higher sense of co-presence in a condition with head movement compared to the other conditions [1]. Garau et al. evaluated participants' responses, including presence, co-presence, and physiological signals, with respect to an IVA's degree of responsiveness. Their results did not show a significant relationship between perceived co-presence and the IVA's degree of responsiveness. However, they did suggest a link between higher levels of co-presence and participants who reported using computers less [11]. We took these findings into consideration while designing the study and analyzing the data.

While there are multiple possibilities for how the sense of social presence or co-presence of an IVA can be improved through modifications to its behavior *during* an interaction [2, 11, 15], the motivation for our work comes from exploring what could be done with the IVA *prior to* such a direct interaction.

Mood and even racial biases can be "contagious", i.e., transferred to other humans via implicit nonverbal behaviors [32, 35]. We wondered if exposure to a social presence priming could also be contagious. In general, *priming* can be seen as the incidental activation of a person's knowledge structure, which can lead the person to specific behaviors and attitudes [3]. It can affect social judgment [31], as well as goal-driven tasks, as Bargh et al. demonstrated by showing that primed participants performed comparatively better in an intellectual task [3]. Dijksterhuis and Bargh indicate that perception itself can prime or activate a behavioral tendency. Apart from perceiving observables of what is literally present, people make trait inferences and activate social stereotypes as forms of social perception that elicit the tendency to imitate in the social perceiver [10]. Qu identified three main elements in a conversation between a real human and an IVA: the surrounding environment, the virtual conversation partner, and the virtual bystanders [28]. Qu used images and videos to prime participants. Primed participants mentioned more keywords related to the priming content. Qu showed that priming with surrounding media content had a guidance effect in both the real world and the virtual world [29]. Similarly, we explore exposing our participants to a social priming and compare the effects on their social presence. Various studies have examined the concept of priming, some related to virtual reality [22, 27], but most of them explore the theory underlying the priming phenomenon. Researchers explored racial biases, gender, and IVA personality in virtual environments [23, 24, 26]. To our knowledge, there are no studies that use priming in the context of supporting social presence of an IVA.

Fig. 1. Experimental setup: Participants were exposed to a brief conversation between the IVA (Katie) on the left and the CVA (Michael) on the right. The virtual elements in the scene were rendered from the participant's viewpoint.

3   Experiment

3.1   Material

We built a room-sized experimental setup (approx. 3m × 3.6m) where a virtual character was presented as sitting behind a shared physical-virtual desk between two bookshelves (see Fig. 1). We modeled and animated a 3D virtual character, named "Katie," in Autodesk Maya. Katie was designed with animations for facial expressions, speaking, and body gestures. She had a mostly neutral, serious, and polite demeanor during the interaction (i.e., designed to not be too warm or cold towards the participant). We then imported the model into Unity3D where we added a graphical user interface allowing an operator to trigger specific body gestures or pre-recorded phrases with corresponding speaking animations, in order to play a game of twenty questions and to carry out other limited responses as needed before or after the game. With this human-in-the-loop experimental setup, the operator pressed buttons behind the scenes to trigger Katie's responses. Katie's image was rear projected onto the screen behind the physical desk using an Optoma TW610ST projector. The participants were recorded using 5 Logitech c920 webcams (2 close ups and 3 wide angles) observing the space from different positions. The CVA, which we call "Michael," was presented on a Panasonic TC-P65VT30 screen.

3.2   Methods

We used a between-participants design for this experiment. To investigate the effect of social priming on social presence with an IVA we defined two groups: (i) *control group* and (ii) *social priming group*. Participants in both groups were asked to play a game of *twenty questions* with the IVA (Katie). Participants in

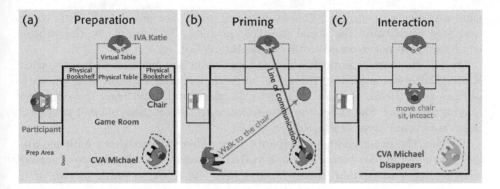

Fig. 2. Setup and procedure in the two experimental conditions. The dotted line around the CVA (Michael) indicates that he was there only in the social priming condition but not in the control condition. The other elements were the same in both conditions.

the social priming group perceived a short interaction between Katie and the CVA before they played the game. Participants in the control group were not primed with this social interaction before playing the game. Figure 2 illustrates the overall procedure which is comprised of three steps: (a) preparation, (b) priming (only for the social priming group), and (c) interaction with a twenty questions game.

In (a), before the participants entered the room, all participants read the informed consent and completed a demographics questionnaire. Then, the experimenter briefed them on the rules of the twenty questions game:

> "You are going to play two games of twenty questions. During the first game, Katie has an object in mind that you have to guess; you can ask her questions that have YES or NO answers. During the game you cannot ask her open ended questions. You have a maximum of 20 questions to guess the object. In the second game, the same rules apply, except that Katie will ask you the YES or NO questions and you have to answer."

Participants were asked to pick their object for the second game from a deck of cards before starting the interaction. They were asked to write down the answers to questions and to record the winner of each game during the interaction with the IVA. While individual interaction times might vary between participants due to the nature of the game (i.e., some people took more time to think before asking questions), the exposure times to the IVA were comparable across both groups.

In (b), the participants in the *social priming condition* saw Katie seated at the table and the CVA (Michael) standing in the corner of the room. They were then exposed to an interaction between Katie and Michael. Michael acted as if he had just finished a game with Katie. As soon as the participant entered, Michael looked at the participant, then at Katie, and said *"Oh, you've got visitors. I'll leave you two to play,"* then Katie and Michael exchanged phrases such as *"It was nice playing with you! Thanks for your time. See you later!"* This short exchange constituted the social presence priming. Participants in the *control condition* were not exposed to this social interaction.

In (c), the participants then entered the room and interacted directly with Katie. Katie was seated at the table, and she initiated the conversation with phrases like *"Hello, how are you? Nice to meet you!"* and then moved on to playing the game. She ended the interaction with *"It was nice playing with you! Thanks for your time. See you later, bye!"*

During the experiment, participants were video recorded from multiple angles and observed for verbal and non-verbal behavior. Specifically, we observed whether the participants waited for the IVA and CVA to finish in (b), or if instead they walked straight to the chair, breaking the line of communication between Katie and Michael.

After completing the experiment, participants were asked to fill out a set of post-questionnaires including a social presence questionnaire [13], a presence questionnaire [36], an affective attraction questionnaire [14], and their subjective emotions state using Wilhelm's Mood Rating Questionnaire which consists of six questions (How did your interaction with the other player (Katie) make you feel: anxious, excited, tense, alert, in control, desire to leave the situation) [34]. Since we used a mixed reality setup rather than an immersive virtual environment (cf. [36]), we used a subset of the original questions, removing those inappropriate for our environment.

The exact questions for social presence dimensions are shown in Table 2 with *Co-Presence* being the degree the participant thinks he/she is not alone, *Attentional Allocation* is the amount of attention the participant allocates to and receives from the IVA, *Perceived Message Understanding* is the ability of the participant to receive a message from the IVA and for the IVA to understand their message, *Perceived affective understanding* is the ability of the participant to understand the IVA's emotional and attitudinal states and for the IVA to understand the participant's emotional and attitudinal states, *Perceived Affective Interdependence* is the extent to which the participant's emotional and attitudinal state affects and is affected by the emotional and attitudinal states of the IVA , *Perceived Behavioral Interdependence* is the extent to which a participant's behavior affects and is affected by the IVAs behavior [13]. The means for each dimension are computed by adding the scores for these questions and dividing by the total number of questions ($N = 6$). The social presence questions are on a 1 to 7 Likert scale. Questions marked with a star were inverted by negating the answer and adding 8. The individual questions from the *presence* questionnaires that showed significantly different answers are shown in Table 1.

3.3   Participants

58 participants (35 males and 23 females from multiple ethnicities) were randomly assigned to the control ($n = 29$) or social priming ($n = 29$) experimental group. Participants were recruited from our university community (students, employees, and alumni from various colleges within the university) via web postings

and email lists. Participants' experience with IVAs varied. Thirteen participants had never interacted with an IVA before, while the others reported varying familiarity with the concept of Virtual Humans (VH), from having encountered some sort of VH at some point, e.g. while playing video games, to four indicating being involved in some type of VH development at some point in their lives.

None of the participants had prior experience with the IVAs used in this experiment.

Table 1. Measurement for select Presence questions regarding Responsiveness, and Involvement that showed significant differences.

Responsive	How responsive were the other player (Katie) and her environment to actions that you initiated (or performed)?
Involved	How much did the visual aspects of the other player (Katie) and her environment involve you?

4   Results

4.1   Qualitative Results

In the social priming condition, most participants commented that they did not pay much attention to the CVA Michael. Fourteen participants acknowledged that they ignored Michael, with comments such as "I didn't pay him much attention," or "I completely ignored him." Five participants did not expect to see the CVA Michael and expressed being surprised or confused. Three participants felt that they "interrupted Katie and Michael's conversation." Six participants expressed positive reactions regarding Michael such as he was "friendly and heartwarming" and that he set the tone as "more realistic." and made participants "more excited," or put them "in a good mood."

Ten participants gave positive comments regarding the IVA Katie's friendliness and expressiveness such as saying she "was expressive" and that she gave off a "friendly vibe," and six participants gave comments suggesting improving the IVA Katie's emotions and expressiveness.

In the control condition, there were more mixed comments regarding the IVA Katie. Nine participants gave positive comments related to Katie's realism and character such as saying she was "very realistic and friendly" while 11 participants gave comments suggesting improvements for the IVA Katie's character, emotions and expressions such as "[she] could have been nicer and more friendly" and that she does not show much "emotion" or "her face doesn't show feeling" or they felt "a little distant" from her.

4.2   Quantitative Results

We decided to use non-parametric statistical tests to analyze the Likert scale ordinal data from the questionnaires [19] comparing the priming condition with

Table 2. Questionnaires for Social Presence including the following dimensions: CoPresence (CoP), Attentional Allocation (Atn), Perceived Message Understanding (MsgU), Perceived Affective Understanding (Aff), Perceived Emotional Interdependence (Emo), Perceived Behavioral Interdependence (Behv).

CoP-Q1	I noticed the other player (Katie).
CoP-Q2	The other player (Katie) noticed me.
CoP-Q3	The other player (Katie)'s presence was obvious to me.
CoP-Q4	My presence was obvious to the other player (Katie).
CoP-Q5	The other player (Katie) caught my attention.
CoP-Q6	I caught the other player (Katie)'s attention.
Atn-Q1*	I was easily distracted from the other player (Katie) when other things were going on.
Atn-Q2*	The other player (Katie) was easily distracted from me when other things were going on.
Atn-Q3	I remained focused on the other player (Katie) throughout our interaction.
Atn-Q4	The other player (Katie) remained focused on me throughout our interaction.
Atn-Q5*	The other player (Katie) did *not* receive my full attention.
Atn-Q6*	I did *not* receive the other player (Katie)'s full attention.
MsgU-Q1	My thoughts were clear to the other player (Katie).
MsgU-Q2	The other player (Katie)'s thoughts were clear to me.
MsgU-Q3	It was easy to understand the other player (Katie).
MsgU-Q4	The other player (Katie) found it easy to understand me.
MsgU-Q5*	Understanding the other player (Katie) was difficult.
MsgU-Q6*	The other player (Katie) had difficulty understanding me.
Aff-Q1	I could tell how the other player (Katie) felt.
Aff-Q2	The other player (Katie) could tell how I felt.
Aff-Q3	The other player (Katie)'s emotions were not clear to me.
Aff-Q4	My emotions were not clear to the other player (Katie).
Aff-Q5	I could describe the other player (Katie)'s feelings accurately.
Aff-Q6	The other player (Katie) could describe my feelings accurately.
Emo-Q1	I was sometimes influenced by the other player (Katie)'s moods.
Emo-Q2	The other player (Katie) was sometimes influenced by my moods.
Emo-Q3	The other player (Katie)'s feelings influenced the mood of our interaction.
Emo-Q4	My feelings influenced the mood of our interaction.
Emo-Q5	The other player (Katie)'s attitudes influenced how I felt.
Emo-Q6	My attitudes influenced how the other player (Katie) felt.
Behv-Q1	My behavior was often in direct response to the other player (Katie)'s behavior.
Behv-Q2	The behavior of the other player (Katie) was often in direct response to my behavior.
Behv-Q3	I reciprocated the other player (Katie)'s actions.
Behv-Q4	The other player (Katie) reciprocated my actions.
Behv-Q5	The other player (Katie)'s behavior was closely tied to my behavior.
Bhv-Q6	My behavior was closely tied to the other player (Katie)'s behavior.

the control condition. While it is common practice in some scientific disciplines to treat Likert-type scales as interval-level measurements [4], we avoid the discussion on whether parametric statistics can be a valid method for the analysis of non-parametric data [16, 17] by using non-parametric (MannWhitney U) tests.

Social Presence: We aggregated scores for the questions per category to cover all dimensions of social presence. We found a significantly higher social presence in the social priming condition for co-presence ($U = 256.0$, $p = 0.009$, $r = -0.664$), attentional allocation ($U = 288.0$, $p = 0.039$, $r = -0.662$), and perceived message understanding ($U = 276.0$, $p = 0.024$, $r = -0.527$). There was no significant difference for perceived affective interdependence ($U = 386.0$, $p = 0.596$, $r = -0.235$), perceived emotion interdependence ($U = 431.0$, $p = 0.876$, $r = -0.016$), and perceived behavioral interdependence ($U = 365$, $p = 0.391$, $r = -0.246$). Figure 3 shows the results for the dependent variables in the experiment.

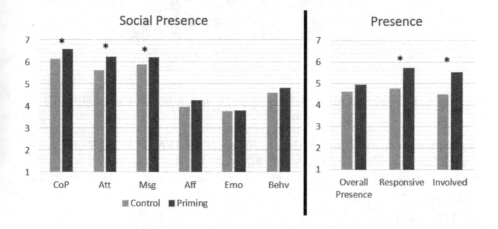

Fig. 3. Results for social presence dimensions (left) and for Presence (right). Star "*" indicates significant results

Mood Rating: Participants were asked to rate their interaction with the IVA Katie for the following Mood Ratings: anxious, excited, tense, alert, in control, and desire to leave the situation. The results show that participants in the social priming condition were more excited ($U = 294.5$, $p = 0.047$, $r = -0.572$) and more alert ($U = 267.5$, $p = 0.017$, $r = -0.651$) compared to those in the control condition. There was no significant difference for feelings of being anxious ($U = 385.5$, $p = 0.586$, $r = -0.182$), tense ($U = 371.5$, $p = 0.442$, $r = -0.134$), in control ($U = 415.0$, $p = 0.944$, $r = 0.000$), or desire to leave the situation ($U = 490.5$, $p = 0.208$, $r = 0.257$).

Presence: When comparing individual Presence questions, the results show that participants in the social priming condition perceived the IVA Katie as more responsive to their actions ($U = 278.5$, $p = 0.024$, $r = -0.641$) and that

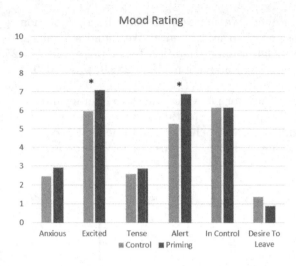

Fig. 4. Results for Mood Ratings. Star "*" indicates significant results.

they were more involved in the visual aspects of the IVA ($U = 254.5$, $p = 0.008$, $r = 0.772$). There was no significant difference for the presence (all $p > 0.05$), affect attraction (all $p > 0.05$), and virtual environment (all $p > 0.05$) questions.

5 Discussion

Overall, our results indicate that subtle social priming, by means of perceiving a short interaction between an IVA and a CVA, can result in a significant increase in social presence (specifically the co-presence, attentional allocation, and perceived message understanding dimensions of social presence), an increase in the sense of feeling more excited and more alert, an increase in the sense of feeling more involved in the visual aspects, and a perception of the IVA as more responsive compared to those who were not primed.

The results are particularly interesting as the social priming in our experiment was a rather short pre-scripted/pre-programmed conversation between our IVA and CVA. Indeed, because the IVA-CVA interaction occurs prior to, and independent of, the participant's interaction with the IVA, the IVA-CVA interaction can be pre-programmed and yet still look spontaneous. One could create a library of such short IVA-CVA vignettes to be invoked periodically when it appears that the circumstances are currently unlikely to yield direct human-IVA interaction. Such vignettes could then also be transferred to other characters and setups, without adding strict requirements in terms of space or interactivity.

Interpretation of the results within the social presence dimensions: We expected *Co-Presence* to be significantly different since Co-Presence is the degree the participant thinks he/she is not alone, and the fact of adding a CVA reinforces this idea. We also expected that the *Attentional Allocation* would be higher as the CVA is expected to draw attention to the unexpected priming conversation. Given that the priming was designed to be the end of the previous player's game, it is possible that the increase in the *Perceived Message Understanding* came from the appearance that the IVA knows what she is doing since she played that game before and it was a pleasant experience for the CVA. We did *not* expect to see a significant change in the dimensions that are related to affect (*Perceived affective understanding*, and *Perceived Affective Interdependence*) as both the IVA and the CVA were designed to have a neutral, polite, and professional character (not too warm, not too cold). The means of the Control and Priming groups were almost identical. We did not design the priming in a way to intentionally affect the behavior (i.e., the CVA did not give a hint about the game, nor did he ask the participant to perform any specific action). We were not surprised that the *Perceived Behavioral Interdependence* was not significantly different. We did notice that *during* the priming, a few participants chose to wait while others chose to keep on walking but that change in behavior did *not* affect the results.

Interpretation of the Mood Ratings results: An argument can be made in either direction whether it is good or bad to be more Alert and more Tense. According to The Positive and Negative Affect Schedule (PANAS), "Excited" and "Alert" are classified as positive affects [33]. According to the Cognitive-Affective Theory of Learning with Media, the multimedia learning process is mediated by the learners mood, and positive mood has a facilitating effect on multimedia learning [18]. We conclude that using social priming can have a positive effect on the mood and possibly on learning using multimedia such as an IVA.

Are there other ways to prime social presence? Other stimuli might also be powerful social presence priming tools. For example, the IVA could exhibit "human-like" traits or characteristics, such as engaging in humor, referencing a recent real world event, or reacting to stimuli in the environment, showing awareness of the person and their surroundings. Likewise, it may be possible to strengthen (or weaken) the priming approach used in this study (e.g., making the perceived conversation appear more exciting). The CVA could engage in an unpleasant conversation such as scolding the IVA which could result in a positive priming (i.e., sympathize with the IVA) or negative priming (take sides with the CVA). Similarly, it may be possible to negatively prime participants if the confederate intentionally ignores the IVA. Future research directions may include experimenting with variations of other aspects of the IVA and CVA, such as attire, gender, or ethnicity as well as replacing the CVA with a real human confederate.

What are the long-term effects? We do not know how long the effects of social priming last or the effectiveness when the same priming situation is re-used multiple times. It may be the case that the effects stay until something else changes them or it could be the case that the effects fade over time and a reminder or "booster" may be periodically required, for which one could pseudo-randomly select one of multiple canned priming sequences. Social priming in this way could be particularly useful to many applications employing IVAs because of its relatively low cost and independence with the actual direct interaction.

6   Conclusion

In this paper we presented a novel method to increase social presence with IVAs. It is generally believed that a higher sense of presence with an IVA has the potential to make applications such as training more effective, which can translate into increased performance in teams in a real environment [9]. Observing the behaviors of another human *prior to* interaction with that human can influence perceptions of that person's intelligence and disposition. To see if this effect could be used to increase the perceived realism of an IVA, we explored what we call *social presence priming*, where we exposed participants to an IVA participating in a seemingly spontaneous but actually pre-programmed socially engaging interaction with a confederate virtual agent *before* the participants interacted directly with the IVA. In the condition where the participants were socially primed, the co-presence, attentional allocation, and perceived message understanding dimensions of social presence were found to be significantly higher compared to the control condition. Participants also felt more excited and alert and perceived the IVA as more responsive. The results of this study are encouraging for the use of relatively low-cost social priming in existing and future IVA applications, since the proposed confederate virtual agents only need a limited functionality to complete a short canned interaction with the IVA.

Acknowledgements
The work presented in this publication is supported primarily by the Office of Naval Research (ONR) Code 30 under Dr. Peter Squire, Program Officer (ONR awards N00014-14-1-0248 and N00014-12-1-1003). We also acknowledge the Link Foundation and the UCF Modeling and Simulation graduate program for their support of co-author Salam Daher via research fellowships. We also acknowledge Florida Hospital for their support of Prof. Welch via their Endowed Chair in Healthcare Simulation.

References

1. Bailenson, J.N., Beall, A.C., Blascovich, J.: Gaze and task performance in shared virtual environments. The Journal of Visualization and Computer Animation 13(5), 313–320 (Dec 2002), http://doi.wiley.com/10.1002/vis.297
2. Bailenson, J.N., Beall, A.C., Loomis, J., Blascovich, J., Turk, M.: Transformed Social Interaction, Augmented Gaze, and Social Influence in Immersive Virtual Environments. Human Communication Research 31(4), 511–537 (2005)
3. Bargh, J.A., Chen, M., Burrows, L.: Automaticity of social behavior: Direct effects of trait construct and stereotype activation on action. Journal of Personality and Social Psychology 71(2), 230–244 (1996)
4. Blaikie, N.: Analyzing quantitative data: From description to explanation. Sage (2003)
5. Blascovich, J.: Social Influence within Immersive Virtual Environments. In: Schroeder, R. (ed.) The Social Life of Avatars, pp. 127–145. Computer Supported Cooperative Work, Springer London (2002)

6. Blascovich, J., Loomis, J., Beall, A.C., Swinth, K.R., Hoyt, C.L., Bailenson, J.N.: Immersive virtual environment technology as a methodological tool for social psychology. Psychological Inquiry 13(2), 103–124 (2002)
7. Bulu, S.T.: Place presence, social presence, co-presence, and satisfaction in virtual worlds. Computers & Education 58(1), 154–161 (jan 2012), http://linkinghub.elsevier.com/retrieve/pii/S0360131511002028
8. Cahrtrand, T.L., Bargh, J.A.: The chameleon effect: The perception–behavior link and social interaction. Journal of Personality and Social Psychology 76(6), 893–910 (1999)
9. De Leo, G., Diggs, L., Radici, E., Mastaglio, T.: Measuring sense of presence and user characteristics to predict effective training in an online simulated virtual environment. Simulation in healthcare: journal of the Society for Simulation in Healthcare 9(1), 1 – 6 (2014)
10. Dijksterhuis, A., Bargh, J.A.: The perception-behavior expressway: Automatic effects of social perception on social behavior. Advances in experimental social psychology 33, 1–40 (2001)
11. Garau, M., Slater, M., Pertaub, D.P., Razzaque, S.: The Responses of People to Virtual Humans in an Immersive Virtual Environment. Presence Teleoperators and Virtual Environments 14(1), 104–116 (2005)
12. Goffman, E.: Behavior in Public Places: Notes on the Social Organization of Gatherings. The Free Press (a Division of Simon and Schuster, Inc.), New York, NY USA (1963)
13. Harms, C., Biocca, F.: Internal consistency and reliability of the networked minds measure of social presence. In: Annual International Presence Workshop. pp. 246–251 (2004)
14. Herbst, K.C., Gaertner, L., Insko, C.a.: My head says yes but my heart says no: cognitive and affective attraction as a function of similarity to the ideal self. Journal of personality and social psychology 84(6), 1206–1219 (2003)
15. Huang, L., Morency, L.P., Gratch, J.: Virtual Rapport 2.0. In: Vilhjálmsson, H., Kopp, S., Marsella, S., Thórisson, K. (eds.) Intelligent Virtual Agents (Lecture Notes in Artificial Intelligence). Lecture Notes in Computer Science, vol. 6895, pp. 68–79. Springer Berlin Heidelberg (2011)
16. Knapp, T.R.: Treating ordinal scales as interval scales: an attempt to resolve the controversy. Nursing research 39(2), 121–123 (1990)
17. Kuzon Jr, W.M., Urbanchek, M.G., McCabe, S.: The seven deadly sins of statistical analysis. Annals of plastic surgery 37(3), 265–272 (1996)
18. Liew, T.W., Su-Mae, T.: The effects of positive and negative mood on cognition and motivation in multimedia learning environment. Journal of Educational Technology & Society 19(2), 104 (2016)
19. Likert, R.: A technique for the measurement of attitudes. Arch. Psychol (22), 5–55 (1932)
20. Lok, B., Chuah, J.H., Robb, A., Cordar, A., Lampotang, S., Wendling, A., White, C.: Mixed-reality humans for team training. IEEE Computer Graphics and Applications (3), 72–75 (2014)
21. Lombard, M., Ditton, T.: At the Heart of It All: The Concept of Presence. Journal of Computer-Mediated Communication 3(2) (Jun 1997), http://doi.wiley.com/10.1111/j.1083-6101.1997.tb00072.x
22. Nunez, D., Blake, E.: Conceptual priming as a determinant of presence in virtual environments. In: Proceedings of the 2nd international conference on Computer graphics, virtual Reality, visualisation and interaction in Africa. pp. 101–108. ACM (2003)

23. Pan, X., Gillies, M., Slater, M.: Male bodily responses during an interaction with a virtual woman. In: International Workshop on Intelligent Virtual Agents. pp. 89–96. Springer (2008)
24. Pan, X., Gillies, M., Slater, M.: Virtual character personality influences participant attitudes and behavior–an interview with a virtual human character about her social anxiety. Frontiers in Robotics and AI 2, 1 (2015)
25. Pan, Y., Steed, A.: A comparison of avatar, video, and robot-mediated interaction on users' trust in expertise. Frontiers in Robotics and AI 3, 12 (2016)
26. Peck, T.C., Seinfeld, S., Aglioti, S.M., Slater, M.: Putting yourself in the skin of a black avatar reduces implicit racial bias. Consciousness and cognition 22(3), 779–787 (2013)
27. Peña, J., Hancock, J.T., Merola, N.A.: The priming effects of avatars in virtual settings. Communication Research 36(6), 838–856 (2009)
28. Qu, C.: Talking with a Virtual Human: Controlling the Human Experience and Behavior in a Virtual Conversation. TU Delft, Delft University of Technology (2014)
29. Qu, C., Brinkman, W.P., Wiggers, P., Heynderickx, I.: The effect of priming pictures and videos on a question–answer dialog scenario in a virtual environment. Presence 22(2), 91–109 (2013)
30. Raij, A.B., Johnsen, K., Dickerson, R.F., Lok, B.C., Cohen, M.S., Duerson, M., Pauly, R.R., Stevens, A.O., Wagner, P., Lind, D.S.: Comparing interpersonal interactions with a virtual human to those with a real human. IEEE transactions on visualization and computer graphics 13(3), 443–457 (2007)
31. Srull, T.K., Wyer, R.S.: The role of category accessibility in the interpretation of information about persons some determinants and implications. Journal of Personality and Social psychology 37(10), 1660 (1979)
32. Sy, T., Côté, S., Saavedra, R.: The contagious leader: Impact of the leader's mood on the mood of group members, group affective tone, and group processes. Journal of Applied Psychology 90(2), 295 – 305 (2005)
33. Watson, D., Clark, L.A., Tellegen, A., Watson, D., Clark, L.A., Tellegen, A.: Positive and negative affect schedule. Journal of Personality and Social Psychology 54(6), 1063 – 1070 (1988)
34. Wilhelm, F.H., Roth, W.T.: Ambulatory assessment of clinical anxiety. In: Ambulatory Assessment: Computer-assisted Psychological and Psychophysiological Methods in Monitoring and Field Studies, pp. 317–345 (1996)
35. Willard, G., Isaac, K.J., Carney, D.R.: Some evidence for the nonverbal contagion of racial bias. Organizational Behavior and Human Decision Processes 128, 96 – 107 (2015), http://www.sciencedirect.com/science/article/pii/S0749597815000291
36. Witmer, B.G., Singer, M.J.: Measuring Presence in Virtual Environments: A Presence Questionnaire. Presence: Teleoperators and Virtual Environments 7(3), 225–240 (Jun 1998), http://www.mitpressjournals.org/doi/abs/10.1162/105474698565686

Predicting Future Crowd Motion Including Event Treatment

Cliceres Mack Dal Bianco[1], Soraia Raupp Musse[1] ✉*, Adriana Braun[1],
Rodrigo Poli Caetani[1], Claudio Jung[2] and Norman Badler[3]

[1] Graduate Program in Computer Science
Pontifical Catholic University of Rio Grande do Sul - PUCRS - Porto Alegre, Brazil
[2] Graduate Program in Computer Science
Federal University of Rio Grande do Sul - UFRGS - Porto Alegre, Brazil
[3] University of Pennsylvania - UPENN -
Philadelphia - USA

Abstract. Crowd simulation has become an important area, mainly in
entertainment and security applications. In particular, this area has been
explored in safety systems to evaluate environments in terms of people
comfort and security. In general, the evaluation involves the execution of
one or more simulations in order to provide statistical information about
the crowd behavior in a certain environment. Real-time applications can
also be desirable, for instance in order to estimate the crowd behavior
in a near future knowing the current crowd state, aiming to anticipate
a potential problem and prevent it. This paper presents a model to estimate crowd behaviors in a future time, presenting a good compromise
between accuracy and running time. It also presents a new error measure
to compare two crowds based on local density.

1 Introduction

Crowd simulation has been investigated in many applications over the last years.
The presence of huge crowds in current games and movies does not surprise the
audience as it did in the first movies, e.g. AntZ [4] and A Bug's Life [5]. In fact,
it is actually a very common Computer Graphics effect nowadays. Despite all
interest in the entertainment area, crowd simulation tools are also important in
security applications. This relevant area aims to investigate the impact of a high
number of people behaving in a specific environment to improve people security
and comfort, as well as to prevent hazardous situations. In this context, many
simulations are typically required to be executed in order to provide statistical
information that can be used by safety engineers. An interesting application is
the possibility of estimating future crowd behaviors in a certain scenario given its
current state. In previous work [2] we proposed a solution which main goal was
to *fast forward* (from now on called FF Model) providing a future estimation.
We presented a model and evaluated its accuracy based on an error measure that

---

* e-mail:soraia.musse@pucrs.br
[4] http://dreamworks.wikia.com/wiki/Antz
[5] https://www.pixar.com/feature-films/a-bugs-life

© Springer International Publishing AG 2017
J. Beskow et al. (Eds.): IVA 2017, LNAI 10498, pp. 101-105, 2017.
DOI 10.1007/978-3-319-67401-8_11

takes into account the relative error in position for each agent in the continuous simulation and in the FF method. This paper presents an extension to [2] in order to provide the estimative for future crowd behavior dealing with the possibility that events can happen and behavioral patterns can change, in addition we also present a new metric to evaluate the FF model using the density information.

2 Related Work

Crowd simulation is the process by which the movement of many agents are calculated for the purpose of animating virtual scenes [3] or verifying the security of real environments [1]. In relation to safety, some works have focused on the prediction of future behavior, as in [6], where the authors estimate the time taken by people to achieve their goals. In a previous work [2], we estimate the future individual position of the people based on a prior information of goals and speeds. In that work, previous positions come from a dead reckoning method and positions are later adjusted. Regarding validation, we propose a way to compare simulation and estimation using densities. However, densities are not new in this context. Density is a feature widely used in crowd simulation work because it allows inferring current and future behavior [5]. In addition the density can be used as an evaluation metric, such as in the work of Lerner et al. [4] where they suggest comparing measures based on crowd densities in the output of a simulator with the observed densities in the experimental date.

3 The FF Model for Estimation of Crowd Behavior

In this section we summarize the previous approach [2] to provide estimation for future crowd behavior. A Pedestrian Dead Reckoning method based on Physics (PDR) is initially used to estimate future positions for agents in the crowd. In addition, crowd position estimation should also take into account the environment complexity (EC), i.e. the free region and presence of obstacles. Also, agents can be affected by others. We called this step as IP (interaction among people), that aims to describe how individual velocities should be affected by the presence of other agents. In this case, the previous approach used Weibull distribution [2]. Finally, the last step, called *Repositioning*, is responsible for fine tuning the agents' positions in the environment avoiding collisions [6].

3.1 The Inclusion of Events in Fast Forward Model (FF-E)

In this paper, we develop a method that can easily and quickly estimate possible future behaviors for crowds when events happen. For proof of concept, we used BioCrowds, as related in [2]. However, the method could be integrated in any crowd simulation platform. An event is given as the possibility of changing the environment by adding, changing or removing obstacles and exits. An event k is defined by $e_k = \{t_k, \Delta t_k, O_k\}$, where t_k is the event start time, Δt_k is the event duration, O_k is defined as $\{o_k, p_k\}$, where o_k is the number of obstacles, and p_k

---

[6] Please refer to [2] for further details.

is the geometry for each obstacle (list of vertices). After having defined an event, we explain how we consider them in our method FF-E. Firstly, we assume that events starting during the simulation, i.e. before the FF behavior, are already dealt with in work proposed by [2]. Hence, we are interested in events that are triggered during the period of time when behaviors are going to be predicted (i.e. not simulated beteen times t and $t + \Delta$). We consider events e_k for which $t < t_k < t + \Delta t$. The endpoint of e_k, given by $t_k + \Delta t_k$, can be greater than $t + \Delta t$. Let us consider a single event e_k, starting at frame t_k. The estimated initial position $(\boldsymbol{X}_{t_k}^i)$ for each agent i is computed using Physics at frame t_k, based on [2], is described in Equation 1:

$$pdr_{t+\Delta t}^i = \boldsymbol{X}_{t_k}^i + \left(s^i \frac{\boldsymbol{g}^i}{||\boldsymbol{g}^i||} \right)(\Delta t), \tag{1}$$

where $\boldsymbol{g}^i = (g_x^i, g_y^i, g_z^i)$ is the agent goal and s^i is its desired speed. An event e_k should impact the environment complexity to be considered. We use an environment complexity function (EC) that works as a speed reduction factor and is modeled as:

$$EC_{t_k} = \min \left\{ 1, \frac{a_k(t_k)A_a + o_k(t_k)}{A_w - A_o(t_k)} \right\}, \tag{2}$$

where A_a is the area of each agent, A_w represents the area of the world (that does not change during the simulation), and $A_o(t_k)$ is the sum of all obstacles areas at frame t_k. If the number of agents and/or area occupied by obstacles are too large and there is no free space to allow individuals to move, then EC_{t_k} is truncated at 1 and no motion is allowed in frame t_k. The reduction factor is applied to all agents i (i.e., EC does not depend on i).

3.2 Proposing a Metric to Compare Crowds

In this paper, we propose a new method to compare the result of FF-E to estimate crowds and the continuous simulation based on local densities in order to provide a global error estimation of crowds. The main idea is to divide the world into uniform regions in the simulated environment, called *cells*. The global crowd comparison metric is an average of the relative differences across cells, given by:

$$Dif(t) = \sum_{c=1}^{N_{cell}} \frac{|s_c(t) - e_c(t)|}{Avg\,(s_c(t))}, \tag{3}$$

where $s_c(t)$ and $e_c(t)$ are the density of agents in each specific cell c in the crowd simulation and in the FF method at frame t and N_{cell} is the number of cells for which either s_c or d_c are different than zero (to avoid computing the relative error at empty cells) and $Avg(\cdot, \cdot)$ is the average operator.

4 Experimental Results and Final Considerations

In order to verify the impact of the events during the simulation, we performed some experiments in one environment with 920sqm (23×40meters) and with populations of $8, 80, 160, 240$ and 320 agents (each one has a diameter of 0.456m). We simulated the crowd from frame 1 to 1000 and compared with FF-E method that estimated the crowd motion from frames 300 and 500. We measured errors, using the metric of the Equation 3, in three different times: frames 500 (time 1), 700 (time 2) and 800 (time 3). The occurred event is described according to definition $e_1 = \{t_1, \Delta t_1, \boldsymbol{O_1}\}$, $\boldsymbol{O_1} = \{o_1, \boldsymbol{p_1}\}$, where $o_1 = 1$ and $p_1 = $ object coordinates - in this case it is a quadrilateral shape of $49m^2$ and where t_1 and Δt_1 are defined depending on the simulated populations: for 8 agents $t_1 = 150$ and $\Delta t_1 = 300$, for 80 ag. $t_1 = 200$ and $\Delta t_1 = 500$, for 160 ag. $t_1 = 300$ and $\Delta t_1 = 600$, and 320 ag. $t_1 = 400$ and $\Delta t_1 = 700$. Two comparisons w.r.t. the computed errors were analyzed. $i)$ Simulation with and without the event; $ii)$ Simulation and FF-E method with event. Figure 1 shows the result of our metric. The error at time 2 in all analysis is larger than at time 1 (during the event) and time 3 (after some time the event finishes). It happens because comparing these three frames, higher impacts exist when more sequential frames propagates the estimation.

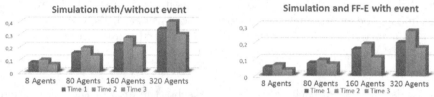

Fig. 1. Error computation observed in two case-studies related

Final Considerations This paper presents two main contributions,the first one is an extension of [2] to estimate crowd motion in a future time (fast forwarding), while treating events. The second one is a new error measure to quantitatively evaluate the error caused by the estimation. The maximum errors observed in the case studies were 30-40%person/sqm.

Acknowledgements

The research is supported by Brazilian Agencies CNPq and CAPES.

References

1. de Almeida, I.R., Cassol, V.J., Badler, N.I., Musse, S.R., Jung, C.R.: Detection of global and local motion changes in human crowds. IEEE Transactions on Circuits and Systems for Video Technology 27(3), 603–612 (March 2017)
2. Bianco, C.M.D., Braun, A., Musse, S.R., Jung, C., Badler, N.: Fast-Forwarding Crowd Simulations, pp. 208–217. Springer International Publishing, Cham (2016)
3. Dal Bianco, C.M., Braun, A., Brasil, J., Musse, S.R.: Preserving the motion features in nonavoiding collision crowds. Comput. Entertain. 15(3), 2:1–2:15 (Apr 2017)
4. Lerner, A., Chrysanthou, Y., Shamir, A., Cohen-Or, D.: Data Driven Evaluation of Crowds, pp. 75–83. Springer Berlin Heidelberg, Berlin, Heidelberg (2009)
5. Van Toll, W.G., Cook, IV, A.F., Geraerts, R.: Real-time density-based crowd simulation. Comput. Animat. Virtual Worlds 23(1), 59–69 (Feb 2012)
6. Yi, S., Li, H., Wang, X.: Pedestrian travel time estimation in crowded scenes. In: 2015 IEEE International Conference on Computer Vision (ICCV). pp. 3137–3145 (Dec 2015)

The Intelligent Coaching Space:
A Demonstration

Iwan de Kok ✉, Felix Hülsmann, Thomas Waltemate, and Cornelia Frank,
Julian Hough, Thies Pfeiffer, David Schlangen, Thomas Schack, Mario Botsch,
and Stefan Kopp

CITEC, Bielefeld University
idekok@techfak.uni-bielefeld.de

Abstract. Here we demonstrate our Intelligent Coaching Space, an immersive virtual environment in which users learn a motor action (e.g. a squat) under the supervision of a virtual coach. We detail how we assess the ability of the coachee in executing the motor action, how the intelligent coaching space and its features are realized and how the virtual coach leads the coachee through a coaching session.

Keywords: Coaching, Virtual Reality, Motor Skill Learning

1 Introduction

This demonstration presents the current state of the ICSPACE (Intelligent Coaching Space) project. In this project we are building an immersive virtual environment in which users are learning a motor action (e.g. a squat) under the supervision of a virtual coach. The project combines expertise from several disciplines such as sport psychology, computer graphics, human computer interaction and computational linguistics.

This short demonstration paper describes how we assess the ability of the coachee to execute the motor action (Section 2), how the intelligent coaching space and its features are realized (Section 3), the virtual coach (Section 4) and finally the demonstration version of the system (Section 5).

2 Coachee Assessment

We have two ways to assess the ability of the coachee to execute the motor action being taught. In the first, we look how the motor action is represented in the coachee's long-term memory (see Section 2.1). In the second, we analyze their performance of the motor action using motion tracking and analysis (see Section 2.2).

2.1 Cognitive representation and neurocognitive diagnostics

As a perceptual-cognitive source for subsequent intelligent virtual coaching based on multilevel analysis of motor action [2], the coachee's memory structure of

© Springer International Publishing AG 2017

J. Beskow et al. (Eds.): IVA 2017, LNAI 10498, pp. 105-108, 2017.

DOI 10.1007/978-3-319-67401-8_12

Fig. 1. The Intelligent Coaching System with virtual mirror and virtual coach.

the motor action to be learned is assessed and analyzed using the structural-dimensional analysis of mental representations (SDA-M) [4]. This splitting method provides psychometric data regarding the coachee's memory structure, revealing the relations and groupings of basic action concepts (BACs) of a complex action in long-term memory. By comparing the coachee's structure to an expert structure, errors are identified and appropriate instructions are chosen based on these errors. This serves as a perceptual-cognitive source for the virtual, intelligent coach to support motor learning and structure formation [1].

2.2 Motion Tracking and Analysis

To track the movement of our coachee we use a 10-camera Prime 13W OptiTrack motion capture system. The Motion Tracker uses information obtained from passive markers attached to a motion capture suit to calculate 20 joint angles / positions of the user.

To segment this data stream of joint angles and positions, recognizing the motor action we are interested in, we use a state machine approach. Each segment of a motor action is defined by a movement primitive. We search our data stream for a posture similar enough to the first key position of the first movement primitive of a given motor action. It will remain in this segment state until a posture is detected that is similar enough to the first key position of the next movement primitive.

Given segmented motor actions, we analyze the execution of the motor action looking for Prototypical Style Patterns (PSPs). These PSPs describe typical errors made during the execution of the motor action. The coaching system is informed of the presence and severity of these PSPs and can use these to make decisions on what feedback to give to the user. This process is explained in more detail in [2].

3   Virtual Coaching Space

The virtual coaching space is located inside a two-sided CAVE (L-Shape, $3\,m \times 2.3\,m$ for each side) with a resolution of 2100 x 1600 pixels per side. Our render engine runs on a single computer equipped with two NVIDIA Quadro K5000 graphics cards. Rendering runs at approximately $60\,fps$ supporting high quality character rendering, shadows, and post-processing and fulfills our low latency requirements [5].

In the virtual coaching space the user, equipped with passive 3D goggles, is located inside a virtual fitness room and stands in front of a *virtual mirror* (see Figure 1). The system maps the user's motion in real time onto an avatar to effect a virtual reflection.

The virtual world is capable of providing visual feedback on motor skill performance in several ways: users are able to observe their own movements inside the virtual mirror; the tint of the mirror adapts depending on the observed performance; and/or the problem area of the movement is highlighted on the mirror character. In our initial setup, feedback was also provided by a summary of the performance as text overlay inside the virtual world.

4   The Virtual Coach

Besides the virtual mirror we also have a virtual coach in the fitness room (see Figure 1). The virtual coach leads the coachee through a coaching session and is there to provide verbal feedback.

Realistic Character Rendering - The coach character and the character in the mirror can be rendered with photo-realistic textures. These characters are created by mapping a texture obtained using photogrammetry techniques onto a model character. Users are placed in a room and surrounded by synchronized cameras. Pictures from these camera are stitched together to form the texture that is then mapped on a model character.

Dialogue and Decision Making - The coaching session follows the dialogue structure of coaching sessions found in human-human coaching interactions [3]. The most important part of the coaching session are the coaching cycles. At the start of each coaching cycle the virtual coach selects the next *Skill-Under-Discussion* (SkUD) based on the assessment of the coachee (see Section 2). SkUD represents the part of the motor action that is currently put in focus to be improved and correspond to BACs and PSPs from the assessment modules. Given this SkUD, the coach selects the coaching act - such as instruction, demonstration or explanation - that is expected to give the most performance gain and does so until the performance on this aspect of the motor action is satisfactory. The multimodal behavior of the virtual coach is driven by AsapRealizer [6].

5 Demonstration System

In the demonstration people will be able to experience our virtual coaching system. In the interaction with our system people will experience a short coaching interaction where the virtual coach will teach the user how to do a perfect squat.

For the demonstration we will bring a downscaled version of our virtual coaching system. The CAVE will be replaced by a HTC Vive head mounted display, while the motion tracking system will be replaced by a Kinect.

Acknowledgements

We like to thank Yannic Wietler and Robert Feldhans helping to implement the HTC Vive renderer. This work was supported by the Cluster of Excellence Cognitive Interaction Technology 'CITEC' (EXC 277) at Bielefeld University, funded by the German Research Foundation (DFG).

References

1. Frank, C., Land, W.M., Schack, T.: Mental representation and learning: The influence of practice on the development of mental representation structure in complex action. Psychology of Sport and Exercise. 14, 353-361 (2013).
2. Hülsmann, F., Frank, C., Schack, T., Kopp, S., Botsch, M.: Multi-Level Analysis of Motor Actions as a Basis for Effective Coaching in Virtual Reality. In: Chung, P., Soltoggio, A., Dawson, C., Meng, Q., Pain, M. (eds.) International Symposium on Computer Science in Sport. Advances in Intelligent Systems and Computing. 392, p. 211-214. Springer (2016).
3. de Kok, I., Hough, J., Frank, C., Schlangen, D., Kopp, S.: Dialogue Structure of Coaching Sessions. Proceedings of the 18th SemDial Workshop on the Semantics and Pragmatics of Dialogue (DialWatt), Posters. p. 167-169. Herriot-Watt University (2014).
4. Schack, T.: Measuring mental representations. In G. Tenenbaum, R. C. Eklund, A. Kamata (eds.), Measurement in sport and exercise psychology. p. 203-214). Champaign, IL: Human Kinetics (2012).
5. Waltemate, T., Hülsmann, F., Pfeiffer, T., Kopp, S., Botsch, M.: Realizing a Low-latency Virtual Reality Environment for Motor Learning. Proceedings of the 21st ACM Symposium on Virtual Reality Software and Technology. VRST '15. p. 139-147. ACM, New York, NY, USA (2015).
6. van Welbergen, H., Yaghoubzadeh, R., Kopp, S.: AsapRealizer 2.0: The Next Steps in Fluent Behavior Realization for ECAs. In: Bickmore, T., Marsella, S., and Sidner, C. (eds.) Intelligent Virtual Agents. Lecture Notes in Computer Science. 8637, p. 449-462. (2014).

Get One or Create One: The Impact of Graded Involvement in a Selection Procedure for a Virtual Agent on Satisfaction and Suitability Ratings

Charlotte Diehl ✉, Birte Schiffhauer, Friederike Eyssel, Jascha Achenbach, Sören Klett, Mario Botsch, and Stefan Kopp

Cluster of Excellence in "Cognitive Interaction Technology" (CITEC), Bielefeld University, P.O. Box 10 01 31, 33501 Bielefeld, Germany
{cdiehl, feyssel, jachenba, sklett, botsch, skopp}@techfak.uni-bielefeld.de, b.schiffhauer@web

Abstract.
N = 86 participants were either confronted with a predefined virtual agent, or could select a virtual agent from predefined sets of six or 30 graphical models, or had the opportunity to self-customize the agent's appearance more freely. We investigated the effect of graded user involvement in the selection procedure on their ratings of satisfaction with the agent and perceived task suitability. In a second step, we explored the psychological mechanism underlying this effect. Statistical analyses revealed that satisfaction with the chosen virtual agent increased with the degree of participants' involvement in terms of more choice, but not in terms of self-customization. Furthermore, we show that this effect was driven by the perceived likeability, attractiveness, and competence of the agent. We discuss implications of our results for the development of a virtual agent serving as a virtual assistant in a smart home environment.

Keywords: technology acceptance, virtual agents, customization, smart home

1   Introduction

Over the last decades, a notable increase in the presence of intelligent virtual agents in daily life as assistive technologies and in smart home contexts could be observed (cf. [1,2]). Such agents provide information services, help in accessing information from the web, or allow for setting up the technical environment through natural language dialogues, and thereby facilitate daily life. However, to date people hold rather negative attitudes towards robots and other assistive technologies in the home context [3,4]. Therefore, it is of major importance that virtual assistants satisfy users' expectations, and elicit positive attitudes towards them. To increase users' acceptance of innovative technologies, psychological aspects and users' needs have to be taken into account [5,6]. Accordingly, we propose a user-centered approach by engaging end users actively in the selection and customization process of virtual assistants. In

© Springer International Publishing AG 2017
J. Beskow et al. (Eds.): IVA 2017, LNAI 10498, pp. 109–118, 2017.
DOI 10.1007/978-3-319-67401-8_13

the present study, we focus on the visual appearance of a virtual agent that would be deployed as a fitness coach within a smart home environment. We explored the effect of user involvement on subsequent evaluations. We did so by investigating whether users would prefer to select the virtual agent's appearance from a predefined set of graphical models or whether they would prefer to self-customize the appearance more freely. Above and beyond, we shed light on the psychological underpinnings of user involvement.

2   Related Work and Background

2.1   The relevance of psychological involvement and self-investment

Phillips and Zhao [7] have identified the lack of user involvement in the selection process of assistive devices as one determinant of technology abandonment. Previous work in the context of assistive technologies has likewise emphasized the need to involve the user to increase satisfaction with technical devices and reduce rejection [8]. Marketing research has shown that consumers prefer products that are tailored to their preferences and that customization has positive effects on people's attitudes towards products [9]. According to Deci and Ryan's *self-determination theory* [10], providing choice or involving people in the decision process on how to carry out a task increases their intrinsic motivation which leads to more satisfaction with the result. Festinger's *dissonance theory* [11] explains the enhancement of satisfaction by two paradigms: The *free-choice-paradigm* proposes that people who are confronted with a difficult choice, will always augment the value of the choose choice, while reducing the value of the un-chosen one, in order to rationally justify their choice. The *effort-justification-paradigm* proposes that when people spent a lot of effort on a task, they value the result more, because they need to justify the effort they put in it. In the domain of marketing research, this effect has been coined the *IKEA effect* [9]. It shows that involving individuals in the product design and customization process leads to a cognitive bias in which consumers place a disproportionately high value on products they partially created. Regarding assistive technologies, these social psychological theories indicate that giving users a choice and the feeling of participation in a selection and customization process is fundamental with regard to the acceptance of the resulting product. We can conclude from self-determination theory and dissonance theory that asking users to invest their time and cognitive resources in certain assistive technologies by involving them in the selection and customization process might lead to a strong identification with the resulting product and result in a greater valuation of the developed technical device.

2.2   The mediating role of agent perception and evaluation

The present research aimed to shed light on the psychological processes underlying the effect of involvement in the selection of a virtual agent on satisfaction with the agent and the perceived suitability for its task. We predicted that the effect should be mediated by user perceptions of the agent. Drawing on previous research on the perception of intelligent virtual agents, the following dimensions are deemed particularly relevant for this mediation process: On the one hand, there is extensive research on perceived agent *likeability and attractiveness* (cf. [12,13]). Furthermore, *warmth and competence*, the two core dimensions of social cognition [14], play a key role in impression formation about humans and nonhuman entities [15]. The dimension of warmth captures friendliness and positive intentions; the dimension of competence captures economical and educational success [14]. Finally, the degree to which persons perceive a virtual agent being *similar to them* seems to be an interesting potential mediator [16]. Going beyond existing research on the perception and evaluation of virtual agents, we propose a mediating function of each of the described variables, perceived likeability, attractiveness, warmth, competence, and similarity, for the relationship between user involvement and satisfaction with the agent as well as the rating of agent's task suitability. As there exists no systematic investigation of variables that mediate the effects of graded involvement of users on their attitudes and cognition (cf. [2]), this is an important step to close this gap.

2.3   Relevant dimensions of agent appearance

A vast body of research documents that the appearance of robots and virtual agents strongly influences their evaluation (e.g. [12], [15]). Research on social categorization emphasizes the relevance of *gender* and *age* as social categories used to form an impression [17]. Furthermore, *hairstyle* seems to be a salient facial cue, especially for determining a target's and even a robot's gender [18,19]. To take this into account, we systematically varied gender, but also age and hairstyle of the virtual agents that were used as stimuli in our study.

3   Present Experiment

Although the relevance of involvement of the end users in the development of assistive technologies is widely acknowledged ([7], [9]), the optimal level of user involvement in the development of virtual agents is yet under-researched. Therefore, we investigate the influence of different degrees of involvement by conducting an experiment with four conditions. One condition represents the control condition without involvement, where participants are confronted with a predefined virtual agent. In the first experimental condition, participants are offered limited choice as they can choose their preferred virtual agent out of a predefined set of six graphical models. In the second experimental condition, they are involved to a greater degree by offering them the choice between 30 predefined models. In the third condition, participants can self-customize the appearance of the virtual agent by individually selecting different graphical features. Primarily, we argue that when people are involved in the selection and customization process for a virtual agent as their smart home assistant, they invest their time and cognitive resources in this process, which they do not when they are confronted with a predefined virtual agent. We assume this self-investment to lead to a more positive evaluation of the chosen or self-customized agent and finally to result in higher satisfaction and in the perception of greater suitability of the agent. Accordingly, we predict a ranking order regarding satisfaction and suitability from the control condition ascending through the three experimental conditions (*Hypothesis 1*). Specifically, we expect the grade of cognitive investment that is needed to choose one agent out of a set of six models to be notably lower than to choose one agent out of 30 models. This assumption fits observations from neuropsychological testing, indicating that six items are easily manageable when it comes to information processing [20]. Second, we argue that self-customization allows individuals to experience a sense of accomplishment following agent creation which increases their valuation of the result. Simply choosing an agent might lead to a far weaker cognitive bias (cf. [8]). Thus, we expect the strongest effects of involvement in the condition where the participants self-customize the intelligent virtual agent. Furthermore, based on the literature about agent perception and social cognition (cf. [12,13,14,15]) we hypothesize that the relationship between freedom of choice in the selection procedure and satisfaction with the virtual agent as well as the rating of agent's suitability for its task would be mediated by the evaluation of the resulting agent in terms of likeability, attractiveness, warmth, competence and participants' perceived similarity to the virtual agent (*Hypothesis 2*). Furthermore, we predict that persons generally request customization of a virtual agent for a smart home context and the possibility to design it themselves (*Hypothesis 3*).

3.1   Method

Participants and design 86 participants (52 females, 31 males, three participants who did not indicate their gender; M_{age} = 25.20; SD_{age} = 8.59; [16; 64]) took part in the online study. The link was shared using social media and snowball sampling. Participants were randomly assigned to one of four conditions resulting from a between subjects design with selection procedure as the independent variable (selection procedure: "no choice" vs. "choice of one out of six virtual agents" vs. "choice of one out of 30 virtual agents" vs. "self-customization of the virtual agent").

Procedure After giving written informed consent, participants were asked to imagine living in a smart home that included a virtual fitness coach. The virtual agent would instruct them while learning new exercises, it would remind them of training goals, and provide information on their general health status. Depending on the condition, participants were then asked to evaluate a predefined, self-chosen, or self-customized virtual agent.

Stimuli Forty-eight virtual agents were built with the Autodesk® Character Generator. Eight "basis" agents were built manually, taking into account both gender and age of the virtual character. The further procedure was automated so that different hair colors and hair lengths were added automatically to each of the basis agents at a time. The resulting virtual agents were pretested in a *pilot study*: Eight participants (two females, five males, one participant who did not indicate his/her gender; M_{age} = 26.62; SD_{age} = 7.17; [22; 44]) selected their first, second and third preference of a virtual agent that should serve as a fitness coach. The most favored agents were chosen for the main study.

Experimental manipulation In *Condition 1*, participants were confronted with the virtual agent that reached the highest preference score in the pilot study (see Figure 1, no. 24). In *Condition 2*, the six virtual agents that reached the six highest preference scores in the pilot study were presented (Figure 1, no. 1, 7, 10, 11, 18, 24). In *Condition 3*, participants chose their most favored virtual agent out of a set of 30, including the stimuli used in Conditions 1 and 2, plus 24 additional agents (see Figure 1). In *Condition 4*, participants could customize the virtual agent by choosing gender, age (i.e., childhood, adolescence, middle age, old age), hair color (i.e., blond, brown, gray) and length (i.e., short, long) of the agent. Finally, a picture of the resulting agent was displayed, and participants were still able to change attributes again. The possible results included all agents presented in the other conditions and 18 additional agents.

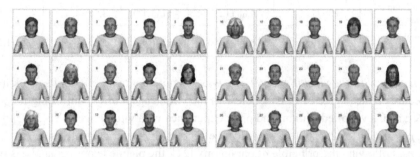

Fig. 1. Stimuli presented in the study.

Measures As *dependent variables*, participants indicated how satisfied they were with the virtual agent, and reported perceived task suitability of the agent. As *potential mediators*, participants evaluated the agent on warmth, competence, likeability, attractiveness, and similarity to themselves. General expectations towards a smart home assistant were assessed by using five items: 'An assistant should...' – 'merely fulfill its task.', 'look visually appealing.', 'be visually unique.', 'be distinct.', 'be customizable.'. As a *control variable*, we measured prior experience with virtual agents using two items. Seven-point Likert scales (from 1 = not at all, to 7 = very much) were used to record participants' responses. Finally, participants indicated their gender, age, and level of education.

5   Results

Descriptive statistics revealed that 40% of the participants in Condition 2 chose agent no. 10. Another 20% of the participants chose no. 7, which is the same agent with blond instead of brown hair. In Condition 3, 21.7% of the participants chose agent no. 1, while 26% of the participants chose agent no. 10, and another 26% of the participants chose no. 7. In Condition 4, 38.5% of the participants ended the design process with agent no. 10, and another 7.7% of the participants ended the process with no. 7.

To test *Hypothesis 1*, a multivariate analysis of covariance (MANCOVA) was conducted to analyze the effect of the selection procedure on satisfaction with the virtual agent and agent's task suitability. Participants' gender, age, level of education, and prior experience with virtual agents were included as covariates. Subsequently, a planned contrast analysis was carried out, which compared each category of selection procedure to the previous category. Descriptive statistics are summarized in Table 1.

Table 1. Means and standard deviations of satisfaction with the virtual agent and agent's task suitability as a function of condition.

Condition	no choice	1 out of 6	1 out of 30	self-customized	total
Satisfaction Mean (SD)	3.29 (1.90)	4.88 (1.20)	5.61 (1.12)	4.96 (1.37)	4.84 (1.53)
Suitability Mean (SD)	4.71 (0.91)	5.04 (1.40)	5.83 (0.98)	5.25 (1.45)	5.26 (1.29)

Satisfaction with the virtual agent There was a significant main effect of selection procedure on the degree of satisfaction with the virtual agent after controlling for gender, age, level of education, and prior experience with virtual agents ($F(3, 75) =$ 7.59, $p < .001$, $\eta^2 = .23$), but no significant effects of the covariates, all $Fs(1, 75) \leq$ 2.56, *ns*. Following the principle of parsimony [21], the planned contrast analysis was carried out without covariates, and revealed that in Condition 1, participants were significantly less satisfied than in Condition 2, $t(18.97) = -2.84$, $p < .05$, $r = .05$ after correcting for unequal variances. Participants in Condition 2 were again significantly less satisfied than in Condition 3, $t(45.99) = -2.18$, $p < .05$, $r = .31$. However, participants' satisfaction did not differ significantly between Conditions 3 and 4, $t(43.93) = 1.79$, $p = .08$.

Task suitability of the virtual agent Contrary to *Hypothesis 1*, there was no main effect of the selection procedure on the degree of task suitability of the virtual agent after controlling for gender, age, level of education, and prior experience with virtual agents, $F(3, 75) = 2.25$, $p = .09$. However, level of education was significantly negative ($F(1, 75) = 4.52$, $p < .05$, $\eta^2 = .06$, $r = -.25$), and prior experience with virtual agents was significantly positive related to agent's task suitability, $F(1, 75) = 5.62$, $p < .05$, $\eta^2 = .07$, $r = .20$. There were no gender nor age effects, $Fs(1, 75) \leq 1.43$, *ns*.

Mediation by the evaluation of the virtual agent To test *Hypothesis 2*, the mediating role of the evaluation of the virtual agent measured by five concepts (likeability, attractiveness, warmth, competence, and perceived similarity) between selection procedure and satisfaction with the virtual agent was established by conducting a mediation analysis using the PROCESS SPSS application provided by Hayes [22] with 5000 bootstrap samples. There were significant indirect effects of selection procedure on satisfaction with the virtual agent through perceived likeability (b = .26, BCa CI [.10, .52]), attractiveness (b = .08, BCa CI [.01, .22]), and competence (b = .09, BCa CI [.01, .27]). There were no indirect effects through warmth and similarity. As no direct effect of selection procedure on agent's task suitability was found, we did not conduct a further mediation analysis for this dependent variable.

Participant's expectations towards a virtual agent To evaluate the general expectations of the participants towards a smart home assistant (*Hypothesis 3*), one-sample t-tests against the neutral scale midpoint (scale value = 4) were conducted using Bonferroni correction for multiple testing. Figure 2 shows significant deviations from the mean value indicating that participants in general favor a smart home assistant that is customizable ($t(85)$= 5.93, p < .001, r = .54), and distinct, $t(85)$= 3.10, p < .01, r = .32. They further favor an assistant that merely fulfills its task ($t(85)$= 3.43, p < .01, r = .35), and that looks visually appealing, $t(85)$= 9.02, p < .001, r = .70. They are rather neutral with regard to visual uniqueness of the agent, $t(85)$= -.80, p = .43.

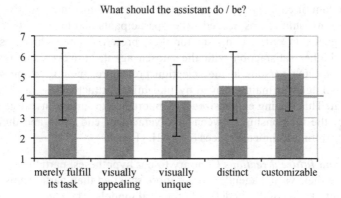

Fig. 2. Means and standard deviations regarding participants' expectations towards a smart home assistant

6   Conclusion and Discussion

Our results show four prominent findings: First, the selection procedure influenced the satisfaction with the virtual agent in the predicted way: Participants were the least satisfied when they had no choice at all, significantly more satisfied when they had the option to choose an agent out of six models, and again more satisfied when they had the option to choose an agent out of 30 models. Above and beyond these effects, there was no increment in satisfaction through self-customization of the virtual agent. Contrary to our predictions, perceived suitability of the virtual agent as a fitness coach was not influenced by the selection procedure. Second, we demonstrated that the relationship between freedom of choice in the selection procedure and satisfaction with the virtual agent is mediated via the evaluation of the chosen agent in terms of perceived likeability, attractiveness, and competence. Third, asking participants for their general expectations towards a smart home assistant as fitness coach, the central features they indicated are customization, fulfillment of its task, and an appealing visual appearance. Fourth, we found person variables such as gender, age, educational level and prior experience with virtual agents to play a rather minor role. Only perceived task suitability was affected by level of education and prior experience with virtual agents in that persons with a higher level of education and less prior experience rated it more discerningly. Built up on related work from robotics and virtual agents ([7], [9]), our results provide further evidence that involving the user in the selection and customization process increases the satisfaction with the present technical device and is needed to enhance technology acceptance. We mainly ascribe this effect to greater self-investment caused by psychological involvement, which is in line with social psychological theories. As predicted by dissonance theory [11], participants were more satisfied with their choice, when they put more effort in the task. We especially found a strong effect occurring, when participants had to choose one out of six versus one out of 30 agents. This is consistent with our assumption that a greater freedom of choice requires more investment of time and cognitive resources. Notably more investment was needed, when participants had to scan 30 compared to six virtual agents, in order to decide for their preferred one, which resulted in a significantly higher satisfaction with the chosen agent. However, our results show that, when involving persons in the selection procedure, their resulting satisfaction with the virtual agent is mainly driven by likeability, attractiveness, and competence attributed to it. This finding emphasizes the importance to further investigate potential mediators for the relationship between involvement of end users and their attitudes towards the resulting technical devices (cf. [12], [15]).

Limitations and future directions Contrary to our hypotheses, participants who could self-customize their virtual agent were not more satisfied than participants who could choose one out of a set of 30 predefined graphical models. There are two explanations for these unexpected results. Although research shows positive effects of having many choices [10], there is also some evidence for the fact that having too many choices can lead to dissatisfaction and regret [23]. According to Iyengar and Lepper [23] this could be due to an initial disengagement process, which should be tested in future studies. A second explanation might be the fact that participants' actual opportunities to design the virtual agent were still rather restricted, and the stimuli might have not matched the expectations of the participants. The graphical models are for instance not perfect in terms of realistic appearance. Since participants in the self-customization condition had no overview of the generally workable solutions, as they had in the choice conditions, they possibly thought that a better solution existed, but they just were not able to create it. Future studies should investigate an even more advanced setting of participatory design, which might more reliably elicit feelings of accomplishment with the self-designed result. Furthermore, perceived warmth and similarity to oneself had no mediating effect on participants' satisfaction. This could be due to the described role of the virtual agent as fitness coach. We would expect more influence of these variables for a virtual agent that functions as a social companion. Further studies could shed more light on this.

Recommendations for the design of virtual agents in the smart home context First of all, directly asking people, they clearly request a possibility to customize a virtual assistant for the smart home context. Based on our results, we can recommend giving persons as much freedom as possible in a selection and design procedure for virtual agents. Especially the set ups of Conditions 3 and 4 turn out to be highly recommendable. Second, in line with previous research (e.g. [12,13], [15]), we could show that virtual agents in the smart home context should appear likeable, attractive, and competent. Interestingly, we found a resounding favorite within the pool of virtual agents over all experimental conditions. The female agent no. 10 and no. 7, was chosen noticeably often. This might indicate that besides the wish of customization and freedom of choice, there might exist agents that fit average standards. However, although Conditions 2 to 4 offered the possibility to choose agent no. 10 or no. 7, we still found differences regarding the satisfaction with the resulting agent between those conditions. Finally, we are confident that our research provides a fruitful basis for future research by showing that involvement of the potential end users seems to be the crucial factor in order to maximize user acceptance and to elicit positive attitudes towards virtual agents that serve as smart home assistants.

Acknowledgements This research was supported by the German Federal Ministry of Education and Research (BMBF) within the project 'KogniHome' and the Cluster of Excellence Cognitive Interaction Technology (EXC 277), Bielefeld University. The authors thank Thies Pfeiffer for conducting the pretest and for programming the present study together with Birte Schiffhauer and with the help of Valerie Bonrath, Melanie Derksen, Lukas Kohlhase, Marco Lau, and Soham Panda within the seminar "Conducting Experiments in Virtual Reality" in 2016.

References

1. Augusto, J.C., Nakashima, H., Aghajan, H.: Ambient intelligence and smart environments: A state of the art. In: Augusto, J.C., Nakashima, H., & Aghajan, H. (eds.) Handbook of ambient intelligence and smart environments, pp. 3-31. Springer US, New York (2010)
2. Dehn, D.M., Van Mulken, S.: The impact of animated interface agents: a review of empirical research. International Journal of Human-Computer Studies 52(1), 1-22 (2000)
3. Reich, N., Eyssel, F.: Attitudes towards service robots in domestic environments: The role of personality characteristics, individual interests, and demographic variables. Journal of Behavioral Robotics 4, 123–130 (2013)
4. Schiffhauer, B., Bernotat, J., Eyssel, F., Bröhl, R., Adriaans, J.: Let the user decide! User preferences regarding functions, apps, and control modalities of a smart apartment and a service robot. In: Proceedings of the 8th International Conference on

Social Robotics (ICSR 2016), pp. 971-982. Springer International Publishing, Cham, Switzerland (2016)

5. Shneiderman, B. Plaisant, C.: Designing the user interface: strategies for effective human computer interaction. Pearson, Boston (2005)
6. Nielsen, J.: Usability engineering. Morgan Kaufmann, San Diego (1993)
7. Philips, B., Zhao, H.: Predictors of Assistive Technology Abandonment. Assistive Technology 5, 36-45 (1993)
8. Hurst, A., Tobias, J.: Empowering Individuals with Do-It-Yourself Assistive Technology. In: 13th international ACM SIGACCESS Conference on Computers and Accessibility (ASSETS), pp. 11-18. ACM, Dundee, Scotland (2011)
9. Mochon, D., Norton, M. I., Ariely, D.: Bolstering and restoring feelings of competence via the IKEA effect. International Journal of Research in Marketing 29(4), 363-369 (2012)
10. Deci, E.L., Ryan, R.M.: Intrinsic motivation and self-determination in human behavior. Plenum, New York, NY (1985)
11. Festinger, L.: A theory of cognitive dissonance. Stanford University Press, Stanford, CA (1957)
12. Buisine, S., Martin, J.C.: The effects of speech-gesture cooperation in animated agents' behavior in multimedia presentations. Interacting with Computers 19, 484–493 (2007)
13. Jin, S.A.A., Bolebruch, J.: Avatar-based advertising in Second Life: The role of presence and attractiveness of virtual spokespersons. Journal of Interactive Advertising 10(1), 51-60 (2009)
14. Fiske, S.T., Cuddy, A.J., Glick, P.: Universal dimensions of social cognition: Warmth and competence. Trends in Cognitive Science 11(2), 77–83 (2006)
15. Bergmann, K., Eyssel, F., Kopp, S.: A second chance to make a first impression? How appearance and nonverbal behavior affect perceived warmth and competence of virtual agents over time. In: International Conference on Intelligent Virtual Agents, pp. 126-138. Springer, Berlin, Heidelberg (2012)
16. Li, L., Forlizzi, J., Dey, A., Kiesler, S.: My agent as myself or another: effects on credibility and listening to advice. In: Proceedings of the Conference on Designing Pleasurable Products and Interfaces (DPPI'07), 194–208. ACM, New York, NY (2007)
17. Fiske, S.T., Neuberg, S.L.: A continuum of impression formation, from category-based to individuating processes: Influences of information and motivation on attention and interpretation. Advances in Experimental Social Psychology 23, 1-74 (1990)
18. Brown, E., Perrett, D.I.: What gives a face its gender?. Perception 22(7), 829-840 (1993)
19. Eyssel, F., & Hegel, F.: (S)he's got the look: Gender stereotyping of robots. Journal of Applied Social Psychology, 42(9), 2213-2230 (2012)
20. Miller, G.A.: The magical number seven, plus or minus two: some limits on our capacity for processing information. Psychological Review 63(2), 81 (1956)
21. Tabachnick, B.G., Fidell, L.S.: Using multivariate statistics. Pearson, Harlow (2014)
22. Hayes, A.F.: Introduction to mediation, moderation, and conditional process analysis: A regression-based approach. Guilford Press, New York [a. o.] (2013)
23. Iyengar, S.S., Lepper, M.R.: When choice is demotivating: Can one desire too much of a good thing?. Journal of Personality and Social Psychology, 79(6), 995 (2000)

Virtual reality negotiation training system with virtual cognitions

Ding Ding[1] ✉, Franziska Burger[1], Willem-Paul Brinkman[1], and Mark A. Neerincx[1,2]

[1] Delft University of Technology, Netherlands,
{d.ding-1, f.v.burger, w.p.brinkman, m.a.neerincx}@tudelft.nl
[2] TNO Human Factors, Netherlands

Abstract. A number of negotiation training systems have been developed to improve people's performance in negotiation. They mainly focus on the skills development, and less on negotiation understanding and improving self-efficacy. We propose a virtual reality negotiation training system that exposes users to virtual cognitions during negotiation with virtual characters with the aim of improving people's negotiation knowledge and self-efficacy. The virtual cognitions, delivered as a personalized voice-over, provide users with a stream of thoughts that reflects on the negotiation and people's performance. To study the effectiveness of the system, a pilot study with eight participants was conducted. The results suggest that the system significantly enhanced people's knowledge about negotiation and increased their self-efficacy.

Keywords: Virtual reality, Negotiation training system, Virtual cognitions

1 Introduction

Negotiations are very commonplace in many kinds of interpersonal relationships and being able to negotiate successfully is hence a crucial social skill. Despite this, people may choose to avoid negotiations because of a lack of skills or motivation. While many self-help books have been published on the topic, electronic solutions, so-called negotiation skills training systems, are becoming a viable alternative due to their accessibility and low cost. Existing training systems seem, however, to focus exclusively on skill development. Learners are typically taught what to do or how to behave in a negotiation situation in a learning-by-doing manner. Although feedback is provided, to the best of our knowledge, no system exists that informs learners about the reasons as to why they should behave in a certain prescribed way. The latter would be beneficial for learners as thoughtful and timely guidance is vital for the effectiveness of the learning experience [8]. Besides understanding, little attention has also been paid to people's self-efficacy, which affects their motivation to engage in negotiation. People's beliefs about their capabilities, e.g. their self-efficacy, determine how they feel, think, behave, and motivate themselves to participate in social interactions [4].

To enhance people's knowledge and self-efficacy, we put forward a virtual reality training system that allows people to passively experience a one-on-one

© Springer International Publishing AG 2017
J. Beskow et al. (Eds.): IVA 2017, LNAI 10498, pp. 119–128, 2017.
DOI 10.1007/978-3-319-67401-8_14

negotiation while being exposed to a stream of thoughts of one of the virtual negotiators. These simulated thoughts, i.e. virtual cognitions, are a set of pre-recorded voice-overs that provide understandable guided learning and motivating statements. Users perceive the negotiation from a first-person perspective, hearing themselves talk and think during the negotiation.

2   Related work

Compared to human-human training or traditional therapy, using a computer-based system for negotiation training is more cost-effective and controllable. There are many examples of negotiation training systems that have the potential to address the limitations of traditional negotiation training (see [13] for a game-based example and [22] for an agent-based example).

These systems aim at skill development by giving users hands-on negotiation experience. In this paper, however, we examine a training phase prior to this, focusing on building negotiation understanding and self-efficacy by using virtual cognitions.

2.1   Self-efficacy

Self-efficacy is one's perceived capability to execute a certain task or reach goals [6]. Multiple sources influence self-efficacy. The primary source is *enactive mastery experience*. If individuals have completed a task in the past, they are more confident in their ability to do it again in the future. Instead of obtaining such mastery experiences in the real world, individuals can also gain experiences by actively performing specific tasks in virtual environments [7,1]. These experiences in virtual environments can affect people's self-efficacy belief in the same way that experiences in the real world do [29].

The second source of influence is a *vicarious experience* provided by social models. Observing people similar to oneself succeed raises observers' beliefs that they can master comparable activities. This effect has also been shown to hold when observing virtual agents perform in a virtual environment [12]. Also, en-active mastery and vicarious experience can be mixed in virtual reality by experiencing a virtual doppelganger from a first-person perspective [16].

Verbal persuasion in the form of encouragement and discouragement about individual's performance or capability to perform [21] is another powerful source to develop self-efficacy. Similar to the real world, when individuals receive encouragement in a virtual environment by listening to a virtual coach or hearing a conversation between virtual avatars, people's beliefs can change [20].

Wood, et al. [28] point out that positive self-statements can backfire if they do not match the person's current belief or need. This can be explained by social judgment theory [23] as it provides a framework for the design of strong persuasive messages. Based on a person's beliefs, messages are classified into latitudes of acceptance, non-commitment, and rejection. Messages that target the latitude of non-commitment can establish the largest belief change, as messages falling into the latitude of acceptance are already close to people's beliefs, and messages falling into the latitude of rejection are likely to be rejected or even strength current beliefs. Therefore, to establish persuasive messages, a system needs to take into account a person's current self-efficacy level and the categorization of potential persuasive messages.

2.2 Stream of consciousness

Psychologist William James [14] coined the term stream of consciousness in 1890, to describe that thoughts can be regarded as a continuous stream and "part of a personal consciousness" (p. 225). In literature, the stream of consciousness is a narrative technique that reproduces people's internal psychological world, presenting mental observations and commentary (e.g. [15]).

Human behavior, attitudes, and cognitions are extensively influenced by people's conscious thoughts. Much research work asserts that inner voice, also known as internal monologue, plays various important roles in cognitive function, such as self-regulation [27], self-reflection [19] and, importantly, learning [25]. Helping learners to use inner voice during learning can contribute to reducing anxiety and increasing both confidence and communicative competence [26].

Based on these considerations, we propose the use of virtual cognitions to work as a kind of inner voice or personalized voice-over to present conscious thought to the user during the negotiation training.

3 System

Table 1 is an excerpt from the scripts of our negotiation dialogs and virtual cognitions that users heard when they were immersed in our VR negotiation training system. The conversations were set between the user, in the role of an employer (ER), and a virtual employee (EE), sitting across from the user. Users heard the external dialog as shown in Lines 1-3. Lines 4-6 show the virtual cognitions that users heard as part of an internal monologue. They introduce the relevant negotiation knowledge, describe the current situation, and reflect what users heard and what they should do and why. Line 5 illustrates a self-motivating statement, which users also heard during the training as one key factor of virtual cognitions. Although users played the role of the employer negotiating with an employee, they did not actively contribute to the negotiation. Instead, they heard pre-recorded audio while seeing a virtual self. For this, they wore a head mounted display. Their body movement was captured to synchronize it with their virtual body which they could see in a virtual mirror to enhance the body ownership illusion and sense of agency over the virtual body [2,24].

The system delivered three training sessions, each addressing different negotiation topics and each set in a specific workplace scenario: (1) stages in negotiations (scenario: continuously being late for work); (2) best alternative to a negotiated agreement (scenario: requesting an immediate holiday); and (3) separate the people from the issue (scenario: quitting one's job). During the training,

Table 1. Excerpt from negotiation scripts between employer (ER) Leon (the user's perspective) and virtual employee (EE) Tom.

---

1. EE: (Talking) Next week is the last week that it is still warm in Spain. After that it will be too cold to enjoy the beach this year. My wife likes the beach very much, and she has already been asking me to take her to a beach for over a year. Next week is the last chance for us to go.

2. ER: (Talking) Ok, I see. So you want to have a holiday immediately next week mainly because you worry that you can't take your wife to the beach later?

3. EE: (Talking) Yes, you can say that.

4. ER: (Thinking-reflection) I gathered a large amount of information about Tom's plan for a holiday and finally figured out the underlying and real reason why Tom wanted to take a vacation immediately. It was not just what he said at the very beginning about being very tried, but instead he wants to take his wife to the beach otherwise the weather could turn cold.

5. ER: (Thinking-self motivation) Leon, the negotiation is going quite well, you are doing a great job in the joint exploration stage.

6. ER: (Thinking-knowledge) Now, the negotiation will come to the next stage: bidding. The teacher emphasized that BATNA should always be kept in mind. I should share more information about my interests with Tom and develop multiple options for him to choose from.

7. ER: (Talking) Fine. I understand. How about you finish your project first, then I arrange for you to go to Egypt for a new project. You can take your wife with you, so during the weekends you can relax and enjoy the sunshine and the beach all the time.

8. EE: (Talking) Um, it sounds great, but I don't have enough money to take my wife to Egypt.

Table 2. Three types of virtual cognitions we used in the system.

Type	Function	Example
Knowledge and principles	Introduce the targeted knowledge and principles	"A successful negotiation usually consists of four major stages: private preparation, joint exploration, bidding, and closing."
Reflection	Describe the current situation, analyze the thoughts, feelings, and behaviors of the other parties and explain what to do and why the user should behave in the proposed manner	"Until now, Mike seems getting into a better mood. I should continue making him feel relaxed and let him know he can talk about everything he wants with me."
Self-motivation	Persuade people of their capability to perform social behaviors and encourage themselves to engage in social interactions	"Yes, great! The negotiation went well. Mike was totally calmed down. I did a great job. [User's name], you are quite good at negotiating."

session users were exposed to three types of virtual cognitions (Table 2) as taken from the idea of social stories theory [18]: knowledge and principles, reflection, and self-motivation.

The knowledge and principles introduced in previous training sessions were reviewed to strengthen users' understanding and recollection. The reflective virtual cognitions in the first training session only focused on observations of the situation at hand. In the second and third sessions, these reflections also included thoughts about the previous negotiation. A similar strategy was followed for the self-motivation cognitions, evaluating the user's performance in current or previous negotiation, stressing feelings of mastery of experience. To target users' latitude of non-commitment towards a higher level of self-efficacy, users' self-efficacy level was measured before each training session, and matching self-reflective cognitions were selected from a validated ranked list of cognitions [10]. These self-motivation cognitions were written in the third-person perspective, which has been shown to be more effective in regulating people's thoughts, feelings and behavior compared to first-person language use [17].

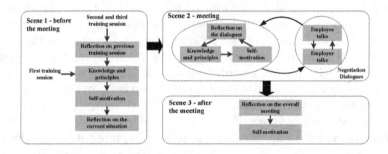

Fig. 1. The flow of virtual cognitions and dialogues in a training session.

Each training session consisted of three scenes (Fig. 1). The first scene was set before the meeting. Here users heard virtual cognitions reflecting on a fictional negotiation course or previous negotiations. These experiences were linked to self-motivation cognitions. The scene ends with reflections on the upcoming negotiation meeting, applying the negotiation knowledge and principle to the situation at hand. In the second scene, users started to experience the virtual negotiation in action, facing a virtual employee, which was gender-matched to the user. When the employee talked, users saw the mouth movement of the employee. When users heard their own external voice, they saw the movement of their virtual mouths in the virtual mirror. When they heard the virtual cognitions, their virtual mouth did not move. To create a natural pause in the dialog, the employee drank from his or her mug when users were hearing an internal monologue. In the closing scene, the users were again alone in the virtual meeting room. Here they heard virtual cognitions that reviewed the process of the past negotiation, their performance and also motivated them affirmatively.

4 Method

To obtain a first evaluation of the system, we conducted a pilot study. To this end, we followed a pretest-posttest design with all participants completing the training and consequently no comparison group. The study was approved by Delft University of Technology Human Research Ethics Committee (ID: 60).

4.1 Participants

Eight participants (1 female) were recruited via e-mail or approached personally throughout the university campus. Their ages ranged from 22 to 29 ($M = 25.5$, $SD = 2$). Participants received a small gift in appreciation of their efforts.

4.2 Materials and Measures

Materials. The system captured the body movements of users with a Kinect, which returned real world distance in meters. For the HMD, an Oculus Rift DevKit 2 with a resolution of 1920*1080 pixels was used, while the virtual environment was created in Unity3D. To strengthen similarity and therefore the effect of this vicarious experience, we gave the virtual employer character the voice of the participants. We recorded all external dialogs and the virtual cognitions, resembling participant's inner voice, by asking participants to read the sentences of the negotiation out loud prior to the training. This was done with a pair of binaural microphones (Roland CS-10EM) worn by the participant.

Self-efficacy. Following Bandura's approach [5], a one-item self-efficacy assessment was conducted. The question was formulated as: "Supposing that now you, as an employer, need to negotiate with your employee about a topic at the workplace, please rate how certain you are that you can successfully negotiate with him/her." The item was rated on an 11-point Likert scale from -5 (highly certain cannot do) to 5 (highly certain can do).

Negotiation knowledge. A validated negotiation knowledge video test [9] was used. This consists of eight negotiation scenarios (female version and male version) each including six video scenes portraying negotiation situations. After each scene, participants are asked: "What is your advice for the employer?". Written answers are scored on the participant's ability to identify key negotiation concepts. The video test has been validated in a study with 128 participants. Mean and standard deviation for each negotiation scenario were hence available to standardize test scores.

Perceived Utility. To investigate how satisfying and useful people found the training, a 7-item utility questionnaire was used, which included three items on the satisfaction of the training process and four items on the effectiveness in improving negotiation performance. This questionnaire was adapted from the one used in a study by Kang [16]. All the items were rated on a 7-point Likert scale from 1 (strongly disagree) to 7 (strongly agree).

4.3 Procedure

On their first visit, participants were informed of the nature of the experiment and signed their consent to participate. The pilot study consisted of three phases: pre-training, training, and post-training. In the first phase, recordings were made of each participant reading out all sentences of the three negotiation training sessions (dialogs and virtual cognitions). The order of sentences was randomized to limit participant understanding and memorization of actual scenarios. After the recording, participants were asked to listen to a part of their recordings and set sound parameters with the instructions to make their recordings sound as they hear their own external voice or as their inner-voice. Participants were also asked to record their names, which were later incorporated into the negotiation dialogs and self-motivation cognitions. After at least one week, we invited participants to complete an online questionnaire collecting demographic information and the pretest measures (self-efficacy question, negotiation knowledge test).

Once the questionnaire was completed, participants started with the training phase. In this phase, they were invited into the lab to receive the negotiation training consisting of three consecutive sessions; each administrated on a separate day. Each training session lasted around 30 minutes, which started with five minutes of immersion into the virtual room, allowing participants to familiarize themselves with the virtual world and their virtual body before the actual scenario started. After each session, participants were asked to finish an online questionnaire to measure their self-efficacy and negotiation confidence. The latter was used to select the self-motivation cognitions in the next training session. Two weeks after entering the second phase, all participants were sent a link for the posttest measurement.

5 Result

5.1 Self-efficacy

Taking participants as a random intercept effect, two multilevel models were fitted to the self-efficacy data: a fixed intercept effect model (baseline model) and extended model that included the moment of data collection as a fixed effect. The analysis revealed a significant model fit improvement for the extended model ($\chi^2(1) = 9.65$, $p = 0.002$), suggesting that, as shown in Fig. 2, over time, self-efficacy increased.

5.2 Negotiation knowledge

Two coders scored the answers obtained from the negotiation knowledge test. With acceptable correlation ($r = 0.95$) between scores of the coders, the average score was taken, which was normalized using the scenario mean, and standard deviation available for each negotiation scenario [9]. A paired-sample t-test, revealed that participants had a significantly higher ($t(7) = 3.19$, $p = 0.015$, $d = 1.13$) negotiation knowledge score after the negotiation training ($M = 1.5$, $SD = 0.94$) than before the training ($M = 0.1$, $SD = 0.90$).

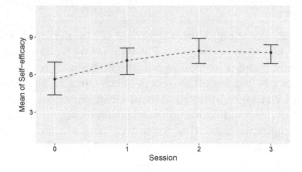

Fig. 2. Mean (error bar 95% CI) self-efficacy score obtained before the training (0) and in the different sessions (1-3).

5.3   Perceived Utility

Cronbach's alpha was calculated for the two subscales of the utility questionnaire, satisfaction of the system ($\alpha = 0.57$) and usefulness of the system ($\alpha = 0.74$), respectively. The mean value of the items within each questionnaire was taken as a single measure of that concept. To investigate if users hold a positive attitude about our training system, one-sample t-tests were conducted comparing scores with a value 4, the neutral position on the scale. Tests did not find significant deviations from the neutral rating, for either the satisfaction-related utility ($M = 4.17$, $SD = 0.99$) or the effectiveness-related utility ($M = 4.66$, $SD = 1.04$).

6   Discussion

We developed a virtual reality negotiation training system that exposes users to an unfolding negotiation, thereby witnessing both the dialog and the thought process of a negotiator. The main findings of the pilot study suggest that the training system can enhance people's negotiation knowledge and their self-efficacy, two key factors influencing a successful negotiation. The results of our pilot study thus encourage further confirmation studies with a control group to control for confounding variables or comparison with groups using other training systems or instruction delivery methods. Although the passive nature of our training might cause less anxiety to enroll, it might also make the experience less engaging and enjoyable, as the perceived utility data of the pilot study indicates. Interesting would, therefore, be to examine the effect of combining this training with existing unguided negotiation training systems where people actively negotiate with a virtual opponent.

Several design choices limit the scope of the results and should be noted to appreciate the findings. First, the format and articulation of the inner voice are very personal, as it has been found to resemble people's voice and regional accent [11]. This might have affected the pilot study as it included non-native English participants, whose everyday inner monologue might not be in English as the virtual cognitions were in the study. Similarly, the sense of agency in the virtual environment might be improved by administering vibrotactile stimulation on the thyroid cartilage when the participants hear the pre-recorded stimulus voice [3]. In our current system, users only passively experience the negotiation. Using eye-tracking in virtual reality offers the possibility to tailor virtual cognitions to people's focus of attention in the virtual environment. It could thus provide more timely guided-learning and more thoughtful motivation. Finally, we received some negative feedback on the audio quality from the participants. The audio of the employee avatar was recorded at close range. This did not match with the spatial distance that participants had to the avatar in the virtual environment.

In conclusion, a system that provides guided learning with the combination of virtual self-experience and virtual cognitions can potentially affect people's knowledge of negotiation and self-efficacy. Further research might investigate the extent to which the system has the potential to change individual's beliefs and behavior in the long run.

Acknowledgements

This research was supported by the China Scholarship Council (CSC), grant number 201506090167. We thank colleagues from Interactive Intelligence Group, TU Delft who carefully prepared the stimuli voice for the virtual employee.

References

1. Laura Aymerich-Franch, René F Kizilcec, and Jeremy N Bailenson. The relationship between virtual self similarity and social anxiety. *Frontiers in human neuroscience*, 8:944, 2014.
2. Domna Banakou, Raphaela Groten, and Mel Slater. Illusory ownership of a virtual child body causes overestimation of object sizes and implicit attitude changes. *Proceedings of the National Academy of Sciences*, 110(31):12846–12851, 2013.
3. Domna Banakou and Mel Slater. Body ownership causes illusory self-attribution of speaking and influences subsequent real speaking. *Proceedings of the National Academy of Sciences*, 111(49):17678–17683, 2014.
4. Albert Bandura. *Self-efficacy: The exercise of control*. Macmillan, 1997.
5. Albert Bandura. Guide for constructing self-efficacy scales. *Self-efficacy beliefs of adolescents*, 5(307-337), 2006.
6. Albert Bandura and EA Locke. Cultivate self-efficacy for personal and organizational effectiveness. *Handbook of principles of organization behavior*, 2:179–200, 2009.
7. Joost Broekens, Maaike Harbers, Willem-Paul Brinkman, Catholijn M Jonker, Karel Van den Bosch, and John-Jules Meyer. Virtual reality negotiation training increases negotiation knowledge and skill. In *International Conference on Intelligent Virtual Agents*, pages 218–230. Springer, 2012.
8. Mark Core, David Traum, H Chad Lane, William Swartout, Jonathan Gratch, Michael Van Lent, and Stacy Marsella. Teaching negotiation skills through practice and reflection with virtual humans. *Simulation*, 82(11):685–701, 2006.
9. Ding Ding. Negotiation knowledge test: videos, validation data and scoring forms - datasets, 2016.

10. Ding Ding. Self-motivation cognitions: validation data and questionnaires - datasets, 2016.
11. Ruth Filik and Emma Barber. Inner speech during silent reading reflects the reader's regional accent. *PloS one*, 6(10):e25782, 2011.
12. Jesse Fox and Jeremy N Bailenson. Virtual self-modeling: The effects of vicarious reinforcement and identification on exercise behaviors. *Media Psychology*, 12(1):1–25, 2009.
13. Marco Greco and Gianluca Murgia. Improving negotiation skills through an online business game. In *Proceedings of the European Conference on Game Based Learning*, pages 97–104, 2007.
14. William James. *The principles of psychology*. Read Books Ltd, 2013.
15. James Joyce. *Ulysses*. Editora Companhia das Letras, 2012.
16. Ni Kang. *Public speaking in virtual reality: Audience design and speaker experiences*. Thesis, 2016.
17. Ethan Kross, Emma Bruehlman-Senecal, Jiyoung Park, Aleah Burson, Adrienne Dougherty, Holly Shablack, Ryan Bremner, Jason Moser, and Ozlem Ayduk. Self-talk as a regulatory mechanism: how you do it matters. *Journal of Personality and Social Psychology*, 106(2):304, 2014.
18. Scott R McConnell. Interventions to facilitate social interaction for young children with autism: Review of available research and recommendations for educational intervention and future research. *Journal of autism and developmental disorders*, 32(5):351–372, 2002.
19. Alain Morin and Breanne Hamper. Self-reflection and the inner voice: activation of the left inferior frontal gyrus during perceptual and conceptual self-referential thinking. *The open neuroimaging journal*, 6(1), 2012.
20. Chao Qu, Yun Ling, Ingrid Heynderickx, and Willem-Paul Brinkman. Virtual bystanders in a language lesson: examining the effect of social evaluation, vicarious experience, cognitive consistency and praising on students' beliefs, self-efficacy and anxiety in a virtual reality environment. *PloS one*, 10(4):e0125279, 2015.
21. Brian Francis Redmond and AC Rupp. Self-efficacy and social cognitive theories. *Retrieved from*, 2013.
22. Avi Rosenfeld, Inon Zuckerman, Erel Segal-Halevi, Osnat Drein, and Sarit Kraus. Negochat: a chat-based negotiation agent. In *Proceedings of the 2014 international conference on Autonomous agents and multi-agent systems*, pages 525–532. International Foundation for Autonomous Agents and Multiagent Systems, 2014.
23. Muzafer Sherif and Carl I Hovland. Social judgment: Assimilation and contrast effects in communication and attitude change. 1961.
24. Mel Slater, Bernhard Spanlang, Maria V Sanchez-Vives, and Olaf Blanke. First person experience of body transfer in virtual reality. *PloS one*, 5(5):e10564, 2010.
25. Luc Steels. Language re-entrance and the'inner voice'. *Journal of Consciousness Studies*, 10(4-5):173–185, 2003.
26. Brian Tomlinson. The inner voice: A critical factor in l2 learning. *The Journal of the Imagination in Language Learning and Teaching, VI*, pages 26–33, 2001.
27. Lev Semenovich Vygotskiĭ, Eugenia Hanfmann, and Gertruda Vakar. *Thought and language*. MIT press, 2012.
28. Joanne V Wood, WQ Elaine Perunovic, and John W Lee. Positive self-statements: Power for some, peril for others. *Psychological Science*, 20(7):860–866, 2009.
29. Ben CB Yip and David WK Man. Virtual reality (vr)-based community living skills training for people with acquired brain injury: A pilot study. *Brain injury*, 23(13-14):1017–1026, 2009.

Do We Need Emotionally Intelligent Artificial Agents? First Results of Human Perceptions of Emotional Intelligence in Humans Compared to Robots

Lisa Fan[1], Matthias Scheutz[1] ✉, Monika Lohani[2,3], Marissa McCoy[3], and Charlene Stokes[3]

[1] Tufts University, Human-Robot Interaction Lab, Medford, MA 02155 USA
[2] University of Utah, Salt Lake City, UT 84112
[3] The MITRE Coorporation, Bedford, MA 01730
matthias.scheutz@tufts.edu

Abstract. Humans are very apt at reading emotional signals in other humans and even artificial agents, which raises the question of whether artificial agents need to be emotionally intelligent to ensure effective social interactions. For artificial agents without emotional intelligence might generate behavior that is misinterpreted, unexpected, and confusing to humans, violating human expectations and possibly causing emotional harm. Surprisingly, there is a dearth of investigations aimed at understanding the extent to which artificial agents need emotional intelligence for successful interactions. Here, we present the first study in the perception of emotional intelligence (EI) in robots vs. humans. The objective was to determine whether people viewed robots as more or less emotionally intelligent when exhibiting similar behaviors as humans, and to investigate which verbal and nonverbal communication methods were most crucial for human observational judgments. Study participants were shown a scene in which either a robot or a human behaved with either high or low empathy, and then they were asked to evaluate the agent's emotional intelligence and trustworthiness. The results showed that participants could consistently distinguish the high EI condition from the low EI condition regardless of the variations in which communication methods were observed, and that whether the agent was a robot or human had no effect on the perception. We also found that relative to low EI high EI conditions led to greater trust in the agent, which implies that we must design robots to be emotionally intelligent if we wish for users to trust them.

Keywords: Human-robot interaction, emotional intelligence, empathetic robot

1 Introduction

With the advances in technology, robots and artificial agents are becoming more prominent in our lives. Virtual personal assistants like Siri and Amazon Echo al-

© Springer International Publishing AG 2017
J. Beskow et al. (Eds.): IVA 2017, LNAI 10498, pp. 129–141, 2017.
DOI 10.1007/978-3-319-67401-8_15

low for frequent interactions in a casual conversational tone. Research has found that virtual therapists and teachers can hold effective sessions with patients and students [22, 2]. To improve the relationship between social artificial agents and their users and increase the effectiveness of their interactions, we must examine the social protocols embedded within our society.

Humans are expected to understand and follow customs and social norms when communicating, while also being aware of others' perceptions of them and appropriately regulating their emotions. Showing empathy is also a highly regarded social skill which can be demonstrated through verbal and nonverbal communication such as words, tone of voice, facial expressions, posture, and physical gestures.

However, people might hold different expectations for artificial agents in social situations. Despite interacting with technology on a daily basis, and oftentimes in a social manner, an artificial agent that can appropriately interact in an emotional capacity may be unexpected (and perhaps unwelcome) to some people. An important open question is whether artificial agents need to be emotionally intelligent in order to be successful at social interactions with humans. Another related question is, whether artificial agents exhibiting emotional intelligence are evaluated differently from agents without EI, and whether such emotionally intelligent agents are considered more trustworthy. Answering these questions is critical for the design of socially interactive artificial agents, not only to ensure smooth interactions, but ultimately to ensure their acceptance and success.

In this paper, we set out to investigate several fundamental questions that can help answer whether artificial agents need EI, including whether humans will even be able to perceive EI in artificial agents compared to their perceptions of EI in other humans, which behavioral factors are critical for perceiving EI, and the extent to which perceptions of EI affect the trustworthiness of artificial agents. The rest of the paper is structured as follows. After a brief review of EI, we introduce our online study together with the specific hypotheses we intended to address. Next we present the results, followed by a discussion about what they imply for the design of artificial agents. Then we conclude with a summary of our findings and a brief outlook of the next steps.

2   Background

Emotions influence thinking, decision-making, relationships and mental health, and success both within and outside of work environments. Emotional intelligence is the capacity to accurately assess one's own and others' emotional state and to use that information to adapt, manage, and guide subsequent thinking and actions [24]. Considerable research has been conducted on EI in the workplace, demonstrating that EI strongly predicts the quality of the organizational climate [20], performance and stress management [7], and teamwork and conflict management [6]. In educational settings, research shows that students with higher emotional intelligence perform better academically [23], have improved

emotion-management skills [4], and experience fewer learning and conduct problems [23]. Likewise, school leaders and teachers who are emotionally intelligent
are more effective leaders and better co-workers [17], are better able to manage
stress and create learning environments that provide greater emotional support,
better classroom organization, and improved instructional support [9].

Enhancing EI skills provides individuals with the capacity to enhance personal growth, performance, problem solving, and relationships [24]. EI screening,
training, and assessment have become a burgeoning business as everyone from
companies, to the military, to educational institutions are hoping to increase pro-
ductivity with workers who are more flexible, adaptable, and skilled at working
in teams [1]. Now, with growing pressure for efficiency and achievement among
workers in a competitive and increasingly technologically advanced global environment, not only is more emphasis being placed on the EI skills of the human
worker, but also on that of the machines in which the workers interact [21].

In artificial intelligence, emotional intelligence is implicitly assumed under
the concept of "relational agents" which are defined as "computational artifacts
designed to build long-term, social-emotional relationships with their users" [3].
One study compares a relational agent with programmed social skills to a non-
relational agent without any such skills. In the development of the relational
agent used in their experiment, the authors gave the agent nonverbal skills, such
as hand gestures, posture shifts, and facial expressions, as well as verbal messages
that conveyed humor, empathy, politeness, and friendliness. When participants
interacted with either the relational or non-relational agent for an extended
period of time, participants reportedly felt closer to and preferred the relational
agent.

The concept of relational agents has further been explored and found to be
effective in a variety of settings, from education to elder care [8] to public areas
like shopping malls [11]. In Baylor's study of virtual educators [2], participants
were able to distinguish between virtual agents with different teaching styles, and
found the agent that exhibited the least relational cues to be less human-like and
less engaging.

The relationship between a human and an artificial agent is not negligible,
since it affects not only the user's perception of the robot, but also the user's
behavior following the interaction. In the aforementioned study on virtual educators, results showed that participants interacting with a more relational agent
had a bigger boost in confidence and performed better on the task taught by the
agent.

While much research has been conducted on what makes an artificial agent
perceived as more emotional, not much has been explored on the perception of
emotional intelligence in an artificial agent, which focuses on how well the agent
comprehends and displays emotions in specific social situations. Moreover, it is
unclear to what extent emotional intelligence, if exhibited by an artificial agent
would engender trust in the agent. In humans, emotions (impacted by EI skills
and training) can exert a significant influence on trust judgments and behavior
[19, 12, 16, 13, 10, 26, 25]. Trust is defined as the willingness to be vulnerable to

the actions of another based on positive expectations [19, 12] and thus a critical factor to consider for human-agent interactions as trust impacts how much humans rely on artificial agents like robots [16, 13, 10, 26, 25]. Previous research has established that numerous factors related to human, artificial agent, as well as the environment in which they interact can impact trust and human-robot team outcomes [16, 13, 25]. For instance, we believe that emotional intelligence of the team-members (human and artificial agent) leads to emergence of team dynamics processes (e.g., human-agent team's rapport, communication, cooperation, team management), which influences trust and team performance [16]. In past work, we have shown that emotional intelligence displays by an artificial agent results in greater trust and reliance on that artificial agent [16, 14, 15]. However, little empirical evidence is currently available to understand how EI levels of both human and artificial agent impact trust and teamwork and whether artificial agents need to display EI. In the present study, we have compared EI displays by an artificial agent versus a human to better understand the role of EI and its influence on trust outcomes.

3 The current study

With the rise of artificial agents in everyday life from personal robots to human-machine teaming in the military to collaborative robots in manufacturing it may be expected that we would want the same EI competencies in our artificial agent counterparts as we have come to expect in our human teammates. Would it not be great, for example, if an artificial agent teammate (perhaps more so than a human teammate) was capable of detecting a certain threshold of stress and in response swiftly relieved a worker of the burdensome task before it became riddled with errors? In this study we focus on empathy, a core competency of EI. While empathy is integral in an interaction between two humans, it is unclear whether we expect artificial agents to also empathize with us during an interaction. It also remains to be seen how we determine that an artificial agent is empathizing with us.

In order to understand human perception of emotional intelligence in artificial agents, we explore the importance of different factors in social behavior, including the content of the message, tone of voice, posturing, and gesturing are also relevant factors in judging an agent's emotional intelligence. We designed our experiment so that we could incrementally evaluate the effect of each of these factors on human perception of an artificial agent's empathy skills.

The study consisted of a participant watching a short workplace scenario between a human and an agent. The agent was either a human or a robot, and either displayed empathy (high EI) or failed to display empathy (low EI). We ran four permutations of this study which varied in the communication methods presented on screen. The communication methods of interest were message content, tone of voice, body posture, and physical gestures. The permutations were phased such that one communication method was removed for each proceeding permutation. We specifically intended to test the following hypotheses:

H1. If robots are not perceived as human-like, then we would expect to see a difference between the human high EI condition and the artificial agent high EI condition, and possibly a difference between the human low EI condition and the artificial agent low EI condition.

H2. If the dynamics of the interactions matter for the perception of EI, then we expect to see a difference in the EI effect between the full video showing all the dynamics of the interaction and the two still images at the beginning and in the middle of the interaction, for both artificial agent and human, with the full video showing overall higher levels of EI than the still images.

H3. If the bodily postures of the two still images convey enough information about the EI of the agent, then we expect a difference between the audio-only condition (with only an initial image of the agent) compared to the condition with the two still images (at critical times during the interaction) and also the full video with the full dynamics of the interaction displayed. Similarly, we would expect a further reduction in the EI assessment for the text-only condition if prosody and other vocal qualities matter for the EI assessment in addition to the semantic content of the utterances.

H4. Overall we expect humans to trust human and artificial agents with high EI more than human and artificial agents with low EI.

3.1 Design

Participants. A total of 395 participants (43% females) were recruited for this study through Amazon Mechanical Turk. Participants were between 18 to 66 years of age (mean age = 33.66, SD = 10.19). The ethnicity distribution for the sample was: White or Caucasian 77.5%, Asian 7.6%, African American 7.8%, Hispanic 5.1%, two or more races 4.5%, and other 2%.

Materials. We used the PR2 robot as the agent, which is physically slightly larger than an average person and has arms that end in a clawed hand. It has 7 degrees of freedom in its arm and wrist, and its head can pan and tilt. In the original videos, the PR2 started at a neutral position, facing the supervisor with arms in front, then moved to a posture reflecting the EI condition as described above. Although the PR2 played the pre-programmed dialogue during filming using its native text-to-speech software, we later dubbed its lines using the "Alex" voice on the Mac OS due to lack of clarity. We filmed a series of videos in which an agent interacted with a workmate who was recently reprimanded by his supervisor. The agent (human or robot) demonstrated empathy (high EI) by showing concern and offering encouragement to his workmate, or failed to demonstrate empathy (low EI) by chastising his workmate. Apart from dialogue, the two EI conditions differed in the posture of the agent. In the high EI condition, the agent faced the workmate with open arms, while in the low EI condition, the agent faced away from the workmate with crossed arms. Naturally, the videos with the human agent had minimal physical gestures and slightly different tones of voice between the EI conditions, while the robot in the robot agent videos did not move once it struck its designated pose, and did not vary its tone of voice between the EI conditions. The supervisor, workmate, and human agent were played by male actors, and a male voice was used for the robot agent.

To do a phased study of the different communication methods, we varied the presentation of the stimuli-type in the following way:

1. *Video*. The video was shown in its entirety, which displayed the agent's message, tone of voice, posture, and movement.
2. *Audio*. The video showed two still images from the original video while keeping the audio (see Fig. 1). The first still in both EI conditions showed the agent and the workmate looking at the supervisor in a neutral position. In the second still, the supervisor has left and the workmate is looking at the agent. The agent is displaying the posture for the given EI condition as described above. By showing stills instead of the video throughout the interaction, this experiment removes physical gestures and other dynamic movements from the participant's evaluation of the human and agent's EI.
3. *Image*. The video showed two head-shot images of the agent and workmate, respectively, in neutral positions prior to the dialogue, then played the audio from the original video against a black background with no images. This removes posture information in addition to gestures from the participant's evaluation.
4. *Text*. The video showed images of the agent and workmate prior to the dialogue, then displayed the text of the dialogue without audio or other visuals. This removed tone of voice from the communication methods the participant observed.

Questionnaires. Prior to viewing the scenario, the participants answered a demographic survey about their age, gender, and ethnicity. After viewing the scenario, to measure how participants perceived the agent's EI, a standardized questionnaire was completed by the participants (24-item, Cronbach's α was .99) [5]. Example items include: "Considerate of others' feelings", "Puts people down". Next, participants reported how much they trusted the agent using a standardized questionnaire (4-item, 5-point Likert scale, Cronbach's α was .76) [18]. An example item is: "I really wish I had a good way to keep an eye on the agent").

3.2 Procedure

Participants from Mechanical Turk were redirected to our website which led them through the experiment. After accepting the consent form, participants completed the demographics and EI questionnaire. The participants were then led to a page that played a video with randomly assigned conditions. The scenario was only played once, and the participant could not pause or skip the video. The participants then answered the agent EI questionnaire, after which they were given a code to redeem payment from Mechanical Turk.

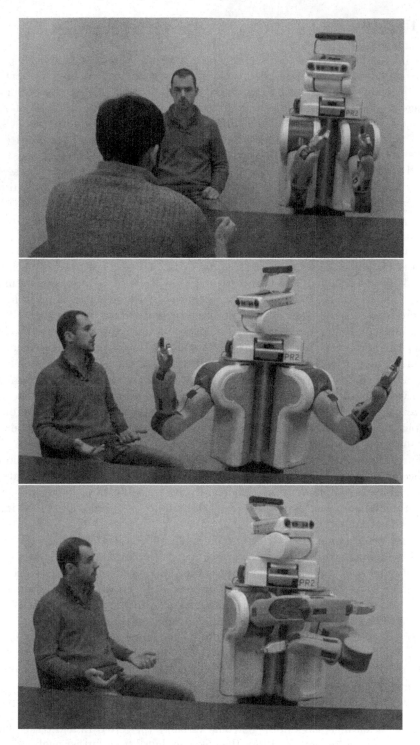

Fig. 1. Three still images from the EI robot scenario (from top to bottom): at the beginning of the interaction, in the high EI condition and the low EI condition after the supervisor left.

4   Results

As a manipulation check, we wanted to make sure that the high EI vs. low EI scenarios that were created for this study actually led to high vs. low EI-related perceptions by the participants. We tested if EI-related perceptions of the agent (dependent variable) was influenced by the EI behavior presented by the agent in the scenario (low vs. high) for each of four stimuli-types (video, audio, image, and text stimuli). Fig. 2 presents the mean and standard error values across the resulting 16 conditions.[4] Simple contrast comparisons confirmed that the manipulation led to significant differences in EI level presented by the human or robot agent across all the stimuli-type was significantly different. For human agent: in video ($F(1, 379) = 46.84, p < .001$), audio ($F(1, 379) = 23.59, p < .001$), image ($F(1, 379) = 45.39, p < .001$), and text ($F(1, 379) = 52.46, p < .001$) stimuli-types, high-EI (than low-EI) behavior displayed by the agent resulted in higher EI perceptions of the agent. Similarly, for robot agent: in video ($F(1, 379) = 41.87, p < .001$), audio ($F(1, 379) = 23.89, p < .001$), image ($F(1, 379) = 44.33, p < .001$), and text ($F(1, 379) = 51.74, p < .001$) stimuli-types, high-EI (than low-EI) behavior displayed by the agent resulted in higher EI perceptions of the agent. These findings suggested that during high-EI scenarios (relative to low-EI), human as well as robot agents were perceived to have higher EI. These analyses were done as a manipulation check to ensure that the stimuli manipulation led to conditional differences in agent's EI perception.

Planned comparisons using one-way ANOVAs were conducted to examine if there were any differences in perceived EI depending upon the agent being a human versus a robot (related to H1). No significant differences for any of the comparisons were found suggesting that the perceived EI were not different for human versus robot agents.

Furthermore, related to H2 and H3, stimuli-type was found to have no difference on perceived EI of robot agent, whereas the stimuli-type influenced perceived EI levels of human agent. Specifically, text stimuli led to higher perceived EI of the human agent than video ($p = .03$), audio ($p < .001$), as well as image ($p = .001$) stimuli.

Next, we examined how trust in the agent (dependent variable) was influenced by the following three factors: *agent-type* (human vs. robot), *agent's EI level displayed in a scenario* (low vs. high), and *different stimuli* (video, audio, image, and text stimuli). Fig. 3 presents the mean and standard error values across the resulting 16 conditions. A between-subjects analyses of variance (ANOVA) model revealed a significant effect of EI-scenario ($F(1, 379) = 121.87, p < .001, \eta_p^2 = .24$), as well as stimuli-type on trust ($F(1, 379) = 3.23, p = .02, \eta_p^2 = .03$). No effect of agent-type was found on trust ($p = .23$).

Planned comparisons using one-way ANOVAs related to H4 suggested that during high-EI scenarios, participants trusted the agent significantly more than the low-EI scenarios, for both human and robot agents, in all conditions. For hu-

---

[4] No significant differences in the outcome variables (perceived EI and trust) due to age or gender were found and thus they were excluded from further analyses.

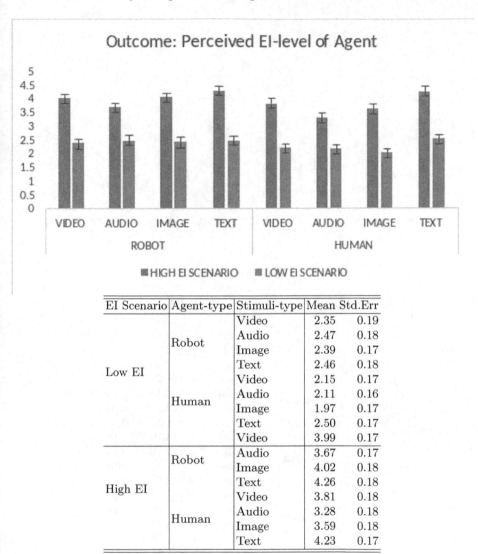

Fig. 2. Mean values and standard errors of perceived EI presented by the agent.

man agent: in *video* $(F(1, 379) = 22.94, p < .001)$, *audio* $(F(1, 379) = 13.19, p <$ .001), *image* $(F(1, 379) = 20.61, p < .001)$, and *text* $(F(1, 379) = 18.45, p < .001)$ stimuli-type, high-EI (than low-EI) behavior by the agent resulted in greater trust on the agent. Similarly, for robot agent: in *video* $(F(1, 379) = 6.65, p = .01)$, *audio* $(F(1, 379) = 11.32, p = .001)$, *image* $(F(1, 379) = 22.89, p < .001)$, and *text* $(F(1, 379) = 11.06, p < .001)$ stimuli-type, high-EI (than low-EI) behavior by the agent resulted in greater trust on the agent.

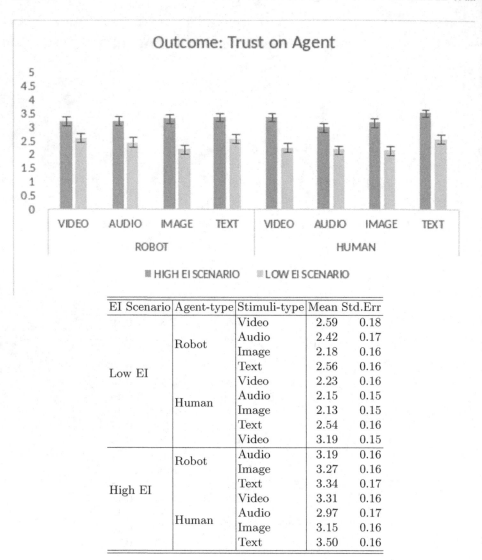

EI Scenario	Agent-type	Stimuli-type	Mean	Std.Err
Low EI	Robot	Video	2.59	0.18
		Audio	2.42	0.17
		Image	2.18	0.16
		Text	2.56	0.16
	Human	Video	2.23	0.16
		Audio	2.15	0.15
		Image	2.13	0.15
		Text	2.54	0.16
High EI	Robot	Video	3.19	0.15
		Audio	3.19	0.16
		Image	3.27	0.16
		Text	3.34	0.17
	Human	Video	3.31	0.16
		Audio	2.97	0.17
		Image	3.15	0.16
		Text	3.50	0.16

Fig. 3. Mean values and standard errors of trust presented by the agent.

Next, we examined differences in trust appraisal when the agent is human versus robot across all conditions (related to H1). These comparisons revealed that there were no differences in trust appraisals when human versus robot agents were used to display EI-relevant behavior.

We conducted planned contrast comparisons using one-way ANOVAs to examine if there were any differences in trust levels in the agent depending upon the stimuli type. Stimuli-type was found to have no difference on trust in robot agent, whereas the stimuli-type was found to influence trust appraisals of human agent in the following two comparisons: Specifically, text stimuli led to greater trust in human agent than audio ($p = .01$) as well as image stimuli ($p = .02$).

5 Discussion

The results revealed that there was indeed no significant difference in how the human and robotic agents were perceived, thus allowing us to reject H1 and providing evidence for the fact that robots can be perceived as showing human-like EI in human-robot interactions. In addition, variation in the stimuli-type had no effect on the perceived EI of the robot agent, thus allowing us to reject H2 and H3 for the artificial agent. In the human case this was not true, as the text stimulus led to even higher perceived EI of the human agent than the video, audio, and image stimuli, thus making an even stronger case for rejecting H2 and H3 for humans. We did find support for H4 in that people did rate the high EI robots and humans as more trustworthy than the low EI robots and humans.

Overall, our findings suggest that regardless of whether the agent is human or robot, people are able to perceive a difference in the agent's EI level. We also found that while the different factors of communication had some effect on the perception of the human's EI, we observed no effects in the different communication methods displayed by the robot. These results suggest that the content of the verbal interaction is essential for humans' perceptions of EI in both humans and robots and not the tone of voice, posture, gesturing or other bodily dynamics. The fact that the high-EI human is rated even higher in the text-based condition compared to all other conditions squarely points to that fact. Hence, when a robot or artificial agent is capable of natural language interactions, it will be critical for the agent to demonstrate EI through the semantics of its utterances rather than its appearance and bodily dynamics. This is all the more important since trust in an artificial (and human) agent is critically linked to the perception of that agent's EI.

While the question of whether we will, in fact, need emotionally intelligent artificial agents is still open and needs much more extensive investigations, including investigations of interactions between humans and artificial agents with different levels of EI (as opposed to the interaction observation experiments we have conducted in this study), the present results provide first evidence that we artificial agents might have to be endowed at least with rudimentary EI capabilities. For if we wish to design robots and other artificial agents to have strong working relationships with their users, they will not succeed at establishing and maintaining human trust without demonstrating that they are capable of being emotionally intelligent and empathetic to the user's emotional state.

6 Conclusion and Future Work

In this paper, we set out to evaluate the perception of emotional intelligence in robots vs. humans. Our study consisted of participants viewing scenarios in which a robot or human acted out a scene with or without empathy, and we had participants rate the agent's EI and trustworthiness. We also varied the presentation of these scenes to see the effect of different facets of communication, such as tone of voice and posture. We found that participants were consistently able to tell the difference between the high and low EI conditions, and that agents with high EI were rated as more trustworthy than agents with low EI. We also found that natural language is the most influential factor in determining an agent's EI, and therefore conclude that in order to design more trustworthy artificial agents, we must focus on designing them with empathetic natural language capabilities. Given the fact that people have different responses to observing a situation and participating firsthand in a situation, we hope to conduct a future study in which participants interact with the robot directly. In addition to empathy, we also wish to investigate the perception of additional EI competencies, such as self-regulation and self-awareness. Although we observed no gender effects in the results of this study, it would also be interesting to investigate whether the gender of the agents in the scenario have an effect on their perceived level of emotional intelligence. By gaining a better understanding of perception in emotional intelligence context, in the future we can design more empathetic robots which will be viewed as more trustworthy.

Acknowledgements
This project was in part supported by ONR MURI grant #N00014-16-1-2278 to the second author.

References

1. Ashkanasy, N., Daus, C.: Emotion in the workplace: The new challenge for managers. The Academy of Management Executive 16(1), 76–86 (2002)
2. Baylor, A., Kim, Y.: Simulating instructional roles through pedagogical agents. International Journal of Artificial Intelligence in Education 15(2), 95–115 (2005)
3. Bickmore, T., Picard, R.: Establishing and maintaining long-term human-computer relationships. ACM Transactions on Computer-Human Interaction (TOCHI) 12(2), 293–327 (2005)
4. Brackett, M., Rivers, S., Salovey, P.: Emotional intelligence: Implications for personal, social, academic, and workplace success. Social and Personality Psychology Compass 5, 88–103 (2011)
5. Caruso, D.: Emotional intelligence scale. in preparation
6. Clarke, N.: Emotional intelligence and its relationship to transformational leadership and key project manager competences. Project Management Journal 41(2), 5–20 (2010)
7. Fariselli, L., Freedman, J., Ghini, M.M., Valentini, F.: Stress, emotional intelligence, and performance in healthcare (Retrieved 07/19/2017)
8. Fasola, J., Mataric, M.: Using socially assistive humanrobot interaction to motivate physical exercise for older adults. Proceedings of the IEEE 100, 2512–2526 (2012)
9. Hagelskamp, C., Brackett, M., Rivers, S., Salovey, P.: Improving classroom quality with the ruler approach to social and emotional learning: Proximal and distal outcomes. American Journal of Community Psychology 51, 530–543 (2013)
10. Hancock, P., Billings, D., Schaefer, K., Chen, J., Visser, E.D., , Parasuraman, R.: A meta-analysis of factors affecting trust in human-robot interaction. Human Factors: The Journal of the Human Factors and Ergonomics Society 53(5), 517–527 (2011)

11. Kanda, T., Shiomi, M., Miyashita, Z., Ishiguro, H., Hagita, N.: An affective guide robot in a shopping mall. In: 4th ACM/IEEE International Conference on Human-Robot Interaction (HRI). pp. 173–180 (March 2009)
12. Lee, J.D., See, K.A.: Trust in automation: Designing for appropriate reliance. Human Factors: The Journal of the Human Factors and Ergonomics Society 46(1), 50–80 (2004)
13. Lohani, M., Stokes, C., Dashan, N., McCoy, M., andS.E. Rivers, C.B.: A framework for human-agent social systems: The role of non-technical factors in operation success. In: Proceedings of Advances in Human Factors in Robots and Unmanned Systems. pp. 137–148 (2017)
14. Lohani, M., Stokes, C., McCoy, M., Bailey, C., Joshi, A., Rivers, S.: Perceived role of physiological sensors impacts trust and reliance on robots. In: Proceedings of 25th IEEE International Symposium on Robot and Human Interactive Communication. pp. 513–518 (2016)
15. Lohani, M., Stokes, C., McCoy, M., Bailey, C., Rivers, S.: Social interaction moderates human-robot trust-reliance relationship and improves stress coping. In: Proceedings of 11th ACM/IEEE International Conference on Human-Robot Interaction. pp. 471–472 (2016)
16. Lohani, M., Stokes, C., Oden, K., Frazier, S., Landers, K., Craven, P., Lawton, D., McCoy, M., Macannuco, D.: A framework for human-machine social systems: The influence of non-technical factors on trust and stress appraisal. ACM Transactions in Interactive Intelligence Systems (forthcoming)
17. Lopes, P., Grewal, D., Kadis, J., Gall, M., Salovey, P.: Evidence that emotional intelligence is related to job performance and affect and attitudes at work. Psicothema 18, 132–138 (2006)
18. Mayer, R.C., Davis, J.H.: The effect of the performance appraisal system on trust for management: A field quasi-experiment. Journal of applied psychology 84(1), 123 (1999)
19. Mayer, R.C., Davis, J.H., Schoorman, F.D.: An integrative model of organizational trust. Academy of management review 20, 709–734 (1995)
20. Momeni, N.: The relation between managers' emotional intelligence and the organizational climate they create. Public Personnel Management 38(2), 35–48 (2009)
21. Picard, R.: Toward machines with emotional intelligence. In: ICINCO (Invited Speakers). pp. 29–30 (2004)
22. Pontier, M., Siddiqui, G.: A virtual therapist that responds empathically to your answers. In: Intelligent Virtual Agents. pp. 417–425. Springer, Berlin/Heidelberg (2008)
23. Rivers, S.E., Brackett, M.A., Reyes, M.R., Elbertson, N.A., Salovey, P.: Improving the social and emotional climate of classrooms: A clustered randomized controlled trial testing the ruler approach. Prevention Science 14(1), 77–87 (2013)
24. Salovey, P., Mayer, J.: Emotional intelligence. Imagination, Cognition and Personality 9(3), 185–211 (1990)
25. Schaefer, K., Billings, D., Szalma, J., Adams, J., Sanders, T., Chen, J., Hancock, P.: A meta-analysis of factors influencing the development of trust in automation: Implications for human-robot interaction. DTIC Document, Tech. Rep. (2014)
26. de Visser, E., Parasuraman, R.: Adaptive aiding of human-robot teaming effects of imperfect automation on performance, trust, and workload. Journal of Cognitive Engineering and Decision Making 5(2), 209–231 (2011)

Pragmatic multimodality: Effects of nonverbal cues of focus and certainty in a virtual human

Farina Freigang ✉, Sören Klett, Stefan Kopp

Social Cognitive Systems Group, Faculty of Technology
Center of Excellence "Cognitive Interaction Technology" (CITEC)
Bielefeld University, P.O. Box 100 131, D-33501 Bielefeld, Germany
farina.freigang@uni-bielefeld.de, sklett@techfak.uni-bielefeld.de,
skopp@techfak.uni-bielefeld.de

Abstract. In pragmatic multimodality, modal (pragmatic) information is conveyed multimodally by cues in gesture, facial expressions, head movements and prosody. We observed these cues in natural interaction data. They can convey positive and negative focus, in that they emphasise or de-emphasise a piece of information, and they can convey uncertainty. In this work, we test the effects on perception and recall in a human user, when those cues are carried out by a virtual human. The nonverbal behaviour of the virtual human was modelled using motion capture data and ensured a fully multimodal appearance. Results of the study show that the virtual human was perceived as very competent and as saying something important. A special case of de-emphasising cues led to lower content recall.

Keywords: Pragmatic modification, utterance marking, linguistic modals, virtual human, motion capture, perception study.

1 Introduction

When humans communicate naturally, a lot more is transferred than just the semantic content. The meaning of an utterance is enhanced by verbal pragmatic markers but also by gestural and other nonverbal and paraverbal signals in order to classify the semantic content of the utterances [1]. Senders want to communicate their convictions, viewpoints, knowledge, attitudes, among others. These signals are not discourse related, they merely support the recipient to arrive at the correct interpretation that was intended by the sender. Recipients perceive those signals on top of to the semantic content and integrate everything into a congruent message. However, albeit its prominence and importance, this meta-communication has not received much attention so far.

We define such signals as *modal (pragmatic) functions*[1] (MPF), a sub-category of pragmatic functions. This notion is related to [3] *modal* functions which "seem

---

[1] We use this terms instead of the previously adopted term "modifying functions" (MF), which refers to modifications on a grammatical level, e.g. adjectives modifying noun phrases [2]. The term "modal" function fits our approach more intuitively since it implies a modification on a semantic-pragmatic level.

© Springer International Publishing AG 2017
J. Beskow et al. (Eds.): IVA 2017, LNAI 10498, pp. 142–155, 2017.
DOI 10.1007/978-3-319-67401-8_16

to operate on a given unit of verbal discourse and show how it is to be interpreted" [p. 225] as, e.g., to "indicate what units are 'focal' for their arguments" [4, p. 276].

Few studies have looked at how modal functions get expressed in single modalities, most notably language, prosody and gesture. In language, lexical items like modal particles and discourse markers, may mark "assumptions about the current speech event", "its evidential status", and "the speakers stance, attitude, emotional state" [5, p. 160]. However, different points of view exist on which markers highlight, understate or make an utterance uncertain. In the field of prosody, [6] examined various dimensions of pragmatic functions of prosodic features, among them are duration, pitch hight and loudness. This analysis forms the baseline for our modification in speech synthesis.

A recent summary of gestures [7] that take up pragmatic functions mentions various gestures with certain recurrent form features/gesture families and the corresponding pragmatic functions, e.g., away gestures [8, p. 1599] "to mark arguments, ideas, and actions as uninteresting and void". However, "no clear notion of pragmatic gesture is available, neither in the area of pragmatics nor in gesture studies" [7, p. 1536]. In previous work [9, 10], we tried to address this shortcoming with a corpus-based approach to empirically obtain ratings of the "modifying functions" that people see in gestures.

In a first theoretical approach, [11, p. 540] tackled multimodal pragmatic markers and identified pragmatic events similar to the ones we will present, e.g. "calling attention", "uncertainty" and "uninterested". However, it is not clear how the different modalities jointly realize modal marking. In this work, we go one step further by selecting various – what we think are decisive – features, based on our natural human data and other findings, to jointly realise the intended modification. To our knowledge, no well controlled study exists, which analyses language, nonverbal and paraverbal cues in combination.

In other previous work, we have demonstrated that pragmatic marking, using speech and/or gesture, is also recognized in virtual humans (VH) [12]. This research is important for the field of developing VH as easily accessible, acceptable, understandable and helpful communication partners, as well as getting more insights into human natural communication behaviour. With the present work, we build on this research and extend it in several ways. Our previous study showed that in most cases words indicating MPF (such as modal particles) together with gestures had a strong effect. Here we complement this by focusing on the contribution of other nonverbal and paraverbal cues in the expressive behaviour of the agent. That is, we aim to investigate the effects of gestures in combination with other nonverbal and paraverbal signals like facial expression and intonation. Additionally, two aspects ensured more natural and human-like stimuli: The enacted motion capture data itself was improved and the post-processing of the motion capture data led to more unfiltered behaviour. Furthermore, based on experiences from our previous study, we carried out some improvements regarding the experimental design and procedure. The recognition of the MPF in a gestural and nonverbal expressive behaviour, as well as the similarity with an prototypical gesture from our corpus data, were pre-tested (cf. Section 2: Non-verbal behaviour). Then, we developed a story with a well-defined information structure (cf. Section 3: Stimulus videos), ensuring that an MPF appears with the new information. And finally, we improved the MPF elicitation questions (cf. Section 4: MPF recognition) and the method for measuring content recall (cf. Section 4: Content recall).

In the present work, we ask how a combination of nonverbal and paraverbal cues alone (gesture, facial expression and prosody), that is without using explicit keywords, can affect the listener's interpretation of a given utterance of a VH. All cues have previously been reported in studies on natural human-human interaction. We present a study investigating how this influences the uptake and recall of the information conveyed verbally by the VH, and how the overall perception of the VH is affected. We start by providing theoretical background and describe our experimental design in Section 2. In Section 3, we explain stimuli and procedure of the present study, before analysing and discussing the results in Section 4.

2   Theory and Experiment Design

We define MPF to have a focusing and an epistemic component, and possible attitudinal layers on top of these modifications. Qualitatively, focusing and epistemic functions can be either positive or negative:

- A *positive focusing* function (Foc+) puts importance and emphasis on an specific aspect of an utterance, it highlights or brings a piece of information to the addressee's attention.
- A *negative focusing* function (Foc-) marks unimportance, irrelevance and accessoriness, it moves a piece of information out of focus.
- A *negative epistemic* function (Epi-) indicates a speaker's uncertainty about the corresponding piece of information.
- A *positive epistemic* function (Epi+) corresponds to a competent speaker and is generally assumed to be the default.

In our previous work, we found evidence that speakers in particular use gestural or verbal cues to mark the first three functions (Foc+, Foc-, Epi-). We thus concentrate on them in the remainder of the paper.

MPF are loosely related to the notion of information structure which describes the way information is organized and distributed within a sentence's syntactic structure [13]. Information structure distinguishes between *topic* (or *theme*, what is talked about) and *comment* (or *rheme*, what is said about the topic). The notion of *focus* is used here to denote the grammatical means of indicating that some information is new or contrastive. Note that this differs from MPF which are not defined in terms of utterance structure, but based on the speaker's mental state and her intentions to influence the recipient's interpretation of the utterance. In consequence, MPFs are assumed to act more at the level of discourse units. For example, a Foc-function can be well placed on the utterance's rheme, e.g. when the speaker makes an utterance but wants to signal that its new information is not particularly important for the larger discourse. Likewise, verbal or nonverbal cues of the Epi-function could be added to the rheme to indicate uncertainty about this information. This analysis also hints to the importance of distinguishing different degrees of communicative intentionality in pragmatic marking. Adopting the notion of [14, 15], we assume that Foc+ and Foc- functions are rather signalled or displayed, i.e. they are intentionally designed to be perceived by the recipient. On the contrary, the Epi- function is rather indicated or displayed, i.e. this function indicates the mental state of the sender and it does not need not be designed specifically for the recipient. In the present study, we aim to test exactly this interpretation of nonverbal cues when produced by a VH.

Nonverbal behaviour. The gestural forms used for the respective MPF are: *abstract deictic* gestures [16–18] for Foc+, *brushing* gestures [19, 20] for Foc- and *Palm Up Open Hand* gestures (PUOH) [21, 3] for Epi-. This nonverbal behaviour has been extracted from previous analyses of natural human interaction data ([9, 12]). The gestures are accompanied by certain body, shoulder and head movements (as depicted in Table 1). These findings and categorisation of features form the baseline for the motion capture recordings carried out specifically for this study. We put a lot of effort into the choice of gestures as well as the recording and post-processing of the motion capture data. The nonverbal behaviour was re-enacted and recorded with a sixteen-camera OptiTrack motion capture system. From a big corpus of gestures recordings, we chose nine recordings for each function, which we perceived to carry the respective function best and fit the gestures in our natural human interaction data. The total of 27 motion capture recordings were tested by four participants (2 female, 2 male) in a pre-study. We asked two questions: whether a gesture fulfils the particular pragmatic function and whether the re-enacted gesture fits the original human gesture, which the participants saw in a video at the beginning of the study. The results of the first question were weighted as most important. We used only those gestures, which functions were recognised by all or at least three of the participants and which at least two (most of the time it was three and four) of the participants matched with the natural gesture in the video. This resulted in six gestures for the Foc+-function, seven gestures for the Foc--function and three gestures of the Epi--function. Since we obtained only a few gestures carrying Epi--functions from the pre-study, we added one gesture to the final corpus of recordings, which was not rated beforehand. The post-processing steps included adding hand shapes designed with the MURML Keyframe editor [22] and merging them with the motion capture data, which was additionally filtered for errors. For proper agent animation, facial expressions, lip movements and blinking was added by modifying the blend shapes. In all conditions, the VH's behaviour was steered by

AsapRealizer [23] and his speech is synthesised by the Text-To-Speech system CereProc[2] with the female voice Gudrun[3].

Table 1. Nonverbal and paraverbal features modified in our VH for the stimulus videos in the three main conditions.

	gesture	wrist	upper body	shoulder	head	eyes
Foc+	abstract deictic	beat	rather forward	–	nod	bigger
Foc-	brushing	beat	–	–	shake	–
Epi-	PUOH	–	rather backward	shrug	tilt	–

	brows	mouth	speech rate	loudness	pitch	speech break
Foc+	raised	smile up	faster	louder	higher	100ms after
Foc-	down	smile up	–	–	–	100ms after
Epi-	down	smile down	slower	quiet	–	200ms before

Pragmatic multimodality. The aim of this study was to test the multimodality of non-speech pragmatic modification. That is, additionally to using nonverbal markers like gesture, body, head and shoulder movements, as well as facial expressions, we added synthetic paraverbal markers to the stimulus videos. These include variations in speech rate, pitch, loudness and added pauses (speech synthesis). In a corpus-based approach, [6] analysed prosodic pragmatic functions and found, e.g., that the loudness correlates with importance and confidence, relevant for Foc+/Foc-, and that the duration of an utterance mirrors the amount of thought a sender needs to express it, indicating the degree of certainty which is relevant for Epi-/Foc+. Our prosodic modifications were based on this analysis, as testing the paraverbal effects in separate conditions was not feasible within this work. Table 1 summarises all nonverbal and paraverbal features that we used to replicate the natural human behaviour with MPF. When interpreting the results it should be kept in mind that the modification of the stimuli are multimodal and do not sorely consist of gestural behaviour.

Few approaches dealt with pragmatic multimodal modification. [24] designed 'believable and expressive' VH with tightly synchronised of verbal and nonverbal signals (facial expressions) to mark certainty, topic and emotion among others. Also, [25] worked on nonverbal behaviour in virtual humans and summarizes head movements and facial expressions which "mark uncertain statements" and "emphasise a particular conversation point." [26] looked at the correspondence between tilts and nods and prosodic features to create "intentions, attitudes and emotions" and summarizes that the "emphasis of a word often goes along with head nodding" and that a greater variation of facial parameters accompany a

---

[2] www.cereproc.com

[3] Since Billie has a childlike appearance, the female voice Gudrun fits best to the behaviour of the character.

focal accent. However, a full approach of multimodal pragmatic marking in VH – to our knowledge – has not been dealt with so far.

Hypotheses. As dependent variables, we asked whether the VH was perceived to modify its narrative as emphasising, de-emphasising or as being uncertain in order to check whether the participants recognised the underlying MPF. Secondly, we captured the content recall with a cloze text. And finally, we measured the VH likeability, competence and human-likeness. Based on our own previous work, our hypotheses were that the VH is perceived as most emphasising and that the content recall would be best in the Foc+-condition. Additionally, we expected the Epi- and Foc- conditions to retrieve least recall, whereas this effect should be stronger in the latter condition due to explicit de-emphasising.

3   Stimuli and Procedure

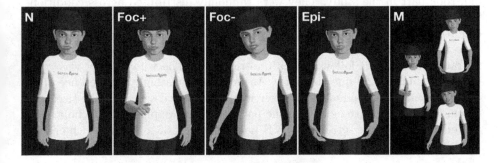

Fig. 1. Stills of the VH carrying out the three MPF in the various conditions. In the N-condition, the VH showed only "idle" behaviour.

Stimulus videos. We developed a story which the VH narrated to the participants during the study. The story consists of 28 sentences, was about the VH and its life at its research institute, included many technical terms and every sentence was designed to have a theme and a rheme[4]. According to the definition above, we placed one multimodal modification on one or more words in the rheme, and thus, the new part of the sentence. Based on the definition of MPF, we were interested in three main conditions: Foc+, Foc- and Epi-. Additionally, we surveyed a neutral condition (N) and a mixed condition (M). The latter condition contains pragmatic cues of all three main functions and is designed to test, whether the MPF can be used when they are collocated within a cohesive narrative. We were curious if MPF are still perceived and understood independently or if there are

---

[4] The story and the stimulus videos can be accessed at:
https://pub.uni-bielefeld.de/publication/2911804

interdependences between the pragmatic cues. This results into five conditions. The N-condition included idle motion capture behaviour, which consists of subtle arm and head movements. In all other conditions, the four to seven recorded nonverbal behaviours from the pre-study (cf. Section 2: Nonverbal behaviour) were equally distributed across the narrative. The M-condition contained markers of all MPF, so we had to make sure that the story of the VH was coherent, i.e., that the VH emphasises or downtones or is uncertain about the same instances throughout the story. Since this requirement was decisive for which MPF was assigned to which sentence, we could not balance the order of MPF strictly. All but the M-condition were carried out by a between-subject design and, thus, participants were exposed to only one condition. Stills of the final stimulus videos are depicted in Figure 1. All five videos were about three minutes long.

Perception study. The study was carried out on seven days between April 7th and 21th, 2017. 56 (28=male, 28=female) university students, on average 24.7 year old, took part in the study. They were randomly distributed across conditions. Twelve participants took part in the N-condition and eleven each in all other four conditions. The duration of the study was about 25 minutes and the students were reimbursed with 3 Euros and chocolate. They saw a video recording of a narration by our VH followed by a questionnaire. The whole study was coded in a SoSci Survey [27] questionnaire. As we aimed at a high felt presence of the VH, the study was conducted on a vertically positioned screen of the size 143 x 81 cm (a diagonal of 164 cm) and the participants were placed on a chair about 120 cm in front of the screen. The VH had the size of 66 x 30 cm which ensured a good visibility. Figure 2 depicts the study setup.

Fig. 2. The setup of the perception study. The photo is staged with a person that was not a participant.

4   Results

We conducted several analyses on the recognition of MPF, on the recalled content of the VH's short story and on the perception of the VH. Responses were captured using 5-point Likert scales (5= "entirely the case" to 1= "not at all the case") in all but the demographic questions. The results were calculated using SPSS[5] and Microsoft Excel.

MPF recognition. To measure whether participants would recognise what kind of pragmatic functions the VH nonverbally and paraverbally expresses during its narrative, we developed a set of questions which we expect to capture the meaning of the pragmatic functions. Foc+ questions surveyed whether the VH wanted to put into focus what it said, underline, emphasize and stress what it said, to express that what the VH said is important for the participant and whether the VH was confident. Foc− items accounted for contrary impressions, namely, whether the VH wanted to put what it said out of focus, discount what it said, express that what it said is unimportant, irrelevant and negligibly. Finally, the negative Epi− items raised whether the VH was unsure with what it said and is vague in its expressions. This was done in conjunction with questions formulated in a negative manner (the VH knows what it is talking about and it knows the topic well), which results we translated into the opposite value. A separate document with the exact wording of the MPF-items (in German and English) can be accessed online[6].

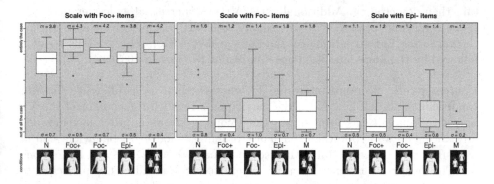

Fig. 3. Three scales with items measuring whether the MPF of the respective condition was recognized.

These MPF-items were merged onto three corresponding scales, justified by Cronbach's Alpha values being above 0.7 for each MPF-scale: Foc+: $a=.74$,

---

[5] IBM Corp. Released 2015. IBM SPSS Statistics for Mac, Version 23.0. Armonk, NY.
[6] The MPF-items can be accessed at:
https://pub.uni-bielefeld.de/publication/2911804

Foc-: $a=.85$ and Epi-: $a=.77$. Conducting a MANOVA using Pillai's trace, there was slightly no overall significant effect of the stimulus video on the perceived MPF, $V=0.36$, $F(12,153)=1.76$, $p=.06$. Individual ANOVAs on each of the dependent variables, however, suggest that there is a significant effect for Foc+, $F(4,51)=2.64$, $p=.044$ but none for Foc- and Epi-. Pairwise comparisons with 95% confidence intervals (CI) for Foc+ using Independent Sample T-tests for normally distributed data meeting equality of variances, slightly failed significance after using Bonferroni corrections on four tests for Foc+ and N ($t(21)=2.502$, $p=.084$, CI=[0.11;1.14]) and Foc+ and Epi- ($t(20)=2.529$, $p=.080$, CI=[0.09;0.97]). Since we found significant results on the Foc+-scale from the quantitative analysis, we turned to a descriptive analysis to shed more light on the underlying trends.

Medians and standard deviations of all five conditions are depicted for each scale of MPF-questions separately in Figure 3. In general, a strong perception of Foc+ is apparent: the VH has been rated as very emphasising in all conditions ($m=4.2$, $\sigma=0.6$). At the same time, the VH was rather not perceived as downtoning (Foc-: $m=1.6$, $\sigma=0.7$) and uncertain (Epi-: $m=1.2$, $\sigma=0.5$). Supporting our hypothesis, the VH was perceived as most emphasising in the Foc+-condition on the Foc+-scale ($m=4.3$, $\sigma=0.5$). This result is tightly followed by Foc- and the mixed condition M. Since the comparison between the three main conditions is most meaningful, we note that there is a small difference between Foc+ and Foc-, and even more so between Foc+ and Epi-. Interestingly, the VH was not perceived as most downtoning in the Foc--condition on the Foc--scale ($m=1.4$, $\sigma=1.0$), compared to both, the Epi-- and the M-conditions ($m=1.8$, $\sigma=0.7$). The result of this Epi--condition shows that the VH was perceived as rather uncertain than downtoning. Additionally, the VH was perceived as less emphasising (Foc+-condition: $m=1.2$, $\sigma=0.4$). Finally, the VH was perceived as most uncertain in the Epi--condition on the Epi--scale ($m=1.4$, $\sigma=0.8$). This result is followed by the Foc+- and the Foc--conditions ($m=1.2$, $\sigma=0.5/0.4$).

Content recall. We were interested in whether there is a difference between conditions regarding how much the participants recalled the content of the VH narrative. Since it has been shown that iconic gestures improve memory performance [28], we hypothesise that Foc+ pragmatic nonverbal behaviour can be helpful as well and, hopefully, that content marked with Foc- and Epi- won't be. The decision was made for a cloze text for true recall of the participants, instead of multiple choice questions, which we surveyed in our previous study. The participants were not told to memorise the story beforehand and the task turned out to be quite challenging for them. In the following, we will present differences between the conditions.

35 individual answers were asked for in the cloze text, which retrieved exactly those items to which the multimodal cues were added. There are two exceptions: one enumeration of seven items and one pair of items, in each case only the first word was accompanied by a cue. As mentioned before, the N-condition was not modified by any cues. The best recall was achieved in the conditions N with $m=9.75/\mu=9.29$ and in Foc+ with $m=9.5/\mu=8.82$ correct answers (out of 35),

followed by Epi- ($m=7/\mu=9.73$), Foc- ($m=7/\mu=9.32$) and M ($m=7/\mu=7.82$). Since condition N precedes Foc+, we cannot verify our hypothesis from these results alone. However, taking a closer look at the data from the condition M, we obtained interesting results.

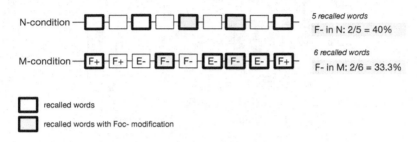

Fig. 4. An example of how we calculated *average recall shares*: Each box represents (a) recalled word(s) in a sentence. In condition M a nonverbal modification was placed on (a) particular word(s) and in the N-condition there was no modification.

We analysed whether adding an MPF cue to specific items is beneficial for the recall of these items. Adding an MPF was, e.g., done in the M-condition, which was our starting point. In this condition, we divided the items that were to be recalled into three categories. That is, the items that received a Foc+ MPF in the mixed condition are called Foc+-items; Foc--items and Epi--items are defined analogously. We then compare the N-condition, which is our baseline, to the M-condition. For each of the conditions and for each participant separately, we considered the overall number of recalled items and determined the share of Foc+-, Foc-- and Epi--items. We then calculated the average over all participants. The procedure of calculating *average recall shares* and our recall study results are visualized in Figure 4 and Figure 5, respectively. For a clean analysis, the two exceptions mentioned above were left out.

In the N-condition, the average recall share of Foc+-items was 36.2%, whereas this share was 39.5% for the M-condition. Hence, adding the Foc+ MPF resulted in a 9.0% increase of the average recall share of Foc+-items. In contrast, the average recall share of Foc--items was 39.7% for the N-condition and 33.2% for the M-condition. Adding the Foc- MPF hence yielded a 16.3% decrease of this share. Finally, the average recall share of Epi--items was 24.0% for the N-condition and 27.3% for the M-condition. Adding the Epi- MPF thus resulted in a 13.5% increase of this share.

Overall, these results give evidence that the Foc+ and Epi- MPF increased the recall and the Foc- MPF decreased the recall. That is, we can identify a tendency that items supported with a Foc- MPF were regarded as irrelevant and thus recalled less often. However, we could not directly confirm that items supported by a Foc- MPF led to a better memorisation. Partly because we

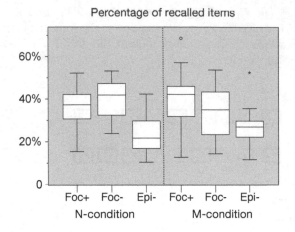

Fig. 5. Recall shares of recalled items over all participants.

got the same result for Epi--items, where we would not have expected a recall increase.

VH perception. In a third analysis, we evaluated whether the VH was perceived as likeable, competent and human-like. We adopted a design by [29], in that 18 adjectives were merged onto three scales, justified by Cronbach's Alpha values being above 0.7 for each VH perception-scale. Items for likeability (a=.87) are pleasant, sensitive, friendly, likeable, affable, approachable and sociable; items for competence (a=.78) are dedicated, trustworthy, thorough, helpful, intelligent, organized and expert; and items for human-likeness (a=.82) are active, human-like, fun-loving and lively.

The results are depicted in Figure 6. The VH was perceived as very competent (m=4.0, σ=0.6), rather likeable (m=3.4, σ=0.7) and intermediate human-like (m=2.8, σ=0.9). Conducting a MANOVA and several post-hoc tests, we did not get any significant results.

The human-likeness-scale shows that the VH is perceived as much more human-like in the Foc--condition than in the others, particularly in contrast to the Epi--condition. This trend is clearly visible in the box plot. However, using an Independent Sample T-test we could not find significant results between the conditions. The neutral condition is perceived as least human-like.

The same is true for the likeability-scale: the VH in the N-condition was perceived as least likeable (m=3.3, σ=0.7). In contrast, in the mixed condition it was perceived as most likeable (m=3.6, σ=0.8), followed by Foc- (m=3.6, σ=1.0), Foc+ and Epi--condition (both m=3.4, σ=0.5). There was almost no difference between the conditions regarding competence. Participants were most confident regarding their ratings in the Foc+-condition (m=4.0, σ=0.6).

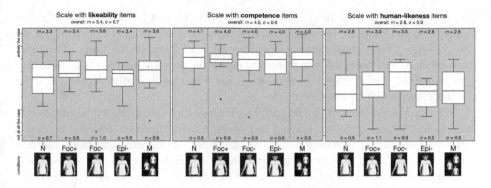

Fig. 6. Three scales of items measuring the perception of the VH.

5 Conclusion

In this paper we have presented a study on how a VH can employ nonverbal
cues in gesture, facial expression, head, or prosody to convey modal (pragmatic)
information to mark focus and uncertainty in its utterances. In all conditions,
the VH was perceived as very competent and as saying something important.
Concerning the different MPF, we can draw several conclusions: First, supporting
our hypothesis, Foc+ was recognized best from the multimodal cues. This led
to higher content recall (together with the N-condition). Second, cues of Epi-
had similar but much lesser effects. Finally, Foc- was not well recognized but
led to the lowest content recall, again supporting our hypothesis. Interestingly,
this also led to the perception that the VH was most human-like and likeable
(latter together with the M-condition), suggesting that the participants perceive
"downtoning" behaviour positively, possibly because it makes the VH appear
less superior. The M-condition tested whether we can use several MPF within one
story. We showed that by adding Foc--items to certain words in this condition,
the content of these words were recalled less. Another anecdotal effect was that
the VH was perceived as having a specific personality by producing various
pragmatic cues and thus appeared more natural overall.

Note, however, that the present study had three biases. First, the gestures
were critical, meaning that always when a gesture and complementary nonverbal behaviour was carried out by the VH, there was a lot of movement; and
possibly the participants were induced to believe that the utterance is relevant,
no matter which MPF was carried out by the agent. This could be an explanation for the fact that the VH was rated as rather communicating something
important (Foc+) across all conditions. And since machines are generally conceived as either functioning well or not at all, it may be difficult for participants
to accept that they do not know something (Epi-). Second, the narrative was
highly technical, possibly leading to the result that the VH has been perceived as
very competent in all conditions, since it was so well-informed. And finally, the
pre-test already indicated that the nonverbal behaviour in the Epi--condition

was not as clear-cut as in the other conditions. In the final stimulus, the VH Epi--gestures could be interpreted as presenting something (important), since the gestures were partly performed rather high in front of the body. This may have resulted in a focusing effect leading to better recall. The results might limit generalizability as participants may have not been as receptive to the, at least partially, quite subtle nonverbal cues.

We introduced (lack of) focus and uncertainty into an expressive artificial system. It is a bigger question driving our research whether the impression that a VH possesses and affects such mental qualities in communication affects human-VH interaction. The present work contributes to this by showing that pragmatic multimodality can be used in VH and that MPF do have an effect. Since the nonverbal behaviour is elicited from natural human data, these results are not only helpful for the field of designing virtual agents, but also provide insights into human behaviour. The next step will be to combine the nonverbal and paraverbal cues explored here with explicit verbal markers (e.g., modal particles) in a systematic model to express pragmatic information gradually and autonomously.

Acknowledgements

This work was supported by the Cluster of Excellence Cognitive Interaction Technology 'CITEC' (EXC 277) at Bielefeld University, funded by the German Research Foundation (DFG), and by the German Federal Ministry of Education and Research (BMBF) in the project KOMPASS (FKZ 16SV7271K).

References

1. Wharton, T.: Pragmatics and non-verbal communication, Cambridge University Press (2009)
2. Smith, M.: Pragmatic functions and lexical categories. Linguistics 48.3: 717–777 (2010)
3. Kendon, A.: Gesture: Visible Action as Utterance, Cambridge Uni. Press (2004)
4. Kendon, A.: Gestures as illocutionary and discourse structure markers in Southern Italian conversation, Journal of pragmatics 23.3, 247–279 (1995)
5. Norrick, Neal R.: Discussion article. Catalan Journal of Linguistics 6, 159–168 (2007)
6. Ward, N.: Pragmatic functions of prosodic features in non-lexical utterances, Speech Prosody 2004 International Conference (2004)
7. Payrató, L. and Teßendorf, S.: Pragmatic gestures, Body Language Communication: An International Handbook on Multimodality in Human Interaction, Handbooks of Linguistics and Communication Science 38.1, 1531–1539 (2013)
8. Bressem, J. and Müller, C.: The family of away gestures: Negation, refusal, and negative assessment, BodyLanguageCommunication, 1592–1604 (2014)
9. Freigang, F. and Kopp, S.: Analysing the Modifying Functions of Gesture in Multimodal Utterances, Proc. of the 4th Conference on Gesture and Speech in Interaction (GESPIN), Nantes, France (2015)
10. Freigang, F. and Kopp, S.: Modal Pragmatic Functions of Gesture - Exploring the Dimensions of Function and Form (in prep.)

11. Hunyadi, L., et al.: Annotation of spoken syntax in relation to prosody and multimodal pragmatics. Cognitive Infocommunications (CogInfoCom), 3rd International Conference on IEEE (2012)

12. Freigang, F. and Kopp, S.: This is whats important using speech and gesture to create focus in multimodal utterance, International Conference on Intelligent Virtual Agents (IVA). Springer International Publishing (2016)

13. Halliday, M. A. K.: Intonation and Grammar in British English, Mouton, The Hague (1967)

14. Allwood, J.: Bodily communication dimensions of expression and content, Multimodality in language and speech systems, Springer Netherlands 7–26 (2002)

15. Allwood, J.: Linguistic communication as action and cooperation, University of Gteborg, Department of Linguistics (1976)

16. McNeill, D.: Hand and mind: What gestures reveal about thought. University of Chicago press (1992)

17. McNeill, D.: Pointing and morality in Chicago, Pointing: Where language, culture, and cognition meet, 293–306 (2003)

18. McNeill, D., Cassell, J. and Levy E. T.: Abstract deixis. Semiotica 95.1-2 5–20 (1993)

19. Bressem, J. and Müller, C.: The family of away gestures: Negation, refusal, and negative assessment, BodyLanguageCommunication, 1592–1604 (2014)

20. Teßendorf, S.: Pragmatic and metaphoriccombining functional with cognitive approaches in the analysis of the 'brushing aside gesture', Bodylanguagecommunication: an international handbook on multimodality in human interaction, 1540–1558 (2014)

21. Müller, C.: Forms and uses of the Palm Up Open Hand: A case of a gesture family, The semantics and pragmatics of everyday gestures 9, 233–256 (2004)

22. Kranstedt, A., Kopp, S., Wachsmuth., I.: MURML: A multimodal utterance representation markup language for conversational agents. Proceedings of the AAMAS02 Workshop on Embodied Conversational Agents (2002)

23. van Welbergen, H., Yaghoubzadeh, R., Kopp, S.: AsapRealizer 2.0: The next steps in fluent behavior realization for ECAs. In: Intelligent Virtual Agents. LNCS, vol. 8637, pp. 449-462. Springer, Berlin, Germany (2014)

24. De Rosis, F., et al.: From Greta's mind to her face: modelling the dynamics of affective states in a conversational embodied agent. International journal of human-computer studies 59.1 81–118 (2003)

25. Lee, J., and Stacy M.: Nonverbal behavior generator for embodied conversational agents, International Workshop on Intelligent Virtual Agents, Springer Berlin Heidelberg (2006)

26. Liu, C., et al.: Generation of nodding, head tilting and eye gazing for human-robot dialogue interaction, Human-Robot Interaction (HRI), 7th ACM/IEEE International Conference on IEEE (2012)

27. Leiner, D. J.: SoSci Survey (Version 2.6.00-i) [Computer software]. Available at http://www.soscisurvey.com (2014)

28. Bergmann, K., and Macedonia, M.: A virtual agent as vocabulary trainer: iconic gestures help to improve learners' memory performance. International Workshop on Intelligent Virtual Agents. Springer, Berlin, Heidelberg (2013)

29. Bergmann, K., Kopp, S., Eyssel, F.: Individualized gesturing outperforms average gesturing: evaluating gesture production in virtual humans. In: Intelligent Virtual Agents. LNCS, vol. 6356, pp. 104-117. Springer (2010)

Simulating listener gaze and evaluating its effect on human speakers

Laura Frädrich[1] ✉, Fabrizio Nunnari[2], Maria Staudte[1], and Alexis Heloir[2,3]

[1] Embodied Spoken Interaction Group, Saarland University, Saarbrücken, DE
[2] SLSI Group, German Research Center for Artificial Intelligence, Saarbrücken, DE
[3] LAMIH, UMR CNRS 8201 / Université de Valenciennes, F

Abstract. This paper presents an agent architecture designed as part of a multidisciplinary collaboration between embodied agents development and psycho-linguistic experimentation. This collaboration will lead to an empirical study involving an interactive human-like avatar following participants' gaze. Instead of adapting existing "off the shelf" embodied agents solutions, experimenters and developers collaboratively designed and implemented experiment's logic and the avatar's real time behavior from scratch in the Blender environment following an agile methodology. Frequent iterations and short implementation sprints allowed the experimenters to focus on the experiment and test many interaction scenarios in a short time.

1 Introduction

Gaze is a very important aspect of social communication as it is closely connected with comprehension, planning, and prediction processes [6]. It furthermore represents a strong cue for the speaker and listener's focus of attention [2]. While the influence of the speaker's gaze and utterances on the listener's gaze has been investigated to some extent [7], the influence of the listener's gaze on the speaker's behaviour is largely unexplored so far. The difficulty of precisely controlling a human being's gaze behaviour might have contributed to the sparse amount of related work. Indeed, in an experimental setup which intends to investigate the speaker's reaction to the listener's behaviour, the manipulated variable, i.e. the listener's gaze behaviour, has to be controllable in a way that minimises the interfering impact of any confounding variables. In human-human interaction, however, the possible sources of interference are manifold. Only recent advances in the development of embodied conversational agents provide a possible solution to overcome these difficulties. Employing an artificial agent as listener makes the experiment substantially more controllable, interrupting the recursive relation between speaker and listener behaviour. Also, even though interacting with a virtual agent is an unusual situation for most, people generally treat agent gaze similarly to human gaze [6]. Our goal is to examine whether listener gaze can be simulated by simple gaze-following (also imitating joint attention) and whether that affects speaker behaviour in terms of speech production and gaze behaviour.

© Springer International Publishing AG 2017
J. Beskow et al. (Eds.): IVA 2017, LNAI 10498, pp. 156-159, 2017.
DOI 10.1007/978-3-319-67401-8_17

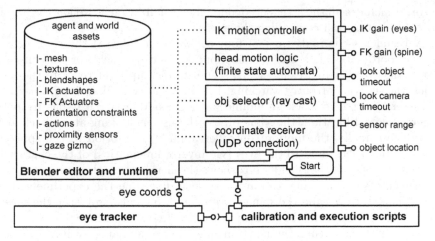

Fig. 1: Software architecture of the virtual agent.

2   Implementation Decisions and Architecture

The avatar-based interactive application supporting the experiment described in this paper capitalises on a previous work experiment [7]. The solution employed back then was comparable to available agent control frameworks [8,9,5,1] and offered a BML [4] interface to the experimenters to interactively control the avatar. This raised a number of issues, the most significant drawbacks being a cumbersome deployment process, a non-trivial compilation and packaging pipeline, and the impossibility for experimenters to interactively edit the scene layout or the assets. These issues hindered the collaboration flow between the multidisciplinary team as well as the experimental setup eventually used in the study.

In this experiment, the interactive agent framework was reimplemented from scratch around the Blender software[4]. Blender indeed provides an integrated full-fledged editing environment tightly coupled with a complete game engine which does not constrain which attributes of the game logic, assets, or real-time controllers can be exposed to the experimenters. Also, because all resources (assets, game logic, and input/output scripts) can be packed in a single .blend file, packaging and deployment becomes as trivial as sharing a single file on a convenient file-sharing service like Dropbox[5]. All assets used in the experiment are covered by the Creative Common (static objects) or the LGPL licence (Mesh, textures and weight maps of the Brad Character from ICT's Smartbody [8]).

Figure 1 depicts the architecture of the interactive setup. The eye tracker machine (bottom left) sends, via local area network, the coordinates of the screen point that the user is watching. The top box represents the content of the Blender

---

[4] https://www.blender.org/ – 18 July 2017
[5] http://www.dropbox.com/ – 18 July 2017

editor. It includes all the assets needed for the visualization as well as the invisible assets animating and controlling the agent.

A Blender scene makes use of four software modules: i) the receiver reads the eye coordinates via a UDP connection; ii) the object selector performs a ray cast of the eye coordinates in the 3D scenes to pick up a reference to the object which the user is currently watching; iii) the logic controller determines if the character has to play back an animation (e.g. nodding) or if it has to look at either a neutral location, the same object the user is looking at, or back at the camera; iv) finally, the motion controller applies the motion to the spine (via forward kinematics) and to the eyes (via inverse kinematics) of the character.

The right side of the Blender box shows the elements which are exposed to the experimenters so that they can autonomously fine-tune the experiment: i) the gain of both the eyes and the spine movements, which also influence the speed of the gazing behaviour; ii) the timeouts used by the state machine to change state, which are needed to tune the reaction speed of the avatar as well as to smooth the avatar's behavior when the subject's inferred gaze trajectory becomes noisy; iii) the range of the sensors used to intercept the ray cast; and iv) the location of the objects, to customise the layout of the scenes. The experimenters were also provided with two commodity scripts to start the calibration procedure and to run the trials.

3   Experimental set-up

We plan to use the avatar to address psycholinguistic research questions, in particular the influence of listener gaze on human-agent interaction. We intend to examine whether simple gaze-following by the avatar, which merely mirrors (after some filtering) the human participants' own gaze, might be enough to create the impression of an intelligent avatar that processes and understands spoken descriptions, and whether this affects the participant's behaviour in terms of speech production and gaze behaviour. In contrast to previous research concentrating, for instance, on the perception of virtual agents [3], we will exploit the actual, real-time gaze behaviour of the participants.

To this end, participants will sit in front of a computer screen displaying the content of the experiment. An eye tracking camera will be positioned directly below the screen. During the experiment, participants will view face and torso of the avatar (introduced as "Brad") with a set of six similar 3D objects arranged on a table in front of it, which they will be asked to describe verbally. The eye tracking technology will be used both as a diagnostic tool to measure the fixation locations as well as as input data for the experiment, endowing the virtual agent with the ability to follow the participant's gaze. Figure 2 depicts the data flow in this set-up.

References

1. Courgeon, M.: MultiModal Affective and Reactive Characters. Springer Lecture Notes in Artificial Intelligence (2011)

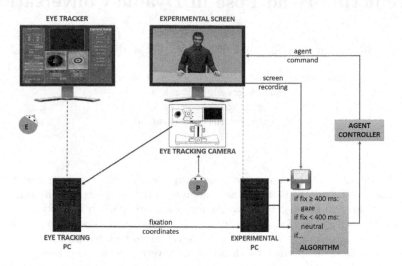

Fig. 2: Architecture of the experimental set-up. Data regarding the eye tracking are marked in blue; data relevant to the agent, in green. The camera records the participant's (P) fixations which are processed by the eye tracker PC. Calibration is done on the experimental PC screen.

2. Courgeon, M., Rautureau, G., Martin, J.C., Grynszpan, O.: Joint attention simulation using eye-tracking and virtual humans. IEEE Transactions on Affective Computing 5(3), 238–250 (2014)
3. Heylen, D., van Es, I., Nijholt, A., van Dijk, B.: Controlling the gaze of conversational agents. In: Advances in Natural Multimodal Dialogue Systems, pp. 245–262. Springer (2005)
4. Kopp, S., B, K., Marsella, S.S., Marshall, A., Pelachaud, C., Pirker, H., Thorisson, K.: Towards a common framework for multimodal generation in ECAs: The behavior markup language. In: Intelligent Virtual Agents 2006. pp. 205–217. Berlin: Springer-Verlag (2006)
5. Mancini, M., Pelachaud, C.: Dynamic behavior qualifiers for conversational agents. In: Intelligent Virtual Agents. pp. 112–124 (2007)
6. Staudte, M., Crocker, M.W.: Investigating joint attention mechanisms through spoken human–robot interaction. Cognition 120(2), 268–291 (2011)
7. Staudte, M., Crocker, M.W., Heloir, A., Kipp, M.: The influence of speaker gaze on listener comprehension: Contrasting visual versus intentional accounts. Cognition 133(1), 317–328 (Oct 2014), http://linkinghub.elsevier.com/retrieve/pii/S0010027714001139
8. Thiebaux, M., Marsella, S., Marshall, A.N., Kallmann, M.: Smartbody: Behavior realization for embodied conversational agents. In: Proceedings of the 7th International Joint Conference on Autonomous Agents and Multiagent Systems-Volume 1. pp. 151–158 (2008)
9. Welbergen, H., Reidsma, D., Kopp, S.: An incremental multimodal realizer for behavior co-articulation and coordination. In: Intelligent Virtual Agents, vol. 7502, pp. 175–188. Springer Berlin Heidelberg, Berlin, Heidelberg (2012)

Predicting Head Pose in Dyadic Conversation

David Greenwood ✉, Stephen Laycock ✉, and Iain Matthews ✉

University of East Anglia, Norwich, United Kingdom
david.greenwood@uea.ac.uk
s.laycock@uea.ac.uk
iain.matthews@uea.ac.uk

Abstract. Natural movement plays a significant role in realistic speech animation. Numerous studies have demonstrated the contribution visual cues make to the degree we, as human observers, find an animation acceptable. Rigid head motion is one visual mode that universally co-occurs with speech, and so it is a reasonable strategy to seek features from the speech mode to predict the head pose. Several previous authors have shown that prediction is possible, but experiments are typically confined to rigidly produced dialogue.

Expressive, emotive and prosodic speech exhibit motion patterns that are far more difficult to predict with considerable variation in expected head pose. People involved in dyadic conversation adapt speech and head motion in response to the others' speech and head motion. Using Deep Bi-Directional Long Short Term Memory (BLSTM) neural networks, we demonstrate that it is possible to predict not just the head motion of the speaker, but also the head motion of the listener from the speech signal.

Keywords: speech animation, head motion synthesis, visual prosody, dyadic conversation, generative models, BLSTM, CVAE

1 Introduction

Speech animation involves transforming and deforming a character model, temporally synchronised to an audible utterance to give the appearance that the model is speaking. Given the close relationship between speech and gesture, the problem is challenging, as human viewers are very sensitive to natural human movement [24]. Practical applications of speech animation, for example computer games and animated films, often rely on motion capture devices or hand keyed animation. Demand for realistic animation within these domains is high and both of these approaches are expensive and time consuming, providing considerable incentive for automation of the process. Embodied Conversational Agents (ECAs) for education, training, entertainment or Human-Computer Interaction (HCI) require realistic motion in both speaking and listening modes. More recently, increasing interest in Virtual Reality (VR) and Augmented Reality (AR) applications provide further stimulus for the development of predictive animation systems.

© Springer International Publishing AG 2017
J. Beskow et al. (Eds.): IVA 2017, LNAI 10498, pp. 160-169, 2017.
DOI 10.1007/978-3-319-67401-8_18

Human discourse essentially flows in two modes: the explicit mode of audible speech, and a more supportive visual mode where non-verbal gestures complement and enhance the audible mode. Research suggests that speech and visual gesture stem from the same internal process and share the same semantic meaning [22, 7]. Speaker head motion is a rather interesting aspect of visual speech. Head motion has been shown to contribute to speech comprehension [25], yet unlike the articulators, it is under independent control. As the audio channel contains the most complete information stream in an utterance, it is a reasonable strategy to seek a mapping from within this modality that might enable plausible predictions of head pose. Indeed, there is significant measurable correlation between speech and speaker head motion [5] that has motivated a number of authors to choose this approach.

2 Previous Work

Initial speech to head motion prediction strategies took the approach of clustering motion patterns and assigning class labels [11, 5]. Hidden Markov Models (HMMs) were trained for each cluster, modelling the relation between the speech features and head motion. These approaches rely on a suitable labelling of motion units, either manually or automatically; a challenging problem in itself.

In recent years, the Graphics Processor Unit (GPU) has enabled efficient training of Deep Neural Networks (DNNs), and within many aspects of speech and language processing, DNNs are now state of the art [19, 10, 9]. DNNs were proposed as a modelling strategy for head motion prediction by Ding et al. [12]. Using a deep Feed-Forward Neural Network (FFN) regression model to predict Euler angles of nod, yaw and roll, they were able to report advantages over the previous HMM based approaches and were able to avoid the problem of clustering motion. Deep FFNs are a powerful modelling tool, capable of learning complex non-linear mappings, however, they are limited in their ability to model long term temporal data.

The Long Short Term Memory (LSTM) network [18], has been used to great effect in many disciplines arguably related to the speech to head pose problem. Graves [16], demonstrated the ability of LSTM networks to model long term structure by predicting discrete text values, and by predicting the real values of hand-writing trajectories. Another example by Sutskever et al. [28] reports state of the art performance for the language translation task. Ding et al. [13] introduced Bi-Directional Long Short Term Memory (BLSTM) networks to the head motion task, noting improvements over their own earlier work [12]. More recently Haag [17] uses BLSTMs and Bottleneck features [14] and noted a subtle improvement.

Yngve [31] introduced the term "backchannels" to describe listener interaction providing acoustic and visual signals that inform turn taking. Later, Allwood et al. [1] suggested this linguistic feedback conveys perception, comprehension and empathy. Ward & Tsukahara [29] gave evidence that audible speaker prosody offers cues for backchannel response from the listener.

There have been a number of listener models described in the literature. Cassel *et al.* [6] report a comprehensive rule-based model that triggers backchannels from multi-modal input. Watanabe *et al.* [30] describe a rule-based speech driven interactive agent. Nishimura *et al.* [26] presented a decision tree model driven by prosodic audio features. Morency *et al.* [23] demonstrated a data driven sequential probabilistic model using HMMs and Conditional Random Fields (CRFs). Bevacqua *et al.* [3] introduced a model with personality traits.

Generative models [20, 27] trainable with back propagation [2], have taken an important step in learning. These models can perform probabilistic inference and make diverse predictions. For example, Bowman *et al.* [4] employed a Variational Autoencoder (VAE) for natural language generation. Given the diverse expectation of head pose during conversation, either as speaker or listener, generative probabilistic models represent an encouraging prospect for head pose prediction.

3   Corpus

Head motion prediction studies typically use data that is not widely available. At the present time there are few significant multi-modal corpora freely available, that are suitable for modelling any rigid gesture with speech. For our own research we developed a corpus as described in this section.

3.1   Data Collection

We invited two actors, one female (speaker A), one male (speaker B) to recite from a scripted set of short conversational scenarios. The actors were encouraged to speak emotively and emphatically in order to provide natural, expressive and prosodic speech. In all, 3600 utterances were captured, giving a total of around six hours of speech.

We used six synchronised cameras, with three cameras aimed at each actor. Video frequency was 59.94 Frames per Second (FPS) and audio was recorded at 48 kHz then down sampled to 16 kHz. Each actor had 62 landmarks distributed about the face, which along with 58 natural feature landmarks such as eyes and lip edges, were tracked with Active Appearance Models (AAMs) [21]. With the cameras arranged such that left and right stereo pairs were formed on each actor, we were able to derive 3D models. The 3D models were stabilised by selecting the least deformed points and, using Procrustes analysis [15], rigid motion was separated from deformation. The rotations are about the X,Y and Z axes of a right handed coordinate system, with Y pointing up.

3.2   Motion Statistics

After data collection, we pre-processed our rigid motion modalities, to leave a global mean of zero and a global unit standard deviation. We took basic statistical measures (standard deviation, maximum and minimum values, and mean) for each individual utterance for head rotation and delta 1 and 2 (first and second derivatives) of head rotation. We were able to identify significant outliers as failed reconstructions which were subsequently removed from the corpus. We show in Figure 1 the delta 1 for X, Y, Z Euler angles, for each actor, during speaking and listening, for the entire corpus. In Table 1, we show the median of the absolute minima and maxima for each rotation mode, to give an overview of the dynamic properties of our corpus.

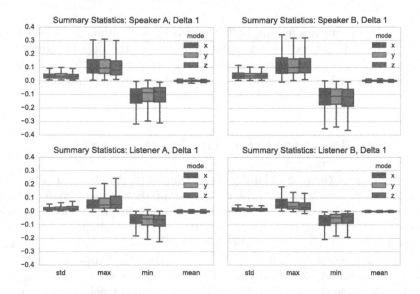

Fig. 1. The standard deviation, maximum, minimum and mean delta 1 for head rotation angles, from our entire corpus. We can observe characteristic differences in each actor, for speaking and listening.

Table 1. For the entire corpus, we summarise the head motion deltas with the median of the absolute minima and maxima for each rotation mode.

	Speaker A			Speaker B			Listener A			Listener B		
	x	y	z	x	y	z	x	y	z	x	y	z
Delta 1	0.15	0.33	0.12	0.18	0.37	0.12	0.06	0.23	0.07	0.07	0.12	0.06
Delta 2	0.06	0.17	0.06	0.10	0.25	0.05	0.03	0.11	0.03	0.05	0.08	0.04

3.3   Audio Feature Extraction

We used a sliding frame over the time domain audio signal of $2/59.94$ s with an overlap of $1/59.94$ s, matching the sampling rate of our motion data. Following convention, each frame was multiplied by a Hamming window. Although we have experimented with many audio features, for this report we use the log of the filter bank values as described by Deng *et al.* in [10]. Under this scenario we have a feature vector temporally aligned with the 3 Euler angles: nod (x), yaw (y) and roll (z). We normalise all features to have unit variance and zero mean.

4   Model Topology

Our modelling strategies feature LSTM networks, and although there are many variations to consider, we use the implementation in the popular Keras framework [8]. We describe each of our modelling strategies in the following subsections, along with our observations for their respective advantages and disadvantages.

4.1   Bi-Directional Long Short Term Memory (BLSTM)

Our application of the BLSTM differs from Ding *et al.* [13]. Instead of predicting one motion coefficient at each time step, we predict a short span: $1 \leq k \leq 29$. This allows observation of frame-wise variation in prediction and permits options on recombining each frame. For this report we simply take the mean at each predicted time step. Notably, we do not apply any post process to the prediction such as smooth filtering. We observed distinct motion events in our data $> 500 \ ms$ and to ensure capturing these events the receptive field was $29 \leq n \leq 129$ time steps, $n/59.94 \ s$. This network works well for a single actor, and less well for multiple actors where we observe greater variation at each predicted time step. We can see in our statistics plots(Figure 1) that each actor has individual motion characteristics, we speculate that a significantly larger corpus might allow this model to separate this variation.

4.2   Conditional Variational Autoencoder (CVAE)

A VAE comprises an encoder and a decoder. The encoder, $Q_\theta(z|x)$, seeks to represent input data x in a latent space z with weights and biases θ, where the encoder outputs the parameters of a Gaussian probability density. The decoder, $P_\phi(x|z)$, with weights and biases ϕ, transforms the parameters to the distribution of the original data. Our Conditional Variational Autoencoder (CVAE) model adds a conditioning element to the VAE, such that the decoder is $P_\phi(x,c|z)$, and we use a deep BLSTM for both the encoder and decoder. Recall, we regard head pose as having a diverse, one to many relationship to any utterance. The generative model here permits sampling from a normal distribution during prediction, giving the option of multiple predictions for any given utterance. Further, this model performs well with multiple actors.

5   Model Training

We trained the networks on our data, split 85% for training, 10% for validation and 5% for testing. Our objective function is Mean Squared Error (MSE), except for the CVAE model which has a custom objective function: the sum of the reconstruction loss and the Kullback-Leibler divergence [20]. Our optimising function is *RMSprop*, and we set an initial learning rate of 10^{-3}. Training continues until no further improvement on the validation set, with a patience of 5 epochs. Model weights are saved at each epoch. We reload the best weights, decrement the learning rate by a factor of 10 until 10^{-5}, finally stopping at the best validation error. We then select the model with the lowest overall validation error. The total number of examples presented to the network at training time depends somewhat on the value of span k and time steps n, and is in a range approximately 7×10^4 to 3×10^5. For this report, we trained models on each single speaker, each individual listener, speaker A and B combined and listener A and B combined.

6   Evaluation

Subjective testing has been commonly used to evaluate speech animation quality. However, such tests are often small scale and can lack statistical significance. Furthermore, for the period of time such systems have been developed, now some decades, the subjective tests invariably confirm the proposed system. This suggests such testing strategies might be unreliable. Empirical measurements utilised so far can also have problems. Previous authors have used point wise measures such as MSE or Canonical Correlation Analysis (CCA) against a true example to assess results. Head motion during speech does not have a deterministic outcome. If a speaker were head shaking to express disagreement, a phase shift would affect MSE, but not necessarily the plausibility of the motion. Conversely, CCA on the X, Y, Z rotations would show strong correlation for head shake against head nod at the same phase and frequency, even though the sentiment is opposite. In the event we had a reliable empirical measure, comparison with existing systems remains difficult, due to the lack of standard multi-modal corpora. Consequentially, we assess our predictions by comparing the dynamic statistics to those of our entire data set, that we show in Figure 1 and Table 1.

7   Results

For each of our models we make predictions using examples from our data that have been randomly and fairly selected. None of the test examples have been involved in the training of any model nor have any been used to select the best model. A further constraint on the test examples is that for each speaker, the corresponding listener is not involved in training or selection. Reconstruction simply involves presenting a test utterance and forward propagating through each network. Each resulting motion coefficient has 1 to k values, from which we take the mean.

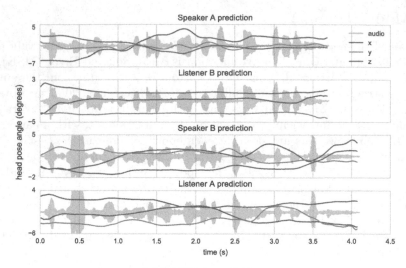

(a) BLSTM predictions.

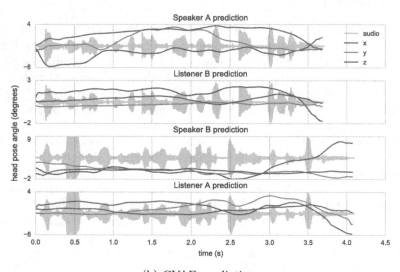

(b) CVAE predictions.

Fig. 2. Example predictions from our models, discussed in Section 7. The BLSTM model is trained on each individual speaker and listener, whereas for the CVAE, we use a single model to predict both speakers, and a single model to predict both listeners.

7.1   BLSTM

We show some example predictions from our BLSTM network in Figure 2a. For speaker A, the utterance: "This is the most ridiculous spiritual quest I've ever been on." and for speaker B the utterance: "It's laughable to me that you assume I have any interest in touching you." The head pose angle is predicted from the same utterance for both speaker and listener. We show a summary of the motion deltas in Table 2. We observe that our results fall within a small factor of the global summary in Table 1. Generally motion is a little smoother than our recorded motion, which we attribute partially to noise in the data collection, and to variation at each predicted time step. We note that head motion corresponds to events in the audio, both for speaker and listener. For these predictions the models were trained for single speaker and single listener, a total of four individual models.

7.2 CVAE

For our generative model, we use the same utterances as in 7.1. Here we train the speaker model on both actors, and the listener model on both actors. We find our trajectory statistics are closest to our corpus for these models (Table 2) and observe the prediction responds very well to the audio, matching key prosodic events of an expressive utterance. We make predictions from this model by sampling from the unit Gaussian space and conditioning with our example audio features. A parameter for this model, not present in the earlier models, is the size of the latent space. For this report we show a model with z in 3 dimensions, which we found to have no disadvantage to larger space.

Table 2. For the predictions from our models discussed in Section 7.1 and 7.2, we summarise the deltas with the median of the absolute minima and maxima for each rotation mode.

	Speaker A			Speaker B			Listener A			Listener B		
	x	y	z	x	y	z	x	y	z	x	y	z
BLSTM Delta 1	0.14	0.13	0.15	0.07	0.07	0.05	0.05	0.10	0.09	0.06	0.03	0.05
BLSTM Delta 2	0.05	0.07	0.06	0.02	0.03	0.02	0.03	0.04	0.04	0.03	0.02	0.02
CVAE Delta 1	0.08	0.15	0.15	0.10	0.12	0.10	0.12	0.11	0.11	0.08	0.06	0.06
CVAE Delta 2	0.03	0.05	0.07	0.05	0.04	0.06	0.05	0.06	0.07	0.03	0.03	0.03

8 Conclusion

The question of what represents appropriate or plausible head motion during speech is unclear. Subjectively, we have observed certain key events support viewer acceptance, but we have not yet been able to identify exactly why this is the case. We do know however, that it is important to have correct motion [25], and also that we can identify when it's not correct [24]. We have taken a decision to offer an alternative assessment for model predictions by showing statistics for the entire utterance. Developing a universal measurement of correct head motion, or indeed more broadly gesture, is an open and difficult problem, and we are actively pursuing this goal.

Our most interesting results come from the CVAE model, that addresses the diverse expectation of speech to head motion. We can predict a number of plausible motion trajectories by choosing new values for z, but with the same audio features. Quicktime movie files are provided in the supplementary material showing examples from our models.

In this paper we have presented our work on predicting head pose in dyadic conversation. We described our corpora, and presented modelling strategies that offer diverse but plausible outcomes for audio input. The LSTM has been a powerful tool in speech and language modelling, and as the encoder-decoder in our CVAE has shown great utility. We feel that generative models offer great promise to this field and we continue working in this area.

References

1. Allwood, J., Nivre, J., Ahlsén, E.: On the semantics and pragmatics of linguistic feedback. Journal of semantics 9(1), 1–26 (1992)
2. Bengio, Y., Laufer, E., Alain, G., Yosinski, J.: Deep generative stochastic networks trainable by backprop. In: Proceedings of The 31st International Conference on Machine Learning. pp. 226–234 (2014)
3. Bevacqua, E., De Sevin, E., Hyniewska, S.J., Pelachaud, C.: A listener model: introducing personality traits. Journal on Multimodal User Interfaces 6(1-2), 27–38 (2012)
4. Bowman, S.R., Vilnis, L., Vinyals, O., Dai, A.M., Jozefowicz, R., Bengio, S.: Generating sentences from a continuous space. CoNLL 2016 p. 10 (2016)
5. Busso, C., Deng, Z., Grimm, M., Neumann, U., Narayanan, S.: Rigid head motion in expressive speech animation: Analysis and synthesis. IEEE Transactions on Audio, Speech, and Language Processing 15(3), 1075–1086 (2007)
6. Cassell, J., Bickmore, T., Billinghurst, M., Campbell, L., Chang, K., Vilhjálmsson, H., Yan, H.: Embodiment in conversational interfaces: Rea. In: Proceedings of the SIGCHI conference on Human Factors in Computing Systems. pp. 520–527. ACM (1999)
7. Cassell, J., McNeill, D., McCullough, K.E.: Speech-gesture mismatches: Evidence for one underlying representation of linguistic and nonlinguistic information. Pragmatics & cognition 7(1), 1–34 (1999)
8. Chollet, F., et al.: Keras. https://github.com/fchollet/keras (2015)
9. Deng, L., Hinton, G., Kingsbury, B.: New types of deep neural network learning for speech recognition and related applications: An overview. In: 2013 IEEE International Conference on Acoustics, Speech and Signal Processing. pp. 8599–8603. IEEE (2013)
10. Deng, L., Li, J., Huang, J.T., Yao, K., Yu, D., Seide, F., Seltzer, M., Zweig, G., He, X., Williams, J., et al.: Recent advances in deep learning for speech research at Microsoft. In: Acoustics, Speech and Signal Processing (ICASSP), 2013 IEEE International Conference on. pp. 8604–8608. IEEE (2013)
11. Deng, Z., Narayanan, S., Busso, C., Neumann, U.: Audio-based head motion synthesis for avatar-based telepresence systems. In: Proceedings of the 2004 ACM SIGMM workshop on Effective telepresence. pp. 24–30. ACM (2004)
12. Ding, C., Xie, L., Zhu, P.: Head motion synthesis from speech using deep neural networks. Multimedia Tools and Applications pp. 1–18 (2014)

13. Ding, C., Zhu, P., Xie, L.: Blstm neural networks for speech driven head motion synthesis. In: Sixteenth Annual Conference of the International Speech Communication Association (2015)
14. Gehring, J., Miao, Y., Metze, F., Waibel, A.: Extracting deep bottleneck features using stacked auto-encoders. In: Acoustics, Speech and Signal Processing (ICASSP), 2013 IEEE International Conference on. pp. 3377–3381. IEEE (2013)
15. Gower, J.C.: Generalized procrustes analysis. Psychometrika 40(1), 33–51 (1975)
16. Graves, A.: Generating sequences with recurrent neural networks. CoRR abs/1308.0850 (2013), http://arxiv.org/abs/1308.0850
17. Haag, K., Shimodaira, H.: Bidirectional lstm networks employing stacked bottleneck features for expressive speech-driven head motion synthesis. In: International Conference on Intelligent Virtual Agents. pp. 198–207. Springer (2016)
18. Hochreiter, S., Schmidhuber, J.: Long short-term memory. Neural computation 9(8), 1735–1780 (1997)
19. Huang, J.T., Li, J., Gong, Y.: An analysis of convolutional neural networks for speech recognition. In: 2015 IEEE International Conference on Acoustics, Speech and Signal Processing (ICASSP). pp. 4989–4993. IEEE (2015)
20. Kingma, D.P., Mohamed, S., Rezende, D.J., Welling, M.: Semi-supervised learning with deep generative models. In: Advances in Neural Information Processing Systems. pp. 3581–3589 (2014)
21. Matthews, I., Baker, S.: Active appearance models revisited. International Journal of Computer Vision 60(2), 135–164 (2004)
22. McNeill, D.: Hand and mind: What gestures reveal about thought. University of Chicago Press (1992)
23. Morency, L.P., de Kok, I., Gratch, J.: Predicting listener backchannels: A probabilistic multimodal approach. In: Intelligent Virtual Agents. pp. 176–190. Springer (2008)
24. Mori, M.: The uncanny valley. Energy 7(4), 33–35 (1970)
25. Munhall, K.G., Jones, J.A., Callan, D.E., Kuratate, T., Vatikiotis-Bateson, E.: Visual prosody and speech intelligibility: head movement improves auditory speech perception. Psychological science : A journal of the American Psychological Society / APS 15(2), 133–137 (2004)
26. Nishimura, R., Kitaoka, N., Nakagawa, S.: A spoken dialog system for chat-like conversations considering response timing. In: International Conference on Text, Speech and Dialogue. pp. 599–606. Springer (2007)
27. Rezende, D.J., Mohamed, S., Wierstra, D.: Stochastic backpropagation and approximate inference in deep generative models. In: Proceedings of The 31st International Conference on Machine Learning. pp. 1278–1286 (2014)
28. Sutskever, I., Vinyals, O., Le, Q.V.: Sequence to sequence learning with neural networks. In: Advances in neural information processing systems. pp. 3104–3112 (2014)
29. Ward, N., Tsukahara, W.: Prosodic features which cue back-channel responses in english and japanese. Journal of pragmatics 32(8), 1177–1207 (2000)
30. Watanabe, T., Okubo, M., Nakashige, M., Danbara, R.: Interactor: Speech-driven embodied interactive actor. International Journal of Human-Computer Interaction 17(1), 43–60 (2004)
31. Yngve, V.H.: On getting a word in edgewise. In: Chicago Linguistics Society, 6th Meeting. pp. 567–578 (1970)

Negative Feedback In Your Face: Examining the Effects of Proxemics and Gender on Learning

David C. Jeong[1] ✉, Dan Feng[2], Nicole C. Krämer[3], Lynn C. Miller[1], and Stacy Marsella[2]

[1] University of Southern California, Los Angeles, CA 90089, USA,
{davidjeo,lmiller}@usc.edu
[2] Northeastern University, Boston, MA 02115, USA,
{danfeng, marsella}@ccs.neu.edu
[3] University Duisburg-Essen, Duisburg, Germany,
nicole.kraemer@uni-due.de

Abstract. While applications of virtual agents in training and pedagogy have largely concentrated on positive valenced environments and interactions, human-human interactions certainly also involve a fair share of negativity that is worth exploring in virtual environments. Further, in natural human interaction as well as in virtual spaces, physical actions arguably account for a great deal of variance in our representations of social concepts (e.g., emotions, attitudes). Proxemics, specifically, is a physical cue that can elicit varying perceptions of a social interaction. In the current paper, we explore the combined and individual effects of proxemic distance and gender in a specifically negative feedback educational context. We pursue this with a 2 (Proxemic Distance) × 2 (Virtual Instructor Gender) between subject design, where participants actively engage in a learning task with a virtual instructor that provides harsh, negative feedback. While this study demonstrates some anticipated negative reactions to negative feedback from a close distance, such as external attribution of failure, we also observe some unexpected positive outcomes to this negative feedback. Specifically, negative feedback from a close distance has raises positive affect and effort, particularly among male participants interacting with a male virtual professor. Objective measures (head movement data) corroborate these same-gender effects as participants demonstrate more engagement when interacting with a virtual professor of their same gender. The results of the present study have broad implications for the design of intelligent virtual agents for pedagogy and mental health outcomes.

Keywords: Virtual Instructor, Attribution Theory, Proxemics, Affect

1 Introduction

Applications of intelligent virtual agents (VA) to facilitate learning has been well-documented [17, 29, 20, 21]. While some research focuses on the agent's appearance [4, 21], others focus on the nature of the agent's communication [24]. That being said, current research on pedagogical agents focuses mainly on the interactions with a positive valence, such as politeness [32] and rapport [31, 26]. A

© Springer International Publishing AG 2017
J. Beskow et al. (Eds.): IVA 2017, LNAI 10498, pp. 170–183, 2017.
DOI 10.1007/978-3-319-67401-8_19

fundamental determinant to how people respond to feedback from virtual agents is the manner in which the feedback is delivered. Research on politeness within [32] and outside [6] the virtual agent research community demonstrate that forms of communication, namely phrasing, are critical. Prior research has shown that both positive phrases [32] and non-verbal behaviors [26] may positively impact the learning outcome.

Real world learning experiences, however, are not necessarily exclusively positive in valence. The effect of negative feedback in educational contexts have long been debated [9]. Kluger and Neulsin [23] argue that negative feedback benefits learning. However, few studies have explored the consequences of a negatively valenced educational context by examining students' reactions and response to a virtual teacher's negative feedback. An exception is the work introduced by Feng et al., (2017) which focuses on explicitly harsh negative feedback, and is discussed further in the related work.

We used a 2 × 2 design (Gender × Approach) in a virtual environment, where a male or female virtual agent (depending on condition) provides an identical series of explicitly harsh negative feedback messages while standing either close or far away from the participant. In manipulating who delivered the negative feedback (i.e., a man or a woman) and how (i.e., with what accompanying proxemics), our research goal for this study was to identify differential patterns participants' attributions and affect. We report a number of findings, with the most compelling of which is an unexpected "bounce-back effect" as male participants curiously report positive affect and effort in response to the harsh feedback.

The paper is organized as follows: In Section 2, we present the theoretical background and related work. Our methods and results will be discussed in section 3 and 4. We conclude and discuss the implications and future directions of this work in Section 5 and 6.

2   Related Work

Negative Feedback.   First introduced by Dweck [9], the effects of negative feedback in educational contexts have long been a topic of discussion in the field of education and psychology. Some argue that negative feedback benefits learning [23] while others argue that it leads to a learned helplessness that hampers learning [10]. At a fundamental level, negative feedback has been shown to lower motivation [30]. That said, students may employ strategies to address the negative feedback, such as increasing effort [8] and lowering goals and expectations [23]. Such goal regulation strategies have been observed both for legitimate and manipulated feedback [19].

Attribution.   A crucial response to negative feedback in an educational context is one's attribution of blame or responsibility. That is, does the student attribute blame to their own poor abilities or do they attribute blame to the instructor's poor teaching abilities? Attribution theory has long been discussed in the field of education [33]. While students' success is often attributed to the self, failures are typically attributed to others [22]. In fact, students tend to ignore negative feedback that contrasts with their own assessments of their performance [7]. What remains to be seen, however, is an understanding of how negative feedback transforms and shifts students attribution tendencies based on the gender of a teacher and the interpersonal distance between the student and the teacher.

Proxemics. Proxemics, or interpersonal distance between communicators, highly impacts the perception of meaning in all forms of human social interaction. Hall (1966) [15] identified 4 types of interpersonal distance zones with varying distances and social meaning: the intimate zone $(0 - 45$ cm), the personal-casual zone (45 - 120 cm), the socio-consultive zone $(120 - 360$ cm), and the public zone $(360 - 750$ cm). Management of and responses to interpersonal distance has also been examined closely among virtual agents [1, 2, 34, 27] and robotics [14]. As Bailenson et al. (2001) note, studies about proxemics have historically been wrought with issues of reliability and validity across participants [1]. Virtual environments offer an opportunity to reliably test precisely defined proxemics while also maximizing realism [5].

2.1   Embodied Agents

Research examining learning within virtual environments have mostly made use of computer-driven embodied agents [1]. To have optimal learning effects using virtual agents, studies have underscored the need to integrate socio-emotional and relational variables such as embodiment and nonverbal behavior [25]. These studies have traditionally focused on the effects of positive feedback from virtual agents in a virtual learning environment [25, 26, 31]. For instance, Wang et al. (2008) found that an agent who uses polite requests had a more positive impact on learning than a more direct agent. Further, Krämer et al. (2016) found a significant improvement on participant's performance when interacting with same-gender virtual agents that rapidly respond to the participants with positive non-verbal behavior.

Departing from these prior work, Feng et al., (2017) focused on students' direct response to purely negative feedback from virtual instructors, and found that students attribute greater self-blame (internal attribution) for their purported poor performance when interacting with the female virtual instructor than when interacting with the male virtual instructor [12]. This was accomplished by comparing students' reactions to negative feedback delivered by a virtual agent that stood still with a virtual agent that approached the student in a somewhat threatening manner. While prominent gender differences were found, a potential limitation of the proxemic stimuli was that the approaching behavior happened at the very end of the experiment, which may have softened its threatening intent, which in turn may have muted the experimental manipulation. In order to account for this potential conflation of experimental conditions, the present study examined the differences in perception of a virtual agent standing still at a near and far distance.

2.2   Hypotheses

Generally, this study explores the role of instructor gender, and potential interaction effects of instructor gender with both instructor proxemic distance and student gender (participant) as they impact participant attribution, affect, judgments of the instructor, and head movements. We anticipate the proxemic distance of the virtual instructor to have a wide impact on participants' experiences in this virtual learning environment. Research on Attribution Theory has noted that in general, men tend to attribute success to internal/stable causes while women tend to attribute failures to internal/stable causes. As such, we hypothesize similar gender differences to emerge in the current study [3, 13, 28]. This study will further examine these gender effects in a negative feedback-based virtual learning environment, but we have no literature-backed predictions for how gender may potentially interact with proxemics in this negative feedback interaction. We do however, predict that the close distance in the negative feedback context will exacerbate feelings of Dweck's [10] "learned helplessness" , which may be associated with perceptions of less personal control and greater external control. In terms of affect, close interpersonal distance is generally associated with greater intimacy [15], but closer interpersonal distance in a negatively valenced context lead us to expect greater negative affect, lower attributional control, and external attributional tendencies. In line with Edney et al 1976 [11], we also predict that this unwanted closer interpersonal distance would lead to greater reactive head movements (HMD) in order to re-establish personal space.

3   Method

3.1   Participants

117 students from two universities (54 men and 63 women), with an average age of 20.94 (SD = 2.77) participated in this study and were randomly assigned to one of 4 conditions in a 2 (Virtual Instructor Gender) × 2 (Close/Far) between-subjects design. Although assignment to conditions was randomized, the distribution of participants across the 4 conditions was slightly uneven. The number of participants in each condition is shown in Table 1

Table 1. Number of participants in each condition

Proxemics	Virtual Instructor Gender	Male Participants	Female Participants
Close	Male	14	14
	Female	13	11
Far	Male	10	19
	Female	17	19

3.2   Measures

To examine the changes of the participants' affect and attribution, we used the same measures introduced in [12], including Positive and Negative Affect Schedule-Expanded Form (PANAS-X), The Revised Causal Dimension Scale II (CDSII) and additional Ad-Hoc Questions about participants' judgments of the experiment.

Another significant factor in the present study was the degree to which participants truly believed that the negative feedback they were receiving was tailored and specific to each person. Although efforts were made to make the virtual environment authentic, some participants could pick up on the actual non-intelligent nature of the virtual environment. As such, a manipulation check was delivered to the participants in the form of two items on a 7-point Likert scale (anchors extremely inauthentic and extremely authentic): "To what extent did you feel that the instructor's feedback was authentic/real?" and "To what extent did you feel that the virtual environment was authentic/real?"

Head Movement Head movement data coordinates for x-, y-, and z-axes were recorded at 25 separate time points over the course of the actual acting experiment. Each time point interval varied as the time points were event-based. That is time points were tagged according to the statements made by Virtual Instructor throughout the experiment. Naturally, the time points were identical across all participants. Head movement were analyzed for aggregate movement (bi-directional) and directional movement (uni-directional).

Aggregate Head Movement (Bi-Directional) was calculated by summing up the absolute values of the differences between each pair of the sequential data points, as shown in Equation (1). In other words, the absolute value of the difference between time 1 and time 2 was added with the absolute value of the difference between time 2 and time 3, and so on up to the absolute value of the difference between time 24 and time 25. By summing up the absolute values of each time point for each axis, we computed aggregate movement variables for each axis. The formulas for the movement variables of each axis are depicted below.

$$Aggregate\ movement = |i_1 - i_2| + ... + |i_n - i_{n+1}| + .. + |i_{24} - i_{25}|),$$
$$i \in \{x - axis, y - axis, z - axis\}, \tag{1}$$

Directional Head Movement (Uni-Directional) was calculated by summing the non-absolute differences between each pair of sequential data points. The output generated by this formula represents the aggregate movement direction that the participants tended to move towards over the course of the experiment for each x-,y-, and z- axes. The formulas for the movement direction variables are depicted in Equation (2).

$$Directional\ movement = (i_1 - i_2) + ... + (i_n - i_{n+1}) + .. + (i_{24} - i_{25}),$$
$$i \in \{x - axis, y - axis, z - axis\}, \tag{2}$$

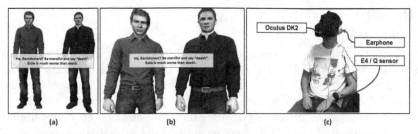

Fig. 1. Screen-shot of the virtual environment in far condition (a) and close condition(b). In far condition(a), the virtual instructor stands far away from the participants at the beginning of the experiment while in closing condition (b), the virtual instructor stands right in front of the participants' face. (c) shows the system apparatus.

3.3 Materials

We created a contextualized virtual environment that aims at invoking the key components of negative feedback, namely, the feeling of helplessness and lack of motivation. Specifically, we simulated an acting rehearsal in an acting class scenario. Participants took the role of an acting student, reading lines from 'Romeo and Juliet' while taking instruction from a virtual instructor. Participants were told that the instructor's feedback was specifically tailored to their performance, but the twist here was that the negative feedback from the virtual instructor was scripted and identical for all participants regardless of their performance. Each time the participant finished reading a line, the virtual instructor provided negative feedback using harsh language along with negative non-verbals. For example,"You sound like a dead fish" and "No no no, that's not right". Participant engaged in the acting rehearsal with a second virtual agent, which took on the role of a fellow acting student (See Fig. 1). In other words, the Instructor virtual agent provided the negative feedback and the Student virtual agent engaged in a rehearsed conversational exchange with the research participant(s). The virtual instructor, however, never provided any feedback to or even directed eye gaze at the virtual student.

3.4 Experiment Procedure

Prior to arrival, participants were randomly assigned to one of four conditions (Male Close, Female Close, Male Far, Female Far). As they began to read the informed consent form, participants were fitted with the E4/Q skin conductance measure bracelet. After completing this briefing session, participants were asked to fill out the PANAS-X (pre-test) and the Rosenberg Self-Esteem Scale. After completing those two questionnaires, participants were fitted with the HMD and headphones at an appropriate distance of about 5 feet from the HMD sensor. Upon completing the experiment, the participants responded to additional questionnaire measurements including the PANAS-X (post-test) and the CDS II. Each session for a given participant lasted no more than 30 minutes.

4 Result

4.1 Data Preparation

CDS II Factor analysis was conducted on individual subscales that make up the Causal Dimension Scale II. Five items under the Locus of causality dimension of the CDSII were examined via principal components analysis using varimax rotation. All five items loaded onto one factor and were retained under a locus of causality composite measure (Cronbachs α = .86). Three items under the personal dimension of the CDSII were examined via principal components analysis and were all found to load on one factor (Cronbachs α = .87). Three items under the stability dimension of the CDSII were examined via principal components analysis using varimax rotation, and all loaded on one factor (Cronbachs α = .73). Six items under the external dimension of the CDSII were examined via principal components analysis using varimax rotation. Three items did not load on the first factor and were dropped from the composite external measure (Cronbachs α = .76).

4.2 Manipulation check

Negative Affect. Critical to the present study was that participants actually perceive the negative feedback messages as negative in affect. As such, we tested the effectiveness of the negative feedback by determining the level of negative affect that the feedback generated. We conducted a series of paired samples t-tests. Significant mean differences between pre- and post-test measurements of PANAS-X were observed for the composited negative affect values, $t(116) = -2.126, p = .036$ as well as individual negative affect items including Upset, $t(114) = -5.74, p < .001$, Guilty, $t(114) = -2.252, p = .026$, Hostile, $t(114) = -4.041, p < .001$, Irritable, $t(114) = -2.52, p = .013$, Ashamed, $t(114) = -4.54, p < .001$, and Nervous, $t(114) = 3.495, p = .001$. Here, we see clear indication that the experimental negative feedback was generally successful in communicating its meaning and intent. Significant mean differences were also observed for the positive affect items of Enthusiastic, $t(114) = 2.62, p = .01$, Proud, $t(114) = 2.82, p = .006$, but the direction of the mean differences indicate a decrease in enthusiasm and pride, providing further support for that the negativity of the feedback was accurately perceived.

Experiment Authenticity. Both items were normally distributed and no outliers were identified, enabling all participants to be included for analysis. Participants generally were mixed in their judgments of the authenticity of the instructor feedback (M= 3.92, SD = 1.7) and generally felt the virtual environment was more authentic than inauthentic (M = 4.43, SD= 1.5). Further, the medians for each of the two items were 5, which corresponds to Slightly authentic on the 7-point Likert scale.

Appearance and Audio. As this experiment only utilized 1 male and 1 female VH, a separate manipulation check was conducted to control for the appearance and voice of the Virtual Instructor. 178 participants were recruited from Amazon Mechanical Turk to judge 5 virtual humans (3 males, 2 females) for threat, likability, and attractiveness of virtual human with different appearances. Each participant was randomly assigned to rate 2 virtual agents repeating the same line, which was taken from the actual main experiment. The affect was evaluated by a Self-Assessment Manikin (SAM) scale and personality was assessed by using the same scale introduced in [18] by adding one more item, 'attractiveness'. We found no significant difference between the appearance and voice of 5 virtual agents which suggests that appearance and vocal quality have no significant impact on the participants' perceptions of explicitly harsh negative feedback.

4.3   Statistical analysis

CDSII. A 2-way MANOVA was conducted examining the effects of Proxemic Distance with the Gender of the Virtual instructor on the factor analyzed composite CDS II Dimensions of Locus of Causality, Personal Control, Stability, and External Control. A multivariate main effect of Proxemic Distance on the CDS Dimensions was observed, $F(4, 117) = 7.15, p < .001, r = .21$. No other main effects or interaction effects were found. Univariate main effects of Proxemic Distance were observed for Stability, $F(3, 117) = 20.69, p < .001, r = .16$, Personal Control, $F(3, 117) = 4.88, p = .029, r = .04$ and External Control, $F(3, 117) = 7.91, p = .006, r = .07$. No other main effects or interaction effects were observed. As each independent variable was limited to 2 levels, post-hoc tests were not conducted.

Regardless of Virtual Instructor Gender, those who interacted with a Close instructor reported significantly higher levels of External Control. In other words, the participants in the Close conditions tended to report that people outside of themselves (the professor) had a more impactful role in their performance. Further, those who interacted with a Close instructor reported significantly lower levels of personal control, or ones own ability to regulate and manage ones performance, as well as significantly higher levels of stability, deeming the current situation of negative feedback to be more permanent, stable, and unchangeable.

PANAS-X. Participant Gender was added to the MANOVA model to examine the 3-way effects of Proxemic Distance, Gender of the Virtual Instructor, and Participant Gender on the individual post-test measurements of PANAS-X. As each independent variable was limited to 2 levels, post-hoc tests were not conducted. Univariate main effects of Participant Gender were found on items such as Interested, Excited, Enthusiastic, Inspired, Determined and Active, as shown in Table 2. That is, male participants generally reported greater positive affect than female participants after receiving the negative feedback. This indicates a presence of a gender-based pattern in which male participants seemingly bounce-back in reaction to harsh negative feedback.

Ad-Hoc Items. A 3-way MANOVA was conducted examining the effects of Proxemic Distance, Virtual Instructor Gender, and Participant Gender on the individual Ad-hoc items. As the Ad-hoc items did not constitute a composite

Table 2. Main effect of Participant Gender on Post-test PANAS-X

Dependent Variable	df	Mean Square	F	Sig.	Partial Eta Sq
Interested	1	4.259	4.521	.036	.04
Excited	1	9.747	7.459	.007	.06
Enthusiastic	1	5.386	4.135	.044	.04
Inspired	1	12.671	8.395	.005	.07
Determined	1	11.032	8.68	.004	.07
Active	1	19.34	13.96	.000	.11

measurement scale, each item was examined at the univariate level. Univariate main effects of Proxemic Distance were observed for the helpfulness of the feedback, the likability of the professor and the level of effort put into the task, as shown in Table 3. That is, participants in the Close condition perceived the feedback to be less helpful, the professor to be less likable, and tried harder to complete the task than participants in the Far condition did. Further, participants in the Close condition attributed the professors reactions to his/her personality more so than those in the Far conditions, $F(3, 117) = 28.23, p < .001$, r = .20.

Table 3. Main effect of Proxemic Distance on Ad-hoc Items

Dependent Variable	df	Mean Square	F	Sig.	Partial Eta Sq
Helpfulness of the instructor's feedback	1	9.078	7.687	.007	.08
Accuracy of the instructor's feedback	1	2.676	2.928	.090	.02
Attribute to professors personality	1	88.264	28.226	.000	.20
Attribute to professor having a bad day	1	5.398	2.424	.122	.03
Level of Effort	1	23.509	27.460	.000	.22
Likability of professor	1	39.971	23.738	.000	.18

An interaction effect of Participant Gender and Proxemic Distance was observed for the level of effort placed on the acting task, $F(3, 117) = 5.304, p = .023$, r = .05. That is, male participants in the Close condition tried much harder on the task than the males in the Far condition. The difference in effort between Close and Far conditions was not as pronounced for the female participants.

Head Movement. A 3-way MANOVA was conducted examining the effects of Proxemic Distance, Virtual Instructor Gender, and Participant Genderthe aggregate and directional HMD movement on the x, y, and z axes.

Aggregate Head Movement (Bi-Directional). A multivariate main effect for Proxemic Distance was observed for HMD movement, $F(3, 105) = 2.983, p = .035$, r = .08. Further, a 2-way multivariate interaction effect was observed between Participant Gender and Virtual Instructor Gender, $F(3, 105) = 5.334, p = .002$. Finally, a 3-way multivariate interaction effect was observed for Proxemic Distance, Participant Gender, and Virtual Instructor Gender, $F(3, 105) = 2.994, p = .034$, r = .13. Univariate analyses revealed main effects of Proxemic Distance on x-axis movement, $F(1, 115) = 8.498, p = .004$, r = .07, and z-axis movement, $F(1, 115) = 4.105, p = .045$, r = .04. In other words, there was a significant difference in side-to-side movement (x) and front-back movement (z) depending on the Virtual Instructors Proxemic Distance. Proxemic Distance also impacted the up-down movement (y), but this main effect was not significant, $F(1, 115) = 3.069, p = .083$, r = .03. A univariate 2-way interaction effect between Participant Gender and Virtual Instructor Gender was observed on only the x-axis movement, $F(1, 115) = 9.598, p = .002$, r = .08. Male participants x-axis head movements shot up in response to interacting with a female virtual instructor, whereas female participants x-axis head movement declined when interacting with a male virtual instructor. No other significant univariate main effects or interaction effects were observed.

Directional Head Movement (Uni-Directional). A univariate main effect was observed for Proxemic Distance on HMD y-axis (up-down) movement direction, $F(1, 115) = 4.461, p = .037$, r = .04. In other words, participants tended to sink down in response to the Close distance conditions relative to the Far distance conditions.

Further, a univariate 3-way interaction for Proxemic Distance, Virtual Instructor Gender, and Participant Gender was observed on HMD z-axis (towards-away) movement direction, $F(1, 115) = 5.41, p = .022$, r = .05. In other words, a two-way interaction varies across different levels of a third variable. Fig. 2(a) depicts the 2-way interaction for Proxemic Distance and Virtual Instructor Gender for Male participants and Fig. 2(b) depicts the 2-way interaction for Proxemic Distance and Virtual Instructor Gender for Female participants. Male participants tended to move forward when they interacted with a male virtual instructor at a close distance relative to those who interacted with a male virtual instructor at a far distance. Conversely, male participants interacting with a female virtual instructor at a close distance tended to move backwards relative to male participants interacting with a female virtual instructor at a far distance. As shown in Fig. 2, this identical pattern of forward-movement in response to same-gendered virtual instructors and backward-movement in response to cross-gendered virtual instructors at a close distance was also observed among female participants. No other main effects or interaction effects were observed for the above variables.

5 Discussion

Attribution and Affect To begin, the current study lent partial support to our attribution-related hypotheses. Negative feedback at a close distance led to greater judgments of external control and less personal control over one's performance, providing support to the prediction that negative feedback at a closer distance would exacerbate feelings of "learned helplessness" [10]. That said, contrary to predictions based on literature [3, 13, 28](Bar Tal, 1978; Frieze, 1975; McMahan, 1973)., no significant gender effects of attribution were observed. A concept closely tied to attribution is motivation. At a fundamental level, negative feedback has been shown to lower motivation [30]. That said, students may employ strategies to counteract the negative feedback, such as increasing effort

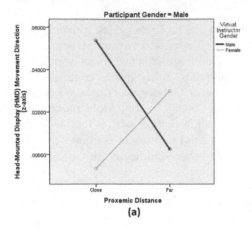
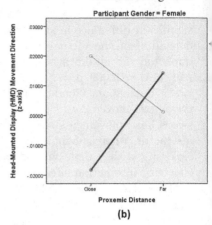

Fig. 2. 2-way Interaction for Proxemic Distance and Virtual Instructor Gender across Male (a) and Female Participants (b) (3-way Interaction)

[8] and lowering goals and expectations [23]. As such, a more complete under-standing of attributional tendencies warranted more detailed ad-hoc analysis of participants' judgments of the instructor and the feedback. Although partici-pants in the close conditions perceived the instructor to be less likable and the feedback to be less helpful, they did report trying harder in the task than did participants in the far condition. As observed as by the PANAS-X and Ad-Hoc Measure results above, the close distance seems to raise the degree of account-ability in the task particularly for male participants, who demonstrate a sizable drop off in effort when interacting with a Far virtual instructor. This pattern of behavior somewhat corroborates the above tendency for the male participants to be being more interested, excited, enthusiastic, determined, and active in response to the instructors negative feedback.

Unexpectedly, however, we found a pattern of mixed affect-related reactions to negative feedback delivered at a close distance– particularly among male par-ticipants. Specifically, we found that that negative feedback at a close distance raised various components of positive affect among male participants, who re-ported significantly higher levels of interest, excitement, enthusiasm, determined, and activity.

While the manipulation check of the negative affect reinforced the notion that participants reported significantly greater negative affect after the exper-iment, male participants exhibited a curious pattern of asserting what may be categorized as a defiant resilience, and a refusal to be negatively impacted by the criticisms. This pattern of behavior may be explained by the tendency of negative feedback to enforce a sense of accountability, thereby generating the attention and motivation needed to complete the task successfully.

A small twist in this affective response of male participants was that male participants seemed to report feeling far more irritated by instructors providing negative feedback at a far distance than close distances, whereas the inverse effect was seen among female participants. The male effect may be attributable to the cognitive dissonance experienced with an extremely critical message coupled with a perception of a less engaged body language (far distance). This irritation experienced by male participants is likely associated with the tendency for male participants to try harder on the task in the close conditions.

Head Movement. Finally, in order to examine the reactionary physical behaviors of participants in response to varying proxemic distance, we examined two types of head movment across 3 different coordinate-planes. We observed gendered differences in Head Movement in reaction to the Close and Far distance conditions. Specifically, male participants cumulative side-to-side head movements shot up in response to interacting with a female virtual instructor, whereas female participants' side-to-side head movement declined when interacting with a male virtual instructor. More interestingly, all participants in Close conditions - regardless of gender - exhibited a tendency to move forward in response to a same-gendered VH while moving backwards in response to a cross-gendered VH. This result adds complexity to our original hypothesis that participants would generally move backwards in response to a Close VH. A forward-movement, or leaning- of the head over the course of the experiment may suggest an in-group/out-group phenomenon where participants are less comfortable and/or less focused when receiving negative feedback from a same-gendered instructor.

Limitations and Future Directions. Future research should be done into examining the specific gender-specific patterns observed here. Notably, head movement has not previously been associated with proxemics/interpersonal distance, but the implicit nature of these fine-grained head movements may be reliable measurement of proxemic effects moving forward – potentially having greater implications for how we study the basic components, effects, and perceptions of social interactions and situations.

Recall that we performed a manipulation check of VH appearance and voice that used video clips as opposed to the experience in the VR experiment. The use of these separate modalities may potentially weaken the impact of the manipulation check. Future studies would ideally run the full VR-environment experiment using a range of virtual human characters that account for the variability in human appearance and voice.

Finally, a significant limitation to this study is a lack of a true control where the negative feedback is more muted or non-existent. The presence of such a control condition could allow for a stronger argument about the effects found in this study – particularly the resilient "bounce-back" effect observed among male participants.

6 Conclusion

Why do drill sargeants and sports coaches often use harsh feedback? All together, this study provides a keener understanding of the varying effects of negative feedback that could potentially have positive outcomes– particularly when delivered from a close proximal distance. Indeed, negative feedback has been observed to act as a motivator for tasks that are required [16]. The findings suggest a gendered pattern in reaction to negative feedback as male participants seem to demonstrate a "bounce-back" effect in response to the negative feedback by trying harder, feeling more positive, and moving even closer to the instructor.

This project has broad implications for pedagogy, mental health, decision-making and skill-based training. For instance, these findings may enable researchers to develop a keener understanding of how participants respond, both verbally and physiologically, to the experience of negative feedback. This information can then be used to create intervention strategies to "buffer" participants against the instructor's negative feedback: These student tactics could be taught through successive iterations of the virtual scene. By simulating a negative feedback teaching situation in a virtual environment, we present the potential for a more precise understanding of the effects of negative feedback on students' learning, emotional state, attribution patterns, and even their nonverbal reactions to the negative feedback. We suggest further inquiry into different social situations and contexts in order to develop and strengthen these arguments.

References

1. Bailenson, J.N., Blascovich, J., Beall, A.C., Loomis, J.M.: Equilibrium theory revisited: Mutual gaze and personal space in virtual environments. Presence: Teleoperators and virtual environments 10(6), 583–598 (2001)
2. Bailenson, J.N., Blascovich, J., Beall, A.C., Loomis, J.M.: Interpersonal distance in immersive virtual environments. Personality and Social Psychology Bulletin 29(7), 819–833 (2003)
3. Bar-Tal, D.: Attributional analysis of achievement-related behavior. Review of educational research 48(2), 259–271 (1978)
4. Baylor, A.L.: Promoting motivation with virtual agents and avatars: role of visual presence and appearance. Philosophical Transactions of the Royal Society of London B: Biological Sciences 364(1535), 3559–3565 (2009)
5. Blascovich, J., Loomis, J., Beall, A.C., Swinth, K.R., Hoyt, C.L., Bailenson, J.N.: Immersive virtual environment technology as a methodological tool for social psychology. Psychological Inquiry 13(2), 103–124 (2002)
6. Brown, P., Levinson, S.C.: Politeness: Some universals in language use (1999)
7. Campbell, J.D., Tesser, A.: Motivational interpretations of hindsight bias: An individual difference analysis. Journal of Personality 51(4), 605–620 (1983)
8. Carver, C.S.: Resilience and thriving: Issues, models, and linkages. J. of social issues 54(2), 245–266 (1998)
9. Dweck, C.S.: The role of expectations and attributions in the alleviation of learned helplessness. Journal of personality and social psychology 31(4), 674 (1975)
10. Dweck, C.S., Davidson, W., Nelson, S., Enna, B.: Sex differences in learned helplessness: Ii. the contingencies of evaluative feedback in the classroom and iii. an experimental analysis. Developmental psychology 14(3), 268 (1978)
11. Edney, J.J., Walker, C.A., Jordan, N.L.: Is there reactance in personal space? The Journal of Social Psychology 100(2), 207–217 (1976)
12. Feng, D., Jeong, D.C., Krämer, N.C., Miller, L.C., Marsella, S.: Is it just me?: Evaluating attribution of negative feedback as a function of virtual instructor's gender and proxemics. In: AAMAS 2017. pp. 810–818. IFAAMAS (2017)
13. Frieze, I.H.: Women's expectations for and causal attributions of success and failure. Women and achievement pp. 158–171 (1975)

14. Gockley, R., Forlizzi, J., Simmons, R.: Natural person-following behavior for social robots. In: HRI 2007. pp. 17–24. ACM (2007)
15. Hall, E.T.: The hidden dimension (1966)
16. Hattie, J., Timperley, H.: The power of feedback. Review of educational research 77(1), 81–112 (2007)
17. Heidig, S., Clarebout, G.: Do pedagogical agents make a difference to student motivation and learning? Educational Research Review 6(1), 27–54 (2011)
18. Hoffmann, L., Krämer, N., Lam-Chi, A., Kopp, S.: Media equation revisited: do users show polite reactions towards an embodied agent? In: IVA. pp. 159–165. Springer (2009)
19. Ilies, R., Judge, T.A.: Goal regulation across time: the effects of feedback and affect. Journal of applied psychology 90(3), 453 (2005)
20. Johnson, W.L., Lester, J.C.: Face-to-face interaction with pedagogical agents, twenty years later. Int. J. of AI in Education 26(1), 25–36 (2016)
21. Kim, Y., Baylor, A.L.: Research-based design of pedagogical agent roles: a review, progress, and recommendations. Int. J. of AI in Education 26(1), 160–169 (2016)
22. Klein, O., Licata, L.: Explaining differences between social groups: The impact of group identification on attribution. Swiss Journal of Psychology/Schweizerische Zeitschrift für Psychologie/Revue Suisse de Psychologie 60(4), 244 (2001)
23. Kluger, A.N., DeNisi, A.: The effects of feedback interventions on performance: a historical review, a meta-analysis, and a preliminary feedback intervention theory. Psychological bulletin 119(2), 254 (1996)
24. Kolkmeier, J., Vroon, J., Heylen, D.: Interacting with virtual agents in shared space: Single and joint effects of gaze and proxemics. In: IVA. pp. 1–14 (2016)
25. Krämer, N.C., Bente, G.: Personalizing e-learning. the social effects of pedagogical agents. Educational Psychology Review 22(1), 71–87 (2010)
26. Krämer, N.C., Karacora, B., Lucas, G., Dehghani, M., Rüther, G., Gratch, J.: Closing the gender gap in stem with friendly male instructors? on the effects of rapport behavior and gender of a virtual agent in an instructional interaction. Computers & Education 99, 1–13 (2016)
27. Llobera, J., Spanlang, B., Ruffini, G., Slater, M.: Proxemics with multiple dynamic characters in an immersive virtual environment. TAP 8(1), 3 (2010)
28. McMahan, I.D.: Relationships between causal attributions and expectancy of success. Journal of Personality and Social Psychology 28(1), 108 (1973)
29. Schroeder, N.L., Adesope, O.O., Gilbert, R.B.: How effective are pedagogical agents for learning? a meta-analytic review. J. of Educational Computing Research 49(1), 1–39 (2013)
30. Vallerand, R.J., Reid, G.: On the causal effects of perceived competence on intrinsic motivation: A test of cognitive evaluation theory. J. of Sport Psychology 6(1), 94–102 (1984)
31. Wang, N., Gratch, J.: Rapport and facial expression. In: ACII. pp. 1–6. IEEE (2009)
32. Wang, N., Johnson, W.L., Mayer, R.E., Rizzo, P., Shaw, E., Collins, H.: The politeness effect: Pedagogical agents and learning outcomes. International Journal of Human-Computer Studies 66(2), 98–112 (2008)
33. Weiner, B., Russell, D., Lerman, D.: Affective consequences of causal ascriptions. New directions in attribution research 2, 59–90 (1978)
34. Wilcox, L.M., Allison, R.S., Elfassy, S., Grelik, C.: Personal space in virtual reality. ACM Transactions on Applied Perception (TAP) 3(4), 412–428 (2006)

A psychotherapy training environment with virtual patients implemented using the Furhat robot platform

Robert Johansson[1,2]✉, Gabriel Skantze[3], and Arne Jönsson[1]

[1] Department of Computer and Information Science, Linköping University, Linköping, Sweden

[2] Eailab AB, Stockholm, Sweden
{robert.johansson, arne.jonsson}@liu.se

[3] KTH Speech, Music and Hearing, Stockholm, Sweden
gabriel@speech.kth.se

Abstract. We present a demonstration system for psychotherapy training that uses the Furhat social robot platform to implement virtual patients. The system runs an educational program with various modules, starting with training of basic psychotherapeutic skills and then moves on to tasks where these skills need to be integrated. Such training relies heavily on observing and dealing with both verbal and non-verbal in-session patient behavior. Hence, the Furhat robot is an ideal platform for implementing this. This paper describes the rationale for this system and its implementation.

Keywords: Psychotherapy, Virtual patients, Social robots.

1. Introduction

For over a decade it has been possible for surgeons and other medical specialists to practice in a simulated environment, for example with the help of virtual reality. This has enabled both students and experienced clinicians to practice complicated procedures systematically. A problem for clinical psychologists and psychologists in training is that there are no available simulators adapted for psychotherapy training. This demo paper introduces such a training environment that has been implemented with the help of the social robot platform Furhat.

2. The Furhat Platform

Furhat is a three dimensional back-projected robot head built for the purpose of multimodal multiparty human-machine interaction systems [1]. It utilizes a computer-animated face with a very high capacity for non-verbal communication and face movement, leading to a very realistic end result. The Furhat platform comes with IrisTK [2], a software framework for building event-based, modular interactive systems. IrisTK has a flexible design and uses a statechart-based XML formalism for designing the dialog flow.

© Springer International Publishing AG 2017
J. Beskow et al. (Eds.): IVA 2017, LNAI 10498, pp. 184-187, 2017.
DOI 10.1007/978-3-319-67401-8_20

3.   Psychotherapy training program

The system is based on a theory of psychotherapy called Intensive short-term dynamic psychotherapy (ISTDP) [3, 4]. This is an emotion-focused form of psychotherapy that explicitly focuses on in-session patient expression of emotion and other clinically relevant behaviors. Furthermore, ISTDP provides a large corpus of knowledge on how verbal and non-verbal behavior are related to therapeutic interventions (see below for examples). Hence, we use the theory of ISTDP to create realistic patient behavior. We aim to create a training environment that is suited for training in any form of psychotherapy. For this, we have been inspired by the general model of psychotherapy training as developed by psychotherapist Jon Frederickson [5].

A core module of the training program is related to the assessment phase of the treatment where a focus for therapy needs to be established. This is typically part of the very beginning of therapy, in where patient and therapist agree on a problem to work on. The process continues with the therapist investigating situations where the problem arises for the patient and exploring whether there are emotional factors contributing to the problem. Importantly, the occurrence of barriers to the process is a rule rather than an exception. Such barriers can broadly be said to be either *anxiety* or *defenses*. If a patient experiences excessive anxiety for example in the form of blurry vision or stomach pain, manifested for example with disorganized talking, then the process cannot continue in a benefical way without regulating the anxiety. A *defense* can be said to be any in-session patient behavior that becomes a blocker for the process. Very briefly, this can be anything from vagueness and overgeneralization to taking a highly passive stance in therapy. Let's say for example that the therapist asks an initial question *"What problem do you want my help with?"*. A patient response such as *"Lots of things"* won't help the process further since it is too general to work with. This calls for the therapist to deal with this blocker for example by saying *"That is quite vague. Can you please be a bit more specific what problem you would like me to help you with?"*. Throughout the whole treatment, i.e. beyond the initial assessment phase, the same principles apply: If there are barriers to engagement in the process, these needs to be dealt with. In the training environment described in this paper, these principles are taught repeatedly with the help of the Furhat robot platform.

4.   Implementation

An initial implementation of the training program has been created uing the Furhat robot. The training program starts by teaching the trainee how to identify various expressions of anxiety and defenses. Importantly, these are both verbal and non-verbal. For example, a barrier in the form of slowing down, looking away, and taking an unengaged position, is mostly non-verbal. Such non-verbal behavior is an example of what is possible to model using the Furhat robot. After initial training on how to spot these patterns, the trainee learns how to deal with these barriers, i.e. dealing with in-session behavior that has become a blocker to the process. This is modeled as part of the dialog flow in the Furhat robot. Using this approach, the trainee gets a direct experience of what it feels like to deal with blockers in therapy and to observe the effects that follow. Later on in the training program, the trainee can practice the assessment phase with several virtual patents. The aim for the trainee in this step is to work with virtual patients with different characteristics and to work through the complete assessment phase with identifying the problem, investigating specific examples and exploring emotional factors driving the problem. As described above, the trainee needs to deal with barriers in therapy in the form of anxiety and defenses throughout the entire process.

Below is an example dialogue between a therapist and a virtual patient in the system. With this, we aim to illustrate how the dialogue progresses when the therapist deals with in-session barriers to engagement:

T: What is the problem you would like me to help you with?

P: I don't recognize myself lately [Defense: vagueness]

T: Could you please be more specific? What specific problem would you like my help with? [Block the defense. As long as we don't have a specific problem to work on, we can't help the patient]

*P: *sigh* Maybe you could say that there are some problems at work.* [Defense: vague and general]

T: How do you mean? What happens at work that becomes a problem for you? [Asking to be more specific]

*P: *sigh* [looking away] I get into a lot of conflicts.* [Still a bit vague, but in the right direction. Move on to asking for a specific example]

T: Do you have a specific example?

P: I would say it's more a general problem. [Defense: vague and general]

T: That description is vague. As long as this remains vague for us, we won't have a clear picture of your problem, and then we won't be able to help you with it. Could we look at a specific example of this? [Explicitly clarify the defense and invite a more specific response]

*P: *sigh* There have been a lot of situations lately.* [Defense: General]

T: That's still vague and general. What can we do about this vagueness? [Challenge the defense of vagueness]

*P: *sigh* OK, I shouted at my boss last week. Then I slammed the door and drove home. I have stayed home since then and I feel really bad.* [The patient has come up with a specific example that seems related to his/her problems. Move on to exploring the situation further.]

T: Could you please tell me more about that situation?

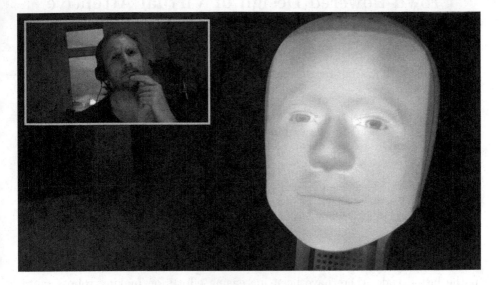

Fig. 1. An example interaction with the training environment

5. Outline of the demonstration

Figure 1 depicts the simulation environment and shows a typical interaction. The presentation conducted at the conference will demonstrate the core features of the application and the implementation in the Furhat robot platform. Focus of the presentation will be on demonstrating our implementation of various virtual patients, with different presenting problems.

Acknowledgements
The development of the application described in this paper was supported by a grant from Vinnova (2017-00727).

References

1. Moubayed, S.A., Beskow, J., Skantze, G., Granström, B.: Furhat: A Back-Projected Human-Like Robot Head for Multiparty Human-Machine Interaction. In: Cognitive Behavioural Systems. pp. 114–130. Springer, Berlin, Heidelberg (2012).
2. Skantze, G., Al Moubayed, S.: IrisTK: A Statechart-based Toolkit for Multi-party Face-to-face Interaction. In: Proceedings of the 14th ACM International Conference on Multimodal Interaction. pp. 69–76. ACM, New York, NY, USA (2012).
3. Davanloo, H.: Intensive short-term dynamic psychotherapy : selected papers of Habib Davanloo. Wiley, Chichester (2000).
4. Abbass, A.: Reaching Through Resistance: Advanced Psychotherapy Techniques. Seven Leaves Press, Kansas City, MO (2015).
5. Frederickson, J.: Co-creating change : effective dynamic therapy techniques. Seven Leaves Press, Kansas City, MO (2013).

Crowd-Powered Design of Virtual Attentive Listeners

Patrik Jonell ✉, Catharine Oertel, Dimosthenis Kontogiorgos, Jonas Beskow, Joakim Gustafson

Department of Speech, Music and Hearing,
KTH Royal Institute of Technology, Stockholm
[pjjonell; catha; diko; beskow]@kth.se, jocke@speech.kth.se

Abstract. This demo presents a web-based system that generates attentive listening behaviours in a virtual agent acquired from audio-visual recordings of attitudinal feedback behaviour of crowdworkers.

1 Introduction

In the last decade, there have been increasing efforts on making robots more human-like. Most of the studies which investigated the design of virtual agents and social robots have used actors or rule-driven approaches in order to design specific social behaviour. These approaches come with certain disadvantages, however. Behaviours that are gathered in an artificial environment will remain, at least to a certain degree, artificial. Furthermore, it is hard to get a natural variation of behaviour using this approach. Various studies have therefore explored crowdsourcing techniques as an alternative or supplement to the more traditional approaches [4, 7, 2, 9, 6].

In this paper we demonstrate our approach of using crowdsourcing techniques in order to collect a wide array of attitudinal backchannel responses in identical conversational context and how we translate them in a virtual agent. Applications where this could be useful are for example virtual agents used in education, counselling and elderly care, where it is important to give the impression of the interlocutor being listened to.

2 The Crowd-Powered Design Tool

2.1 Data collection

The Crowd-Powered Design Tool was designed for rapid collection of rich multimodal data. It allows for collecting demographically varied data as the crowdsourcing platforms reach a wide audience. Additionally these platforms often provide very detailed demographic data about each participant. It also gives researchers the capabilities to control for experimental factors. The tool is a web-based application which utilises modern web technologies in order to access the participant's webcamera and microphone. No particular technical skills are required from the participants and no installation of software is required. The main features of the tool are presented below.

© Springer International Publishing AG 2017
J. Beskow et al. (Eds.): IVA 2017, LNAI 10498, pp. 188-191, 2017.
DOI 10.1007/978-3-319-67401-8_21

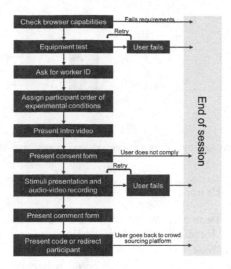

Fig. 1. Flow diagram depicting the data collection process.

User flow As can be seen in Fig. 1, the participants go through several steps during the session. If a participant does not successfully complete a step, the session ends and the data recording is dismissed.

Initial quality control Participants are asked to perform the recordings in a quiet environment, and an automatic process makes sure that the user's equipment is working, and that no background sounds are collected when the participant is silent. The system also makes sure that no cross-talk occurs by playing audio while asking the participant to be silent.

Stimuli presentation through video stream Participants are presented with stimuli which are streamed over the internet. Both pre-recorded and live audio-video stimuli are supported and can be assigned to experimental conditions.

Automatic quality control after stimuli presentation As with any crowd-sourcing application, quality control is essential. In addition to the general recording environment requirements detailed above, it is necessary to ensure that the crowdworkers actually do the task as intended.

In order to be able to make an automatic quality control, we implemented the following simple but efficient procedure; (1) Record a test recording where a participant responds to each stimuli and (2) aggregate the duration of the speech. Then (3) set a generous lower and upper duration limit for each stimuli. If participants are too far outside the time-span, the participant is notified about it and given the option to repeat the recording.

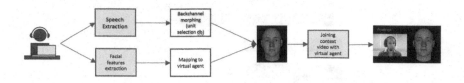

Fig. 2. Crowdworker recording being processed and transformed into a virtual agent.

2.2 Audio-Visual Processing

Audio Processing We processed the audio files in the following way. We used the ProMo (Prosody Morph) library [8] in order to morph a backchannel from our unit-selection database towards the duration and pitch of a crowdworker's backchannel. In order to do so, we first selected a backchannel token from our database by filtering on backchannels that shared the same lexical form. We then picked the one with the smallest difference in duration with the crowdworker's backchannel. Finally, we morphed the duration and then the pitch.

Video Processing In order to transform the video of the crowdworker into the face of the animated agent we did the following: we used OpenFace [1] in order to extract the visual features from the video. We extracted head pose, facial landmarks, and FACS action units [3]. We mapped these features onto a 3D-model (generated by FaceGen[1]) using morph targets for the corresponding action units. In addition, we smoothed the signal and normalised the pose of the participant; they were all normalised to face forwards towards the camera. The face was then generated through Open Scene Graph[2].

Finally, the generated face of the agent and the morphed audio were merged and either used interactively or saved to a video file. This audio-visual processing pipeline is detailed in Fig. 2

3 Studies

In an initial study [5] we wanted to investigate whether it was possible to learn lexical and prosodical backchannel generation models for different attitudes when using the approach described above. We found significant differences in the distribution of both lexical token and prosodic features in backchannels across attitudinal data. For an initial evaluation we presented crowdworkers with a dialogue in which a robot took on the role of a supportive or sceptical listener and could show that crowdworkers were able to perceive the attitudinal state of the robot with an accuracy of 63%.

---

[1] https://facegen.com/
[2] http://www.openscenegraph.org/

4   Conclusions and future work

Despite many advantages of using our proposed approach there are some limitations, such as not providing the researcher with full control of the environment nor the equipment being used. But as each recording is relatively cheap to perform, participants who do not meet a desired quality criteria can easily be discarded. The crowdsourcing platforms often provide good pre-screening.

Future research should investigate how the data collected through the presented tool compares to data collected in an in-lab high quality environment.

Acknowledgements

The authors feel particularly thankful to Joseph Mendelson and Todd Shore for making the data recordings possible. The authors would also like to acknowledge the support from the Swedish Research Council Project InkSynt (2013-4935), the EU Horizon 2020 project BabyRobot (687831) and the Swedish Foundation for Strategic Research project EACare (RIT15-0107).

References

1. Baltrušaitis, T., Robinson, P., Morency, L.P.: Openface: an open source facial behavior analysis toolkit. In: Applications of Computer Vision (WACV), 2016 IEEE Winter Conference on. pp. 1–10. IEEE (2016)
2. Breazeal, C., DePalma, N., Orkin, J., Chernova, S., Jung, M.: Crowdsourcing human-robot interaction: New methods and system evaluation in a public environment. Journal of Human-Robot Interaction 2(1), 82–111 (2013)
3. Ekman, P., Friesen, W.V.: Facial action coding system (1977)
4. Leite, I., Pereira, A., Funkhouser, A., Li, B., Lehman, J.F.: Semi-situated learning of verbal and nonverbal content for repeated human-robot interaction. In: Proceedings of the 18th ACM International Conference on Multimodal Interaction. pp. 13–20. ACM (2016)
5. Oertel, C., Jonell, P., Kontogiorgos, D., Mendelson, J., Beskow, J., Gustafson, J.: Crowd-sourced design of artificial attentive listeners. In: accepted at Interspeech 2017 (2017)
6. Oertel, C., Lopes, J., Yu, Y., Mora, K.A.F., Gustafson, J., Black, A.W., Odobez, J.M.: Towards building an attentive artificial listener: on the perception of attentiveness in audio-visual feedback tokens. In: Proceedings of the 18th ACM International Conference on Multimodal Interaction. pp. 21–28. ACM (2016)
7. Orkin, J., Roy, D.: Automatic learning and generation of social behavior from collective human gameplay. In: Proceedings of The 8th International Conference on Autonomous Agents and Multiagent Systems-Volume 1. pp. 385–392. International Foundation for Autonomous Agents and Multiagent Systems (2009)
8. Tim   Mahrt: ProMo: The   Prosody-Morphing   Library. https://github.com/timmahrt/ProMo (2016), online; accessed 15 May 2017
9. Yu, Z., Xu, Z., Black, A., Rudnicky, A.: Chatbot evaluation and database expansion via crowdsourcing. In: Proc. of the chatbot workshop of LREC. 2016 (2016)

Learning and Reusing Dialog for Repeated Interactions with a Situated Social Agent

James Kennedy[1] ✉, Iolanda Leite[1,2], André Pereira[1], Ming Sun[1],
Boyang Li[1], Rishub Jain[1,3], Ricson Cheng[1,3], Eli Pincus[1,4],
Elizabeth J. Carter[1], and Jill Fain Lehman[1]

[1] Disney Research, Pittsburgh, PA 15213, USA,
[2] KTH Royal Institute of Technology, SE-100 44, Stockholm, Sweden
[3] Carnegie Mellon University, Pittsburgh, PA 15213, USA,
[4] USC Institute for Creative Technologies, Los Angeles, CA 90094, USA
james.kennedy@disneyresearch.com, jill.lehman@disneyresearch.com

Abstract. Content authoring for conversations is a limiting factor in creating verbal interactions with intelligent virtual agents. Building on techniques utilizing semi-situated learning in an incremental crowdworking pipeline, this paper introduces an embodied agent that self-authors its own dialog for social chat. In particular, the autonomous use of crowdworkers is supplemented with a generalization method that borrows and assesses the validity of dialog across conversational states. We argue that the approach offers a community-focused tailoring of dialog responses that is not available in approaches that rely solely on statistical methods across big data. We demonstrate the advantages that this can bring to interactions through data collected from 486 conversations between a situated social agent and 22 users during a 3 week long evaluation period.

Keywords: Verbal chat; social robot; repeated interactions; borrowing dialog

1   Introduction

Traditional dialog systems rely on domain experts to manually define structure, rules, and goals to navigate through conversations, e.g., [2], imposing considerable costs for content authoring. Hand-crafted dialog knowledge also risks the introduction of personal bias – while system builders may have absolute certainty about what the agent can do, they may not fully anticipate what people will say to effect action or what the agent should say to keep people on task. As a result, statistical techniques with big data have been an increasing focus for learning dialog without the content authoring expense [11,12]. Not surprisingly, statistical techniques are most successful when the distribution of language phenomena in the underlying data match the distribution of language phenomena in the desired interaction. Such approaches are promising for a number of important applications, however they do not address the problem of efficiently authoring content when prior corpora do not exist. This work makes a contribution toward

© Springer International Publishing AG 2017
J. Beskow et al. (Eds.): IVA 2017, LNAI 10498, pp. 192–204, 2017.
DOI 10.1007/978-3-319-67401-8_22

a scenario that remains a challenge for purely statistical approaches: conversation situated in natural environments with relationships that persist over time.

The current work seeks to explore this scenario by creating a Persistent Interactive Personality (PIP) that can engage in verbal social chat interactions as part of a community. Although the particular agent we focus on here, Kevin, engages only in social chat, the mechanisms used for self-authoring dialog build on existing techniques for task-driven discourse introduced in an earlier PIP; specifically, the generation of narrative descriptions of future task situations to elicit dialog lines from crowdworkers [6]. Kevin learns new dialog through face-to-face interaction and the crowdworking pipeline, then generalizes the conditions of use by borrowing across dialog states. In the following, we briefly review previously described capabilities as they occur in Kevin, then focus on when and how borrowing occurs as a function of experience. The paper contributes a description of the implemented system, with an evaluation used as a proof-of-concept. We demonstrate that the technique has a number of advantages for users during interactions, particularly in the context of repeated interactions within a community. In addition, we posit that the combination of mechanisms offers analysis opportunities for understanding natural language that are not possible with purely statistical approaches.

2   Related Work

Manual definition of dialog structure, rules or action space [2,13] incurs high cost and tends to work well when domains are small, i.e., task-oriented dialog such as when an agent has to guide users in a shopping mall [4] or interact in limited virtual worlds [1]. The less cumbersome and increasingly popular approach to learning dialog structure is to use machine learning techniques. Machine learning techniques are commonly used to translate user input directly into a system response [11, 12]. Models are typically trained on huge amounts of data that is difficult to adapt to specific situations. For example, a model trained using hundreds of movie scripts is unlikely to be applicable when talking to a close friend in an office setting. Such systems may also have problems in generating a variety of responses, and in utilizing history over repeated interactions with the same users. As a solution, Mori and Araki [9] propose a method that combines a statistical model with rule-based and transition-oriented approaches. Each of the three methods seeks to cover for shortcomings in another. For example, the rule-based element generates appropriate responses, but over a narrow set of inputs, whereas the machine learning element is broad but sometimes inappropriate in response. All three methods are employed, with utterance selection based on an approximation of naturalness and the likelihood of conversation continuation. The approach we take is similar in combining both statistical and non-statistical methods, but supplants rule authoring with a kind of learning from examples via autonomous deployment of human crowdworkers.

Commercial approaches that mix rule-based systems with machine learning approaches from leading artificial intelligence companies are also starting to power several question/answering chatbots for specific domains. However, in socially-oriented conversations where there are various ways to address user input depending on the current situation, these systems are still not very capable. For example, in response to "Good morning!", one may say "Good morning. My name is __" (a new hire greets a colleague), "How was your weekend?" (a friend greets another on Mondays), or simply "Hi!" (one greets a stranger on the street). Accounting for the context of the interaction becomes an important part of the content to be generated; in the work presented here, we use an explicit dialog state to explore and generalize language use across contexts, as defined by our state variables.

In social chat domains, where people generally possess sufficient knowledge to continue a conversation, we suggest that crowdworkers could be a useful resource to tailor the responses. The approach taken in [5] also uses crowdworkers but in a 'live' interaction, providing dialog responses to users in the moment. The content is ephemeral, requiring continual access to crowdworkers and the associated cost. It is also likely that to sustain interactions with users, some use of user history will be required to build rapport, as suggested by [7]. Guo et al. [3] describe a system where a concierge robot systematically improves its dialog capabilities in a set of categories. The robot automatically updates thresholds to decide when to respond to a user or when to ask for clarification. After asking for clarification if the user's utterance can still not be understood, it is marked for further processing. In these cases, the development team or crowdworkers can help the system to add new utterances to existing classes or to create new ones. This work is similar to ours as we propose an agent that can learn from crowdworkers, that engages in face to face interactions and that draws on prior experience to select dialog responses. However, our work differs in several key aspects. Our agent is not a question/answering system, but is solely interested in social chit chat. We therefore do not restrict the categories that users can talk about; the dialog is completely open. Also, it does not ask the users or the development team for additional clarification, but improves its dialog capabilities in an autonomous manner using generalization or crowdworkers as necessary.

3   System Design

The goal for Kevin was to create an embodied agent capable of engaging in social chit-chat over repeated interactions with users in an office. When a valid response was available, he would continue a conversation; otherwise, the conversation would fail. The failure point was then used to drive expansion and acquire a response, so failure never occurred twice at the same point. Kevin was introduced to our user community as a casual acquaintance at work. Users were requested to be natural but 'benevolent' in conversations, i.e., not to try to intentionally cause dialog failure. This section will describe the system implementation, including the two methods used for generating dialog, the instantiation of the agent, and the technologies used to enable smooth human-agent interactions.

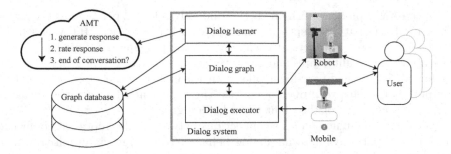

Fig. 1. System diagram showing key components and the flow of information between them. The dialog components are independent of the agent instantiation.

3.1 AMT Expansion

Kevin's dialog graph was learned both by the agent's autonomous deployment of a pipeline of Human Intelligence Tasks (HITs) on Amazon Mechanical Turk (AMT) and through face-to-face interactions with users. The full AMT pipeline consisted of three stages: generating a line of dialog, rating the line, and evaluating the line as a conversational ending (as in [6]). Crowdworkers' decisions were contextualized by a story narrative that described some or all of the agent's state and up to 5 lines of previous dialog (details below). Dialog graph nodes that arose from face-to-face interaction did so either through *direct addition* of an Automatic Speech Recognition (ASR) transcription or by *borrowing*, both described more fully below and in Fig. 2. Because each source could introduce errors – due to poor ASR or inappropriate generalization – nodes that arose from fully-situated face-to-face interaction were evaluated for quality control by Kevin's autonomous deployment of the latter two portions of the AMT pipeline.

The initial dialog graph was generated by situating AMT workers with a story narrative that conveys the values of a small number of state variables: time of day, day of week, and familiarity. For example, "Mai is a friendly person who enjoys her job in an office downtown. It's Wednesday afternoon. Kevin and Mai have never met. They run into each other at the office". The values for the variables are as follows: time of day - morning/afternoon; day of week Monday/Wednesday/Friday[5]; familiarity: never met/known each other for a few weeks. The state and number of situational features was intentionally small in order to be explicit in representation, enabling straightforward attribution of changes in the graph. All names in the exposition were changed to protect participant anonymity.

To create the initial graph, root nodes were generated for all combinations of the state variables. Then, each root node was expanded breadth-first by repeated

---

[5] Pilot studies informed us that this constituted a minimal set of states to begin social chat with some linguistic variety. These studies also indicated that Tuesday and Thursday contained similar language to Wednesday, so the state space was reduced and these days would resolve to using the state of Wednesday.

use of the AMT pipeline with one node randomly selected per level as the graph grew, until one path of depth 9 existed for each root. Each HIT was sent to 5 independent crowdworkers at each stage of the pipeline. Authored lines that were above the quality threshold given the editors' ratings were grouped into a single node if they had near-identical semantic similarity scores (see below). This grouping both helps to provide linguistic variation when the agent is speaking and greater coverage of the input when listening.

Nodes contain dialog and the connections between nodes represent confirmed continuation pathways allowing dialog behavior to emerge via graph traversal. When approached, Kevin randomly chooses whether to initiate a conversation or wait, but uses the same graph independent of speaking and listening roles. Thus, the simplest form of generalization occurs when Kevin acquires and speaks lines it earlier heard from a user, in situ. A conversation in which Kevin said, "How you doing?" and heard "I'm good, how about you?" as a reply, may later produce the reply "I'm good, how about you?" to the human's "How's it going today?". Given multiple options for speech at a turn, a random choice of responses is made in order to encourage growth of the graph (a strategy such as always picking the highest rated response would force growth in some graph areas to the detriment of others).

Kevin had 632 nodes in the initialized graph prior to beginning face-to-face interactions. Once deployment began, all conversation failure points (i.e., no response available yet) were marked for expansion during an overnight AMT run so that 5 responses would be available at those points the next morning. Thus, Kevin would progress further in the chat over time.

3.2   Dialog Borrowing and Selection

Dialog utterances can be 'borrowed' across state space within the graph as a form of generalization. This is done by replicating a node and updating the vertices to connect the copy to the previous point in the conversation. Borrows were rated using 3 workers and were made permanent if they made sense or, if not, stored as unusable to avoid repeating the work in the future. Although borrowing does not introduce new language to Kevin's repertoire, the mechanism does provide a way to both continue the conversation in the moment and expand dialog behavior at lower cost than a full AMT expansion. The same process is applied to utterances added from transcribed user speech.

Borrowing is based on a calculation of semantic similarity between utterances. Similarity was computed by $1 - cos(\theta)$, where θ is the angle between two feature vectors utt_1 and utt_2 that represent utterances. To compute an utterance vector representation, we started by training a Word2vec model [8] on a corpus containing over 6,500 scripts of soap operas and TV series (approximately 43 million words). Using the Gensim package [10], we trained a Skip-gram model – more appropriate for predicting the surrounding words in a sentence – with window size 5 and excluding words with frequency less than 10. The extracted feature vector for an utterance was computed by the average vectors of each word present in that utterance, excluding the vectors of stop words such as

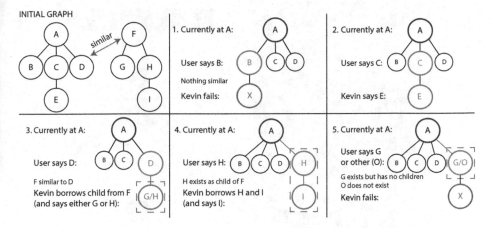

Fig. 2. To select the next utterance for Kevin to say, the dialog tree is traversed from the current node (node A in the example). Depending on the user utterance, five scenarios are possible. Two of these result in failure (red X node), one results in following a confirmed pathway, and the final two borrow from elsewhere in the graph to continue the conversation. The temporary modifications (indicated through gray dotted boxes) are marked for validation in the last two stages of the AMT pipeline.

On Monday
Kevin : How was your weekend?
User : It was great.
Kevin : What did you do?
User : Went to the movies with friends.

On Wednesday
User : Do anything after work yesterday?
Kevin : Went to the movies with friends.

Fig. 3. Example of how Kevin may borrow a user utterance.

"the" or "and"[6]. The threshold for two utterances to be considered similar was 0.6 (based on experimenter judgment of data collected from pilot studies). This cosine similarity metric is also used to determine whether what the user says is similar to any of the child nodes of the node used by the agent in the non-failure cases (see Fig. 2).

Combining the borrowing technique with the existing learned graph structure provides three possible successful routes to a response from a user utterance, along with 2 failure routes. Whenever possible, the utterance Kevin selects as a response is from the current context, based on traversing the graph from the root note that instantiates that context. If the user utterance is already in that context and it has one or more children, then Kevin will respond from that set (Fig. 2: 2). If the utterance exists in the current context, but nothing is similar according the the similarity metric just described, then Kevin will fail

---

[6] We started our experiments with a pre-trained Word2vec model based on the Google-News dataset, but the performance of that model for computing semantic similarity between social dialog lines was substantially worse.

Fig. 4. Our agent, Kevin, in both robot (*left*) and mobile app (*right*) embodiments.

(Fig. 2: 1). Failure will also occur if the user says something that exists in another context, but that does not have children, or if something new is said that has no similarity to something already in the graph (Fig. 2: 5). In cases where the user says something from the current context that has no response, but is similar to something elsewhere in the graph with children, then a child will be borrowed as a response (and later validated; Fig. 2: 3). In the pair of conversations in Fig. 3, for example, a line from the user that is originally tied to the day after the weekend is borrowed to a different portion of the week via the semantic similarity of "What did you do?" and "Do anything after work?".

In the final case, (Fig. 2: 4) if the user utterance does not exist in the current context, but is similar to an utterance from another context, then the parent and child pair can be borrowed from that context. In all conversations, Kevin continues to select a dialog response until two simultaneous utterances (i.e., one from Kevin and one from the user) are both suitable 'end-of-conversation' points, based on crowdworker evaluations when the dialog was added to the graph.

3.3 Agent Instantiation

The agent was embodied as both a robot head and a virtual character in a mobile phone app that displayed the head (Fig. 4). Kevin was placed in a public space in an office for 12 days; members of the office could also choose to have the Kevin app on their phones to verbally chat with him. Kevin randomly either waited for the user to start talking or initiated the conversation himself. When the interaction began, the state was resolved based on the current time, day, and user history to provide the starting root node for dialog graph traversal. When the user said an utterance, Kevin sought to match this to something in the graph, prioritizing by the previous position as described above, borrowing if necessary. If no response was found, Kevin would fail and say "Oops, gotta go!".

The social robot version of Kevin is a Furhat retro-projected robot head, augmented with a Microsoft Kinect v2, a webcam, and a long-range RFID reader. The Kinect is used for skeleton tracking, allowing the robot to detect when a user is approaching. Users were provided with RFID badges to wear when interacting with the robot, enabling seamless user identification as well as storage and retrieval of information pertaining to that user. The webcam was used to record video logs of all interactions, and to provide an audio input for automatic speech recognition (ASR) provided by Microsoft Cognitive Services.

The mobile version of Kevin was implemented using Unity3D to provide a cross-platform mobile front-end to the dialog system. The phone used speech-to-text from IBM Watson, available as a Unity3D plug-in. Both the robot and mobile versions of the system connected to the same server running the dialog logic code and the graph database where the structure was stored. All conversations were logged in the graph database for recall in resolving starting conversation states and for subsequent analysis.

4   Evaluation and Results

The overall aim of the evaluation was to provide a proof-of-concept that an agent utilizing the expansion and borrowing capabilities described above could indeed have longer conversations with less failures over time. In addition, the evaluation allowed the collection of data to study how language was used within the user community, demonstrating the value of the approach and providing insights into improvements in the system design moving forwards.

4.1   Participants

Kevin was deployed in an office for 12 days with 22 users (age $M(SD)$=32.5(9.0) years). The study was conducted with IRB approval; participants provided informed consent and were paid. Participants were asked to interact multiple times daily; the robot was located in the kitchen to make this a convenient occurrence. User name, gender and time of participation was stored along with each conversation; names were replaced in the AMT hits and all narratives were generated for both genders. Participants averaged 22.1 interactions $(SD$=13.6), for a total of 486 conversations. The initialized graph grew from 632 to 4292 nodes.

4.2   Graph Expansion and Utterance Use

Over time, significantly more conversations were completed successfully; day 12 failure (82%) was significantly lower than day 1 failure (100%); $z = 2.913, p = .004$. Interactions also showed a trend of increasing length (Fig. 5), indicating that the approach achieved the main goal of extending conversations based on learned material. The system instantiation was intentionally designed to allow explicit exploration of how the graph expanded and the impact that this had on conversations (and vice versa). Through examining the graph node origins (user

Origin	Created	Created Used	Borrowed	Borrowed Used
ASR	270	293	207	230
AMT	2751	362	599	814
Total	3021	655	806	1044

Table 1. Origin of nodes in the final graph, with the number of times each type was used subsequent to its initial creation. The full graph consists of 4292 nodes: 3021 'created' via AMT, 806 'borrowed' across contexts, 13 roots, and 452 nodes that were rejected or borrowed to a position below a temporary node before it was rejected.

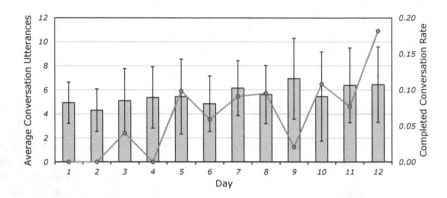

Fig. 5. Over time, our approach leads to longer conversations *(primary vertical axis; bars)*. The completed conversation rate is calculated from the number of conversations ended by the agent based on both the user and the agent saying an utterance that could end the conversation in sequence. The rate of successful conversations increases over time *(secondary vertical axis; line)*. Error bars show *SD*.

speech transcriptions – ASR nodes – and AMT expansions, and borrowing of both), evidence suggests that both of the learning mechanisms were beneficial to extending the conversations. Table 1 shows the breakdown of node origins and the times they were used at the completion of the study. Average use of ASR nodes ($M=1.09$, $SD=0.38$) was greater than the use of AMT nodes ($M=0.13$, $SD=0.88$), however 5 AMT nodes at a time were generated at a failure point, compared to 1 ASR node.

Our method of generalization (dialog borrowing) is supported by examining how individuals interact with Kevin. *Idiosyncrasy* is calculated as the proportion of times an individual re-visits a node that was created by him/her as opposed to other users or the agent (via AMT). Users had a tendency to revisit nodes they created, with the mean idiosyncrasy equal to 0.71 ($SD=0.21$). Thus, 71% of ASR node visits were by the user that created them. This suggests that users like to follow up on topics that were previously discussed and encourages personalization for users that cannot be gained through big data use.

Generated by:	this user	any user	AMT	combined
First heard	11	119	809	939
Heard before	1	2	45	48
Combined	12	121	854	987

Table 2. Utterances heard by users (i.e., only considering nodes spoken by Kevin, not heard by Kevin) split by the origin of the utterance and excluding "Oops, gotta go!".

Depth difference	-4	-3	-2	-1	0	1	2	3	4
Borrow count	27	33	74	128	196	161	117	44	40
Success rate (%)	89	85	92	94	94	94	91	77	90
SD (%)	6	6	3	2	2	2	3	6	5

Table 3. Borrow counts and success by depth difference in the graph. Most borrows go to a graph depth within 1 level of the borrow origin. This suggests a semantic structure to conversations based on depth.

The content that Kevin learns from users is made permanent if it makes sense (as judged using the rating portion of the AMT pipeline). As a result, users can hear back things that they have said to Kevin, or that other users have said to Kevin. This aspect of the system is particularly advantageous as it results in Kevin gradually acquiring utterances that are well-suited for use in the context in which interactions are taking place (as the utterances originate directly from those interacting in this context). Table 2 summarizes the utterances that users hear during interactions, separated by their origin. It can be seen that novel utterances are typically used, with a favorable proportion stemming from user input (13.5%) considering the overall portion of nodes originating from ASR input (9.8%). This further supports the idea that users follow up on previously discussed topics, as ASR nodes are more likely to be part of previously raised topics.

4.3 Emergent Graph Structure

Analyzing the depth relationships between borrows (which are performed based on semantic similarity), it is clear that most borrows occurred at equivalent depths in interactions (Table 3). This suggests that the conversations take some kind of structure; semantically similar utterances were produced at roughly the same depth in the conversations. This is likely to be in part a product of the shorter length of conversations occurring in this context; most of the conversations covered a greeting and health inquiry near the beginning. However, when conversations became longer, successful borrowing across depths could be used to help further generalize responses, thereby improving the efficiency of expanding dialog options and again offering analysis approaches not available using purely statistical methods.

Day 1, Interaction 1
Kevin : Hello, my name is {{ speakerA }}.
User : Hi, how are you?
Kevin : I'm good, how about you?
User : I'm very good, what do you think
        about the weather today?
Kevin : Oops, gotta go!

Day 4, Interaction 9
Kevin : Good afternoon <user name>.
User : How are you today Kevin?
Kevin : I'm good, How are you?
User : I'm good.
Kevin : You sounded hesitant. You sure?
User : Yes
Kevin : Oops, gotta go!

Day 8, Interaction 25
User : Hi Kevin.
Kevin : Hello <user name>.
User : How was your weekend?
Kevin : It was great
User : What did you do?
Kevin : Went Christmas shopping.
User : Did you buy anything fun?
Kevin : I was mostly shopping for others.
User : Or what. <asr error>
Kevin : Oops, gotta go!

Day 12, Interaction 33
User : Hi Kevin.
Kevin : Hello <user name>.
User : Would you like a cup of coffee?
Kevin : That would be great, thanks.
User : What's your plan for Christmas?
Kevin : I have some family flying in, so just
        spending it with them, you?
User : Do you have any plans this weekend?
Kevin : Not really.
User : OK enjoy your holidays.
Kevin : Oops, gotta go!

Fig. 6. Examples of conversations with the same user over the course of the evaluation. The conversations increase in length, nearing a natural conclusion by the final example, but also vary in content. Minor punctuation corrections have been made in ASR transcriptions to ease readability.

5   Discussion

Conversations were extended over time and conversations increasingly ended through reaching crowdworker marked 'end-of-conversation' points, rather than through failure (Fig. 5; Sec. 4.2). Given the completely open nature of the dialog, this kind of improvement was not necessarily guaranteed despite it being the goal of the system design. Fig. 6 shows an example of how turns evolve as the agent learns. This improvement provides the proof-of-concept for the system design that the evaluation sought to demonstrate. The results show that the application of Kevin in a persistent user community allows reuse of material generated by users through the borrowing mechanism. This can be an advantage in producing dialog responses that are well-suited to the environment. Simultaneously, the crowdworking pipeline broadens the response range and can be used to validate borrowed responses.

Kevin's use of explicit state provides the semantic anchors for organizing the dialog knowledge acquired. The state is used to generate the narratives in the AMT pipeline, thereby eliciting responses that are indexed for future use in exactly the ways that Kevin senses and represents his world. The same state descriptions are extant when Kevin acquires language through face-to-face interaction. While the result is a contextualization of language that is stronger than that which can be achieved by methods whose only representation of context is the co-occurrence statistics of words, it is by no means perfect. In particular, it will invariably be the case that small, engineered states will fail to include features that always make relevant distinctions among subsets of utterances. The current implementation of Kevin does not, for example, include any notion of time of year. With a December deployment, it is not surprising that some of the language learned is quite specific to the holiday season. As these utterances are contextualized only with respect to day of week, time of day, and length of relationship between conversants, they may well be used again in June. The decision to restrict the state to a small number of relevant features would lead to a less-coherent experience for users in this instance, one that might or might not have occurred in a purely statistically-driven approach.

Interestingly, we have some evidence that Kevin's simple mechanisms ameliorate the small-state problem to a degree, at least in a limited community setting. An early implementation decision was to not include gender of the conversant as part of the state. Nevertheless, narrative generation requires instantiating the dialog partners and assigning gender implicitly through names or pronoun choice. Because Kevin uses his dialog model in both speaker and listener roles, the lack of gender feature resulted in acquiring a response to "How are you today?" of "Great! I just found out I am pregnant". Kevin's pregnancy became enough of a topic within the office community that subsequent interactions with different users pursued the topic until, finally, Kevin's failure-driven learning resulted in an AMT-authored response that resolved the situation: "it was just a joke <user name>, guys can't get pregnant". Whether Kevin can learn to recognize such paths through his knowledge graph as opportunities for discovering important distinctions is a topic for future work, but one that is made possible by being able to inspect the dialog traces and their accompanying states over time.

In the future, we intend to reintroduce explicit goal structure to Kevin, including both conversational and non-conversational task goals. Furthermore, we will explore the trade-off between exploitation of re-using utterances that are known to be valid, against exploring a greater number of the available but untested utterances. We also expect to replace the current "copy and paste" method for growing the graph with a more efficient dialog representation in which utterance nodes store vertices connected to the states in which they have been validated. Such a change would still permit observing relationships between state variables and their effects on dialog use.

6   Conclusion

Our agent, Kevin, uses face-to-face dialog, semi-situated elicitation of dialog, and generalization of dialog context via semantic similarity to bring about advantages for users during interactions. The generalization method enables the agent to continue conversations in the moment, whilst the AMT pipeline provides breadth in responses to help further extend conversations over time. The generalization method additionally enables reuse of user spoken utterances, allowing idiosyncrasy and appropriateness in conversations with individual users, and with the larger user community. This paper described the system design in detail and provided a proof-of-concept for the approach. An evaluation consisting of 486 conversations with 22 users over a 3 week period demonstrated that while the generalization is not perfect, it provides a practicable and beneficial option when large corpora are not available to use with purely statistical approaches in an interaction scenario.

References

1. Aylett, R.S., Louchart, S., Dias, J., Paiva, A., Vala, M.: FearNot!–an experiment in emergent narrative. In: Proc. of the 5th International Conference on Intelligent Virtual Agents. pp. 305–316. Springer Berlin Heidelberg (2005)
2. Bohus, D., Rudnicky, A.: The RavenClaw dialog management framework: Architecture and systems. Computer Speech & Language 23(3), 332–361 (2009)
3. Guo, S., Lenchner, J., Connell, J., Dholakia, M., Muta, H.: Conversational Bootstrapping and Other Tricks of a Concierge Robot. In: Proc. of the 2017 ACM/IEEE International Conference on Human-Robot Interaction. pp. 73–81. ACM (2017)
4. Kanda, T., Shiomi, M., Miyashita, Z., Ishiguro, H., Hagita, N.: An affective guide robot in a shopping mall. In: Human-Robot Interaction (HRI), 2009 4th ACM/IEEE International Conference on. pp. 173–180. IEEE (2009)
5. Lasecki, W., Wesley, R., Nichols, J., Kulkarni, A., Allen, J., Bigham, J.: Chorus: a crowd-powered conversational assistant. In: UIST 2013. pp. 151–162. ACM (2013)
6. Leite, I., Pereira, A., Funkhouser, A., Li, B., Lehman, J.F.: Semi-situated Learning of Verbal and Nonverbal Content for Repeated Human-robot Interaction. In: ICMI 2016. pp. 13–20. ACM, New York, USA (2016)
7. Matsuyama, Y., Bhardwaj, A., Zhao, R., Romero, O.J., Akoju, S.A., Cassell, J.: Socially-aware animated intelligent personal assistant agent. In: 17th Annual Meeting of the Special Interest Group on Discourse and Dialogue. p. 224 (2016)
8. Mikolov, T., Sutskever, I., Chen, K., Corrado, G.S., Dean, J.: Distributed representations of words and phrases and their compositionality. In: Advances in neural information processing systems. pp. 3111–3119 (2013)
9. Mori, H., Araki, M.: Selection method of an appropriate response in chat-oriented dialogue systems. In: 17th Annual Meeting of the Special Interest Group on Discourse and Dialogue. p. 228 (2016)
10. Řehůřek, R., Sojka, P.: Software Framework for Topic Modelling with Large Corpora. In: Proc. of the LREC 2010 Workshop on New Challenges for NLP Frameworks. pp. 45–50 (2010)
11. Shang, L., Lu, Z., Li, H.: Neural Responding Machine for Short-Text Conversation. CoRR abs/1503.02364 (2015)
12. Vinyals, O., Le, Q.: A neural conversational model. arXiv preprint arXiv:1506.05869 (2015)
13. Young, S., Gašić, M., Thomson, B., Williams, J.D.: POMDP-based statistical spoken dialog systems: A review. Proc. of the IEEE 101(5), 1160–1179 (2013)

Moveable Facial Features in a Social Mediator

Muhammad Sikandar Lal Khan[1], Shafiq ur Réhman*✉[1,2], Yongcui Mi[1],
Usman Naeem[2], Jonas Beskow[3], and Haibo Li[3]

[1] Umeå University, SE-90187 Umeå, Sweden.
[2] University of East London, E16 2RD, United Kingdom.
[3] The Royal Institute of Technology (KTH), SE- 114 28 Stockholm, Sweden.

Abstract. Human face and facial features based behavior has a major
impact in human-human communications. Creating face based personality traits and its representations in a social robot is a challenging task.
In this paper, we propose an approach for a robotic face presentation
based on moveable 2D facial features and present a comparative study
when a synthesized face is projected using three setups; 1) 3D mask, 2)
2D screen, and 3) our 2D moveable facial feature based visualization. We
found that robot's personality and character is highly influenced by the
projected face quality as well as the motion of facial features.

1   Introduction

When it comes to judging the human personality traits, the certain face regions and their motions may contain more information than others; for instance
the eyes and the lips regions [5, 4]. Therefore, human face with moveable facial
features modeling as an interface has always been a major interest for human-
robot interactions. Social information (e.g., personality traits) can be accurately
perceived from dynamic body motion [6], however it is *unclear* how the motion of facial features are related to the perceived personality and/or projected
face. In this work, we consider *how well can a human observer recognize a presented face?* To investigate this, we have prototyped a moveable facial feature
robotic (MFFR) system and performed a comparative study of face (personality)
recognition considering various faces (and moveable facial features) projection
methods; 1) 3D facial mask based Furhat [1], 2) 2D screen, and 3) our proposed
moveable facial feature robotic (MFFR) system.

2   Moveable Facial Feature Robotic (MFFR) System

We have designed a moveable facial feature robotic (MFFR) system which represents a brief moveable display of non-verbal facial feature behavior. It has
three components; i) a mechanical platform, ii) facial features capturing module
and iii) a control module. The MFFR system is designed to represent a pilot
users facial features in different social settings. The developed electromechanical
setup mimics the eyes and lips motion of a pilot user as shown in Fig. 1. The

---

* Corresponding authors: shafiq.ureheman@umu.se

J. Beskow et al. (Eds.): IVA 2017, LNAI 10498, pp. 205-208, 2017.
DOI 10.1007/978-3-319-67401-8_23

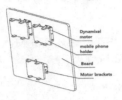

(b) A View of Electrome- (c) Back View of our pro-
(a) A CAD model.   chanical platform.   totype.

Fig. 1: The Moveable Facial Feature Robotic (MRRF) system which provides an active 'visualization' - a synchronous and simultaneous display of eyes and lips regions to represent a human face.

(a) Furhat [1] - a 3D pro-   (b) 2D screen - a flat pro-   (c) MFFR - a moveable
jection.   jection.   feature projection.

Fig. 2: An Experimental Setup for three projection methods.

smart phones 2D screens are used to display vital parts of a human face. These 2D screens are attached to actuators for mimicking the facial expressions. To project the facial expressions of a person on our MFFR system, the head pose estimation algorithm [3] and facial features (such as eyes, nose, lips, eye-brows, and face boundary)segmentation using Haar-feature based cascade classifiers for human face detection [7] and w Constrained Local Model (CLM) approach [2]. We then present the most important face regions, more specifically eyes and lips regions on to the MFFR system.

3   Experimental Study

In this work, we consider a comparative experiment among three systems, i) 3D Furhat, ii) 2D screen and iii) MFFR system. The experiment consisted of three sessions in which participants were asked to recognize the projected face representations. The session 1 and 2 were held at the Royal Institute of Technology (KTH), Sweden, and the 3rd session was conducted at Umeå University, Sweden. The three setups for this experiment are shown in Fig. 2. We had n=20 participants (ranging in age from 18 - 40) for each session of an experiment. The participants were briefed about the experimental setup and aim of the study. The participants were also explained how the face projection/visualizations would be displayed. Each session of our experiment is divided into two phases, i) training phase and ii) testing phase.

During the training phase, the participants were presented with 8 *known* projected faces with 3 orientations - Left (L), Center (C), Right (R); i.e., *24 known*

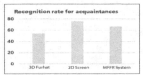 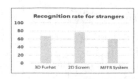 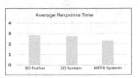

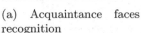

(a) Acquaintance faces recognition
(b) Stranger (non-familiar) faces recognition
(c) The Average time for one face.

Fig. 3: Face recognition Accuracy and Response time of three face presentations.

stimuli. For memory building, these projected faces were repeated 3 times. In total we had 8 x 3 orientations x 3 repetitions = 72 projected face presentations. Each face presentation is about 3 seconds. The time of training phase was 72 x 3 seconds = 216 sec for each participant. During testing phase, 24 known presentations (from training phase 8C, 8L, 8R) were mixed with 24 unknown presentations (8C, 8L, 8R)) and were presented randomly to the participants and asked to press 'Y' for "Yes"- for already seen face, otherwise 'N' for "No"- not seen.

4   Results and Concluding Remarks

The participants completed the experimental study in a reasonable time duration and response rate was 100%. Our parameter of interest are *the accuracy of face-recognition* and *the response time of each participant.* The accuracy measure indicates how accurately a participant can recognize a projected face (Tab. 1). Response time indicates how long time a participant takes in making his/her decisions (Tab. 2). It turns out that the recognition rate of the MRRF is between 3D Furhat and 2D screen when it comes to acquaintances. The recognition rate of MRRF is lower than both 3D Furhat and 2D screen for strangers (to successfully say that they have not seen this presentation during training phase). It is very interesting that the moveable features help the users to make the decision faster as the response time drops as seen in Fig. 3c. From the Fig. 3a, it is clear that 2D screen performs better in face recognition compare to 3D face mask and MRRF system. Despite 2D screen performs better in face recognition, it is abortive in presenting different social cues (such as head gesture, gaze direction, etc.) which are important for different applications such as, video teleconferencing. The 3D face mask presents better social cues compare to 2D screen but it lacks the property of face recognition which is an important feature of social settings. However, the introduction of our MRRF system contains the properties of both systems. However, when it comes to the strangers (unknown presentations), the face recognition rate drops as compared to acquaintances as shown in Fig. 3b. In future studies, we will address this issue. It is very interesting that the moveable features help the users to make the decision faster as there is a decrease in response time (Fig. 3c).

The motivation of this work was to examine how well can a human observer recognize a presented face and what is an impact of moveable facial features in

Visualization Method	Faces	Test		Rate (%)
3D Furhat	ACQ (525)	YES	283	54
		NO	242	46
	STR (435)	YES	141	32.4
		NO	294	67.9
2D-Screen	ACQ (519)	YES	394	76
		NO	125	24
	STR (441)	YES	102	23.1
		NO	339	76.9
MFFR System.	ACQ (480)	YES	319	66.5
		NO	161	33.4
	STR (480)	YES	188	39,2
		NO	292	60.8

Time (s)	Face mask	2D 2D	MFFR System
Total	2755	2666	2225
Average	2.87	2.78	2.31

Table 1: Projected face recognition accuracy for three Systems. ACQ= Acquaintances, STR = Strangers

Table 2: All participants' Response time for all three systems.

social settings. This work presented a design of novel MFFR system. MFFR not only presents the important social gestures and cues (which 2D screen is *not* capable of) but also helps in face recognition (which 3D mask is *not* capable of). In our future work, we will optimize the program to reduce the response time of a system and employ an eye-tracker sensor to improve the accuracy of the eyes movements. Furthermore, we are also interested in identifying the key components for humanizing (human-like interface) the social robot when it comes to face and facial expressions.

References

1. Al Moubayed, S., Beskow, J., Skantze, G., Granström, B.: Furhat: a back-projected human-like robot head for multiparty human-machine interaction. Cognitive behavioural systems pp. 114–130 (2012)
2. Cristinacce, D., Cootes, T.F.: Feature detection and tracking with constrained local models. In: British Machine Vision Conference (BMVC). p. 3. No. 2 (2006)
3. Khan, M.S.L., ur Réhman, S., Lu, Z., Li, H.: Head orientation modeling: Geometric head pose estimation using monocular camera. In: IEEE/IIAE Int'l Conf. Intelligent Sys. and Image Proc. pp. 149–153 (2013)
4. ur Réhman, S., Liu, L.: ifeeling: Vibrotactile rendering of human emotions on mobile phones. In: Mobile multimedia processing, pp. 1–20. Springer (2010)
5. Schurgin, M., Nelson, J., Iida, S., Ohira, H., Chiao, J., Franconeri, S.: Eye movements during emotion recognition in faces. Journal of vision 14(13), 14–14 (2014)
6. Thoresen, J.C., Vuong, Q.C., Atkinson, A.P.: First impressions: Gait cues drive reliable trait judgements. Cognition 124(3), 261–271 (2012)
7. Viola, P., Jones, M.J.: Robust real-time face detection. International journal of computer vision 57(2), 137–154 (2004)

Recipe Hunt: Engaging with Cultural Food Knowledge using Multiple Embodied Conversational Agents

Sabiha Khan[1] ✉, Adriana Camacho[2], and David Novick[3]

[1]Dept. of Communications, The University of Texas at El Paso, El Paso, TX USA
[2]Dept. of Computer Science, The University of Texas at El Paso, El Paso, TX USA
[3]Dept. of Eng. Educ. and Leadership, The University of Texas at El Paso, El Paso, TX USA
{skhan2, novick}@utep.edu, caro4874@gmail.com

Abstract. The popularity in recent years of food media, particularly in the domain of documentary films, has brought the communicative potential of food to the fore. Recipe Hunt is an interactive documentary that simulates the cultural experience of connecting over food by sharing recipes. Embodied conversational agents (ECAs) are used to engage users with cultural food heritage from the U.S.-Mexico border. Recipe Hunt aims to use a distributed and participatory model of cross-cultural learning for users to engage with the culinary heritage from this region of the United States.

Keywords: Embodied Conversational Agents, cultural heritage, interactive documentary.

1   Introduction

In this paper, we describe an approach to storytelling about the culture of food [1] through a docu-game, implemented through verbal interaction with virtual agents, that teaches users about regional traditions through food. Our approach reflects that of many documentary film about food, which take pains to actively engage the viewer through diverse approaches, including: political narratives of the food-industrial complex, such as *Food, Inc.* [2]; highly aesthetic treatments of culinary traditions, such as *Jiro Dreams of Sushi*; participatory endeavors to understand the agricultural system, such as *King Corn*; and personal narratives of food justice such as *Soul Food Junkies*. As these examples show, many documentary films draw in their viewership by taking otherwise dry subjects and enlivening them with a political, aesthetic, or personal angle that appeals to the emotions [3]. We describe a pilot application, *Recipe Hunt*, and the process of creating naturalistic dialog using our system for the application. We also discuss how we added handling agent-agent interaction and multi-agent-to-human interaction to our system.

Recipe Hunt is an interactive documentary about Borderland culture that employs embodied conversational agents (ECAs) to engage users with that culture through the familiar medium of food. The premise of *Recipe Hunt* is that a college student from the U.S.-Mexico border is far away from home and missing the food of her

© Springer International Publishing AG 2017
J. Beskow et al. (Eds.): IVA 2017, LNAI 10498, pp. 209-212, 2017.
DOI 10.1007/978-3-319-67401-8_24

hometown. She remembers some aspects of each recipe, but not all. She is a bit shy, so she enlists the user, her roommate, to help her roam around the city and ask for help locating the missing ingredients for chile con queso. Luckily, teleportation and time travel are possible in this game world, so the agent and the user potentially have the option of going to foreign countries and into the past as well. The roommate agent trusts that the user will help her, so will provide clues along the way to guide the user.

The underlying conflict in this scenario however is that the user is an outsider to the roommate's culture. That means the user must measure her responses to avoid offending both the roommate and other agents. This feature of the game enables the user to interact with the agents beyond the merely transactional business of hunting down missing ingredients. By making the agents' communication dependent on the politeness and sincerity of the user, *Recipe Hunt* engages the user as the best documentary films do: through both intellect and affect. The emotional engagement of the user with the agents in this way would eventually allow for a more natural interaction with the agents through subsequent stages of game play.

2   UTEP AGENT System

Recipe Hunt is based on the UTEP AGENT system for creating scripted interactions between embodied conversational agents (ECAs) and humans using XML-style scripting and the Unity game engine [4]. *Recipe Hunt's* design extended the existing system by featuring multiple agents interacting with the user. Its ECAs are fully automated rather than reliant on a Wizard of Oz (WoZ) scenario in which a human controls the agent behind the scenes. As *Recipe Hunt* portrays a specific culture, sustaining multivocality in the agents' representation of the culture in question becomes important. To assuage any potential awkwardness between user and agents, the game starts with a series of brief instructions to orient the user in the proper use of the system.

In this pilot version of *Recipe Hunt,* the agents lead the user through a series of activities and conversations while playing a game. We simulate a roommate relationship, where the user must collaborate with a set of agents to uncover the ingredients and preparation details of a traditional family recipe from the U.S-Mexico border. This simulation is built to be engaging, where both the user and the agent can interact with the same objects in virtual space. The storyline provides the necessary flexibility and decision making, without creating a completely open environment where tasks would otherwise be difficult to set up and evaluate.

The scenario comprises six scenes, each of which lasts approximately one to two minutes, depending on the player's choices and interaction speed. The first scene focuses on the user learning the environment and interaction style. There are no text, heads-up display, buttons, or notifications of any kind, and all interaction occurs through verbal speech [Fig. 1a]. Throughout every scene, each player is offered the same decision-making opportunities and asked the same personal questions. However, scenario choices, animations, and some agent responses depend on each player and can affect the behavior of the agent. *Recipe Hunt* involves agent-to-agent interaction as well as multi-agents-to-human interaction, automated and in real-time [Fig. 1b].

Fig. 1. (a) The first scene of *Recipe Hunt*, in the apartment shared between the agent and the user. (b) A scene in which the roommate agent debates with the shopkeeper agent over the ingredients used in a well-known dish form the U.S.-Mexico border.

Each agent is independently controlled through the XML script and can recognize and react to the user's speech accordingly. One of the major limitations is the ability to recognize to whom the user is speaking when there are multiple agents in the scene. Currently we address this problem by having the agent who last spoke to the user be the agent that is spoken to [see, e.g., Fig. 2].

```
<!--Shopkeeper to Roommate-->
<event id="s2a9" agent="Shopkeeper">
   <animation> telling_a_secret </animation>
</event>
<event id="s2e13" agent="Shopkeeper">
   <dialog>Well, yes actually. Sometimes I see people buying Velveeta cheese and
   RoTel tomatoes with chiles.</dialog>
</event>
<event id="s2e14">
   <dialog>It seems like those would go together pretty well.</dialog>
</event>
<!--Roommate to user-->
<event id="s2a10" agent="Roommate">
   <animation>talking</animation>
</event>
<event id="s2e14" agent="Roommate">
   <dialog>mmm...that's not what I expected, but it seems worth a shot.</dialog>
</event>
<!--Roommate to shopkeeper-->
<event id="s2e15" agent="Roommate"><dialog>Thanks</dialog></event>
<!--Roommate to user-->
<event id="s2e16" agent="Roommate"><dialog>Lets keep going.</dialog></event>
```

Fig. 2. Example of XML script for the market scene, during which two agents speak both to one another and to the user.

2.1 Creating a Naturalistic Dialog

When creating a dialog for the system, our process is like writing a story with a protagonist who has a goal, goes through a conflict, and eventually reaches a resolution. The system works with a declarative XML-style script which is parsed through C# code inside Unity and which in turn controls the 3D models inside a scene (including our agents and the environment) such as how to behave in terms of animation, speech recognition, sounds inside the environment, whether the agent's voice is synthesized

or recorded wav files, etc. In this version of the system, in addition to having information regarding one agent and a few triggers for the environment, we now have to
specify to which agent the voice belongs and which agent is activated for a specific
animation. Our team first writes a mock-up script without the technicalities of an
XML script and performs the script to ensure that expected responses from the user
are induced and anticipated. Our aim is to induce the user to respond within a known
range of possibilities and to make it unambiguous for users whether the system expects a response from them. One way of doing this is by asking users specific questions but avoiding rhetorical questions, which could lead to interruptions of the agent
when the user responds and the agent was expecting an answer.

3   Limitations and Future Work

Recipe Hunt is currently in its pilot stage and limited to a basic recipe played out
over a few scenes. Further work will require developing scripts and scenarios based
on extensive oral histories, interviews, and archival research. Future scenes may involve more involved actions, such as walking the user through the actual process of
cooking a meal and more culturally specific environments that would place *Recipe
Hunt* squarely in the docu-game genre. Beyond transmitting the basics of Borderland
culinary heritage, *Recipe Hunt* promises to serve as a food-based, participatory model for cross-cultural engagement both within the field of interactive documentary and
beyond to domains such as museum curation and education.

Acknowledgments

This material is based upon work supported by a National Science Foundation Graduate Research Fellowship under grant 2015195909. Any opinion, findings, and conclusions or recommendations expressed in this material are those of the authors and do
not necessarily reflect the views of the National Science Foundation. We thank In-
merssion for an updated xml interpreter based on the UTEP AGENT system.

References

1. Barthes, R. Toward a Psychosociology of Contemporary Food Consumption. In: Food and
   Culture: A Reader (pp. 23-30). Routledge (2013).
2. Carson, D. Baron, C., and Bernard, M. Appetites and Anxieties: Food, Film, and the Poli-
   tics of Representation. Wayne State University Press (2014).
3. Miles, A. Interactive Documentaries and Affective Ecologies. In: New Documentary Ecologies: Emerging Platforms, Practices, and Discourses. Palgrave Macmillan (pp. 67-82)
   (2014).
4. Novick, D., Gris Sepulveda, I., Rivera, D. A., Camacho, A., Rayon, A., & Gutierrez, M.
   (2015, November). The UTEP AGENT System. In : Proceedings of the 2015 ACM on International Conference on Multimodal Interaction (pp. 383-384). ACM.

Development and Perception Evaluation of Culture-specific Gaze Behaviors of Virtual Agents

Tomoko Koda[1,2] ✉, Taku Hirano[1], and Takuto Ishioh[2]

[1] Faculty of Information Science and Technology, Osaka Institute of Technology, Osaka, Japan
[2] Graduate School of Information Science and Technology, Osaka Institute of Technology, Osaka, Japan

tomoko.koda@oit.ac.jp, m1m16a03@st.oit.ac.jp

Abstract. Gaze plays an important role in human-human communication. Adequate gaze control of a virtual agent is also essential for successful and believable human-agent interaction. Researchers on IVA have developed gaze control models by taking account of gaze duration, frequency, and timing of gaze aversion. However, none of this work has considered cultural differences in gaze behaviors. We aimed to investigate cultural differences in gaze behaviors and their perception by developing virtual agents with Japanese gaze behaviors, American gaze behaviors, hybrid gaze behaviors, and full gaze behaviors. We then compared their effects on the impressions of the agents and interactions. Our experimental results with Japanese participants suggest that the impression of the agent is affected by participants' shyness and familiarity of the gaze patterns performed by the agent.

Keywords: gaze, shyness, intelligent virtual agents, non-verbal behavior, cross-culture, perception, evaluation

1 Introduction

Intelligent virtual agents (IVAs) that interact face-to-face with humans are beginning to spread to general users across cultures, and IVA research is being actively pursued. IVAs require both verbal and non-verbal communication abilities to achieve natural interaction with humans. Among those non-verbal behaviors, gaze plays an important role in our social interactions, including controlling the flow of a conversation, indicating interest and intentions, and improving the listener's attention and comprehension [1, 2]. As in humans, a virtual agent's gaze behavior is important for facilitating natural interaction. Previous research on modelling gaze behavior of virtual agents has investigated appropriate turn management [3], where to look [4], making idle gaze movements [5], expressing social dominance by gaze [6], and the appropriate amount of gaze to facilitate interaction [7, 8]. All of these studies have modelled realistic human gaze behavior to an agent, resulting in more natural and smooth interaction.

Gaze perception and preferences are also affected by personality. For example, being gazed at can lead to discomfort from feeling observed, especially for shy people [9]. Shyness is defined as "discomfort and inhibition in the presence of others, where

[Tapez ici]

© Springer International Publishing AG 2017
J. Beskow et al. (Eds.): IVA 2017, LNAI 10498, pp. 213-222, 2017.
DOI 10.1007/978-3-319-67401-8_25

these reactions derive directly from the social nature of the situation" [9]. Shy people tend to avert gaze and engage in more self-manipulation [10, 11]. Thus, shy people might not prefer to interact with a virtual agent that exhibits the realistic social human gaze behavior that is believed to facilitate smooth interaction. Our previous research investigated how shy people perceive different amounts of gaze from a virtual agent and how their perception of gaze affects the comfortableness of the interaction [12]. The results indicated that shy people are sensitive to even a very low amount of gaze from the agent. However, contrary to our expectations, as the amount of gaze from the agent increased, shy people had a more favorable impression of the agent, and they did not perceive the typically adequate amount of gaze (66%) as most comfortable. On the other hand, non-shy people perceived the gaze condition and recognized the adequate amount of gaze as most friendly.

None of the above IVA research, however, has addressed cultural differences in gaze behaviors, despite researchers in psychology having reported cultural difference in gaze behaviors and their perception. We believe there is a strong need to develop enculturated agents by making them exhibit culture-specific non-verbal behaviors such as gaze. Although this study focused on gaze behaviors, the importance of culturally adaptive IVAs for successful agent interactions has been suggested by Rehm and Nakano [13], who focused on gestures and postures, by Koda [14] in an investigation of facial expressions, and by Kuhne and Finkelstein [15, 16] in research on linguistic alignment. Culturally aware agent applications have been implemented as a culture training system [17] and to raise cultural awareness [18].

In terms of culture-specific gaze behaviors, there are findings from observation and video analysis of human-human and human-agent interactions that show cultural differences. Mayo [19] found that gaze patterns differ according to the culture of the conversant by analyzing gaze behaviors in video recordings of human-human conversations. Elzinga [1] reported that Japanese individuals had "more frequent and shorter lasting other-directed gazes" than did Australian participants, and that English-speaking participants looked at the other person to signal turns, while Japanese participants did not [20]. Argyle found that Swedes gaze at their conversation partner more than English participants do (50% vs. 38% of the time) [1].

In terms of perception of gaze behaviors, studies have indicated cultural preferences in the gaze amount that one receives. According to Cook [21], favorableness of impression is a linear function of the amount of gaze a person receives, and 50% of gaze amount gave the most favorable impression toward the human gazer in an experiment conducted in UK. Fukayama et al. [22] changed the amount of gaze from a virtual agent by 25%, 50%, 75%, and 100% and compared the agent's impressions by Japanese evaluators. The results showed that 50% gaze was perceived as most friendly, followed by 75%, then 25%. Impressions of friendliness plummeted in the full gaze (100%) condition.

If there are cultural differences in performing gaze behaviors, there should also be cultural differences in perceiving gaze behaviors of other cultures. We aimed to investigate cultural differences in gaze behaviors and their perception by developing virtual agents with Japanese gaze behaviors, American gaze behaviors, their hybrid gaze behaviors, and full gaze behaviors, and to compare their effects on the impressions of the agents and interactions. In our previous work [12], non-shy people recognized the adequate amount of gaze (66%) and perceived the condition as most comfortable, while shy people did not. Accordingly, it is possible that the impression of the agent is affected by participants' shyness and the familiarity of the gaze patterns performed by the agent. Considering our findings that shy people's sensitivity to gaze amount and non-shy people's recognition of an adequate amount of gaze [12], we formed the following two hypotheses: H1) Shy people form worse impressions of agents whose gaze model does not originate from the same culture; H2) Non-shy people are more tolerant of gaze models from other cultures. This paper reports our experimental results with Japanese participants.

2   Gaze Models

We implemented American gaze behaviors (AG), Japanese gaze behaviors (JG), hybrid gaze behaviors (HG), and full gaze behaviors (FG) in our virtual agent in order to compare the impression of different cultural gaze behaviors.

AG was implemented in accordance with the gaze model proposed by Cassell et al. [23]. Their model shows American gaze patterns by analyzing video recordings of human dyad conversations. The model shows the probability of "looking away" at the beginning (44%) and end (84%) of an utterance. Fig. 1a shows the state transition diagram of AG at the beginning of an utterance, and Fig. 1b shows the AG at the end of an utterance as implemented in our AG model. Our AG also includes a gaze pattern at the end of a question, where the agent "gazes at" the user (human participant). The agent "looks away" from the user for 0.5 seconds 44% of the time at the beginning of an utterance, then shifts toward a "gaze-at" state. The agent keeps its gaze toward the user during the utterance. The agent "looks away" from the user for 2 seconds 84% of the time at the end of the utterance. The "look away" timing at the end of the utterance is calculated by estimating the duration of the synthesized speech. The agent keeps its "gaze-at" state toward the user while listening.

JG was implemented in accordance with the gaze model proposed by Ishii et al. [7, 8]. Their model shows Japanese gaze patterns by analyzing video recordings of three-way human conversations. We implemented JG by modifying their gaze model for dyad conversations by eliminating the state transitions to the third person. Fig. 2a shows the state transition diagram of JG. The agent "gazes at" the user at the beginning of an utterance, maintains the gaze for 1.1 to 3.1 seconds, and then shifts its gaze to "vague gaze" (described in section 3) for 3.2 to 7.9 seconds. The agent shifts its gaze pattern to "gaze-at" state 67% of the time or to "averted gaze" for 2.0 seconds 33% of the time after the "vague gaze." "Gaze aversion" is continued 13% of the time or shifted to the "gaze-at" state 87% of the time at the end of gaze aversion. The agent follows the gaze transitions during its utterance and while it is listening.

HG was implemented by combining JG and AG. As gaze behaviors and patterns are dependent on culture [19], we implemented HG as a culture-independent model that was neither American nor Japanese. Fig. 2b shows the state transition diagram at the beginning of and during an utterance. The agent follows the transition of AG at the beginning of an utterance, and then follows JG during the utterance. The agent follows the state transition diagram of AG while listening. In addition to AG, JG, and HG, we implemented FG, a full gaze model, as a control gaze condition.

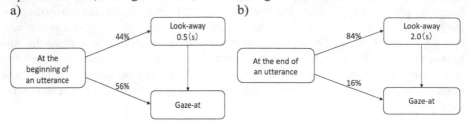

Fig. 1. a) State Transition Diagram of American Gaze Behavior at the Beginning of an Utterance, b) at the End of an Utterance

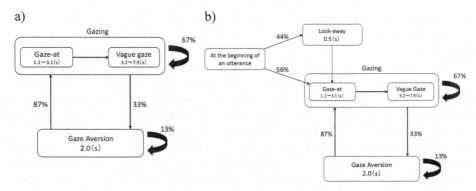

Fig. 2. a) State Transition Diagram of Japanese Gaze Behavior, b) Hybrid Gaze Model

3   Virtual Agent and Gaze Animations

The agent's appearance and gaze animations were developed by Unity 5.2.1fl (https://unity3d.com/) and Taichi Character Pack asset (https://www.assetstore.unity3d.com/jp/#!/content/15667). The agent's voice was synthesized with AITalk (http://www.ai-j.jp/english/). The gaze behaviors implemented in the agent were the four types described in section 2, namely, "gaze-at," "vague gaze," "look-away," and "gaze-aversion".

   "Gaze at" is a state in which the agent keeps gazing at a user (shown in Fig. 3a: left, b: top). "Vague gaze" is described as follows: "in order to express less-face-threatening eye-gaze in virtual space avatars" [7, 8], which was implemented with the agent looking five degrees lower than the user's eye position (shown in Fig. 3a: right, b: bottom). "Look-away" was implemented as an animation in which the agent discontinues its gaze for 0.5 seconds and looks up, as in Gambi's agent [24], which was implemented in accordance with Cassell's American game model [23]. The agent looks up (in "look-away" state for 0.5 seconds) before an utterance (shown in Fig. 4a). "Gaze aversion" was implemented in two directions, to the right and left, and each aversion lasts for 2 seconds, as described in [8] (shown in Fig. 4b). A validation check for each gaze animation was conducted by 8 university students. The agent performs blinks, head rotation, lip sync, and the gaze patterns. The gaze behaviors are fully automated according to a dialogue the agent speaks. The amount of gaze in each condition is not fixed, as it is affected by the duration of utterance from the agent and a participant, as well as randomized transition processes of each model. However, we can estimate that the amount of gaze becomes greater, in order, for HG, JG, AG, and FG.

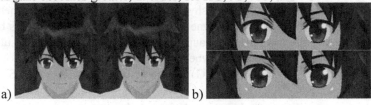

Fig. 3. Agent's Gaze-at State (a: left, b: top) and Vague Gaze State: 5 degrees lower than gaze-at (a: right, b: bottom)

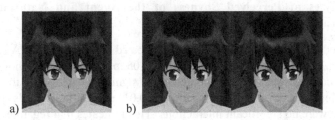

Fig. 4. a) Agent's Look-away state, b) Agent's Gaze Aversion States (to left and right, in either direction)

4   Experiment

4.1   Experimental Procedure

The experiment was conducted as a Wizard of Oz experiment. Participants were asked to have four formal conversational sessions with a conversational virtual agent to assess its functions. The true purpose of the experiment was not explained to the participants during the experiment. The agent's gaze models and conversational topics were randomly assigned in each of four conversation sessions in order to minimize the effect of conversational content. The topics included the US Election, Senior Driving, Pokémon GO, and POP Icons. Each conversation lasted about 2 minutes. The agent brought up the issue at asked the participants for their opinions. The agent's reply was controlled by a Wizard. The distance between the agent and participant was set to 1.8 meters, which is defined as an appropriate social distance by Hall [25]. The agent's upper torso was displayed on a 42-inch display, and the display's height was adjusted to the eye level of each participant. The participants were asked to answer a questionnaire after each session, indicating the agent's perceived shyness, perceived friendliness, their friendly feelings toward the agent, and comfortableness and naturalness of the conversation.

In this experiment, we recruited 18 Japanese university students (15 men and 3 women, 19 to 23 years old). Their shyness level was measured by the Shyness Scale [26] beforehand. We divided the 18 participants into three groups according to their shyness scores. The average shyness score of Japanese university students in engineering was reported in a previous study to be 47.56 [26]. Seven participants with scores above 51 were categorized as the high shyness group (HS), 4 with scores between 45 and 48 were categorized as the mid shyness group (MS), and 7 with scores below 41 were categorized as the low shyness group (LS). We only analyzed the results of HS and LS to investigate the effects of shyness. The experimental conditions were gaze model (four models: FG, AG, JG and HG) and participant's shyness (HS/LS).

5   Results

5.1   Analyses of Perceived Shyness of the Agent and Naturalness of the Interaction

For perceived shyness of the agent, a 2-way repeated measures ANOVA showed a significant main effect of gaze condition ($F = 11.105$, $p < 0.01$). Fig. 5 shows the results of multiple comparisons. AG was perceived as significantly less shy than were other gaze conditions by both the HS ($F = 5.45$, $p < 0.01$) and LS individuals ($F = 5.69$, $p < 0.01$). There were no significant interactions. This indicates that regardless of the shyness of the participants, AG was perceived as less shy than were the other gaze models. It is interesting that FG was not perceived as least shy, when the amount of gaze was 100%. As for perceived naturalness of the interaction, a 2-way repeated measures ANOVA showed no significant main effects or interactions. This indicates that all interactions are perceived as equally natural regardless of the gaze conditions and participants' shyness (ratings of 4–5 on a 1–7 scale).

5.2   Analyses of Friendliness from / toward the Agent and Comfortableness of the Conversation

Regarding perceived friendliness from the agent, a 2-way repeated measures ANOVA showed a significant main effect of gaze condition ($F = 4.462$, $p < 0.01$). Fig. 6 shows the results of multiple comparisons. The HS group perceived JG and FG as significantly more friendly as compared to AG and HG (JG–AG: $F = 5.770$, $p < 0.05$; JG–HG: $F = 7.296$, $p < 0.01$; FG–AG: $F = 7.705$, $p < 0.01$; FG–HG: $F = 6.573$, $p < 0.05$). However, the LS group perceived AG to be equally as friendly as JG and FG, and significantly more friendly than HG ($F = 5.517$, $p < 0.05$). The perceived friendliness of AG showed a significant difference by participants' shyness. Specifically, the LS group evaluated AG as significantly more friendly than did the HS group ($F = 6.229$, $p < 0.05$).

These results indicate that HS individuals are sensitive to the change of gaze patterns and perceived less friendliness from gaze patterns with which they are not familiar (i.e., AG and HG). LS individuals are more tolerant of the change in gaze patterns and perceived equal friendliness from gaze patterns with they are not familiar, except for HG. These results are in accordance with the result of our previous study, which suggested that HS individuals are sensitive to even a very small amount of gaze from the agent as well as changes in gaze amount [12].

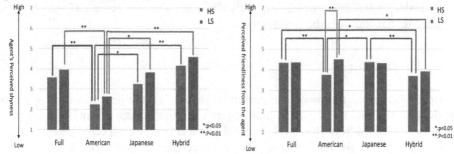

Fig. 5. Agent's Perceived Shyness   Fig. 6. Perceived friendliness from an agent

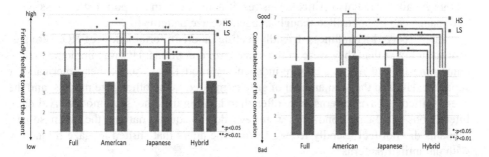

Fig. 7. Friendly feeling toward the agent   Fig. 8. Comfortableness of the Conversation

As for friendly feelings toward the agent, a 2-way repeated measures ANOVA showed a significant main effect of gaze (F = 7.728, p < 0.01) and shyness (F = 4.151, p < 0.05). The result of multiple comparisons is shown in Fig. 7. HS individuals felt significantly more friendly toward JG (F = 8.565, p < 0.01) and FG (F = 6.31, p < 0.05) as compared to HG. While LS individuals had more friendly feelings toward JG and AG as compared to FG and HG (JG–HG: F = 9.443, p < 0.01; JG–FG: F = 4.345, p < 0.05, AG–HG: F = 12.747, p < 0.01, AG–FG: F = 4.356, p < 0.05). Friendly feelings toward AG showed a significant difference between shyness groups. LS individuals had significantly more friendly feelings toward AG than did HS individuals (F = 8.649, p < 0.01).

HS individuals tended to have less friendly feelings toward AG (although not significant) and HG as compared to FG and JG, while LS individuals felt friendly feelings toward AG and JG. HS individuals' overall friendly feelings toward the agent were lower than were those of LS individuals. These results show similar trends to the results for agent's perceived friendliness.

As for comfortableness of the conversation, a 2-way repeated measures ANOVA showed a significant main effect of gaze condition (F = 7.979, p < 0.01). Fig. 8 shows the results of multiple comparisons. HS individuals felt less comfort than did LS individuals in all gaze models. In particular, AG was evaluated as less comfortable by HS than by LS individuals ($F = 5.355$, $p < 0.05$), a similar trend to that for friendly feelings. HG was evaluated as less comfortable than were other gaze models by both HS and LS individuals ($p < 0.05$). The agent frequently changed its gaze states in HG, which might have led to discomfort in the conversation.

6   Discussion

Our previous research showed that perceived shyness of an agent was inversely proportional to the amount of gaze from the agent [12]. In this experiment, the amount of gaze was increased from HG to JG, AG, and FG, and thus, we expected perceived shyness to increase in the inverse order. However, contrary to our expectation, AG was perceived as significantly less shy than were other gaze models. One possible reason is that amount of gaze is not the only factor that affects an agent's perceived shyness, and that gaze patterns are also critical. This result is in line with a report that expression of dominance can be controlled though an agent's gaze patterns [6].

The perceived friendliness, friendly feeling, and comfortableness of HG were significantly lower than they were in the other gaze conditions. HG was implemented by combining JG and AG as a culture-independent model that was neither American nor Japanese. HG had the least amount of gaze compared to the other gaze models, and the agent shifted its gaze patterns more often than it did in the other gaze models. Although interactions in all gaze conditions were regarded as equally natural, the Japanese participants did not feel friendly feeling toward the agent that shifted its gaze frequently with unfamiliar patterns.

FG was perceived as equally friendly and comfortable by both shyness groups (HS and LS). FG was perceived as equally friendly and comfortable as was JG by HS individuals. One possible reason for this result is that the Japanese participants were familiar with agents or computer characters that do not move their eyes and keep staring at them, as many virtual agents are not programmed to shift their gaze.

JG was perceived as equally friendly and comfortable by both shyness group, although there was an overall tendency for LS individuals to form more positive impressions of the agents and interactions as compared to HS individuals. This result is reasonable, as the participants were familiar with JG patterns.

In order to verify whether our hypotheses were supported, we compared perceptions of AG evaluated by both shyness groups. The hypotheses were as follows: H1) Shy people form worse impressions of agents whose gaze model does not originate from the same culture; and H2) Non-shy people are more tolerant of gaze models from other cultures.

HS individuals formed worse impressions of AG than they did of FG and JG, as low as their impressions of HG. This suggests that HS individuals' perceptions and impressions of AG are as unfriendly and uncomfortable as their impressions of HG are. One possible explanation is that this poor impression is caused by unfamiliarity of gaze patterns in AG, in addition to HS individuals' reduced tolerance or adaptation skills for unfamiliar gaze patterns. HS individuals had similarly positive impression of FG and JG, demonstrating the same tendency as a previous study [12]. HS individuals had more favorable impressions of the agent as the amount of gaze from the agent increased. Other characteristics of HS individuals include their sensitivity to changes in gaze patterns, as their perception of friendliness changed significantly across the four gaze patterns. These results are in accordance with previous findings [12]. HS individuals' evaluations of friendliness and comfort were lower than were those of LS individuals in general. In particular, their impressions of AG were significantly lower than the ones made by LS individuals. These results support H1.

LS individuals showed the opposite impressions of AG. They maintained a stable positive impression of AG, which was as positive as their impression of JG. Their friendly feeling toward the agent in AG was higher than it was for FG. LS individuals' impressions of HG were consistently lowest. These results support H2. The findings suggest that LS individuals are more tolerant to unfamiliar gaze patterns from different cultures because of their social skills.

7   Conclusion

We aimed to investigate cultural differences in gaze behaviors and their perception by developing virtual agents with Japanese gaze behaviors, American gaze behaviors, hybrid gaze behaviors, and full gaze behaviors. We then compared their effects on impressions of and interactions with the agents. Our experimental results with Japanese participants suggest that impressions of the agent are affected by participants' shyness as well as the familiarity of the gaze pattern performed by the agent.

We will continue the experiment with participants from the US and other cultures. The limitations of this study include the agent's appearance, and that most participants were male, with a limited sample size. Our follow-up study should include a female agent and more female participants, with a larger sample size, people with mid-level shyness. Finally, the agent should exhibit non-verbal behaviors other than gaze.

We believe this study will draw more attention to awareness of cultural differences of gaze behaviors, which we usually control unconsciously. One potential application of this outcome is cultural training for the typical gaze behaviors of different cultures in order to facilitate mutual understanding and decrease the likelihood of misunderstandings through misinterpretation of other cultures' gaze behaviors.

Acknowledgements
This research is supported by JSPS KAKENHI JP26330236 and JP17K00287.

References

1. Argyle, M., Cook, M. Gaze and mutual gaze. Cambridge University Press Cambridge, 1976.
2. Bayliss, A.. Paul. M., Cannon, P, and Tipper, S. Gaze cuing and affective judgments of objects: I like what you look at. Psychonomic bulletin & review 13, 6, pp. 1061-1066, 2006.

3. Pelachaud, C., and Bilvi, M. Modelling gaze behavior for conversational agents. In IVA2003, Springer, pp. 93-100, 2003.
4. Lee, J., Marsella, S., Traum, D., Gratch, J., and Lance, B. The rickel gaze model: A window on the mind of a virtual human. In IVA2007, Springer, pp. 296-303, 2007.
5. Cafaro, A., Gaito, R., and Vilhjrilmsson, H. Animating idle gaze in public places. In IVA2009, Springer, pp. 250-256, 2009.
6. Bee, N., Pollock, C., André, E., Walker, M. Bossy or Wimpy: Expressing Social Dominance by Combining Gaze and Linguistic Behaviors. In IVA2010, Springer, pp 265-271, 2010.
7. Ishii, R, et al. Avatar's gaze control to facilitate conversational turn-taking in virtual-space multi-user voice chat system. In IVA2006, Springer, pp.458-458, 2006.
8. Ishii, R, et al. Avatar's Gaze Control to Facilitate Conversation in Virtual-Space Multi-User Voice Chat System, in J. of Human Interface, 10 (1), pp. 87-94, 2008. (in Japanese)
9. Jones, Warren H., and Dan Russell. The social reticence scale: An objective instrument to measure shyness. Journal of personality assessment 46.6, pp. 629-631, 1982.
10. Cheek, J. M., & Buss, A. H. 1981 Shyness and sociability. Journal of Personality and Social Psychology, 41, pp.330-339, 1981.
11. Daly, S. Behavioral correlates of social anxiety. British Journal of Social and Clinical Psychology, 17, pp. 117-120, 1978.
12. Koda, T., Ogura, M, and Matsui, Y. Shyness Level and Sensitivity to Gaze from Agents. - Are Shy People Sensitive to Agent's Gaze? In IVA 2016, Springer, pp. pp 359-363, 2016.
13. Rehm, M. et al. From Observation to Simulation - Generating Culture Specific Behavior for Interactive Systems. AI & Society 24, Springer, pp. 267–280, 2009.
14. Koda, T. et al. Avatar Culture: Cross-Cultural Evaluations of Avatar Facial Expressions. AI & Society, Springer, pp. 237–250, 2009.
15. Kühne, V. et al. Using linguistic alignment to enhance learning experience with pedagogical agents: the special case of dialect. In IVA2013, Springer, pp. 149-158, 2013.
16. Finkelstein, S. et al. The effects of culturally congruent educational technologies on student achievement. AIED2013, Springer, pp. 493-502, 2013.
17. Johnson, L., et al. Tactical language and culture training systems: Using artificial intelligence to teach foreign languages and cultures. In: Proc of IAAI, pp,73-83, 2008.
18. Aylett, R. et al. But that was in another country: agents and intercultural empathy. In: Proceedings AAMAS, pp. 329–336, 2009
19. Mayo, C., and La France, M. Gaze Direction in Interracial Dyadic Communication. In Harper, R.G. et al.(ed.) Meeting of Eastan Psychological Association. 1978.
20. Elzinga, R.H. Temporal Organization of Conversation, Sociolinguistics Newsletter, 9, 2 (summer), pp.29-31, 1978.
21. Cook, M. and Smith, M.C. The Role of Gaze in Impression Formation, Br. J. Clinical Psychology, Vol.14, pp.19-25, 1975.
22. Fukayama, A. et al.. Messages embedded in gaze of interface agents - impression management with agent's gaze. Proc. of the SIGCHI (CHI '02). ACM, New York, pp.41-48, 2002.
23. Cassell, J., Obed E. T., and Prevost, S. Turn taking versus discourse structure. Machine conversations. Springer US, pp.143-153, 1999.
24. Gambi, C., Staudte, M., and Torsten, J. The role of prosody and gaze in turn-end anticipation. Procs. of the Annual Conference of the Cognitive Science Society. 2015.
25. Hall, E.T. The hidden dimension, Doubleday and Company, 1966.
26. Aikawa, A. A study on the reliability and validity of a scale to measure shyness as a trait. The Japanese Journal of Psychology, 62(3), pp.149-155, 1991. (in Japanese)

A demonstration of the ASAP Realizer-Unity3D Bridge for Virtual and Mixed Reality Applications

Jan Kolkmeier ✉, Merijn Bruijnes, and Dennis Reidsma

Human Media Interaction, University of Twente, The Netherlands
[j.kolkmeier; m.bruijnes; d.reidsma]@utwente.nl

Abstract. Modern game engines such as Unity make prototyping and developing experiences in virtual and mixed reality environments increasingly accessible and efficient, and their value has long been recognized by the scientific community as well. However, these game engines do not easily allow control of virtual embodied characters, situated in such environments, with the same expressiveness, flexibility, and generalizability, as offered by modern BML realizers that generate synchronized multimodal behavior from Behavior Markup Language (BML). We demonstrate our integration of the ASAP BML Realizer and the Unity3D game engine at the hand of an Augmented Reality setup. We further show an in-unity editor for BML animations in the same system.

Keywords: BML, SAIBA, Virtual Agents, Unity, Virtual Reality, Mixed Reality

1 Introduction

The Articulated Social Agent Platform (ASAP) provides a collection of software modules for building social robots and virtual humans [3, 5]. ASAP is a SAIBA compliant, OS independent behavior realizer, enhanced with two features that allow for fast and fluent virtual human behaviors: a close bi-directional coordination between input processing and output generation, and incremental processing of both input and output. The default virtual embodiment in ASAP is for the Armandia ECA. It is implemented as a Java OpenGL application that is controlled by directly binding to the ASAP platform code.

In our demo, we show the integration of the ASAP BML Realizer and the Unity3D game engine[1]. For more details and background, we refer to the main paper [1]. This demo is meant to showcase the technology itself, invite others to use it and help solving similar problems for their own engines or realizers. The main software component used in this demo will be made publicly available[2]. In the following we describe what we demonstrate as well as previous work that made use of this technology, illustrating different use cases in which it can be employed.

---

[1] Developed by Unity Technologies: https://unity3d.com
[2] https://github.com/hmi-utwente/AsapUnityBridge

© Springer International Publishing AG 2017
J. Beskow et al. (Eds.): IVA 2017, LNAI 10498, pp. 223-226, 2017.
DOI 10.1007/978-3-319-67401-8_26

2 Virtual Agents in the HoloLens

We demonstrate the ASAP Realizer-Unity3D Bridge at the hand of a prototype shown in Fig. 1. We use the Microsoft HoloLens[TM,3] running a 'client' Unity scene to the ASAP backend where the agent behavior is being realized. Virtual Agents can be placed in the real world using a uniquely identifying augmented reality marker using the Vuforia augmented reality SDK[4].

Fig. 1. Left: Using the ASAP Realizer-Unity3D Bridge and HoloLens AR glasses to create a situated embodied agent in our hallway. Right: The Animation Editor view in Unity. A: The skeleton hierarchy. B: The character and the ASAP Animation rig. C: The time-line editor with sync-points as animation events. D: The exported BMLT.

3 Animation Editor for BML

We further demonstrate our unity extension to create BML-animations. Natural behaviors for a virtual agent depends in large part on realistic and appropriate animations. Currently, the ASAP is lacking a flexible pipeline for creating new animations for gestures and postures. For this purpose we extended the Unity editor with a work flow for creating and exporting keyframe animations using the animation time-line (see Fig. 1). These animations can be exported in the *<bmlt:keyframe>* format as described in ASAP's BML Twente-extensions[5] (BMLT).

Animations and poses are created by animating the H-Anim[6] skeleton – currently using forward kinematics only. The H-Anim skeleton is the same as the one that is used for re-targeting between ASAP and Unity (see above), hence the resulting poses are consistent between the 'preview' in the editor and what is produced by ASAP when the generated BML is realized. New BMLs can be used by ASAP to control also other characters in any H-Anim-compatible embodiment.

---

[3] https://www.microsoft.com/en-us/hololens
[4] https://www.vuforia.com
[5] asap-project.ewi.utwente.nl/wiki/BMLT
[6] http://h-anim.org/Specifications/H-Anim1.1

The BML standard supports the synchronisation between different multimodal behaviors. During realisation, the agent's behaviors can be broken down into phases making it easy to specify alignment of behaviors at meaningful boundaries: at sync-points. To allow this synchronisation with the new animations, named sync-points for gesture animations can be added in the Unity time-line (see Fig. 1 C).

4   Other Use-cases & Projects

The technology presented in this demo is a SAIBA compliant BML realizer in Unity. Besides the demo described above, we have applied the Unity embodiment in several recent projects, three of which we discuss briefly here, highlighting some aspects of the system.

The AVATAR project. In the AVATAR project, a partner developed a Unity environment where a policeman and a witness could interact with the user. The aim was to create an educational setting where social skills could be trained using virtual agents. The behaviors of the agent was driven by ASAP and realized in the Unity world. The facial expressions and lip-sync were procedurally generated by ASAP and combined with animations that were specified in Unity by the partner. The animations were mapped to descriptive BML commands, demonstrating the flexibility of our approach.

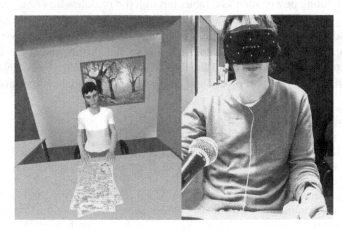

Fig. 2. The R3D3 robot (left) with a mixed-modality agent and the Moral Competence Training experiment setup in immersive VR (right)

The R3D3 project. In the Rolling Receptionist Robot with Double Dutch Dialogue (R3D3) project, a robot drives around in a reception area and a virtual agent on a screen in the robot's hands could help people find their way in the building. In this project, ASAP controlled the robot body as well as the virtual agent on the screen (see Fig.

2 left and [4]). In early versions of the system, the agent was situated in an Android tablet using the Unity embodiment. Calculations for the robot's perception as well as the ASAP realizer were executed on a more powerful PC. The tablet only rendered the agent based on the received output of the Unity embodiment over the middleware. This shows the capability of ASAP to run distributed and to control a variety of mixed-modality embodiments.

Training for Moral Competences. This project investigates the possibilities of developing a training agent that help teachers to develop their moral and ethical competences through simulating conflicts. A prototype of this training agent was developed using the Unity embodiment (see Fig. 2 right and [2]). It was necessary to use Unity as we employed a VR headset with integrated eye-tracker, the FOVE 0[7], that was not supported in other 3D engines for ASAP. In this prototype, we made use of the world environment by keeping ASAP informed of the user's head position (which was available in the Unity world frame from the VR headset). This way ASAP could reliably generate mutual and averted gaze behaviors through its IK system.

5 Conclusion

The integration we present here makes it possible to drive characters in Unity with the ASAP BML realizer. It is also possible to control virtual agents on a system with limited computing power such as a tablet through the middleware connection. We demonstrate this specifically with our augmented reality setup. An agent is situated in the real world, rendered through the HoloLens in a Unity scene, while the behavior is computed using the ASAP back-end in a remote location. We further showcase the Unity animation editor as way of quick and flexible creation of reusable BML gesture animations and postures that support procedural change for multimodal synchronization.

References

1. Kolkmeier, J., Bruijnes, M., Reidsma, D., Heylen, D.: An asap realizer-unity3d bridge for virtual and mixed reality applications. In: International Conference on Intelligent Virtual Agents. Springer (2017)
2. Kolkmeier, J., Lee, M., Heylen, D.: Moral conflicts in vr: Addressing grade disputes with a virtual trainer. In: International Conference on Intelligent Virtual Agents. Springer (2017)
3. Kopp, S., van Welbergen, H., Yaghoubzadeh, R., Buschmeier, H.: An architecture for fluid real-time conversational agents: integrating incremental output generation and input processing. Journal on Multimodal User Interfaces 8(1), 97–108 (2014)
4. Linssen, J., Berkhoff, M., Bode, M., Rens, E., Theune, M., Wiltenburg, D.: You can leave your head on - attention management and turn-taking in multi-party interaction with a virtual human/robot duo. In: International Conference on Intelligent Virtual Agents. Springer (2017)
5. Van Welbergen, H., Yaghoubzadeh, R., Kopp, S.: Asaprealizer 2.0: the next steps in fluent behavior realization for ecas. In: International Conference on Intelligent Virtual Agents. pp. 449–462. Springer (2014)

---

[7] getfove.com

An ASAP Realizer-Unity3D Bridge for Virtual and Mixed Reality Applications

Jan Kolkmeier ✉, Merijn Bruijnes, Dennis Reidsma, and Dirk Heylen

Human Media Interaction, University of Twente, The Netherlands
[j.kolkmeier; m.bruijnes; d.reidsma; d.k.j.heylen]@utwente.nl

Abstract. Modern game engines such as Unity make prototyping and developing experiences for virtual and mixed reality contexts increasingly accessible and efficient, and their value has long been recognized by the scientific community as well. However, these game engines do not have the capabilities to control virtual embodied characters, situated in such environments, with the same expressiveness, flexibility, and generalizability, as offered by modern BML realizers that generate synchronized multimodal behavior from Behavior Markup Language (BML). We implemented a Unity embodiment bridge to the Articulated Social Agents Platform (ASAP) to combine the benefits of a modern game engine and a modern BML realizer. The challenges and solutions we report can help others integrate other game engines with BML realizers, and we end with a glimpse at future challenges and features of our implementation.

Keywords: BML, SAIBA, Virtual Agents, Unity, Virtual Reality, Mixed Reality

1 Introduction

Natural multimodal behavior for an embodied conversational agent requires producing, at the right moment, utterances combined with appropriate non-verbal behaviors and the capability to 'color' these behaviors to adapt to the social situation [1]. In a SAIBA system [3], an *Intent Planner* produces intents composed of speech acts and communicative functions that are translated into expressive multimodal behavior by a *Behavior Planner*. In the Articulated Social Agent Platform (ASAP [4]), *embodiment* modules are tasked with the timely realization of planned behavior. This modularization allows control of both virtual and robotic embodied agents, as well as control of agents with embodiments situated in multiple environments, such as a robotic platform with a virtual head on a screen [8]. Furthermore, ASAP specializes in on-the-fly adaptation of the timing of the realized behavior, for mutually coordinated fluent interaction with an interlocutor [7].

In the following we present our work towards an integration of the ASAP platform and the popular Unity[1] game engine and editor through a *Unity embodiment*[2]. Although integrations with other 3D engines already exist, the Unity game engine is an attractive

---

[1] Developed by Unity Technologies: https://unity3d.com
[2] All software discussed in this work is publicly available at this repository: https://github.com/hmi-utwente/AsapUnityBridge

© Springer International Publishing AG 2017
J. Beskow et al. (Eds.): IVA 2017, LNAI 10498, pp. 227–230, 2017.
DOI 10.1007/978-3-319-67401-8_27

addition to this list. It is becoming a popular tool for creating 3D and Virtual Reality environments also in scientific circles and among students, making collaboration and re-production easier. What is more, Unity is currently one of the first engines offering API support for consumer and scientific grade MR and VR products, thus reducing the effort needed to incorporate these new technologies into existing systems. It further supports importing existing assets in various formats and has a wide range of assets – including virtual characters – available through the asset store, allowing for fast prototyping of virtual environments.

While Unity also provides a powerful animation engine, it does not aim to satisfy the same requirements that a BML realization engine does, such as multimodal behavior planning and synchronization and lip-sync. BML realizers provide an important missing set of functions not present in Unity or standard game engines. The Virtual Human Toolkit (VHTK) [2] already comes with a Unity integration of another popular BML realizer: SmartBody [9]. While this is a good option, it is always beneficial to have more choices, as there are strengths and weaknesses to different BML realizers. As mentioned above, one of the strengths of ASAP lies in its flexibility when looking to control agents with heterogeneous embodiments. This is useful, for example, in mixed reality settings, where agents and their modalities are situated in both the virtual and physical world.

2 Related work

ASAP provides a collection of software modules for building social robots and virtual humans [10]. SAIBA makes a distinction between the communicative intent and be-havior descriptions of the Embodied Conversational Agent (ECA) with XML based in-terfaces, Functional Markup Language (FML) and Behavior Markup Language (BML) respectively [3]. ASAP is a SAIBA compliant, OS independent behavior realizer, en-hanced with two features that allow for fast and fluent virtual human behavior: a close bi-directional coordination between input processing and output generation, and incre-mental processing of both input and output. The default virtual embodiment in ASAP is for the Armandia ECA. It is implemented as a Java OpenGL application that is con-trolled by directly binding to the ASAP platform code. Implementation of new embodi-ments is described in [8]. ASAP has been used not only for virtual humans, but also for controlling social robots, such the Zeno R25[3] in the EASEL project [6].

The Greta platform realizer supports controlling both virtual and robotics agents through MPEG4 BAP-FAP *players* [5]. The default player for virtual agents uses the Ogre engine[4]. There is mention of an experimental Greta branch[5] with Unity integration using thrift[6].

The VHTK [2] uses SmartBody [9] as BML realization engine. To our knowledge, there is no work on controlling heterogeneous or robotic agent platforms with Smart-

---

[3] hansonrobotics.com/robot/zeno, former Robokind
[4] ogre3d.org
[5] https://trac.telecom-paristech.fr/trac/project/greta/wiki/
   GretaUnity
[6] https://thrift.apache.org

Body. Written in C++, it can be compiled and thus included natively in various platforms (including Unity).

3 Implementation Summary

Several things are needed to integrate a BML realizer (ASAP) with a new embodiment (Unity). We follow the overall steps to extend ASAP with a new embodiment as described in [8]. First, ASAP needs the capability to control the Unity embodiment for animation of posture, gesture and facial expressions. This requires an implementation of the face and skeleton embodiment interface in ASAP, whereas in Unity the character needs to be configured to expose the right animation controls to be able to execute the requested behavior. Communication between the two processes (Unity and ASAP) is implemented with a generic middleware implementation, allowing for a distributed setup. ASAP needs to have access to information about the Unity character that is being controlled, such as the composition of the skeleton and the face. We refer to this as the *AgentSpec*. The AgentSpec is requested by ASAP upon initialization of the Unity embodiment loader. Now, when ASAP receives a BML to be realized, it can compute both skeleton and face data internally. Resulting bone transforms and morph targets are shared through *AgentState* messages with Unity at a desired frame rate.

To realize lip-sync, mouth shapes need to be defined in a *facebinding* using the facial controls that the Unity character exposes.

ASAP is capable of using Inverse Kinematics (IK) for pointing or directed gaze. However, to do this the locations of the relevant objects in the Unity environment need to be made available to ASAP. This is done by the implementation of the WorldObjectEnvironment interface.

As part of this work, we further provide a Unity editor extension to create forward kinematic animations that can be exported to BML keyframe animations that can be used in the ASAP gesture binding. These animations support procedural changes for multimodal synchronization using named sync points.

4 Conclusion and Future work

The integration we present makes it possible to drive characters in Unity with the ASAP BML realizer. The implementation allows re-use of most existing agent behaviors that were defined in BML in earlier work. This includes automatically generated BML through SAIBA-compliant agent architectures. Through the distributed implementation, it is possible to run an embodied conversational agent on a system with limited computing power such as a tablet. Additionally, mixed-modality agents, such as a robot with a virtual face on a screen, are supported by ASAP. The Unity integration with ASAP, combined with novel AR technology such as the HoloLens, offers the exciting possibility to place persistent virtual conversational agents throughout the persistent mixed reality world that the HoloLens offers.

The possibility to export BML from the Unity animation editor is a promising approach for quick and flexible creation of reusable animations and postures.

Some challenges remain, for instance, TTS engine output uses the default audio system, and is not streamed through a virtual audio source in Unity's 3D environment. Thus, the 3D localization of the sound of the agent's speech in virtual space is not possible. This is important for making the experience immersive in VR settings. An exciting next step is the integration of mo-cap systems to allow for agents mirroring posture or behaviors of the agent. Some of the challenges that we faced in the implementation of the Unity embodiment, such as animation re-targeting and the generation of BML in the Unity Animation editor contribute in making this possible in the future.

Acknowledgements

This work has been supported by the following projects: EU-projects ARIA-VALUSPA-H2020, No 645378; EASEL-FP7, No 611971; And the Dutch projects COMMIT/R3D3 and Project Avatar.

References

1. Bruijnes, M.: Believable suspect agents: response and interpersonal style selection for an artificial suspect. Ph.D. thesis, University of Twente, Enschede (October 2016), http://doc.utwente.nl/101371/, sIKS dissertation series no. 2016-39
2. Hartholt, A., Traum, D., Marsella, S.C., Shapiro, A., Stratou, G., Leuski, A., Morency, L.P., Gratch, J.: All Together Now: Introducing the Virtual Human Toolkit. In: 13th International Conference on Intelligent Virtual Agents. Edinburgh, UK (Aug 2013), http://ict.usc.edu/pubs/All%20Together%20Now.pdf
3. Kopp, S., Krenn, B., Marsella, S., Marshall, A.N., Pelachaud, C., Pirker, H., Thórisson, K.R., Vilhjálmsson, H.H.: Towards a common framework for multimodal generation: the behavior markup language. In: Proceedings of the 6th international conference on Intelligent Virtual Agents. pp. 205–217. Springer-Verlag, Berlin, Heidelberg (2006)
4. Kopp, S., van Welbergen, H., Yaghoubzadeh, R., Buschmeier, H.: An architecture for fluid real-time conversational agents: integrating incremental output generation and input processing. Journal on Multimodal User Interfaces 8(1), 97–108 (2014)
5. Niewiadomski, R., Bevacqua, E., Mancini, M., Pelachaud, C.: Greta: an interactive expressive eca system. In: Proceedings of The 8th International Conference on Autonomous Agents and Multiagent Systems-Volume 2. pp. 1399–1400. International Foundation for Autonomous Agents and Multiagent Systems (2009)
6. Reidsma, D., Charisi, V., Davison, D., Wijnen, F., van der Meij, J., Evers, V., Cameron, D., Fernando, S., Moore, R., Prescott, T., et al.: The EASEL project: Towards educational human-robot symbiotic interaction. In: Conference on Biomimetic and Biohybrid Systems. pp. 297–306. Springer (2016)
7. Reidsma, D., Van Welbergen, H.: Multimodal plan representation for adaptable bml scheduling. In: In: Autonomous Agents and Multi-Agent Systems. Citeseer (2013)
8. Reidsma, D., van Welbergen, H.: AsapRealizer in practice–a modular and extensible architecture for a bml realizer. Entertainment computing 4(3), 157–169 (2013)
9. Shapiro, A.: Building a character animation system. In: International Conference on Motion in Games. pp. 98–109. Springer (2011)
10. Van Welbergen, H., Yaghoubzadeh, R., Kopp, S.: AsapRealizer 2.0: the next steps in fluent behavior realization for ECAs. In: International Conference on Intelligent Virtual Agents. pp. 449–462. Springer (2014)

Moral Conflicts in VR:
Addressing Grade Disputes with a Virtual Trainer

Jan Kolkmeier[1] ✉, Minha Lee[2], and Dirk Heylen[1]

[1] Human Media Interaction, University of Twente, The Netherlands
[j.kolkmeier; d.k.j.heylen]@utwente.nl
[2] Human Technology Interaction, the Technical University of Eindhoven, The Netherlands
m.lee@tue.nl

Abstract. A Virtual Trainer (VT) for moral expertise development can potentially contribute to organizational and personal moral well-being. In a pilot study
a prototype of the VT confronted university employees with a complaint from an
anonymous student on unfair grading: a plausible scenario. Addressing criticisms
from students may be a stressful situation for many teaching professionals. For
successful training, adapting the agent's strategy based on the performance of the
user is crucial. To this end, we further recorded a multimodal dataset of the interactions between the participants and the VT for future analysis. Participants saw
the value in a VT that lets them practice such encounters. What is more, many
participants felt truly taken aback when our VT announced that a student was
unhappy with them. We further describe a first look at the multimodal dataset.

Keywords: VR, skill training, moral expertise, moral conflict, gaze, multimodal

1 Introduction

An experienced teacher knows how to solve moral conflicts, and can do so with little mental effort and a good conscience. Those with less experience might experience
uncertainty when facing such conflicts, which causes moral stress [10]. In the workplace, moral stress has been shown to increase fatigue, lower job satisfaction, and lead
to higher turnover [4]. In the following we present the idea of a virtual trainer (VT) for
practicing moral conflicts to improve moral competences. In particular, we investigate
this in the context of teachers and supervisors in an academia.

A first evaluation of the concept was in the form of a pilot study using a Wizard-
of-Oz prototype. Qualitatively, we investigated how participants perceived the training
throughout several stages, and to what extent they could see themselves using such
a system at work. A second research question is in what ways we can automatically
determine the user's performance during such a training. How people react to the possibility that others view their actions as morally questionable may elicit emotional and
stress responses, the extent of which may be used as one dimension of their *performance*. While the reasoning process alone is often prioritized in moral decision-making
research, affective features that accompany moral reasoning are equally important and
mostly under-represented [7]. To this end, the interaction with the VT during the pilot
study also serves as a multimodal data-collection for future analysis, including gaze,
physiological signals and verbal and non-verbal aspects of speech.

© Springer International Publishing AG 2017
J. Beskow et al. (Eds.): IVA 2017, LNAI 10498, pp. 231–234, 2017.
DOI 10.1007/978-3-319-67401-8_28

2   Ethical Competences Training

Acquiring ethical expertise for work requires convergent and divergent experiences [3]. Convergent experiences depend on topically similar moral situations, such as a repeated experience of assessing students fairly. Divergent experiences are based on different ethical scenarios, such as in individual coaching, classroom conflict resolution or multi-cultural education. However, necessary experiences to build one's moral expertise are often limited, especially for those who are in early stages of their careers. A common conflict for university teaching staff is on grading students fairly. Quality feedback is important for progress and it is a prerequisite for academic assessment of students [1]. University tutors tend to believe that their feedback is more helpful than students who receive them [1], leading to grading conflicts [8].

A moral conflict is experienced when there are simultaneously competing obligations or principles that cannot all be fulfilled [9]. Moral stress occurs when decision makers face uncertainty on actions to take on ethical matters [10]. Workplace moral stress has been shown to increase fatigue, lower job satisfaction, and lead to higher turnover [4].

3   The Virtual Trainer Prototype

A prototype of the VT was developed that could be controlled in a Wizard-of-Oz setup (WoZ, [2]). With the prototype, users were lead through a natural conversation of three parts, as shown in Table 1. After some small talk on personal and work related matters, the goal was to expose users to relatable moral conflicts pertinent to their work as teachers or supervisors. Extra utterances were included to help elicit more elaborated responses (*How do you feel about that?*). The VT speaks with a TTS module and head-tilt and gaze behavior was implemented as described in [5] for the *accommodating* agent personality. Besides blinking, the agent would exhibit no other nonverbal behaviors.

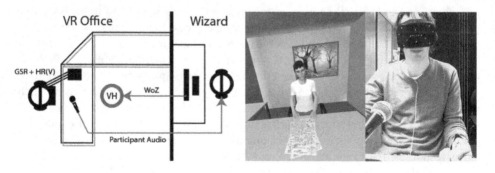

Fig. 1. The experiment setup (left). The participant is immersed in a virtual office that matches the real room, with the VT located across the desk (shown right).

Table 1. Some of the Agent's utterances in the WoZ setup per part of the conversation.

Part	Utterances
Small talk	What are you currently working on?; Could you describe a typical work day?
Teaching	Have you given lectures?; Can you tell me more about a recent student project?; How do you feel about being in a teaching position?
Conflict	According to the student you did not give timely feedback.; Have you had such complaints from students before?

4 Pilot Study & Data Collection

In the pilot study, participants engaged in a brief (8-10 minutes) interaction with our prototype. Exit interviews were conducted on how the VT was perceived throughout interaction. During the interaction, the topic of the conversation changed as a within subject variable from 'small-talk' to 'teaching' to 'grading', as described in Section 3. With several sensors, we recorded participants activity: Voice and video using a web-cam and studio microphone; Participants eye-gaze in the virtual world using the *FOVE* HMD; Heart rate and electrodermal activity using the *BioSemi ActiveTwo* system.

In total we recruited *42* participants (Age $M=31.19$ $SD=8.52$), of which twelve were female. All but one finished the entire experiment, questionnaire (not discussed in this work) and interview and were included in the qualitative analysis. In the resulting dataset, recordings of *32* participants (seven female) were completely successful in all modalities.

Exit Interviews Preparing for job-related morally stressful situations with a VT was seen as helpful. VTs were not seen to have the privilege of attributing blame on humans, while facilitating human communication and ethical expertise training was allowed. VTs that conversationally frame ethical dimensions of what is unacceptable or acceptable behavior was unfamiliar and thus confusing for many. In contrast, VTs that introduce moral situations as uninvolved third-parties were more likely to be accepted. When our VT pointed out that a student viewed a participant as unprofessional or unfair, participants shared that the experience became 'more realistic' or 'immersive', with the VT being 'critical' and trying to give 'blame', and many had to think back on their experiences with former students. This signified that both cognitive and moral aspects were essential to participants' thought processes.

Gaze Analysis We performed a first analysis on the eye-tracking data. Based on our previous work [6], our hypothesis was that participants' gaze behavior would be increasingly avoidant between the non-conflict and conflict parts of the dialog, due the personal, accusative nature of the scenario. We tested this with two measures: First, the proportions of time spent by participants fixated on agent's face (rather than averting gaze), and second, the duration of participants' fixations on the VT's face before avert-ing their gaze. We expected the turn of speech to primarily determine gaze behavior, thus, we looked at the gaze data within participants and VT turns respectively.

Indeed, we found that when the VT was talking, participants mostly looked directly at the agent ($M=.93$, $SD=.10$), whereas during their own turn, participants also spent some proportion of the time averting their gaze, ($M=.67$, $SD=.21$). When the VT was talking, participants also had longer continuous fixations on the agent's face ($M=4.33s$,

$SD=2.40s$). During their own turn, fixations on the VT were shorter ($M=1.86s$, $SD=1.14s$). Comparing the means between the three topics of conversation of the conversation however, we find little difference. A repeated measures ANOVA with a Greenhouse-Geisser correction confirmed this for both the proportion and duration measure.

5 Discussion & Conclusion

We introduced the concept of a virtual trainer for helping university teachers to develop and hone moral expertise. A qualitative evaluation based on exit interviews was made and a multimodal dataset of the interactions was recorded for future analysis. We further took a first look at the eye-tracking data.

The overall findings from the qualitative exit interviews suggest that future research on VTs as morally equal counterparts may be enlightening. In the interaction participants were engaged, albeit surprised. User-acceptance of technology has mostly envisioned friendly, cooperative agents, yet ethical competence development may involve stressful or conflicting situations in which users do not always have the upper hand.

We expected increased frequency of gaze aversion and overall less eye-contact with the agent when addressing the conflict. The preliminary analysis did not reveal any significant differences between the non-conflict and conflict related parts of the conversation. Future analysis of the dataset incorporating other modalities may lead to a better understanding to what extent the recorded cues may be used to determine performance of users of such a system.

References

1. Carless, D.: Differing perceptions in the feedback process. Studies in higher education 31(2) (2006) 219–233
2. Dahlbäck, N., Jönsson, A., Ahrenberg, L.: Wizard of Oz studies—why and how. Knowledge-based systems 6(4) (1993) 258–266
3. Dane, E., Sonenshein, S.: On the role of experience in ethical decision making at work: An ethical expertise perspective. Organizational Psychology Review 5(1) (2015) 74–96
4. DeTienne, K.B., Agle, B.R., Phillips, J.C., Ingerson, M.C.C.: The impact of moral stress compared to other stressors on employee fatigue, job satisfaction, and turnover: An empirical investigation. Journal of Business Ethics 110(3) (2012) 377–391
5. Gebhard, P., Baur, T., Damian, I., Mehlmann, G., Wagner, J., André, E.: Exploring interaction strategies for virtual characters to induce stress in simulated job interviews. In: Proc. of the 2014 int. conf. on Autonomous agents and multi-agent systems, Int. Found. for Autonomous Agents and Multiagent Systems (2014) 661–668
6. Kolkmeier, J., Vroon, J., Heylen, D.: Interacting with Virtual Agents in Shared Space: Single and Joint Effects of Gaze and Proxemics. In: International Conference on Intelligent Virtual Agents, Springer, Springer (2016) 1–14
7. Monin, B.B., Pizarro, D.A., Beer, J.S.: Deciding versus reacting: Conceptions of moral judgment and the reason-affect debate. Review of General Psychology 11(2) (2007) 99
8. Roosevelt, M.: Student expectations seen as causing grade disputes. The New York Times (2009) 12–13
9. Sinnott-Armstrong, W.: Moral dilemmas. Wiley Online Library (1988)
10. Waters, J.A., Bird, F.: The moral dimension of organizational culture. Journal of Business Ethics 6(1) (1987) 15–22

Evaluated by a Machine. Effects of Negative Feedback by a Computer or Human Boss

Nicole C. Krämer[1]✉, Lilly-Marie Leiße[1], Andrea Hollingshead[2] & Jonathan Gratch[2]

[1]University of Duisburg-Essen, Forsthausweg 2, 47057 Duisburg, Germany; [2]University of Southern California, USA
Nicole.kraemer Lilly-Marie.leisse @uni-due.de; aholling@usc.edu; gratch@ict.usc.edu

Abstract. In today´s remote working environments that include tasks given and performed via the Internet, people will encounter computer bosses that supervise their work. There is no knowledge on whether people will accept (negative) feedback that is given by an autonomous agent instead of a human. In a 2x2 between subject online experiment 183 participants performed a proofreading task and received either emotional or factual feedback by a human or computer boss. Results indicate that while the bosses´ behavior affects perceived warmness, human likeness and perceived psychological safety in the sense that factual feedback is perceived as more positive, there was only one significant result for the manipulation of the boss with regard to the perception of human-likeness.

Keywords: Feedback, media equation, CASA, work, computer boss

1 Differential effects by Human and Computer Bosses?

Intelligent technical applications are entering our lives: Smart home applications, robots for medical healthcare or as co-workers in our jobs are only a few examples. Especially the emerging application of artificial entities in organizational and operational contexts and their effects when they take the role of a supervisor needs to be scrutinized. It has to be examined whether from the perspective of the employee, a computer boss is suited better or worse to master fragile interactions such as giving negative feedback. As early as 1999, it was argued that interactions with computers could result in beneficial consequences such as increased psychological safety (i.e., the certainty that the other will respond in a favorable way when one reports a mistake) [1].

Several findings demonstrate differences between the interaction with a computer and a real human. For example, some studies [2] reveal that people self-disclose more towards a computer than towards a real person. The fear of being judged is lower and people deliver more honest answers. Further studies show that participants experience less negative emotions and report less desire for revenge and retaliation [3]. On the

J. Beskow et al. (Eds.): IVA 2017, LNAI 10498, pp. 235-238, 2017.
DOI 10.1007/978-3-319-67401-8_29

other hand, numerous studies following the media equation approach find that people´s social reactions to computers and humans are very much alike [4]. Additionally, other findings indicate that a social reaction towards a computer is rather dependent on the amount of social cues displayed by the computer than on the knowledge whether one interacts with a human or a computer [5]. In order to contribute to the controversy on computer agents´ abilities to evoke social effects and to provide insights for the emerging applied area of computer bosses, the present research analyzes whether computer and human bosses evoke similar or different effects and/or whether it is their behavior that matters.

2   Method

Participants. 183 participants (74 females, Mage = 34.20, age range: 20-69 years) were considered for analysis (after excluding 19 due to lack of understanding).

Design. A 2x2 between-subjects design was used. The first manipulation concerned the nature of the supervisor: in one condition participants were instructed that they were interacting with a mediated real human boss, people in the other condition were led to believe their boss was an autonomously acting computer agent. The second manipulation was a distinction between factual and emotional feedback in reaction to the performance in a proofreading task. In all conditions, participants received the same negative, bogus feedback. The communication between the employee and the supervisor proceeded only via text messages. A picture of the particular boss was included in order to remind the participants of their interlocutor during the procedure and increase social presence (Figure 1). Two different pictures were used in each condition to guarantee generalizability.

Fig. 1. Fictitious pictures of the human bosses (left) and computer bosses (right)

Procedure. The whole study was processed online. Depending on condition, participants received different instructions: "Today, you are being supervised by another person over the web [computer boss]. This is another Turker [an artificially intelligent program] that has been trained to execute all the tasks and functions that a normal boss would do. [...] Please attend to your [computer] bosses instructions."

After this description of the situation, the remainder of the survey was supervised by the [computer] boss. The participants received a text with numerous spelling errors and were asked to detect all errors. After this, the participants received a graphical presentation of their performance on a scale (with a low score of 3.5 of 10 possible points). Additionally, the boss commented on the performance either in an emotional or factual way. "[...] As you can already see at the chart, your performance was not that good at all. *It is vividly shown there.* [*I am really upset.*] Actually you are just above the lower third. [...] *Many things went wrong.* [*You disappoint me a lot.*] Seems you did not work hard enough and *that was not the aim of this task* [*that is embarrassing*]. [...]. *Take my advice* [*Don't blame yourself.*]." Afterwards, participants filled in the questionnaires.

Measures. All questions were directly administered by the boss.

Evaluation of the boss. Two questionnaires were included to gain information about the perception concerning the boss. Twelve items measured the leading ability of the boss (e.g., "I create a good working atmosphere for you".) The items were rated on a seven-point scale from strongly disagree (1) to strongly agree (7) ($\alpha = .961$; M = 2.61, SD = 1.257). In the second questionnaire, participants were asked to rate the personality of their boss with 13 item pairs (e.g., warm – cold, helpful – hindering; $\alpha = .891$; M = 4.85, SD = 1.035). A factor analysis yielded three factors (warmness, efficiency, human-likeness, 70.80% of variance).

Social presence. The interaction were evaluated by four statements of the Social Presence Scale [6] such as: "During the interaction, how much did you feel as if someone was talking to you?" The statements were rated on a nine-point Likert scale from not at all (1) to very much (9) ($\alpha = .768$; M = 6.24, SD = 1.704).

Psychological safety. A slightly reworded version of the Psychological Safety Scale [7] was included (e.g., "I value others' unique skills and talents"). Each statement was evaluated on a seven-point scale from strongly disagree (1) to strongly agree (7) ($\alpha = .865$; M = 3.05, SD = 1.144).

3   Results

Concerning the evaluation of the boss, there was no significant main of the nature of the boss nor of the nature of the feedback (nor an interaction effect). There was, however, an effect on the perceived personality of the boss: Concerning the first factor "warmness", one significant main effect was found for the feedback condition ($F(1, 163) = 7.497$, $p = .007$, $\eta2 = .044$): Participants in the emotional feedback condition (M = 4.93, SD = 1.27) rated the warmness of the boss significantly lower than in the factual feedback condition (M = 5.46, SD = 1.06). However, no significant main effect was found for the boss condition. Also, there were two main effects for the factor "human likeness": The first one ($F(1, 163) = 27.557$, $p < .001$, $\eta2 = .145$) showed that the computer boss (M = 5.35, SD = 1.387) was rated significantly less human-like than the human boss (M = 4.21, SD = 1.520). The second main effect referred to a significant difference between the two kinds of feedback ($F(1, 163) = 6.224$, $p = .014$, $\eta2 = .037$). Participants in the factual feedback condition (M = 4.5, SD = 1.61) rated the human likeness of the boss significant lower than participants in the emotional feedback condition (M = 4.99, SD = 1.49).

For psychological safety, a two-way independent analysis of variance revealed a significant main effect for the feedback condition ($F(1, 166) = 6.649$, $p = .011$, $\eta2 = .039$). Participants in the factual feedback condition (M = 3.27, SD = 1.212) reported a significant higher amount of psychological safety compared to participants in the emotional feedback condition (M = 2.82, SD = 1.024). There was no main effect for the boss condition nor an interaction effect.

Both, nature of the boss and nature of the feedback had no influence on perceived social presence. Finally, the nature of the boss did not influence participants' performance.

4 Discussion

The present study focused on the question whether a computer boss supervising a task and providing negative feedback will be perceived differently from a human boss. To this aim we had people in an M-Turk setting perform a task on which they were subsequently given negative feedback in either an emotional or factual way by either a human or computer boss. As was already observed in prior studies [5] the information on whether the boss was a human or a computer did not make a difference. After the reception of negative feedback the human and the computer boss were evaluated similarly – in general and also with regard to the sub-factors warmth and efficiency. Also, the perceived psychological safety and performance did not differ, indicating that a human boss is not per se perceived as providing more psychologically safe behavior in times of need. However, this also implies that a computer boss is not automatically perceived as a "better boss" as other prior studies seemed to suggest. The study again demonstrated that behavior matters and yields more effects than the nature of the interlocutor. Results indicate that independent of whether the boss is human or artificial factual feedback is perceived as more beneficial as emotional feedback – in the sense that people perceived the boss warmer, more human-like and felt more psychological safety.

References

1. Edmondson, A.: Psychological Safety and Learning Behavior in Work Teams. In: Administrative Science Quarterly, 44(2), 350 (1999)
2. Lucas, G. M., Gratch, J., King, A., & Morency, L.-P.: It's only a computer: Virtual humans increase willingness to disclose. In: Computers in Human Behavior, 37, 94-100 (2014)
3. Kim, D., Frank, M. G., & Kim, S. T.: Emotional display behavior in different forms of Computer Mediated Communication. In: Computers in Human Behavior, 30, 222-229 (2014)
4. Reeves, B., & Nass, C. I.: The media equation: How people treat computers, television, and new media like real people and places. Stanford, Calif., New York: CSLI Publications; Cambridge University Press (1996)
5. von der Pütten, A. M., Krämer, N. C., Gratch, J., & Kang, S.-H.: "It doesn't matter what you are!" Explaining social effects of agents and avatars. In: Computers in Human Behavior, 26(6), 1641-1650 (2010)
6. Lee, K. M., & Nass, C.: Designing social presence of social actors in human computer interaction. Conference on Human Factors in Computing Systems - Proceedings, 289-296 (2003)
7. Baer, M., & Frese, M.: Innovation is not enough: Climates for initiative and psychological safety, process innovations, and firm performance. In: Journal of Organizational Behavior, 24(1), 45-68 (2003)

A Web-Based Platform for Annotating Sentiment-Related Phenomena in Human-Agent Conversations

Caroline Langlet[1] ✉, Guillaume Dubuisson Duplessis[1], and Chloé Clavel[1]

LTCI, Télécom ParisTech, Université Paris-Saclay, 75013, Paris, France,
caroline.langlet@telecom-paristech.fr

Abstract. This paper introduces a web-based platform dedicated to the annotation of sentiment-related phenomena in human-agent conversations. The platform focuses on verbal content and deliberately sets aside non-verbal features. It is designed for managing two dialogue features: adjacency pair and conversation progression. Two annotation tasks are considered: (i) the detection of sentiment expressions, (ii) the ranking of user's preferences. These two tasks focus on a set of specific targets. With this demonstration, we aim to introduce this platform to a large scientific audience and to get feedback for future improvements. Our long-term goal is to make the platform available as open-source tool.

Keywords: verbal content annotation, virtual agent, sentiment analysis

1 Introduction

In the research field of embodied conversational agents, the detection of sentiment-related phenomena is a challenging task contributing to the improvement of human-agent interactions. Verbal content is more and more integrated [4]. Developing a detection system of verbal expressions of sentiments in human-agent conversations requires annotated corpora. Such corpora are rare and managing annotation campaigns appears as the first step in the development of a detection system. In order to make easier the implementation of datasets, we have created a web-based platform focusing on the verbal expression of sentiment and suited to transcriptions of human-agent conversations.

2 A Platform Focusing on Verbal Content and Conversational Structure

Focus on Verbal Content. Our annotation platform deals with verbal content, without non-verbal context. The annotator has only access to manually transcribed conversations. In this way, we aim to get information about the verbal form of the sentiment-related phenomena, for helping the design and evaluation of algorithms grounded on either machine learning or rule-based models.

© Springer International Publishing AG 2017
J. Beskow et al. (Eds.): IVA 2017, LNAI 10498, pp. 239–242, 2017.
DOI 10.1007/978-3-319-67401-8_30

Dealing with Conversational Structure. To the best of our knowledge, the sentiment analysis research does not provide annotation sets in human-agent conversation context. The existing annotation tools are mostly designed for non-conversational texts and do not deal with the specific features of conversation (see [6] and [7]). In order to fill this gap, we give attention to two important dialogue features: adjacency pairs and conversation progression. First, adjacency pairs are defined as the minimal annotation context (see Area 2 in Figure 1). Second, the annotator has the previous speech turns and their annotation (see Area 1 in Figure 1). She/he can keep in mind past information of the conversation progress while annotating a specific adjacency pair.

Simplifying the Annotation Task. Annotating sentiment-related phenomena is a challenging task. It depends on the personal subjectivity and interpretation of verbal content. This platform provides a frame which guides the annotator and simplifies the annotation process. No span of text or complex semantic features have to be defined: each adjacency pair is displayed with questionnaires asking information about sentiment expressions.

A Generic Framework. The framework relies on standard web technologies (PHP, HTML, JAVASCRIPT) and can deal with various dyadic human-agent conversation corpora. For using our annotation platform, a simple pre-processing of the data is needed to: (i) uniquely identify conversations (via a unqiue ID), (ii) turn each conversation into a sequence of adjacency pairs (first, the agent's speech turn, then the user's speech turn), (iii) in the transcription, no paralinguistic annotations are allowed, (iv) a specific set of targets must be defined (the targets can be either artefacts or animated entities).

3 Annotating User's Sentiments and Preferences

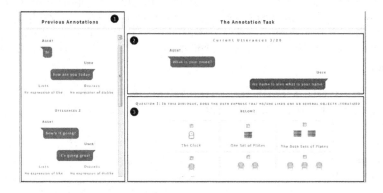

Fig. 1. Platform Overview

The platform deals with two different annotation tasks which are both key tasks in the research field of virtual agent (see [1] and [3]): (i) the detection of sentiments related-phenomena toward specific objects; (ii) the ranking of user's preferences. As we consider that it is too difficult for a single annotator to concurrently decide which object is the target of a sentiment and which one is the most liked, the two tasks are strictly independent from each other and are assigned to different annotators. For each task[1], the framework is divided in two parts: first, the current annotation task which concerns a specific pair (Area 2 and 3 in Fig. 1); second, the history (Area 1 in Fig. 1) which comprises all the previous pairs and the related annotations.

Task 1. At each adjacency pair, the annotator has to detect an expression of sentiment targeting specific objects by filling in a questionnaire, split in two questions. The first question (see Figure 2) concerns presence of positive sentiment-related phenomena, the second, the presence of negative sentiment-related phenomena.

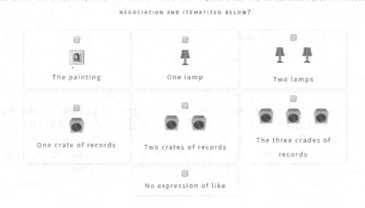

Fig. 2. First questionnaire of Task 1

The user's sentiments related phenomena toward an object may change during the conversation. As the task is to find expressions of sentiment within a specific pair, the annotator can check a positive expression of sentiment toward an object even if a negative sentiment toward the same object was previously noted. In this way, we will be able to analyse user's sentiments along the conversation.

Task 2. For ranking preferences, each object needs to be scored. The score depends on the number of objects comprised in the set. In the demonstration, we

---

[1] perso.telecom-paristech.fr/ langlet/annotationNegociation/task1, the task 2 at perso.telecom-paristech.fr/ langlet/annotationNegociation/task2

use a score from 1 to 3 because the annotator has to rank preferences toward three different objects. Each score indicates the position of the object in the scale of the user's preferences. For example, when the user verbally expresses a preference for a painting over records and lamps, the annotator can attribute to the painting the score 3 and to the lamps and the records, the score 1. Similarily to Task 1, user's preferences may change during the conversation. As an annotation is asked for each pair, the annotator will be able to make modifications, that could be appropriate, to any score. In this way, we can follow the evolution of user's preferences throughout the conversation.

Demonstration Outline. The demonstration will be an opportunity to test the platform with native English speakers and non-expert annotators. The visitors will be invited to annotate few adjacency pairs of a human-agent corpus [2]. In this corpus, the user and the virtual agent are negotiating over six valuable objects. "They are told that their task is to decide how to divide up these six items with another participant" [5]. Finally, by presenting the platform to an international and experienced audience, we aim to get feedback about usability and genericity of the platform.

Acknowledgements

We warmly thank Jonathan Gratch and David DeVault for sharing the negotiation corpora.

References

1. Clavel, C., Callejas, Z.: Sentiment analysis: from opinion mining to human-agent interaction. In: Affective Computing, IEEE Transactions on. vol. PP (2015)
2. DeVault, D., Mell, J., Gratch, J.: Toward natural turn-taking in a virtual human negotiation agent. In: AAAI Spring Symposium on Turn-taking and Coordination in Human-Machine Interaction. AAAI Press, Stanford, CA (2015)
3. Glas, N., Pelachaud, C.: User engagement and preferences in information-giving chat with virtual agents. In: Workshop on Engagement in Social Intelligent Virtual Agents (ESIVA). pp. 33–40 (2015)
4. Langlet, C., Clavel, C.: Grounding the detection of the users likes and dislikes on the topic structure of human-agent interactions. Knowledge-Based Systems 106, 116–124 (2016)
5. Nazari, Z., Lucas, G.M., Gratch, J.: Opponent Modeling for Virtual Human Negotiators. In: Intelligent Virtual Agents. vol. 9238, pp. 39–49. Springer International Publishing, Delft, Netherlands (Aug 2015)
6. Poignant, J.: The CAMOMILE Collaborative Annotation Platform for Multi-modal, Multi-lingual and Multi-media Documents. In: LREC 2016 Conference. Portoroz, Slovenia (May 2016)
7. Stenetorp, P., Pyysalo, S., Topić, G., Ohta, T., Ananiadou, S., Tsujii, J.: Brat: A web-based tool for nlp-assisted text annotation. In: Proceedings of the Demonstrations at the 13th Conference of the European Chapter of the Association for Computational Linguistics. pp. 102–107. EACL '12, Association for Computational Linguistics, Stroudsburg, PA, USA (2012)

Does a robot tutee increase children's engagement in a learning-by-teaching situation?

Markus Lindberg[1] ✉, Kristian Månsson[1], Birger Johansson[1], Agneta Gulz[1], and Christian Balkenius[1]

[1] Lund University Cognitive Science, Lund, Sweden
markus.lindberg.340@student.lu.se; tkman85@gmail.com; {birger.johansson, agneta.gulz,christian.balkenius}@lucs.lu.se

Abstract. This paper presents initial attempts to combine a humanoid robot with the teachable agent approach. Several design choices are discussed, including the decision to use a robot instead of a virtual agent and which behaviours to implement in the robot. A pilot study explored how the interaction with a robot seemed to influence children's engagement as well as their attribution of mental states to a robot and to a virtual agent. Eight children participated and the interaction was measured via an observational protocol and a conversational interview. A main outcome was large individual differences between the children's interaction with the robot compared to the virtual agent.

Keywords: · Learning-by-teaching · Virtual agent · robot

1   Introduction/Background

The observation that teaching is a way of learning is at least 2000 years old [1]. About twenty years ago this approach – learning-by-teaching – was implemented in a digital form, where human students take on the teacher role and instruct a digital tutee or so called teachable agent, TA. There is rich evidence for the effectiveness of this pedagogical approach, both in terms of learning outcomes and motivational effects.

TA-based software seems to draw on socio-cognitive mechanisms that increase engagement in the task [2,3] Importantly, students seem to take responsibility for their TA's learning. In a study by [2] both 10-11- and 13-14-year-olds spent more time on learning activities when their task was to teach a TA compared to when learning for themselves. The study also provided evidence that the 10-11-year-olds treated their TAs as social entities by attributing mental states and responsibility to them.

In addition, results from several studies indicate that the central educational phenomenon of metacognition can be boosted by LBT-software. Students are encouraged to reflect on their TA's thinking and accuracy, and subsequently also apply metacognition to their own understanding [3,4].

In recent years learning-by-teaching with a robot, instead of a virtual agent, has attracted increasing interest. It has been theoretically discussed [5,6], and the pedagogical potentials of robot tutees have been highlighted. A robot is obviously more suita-

© Springer International Publishing AG 2017
J. Beskow et al. (Eds.): IVA 2017, LNAI 10498, pp. 243-246, 2017.
DOI 10.1007/978-3-319-67401-8_31

ble than a virtual agent for learning fields with a physical or mechanical component such as table tennis or handwriting, but there are also other potential advantages to be gained from the physical embodiment of a robot. Both authors [5,6] discuss how robots have a greater possibility to use nonverbal channels for communication, such as posture, personal space, gaze, pointing and touch. Lemaignan et al. [7] carried out a study where children taught handwriting to a robot. A first study in a larger school-class indicated that the robotic system was accepted by the students and kept them focussed and engaged for short sessions. Later case studies showed that the system could be used as a tool for children with different attentional impairments, as they would accept the robot, could carry out longer learning sessions, and adapted themselves to the role as a teacher.

Our pilot study regards a comparison between a robot tutee and a virtual agent tutee with respect to effects on learners (in the role as teachers). Engagement and attribution of mental states were key areas of interest.

2   System and study design

The study made use of the play-and-learn-game Magical Garden [4,8] where young children learn early math by teaching a virtual agent in animal shape, for instance the panda Panders (Fig 1). In the robot version, Panders was replaced by Epi, a humanoid robot developed at Lund University Cognitive Science (Fig 2). The robot was designed to give the impression of being a child while still being decidedly robotic. Consequently, a simple geometric, almost rectangular, shape has been use as the basis for the head. The eyes are relatively large, suggesting child like proportions. The head has four degrees of freedom in the neck and eyes and it can also change eye-color and pupil size to identify different moods.

Fig 1. A virtual TA, thinking about a problem.

Fig 2. The robot, thinking about a problem.

In the robot version the virtual agent was blanked out, and the behaviours of the agent was sent as commands via http requests. This allowed for a simple solution to behavioural timing, as the robot only needed to receive all commands and synchronize each one with a predetermined behavioural pattern. The same was done with sounds, so that any command that should have triggered a sound made by the virtual agent instead triggered the activation of a sound file in the robot. The following seven behaviours were identified as relevant to re-implement in the robot:

Idle was designed to be the most basic mode in the robot, used whenever nothing else was displayed. This included pale blue eyes, random gaze shifts and changes in pupillary size, and movement of the eyes. *Speech* caused the robot to turn its head towards the participant and produce a synchronized blinking pattern with its mouth. *Acknowledgement* made the robot turn to the participant with yellow eyes. *Content, happy,* and *exhilarated* all built on the same base behaviour, which included yellow eyes and pupillary dilation. While *content* only used the baseline behaviour, *happy* added simple movements of the head, and e*xhilarated* used the baseline and even wider movements than *happy*. Finally, *sad* involved changing the eye-colour to a darker blue, moving the head down, and turning both eyes inwards.

The system architecture was primarily the same for both the robot and virtual agent designs. There were, however, dimensions that could not be kept the same. An example of this is the positioning of the agent. The virtual agent was always turned towards the student, but the robot had to be midway between both the participant and the game. This was necessary for allowing attention to be directed between both the game and the participant.

Eight children, age 5-9 (mean age 7), two girls and six boys, participated in the study. Each child taught both the robot and the virtual agent systems, with the order being randomized. They started playing the game and teaching their tutee – robot or agent – while the examiner filled out an observational protocol. After finishing two games, the game was closed and a conversational interview was carried out. Following the interview, the child started teaching the other tutee.

The interaction was measured using an observational protocol according to which the following was noted: Willingness to continue for another five minutes after an initial trial; displayed positive emotions during the interaction (e.g. happiness) and/or displayed negative emotions (e.g. irritation); overall attention and focus; displayed changes in teaching methodology; utterances regarding success and failure of the robot or agent as it tried on its own; utterances regarding success and failures in teaching the agent or robot; manner of talking about and addressing the agent/robot.

Another tool used in the study was a conversational interview. The questions used in the interview were based on a translated version of the godspeed questionnaire [9], with the goal to measure attitudes towards the tutee – robot and/or agent. The questionnaire is used to evaluate questions like: whether one finds the robot/agent to behave human-like versus machinelike (anthropomorphism); whether it seems lively versus lazy (animacy); whether it is nice versus not nice (likeability); if it is knowledgeable versus ignorant (perceived intelligence); whether it feels relaxing to be around the agent/robot versus tense (perceived safety).

3   Results and discussion

Some interesting differences were noted between children interacting with a robot TA and a virtual TA appear. Based on the observational data, the robot seems capable of attracting attention, something which should be useful for engagement. It does, however, also tend to lose it partway into the interaction. As for the ability to convey mental states, the robot at least seems to be comparable to that of the virtual agent, with certain children choosing to speak to it in a teaching manner. It is, however, possible that there is a dissonance between picturing the robot as a student and the idea that a robot is like a computer in that it has access to a multitude of information. Individuality appears to be central here, with children showing large variations in both engagement and ability to attribute mental states. Data from the conversational interview showed overall positive judgments for both the robot and the virtual agent. Individual differences were also observed here, especially in judgments of perceived intelligence. It was observed that the robot received lower score for anthropomorphism compared to the agent, but the high scores on animacy make these results harder to interpret. For more details on the study and its results, see [10].

Some improvements on the robotic systems as well as the study design are called for. Using motion capture technology, it should be possible to make more fitting and natural behaviors for the robot. Gaze behaviors such as gaze aversion could also be used to improve the interaction. Notably, the virtual agent displays a simple form of joint attention. A fuller study should also involve more children and longer player sessions, as well as children of a younger age-group.

References

1. Lucius Annaeus Seneca, Moral letters to Lucilius I, 7. 8
2. Chase, C., Chin, D., Oppezzo, M., & Schwartz, D. (2009). Teachable agents and the protégé effect: Increasing the effort towards learning. *J. of Science Education and Technology, 18*, 334– 352.
3. Lindström, P., Gulz, A., Haake, M., & Sjödén, B. (2011). Matching and mismatching between pedagogical design principles and actual practices of play. *J. of Computer Assisted Learning, 27*, 90–102.
4. Haake, M., Axelsson, A., Clausen-Bruun, M., & Gulz, A. (2015). Scaffolding mentalizing via a play-&-learn game for preschoolers. *Computers & Education*, 90, 13-23.
5. Werfel, J. (2013). Embodied teachable agents: Learning by teaching Robots. In *Proc. 13th Int. Conf. on Intelligent Autonomous Systems*.
6. Pareto, L. (2017). Robot as Tutee. In *Robotics in Education* (pp. 271-277). Springer International Publishing.
7. Lemaignan, S., Jacq, A., Hood, D., Garcia, F., Paiva, A., & Dillenbourg, P. (2016). Learning by teaching a robot: The case of handwriting. *IEEE Robotics & Automation Magazine, 23*(2), 56-66.
8. Husain, L., Gulz, A., & Haake, M. (2015). Supporting Early Math – Rationales and Requirements. *J. of Computers in Mathematics and Science Teaching*, 34(4), 409-429.
9. Bartneck, C., Croft, E., & Kulic, D. (2008, March). Measuring the anthropomorphism, animacy, likeability, perceived intelligence and perceived safety of robots. In *Metrics for HRI workshop, technical report* (Vol. 471, pp. 37-44).
10. Lindberg, M. (2017). Design and Influence of a Robot as Teachable Agent in an Educational Game. Master thesis. Lund University.

The Expression of Mental States in a Humanoid Robot

Markus Lindberg, Hannes Sandberg, Marcus Liljenberg, Max Eriksson, Birger
Johansson, and Christian Balkenius ✉

Lund University Cognitive Science, Sweden
christian.balkenius@lucs.lu.se

Abstract. We explore to what degree movement together with facial
features in a humanoid robot, such as eyes and mouth, can be used to
convey mental states. Several animation variants were iteratively tested
in a series of experiments to reach a set of five expressive states that
can be reliably expressed by the robot. These expressions combine biologically motivated cues such as eye movements and pupil dilation with
elements that only have a conventional significance, such as changes in
eye color.

Keywords: mental states, emotions, humanoid robot

1 Introduction

What features of a robot facilitate natural interaction with humans? It has been
claimed that a human appearance is easier to interact with [3]. Features such
as eyes and mouth convey much information, and these can be used by humans
to infer different mental states and alter human perception [2]. For example.
robots with big round irises are judged as more friendly by humans [4] and
gaze has a strong influence on a human interacting with the robot [1]. In a
series of experiments, we developed and evaluated a number of expressions of
mental states in the humanoid robot Epi. This robot has been designed to give
a childlike impression while still being decidedly robotic. The robot has two
degrees of freedom in the neck and each eye can move laterally. In addition, the
irises can change color and the pupils can dilate and contract. There is also a
grid of LEDs that resembles a mouth that can be animated by changing their
colour and intensity.

2 Methods

A set of candidate mental states were selected to be tested in the robot: The **neutral** state was designed to include a minimal amount of communicative features.
The eyes used white for color at 50% intensity. No light or color was used in the
mouth. Pupils were kept at an initial state, with no change in size. No movement

© Springer International Publishing AG 2017
J. Beskow et al. (Eds.): IVA 2017, LNAI 10498, pp. 247-250, 2017.
DOI 10.1007/978-3-319-67401-8_32

was included in either neck or eyes. Blinking was included. (Fig. 1A). A throbber effect in the eyes of Epi was used to convey the mental state of **thinking**.
Throbber was implemented by lighting blue LEDs with different intensity in a
serial manner. The pupils were held at constant size and that blinking was not
used. This mapping relates to computers rather than humans. This mental state
also included an upwards movement of the entire head. **Anger**, was displayed
by constricting the pupils. In addition, red eyes convey anger more effectively
than white. Although this has no biological counterpart, angry robots are con-
ventionally shown with red eyes. Intensity was kept at the baseline value at 50%.
Color in the mouth was not used, but blinking was included. In addition, the
head moved back and fourth sideways (Fig. 1D & 2A). The third mental state,
happy, followed the same principles as the design of angry. Pupils were programmed to dilate. The color used was green, on the basis that it was opposite
of red in the sense of traffic light coding. Mouth color was excluded again. No
movement was used for the eyes but the neck moved upwards. Blinking was also
included (Fig. 1C). For the fourth state, **confused**, the eye colors were changed
to red, relying on the mapping that red means something has gone wrong. In
combination with this, movement of the neck from left to right in a head-shaking
manner were used to further display that a problem had taken place. Blinking
and pupillary change was not included. The final mental state, **sad**, directed
both eyes so they focused inwards to make the robot appear sad. Blue eyes with
an with average intensity was used. A movement of the neck, directed right and
down, was used. Blinking was also included (Fig. 1B).

To test the different behaviors, 20 participants were recruited, all of which
were found on the university grounds at Lunds University. No reward was promised
for participating. Participant were asked to sit in a chair facing Epi. Between
Epi and the participant was a paper with different mental states written on it,
and five pieces of paper with the numbers one to five written on them. The
participant was asked to display a number, and then watch Epi as a behavioral
pattern was presented. Following this, the participant was asked to place the
piece of paper at the written mental state that they felt corresponded best with
Epi's behavioral pattern. Participants were allowed to display the same number
several time before making a decision, and could change their choices during the
test. Once all five pieces of papers had been placed on the paper with mental

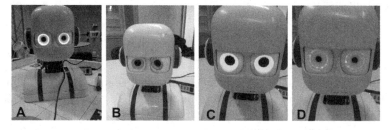

Fig. 1: The robot Epi. A: neutral. B: sad. C: happy. D: angry.

states, the second part of the experiment started where the participants were asked to judge to what degree they felt each behavior captured the mental state they had attributed to it. This judgment was made on a 1 to 5 scale.

3 Results and Discussion

The results showed that at least two of the five designed mental states can be easily identified and have a high degree of distinctness (Fig. 3). Both *angry* and *sad* were correctly identified by all 20 participants, and received values of distinctness close to 5. The variability regarding distinctness was also kept reasonably low for both states, indicating that close to all participants considered these states to be very distinct. The majority of participants were able to identify *thinking*, *happy* and *confused*, but judgment of distinctness was about average. The variability in participants judgment of distinctness is also very large, which shows that the mental states created likely won't be universally useful. Some participants, however, considered these states to be highly distinct, and further testing might reveal that some features included in these states can be used to infer the mental state. An example of this was observed when testing the mental state *happy*, which several people mentioned became much more distinct once they had come to realize that the mouth was indeed lit. The mouth used in this experiment was very limited in its design, and even when the robot was looking up it was often difficult to notice the light. For *thinking*, the computer metaphor used in the current design is limited. Adding another feature frequently associated with loading, in the form of a loading bar, did not increase its usefulness as a tool for conveying thinking in the robot. Unfortunately, *confused* is not efficient in conveying the mental state. After trying three significantly different designs and still not getting any improvements to the results, it seems reasonable to assume that this mental state is difficult to display with the tools available.

While the results are very positive, it is important to mention that the test allowed for different methods of exclusion. The participants knew beforehand which mental states were to appear, and they could only connect one behavioral pattern to one mental state. Even if a mental state was not very clear it would

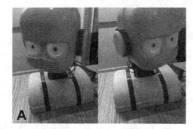

Fig. 2: A: The implementation of a shaking head movement in the mental state *angry*. B, C: Two different designs of smiling. The left one was superior and therefore used in later experiments.

 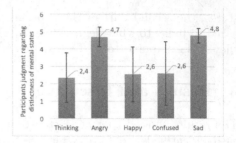

Fig. 3: Left: Results from the experiment. Each bar represents a correct mapping between designed mental state and interpreted mental state. Right: The mean value of the participants judgment regarding distinctness of the five mental states represented with a numeric rating scale, where 5 was very distinct and 1 was indistinct. Also including standard deviation.

still be possible for the participant to reach a correct conclusion by excluding behaviors that had already been mapped to another state. Considering that the participants were also allowed to change their decisions after having seen all mental states, and could see each mental state more than once, it seems likely that this method could be used. Not knowing if the mental states could be identified without methods of exclusion makes the gathered results less useful. It is possible that the mental state can not be properly distinguished on their own, and if this is the case they would be much less useful in a more natural situation. An attempt to reduce this problem was to include the scale of distinctness. If a mental state is rated as highly distinct by the participants, it seems more likely that it would be able to convey the correct mental state in a natural setting. These ratings might arguably also be affected by knowing which states exist beforehand, but it seems likely that state which received both high values for identification and distinctness should be employing a good design.

References

1. Breazeal, C.: Toward sociable robots. Robotics and autonomous systems 42(3), 167–175 (2003)
2. Foerster, F., Bailly, G., Elisei, F.: Impact of iris size and eyelids coupling on the estimation of the gaze direction of a robotic talking head by human viewers. In: Humanoid Robots (Humanoids), 2015 IEEE-RAS 15th International Conference on. pp. 148–153. IEEE (2015)
3. Gielniak, M.J., Liu, C.K., Thomaz, A.L.: Generating human-like motion for robots. The International Journal of Robotics Research 32(11), 1275–1301 (2013)
4. Onuki, T., Ishinoda, T., Tsuburaya, E., Miyata, Y., Kobayashi, Y., Kuno, Y.: Designing robot eyes for communicating gaze. Interaction Studies 14(3), 451–479 (2013)

You Can Leave Your Head On

Attention Management and Turn-Taking in Multi-party Interaction with a Virtual Human/Robot Duo

Jeroen Linssen ✉, Meike Berkhoff, Max Bode, Eduard Rens,
Mariët Theune ✉, and Daan Wiltenburg

Human Media Interaction
University of Twente
Drienerlolaan 5, 7522 NB Enschede
The Netherlands
J.M.Linssen@utwente.nl, M.Theune@utwente.nl

Abstract. In two small studies, we investigated how a virtual human/ robot duo can complement each other in joint interaction with one or more users. The robot takes care of turn management while the virtual human draws attention to the robot. Our results show that having the virtual human address the robot, highlights the latter's role in the interaction. Having the robot nonverbally indicate the intended addressee of a question asked by the virtual human proved successful in all cases when the robot was first addressed by the virtual human.

1 Introduction

In this paper, we investigate attention management and turn-taking in interactions with R3D3: the Rolling Receptionist Robot with Double Dutch Dialogue, which is intended to serve as an assistant to visitors of public places. R3D3 consists of a robot and a virtual human, which is carried on a tablet by the robot (see Fig. 1a). The virtual human can interact with people using Dutch spoken language. The robot does not speak, but takes on a supportive role by providing nonverbal cues with its eyes and head. However, our initial experiences with R3D3 showed that when talking to the virtual human, users tended to ignore the robot, putting the robot's added value for the conversation into question [3].

Our main research question for this paper is therefore how we can give the robot a clear role in the interaction. Specifically, we investigate how the virtual human can draw attention to the robot and how the robot can manage turn taking in multi-party conversation. Turn-taking, between humans [6] as well as between humans and both virtual characters [1] and social robots [2], is seen as an important factor in managing fluent interactions. Especially in crowded places, interactions between robots and multiple users can benefit from turn management through gaze, both for enabling a robot to express its intentions and controlling users' attention [2, 7].

Below we describe two small studies we carried out to investigate attention management and turn-taking with our virtual human/robot duo.

© Springer International Publishing AG 2017
J. Beskow et al. (Eds.): IVA 2017, LNAI 10498, pp. 251-254, 2017.
DOI 10.1007/978-3-319-67401-8_33

2 Study 1: Attention Management

The first study involved interactions between the virtual human (VH), the robot and a single user. The VH talked to the user about the research topics of our department, while the robot nonverbally supported the VH's utterances, nodding in confirmation and showing emotions in line with what the VH said. We used a Wizard-of-Oz setup, with a hidden experimenter controlling R3D3's behaviour.

The interactions took place in one of two conditions. In Condition 1 (C1), the robot nonverbally reacted to the participant's answers before the VH replied. In Condition 2 (C2), the VH explicitly addressed or referred to the robot before the robot showed its nonverbal behaviour. This is illustrated in Table 1. In each condition, five participants (students aged 18 to 25 years) interacted with R3D3.

Table 1. Excerpts from the interaction of Study 1 (translated from Dutch), with the difference between the conditions shown underneath the line.

VH: *If you had to choose, which of the following research topics would you like to hear more about: [...]?*

Participant mentions one of the topics.

C1	Robot nods enthusiastically. VH: *Good choice, I think that is very interesting too.*	C2	VH: *Good choice, Robot and I think that is very interesting too.* Robot nods enthusiastically.

Analysis of the participants' gaze behaviour showed that although they did not pay less attention to the robot in C2 compared to C1, their attention was better timed. In C2, the participants tended to gaze at the robot after it had been mentioned or addressed by the VH, and also at pauses in the speech of the VH. The latter suggests that they saw the robot as a side-participant in the conversation from whom they expected backchannelling behaviour at the appropriate places (see, e.g., [8]). In C1, the participants tended to look at the robot only after it had already started performing its nonverbal behaviour. They may have been alerted to this by the slight noise caused by the robot's head movements.

3 Study 2: Turn Allocation

In the second study we gave a bigger role to the robot by having it use gaze and head movement to allocate turns in interactions with two users. The intentional direction of gaze [5] has been shown to be a highly effective turn-taking mechanism in human-robot interaction [4].

As in Study 1, we used a between-subjects design with two conditions. In each condition, five pairs of participants (students aged 18-25 years) had a short conversation with R3D3, which was again controlled by a wizard. During each interaction, one of the participants was given a cap to wear; see Fig. 1b.

Fig. 1. (a) R3D3 at the time of the studies. (b) The setup of Study 2, with two participants standing in front of R3D3. The robot gazes at the person without the cap.

Table 2 shows the interaction scenarios for the two conditions. In both conditions, the final question was meant to be answered by Participant 2, the one without the cap. This addressee could not be derived from the VH's utterance. Instead, the robot's gaze was used to disambiguate the addressee, while the gaze direction of the VH remained neutral. In C2 but not in C1, the VH explicitly addressed the robot to draw the participants' attention to it before posing the final question.

Table 2. The interaction scenarios of Study 2 (translated from Dutch), excluding closing sequences. The difference between conditions is shown between the two lines.

Robot gazes at Participant 1 (with cap)

VH: *Hello, does the cap fit well?*

Participant 1 responds.

VH: *It looks great on you.*

C1	Robot gazes at Participant 2 (without cap). VH: *What do you think?*	C2	VH looks up at robot (called EyePi). VH: *What do you think, EyePi?* Robot nods and gazes at Participant 2. VH: *Would you agree?*

Either Participant 1 or Participant 2 (the intended addressee) responds.

In C1, in which the robot was not explicitly addressed by the VH, the intended addressee (Participant 2) responded only two out of five times. Participant 1 responded the other three times. The two participants who correctly took the turn in C1 clearly responded when they saw the robot head turning in their direction. The others did not look at the robot when the question was asked (or slightly after). In C2, in which the robot was addressed before gazing at Participant 2, this participant responded in all five cases. This confirmed our expectation that using the robot's gaze for turn allocation would be more effective in combination with explicit addressing of the robot by the VH (C2) than without (C1).

4 Conclusion

We conducted two studies to investigate turn management with R3D3, a virtual human/robot duo. We found that by having the virtual human address or refer to the robot, the users' attention could be drawn to the robot as a participant in the conversation. We also found that this helped the robot to assign turns in interactions with multiple users. Although too small scale to draw strong conclusions, our studies suggest that the robot head can be used successfully to complement the behaviour of the virtual human, if proper attention is drawn to it. For the ongoing development of R3D3, this means it can leave its head on.

Acknowledgements

This publication was supported by the Dutch national program COMMIT.

References

1. Bohus, D., Horvitz, E.: Models for multiparty engagement in open-world dialog. In: Proceedings of SIGDIAL '09. pp. 225–234 (2009)
2. Leite, I., Hajishirzi, H., Andrist, S., Lehman, J.: Managing chaos: Models of turn-taking in character-multichild interactions. Proceedings of ICMI '13 pp. 43–50 (2013)
3. Linssen, J., Theune, M.: R3D3: the Rolling Receptionist Robot with Double Dutch Dialogue. In: Proceedings of the Companion of HRI '17. pp. 189–190 (2017)
4. Mutlu, B., Kanda, T., Forlizzi, J., Hodgins, J., Ishiguro, H.: Conversational gaze mechanisms for humanlike robots. ACM Transactions on Interactive Intelligent Systems 1(2), 1–33 (2012)
5. Ruhland, K., Peters, C.E., Andrist, S., Badler, J.B., Badler, N.I., Gleicher, M., Mutlu, B., McDonnell, R.: A review of eye gaze in virtual agents, social robotics and HCI: Behaviour generation, user interaction and perception. Computer Graphics Forum 34(6), 299–326 (2015)
6. Sacks, H., Schegloff, E.A., Jefferson, G.: A simplest systematics for the organization of turn taking for conversation. Language 50(4), 696–735 (1974)
7. Shiomi, M., Kanda, T., Koizumi, S., Ishiguro, H., Hagita, N.: Group attention control for communication robots with wizard of oz approach. In: Proceedings of HRI '07. p. 121 (2007)
8. Yamazaki, A., Yamazaki, K., Kuno, Y., Burdelski, M., Kawashima, M., Kuzuoka, H.: Precision timing in human-robot interaction. In: Proceedings of CHI '08. pp. 131–139 (2008)

Say Hi to Eliza
An Embodied Conversational Agent on the Web

Gerard Llorach[1,2,3]✉ and Josep Blat[1]

[1] Interactive Technologies Group, Universitat Pompeu Fabra, Barcelona, Spain
{gerard.llorach, josep.blat}@upf.edu
[2] Medizinische Physik and Cluster of Excellence Hearing4all', Universität Oldenburg
[3] Hörzentrum Oldenburg GmbH, Oldenburg, Germany

Abstract. The creation and support of Embodied Conversational Agents (ECAs) has been quite challenging, as features required might not be straight-forward to implement and to integrate in a single application. Furthermore, ECAs as desktop applications present drawbacks for both developers and users; the former have to develop for each device and operating system and the latter must install additional software, limiting their widespread use. In this paper we demonstrate how recent advances in web technologies show promising steps towards capable web-based ECAs, through some off-the-shelf technologies, in particular, the Web Speech API, Web Audio API, WebGL and Web Workers. We describe their integration into a simple fully functional web-based 3D ECA accessible from any modern device, with special attention to our novel work in the creation and support of the embodiment aspects.

Keywords: embodied conversational agents, web technologies, virtual characters

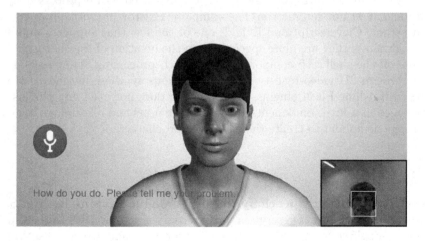

Fig. 1. Interface of the web application

J. Beskow et al. (Eds.): IVA 2017, LNAI 10498, pp. 255-258, 2017.
DOI 10.1007/978-3-319-67401-8_34

255

1 Introduction

We present an implementation where our main contribution is the support of the 3D embodiment and the integration of web technologies. We demonstrate that a 3D ECA in the web browser is feasible using the right tools and libraries, with the work of one or two experts during two weeks. In addition, our system is open and standars based, so that better/alternative artificial intelligence or other components, can be easily connected. Indeed, our web-based ECA uses the following web/open source components:

1. **Listening and Speaking**: speech recognition and synthesis with the Web Speech API.
2. **Understanding, thinking and replying**: ELIZA [1] as artificial conversational entity; rule-based nonverbal behaviors described in [2] for gaze and head motions.
3. **Embodiment**: creation of virtual characters with Makehuman and Blender; support, real-time rendering and animations with WebGLStudio [3]; facial tracking with javascript libraries (jsfeat) [4] within a Web Worker allowing the agent to follow the user with the gaze.

Currently there are no WebGL-based ECAs with 3D virtual characters with the advanced features we present to the best of our knowledge.

2 Related Work

RAG LiteBody [8] was one of the first web implementations but the ECAs only allowed the user to choose from a set of sentences as input and the embodiment was 2D and based on Adobe Flash. A first WebGL implementation of a talking head can be seen in [12], but the facial features need to be processed by the server and it is not interactive. The company Existor [9] with products such as Cleverbot, Cleverscript and Evie, is one of the few that supports web-based ECAs, although they are more specialized on the creation of the chatbot system and use off-the-shelf web components for speech processing. They embody the agent through 2D video-realistic facial expressions synthesis by means of morphing with Adobe Flash plugins. Our approach does not need any plugins, it is based on open source components and allows the users and researchers to modify any components and to create their own virtual characters.

3 Components

Speech Recognition, Speech Synthesis, Dialogue System The Web Speech API permits to use local OS services and external services by URI. In the Chrome browser, Google services are the default configuration, and provide real-time, incremental speech recognition in several languages and dialects with high accuracy as well as speech synthesis through a few lines of code.

For demonstration purposes we used one of the first chatbots: ELIZA from the mid 60s. We integrated the chatbot as a script on the web client [13], adding some nonverbal behavior such as shaking the head when negation words (no, not, n't) are spoken by the agent and head nods while listening and speaking [2]. It is important to note that more sophisticated dialogue systems can be as easily connected, and provide a more conversationally capable ECAs.

Embodiment Among the tools to create 3D humanoid characters, Makehuman, Autodesk Character Generator, Poser, Mixamo (Fuse) and Daz Studio, we used Makehuman to create virtual characters and Blender to add the blend shapes and optimize the models.

Applications such as Unity3D and Unreal Engine permit to rapidly create, visualize and export 3D scenes and games with little coding and compatibility problems for different OSs. However, web plugins are becoming unsupported by some browsers, in particular the Unity Web Player by Chrome. We chose WebGLStudio, a 3D scene editor and game engine, as it has better tools and components to easily to integrate virtual characters than other web engines such as PlayCanvas [10] and Clara.io [11] and it is supported in Chrome.

Our implementation supports some basic BML commands such as gaze and head nods in WebGLStudio; uses a web-based system which automatically generates facial expressions based on the two values of valence and arousal as proposed in [12] and a web-based lip-syncing implementation proposed in [13]. Only eight blend shapes are needed for facial expressions, where three of them are used for the lip-sync, which is quite cost-effective when creating new characters.

We used a facial tracking library [4] and implemented it in Web Workers to extract the position of the user's face relative to the camera so that the ECA directs its gaze at the user. Facial expression analysis libraries and algorithms could also be implemented using such Web Workers, so that the nonverbal behavior of the user could be extracted and used in the dialogue.

4 Results, Discussion and Future Work

A novel web-based ECA was implemented successfully, fulfilling all basic requirements. The timing performance of each component was tested over 100 interactions on a PC (Windows 8 x64 2.50GHz, NVIDIA GeForce GT 750M) with Google Chrome v56.0.2924.87 and a internet connection of 45Mbps with the following results: SST $mean = 166.67ms$ ($sd = 86.47$); TTS $mean = 233.01ms$ ($sd = 251.39$); ElizaAI $mean = 3.72ms$ ($sd = 1.88$); Total processing time $mean = 392.66ms$ ($sd = 254.09$). Thus, the processing time of an interaction with the system (STT, TTS and AI) is less than a second, an acceptable pause in natural human conversations [14]. The system was developed in two weeks of work, using WebGL, BML and facial tracking libraries.

Open web-based ECAs such as ours will allow researchers to carry out large user studies more easily and possibly in a more standardized way, a contribution to advance in the ECAs research field.

Acknowledgements

This research has been partially funded by the Spanish Ministry of Economy and Competitiveness (RESET TIN2014-53199-C3-3-R), by the DFG research grant FOR1732 and by the European Commission under the contract number H2020-645012-RIA (KRISTINA) and under the the the Marie Sklodowska-Curie grant agreement No 675324 (ENRICH). Special thanks to Volker Hohmann and Sergio Sagayo for revisions and counseling and to Javi Agenjo for developing WebGLStudio and helping out with all the technical challenges.

References

1. Weinzembaum, J.: ELIZA A Computer Program for the Study of Natural Language Communication Between Man And Machine. In: Communications of the ACM, 9 (1), pp. 36–45 (1966)
2. Ruhland K., Peters C. E., Andrist S., Badler J. B., Badler N. I., Gleicher M., Mutlu B., McDonnell R.: A Review of Eye Gaze in Virtual Agents, Social Robotics and HCI: Behaviour Generation, User Interaction and Perception. In: Computer Graphics Forum 34, 6, 299–326. (2015)
3. Agenjo, J., Evans, A., Blat, J.: WebGLStudio: a pipeline for WebGL scene creation. In: Proceedings of the 18th International Conference on 3D Web Technology, 79–82. (2013)
4. Zatepyakin E.: JavaScript Computer Vision library (jsfeat), `https://github.com/inspirit/jsfeat`
5. Romeo, M.: Automated Processes and Intelligent Tools in CG Media Production. PhD thesis, 119-148 (2016)
6. Llorach, G., A. Evans, J. Blat, G. Grimm, V. Hohmann. Web-based live speech-driven lip-sync. In: 8th International Conference on Games and Virtual Worlds for Serious Applications (VS-Games) (2016)
7. Kopp S., Krenn B., Marsella S., Marshall A.N., Pelachaud C., Pirker H., Thrisson K. R., Vilhjlmsson H.: Towards a Common Framework for Multimodal Generation: the Behavior Markup Language. In: Proceedings of the 6th international Conference on Intelligent Virtual Agents (IVA'06), Gratch J., Young M., Aylett R., Ballin D., Olivier P. (Eds.). Springer-Verlag, Berlin, Heidelberg, 205–217, (2006)
8. Bickmore T., Schulman D., Shaw G.: DTask and LiteBody: Open Source, Standards-Based Tools for Building Web-Deployed Embodied Conversational Agents. In: Ruttkay Z., Kipp M., Nijholt A., Vilhjlmsson H.H. (eds) Intelligent Virtual Agents. IVA 2009. Lecture Notes in Computer Science, vol 5773. Springer, Berlin, Heidelberg (2009)
9. Existor, `http://www.existor.com/`
10. PlayCanvas, `http://playcanvas.com/`
11. Clara.io, `https://clara.io/`
12. Leone G. R., Cosi P.: LUCIA-webGL: a web based Italian MPEG-4 talking head, In AVSP-2011, 123-126 (2011).
13. Landsteiner, N., `http://www.masswerk.at/elizabot/`, (2005)
14. Sacks, H., Schegloff, E., Jefferson, G.. A Simplest Systematics for the Organization of Turn-Taking for Conversation. In Language, 50(4), 696–735 (1974)

A computational model of power in collaborative negotiation dialogues

Lydia Ould Ouali[1]✉, Nicolas Sabouret[1]✉ and Charles Rich[2]

[1] LIMSI-CNRS, UPR 3251, Orsay, France
Université Paris-Sud, Orsay, France
{ouldouali, nicolas.sabouret}@limsi.fr
[2] Worcester Polytechnic Institute
Worcester, Massachusetts, USA
rich@wpi.edu

Abstract. This paper presents a conversational agent that can deploy different strategies of negotiation based on its social power. The underlying computational model is based on three principles of collaborative negotiation from the literature in social psychology. The social behavior of the agent is made visible through its dialogue strategy. We evaluated our model by showing that these principles are correctly perceived by human observers on synthetic dialogues.

1 Introduction

As they rise in popularity, artificial conversational agents become more present in daily applications in which they play different roles such as pedagogical robots, companion robots for children or for the elderly, etc. In these situations, agent and user have to collaborate through their interaction in order to achieve shared goals. Such example of collaboration can be found in intelligent tutoring agents [14], where agent and learner collaborate to achieve exercises. They compare their respective knowledge on the problem to be solved and discuss possible solutions. Such confrontation offers a personalized teaching to the learner.

As illustrated in the above example, user and the agent typically negotiate in a collaborative manner about the way to achieve the shared goal, depending on individual expertise and preferences. This specific type of discussion is called *collaborative negotiation*. Unlike adversarial negotiation [3], collaborative negotiation assumes that each participant is motivated by the goal of finding a trade-off that best satisfies the interests of both participants, instead of one that maximizes his own interest [22, 5].

Our goal is to build conversational agents capable of credible collaborative negotiation with a human user. To this end, we need to understand how human beings behave in such situation. Indeed, as stated by [3], negotiation is a multi-faceted process which involves social interaction and affects as well as personal preferences and opinions. Therefore, it is crucial to understand the impact of social aspects of the negotiation process. Researchers in social psychology and

© Springer International Publishing AG 2017
J. Beskow et al. (Eds.): IVA 2017, LNAI 10498, pp. 259-272, 2017.
DOI 10.1007/978-3-319-67401-8_35

communication [8, 7] showed that *social power* directly affects the strategies of negotiators. Therefore, we claim that conversational agent which is able to negotiate with a user must be able to adapt their negotiation strategies to different levels of power.

In this paper, we present a conversational agent that aims to contribute to essentials aspects of conversation agents in terms of negotiation and social behaviors. We propose an agent capable of negotiating with the user. In addition, it can deploy different strategies of negotiation based on the social power it wants to express.

In the next section, we discuss existing works on interpersonal power in the domain of social psychology and affective computing. Section 3 presents the computational model of negotiation, based on a set of utterance types and a model of preferences. It implements a general model of negotiation based on three principles of collaborative negotiation from the literature in social psychology. In section 4, we present an experiment conducted with two virtual agents on a negotiation about restaurants showing that the principles are correctly perceived by human observers.

2   Related work

The notion of social power has been widely studied in the fields of interpersonal communication and psychology [13]. It can be defined as the capacity to produce intended effects and to influence the behavior of the other person in the conversation [8]. In the context of communication and negotiation, power is a dyadic variable that takes place during the dialogue. Behaviors related to power can contribute either positively or negatively to the dialogue. Positive contributions include keeping the conversation going and making quick decisions. Negative contributions include not considering the partner (*e.g.* not giving the occasion to express his opinion) and appearing offensive. In our work, we focus on negotiation dialogues, in which several researchers have already shown the impact of social power[6, 4].

2.1   Behaviors of power in dialogue

During a dialogue, power can manifest through verbal and nonverbal behaviors. At the nonverbal level, a wide range of behaviors have been associated with the relation of power in kinesthetic behaviors (facial expression, body movements and gestures) and voice (speaking duration, speaking intensity, voice control and pitch) [4]. Based on this work, several conversational agents have been developed with the ability to exhibit social power through nonverbal behavior, such as gaze [16], body movements [19] or head tilt [11] in relation to high-power and low-power perception.

However, power is also expressed through verbal behaviors. A considerable body of research in social science and communication has documented the effects of power on negotiation behaviors and outcomes. De Dreu [7] demonstrated that high-power negotiators have higher aspirations, demand more and concede less. Galinsky [10] affirms that power increases the action orientation: high-power negotiators control the flow of the negotiation. In addition, high power increase task orientation and goal-directed behavior. Giebels [12] shows that this leads powerful negotiators to end up with the larger share of the pie.

Furthermore, power affects the way that negotiators gather information about their partners [6]. Low-power negotiators have a stronger desire to develop an accurate understanding of their negotiation partner, which leads them to ask more *diagnostic* rather than *leading* questions.

It was also shown that high-power negotiators are self-centered and tend not to pay attention to the preferences of the less powerful negotiators [9, 7].

Our goal is to develop a model of dialogue for Virtual Agents which considers these properties related to social power. We want to make visible *the strategies* deployed during the negotiation depending on the power. In order to implement these different behaviors, we identified three principles related to the relation of power and their impact on the strategy of negotiation

1. **Level of demand and concession:** High-power negotiators show a higher level of demand than the low-power ones. In addition, low-power negotiator's demand decrease over time and the negotiator tends to make larger concessions than high-power negotiators. [7]
2. **Self vs other:** Low-power negotiators consider the preferences of the other in the negotiation, whereas high-power negotiators are self-centered and only interested in satisfying their own preferences. [9, 7]
3. **Controlling the flow of the negotiation:** High-power negotiators tend to make the first move [17] and take the lead in the negotiation. Low-power negotiators aim to construct an accurate model of other preferences, which leads them to ask more questions about other preferences rather than keeping the negotiation going (*e.g* by making proposals)[6].

In the context of collaborative negotiation, we must combine these principles with the goal of finding a trade-off that satisfies both negotiators.

2.2   Similar work in the literature

Only a few researchers have considered the expression of power in the verbal behavior of a conversational agent. [1] developed an agent that expresses social power through gaze and linguistic features. They demonstrated that linguistic personality traits influence the perception of power. However, this work does not consider how power affects the strategies of negotiation in dialogue. More recently, [3, 18] consider trust, expression of emotions as anger and happiness as dimensions of the negotiation strategy of a virtual agent. However, this research focuses more on the negotiation aspect than on the expression of social power. In our work, we want to investigate the expression of power through the dialogue strategy, which has not been considered by previous work.

In a different context, [20] studied how the communication of preferences in a negotiation with a human can impact the negotiation outcomes. They consider situations in which negotiators can use deception to gain an unfair advantage and can hide their intentions. We do not consider this case in our work. Our agents are not only collaborative, but they also give correct information about their preferences and they do not try to hide any information. Previous work such as [23] showed that, even in collaborative negotiation, it is not always possible or advisable to give information about all preferences.

3 Model of negotiation based on the relation of power

In this section, we present our model of dialogue for a Virtual Agent in the context of collaborative negotiation based on power. First, we present the data structure for the agent's preferences and the topics of the negotiation. Second, we present the implementation of the principles of behaviors of power in negotiation discussed in this section 2.1.

3.1 Domain model

The overall goal of a negotiation is to choose an **option** in a set of possible options $\mathcal{O}$. The evaluation of each option by participants is based on a set of **criteria** that reflect the option's characteristics. Let us consider a set $\mathcal{C}$ of n criteria and let $C_1, \ldots, C_n$ be their respective domains of values. $\mathcal{O}$ can be simply defined as the cross-product $C_1 \times \ldots \times C_n$ and each option $o \in \mathcal{O}$ is a tuple $(v_1, \ldots, v_n)$, making the simplifying assumption that all options are available. For instance, in a dialogue about restaurants, the criteria might be the type of cuisine and the price, we could have the option: $(\mathsf{French}, \mathsf{expensive})$.

3.2 Preference model

The conversational agent is defined with a set of preferences, formalized as a set of partial orders $\prec_i$ on each C_i. For instance, if the agent prefers French food to Italian, $\mathsf{Italian} \prec_{\mathsf{cuisine}} \mathsf{French}$.

For a given criterion $i \in \mathcal{C}$, for a given value $v \in C_i$, the agent computes its *satisfaction* $\mathsf{sat}_{\mathsf{self}}(v \prec_i)$ for this value as the number of values it prefers less in the partial order $\prec_i$, normalized in $[0,1]$:

$$\mathsf{sat}_{\mathsf{self}}(v, \prec_i) = 1 - \left(\frac{|\{v' : v' \neq v \ \wedge \ (v \prec_i v')\}|}{(|C_i| - 1)} \right) \tag{1}$$

This notion of satisfaction is generalized to any option $o = (v_1, \ldots, v_n) \in \mathcal{O}$ as a simple average[3]:

$$\mathsf{sat}_{\mathsf{self}}(o, \prec) = \frac{\sum_{i=1}^{n} \mathsf{sat}_{\mathsf{self}}(v_i, \prec_i)}{n} \tag{2}$$

The satisfaction represents the tendency for an agent to accept or to propose a possible value or option in the negotiation dialogue: the closer to 1, the more it will be selected early in the negotiation.

---

[3] There exists a great amount of literature in theoretic decision making on how to combine multiple criteria using Order Weight Averages or Choquet's integrals, for instance. We are not concerned with this question of criteria aggregation in this paper.

3.3   Dialogue model

Negotiators communicate during the negotiation via *utterances*. Each utterance type has a specific set of arguments and is associated with a specific expression in natural language (NL). We use five utterance types, based on the work of Sidner [22] and two additional utterances to close the negotiation. Table 1 summarizes these generic utterance types. Only the NL generation of these utterances has to be specialized in the application domain. In this paper, we will illustrate this model on a collaborative negotiation about restaurants. The value /v/ in Table 1 refers to this NL format to express a value.

Each utterance type takes as parameter either a criterion value $v \in C_i$, an option $o \in \mathcal{O}$ or a criterion type $i \in \mathcal{C}$. They can be separated into three groups. Information moves (*AskValue/AskCriterion* and *StateValue*) are used to exchange information about the participant's likings. In human-human negotiation dialogue, we observed that partners tend to express what they like or do not like (*e.g I (don't)like Chinese restaurants*) rather than binary comparison (*e.g I like Chinese more than French*). This is the reason we use unary operators for the information utterances.

Negotiation moves (*Propose*, *Accept* and *Reject*) allow the agent to make or to answer to proposals. The agent can propose, accept and reject both values ("Let's go to a Chinese restaurant") or options ("Let's go to *Chez Francis*").

Closure moves (*NegotiationSuccess* or *NegotiationFailure*) are used to end the dialogue. Examples of dialogues for restaurants are given in section 4.

The decision process for utterance selection is based on our three principles and is described in section 3.4. To perform this utterance selection, the agent keeps track of all statements and proposals during the dialogue. For each criterion $i \in \mathcal{C}$, we build the set $S_i \subseteq C_i$ of statements that the agent has made about this criterion. This avoids restatements of previous information. We also build the sets $A_i \subseteq C_i$ and $U_i \subseteq C_i$ of values which have been stated by the interlocutor as liked or disliked through *StateValue* utterances. We assume that $A_i \cap U_i = \emptyset$.

We also maintain the sets $P_i \subseteq C_i$, $T_i \subseteq C_i$ and $R_i \subseteq C_i$ of all proposed, accepted and rejected values for each criteria. These will be used to make relevant proposals. Similarly, we consider $P \subseteq \mathcal{O}$, $T \subseteq \mathcal{O}$ and $R \subseteq \mathcal{O}$ the sets of all proposed, accepted and rejected options in the dialogue.

Satisfiability Using the sets A_i and U_i that represent the interlocutor's likings, the agent can compute the satisfiability of a value $v \in C_i$ for the interlocutor (*i.e.* the *other* person) using the following formula:

$$\text{sat}_{\text{other}}(v) = \begin{cases} 1 & \text{if } c \in A_i \\ 0 & \text{if } c \in U_i \\ 0.5 \text{ otherwise} \end{cases} \tag{3}$$

Note that some values might remain unknown: in a collaborative negotiation, they can be considered as being potentially satisfiable. Therefore, we give them an arbitrary value fixed to 0.5.

Utterance type	NL generation	Postcondition
StateValue(v)	I (don't) like /v/.	Speaker : $v \in S_i$ Hearer: $v \in A_i$ is likable, $v \in U_i$ otherwise
AskValue(v) AskCriterion(i)	Do you like /v/ ? What kind of /i/ do you like ?	
ProposeOption(o) ProposeValue(v)	Let's go to /o/. Let's go to a /v/.	$o \in P$ $v \in P_i$
AcceptOption(o) AcceptValue(v)	Okay, let's go to /o/. Okay, let's go to a /v/.	$o \in T$ $v \in T_i$
RejectOption(o) RejectValue(v)	I'd rather choose something else. I'd rather choose something else.	$o \in R$ $v \in R_i$
NegotiationSuccess	We reached an agreement.	
NegotiationFailure	Sorry, but I no longer want to discuss this.	

Table 1: List of utterance types in the model of dialogue.

This function is generalized to any option $o = (v_1, \ldots, v_n) \in O$:

$$\text{sat}_{\text{other}}(o, A, U) = \frac{\sum_i^n \text{sat}_{\text{other}}(v_i, A_i, U_i)}{n} \quad (4)$$

The satisfiability represents the expectation an agent has about the other accepting or rejecting a proposal. It will be used to select the most tolerable offer to make in the negotiation. The concept of tolerable is presented in the next section.

3.4 Decision based on power in negotiation

In section 2.1, we identified three principles related to the relation of power which affects negotiators strategies and behaviors. In this section, we present the computational theory implementing each principle.

We denote the agent's belief of its power $\text{pow} \in [0, 1]$. It is a constant for a given agent in a given interaction.

Level of demand and concession In collaborative negotiation, both participants reduce their level of demand over time because they want to reach an agreement. However, according to our first principle, the level of demand should be higher for high-power agent and concessions should be greater for low-power ones. To model this behavior, we use a *concession curve* illustrated in Figure 1.

Let $\text{self}(\text{pow}, t)$ be a time varying value, following the concession curve:

$$\text{self}(\text{pow}, t) = \begin{cases} \text{pow} & \text{if } (t \leqslant \tau) \\ \max(0, \text{pow} - (\frac{\delta}{\text{pow}} \cdot (t - \tau))) & \text{otherwise} \end{cases} \quad (5)$$

where is $t \geqslant 0$ is the number of open or rejected proposals, $\tau > 0$ is the minimum number of proposals before the concession begins and $\delta > 0$ is a computational parameter of the concession slope.

The value $self(pow, t)$ represents the weight an agent gives to its self-satisfaction relative to the satisfaction of its partner. The higher the agent's power gets, the higher its demands get. In addition, the slope decreases faster for low values of power.

These behaviors of demand and concession are implemented in the computation of an *acceptability* value. Based on the value of satisfiability, the agent is able to tell if it likes a value or not.

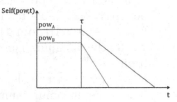

Fig. 1: Concession curve

The acceptability of a value $v \in C_i$ is defined as a boolean function:

$$acc(pow, v, t) = sat_{self}(v, \prec_i) \geqslant (\beta \cdot self(pow, t)) \tag{6}$$

where $\beta > 0$ is a parameter of the theory that defines the weight given to the level of demand.

This boolean function is generalized to any option $o \in O$: $acc(pow, o, t) = sat_{self}(o, \prec) \geqslant (\beta \cdot self(pow, t))$. This acceptability is used by the agent to decide whether he accepts a proposal or not.

Self vs other According to our second principle, high-power negotiators give more weight to their own satisfaction. To implement this principle in the context of collaborative negotiation, we compute how much a given proposal is *tolerable* considering the satisfiability for both the agent and its partner.

For a given criteria $i \in C$, let us consider the subset $V_i \subseteq C_i$ of values that are acceptable for the agent:

$$V_i(pow, t) = \{v \in C_i : acc(pow, v, t)\} \tag{7}$$

This set corresponds to all the proposals an agent could make at a time of the negotiation.

We compute the tolerability of a given value $v \in V_i(pow, t)$ by balancing between the agent's preferences and the likings of its partner. We assume that the agent gives a weight to its partner satisfaction which is complementary to its self-satisfaction:

$$
\begin{aligned}
tol(v, t, \prec_i, A_i, U_i, pow) &= self(pow, t) \cdot sat_{self}(v, \prec_i) \\
&+ (1 - self(pow, t)) \cdot sat_{other}(v, A_i, U_i)
\end{aligned} \tag{8}
$$

And we generalize this function to any option $o = (v_1, \ldots, v_n) \in O$:

$$tol(o, t, \prec, A, U, pow) = \frac{\sum_i^n tol(v_i, t, \prec_i, A_i, U_i, pow)}{n} \tag{9}$$

The agent will always propose the most tolerable element in V_i:

$$propose(V_i, \prec_i, pow) = \arg\max_{v \in V_i}(tol(v)) \tag{10}$$

Summary of general parameters

- $\pi \in [0,1]$: boundary between submissive and dominant used in choosing an utterance type
- β: a value that represents the minimum score that a value has to get to be positively satisfiable to the agent preferences in the negotiation. Note that $\beta = \text{const} \times \text{self}(\text{dom}, t)$.
- $\tau > 0$: the minimum number of open or rejected proposals before concession begins
- $\delta > 0$: parameter in slope of concession curve.
- $\alpha > 0$: the maximum number of successive statement moves.

Controlling the flow of the negotiation According to our third principle, high-power negotiators tend to lead the negotiation. We implemented this principle through the choice of utterance types presented in Table 2. We defined a threshold π to split the spectrum of power in two.

Depending on the power, the previous utterance u^{-1} type and the current dialogue state, the agent selects the first utterance type in Table 2 for which the condition is satisfied. For instance, a high-power agent will stop the negotiation as soon as all the remaining options are unacceptable (line 2). A low-power agent will reject and state a preference, so as to explain why the proposal is not acceptable (line 14). If there is no open proposal, the low-power agent will ask for new information (line 18 -19).

In our model, an agent can express more than one utterance during his speaking turn. This is modeled with the sign "+" in Table2.

Note that a high-power agent will focus on keeping the negotiation going by choosing *negotiation moves* (ProposeValue /ProposeOption, RejectValue /RejectOption, AcceptValue/ AcceptOption) as presented in lines (4 to 10). The agent prioritizes the negotiations moves rather than exchanging information about the preferences. Indeed, as presented in line 3, after α speaking turns dedicated to sharing information, the agent will rather make proposals than stating his likes. An example is presented in the dialogue 2.

On the contrary, a lower power negotiator will focus on building an accurate model of its partner's likings in order to take the fairest decision. It will focus more on *information moves* (StateValue or AskValue/ AskCriterion) as seen in line(18-20). Moreover, the negotiation moves are restricted by conditions which ensure that the agent gathered enough information about its partner likes before to express a proposal (line 16-17).

4 Evaluation

In order to evaluate our model, we conducted a controlled study in which participants judge the behaviors of two agents implemented using our model. Our system is written in Java using the DISCO platform [21]. This allowed us to produce synthetic dialogues between two artificial agents with different values of power and varying preferences.

	Line nb	Utterance type	Condition
pow $\wedge$ π	1	NegotiationSuccess	$\exists o \in T \cup P, acc(pow, o, t)$
	2	NegotiationFailure	$\forall o \in \mathcal{O}, \neg acc(pow, o, t)$
	3	StateValue(v)	$type(u^{-1}) = AskPreference \wedge n < \alpha$ where n is the number of successive statement moves
	4	AcceptValue(v)+ ProposeValue(c)	$\exists v \in P_i \ / \ acc(pow, v, t) \wedge \exists i \in \mathcal{C}, acc(pow, c, t)$
	5	AcceptValue(v)+ ProposeOption(o)	$\exists v \in P_i \ / \ acc(pow, v, t) \wedge \exists o \in \mathcal{O}/ \ v \in o \wedge acc(pow, o, t)$
	6	RejectValue(v)+ ProposeValue(c)	$\exists v \in P_i \ / \ \neg acc(pow, v, t) \wedge \exists i \in \mathcal{C}, acc(pow, c, t)$
	7	RejectValue(v)+ ProposeOption(o)	$\exists v \in P_i \ / \ \neg acc(pow, v, t) \wedge \exists o \in \mathcal{O}/ \ acc(pow, o, t)$
	8	RejectOption(o_1)+ ProposeOption(o_2)	$\exists o_1 \in P \ / \ \neg acc(pow, o_1, t) \wedge \exists o_2 \in \mathcal{O}, acc(pow, o_2, t)$
	9	ProposeValue(v)	$\exists v \in C_i \ / \ tol(v, t, \prec_i, A_i, U_i, pow)$
	10	ProposeOption(o)	$\exists o \in \mathcal{O} \ / \ tol(o, t, \prec_i, A_i, U_i, pow)$
pow $\vee\!\!\vee$ π	11	Negotiation success	$\exists o \in T$
	12	AcceptValue(v)	$\exists i \in \mathcal{C}, \exists v \in P_i, acc(pow, v, t)$
	13	AcceptOption(o)	$\exists o \in P, acc(pow, o, t)$
	14	RejectValue(v)+ StateValue(v)	$t < \tau \wedge (\exists i \in \mathcal{C}, \exists v \in P_i, \neg acc(pow, v, t))$.
	15	RejectOption(o)+ StateValue(v)	$t < \tau \wedge (\exists o \in P, \neg acc(pow, o, t) \wedge \exists v \in o, \neg acc(pow, v, t))$.
	16	ProposeValue(v)	$\exists i \in \mathcal{C}, \exists v \in C_i, v \in A_i \wedge acc(pow, v, t)$
	17	ProposeOption(o)	$\forall i \in \mathcal{C}, \exists v \in C_i, v \in T_i \wedge v \in o$
	18	AskValue(v)	$t > \tau \wedge \exists i \in \mathcal{C}, \exists c \in P_i, \neg acc(c, t)$
	19	AskCriterion(i)	$\exists i \in \mathcal{C}, A_i \cup U_i = \emptyset$
	20	StateValue(v)	$\exists i \in \mathcal{C}, C_i \cap S_i \neq \emptyset$
	21	ProposeValue(v)	$\exists v \in C_i \ / \ tol(v, t, \prec_i, A_i, U_i, pow)$
	22	ProposeOption(o)	$\exists o \in \mathcal{O} \ / \ tol(o, t, \prec_i, A_i, U_i, pow)$

Table 2: Selection of utterance types

4.1 Study design

We simulate a collaborative negotiation for choosing a restaurant using four criteria (cuisine, ambiance, price and location) for a total of 420 options. An example of dialogue is given in the figure 2. The following parameter values were used in our simulation: $\tau = 2$, $\pi = 0.5$, $\alpha = 2$, $\beta = 1$ and $\delta = 0.1$. We generated three preferences sets and we measured the difference between the preference sets using Kendall's distance [2]. We manipulated two simulation parameters: the power of both agents (named *pow-a* and *pow-b*) and the preference sets. This later affects the generation of dialogues in term of values and length. Table 3 summarizes the 4 experimental conditions that results from this combination. Note that we only consider one configuration of social power for the similar preference sets condition, because the produced dialogues with other values of power are all very similar in this case. The first speaker (Speaker A) is always the high-power agent, as stated by our third principle of leading the dialogue.

Our goal is to show these dialogues to human observers so as to evaluate how the relation of power is perceived in the different dialogues.

Preferences	A	B	Label
	0.9	0.4	Dialogue 1
Different preferences (Kendall's tau = 0.96)	0.7	0.4	Dialogue 2
	0.7	0.2	Dialogue 3
Similar preferences (Kendall's tau = 0.46)	0.7	0.4	Dialogue 4

Table 3: Initial condition's setting for generating dialogues

```
A: "Let's go to a Chinese restaurant."
  B: "I don't like Chinese restaurants, let's choose something else."
A: "Let's go to a cheap restaurant."
  B: "Do you like expensive restaurants?"
A: "I don't like expensive restaurants."
  ...
  B: "What kind of atmosphere do you like?"
A: "Let's go to a cheap restaurant."
  B: "Okay, let's go to a cheap restaurant."
A: "Let's go to Sap. It's a quiet, cheap Japanese restaurant on the south side."
  B: "Okay, let's go to Sap.
```

Fig. 2: Excerpt of Dialogue 2.

4.2 Hypotheses

Based on our three principles and the literature on the perception of social power in negotiation, we investigated four hypotheses:

- **H1:** The higher-power speaker will more strongly be perceived as self-centered than the lower-power speaker.
- **H2:** The lower-power speaker will be more strongly perceived as making larger concessions than the higher-power speaker.
- **H3:** The higher-power speaker will more strongly be perceived as demanding than the lower-power speaker.
- **H4:** The higher-power speaker will more strongly be perceived as taking the lead in the negotiation than the lower-power speaker.

4.3 Experimental Procedure

We conducted a between-subject study using the online crowdsourcing website *CrowdFlower*[4]. Each participant was shown only one dialogue. Speaker A and B were described as two friends trying to negotiate a restaurant to have dinner. Participants were asked to read the assigned dialogue and answer a questionnaire.

We defined two questions for each hypothesis. Two test questions were included to check the sanity of the answers. We eliminated participants providing wrong answers to those questions. Each one of these questions was to be answered on a 5 points Likert scale ranging from "I totally disagree" to "I totally agree".

---

[4] https://www.crowdflower.com/

Hypothesis	question 1	question 2
H1	Speaker (A/B) is self-centered.	Speaker (A/B) takes his friend's preferences into account in the choice of the restaurant.
H2	Speaker (A/B) makes concessions in the negotiation.	Speaker (A/B) gives up his position in the negotiation
H3	Speaker (A/B) is demanding	Speaker (A/B) presses his position in the negotiation.
H4	Speaker (A/B) takes the lead in the negotiation.	Speaker (A/B) takes the initiative in the negotiation

Table 4: Questions asked on the questionnaire.

A total of 120 native English subjects participated in the experiment (30 for each condition). Each subject received *25 cents* and we excluded 15 participants because they failed the sanity check.

4.4 Results and discussion

Table 5 summarizes the results of our study, which strongly support all of our four hypotheses. The higher-power speaker was correctly perceived as more self-centered (**H1**), making less concessions (**H2**), more demanding (**H3**) and leading the negotiation (**H4**).

We first computed the correlation for each pair of questions corresponding to a given hypothesis (the average correlation is .5). Since there is a strong correlation, we can use the data to compare the speakers' behaviors on each dialogue. Note that our data are not normally distributed. This is the reason why we used a non-parametric Wilcoxon signed-rank test to verify that our paired sets of data significantly different from each other.

The higher-power speaker was largely perceived as more self-centered, as assumed by hypothesis **H1**, with a large effect size. For instance, if you consider dialogue 1 on Table 5, the statistical test indicates that the higher-power agent was significantly perceived as more self-centered with ($Z=-5.28$ and $p<0.001$).

In addition, a significant difference in the level of concessions expressed in all the dialogues was revealed (**H2**). Indeed, the high-power agent was perceived as making less concessions. The effect size showed a medium effect for dialogues 2 to 4, and a large effect for Dialogue 1 with ($Z=-5.34$ and $p<0.001$).

Hypothesis **H3** was also confirmed by the *Wilcoxon signed-rank test*, where the higher-power agent was defined as the most demanding negotiator, with a large effect size observed for all the dialogues.

The (**H4**) hypothesis was confirmed. The Wilcoxon ranked test revealed that the high-power agent was perceived as significantly more leading the dialogue than the low-power agent, with a large effect size for the dialogues 1, 2 and 4, and a medium effect size for Dialogue3 as depicted in Table 5.

Finally, we made a post-study analysis by comparing the participants' judgments on the behaviors of Speaker A across different dialogues. We computed the differences between the evaluations of Speakers A and B in Dialogue 1 and Dialogue 2 (power of Speaker B remains unchanged at 0.4 whereas the power of Speaker A changes from 0.7 to 0.9).

		Dialogue1		Dialogue2		Dialogue3		Dialogue4	
		SpeakerA	SpeakerB	SpeakerA	SpeakerB	SpeakerA	SpeakerB	SpeakerA	SpeakerB
H1	Mean ± SD	3.9 ± 1.1	2.2± 0.9	3.6 ±0.9	2.2 ±0.8	2.8 ±1.1	2.13± 0.7	3.4 ± 1	2 ±0.9
	p-value	$9.75E^{-08}$		$5.14E^{-08}$		0.002		$6.23E^{-08}$	
	Z-Wilcoxon test	−5.28		−5.34		−3		−4.93	
	Effect size	0.51		0.52		0.3		0.47	
H2	Mean ± SD	2.2 ± 1.1	4.3± 0.8	2.5 ±1.2	3.8 ±1.04	2.7 ±1.2	3.6± 0.8	2.3 ± 1	3.2 ±1.2
	p-value	$7.07E^{-08}$		$3.71E^{-05}$		= 0.01		$1.73E^{-04}$	
	Z-Wilcoxon test	−5.34		−4.05		−3.13		−3.69	
	Effect size	0.52		0.39		0.32		0.35	
H3	Mean ± SD	4.1 ± 0.8	2.6± 1.1	4.03 ± 0.8	2.7 ±0.9	3.5 ±1.1	2.3± 1	3.8 ± 1.8	1.8 ±0.8
	p-value	$2.93E^{-08}$		$4.77E^{-07}$		$1.19E^{-04}$		$2.56E^{-09}$	
	Z-Wilcoxon test	−4.62		−4.96		−3.80		−5.86	
	Effect size	0.45		0.49		0.39		0.56	
H4	Mean ± SD	4.2 ± 0.9	2.3± 1.1	3.8 ±0.9	2.6 ±1.07	3.8 ±0.9	2.8± 1.1	4.5 ±0.5	1.9 ± 0.9
	p-value	$2.44E^{-07}$		$3.28E^{-05}$		0.03		$7.04E^{-10}$	
	Z-Wilcoxon test	−5.11		−4.08		−2.86		−6.09	
	Effect size	0.5		0.4		0.29		0.57	

Table 5: Summary of the obtained results for each hypothesis

Our hypothesis was that a greater difference in power would lead to a better perception of behaviors related to power. However, power in the dialogue is interpersonal by nature, which means that participants rate the power of Speaker A as opposed to the behavior of Speaker B. For this reason, aggregating the evaluations from different dialogues does not make sense. This explains why we obtained mixed results on this aspect. Indeed, a tendency was observed (p $\simeq$ 0.1) for self-centeredness, concessions and the level of demand. Only the lead of dialogue was clearly better perceived (p = 0.043) when the power increases.

Also note that in this experiment, we studied the perception of all the principles related to power simultaneously. This could be seen as a limit of this study: we did not investigate the perception of each principle individually. However, during previous experiments, we detected that the principles are interdependent, which makes a separate evaluation of each of them in a dialogue difficult to perform.

We focus in this study on situations where agents have a complementary relation of power (A high-power side and low-power side). We did not study situations in which both agents are high-powered or low-powerful. The reason is that we want to assess whether the social power is perceived by human observers. This supposes that we aim to analyze the relation of dominance, as defined by [4] in the context of collaborative negotiation. Indeed, [4] defines the relation of dominance as the ability to exert behaviors of power. It refers to context and relationship-dependent interactional patterns in which one actors assertion of control is met by acquiescence from another. Therefore, in the relation of dominance, one actor plays the dominant role and expresses high-powered's behaviors whereas, the other actor plays the submissive role and exerts behaviors of low-power individual.

4.5 Conclusion

Our research aims to model a conversational agent which is able to deploy different strategies of negotiation depending on its representation of social power. Based on research in social psychology, we defined three behavioral principles related to power in collaborative negotiation. We proposed a model of utterance selection based on modeling of preferences and the implementation of these principles. We showed that the behaviors related to social power are correctly perceived in the resulting dialogues. Our findings validate our model of dialogue in general and specifically confirmed the coherence of the generated behaviors of power.

Future works will focus on using this model in a human-agent interaction. It was shown by [15] that having a model of the other impacts the negotiation strategy and improves the outcomes. Therefore, we aim to use our dialogue model to build a representation of the interlocutor's social power, following a theory of mind approach. We hope to show that an agent that adapts its own strategy to the perceived power of its interlocutor will be a better collaborative negotiator.

References

1. Bee, N., Pollock, C., André, E., Walker, M.: Bossy or wimpy: expressing social dominance by combining gaze and linguistic behaviors. In: Proc. IVA 2010. pp. 265–271 (2010)
2. Brandenburg, F.J., Gleißner, A., Hofmeier, A.: Comparing and aggregating partial orders with kendall tau distances. Discrete Mathematics, Algorithms and Applications 5(02), 1360003 (2013)
3. Broekens, J., Jonker, C.M., Meyer, J.J.C.: Affective negotiation support systems. Journal of Ambient Intelligence and Smart Environments 2(2), 121–144 (2010)
4. Burgoon, J.K., Dunbar, N.E.: Nonverbal expressions of dominance and power in human relationships. The Sage handbook of nonverbal communication. Sage 2 (2006)
5. Chu-Carroll, J., Carberry, S.: Response generation in collaborative negotiation. In: Proceedings of the 33rd annual meeting on Association for Computational Linguistics. pp. 136–143. Association for Computational Linguistics (1995)
6. De Dreu, C.K., Van Kleef, G.A.: The influence of power on the information search, impression formation, and demands in negotiation. Journal of Experimental Social Psychology 40(3), 303–319 (2004)
7. De Dreu, C.K., Van Lange, P.A.: The impact of social value orientations on negotiator cognition and behavior. Personality and Social Psychology Bulletin 21(11), 1178–1188 (1995)
8. Dunbar, N.E., Burgoon, J.K.: Perceptions of power and interactional dominance in interpersonal relationships. Journal of Social and Personal Relationships 22(2), 207–233 (2005)
9. Fiske, S.T.: Controlling other people: The impact of power on stereotyping. American psychologist 48(6), 621 (1993)
10. Galinsky, A.D., Gruenfeld, D.H., Magee, J.C.: From power to action. Journal of personality and social psychology 85(3), 453 (2003)

11. Gebhard, P., Baur, T., Damian, I., Mehlmann, G., Wagner, J., André, E.: Exploring interaction strategies for virtual characters to induce stress in simulated job interviews. In: Proc. AAMAS 2014. pp. 661–668 (2014)
12. Giebels, E., De Dreu, C.K., Van De Vliert, E.: Interdependence in negotiation: Effects of exit options and social motive on distributive and integrative negotiation. European Journal of Social Psychology 30(2), 255–272 (2000)
13. Kecskés, I., Romero-Trillo, J.: Research trends in intercultural pragmatics, vol. 16. Walter de Gruyter (2013)
14. Kerly, A., Ellis, R., Bull, S.: Calmsystem: a conversational agent for learner modelling. Knowledge-Based Systems 21(3), 238–246 (2008)
15. Klatt, J., Marsella, S., Krämer, N.C.: Negotiations in the context of aids prevention: an agent-based model using theory of mind. In: Proc. IVA 2011. pp. 209–215 (2011)
16. Lance, B., Marsella, S.C.: The relation between gaze behavior and the attribution of emotion: An empirical study. In: Proc. IVA 2008. pp. 1–14 (2008)
17. Magee, J.C., Galinsky, A.D., Gruenfeld, D.H.: Power, propensity to negotiate, and moving first in competitive interactions. Personality and Social Psychology Bulletin 33(2), 200–212 (2007)
18. de Melo, C.M., Gratch, J., Carnevale, P.J.: Humans versus computers: Impact of emotion expressions on people's decision making. IEEE Transactions on Affective Computing 6(2), 127–136 (2015)
19. Mignault, A., Chaudhuri, A.: The many faces of a neutral face: Head tilt and perception of dominance and emotion. Journal of nonverbal behavior 27(2), 111–132 (2003)
20. Nazari, Z., Lucas, G.M., Gratch, J.: Opponent modeling for virtual human negotiators. In: International Conference on Intelligent Virtual Agents. pp. 39–49. Springer (2015)
21. Rich, C., Sidner, C.L.: Robots and avatars as hosts, advisors, companions, and jesters. AI Magazine 30(1), 29 (2009)
22. Sidner, C.L.: An artificial discourse language for collaborative negotiation. In: AAAI. vol. 94, pp. 814–819 (1994)
23. Swartout, W.R., Gratch, J., Hill Jr, R.W., Hovy, E., Marsella, S., Rickel, J., Traum, D., et al.: Toward virtual humans. AI Magazine 27(2), 96 (2006)

Prestige Questions, Online Agents, and Gender-Driven Differences in Disclosure

Johnathan Mell[1]✉, Gale Lucas[2], and Jonathan Gratch[3]

[1] University of Southern California, Los Angeles CA, USA
[1] mell@ict.usc.edu
[2,3] USC Institute for Creative Technologies, Los Angeles CA, USA
[2] lucas@ict.usc.edu
[3] gratch@ict.usc.edu

Abstract. This work considers the possibility of using virtual agents to encourage disclosure for sensitive information. In particular, this research used "prestige questions", which asked participants to disclose information relevant to their socioeconomic status, such as credit limit, as well as university attendance, and mortgage or rent payments they could afford. We explored the potential for agents to enhance disclosure compared to conventional web-forms, due to their ability to serve as relational agents by creating rapport. To consider this possibility, agents were framed as artificially intelligent versus avatars controlled by a real human, and we compared these conditions to a version of the financial questionnaire with no agent. In this way, both the perceived agency of the agent and its ability to generate rapport were tested. Additionally, we examined the differences in disclosure between men and women in these conditions. Analyses reveled that agents (either AI- or human-framed) evoked greater disclosure compared to the no agent condition. However, there was some evidence that human-framed agents evoked greater lying. Thus, users in general responded more socially to the presence of a human- or AI-framed agent, and the benefits and costs of this approach were made apparent. The results are discussed in terms of rapport and anonymity.

Keywords: Virtual Agents; Human-Agent Experimentation; Disclosure.

1 Introduction

Any automated system that aims to understand or interact with humans needs to have a good model of how those humans will interact with it. Critically, when such a system's function is to collect data, it is imperative that the data it collects are accurate and readily reported. This is especially important in medical fields, where information may be critical in correctly diagnosing patients. Indeed, failure to provide fully honest responses in medical interviews can result in serious consequences for patient health. Therefore, much research has considered how to gain more detailed and honest medical histories, especially sensitive information, from patients [1].

It is also helpful in other, less life-threatening domains—specifically, disclosure of honest financial data allows automated systems to provide helpful information to

© Springer International Publishing AG 2017
J. Beskow et al. (Eds.): IVA 2017, LNAI 10498, pp. 273–282, 2017.
DOI 10.1007/978-3-319-67401-8_36

users to aid them in financial planning and other tasks. However, these kinds of information are often difficult to gather due to social effects that may encourage people to misrepresent or refuse to answer questions about their health or finances [2]. These so-called "prestige questions" are ones that many users may be reluctant to answer, or, when they do, to answer truthfully.

Generally, work has found that rapport and anonymity both foster more honest disclosure on sensitive topics, and indeed, even the most basic of relational agents can have large effects on trust [3]. Honest disclosure requires both 1) willingness to answer sensitive questions, and, if willing to report on such sensitive questions, it then requires 2) answering those questions honestly. However, little to no research has explicitly disentangled honest disclosure of sensitive information in this way: by examining willingness to simply answer sensitive questions *separately* from willingness to answer such questions honestly. Furthermore, most research has focused on reporting of stigmatized health related information, leaving the issue of reporting sensitive information related to socioeconomic status unexplored.

To address these issues, we presented a series of prestige questions, where we asked participants to answer questions about their financial status. These prestige questions are so named due to their relevant to the concept of social prestige—in short, they are questions relating to personal information that directly relates to how an individual is perceived in a social context. Social prestige has been previously studied in the obviously social context of dating [4, 5], but also in terms of occupational prestige—how much a person ties his or her social worth to his or her career, and the reputation of his or her employer [6].

After a series of required questions, participants were asked if they were willing or unwilling to answer more sensitive questions that would directly reveal their socioeconomic status, and thus their level of social prestige. Later, they were asked if they were honest on the required questions. This allowed us to disentangle honest disclosure of sensitive information as well as address disclosure in the domain of socioeconomic status.

The value of automated agents to influence these issues should not be overlooked, given the ubiquitous nature of online interactions. Indeed, the positive effect of agents on the generation of trust when discussing finance has been demonstrated [7]. Previous work [8] provides early models for predicting disclosure based on trust of various commercial websites and aims to model different users. However, this work does not condition on the basis of a virtual human partner, something explicitly shown to affect disclosure in other contexts [9]. In this context, we consider the effect of rapport (even minimal rapport) by examining the presence of an agent (vs. a standard web form). We consider the effect of anonymity by comparing AI-framed agents to human-framed agents. This work thus expands the body of knowledge on human behavior in conjunction with virtual partners into the financial domain.

2   Related Work

2.1   Disclosure, Rapport, and Anonymity

Financial disclosure is a relatively untested domain, and even less work has been done therein that attempts to utilize virtual human partners to effect desired outcomes. Although the use of computer agents to increase disclosure has been examined, previous studies have focused on intimate self-disclosure, rather than on financial or prestige questions [10]. And yet, automated "tele-operator" systems have been in use for years, and their importance has been well established [11]. Indeed, these systems are often seen as critical, complicated, and often protected by various patents [12].

Yet, the effects of *how* these systems influence user behavior, and if there are design principles that improve outcome measures (such as disclosure), are still relatively untested. The decision on whether to provide live phone support, automated telephone systems, chat-bots, or more realistic agents is an important one. Since these decisions are likely to affect the level of rapport generated between an agent/service provider and the user, care must be taken to understand the effects on user behavior [13].

Current evidence suggests that different types of interaction produce different levels of disclosure by affecting two key psychological factors: rapport and anonymity – or the sense that one's identity is protected. Generally, research has shown that greater feelings of rapport lead people to disclose more [9, 14, 15]. Indeed, because computer- and self-administered assessment lack any human element, these traditional assessments do not evoke the same feelings of rapport or social connection. Specifically, when there is not a human or human-like agent present in some way, shape, or form, people feel less socially-connected during the assessment [13, 16, 17].

Besides rapport, anonymity is another psychological factor that leads to differences in disclosure. Indeed, much of the research exploring the effect of anonymity on disclosure has done so by contrasting different assessment methods such as computer-mediated interviews, face-to-face interviews, computer-administered assessment, and standard self-assessment. Research shows that computer-mediated interviews are felt to be more anonymous than face-to-face interviews, just as computer-administered assessment is when compared to self-administered assessment by paper-and-pencil, and this resultant anonymity leads to increased disclosure [18].

2.2   Gender-Based Differences in Behavior

It is important to realize that, although individual differences in user experience are always to be expected, there may be systemic differences based on user gender (and often, based on gender match/mismatch with the perceived gender of the agent). Features such as social distance also often play a role in changing the rapport and behavior of users with others [19]. Often, these system design decisions can make huge differences in the usability and effectiveness of that system [20]. Specifically, the gender of a partner can have substantial effects in social situations, especially ones in which prestige questions are likely to be involved [21].

These predictions are quite distinct between men and women. Evidence suggests that having an opposite-gendered tutor (among heterosexual participants) may increase rapport behavior in certain instructional interactions. This was found to be especially true for female users interacting with a male instructor [22]. Furthermore, in conversations when financial questions were involved—and thus earning potential was discussed—women were far more concerned than men in considering their partners [23]. Expectedly, this can lead to increased deception on the part of males when presenting this information, especially in situations where that information is often shared (such as online dating) [24]. In essence, these works lead us to the idea that if our goal is to increase disclosure of financial information, it pays to be cognizant of the gender-based differences that may arise.

3   Experimental & System Design

To approach these questions of disclosure, we designed a 3-condition study to determine the effects of a virtual assistant when users were asked various financial questions. In all conditions, users were merely told that they would be asked some questions about their finances as part of a study to determine how best to provide information for financial planning. This survey was designed using the Qualtrics survey software. The survey involved a series of questions that were determined to be prestige questions due to the social nature of the queries.

The questions were divided into 5 sections, of which users saw a subset based on their prior answers. The sections were: 1) House ownership, 2) Apartment rental, 3) Past education, 4) Current education, and 5) Credit history. At the start of several sections, users were asked questions that determined which of the subsequent sections they would view. For example, before starting section one, they were asked if they lived in a home, apartment, or dorm room. Users that answered "home" would see section 1 but not section 2. Users that answered "apartment" would see section 2 but not section 1. And users that answered "dorm room" would see neither of those sections. Similar questions gated sections 3 and 4 (Are you attending college/have you previously attended college?) and section 5 (Do you currently have any credit cards?).

Each of these sections contained a number of questions designed to be somewhat uncomfortable but anonymous. For example, the house section asked about current mortgage payments, their amounts and interest rates, and the total value of the home. Near the end of each section, there was also a question that was designed to break the anonymity. These questions were considered the disclosure questions for the purposes of this study. In the house section, this question was "Will you give us your address so we can check the value of the house using Zillow (an online service) to verify this? (If yes, we'll ask you for that information later)." Note that regardless of their answer, this data was *never* collected, and we did not violate the anonymity of the participants. A summary of the sections and questions is listed in Table 1.

Table 1. Survey Disclosure Questions

Section	Disclosure Question
Home ownership	Address of home?
Apartment rental	Address of apartment?
Past school	School name?
Current school	School name?
Credit history	Approval to run a credit check?

At the conclusion of these 5 sections, all participants were debriefed and asked another set of questions regarding whether or not they had previously lied on any of the previous questions (as in [8]), as well as some basic demographic information, including their gender. Due to the nature of the experiment, all demographic information and information about previous lies was, necessarily, self-reported. However, our primary measures—whether the participant agreed to reveal information at all—did not rely on self-report.

Our experimental manipulation took place during the 5 primary sections. In the control condition, there was nothing added to the survey, and it was simply a regular online form. In the "Agent" and "Human" conditions, the survey was augmented with a simple virtual agent that remained at the top of the survey. This agent can be seen in Figure 1. The left image depicts the agent in the "Agent" condition, wherein the photo was made to look like a drawing. The right image depicts the agent in the "Human" condition, wherein the photo remained lifelike (both photos were simple stock photos freely available without copyright).

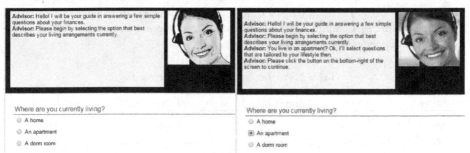

Fig. 1. "Agent" framing condition with automated remarks (left), and "Human" framing condition with additional remarks after a choice has been made (right)

The behavior of the agent in the "Agent" and "Human" conditions was identical. The agent regularly sent messages in the chat window, providing additional explanation about the questions. They also reacted to the user's actions, providing context-specific information based on the user's choices. An example of this can be seen in Figure 2, which takes place after the user has clicked the "Home" option. This behavior was accomplished using the Qualtrics JavaScript API.

The only differences between the two experimental conditions were, (as stated previously) the pictures, and an initial framing description that users saw at the beginning of the survey. In the "Agent" condition, users were told that they were about to interact with an "artificial intelligence (AI) agent", and in the "Human" condition, they were told that they would interact with a "live support representative". Participants experienced a brief "connection delay" in both conditions as they were "matched" with their agent or representative. All participants were debriefed regarding the deception following the study.

4   Results

We recruited 381 participants (241 male, 140 female) using Amazon's Mechanical Turk (MTurk) service as subjects for our study. Their average age was 35.13 (SD = 10.40). Participants were recruited only from the United States (verified using IP address), and were required to have a 98% or higher approval rating using MTurk's reporting system.

Participants completed a manipulation check; specifically, they were asked to identify whether they completed the answers with a human, an agent, or just completed the form themselves. From the original 381 participants, 52 failed the manipulation check. These participants were excluded, leaving 329 for analysis.

4.1   Willingness to answer sensitive questions

A one-way ANOVA revealed a significant difference between conditions ($F(2, 326) =$ 3.38, $p = .04$; see Table 2). Follow-up contrasts indicate that, out of the 4 possible questions, participants were willing to provide significantly more answers to either a human ($t(326) = 2.05$, $p = .04$) or an agent ($t(326) = 2.10$, $p = .04$) than a form. However, human and virtual agents did not elicit different levels of willing to provide these answers ($t(326) = 0.22$, $p = .82$). In a 3 (Condition: Form, Agent, or Human) x 2 (Gender: Male or Female) ANOVA to test gender, there was no main effect or interaction with gender (Fs < 1.47, ps > .23) overall.

Table 2. Proportion of Answers Disclosed

Condition	Form (Control)	Agent Framing	Human Framing
Percentage of possible questions answered	47.5%	55%	55%

However, to investigate whether there was an effect of gender on any of the 4 individual questions, we ran log-linear analyses on participants' willingness to answer each of the 4 questions separately. These analyses revealed that women's responses drove the above effects more than men's for 3 of the 4 questions, but men's responses drove the effect more than women's for the final question. These following results are summarized in Table 3. Generally speaking, it was found that there was an *overall* effect of condition on willingness to disclose, but no *overall* interaction with gender. There were, however, numerous interactions with gender for the individual questions, for which the analysis is detailed below.

First, considering participants' willingness to allow the system to do a credit check, the analysis revealed a significant interaction with gender ($G2(7) = 14.78$, $p = .04$). Indeed, women tended to consent to credit checks more with an agent (14%) or human (13%) than on a form (6%; $\chi^2(2) = 1.72$, p = .42); however, men tended to show the opposite: they consented to credit checks on the form (15%) more than with an agent (6%) or human (7%; $\chi^2(2) = 4.29$, p = .12). While neither of these individual effects for gender are in themselves significant, the interaction effect is—this result is shown in Figure 2.

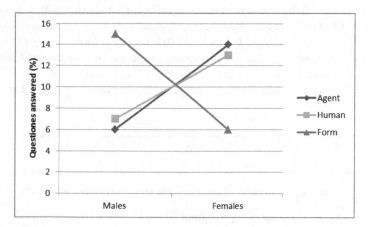

Fig. 2. Percentage of participants willing to disclose credit information, showing interaction between gender and condition.

Similarly, the effect of condition on participants' willingness to provide the name of their former college or university also depended on gender (G2(7) = 17.40, p = .02). Women tended to be more willing to share the name of their former school with an agent (35%) than a human (29%) or on a form (31%; $\chi^2(2) = 1.38$, p = .50). Again, this individual tendency was non-significant, but contributes to the interaction effect observed. Men, however, were *significantly* more willing to provide the school name on the form (54%) than to an agent (34%) or human (29%; $\chi^2(2) = 6.08$, p = .048).

There was also a non-significant trend for a condition by gender interaction on participants' willingness to provide the name of the current school (G2(7) = 10.12, p = .18). Again, women tended to be more willing to provide the name of their current school to a human (43%) or agent (39%) than on a form (12%; $\chi^2(2) = 2.10$, p = .35), whereas men tended to show the reverse: they were less willing to provide the name to a human (12%) than on the form (44%) or to an agent (38%; $\chi^2(2) = 2.80$, p = .25). None of these interactions were statistically significant.

In contrast, while the effect of condition on participants' willingness to provide their address was also significantly qualified by gender (G2(7) = 16.84, p = .02), the effect this time was more driven by men. Men were significantly more willing to provide their address to a human (90%) or agent (72%) than on a form (62%; $\chi^2(2) = 9.24$, p = .01), whereas women were equally willing across conditions (74% vs 72% vs 70%, respectively; $\chi^2(2) = 0.21$, p = .90).

4.2 Reported lying on questions

Additionally, chi-squared tests were run to test the effect of condition on reported lying on each item. Participants were significantly more likely to lie about their credit limit when asked by a human (8%) then when asked by an agent (1%) or on a form (2%; $\chi^2(2) = 6.93$, p = .03). Again, this effect was again driven by female participants more than males. There was a marginally significant interaction with gender (G2(7) = 12.44, p = .087), whereby women were marginally more likely to say they lied to a human (9%) then when asked by an agent (0%) or on a form (2%; $\chi^2(2) = 5.60$, p = .06), and men just showed a non-significant trend to lie more to a human (6%) than an agent (2%) or on a form (2%; $\chi^2(2) = 1.79$, p = .41). The effect of condition failed to reach statistical significance for lying on the remaining items (χ^2s < 2.88, p > .23).

Table 3. Disclosure Results Summary

Question	Overall, more likely to provide answer to:	Males only:	Females only:	Gender interaction?
Total number of answers	Agents and humans*	Agents and humans	Agents and humans	No
Credit Check	Agents and humans	Web form	Agents and humans	Yes*
Past school name	Agents and humans*	Web form*	Agents and humans	Yes*
Current school name	Agents and humans	Web form	Agents and humans	Trend only
Address	Agents and humans*	Agents and humans*	Equally likely	Yes*

*Significant at p < 0.05

5   Discussion

These results suggest not only that there is a substantial benefit to providing an agent or human-controlled avatar to increase user experience and disclosure, but also that gender-based differences are very significant.

The core result of these findings is that the use of a virtual human partner increases disclosure in the domain of financial questions. This result, already shown with agent-assisted disclosure in the medical domain, is another, stronger statement on the usefulness of virtual agent assistants. Generating rapport with a virtual agent—even a relatively simple one like the agent used in this study—will yield actionable results when attempting to get answers to prestige questions that may be hard to get otherwise.

But this result is also tempered by demographic effects—increasing the social presence of a task has both benefits and drawbacks. The agent/avatar used in this study was clearly female, and its gender may have had a large effect on the perceptions and actions of the users according to their own genders—manipulating the gender of the agent is a good target for future work. As previous research has suggested, prestige questions that reveal information about financial security are often very important for females looking for a long-term partner in dating contexts [25]. Speculatively, this social context may have influenced the male participants in our study. It should not be surprising that the males in our study were reluctant to reveal the answers to questions like their credit history and school history to the female agent/avatar. However, the males in this study were willing to reveal their addresses to the agent/avatar. While this result is somewhat unexpected, it is possible that the address is seen as a "safer" option—whereas the very mention of a credit score or school name invites immediate social judgment, determining social status using merely an address does require additional steps (someone would have to search the address using an online service, judge the neighborhood, etc.). Therefore, this question may be perceived as less potentially damaging to males looking to impress.

Indeed, the results on lying do seem in line with this hypothesis. It was the question on credit, not on housing addresses, that prompted lying behavior. When speaking to a human that could potentially judge the users for their perceived poor credit, users lied more than they did to either an agent or a web form. Since none of the other questions prompted (self-reported) lying behavior to a large degree, one possible conclusion is that the credit limit question is seen as potentially the most socially damaging. This is in line with previous research on loss of anonymity.

But, *regardless* of the underlying cause of this lying behavior, it should be concluded that there are serious gender-driven effects when asking prestige questions that should be taken into account. While it is still true that the use of an automated agent/avatar clearly increased disclosure overall in this study, that effect may backfire when used on males. In future work, androgynous or male agents could be used to further determine if female agents drive this behavior, or if gender match/mismatch does.

In sum, the addition of a very simple automated agent was able to produce dramatic changes in the behavior of users on an online form. Prestige questions, much as other questions that people may be reluctant to answer, are often a critical point in data collection. This method paves to the way to collect more data, more accurately, and to target different demographics with data-driven, intelligent techniques.

Acknowledgments
This work was supported the U.S. Army. Any opinion, content or information presented does not necessarily reflect the position or the policy of the United States Government, and no official endorsement should be inferred.

References

1. Maguire, Peter, et al. "Helping cancer patients disclose their concerns." European Journal of Cancer 32.1 (1996): 78-81.
2. Gabler, Neal. "The Secret Shame of Middle-Class Americans." The Atlantic (May 2016).
3. Bickmore, Timothy, and Justine Cassell. "Relational agents: a model and implementation of building user trust." Proceedings of the SIGCHI conference on Human factors in computing systems. ACM, 2001.
4. Larson, Richard F., and Gerald R. Leslie. "Prestige influences in serious dating relationships of university students." Social Forces 47.2 (1968): 195-202.
5. Rogers, Everett M., and A. Eugene Havens. "Prestige rating and mate selection on a college campus." Marriage and Family Living 22.1 (1960): 55-59.

6. MacKinnon, Neil J., and Tom Langford. "The meaning of occupational prestige scores." The Sociological Quarterly 35.2 (1994): 215-245.
7. Bickmore, Timothy, and Justine Cassell. "Relational agents: a model and implementation of building user trust." Proceedings of the SIGCHI conference on Human factors in computing systems. ACM, 2001.
8. Metzger, Miriam J. "Privacy, trust, and disclosure: Exploring barriers to electronic commerce." Journal of Computer-Mediated Communication 9.4 (2004): 00-00.
9. Lucas, Gale M., et al. "It's only a computer: virtual humans increase willingness to disclose." Computers in Human Behavior 37 (2014): 94-100.
10. Moon, Youngme. "Intimate exchanges: Using computers to elicit self-disclosure from consumers." Journal of consumer research 26.4 (2000): 323-339.
11. Bose, Ranjit. "Customer relationship management: key components for IT success." Industrial management & Data systems 102.2 (2002): 89-97.
12. Fawcett, Philip E., and Christopher Blomfield-Brown. "System and method for providing automated customer support." U.S. Patent No. 5,678,002. 14 Oct. 1997.
13. Gratch, Jonathan, et al. "Creating rapport with virtual agents." International Workshop on Intelligent Virtual Agents. Springer Berlin Heidelberg, 2007.
14. Burgoon, Judee K., Laura K. Guerrero, and Kory Floyd. Nonverbal communication. Routledge, 2016.
15. Hall, Judith A., Jinni A. Harrigan, and Robert Rosenthal. "Nonverbal behavior in clinician—patient interaction." Applied and Preventive Psychology 4.1 (1995): 21-37.
16. DeVault, David, et al. "SimSensei Kiosk: A virtual human interviewer for healthcare decision support." Proceedings of the 2014 international conference on Autonomous agents and multi-agent systems. International Foundation for Autonomous Agents and Multiagent Systems, 2014.
17. Gratch, Jonathan, et al. "Creating rapport with virtual agents." International Workshop on Intelligent Virtual Agents. Springer Berlin Heidelberg, 2007.
18. Weisband, Suzanne, and Sara Kiesler. "Self disclosure on computer forms: Meta-analysis and implications." Proceedings of the SIGCHI conference on human factors in computing systems. ACM, 1996.
19. Hoffman, Elizabeth, Kevin McCabe, and Vernon L. Smith. "Social distance and other-regarding behavior in dictator games." The American Economic Review 86.3 (1996): 653-660.
20. Howell, Mark, Steve Love, and Mark Turner. "User characteristics and performance with automated mobile phone systems." International Journal of Mobile Communications 6.1 (2008): 1-15.
21. Evers, Catharine, et al. "Anger and social appraisal: a" spicy" sex difference?." Emotion 5.3 (2005): 258.
22. Krämer, Nicole C., et al. "Closing the gender gap in STEM with friendly male instructors? On the effects of rapport behavior and gender of a virtual agent in an instructional interaction." Computers & Education 99 (2016): 1-13.
23. Buss, David M., and David P. Schmitt. "Sexual strategies theory: an evolutionary perspective on human mating." Psychological review 100.2 (1993): 204.
24. Toma, Catalina L., Jeffrey T. Hancock, and Nicole B. Ellison. "Separating fact from fiction: An examination of deceptive self-presentation in online dating profiles." Personality and Social Psychology Bulletin 34.8 (2008): 1023-1036.
25. Buss, David M. "Sex differences in human mate preferences: Evolutionary hypotheses tested in 37 cultures." Behavioral and brain sciences 12.1 (1989): 1-14.

To Tell the Truth: Virtual Agents and Morning Morality

Sharon Mozgai ✉, Gale Lucas, and Jonathan Gratch

University of Southern California,
Institute for Creative Technologies, USA
smozgai@post.harvard.edu

Abstract. This paper investigates the impact of time of day on truth-fulness in human-agent interactions. Time of day has been found to have important implications for moral behavior in human-human interaction. Namely, the morning morality effect shows that people are more likely to act ethically (i.e., tell fewer lies) in the morning than in the afternoon. Based on previous work on disclosure and virtual agents, we propose that this effect will not bear out in human-agent interactions. Preliminary evaluation shows that individuals who lie when engaged in multi-issue bargaining tasks with the Conflict Resolution Agent, a semi-automated virtual human, tell more lies to human negotiation partners than virtual agent negotiation partners in the afternoon and are more likely to tell more lies in the afternoon than in the morning when they believe they are negotiating with a human. Time of day does not have a significant effect on the amount of lies told to the virtual agent during the multi-issue bargaining task.

Keywords: morning morality, virtual humans, honest responding, multi-issue bargaining

1 Introduction

If you really want the truth, should you ask for it, via virtual agent, in the morning? As the number of applications of virtual agents grows, particularly in domains that depend on honest disclosure for success (e.g., healthcare and experiential learning), it is important to consider what conditions lead people to act unethically when engaging with virtual agents and what advantages virtual agents may have in eliciting honest and ethical behaviors. In addition, interest in how people respond to intelligent virtual agents versus how they respond to people has increased considerably [6, 4]. In human-human interaction, time of day has been shown to have important implications for ethical behavior. Specifically, the *morning morality effect* suggests that time of day can lead to a systematic failure of "good people" to act morally showing that individuals engage in less ethical behavior (i.e., more lying) on tasks performed in the afternoon than on tasks performed in the morning [3]. This current work considers whether the morning morality effect impacts human-agent interactions and posits that one distinct advantage of virtual agents may be inoculation against the morning morality effect.

© Springer International Publishing AG 2017
J. Beskow et al. (Eds.): IVA 2017, LNAI 10498, pp. 283-286, 2017.
DOI 10.1007/978-3-319-67401-8_37

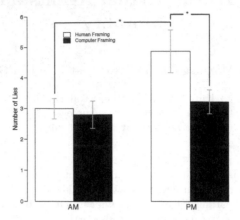

Fig. 1. Comparison between number of lies with respect to both AM and PM as well as human and computer framing conditions. Visualized are mean values with standard error bars. Brackets with * indicate significant differences at $p < 0.05$.

Initial theories regarding human-computer interaction maintained it was possible to replicate any psychological finding on how people interact with one another by replacing the word human with computer [8]. Subsequent work has shown that individuals interact differently with virtual agents, particularly in social settings, where they can exhibit lower social presence [1], arousal [8], and engagement [7]. But recent research has also identified contexts in which virtual agents outperform humans, specifically in overcoming barriers to obtaining truthful information. Lucas et al. [5] have shown that when people believe that a virtual agent was automatically-operated by a computer algorithm rather than tele-operated by a human they reported lower fear of self-disclosure, lower impression management and were rated by observers as being more willing to disclose truthfully.

We contribute to this work on obtaining truthful information via virtual agents by examining the impact of time of day on human-human and human-agent interaction in a multi-issue bargaining task. We predict individuals who lie will be less deceitful with their bargaining partner regardless of time of day when they believe they are interacting with an autonomous virtual agent than when they believe they are interacting with a human. Moreover, we predict that the morning morality effect can still be found when individuals who lie believe they are bargaining with another human but will be diminished when they believe they are negotiating with an autonomous virtual agent.

2   Current Work

This analysis was conducted on the Conflict Resolution Agent (CRA) dataset made available by the authors [2]. The CRA is a semi-automated virtual human that negotiates with people via natural language. The CRA dataset is comprised of ninety three participants (52 female) who were recruited from an on-line job service and who completed two multi-issue negotiations. All participants interacted with both the male and female versions of the virtual agent. Following a wizard-of-Oz paradigm, all participants interacted with an agent that was controlled by a human wizard. Further, participants were randomly assigned to a framing condition, where they were either told that the agent was operated by a human or a computer (artificial intelligence). The wizards followed a predetermined script: the wizard acted as if the participants preferences were unknown, the wizard avoided making the first offer and the wizard avoided volunteering their own preferences unless the participants used reciprocal information exchange. This script was followed across both framing conditions and both negotiations. As an incentive, participants received tickets to a $100 lottery based on how well they performed in the negotiations. The number of tickets each participant received was based on the value of the items they won in the negotiation. The data was transcribed, time stamped, and annotated for lie counts.

3 Results

Out of the 93 participants 12 were not annotated for lies and participants that did not lie at all were excluded from the analyses. In total this leaves 64 participants for the evaluations shown below. Sessions were classified as morning (between 9 a.m. and noon) or afternoon (between noon and 6 p.m).

Correlation analyses results. We observe a significant correlation with respect to number of lies told and time of day (Pearson's $r = 0.296$; $n = 64$; $p = 0.017$). The effect is carried by the human framing ($r = 0.366$; $n = 31$; $p < 0.05$) rather than the computer framing ($r = 0.204$; $n = 33$; $p = 0.25$). In other words, the effect of morning morality is stronger in the human framing.

Morning vs. Afternoon. Similar to the correlation analyses we observe a significant difference in observed lies with respect to AM vs. PM participants. Specifically, subjects participating in the afternoon ($M = 4$, $SD = 2.685$) lie more than those participating in the morning ($M = 2.9$, $SD = 1.210$; $t(62) = -2.256$, $p = 0.027$, $d = -0.471$). Further, we observe that the effect is again carried by the human framing condition (AM: $M = 3$, $SD = 1.054$ vs. PM: $M = 4.857$, $SD = 3.198$; $t(29) = -2.401$, $p = 0.024$, $d = 0.936$). We do not observe a significant effect for the amount of lies expressed in the computer framing between morning and afternoon (AM: $M = 2.8$, $SD = 1.398$ vs. PM: $M = 3.217$, $SD = 1.858$; $t(31) = -0.710$, $p = 0.485$).

Computer vs. Human Framing. While the result is not significant, participants seem to lie more in the human framing condition ($M = 4.258$, $SD = 2.816$) than the computer framing condition ($M = 3.091$, $SD = 1.721$; $t(62) = 1.986$, $p = 0.053$, $d = -0.497$). When comparing the lies between the framing conditions during the morning and afternoon separately we see a significant difference for the afternoon (human framing: $M = 4.857$, $SD = 3.198$ vs. computer framing: $M = 3.217$, $SD = 1.858$; $t(42) = 2.054$, $p = 0.048$, $d = 0.635$) while there is no difference in the morning (human framing: $M = 3$, $SD = 1.054$ vs. computer framing: $M = 2.8$, $SD = 1.398$; $t(18) = 0.361$, $p = 0.722$). The results are summarized in Figure 1.

4 Conclusions

As previous work on disclosure and virtual agents has found, people seem to be more truthful when interacting with virtual humans than when interacting with other people. The current work extends this research to show that not only are people more truthful with virtual agents, they are more truthful despite situational variables, namely time of day, that can significantly affect ethical behavior. This is useful information regarding the utility of virtual agents in contexts where honest disclosure is essential. If people behave more or less ethically depending on time of day, employing a virtual agent for truthful disclosure, particularly in the afternoon and evening, may be preferred to overcome barriers to honesty. Additional inquiry is necessary to fully unpack what might be mediating this phenomenon. One potential theory is that humans engaged in a task with a virtual agent assume the agent has more or perfect information and therefore determine that any lie will be in vain. There might also be an effect of novelty; as people become more accustomed to interacting with virtual agents, this effect may extinguish. Longitudinal investigation is suggested to evaluate whether or not the novelty of interacting with a virtual agent can account for these behaviors.

Acknowledgements

This work was supported by the National Science Foundation under grants IIS-1211064 and BCS-1419621, and the U.S. Army. Any opinion, content or information presented does not necessarily reflect the position or the policy of the United States Government, and no official endorsement should be inferred.

References

1. Gajadhar, B., de Kort, Y., IJsselsteijn, W.: Shared fun is doubled fun: player enjoyment as a function of social setting. Fun and games pp. 106–117 (2008)
2. Gratch, J., DeVault, D., Lucas, G.: The benefits of virtual humans for teaching negotiation. In: International Conference on Intelligent Virtual Agents. pp. 283–294. Springer (2016)
3. Kouchaki, M., Smith, I.H.: The morning morality effect: The influence of time of day on unethical behavior. Psychological science 25(1), 95–102 (2014)
4. Krämer, N.C., von der Pütten, A., Eimler, S.: Human-agent and human-robot interaction theory: Similarities to and differences from human-human interaction. In: Human-computer interaction: The agency perspective, pp. 215–240. Springer (2012)
5. Lucas, G.M., Gratch, J., King, A., Morency, L.P.: Its only a computer: virtual humans increase willingness to disclose. Computers in Human Behavior 37, 94–100 (2014)
6. de Melo, C.M., Gratch, J.: Beyond believability: quantifying the differences between real and virtual humans. In: International Conference on Intelligent Virtual Agents. pp. 109–118. Springer (2015)
7. Ravaja, N.: The psychophysiology of digital gaming: The effect of a non co-located opponent. Media Psychology 12(3), 268–294 (2009)
8. Reeves, B., Nass., C.: The media equation: How people treat computers, television, and new media like real people and places. Cambridge University Press (1996)

Fixed-pie Lie in Action

Zahra Nazari ✉, Gale Lucas, Jonathan Gratch
University of Southern California,
Institute for Creative Technologies, Los Angeles, California
Email: znazari@usc.edu, {lucas, gratch}@ict.usc.edu

Abstract. Negotiation is a crucial skill for socially intelligent agents. Sometimes negotiators lie to gain advantage. In particular, they can claim that they want the same thing as their opponents (i.e., use a "fixed-pie lie") to gain an advantage while appearing fair. The current work is the first attempt to examine effectiveness of this strategy when used by agents against humans in realistic negotiation settings. Using the IAGO platform, we show that the exploitative agent indeed wins more points while appearing fair and honest to its opponent. In a second study, we investigated how far the exploitative agents could push for more gain and examined their effect on people's behavior. This study shows that even though exploitative agents gained high value in short-term, their long-term success remains questioned as they left their opponents unhappy and unsatisfied.

Keywords: Human-Agent Negotiation, Behavioral Game Theory, Deception

1   Introduction

Negotiations are an essential part of our everyday social interactions. Any socially intelligent entity must consider negotiation as an important domain to perform successful interactions with humans. Virtual humans with negotiation capabilities can support novel forms of electronic commerce [1], teach people how to improve their negotiation skills [2][3][4] and, more generally, serve as a challenge problem to advance intelligent virtual agent research [5].

One of the key social skills in human negotiations is how to exchange information about what each side wants. Unlike the rational analysis of negotiation in game theory [6] (where such communication is often considered "cheap talk" that can't be verified and thus be ignored), or most computational approaches to negotiation (where agents simply exchange offers [7] and must indirectly infer what the other side wants), human negotiators talk directly about their goals and interests in a negotiation. In general, information exchange helps human negotiators better understand each side's perspective, often leading to better deals on both sides [8]. Unfortunately, this exchange of information provides an opportunity for malicious actors to use deception for gaining disproportionate advantage.

Research has recently explored the potential of agent technology to understand and model how people use deceptive information exchange to maximize their own self-interest. For example, Gratch and colleagues [9] introduced the *misrepresentation*

© Springer International Publishing AG 2017   287
J. Beskow et al. (Eds.): IVA 2017, LNAI 10498, pp. 287-300, 2017.
DOI 10.1007/978-3-319-67401-8_38

game, a game theoretic analysis of how a deceptive party could misrepresent its preferences to gain benefit, while seeming fair and honest. They proved a particular communication strategy, called the *fixed pie lie*, is the optimal solution to the misrepresentation game and provided some evidence that the technique was effective against human participants. Their proof and evidence, however, rely on assumptions that are unlikely to hold in real-world situations. The liar asks questions about preferences of the user in a one-way information exchange and ends with an ultimatum-type take-it-or-leave-it complete offer. In more realistic negotiations, however, parties are free to ask any questions they like, make tentative offers, and make counter-proposals to offers they receive. Also, both parties are free to lie. Thus, it is unclear if an agent can use this strategy in more realistic settings. In this paper, we explore the misrepresentation game in a more realistic context. Building on a platform that supports human-agent negotiation [10], we investigate Gratch and colleagues' solution to the misrepresentation game under far less restrictive conditions. We show that the fixed-pie lie is surprisingly effective in practice. These results give insight into how people use deceptive communication. They also highlight ways that people (and potentially automated agents) can exploit naïve negotiators. Ultimately, such models facilitate techniques to recognize and protect against such practices.

2   Misrepresentation Game

Gratch and colleagues [9] introduced the *misrepresentation game* to analyze how a deceptive actor could best lie to gain advantage. In negotiations, parties try to decide over several issues under discussion. Each of the parties have their own priorities and preferences, and they should consider the interests of their opponent to come up with an agreement that is acceptable to both. Negotiators, however, are usually not aware of their opponent's preferences and must infer them through exchange of information and offers. Discovering preferences of the opponent is a challenge for both human and automated negotiators [11], [12]. This information exchange provides the opportunity for malicious actors to misrepresent their own preferences to gain advantage. The misrepresentation game uses a game theoretic analyses of how a deceptive agent could best lie, and provides an optimization solution to this problem. Here, we briefly describe this game.

The *misrepresentation game* is defined in the following model of negotiation, known as bilateral multi-issue bargaining. There are two parties that must reach agreement over a set of issues. Each issue can have one of many possible levels, and the value that each party derives from the agreement can be written as a utility function over the assigned levels for the issues. In the misrepresentation game [9], the party under consideration (called the *deceiver*) tries to claim a false set of preferences such that a personally-advantageous solution appears as a fair and efficient solution to the opponent. More formally, let a_i be the deceiver's true preferences for issue i, b_i be the true preference of the opponent for this issue, and x_i and y_i be the agreed upon levels for these players. The objective is to find a 'false' preference $\bar{a}_i$ that maximizes the deceiver's utility, given that the negotiated solution appears to be efficient and fair if $\bar{a}_i$ is believed. This can be written as the following optimization problem (under the assumption that issues are independent).

$$\max_{\bar{a}_i} \sum_{i=1}^{n} a_i \cdot x_i \qquad (1)$$

where x_i is the optimal solution of

$$\max_{x_t, y_t} \bar{a}_i \cdot x_i \qquad (2)$$

such that :

$$\sum_{i=1}^{n} \bar{a}_i \cdot x_i \leq \sum_{i=1}^{n} b_i \cdot y_i \qquad (3)$$
$$\forall i : x_i + y_i \leq L_i \qquad (4)$$
$$0 \leq x_i, y_i \leq L_i \qquad (5)$$

Here L_i is the total number of levels (discrete case) or amount of resource (continuous case). The optimization program (2-5) capture the problem of finding the optimal solution under the fairness constraint (3), known as Kalai's fairness. It can be shown that this optimization problem can be solved by mixed integer-linear programming [13].

Gratch and colleagues [9] showed that the deceiver's best strategy in the misrepresentation game is to always pretend that the negotiation has a distributive structure (i.e., the two parties have the same valuation on issues), even if it does not. That is, honesty is the best policy in distributive negotiations, but in an integrative negotiation a malicious player can gain advantage from a "fixed-pie lie." Either way, a malicious player should simply pretend the same preferences as their opponent's. After building a sufficiently complete model of the opponent, the deceiver then proposes a deal that gives the opponent a disproportionate amount of the opponent's favorite issue, and keeps a disproportionate amount of the rest. This deal appears fair but benefits the deceiver.

Gratch and colleagues [9] provided evidence for effectiveness of this strategy in a simplified setting. In their setting, the agent started by asking questions about preferences of the user in a one-way information exchange and ended with an ultimatum type take-it-or-leave-it complete offer. In more realistic negotiations, however, parties are free to ask any questions they like, make tentative offers, and make counterproposals to offers they receive. Also, both parties are free to lie. Thus, it is unclear if an agent can use this strategy in more realistic settings.

In this paper, we aim to answer this question using a publicly available platform called IAGO [10] that provides a realistic environment for negotiations between agents and humans. A few characteristics that make IAGO a great choice for our purpose are: 1) It supports partial offers, 2) Offer exchange is not limited to alternative offer protocol, 3) Visual representation of emotional signals are provided and 4) Communication of preferences are made possible. This platform is used in human-agent competitions in the IJCAI conference and is a powerful framework to conduct human-agent negotiations.

3   Framework and Implementation

The goal of this work is to investigate if virtual agents can successfully use fixed-pie lie strategy in realistic negotiation settings. We use IAGO which is the only agent-human negotiation platform that provides many characteristics of natural human-human negotiation settings. In this section first we briefly describe the IAGO platform, and next we explain the architecture of our agent that was used to implement and test the fixed-pie lie strategy.

3.1   IAGO Platform

IAGO is a web-based platform proposed for conducting negotiations between agents and humans. It consists of a user interface that human users can interact with and an API that agent designers can use for their agent implementation.

Fig. 1. IAGO's User Interface

IAGO provides a web-based interface that could be displayed on a web browser via a link. The user then can interact with the implemented agent using the environment shown in Fig. 1. The window on right shows the conversation between the agent and the user. Negotiation partners can exchange full or partial offers (e.g., I'll offer you 1 bars of iron and take 3), ask and exchange information about preferences (e.g., "what do you like best? I like iron more than copper") and exchange emoji' that to convey emotional state.

3.2   Agent design

To successfully apply and examine "fixed-pie lie" strategy and compare it to control conditions, our agents must be able to handle three critical requirements: 1) They must make an accurate model of the opponent's preference profile (User Modeling), 2) communicate an intended preference profile (User Influence) and 3) evaluate the utility of deals to come up with desired offers, or accept/reject received offers (Decision Making). In this section, we briefly present the mechanisms by which our agents implement each of these three components.

User Modelling. The agent starts with no information about users' preference profile and attempts to acquire maximal information through communication with them. The agent explains to the user about the importance of communication and asks questions about user's preferences. At each point in the negotiation the agent saves a space of possible preferences for the user based on the information it has gathered up to that point. For example, in the beginning and for a three issues negotiation over bars of gold, silver, and iron, this space is constructed of six possible preferences (Table 1.a). If the user expresses that she likes gold best, then only two possible preference profiles remain (Table 2.b), and after user's answer to if she likes silver or iron more (Table 1.c for iron), the agent has a solid estimation of the user preference profile.

Table 1. tables show the space of possible utility weights for all issues under negotiation.

Gold	Silver	Iron
1	2	3
1	3	2
2	1	3
2	3	1
3	1	2
3	2	1

Gold	Silver	Iron
3	1	2
3	2	1

Gold	Silver	Iron
3	1	2

1.a   1.b   1.c

When asked about preferences, users may provide contradictory information. This could be due to laziness, lying or just unintentional errors. To detect such incidents and keep the user expressions consistent, we implemented a "contradiction check" element that is called after each preference expression made by the user. If the new expression was consistent with the previous ones, the knowledge base gets updated; otherwise, the user is informed about the inconsistency and asked for correction. The following is a description of how contradiction check works in our agents.

Contradiction Check.
To verify that a user's preference expression is consistent with her previous statements, the agent keeps a graph representation of preferences expressed by the user. Each node in this graph represents an issue, and each edge represents a relative connection. The method will add a new expression (and the corresponding edges) only if

it does not create a loop in the graph. Otherwise, the contradiction check fails and the user is notified. For example, in a negotiation over three issues of gold, iron, and silver, the graph has three nodes, one for each issue. If a user states "I like gold the best", edges are is added from all other issues to gold (here, iron and silver). If the user then expresses "I like silver more than gold", adding this new edge could create a loop in the graph (from gold to silver, and silver to gold); The agent will inform the user about the inconsistency and asks for correction.

Shaping the User's Model of the Agent. During the negotiation, the agent provides the user with information about the agent's preferences. This information could be in the form of voluntary information exchange in return for users' similar behavior, or by answering questions asked by the user. A variable "Honesty" specifies how to shape the user's model of the agent. A truthful agent will communicate its actual preference profile; however, a liar agent would communicate the same preference profile as the user.

Decision Making. Once an agent has a proper model of the user's preferences, along with its own preference profile, the agent can calculate how much each deal is worth for itself and how much for the user. The percentage of the joint outcome value that the agent receives is the criterion evaluating each deal. For example, if a deal is worth 22 points for the agent and 22 points for the user, a fair agent will accept it, but an exploitative one will reject it. The same module is used to pick an offer to propose from the agent side.

3.3   Negotiation Task

The misrepresentation game illustrates how a negotiator can use the integrative potential in a multi-issue negotiation task to gain advantage while seeming fair. Even though this "fixed-pie lie" strategy works best when the task is fully integrative, we use a partial integrative task to demonstrate the generalizability of the strategy[1]. The negotiation was framed as a "Resource Exchange Game" where opponents negotiated over four issues of gold, silver, copper and iron. In this task, negotiators should distribute four bars from each issue (overall 16 bars) between themselves. The preference profiles for the agent and the user (shown in Table 2) are used as weights to calculate the gained utility value for each party. For example, if an agent receives four bars of iron, two bars of silver and two bars of copper, the utility value will be calculated as: $(4*4) + (2*3) + (2*2) = 26$. User receives the remaining bars (two bars of silver, two bars of copper and four bars of gold) which gets her $(4*4) + (2*2) + (2*3)$

---

[1] In a fully distributive negotiation, stating that the situation is "a fixed-pie" is the truth. Therefore, the fixed-pie lie strategy would not gain negotiators any advantage in such a situation.

= 26 points. If they fail to reach an agreement, each party receives 4 points, which makes this their BATNA (Best Alternative To Negotiated Agreement) value.

Table 2. Preference profile for the considered negotiation task.

	Gold	Silver	Copper	Iron
User	4	3	2	1
Agent	1	3	2	4

4   Methods

4.1   Study 1

We used a 2 (Agent Fairness: Fair vs Exploitative) x 2 (Agent Honesty: Truthful vs Liar) design to examine the effects of the agent's fairness and honesty on the participant's behavior in our designed negotiation task.

Fairness (fair vs. exploitative) specifies the value threshold of the deals that are acceptable to the agent. Fair agents would only accept deals that give the agent 50% of the total joint value, and exploitative agents would only settle for 60% or more of the overall joint value.

Honesty (truthful vs. liar) specifies the type of information the agent will provide to the participant. A truthful agent would provide truthful information about its own preferences and a liar will pretend the same preferences as the opponent (fixed-pie lie).

We hypothesized that

H1: Fair agents should require that users make fewer offers to reach agreement compared to exploitative ones.

H2: Liar agents should require that users make fewer offers to reach agreement compared to truthful ones.

We recruited 223 participants using Amazon's Mechanical Turk (MTurk) service as subjects for our study. Participants were presented with a demographic survey followed by instructions on the negotiation task, their preferences, BATNA, and how to interact with the IAGO agent. Next, they were given 10 minutes to negotiate with the agent and come up with an agreement or walk out of the negotiation. Following the negotiation, they were asked to rate how satisfied they were with the results, as well as rate the agent's level of honesty, fairness and strategy.

To ensure that participants understood their priorities in the negotiation, they also completed a manipulation check. Specifically, they were asked to report which items were the most and least valuable for them. From the original 223 participants, 11 failed the manipulation check. These participants were excluded, leaving 212 for analysis.

4.2   Study 2

In this study, we investigated the effectiveness of more exploitative agents. We used a 2 (Agent Fairness: More Exploitative vs Most Exploitative) x 2 (Agent Honesty: Truthful vs Liar). Honesty was manipulated as in study1. Fairness, however, was operationalized in this study as more exploitative (asked for 69% of the overall joint value) and most exploitative (asked for 76% of the overall joint value).

In addition to testing H2 again, we also extent hypothesis H1 to predict that

H3: The more exploitative agent should require that users make fewer offers to reach agreement compared to most exploitative one.

Study flow was the same as the first study and 114 participants were recruited using Amazon's Mechanical Turk (MTurk) service as subjects for this study. From the original 114 participants, 1 failed the manipulation check. This participant was excluded, leaving 113 for analysis.

4.3   Measures

Two main types of measures were considered for evaluating effectiveness of the agent when negotiating with humans: behavioral measures and self-report measures.

Behavioral Measures. The low value of alternative to no agreement (BATNA) in our negotiation task encourages participants to agree on some deal rather than leaving the negotiation with no agreement. However, these agents in only propose (and ultimately accept) deals that gain them equal or more than a specific threshold value (depending on fairness condition). To the extent that participants find this value acceptable, they will propose fewer counter offers. Therefore, the number of counter offers proposed by the participants indicates their dissatisfaction with the agent's proposed value.

Self-report measures. We used self-report measures to assess satisfaction and perceptions of the agent's level of honesty, fairness and strategy. After the negotiation, participants reported their satisfaction with the outcome using a 7-point scale that ranged from 1 (very dissatisfied) to 7 (very satisfied). Then participants rated the agent on honesty, fairness and strategy using 1-7 scales that ranged from 1 (dishonest, unfair, or not-strategic) to 7 (honest, fair, or strategic, respectively).

5   Results

5.1   Study 1

Out of 212 analyzed negotiations, only 6 failed to reach an agreement and settled for their BATNA value. A 2 (Agent Fairness: More Exploitative vs Most Exploitative) x 2 (Agent Honesty: Truthful vs Liar) ANOVA shows that, while there were significant main effects of agent fairness and honesty on user offers ($F(1, 208) = 6.82, p = .01$, d $= .36$ and $F(1, 208) = 3.92, p = .049$, d $= .29$, respectively), these were qualified by a significant interaction (F(1, 208) = 6.68, *p* = .01, d = .36). As depicted in Fig. 2, both main effects were driven by users' reactions to the honest exploitative agent compared to the other conditions.

Likewise, the main effects of agent fairness and honesty on satisfaction were either significant (F(1, 208) = 17.61, *p* < .001, d = .59) or at least trend-like (F(1, 208) = 2.26, *p* = .13, d = .21), respectively, but again they were qualified by a significant interaction (F(1, 208) = 14.88, *p* < .001, d = .55). As depicted in Fig. 3, both main effects were again driven by users being less satisfied with the honest exploitative agent compared to the other conditions.

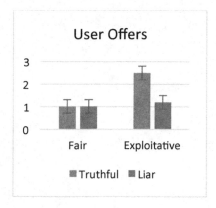

Fig. 2. The number of offers made by users in each condition

Fig. 3. Self-assessed rating on how satisfied the users were at the end of negotiation

In contrast, users' perceptions of the agent's honesty were unaffected by actual honesty (F(1, 208) = 1.55, *p* = .22, d = .17) or fairness (F(1, 208) = 0.86, *p* = .36, d = .13). However, there was a significant interaction (F(1, 208) = 19.61, *p* < .001, d = .63); as depicted in Fig. 4, the liar fair agent and the honest exploitative agent were both perceived as less honest than the other conditions. Perhaps either appearing to give too much or too little, respectively, can reduce perceived honesty.

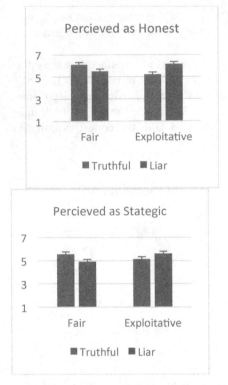

Fig. 4. How honest (left) and strategic (right) agents were perceived by the user (Study 1)

Similarly, users' perceptions of the agent's strategy were unaffected by honesty $(F(1, 208) = 0.39, p = .53, d = .09)$ or fairness $(F(1, 208) = 0.15, p = .70, d = .06)$, but there was a significant interaction $(F(1, 208) = 7.37, p = .007, d = .40)$. As depicted in Fig. 4, the liar fair agent and the honest exploitative agent were also both perceived as less strategic than the other conditions, again perhaps because users thought that either giving too much or too little was not particularly strategic.

5.2   Study 2

Out of 109 analyzed negotiations, 18 failed to reach an agreement and settled for their BATNA value. A 2 (Agent Fairness: More Exploitative vs Most Exploitative) x 2 (Agent Honesty: Truthful vs Liar) ANOVA revealed a significant effect of agent honesty on user offers $(F(1, 109) = 7.89, p = .006, d = .54)$, such that users made fewer offers to agents that lied $(M = 1.90, SD = 1.90)$ than those that told the truth $(M = 3.22, SD = 2.94)$. The main effect of agent fairness and the interaction effect both failed to approach significance $(Fs < .14, ps > .71, ds < .06)$.

However, in this study, participants were no more likely to report feeling satisfied based on the honesty of the agent $(F(1, 109) = 0.55, p = .46, d = .14)$. Instead, there was a trend for participants to report greater satisfaction with the less exploitative of the two agents in this study $(M = 4.41, SD = 2.12 \text{ vs } M = 3.77, SD = 2.00; F(1, 109) =$

2.73, p = .10, d = .31). The interaction effect did not approach significance (F(1, 109) = 0.33, p = .57, d = .11).

Likewise, users' perceptions of the agent's honesty were unaffected by actual honesty of the agent (F(1, 109) = 1.05, p = .31, d = .19). Instead, participants perceived the less exploitative of the two agents in this study as marginally more honest (M = 4.67, SD = 1.86 vs M = 4.08, SD = 1.71; F(1, 109) = 3.08, p = .08, d = .33). Again, the interaction effect did not approach significance (F(1, 109) = 0.85, p = .36, d = .18).

In contrast, while there were also trends for main effects of agent fairness and honesty on perceptions of how strategic the agent was (F(1, 109) = 2.03, p = .16, d = .27 and F(1, 109) = 2.56, p = .11, d = .31, respectively), these were qualified by a significant interaction (F(1, 109) = 7.83, p = .006, d = .54). As depicted in Figure 5, both main effects were driven by users perceiving the truthful agent that is relatively less exploitative as more strategic than the other conditions.

6   Discussion and Conclusion

The misrepresentation game is a game theoretic analyses of how a deceptive agent should lie best to gain advantage in a negotiation. Gratch et al. [9] proposed a solution to this problem that the deceiver should feign similar preferences to the opponent for best outcome (fixed-pie lie). This strategy is theoretically proven to be optimal, however, the feasibility of utilizing it by agents in a realistic environment was never tested. Here, we used a publicly available negotiation platform, IAGO, to test this strategy in realistic negotiations with humans.

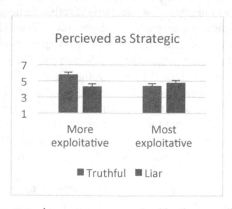

Fig. 5. How strategic agents were perceived by the users (Study 2)

In the first study, we examined the effect of honesty and fairness on user's behavior. We hypothesized that fair agents would require users to make fewer offers to reach agreement compared to the exploitative agent (H1). This hypothesis was confirmed. However, the effect was specifically driven by the truthful exploitative agent, with which users had the hardest time reaching agreement.

Our next hypothesis was that liar agents would require users to make fewer offers to reach agreement compared to truthful agents (H2). Although this hypothesis was confirmed in exploitative condition, participants treated the liar and truthful agents in the fair condition similarly. In exploitative condition, participants also found the liar agent more honest and fairer than the truthful agent, suggesting that there might be a "sweet spot" for deceptive agents. That is, the liar exploitative agent gained the most value, while appearing fair and honest. This result confirms the effectiveness of "fixed-pie lie," particularly in a partially integrative task. In fair condition, however, we found an interesting effect. Even though the liar agent appears to give up a larger share of the overall value, there was a trend for users to be less satisfied with the outcome and find the agent less strategic and less honest. People do not seem to trust an agent who gives up too much or too little, emphasizing the importance of appearing fair (but not too fair) when using "fixed-pie lie" strategy.

Study 1 confirmed the effectiveness of "fixed-pie lie" in partially integrative situations. However, because users showed high levels of satisfaction across the board, we conducted a second study that pushed the boundaries of fairness by using more exploitative agents. We expected the more exploitative agents to require fewer offers from users to reach agreement compared to the most exploitive agents (H3). However, we did not find such effect. It is possible that pushing the boundaries of fairness in this way led to general dissatisfaction. However, Study 2 replicated the finding that liar agents require users to make fewer offers to reach agreement compared to the truthful agent.

Although agents in Study 2 achieved higher gain (only 18 participants walked out of the negotiation out of 109, even though the agents were selfishly asking for 69% or 76% of the overall value), this is probably unrealistic for how agent would do in practice. Since in real-world negotiations users might refuse to negotiate with such agents after this initial exchange, because they were generally dissatisfied, these gains would likely be short-term. In contrast, the liar agent who appears to be fair makes people feel good while gaining more value. The smaller sample size in Study 2 contributed to the effects not reaching traditional levels of significance. For example, three of the trend-like or marginally significant effects would have reached significance if Study 2 had been powered as well as Study 1 (higher satisfaction with the less exploitative agents, higher ratings of honesty for the less exploitative agents, and higher ratings of strategic for the honest agents). Likewise, one trend would have would have been on edge of significance if Study 2 had the sample size of Study 1 (higher ratings of strategic for the less exploitative agents).

These findings emphasize there are clear incentives to creating deceptive agents. An obvious next question is how to avoid or defend against the proliferation of such methods. One often discussed approach is to create ethical guidelines to prevent their creation, yet this is not so simple as it may appear. For example, the type of deception explored in this paper is not actually considered lying by the ethical guidelines that govern human negotiations (see discussion at the end of [9]). Further, the value a negotiator assigns to specific issues is often subjective and difficult to objectively verify. As a result, some negotiation ethicists argue that ethical proscriptions will certainly fail and the only realistic approach is to give people the skills required to detect and defend against such techniques [14]. Indeed, one approach to defeat the fixed-pie lie is to give the opponent what they claim they want to force them to reveal the deception or take a loss to save face. Unfortunately, few of our human participants employed this tactic, and suggests a strong opportunity for using this technology for teaching better skills.

Acknowledgements

This work was supported by the National Science Foundation under grants IIS-1211064 and BCS-1419621, and the U.S. Army. Any opinion, content or information presented does not necessarily reflect the position or the policy of the United States Government, and no official endorsement should be inferred.

References

1.   T. Baarslag, M. Kaisers, E. H. Gerding, C. M. Jonker, and J. Gratch, "When will negotiation agents be able to represent us The challenges and opportunities for autonomous negotiators," in *Proceedings of the Twenty-sixth International Joint Conference on Artificial Intelligence*, 2017.

2.   R. Lin, Y. Oshrat, and S. Kraus, "Investigating the benefits of automated negotiations in enhancing people's negotiation skills," in *Proceedings of The 8th International Conference on Autonomous Agents and Multiagent Systems-Volume 1*, 2009, pp. 345–352.

3.   M. Core, D. Traum, H. C. Lane, W. Swartout, J. Gratch, M. van Lent, and S. Marsella, "Teaching negotiation skills through practice and reflection with virtual humans," *Simulation*, vol. 82, no. 11, pp. 685–701, 2006.

4.   J. Broekens, M. Harbers, W.-P. Brinkman, C. M. Jonker, K. den Bosch, and J.-J. Meyer, "Virtual reality negotiation training increases negotiation knowledge and skill," in *International Conference on Intelligent Virtual Agents*, 2012, pp. 218–230.

5.   J. Gratch, D. DeVault, G. M. Lucas, and S. Marsella, "Negotiation as a challenge problem for virtual humans," in *International Conference on Intelligent Virtual Agents*, 2015, pp. 201–215.

6.   M. J. Osborne and A. Rubinstein, *A course in game theory*. MIT press, 1994.

7.   N. R. Jennings, P. Faratin, A. R. Lomuscio, S. Parsons, M. J. Wooldridge, and C. Sierra, "Automated negotiation: prospects, methods and challenges," *Gr. Decis. Negot.*, vol. 10, no. 2, pp. 199–215, 2001.

8.   L. L. Thompson, "Information exchange in negotiation," *J. Exp. Soc. Psychol.*, vol. 27, no. 2, pp. 161–179, 1991.

9.   J. Gratch, Z. Nazari, and E. Johnson, "The Misrepresentation Game: How to win at negotiation while seeming like a nice guy," in *Proceedings of the 2016 International Conference on Autonomous Agents & Multiagent Systems*, 2016, pp. 728–737.

10. J. Mell and J. Gratch, "IAGO: Interactive Arbitration Guide Online," in

Proceedings of the 2016 International Conference on Autonomous Agents &
Multiagent Systems, 2016, pp. 1510–1512.

11.   Z. Nazari, G. Lucas, and J. Gratch, "Opponent Modeling for Virtual Human
       Negotiators," in *Intelligent Virtual Agents*, 2015.
12.   T. Baarslag, M. Hendrikx, K. Hindriks, and C. Jonker, "Predicting the
       performance of opponent models in automated negotiation," *Proc. - 2013
       IEEE/WIC/ACM Int. Conf. Intell. Agent Technol. IAT 2013*, vol. 2, pp. 59–66,
       2013.
13.   J. Gratch and T. Nguyen, "Misrepresentation Negotiation Games." , Univ.
       South. Calif. Inst. Creat. Technol. Play. Vista, CA, 2016.
14.   P. R. Reilly, "Was Machiavelli right? Lying in negotiation and the art of
       defensive self-help," 2008.

Generation of Virtual Characters from Personality Traits

Fabrizio Nunnari[1,3]✉ and Alexis Heloir[2,3,4]

[1] fabrizio.nunnari@dfki.de
[2] alexis.heloir@dfki.de
[3] DFKI-MMCI, SLSI group, Saarbrcken, Germany
[4] LAMIH UMR CNRS/UVHC 8201, Valenciennes, France

Abstract. We present a method to generate a virtual character whose physical attributes reflect public opinion of a given personality profile. An initial reverse correlation experiment trains a model which explains the perception of personality traits from physical attributes. The reverse model, solved using linear programming, allows for the real-time generation of virtual characters from an input personality. The method has been applied on three personality traits (dominance, trustworthiness, and agreeableness) and 14 physical attributes and verified through both an analytic test and a subjective study.

1 Introduction

In narrative contexts, such as motion pictures, as well as in interactive contexts, such as video games or conversational agents, a virtual character feels authentic when it fulfills the audience's expectations: the character's appearance should match her/his personality as well as her/his behavior [7]. It has been shown that the better a character looks the part, the more believable and effective she/he will be in the narrative [9,3].

This paper presents a *traits-to-attributes* mapping methodology to generate a virtual character whose physical attributes comply with most people's expectations regarding its assumed personality. The method relies on the use of attributes-based character generation software such as MakeHuman[5] (Figure 1, right), Adobe/Mixamo Fuse[6], Daz3D[7], and Poser[8]. These editors account for the customization of a default character through a set of sliders. Each slider controls the deformation of a physical attribute, such as gender, age, height, torso width, finger length, distance between eyes, and the like.

A personality model is a list of traits (dimensions), and the personality profile of an individual is expressed as the quantification, in a closed range, of each trait. The generation method that we propose has been applied to three personality traits: *dominance*, *trustworthiness*, and *agreeableness*. The *dominance*

---

[5] http://www.makehuman.org/ − 10 July 2017
[6] http://www.adobe.com/products/fuse.html − 10 July 2017
[7] http://www.daz3d.com/ − 10 July 2017
[8] http://my.smithmicro.com/poser-3d-animation-software.html − 10 July 2017

J. Beskow et al. (Eds.): IVA 2017, LNAI 10498, pp. 301–314, 2017.
DOI 10.1007/978-3-319-67401-8_39

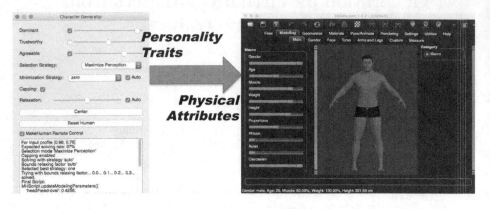

Fig. 1. Our character generation tool (left) allows a designer to provide a personality profile as input. It automatically modulates (some of the) physical attributes of a character editor (MakeHuman, right) so that the resulting character's appearance matches the personality profile given as input.

and *trustworthiness* traits were selected because of their wide acceptance as orthogonal components in the judgment space for first encounters with zero acquaintance [12,4]. Additionally, since there is evidence that people formulate a judgment in less than a second [16], these two traits are suitable candidates for experiments which need to crowd-source many votes in a limited amount of time. We extended the original setup of Oosterhof and Todorov [12] by exposing users to full-body pictures and by adding an additional trait taken from the well established OCEAN model [11] (namely: openness to experience, conscientiousness, extraversion, agreeableness, and neuroticism). We selected agreeableness because there is evidence that people often rely on this trait to guess at the supposed personality of newcomers they meet [1]. This last choice gave us the possibility to investigate how the system behaves with non-orthogonal trait combinations.

Since both the description of a character and a personality profile can be mathematically expressed as points in a closed multi-dimensional space, the *traits-to-attributes* generation consists of mapping a point into a target space with different dimensions. The *traits-to-attributes* generation method accounts for two phases: off-line training and real-time generation. The training phase (Section 3) aims at extracting people's convictions about the association of personality to physical appearance. This knowledge gathering is performed via *reverse correlation* experiments. The generation phase (Section 4) uses linear programming to generate a virtual character from a personality profile. In the remainder of the paper, Section 2 provides an overview of the related work using reverse correlation to support character generation from personality descriptors. Section 5 presents a selection of examples demonstrating the versatility of our approach and the results of a subjective evaluation. Finally, Section 6 concludes the paper.

2 Related work

Reverse Correlation (RC) is an experimental method aiming at highlighting which features of a large set of stimuli better predict judgments. In the field of social perception, it was introduced by Mangini et al. [8] to find out which elements of the human face influence the perception of gender, and discriminate among expressions (happy, sad). An RC perception experiment usually consists of presenting a set of pictures, each one showing a person or an avatar, to a number of subjects and asking them to rank the pictures using Likert scales, along one or more traits. When the synthetic images are parameterized using a set of morphological descriptors, it is possible to highlight the relationship between the perception of an abstract trait (e.g., dominance) and the underlying morphological parameters describing the test images.

The work presented above delivers models able to predict the judgment of an image from the descriptors of the image. Conversely, for authorial purposes, prediction models should be reverted and allow for the creation of a reliable stimulus for an expected judgment. This approach has recently been a subject of few, but promising, investigations. For example, Durupinar et al. [5] developed a system to alter the style of an animation of a virtual character based on the input of an OCEAN personality profile.

As for the creation of the characters' mesh, Vernon et al. [15] developed a system capable of generating new face illustrations from three personality traits: dominance, approachability, and youthful-attractiveness. Similarly to our approach, they gather votes to bootstrap a set of linear models predicting the traits which maximize the perception of the three traits. They later reverse the model using a multi-layered perceptron so they can generate plausible faces from a set of desired traits. However, since the training is based on the location of facial landmarks, rather than high-level morphological parameters, the resulting faces (cartoon-style representation of the key areas that influence the perception of the traits) are usable for illustrative purpose but not for practical authoring.

Recently, Streuber et al. [13] proposed a system for the generation of virtual characters from a set of more than 30 words describing the body shape. Their system is again based on an initial training phase and generation via reverse modeling. It generates bodies belonging to a vector space defined by height principal components obtained from a large collection of scanned human meshes. In contrast, our method focuses on supporting a high degree of uncorrelated physical attributes, leading to a significant difference in the ratio between the cardinalities of the input and the output (e.g., in our work, 3 traits to determine 14 body/face descriptors).

All the works which we surveyed so far conduct RC experiments using Likert ratings. However, Likert scales present several limitations, such as the reluctance of subjects to vote at the extremes of a scale, the subjective variation of votes across sessions, and the need to re-scale previous votes when new absolute references are met [10]. For these reasons, our RC experiments are based on the paired comparison (PC) voting system [2].

Table 1. The attributes modulating the shape of the virtual characters.

MakeHuman ID	Short Name	Description	min	max
chin/chin-bones-in—out	Chin bones	Chin lateral bones extension	0.5	1
chin/chin-height-min—max	Chin height	Distance between chin and lips	0.2	0.8
eyebrows/eyebrows-angle-up—down	Eyebrow angle	Eyebrow inclination	0.2	0.8
eyes/r-eye-size-small—big	Eye size	Size of both eyes	0.1	0.9
head/head-oval	Head ovality	Hard/soft forehead corners	0	0.8
macrodetails-height/Height	Height	From ca. 149cm to 201cm	0.25	0.75
macrodetails-universal/Muscle	Muscularity	Muscular tone of the body	0.2	0.8
macrodetails-universal/Weight	Weight	Overall mass of the body	0.2	0.8
mouth/mouth-scale-horiz-incr—decr	Mouth hscale	Mouth and lip width	0.1	0.9
mouth/mouth-scale-vert-incr—decr	Mouth vscale	Mouth and lip height	0.1	0.9
neck/neck-scale-horiz-less—more	Neck hscale	Neck width	0	1
nose/nose-scale-horiz-incr—decr	Nose hscale	Nose width	0.1	0.9
stomach/stomach-tone-decr—incr	Stomach tone	Belly in/out	0.2	1
torso/torso-vshape-less—more	Torso V-shape	Affects shoulder width	0	0.8

3   Training the model

The training phase aims at building a linear model which, given the physical aspect of a virtual character, predicts how observers would grade its personality traits. The training consists of:

- *Data collection.* Given a set of randomly generated virtual characters, and a number of traits to judge, a pool of human subjects is called to judge on the perception of each trait on each character. Each virtual character is then associated to a numerical quantification of the perception of each trait;
- *Building a prediction model.* A linear regression is run to build a model for the prediction of a trait value from the physical appearance of the character;
- *Simplifying the model.* The full linear models are simplified in order to discard the physical attributes which do not significantly contribute in the perception of a trait. The simplification is performed using two strategies: the first (p-minimization) minimizes the number of attributes, while the second (R-maximization) maximizes the prediction power for a trait.

Data collection. We collected information about the perception of personality traits in relation to physical appearance with a reverse correlation user study based on a paired comparison voting mode. The paired comparison is a preference learning technique which aims at ranking a set of items by asking a preference between two items at a time. Given N items, the number of possible pairs is $P = N * (N - 1)/2$. As output, the paired comparison associates an *estimate* value to each of the items, allowing for their relative ranking.

A set of 50 randomly generated virtual characters was judged by a panel of 50 volunteers on three personality traits: dominance, trustworthiness, and agreeableness. The pictures of the virtual characters were generated using the open source software MakeHuman. MakeHuman allows for the customization of a default character using more than 200 sliders. Each slider modulates the influence of a morph target. For the generation of the characters we selected 14 attributes (listed in Table 1) which visibly alter the appearance of the character

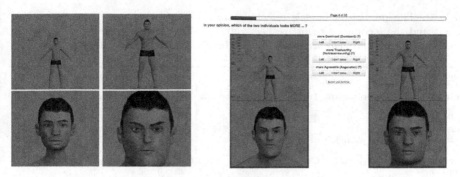

Fig. 2. Left: The characters generated by simultaneously fully minimizing (left) and maximizing (right) all the 14 physical attributes. Right: An example of the voting page shown during the data collection.

in frontal view. In addition, in order to limit biases related to gender or ethnicity discrimination, we locked the *gender* slider to fully masculine and the *ethnicity* to fully Caucasian. Figure 2, left, shows the extreme virtual characters that can be generated by minimizing or maximizing all the 14 physical attributes at once.

Each of the 50 participants voted on 50 pairs of virtual characters through an interface shown in Figure 2, right. Participants were university students from various faculties belonging to different nationalities (30 DE, 5 IN, 3 RU, 2 MEX, 2 IT, 8 not listed); mean age 23.44 years (sd=3.86); level of education: 26 high-school diploma, 11 bachelor's degree, and 13 master's degree. The experiment was conducted in a German university. The experimenters provided instructions in either German or English and supervised the voting session. Each voting session lasted up to 15 minutes. Each voter was rewarded with a meal coupon with a value of 2.85 Euros. On average, the time needed to vote on a pair was 11.38 secs (sd=6.49), and each of the 1225 possible pairs was voted 2.04 times.

The computation of the PC estimates associates each virtual character to a triplet of values, which indicate how much an observer perceives the character as *dominant, trustworthy,* and *agreeable*. For each trait t, the minimum and maximum estimates (E_t^{min}, E_t^{max}) are used to normalize the input traits in a range $[0, 1]$. The estimates were computed using the *prefmod* [6] R module. All the experiments were conducted on the online DeEvA platform[9].

Building the prediction model. We derive three separate linear models, one for each of the three personality traits $t \in T$, by performing a **linear regression** between the character's attributes (predictors) and the trait estimates (measured variable). The output of each regression is: i) an intercept value i_t, and ii) a row vector of coefficients C_t. Given a set of attribute values as column vector $X = \{x_a, a \in A\}$, where A is the set of physical attributes, the formula to estimate the value p_t of the personality trait t is:

$$p_t = i_t + C_t \times X \tag{1}$$

---

[9] https://deeva.mmci.uni-saarland.de/ – 10 July 2017

Table 2. The prediction models selected via p-minimization and R-maximization. The C_x and the p columns report respectively the slope and the p-value of the linear regression for each physical attribute (*=< 0.05, **=< 0.01, ***=< 0.001).

Selection	p-minimization			R-maximization		
Trait (t)	Dominant	Trustworthy	Agreeable	Dominant	Trustworthy	Agreeable
#selected attr.	6	4	4	12	7	9
adjusted R^2	0.903	0.726	0.747	0.917	0.749	0.769
intercept (i_t)	-2.156	0.129	0.316	-2.174	-0.241	-0.012
Attribute Name	C_D p	C_T p	C_A p	C_D p	C_T p	C_A p
Chin bones	- -	- -	- -	0.223 0.196	- -	- -
Chin height	- -	- -	- -	0.344 *	0.601 *	- -
Eyebrow inclination	2.100 ***	-2.080 ***	-2.234 ***	2.092 ***	-2.258 ***	-2.313 ***
Eye size	- -	0.451 *	0.432 *	- -	0.455 *	0.328 0.094
Head ovality	- -	-0.661 ***	-0.782 ***	-0.178 0.077	-0.740 ***	-0.675 ***
Height	1.688 ***	0.829 **	0.897 **	1.846 ***	1.131 ***	0.970 **
Muscularity	0.335 *	- -	- -	0.326 *	0.314 0.165	0.324 0.166
Weight	0.605 ***	- -	- -	0.538 ***	- -	- -
Mouth/lip width	- -	- -	- -	-0.124 0.239	- -	0.284 0.130
Mouth/lip height	- -	- -	- -	-0.110 0.273	- -	0.221 0.197
Neck width	0.521 ***	- -	- -	0.483 ***	- -	- -
Nose width	- -	- -	- -	-0.212 0.065	- -	0.210 0.298
Stomach tone	- -	- -	- -	- -	- -	-0.287 0.089
Torso V-shape	0.524 ***	- -	- -	0.409 ***	-0.251 0.180	- -

Simplifying the prediction model. Each of the three linear models is simplified into two simpler models using a **backward elimination**. The backward elimination approach is an iterative model selection technique which reduces the number of predictors (here, the physical attributes) explaining a variable. We apply the backward elimination with two selection strategies: *p-value minimization* and *R-correlation maximization*.

The model selection based on **p-minimization** considers the p-value associated to each variable as a result of the regression and discards the variable with the higher p-value above the threshold α. The algorithm iterates using the reduced variable set until there are no variables with p-value $\geq \alpha$. In this work, we use $\alpha = 0.05$. In contrast, the model selection based on **R-maximization** takes into account the correlation factor R of the initial regression. Then it computes how the correlation varies by removing each variable, one at a time. The algorithm removes the variable which causes the lowest increment of R and iterates until no removal increases the correlation factor. The selection by p-minimization leads to models with a minimal set of variables, while the selection with R-maximization leads to models with the highest prediction power. The former method allows us to trigger the perception of a trait using the smallest possible number of attributes, leaving more freedom to the author for further customization, while the latter method is more suitable to maximize the perception of the trait. The linear regressions and the model selection were computed in the R programming environment using the default `lm` function. The maximization was based on the adjusted-R-squared correlation factor.

Table 2 shows the results for all of the six models selected using both p-minimization and R-maximization strategies for each trait. As expected, in the p-minimization mode there are fewer attributes compared to the R-maximization. Since the correlation of the estimates between trustworthiness and agreeableness is very high (r=0.965), they share the same attributes. On the other hand, the correlation is lower for dominance vs. trustworthiness (r=-0.402) (confirming the findings of Oosterhof et al. [12]) and for dominance vs. agreeableness (r=-0.400). These finding match with previous research. Concerning the perception of dominance, Toscano et al. [14] already reported on the importance of the inclination of the eyebrows, and Windhager et al. [17] reported the relevance of the rectangularity of the face and of the chin bones. Furthermore, both of the aforementioned works recognized the influence of lip thickness, mouth width, and the eyes' aperture. This experiment, which includes full-body pictures, adds the relevance of the height, weight, muscularity, neck and shoulder width, and stomach tone to the perception of these three traits.

4   Character generation model

The generation of the character takes as input a set of traits and a quantification of their desired level of perception for an observer. The output consists of the values of the physical attributes needed to build an avatar whose appearance triggers the perception of the input personality. In the rest of this section:

- *Problem statement* describes how the generation problem is posed as a linear programming problem;
- *Filter by solvability rate* addresses the issue of unsolvability of a linear problem for some trait combination. It shows how to estimate the solvability chances through simulation;
- *The objective function* illustrates why we need to define several objective functions and how to find, for each trait combination, the function which minimizes prediction errors;
- *Coerce attribute progression* illustrates an additional pair of constraints which improve the smoothness of the solution space; and
- *Evaluating the coercion* presents a quantitative measurement of the improvements introduced by the coercion mechanism.

Problem statement. The linear models derived in the previous section can be combined into a single linear system which can be reverted to calculate the expected physical attributes from a set of personality trait values. Given a personality profile $P = \{p_t, t \in T, E_t^{min} \leq p_t \leq E_t^{max}\}$, the values of X (physical attributes) that lead to the perception of P can be calculated by solving the linear problem:

$$\arg \min_{X} \{G * X\} = \arg \min_{X} \{g_a x_a, a \in A\} \tag{2}$$

subject to:

$$P - I = \mathbf{C} * X \tag{3}$$

Table 3. For each trait combination, the table shows a *solvability rate*, i.e., the chance of being able to generate a character from a given personality profile.

Selection Traits	p #Attrs	#Coeffs	Solve Rate	R #Attrs	#Coeffs	Solve Rate
D	6	6	100.0%	12	12	100.0%
T	4	4	100.0%	7	7	100.0%
A	4	4	100.0%	9	9	100.0%
D,T	8	10	91.1%	13	19	99.7%
D,A	8	10	90.0%	14	21	97.2%
T,A	4	8	3.3%	11	16	62.7%
D,T,A	8	14	4.1%	14	28	55.8%

$$a^{min} \leq x_a \leq a^{max}, a \in A \qquad (4)$$

where $G = \{g_t, t \in T\}$ is the row vector of coefficients of the *objective function*, and $I = \{i_t, t \in T\}$ is the vector of intercepts. The matrix $C = (c_{t,a})$ contains on each line the coefficients C_t of the linear model of a trait (see Table 2): each column is associated to an attribute, and $c_{t,a} = 0$ if the attribute has been eliminated from the trait during the model selection. Finally, each $x_a \in X$ is bound to its min/max values, as documented in Table 1. As for the dimensions: $|P| = |I| = |T|$, the number of traits; $|X| = |A|$, the number of attributes; and the matrix C has $|T|$ rows and $|A|$ columns.

For convenience, the input is provided as normalized personality profile vector $\hat{P} = \{\hat{p}_t \in [0,1], t \in T\}$. The non-normalized vector P of estimates is calculated as: $P = \{E_t^{min} + (E_t^{max} - E_t^{min}) * \hat{p}_t, t \in T\}$, where E^{min} and E^{max} are the vectors of minimum and maximum estimates for each trait. In this work, we solve linear problems using the simplex method as implemented in the `linprog` function exposed by the `scipy.optimize`[10] python module.

Filter by solvability rate. A linear problem might be impossible to solve. In order to provide feedback to the user about the feasibility of a request, we precompute a *solvability rate* for each trait combination for both p and R selection. As can be seen in Table 3, the percentage of solvability drops when the model combination contains highly correlated traits (trustworthiness and agreeableness). The DTA combination in R-maximization rises to 55.8% thanks to the fact that the (higher number of) attributes distribute differently between the T and A traits. Further analysis will consider only trait combinations where the success rate is above 90%, plus the combination of all the three traits (DTA) in R-maximization selection, because it provides the most interesting study case.

The objective function. In linear programming, each coefficient $g_a \in G$ of the objective function (Equation 2) is ideally associated to a *cost*. Among an infinite number of possible solutions, the solver will choose a vector X which minimizes the overall cost.

However, in our case there is not an obvious cost associated to a physical attribute. Hence we conceived and tested six different strategies to assign, for

---

[10] `https://www.scipy.org/` – 10 July 2017

Table 4. Top: The average MSE for each objective function in different selection/trait combinations. The bold text highlights the minimum value(s) for each condition.

Selection	Traits	Minimization Strategy						Solve Rate
		zero	one	minus_one	sign_count	sum_coeff	sum_coeff_over_p	
p	D	0.289	0.290	0.301	0.301	0.289	**0.286**	100%
	T	0.244	0.244	0.261	**0.233**	0.244	0.251	100%
	A	0.239	0.239	0.259	**0.236**	0.239	0.245	100%
	D,T	0.252	0.252	0.263	0.262	0.252	**0.248**	100%
	D,A	0.251	0.251	0.255	0.256	0.251	**0.245**	98%
R	D	0.311	**0.310**	0.332	0.319	0.311	0.318	100%
	T	**0.287**	**0.287**	0.311	0.300	**0.287**	0.290	100%
	A	**0.291**	**0.291**	0.324	0.310	**0.291**	0.300	100%
	D,T	**0.287**	0.291	0.307	0.289	**0.287**	0.299	100%
	D,A	0.285	**0.284**	0.306	**0.284**	0.285	0.294	100%
	D,T,A	0.266	**0.264**	0.289	0.275	0.266	0.278	100%

each attribute $a \in A$, the corresponding coefficient $g_a \in G$:

zero: $g_a = 0$. The solver is subject only to the equality (Equation 3) and to the variable boundaries (Equation 4).

one: $g_a = 1$. The solver will push all variables to their minimum value.

minus_one: $g_a = -1$. The solver will push all variables to their maximum value.

pos_neg_usage_count: $g_a = \sum_{t \in T} -sgn(c_{t,a})$. The solver will maximize variables with a high number of positive coefficients (vice versa for negative ones).

sum_coeff: $g_a = \sum_{t \in T} -c_{t,a}$. The higher the overall coefficients sum, the more the variable will be favored in the maximization. The aim is to give a higher priority to maximization of variables with stronger positive correlations (vice versa for negative correlations).

sum_coeff_over_p: $g_a = \sum_{t \in T}(-c_{t,a}/p_{t,a})$. As the sum_coef strategy, plus each coefficient will be divided by its p-value resulting from the linear regression. The smaller the p-value, the higher the absolute value of the cost. This strategy increases the influence for variables with higher significance.

In order to assess the efficacy of each minimization strategy, we solved the *traits-to-attributes* problem using the same data used for training. In practice, we took the personality triplet associated to each of the 50 virtual characters and back-calculated their physical attributes. Then, we measured the mean squared error (MSE) for each attribute and averaged all of them together. The MSEs are normalized on each attribute min/max range. Table 4 shows the MSE of each minimization strategy for each condition. More elaborate strategies, taking into account the coefficient and the significance of an attribute, helped in reducing the error only for the p-minimization mode (fewer attributes). Given a trait combination, the *traits-to-attributes* model will use this table during the generation phase to select the minimization strategy which leads to the smallest error.

The average error among all conditions, in percentage ($\sqrt{MSE}*100$), is 51.9% (min 48.3%, max 55.6%, sd 2.5%). The next paragraph explains the reason for such high error and presents a strategy to reduce it.

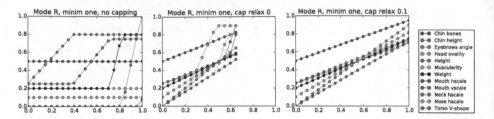

Fig. 3. Variation of the attribute values (y) as a function of the level of *dominance* (x). Left: unbounded; Center: capped with no relaxation; Right: capped with relax, at 0.1.

Coerce attribute progression. As defined so far, the *traits-to-attributes* model provides solutions with an uneven increment of the attribute values over the input range. For example, as can be seen in Figure 3 (left), as the level of dominance increases, the solver maximizes the attribute values one by one, and some of the attributes are locked at their maximum/minimum value. Overall, this increments the error rate of the solver. Also, for authorial purposes a smoother and more evenly distributed increment of all attributes over the trait range would be preferred.

Hence, we introduced a *capping* mechanism to drive the attributes towards a smoother increment. The capping mechanism is based on the sign of the coefficients of the objective function: if a coefficient g_a is negative (i.e., the solver tends to maximize the variable) we impose as upper bound to the variable x_a the same value of the input trait. Vice versa, the bound is on the lower value when g_a is positive. In the case of multiple input traits, the upper and minimum bounds are set to the maximum and minimum value among all traits. Figure 3 (center) shows the result of this strategy: the behavior of the attributes has improved, but the bounding restriction leads more easily to unsolvable problems. Hence, we introduce a relaxation factor $R \in [0, 1]$ which softens the capping constraints. The resulting capping strategy is formally expressed as:

$$\begin{cases} x_a \leq a^{max} - (a^{max} - a^{min}) * \max\{p \in \hat{P}\} * (1 - R) & g_a < 0 \\ x_a \geq a^{min} + (a^{max} - a^{min}) * \min\{p \in \hat{P}\} * (1 - R) & g_a > 0 \end{cases}$$

If the coefficient g_a is 0, the variable bounds are in any case constrained to $a^{min} \leq x_a \leq a^{max}$, as defined in the basic model. With $R = 0$ the bounds are strict and the linear problem is harder to solve, while with $R = 1$ there is no more effect of the capping and the "one-by-one increment" behavior arises. Figure 3 (right) shows the behavior with $R = 0.1$. To verify that the capping mechanism improves the precision, we recomputed the MSEs table with the *capping* enabled and a relaxation set at 0.25. Although the solve rate decreased from 99.8% to 84.3%, the average error decreased from 51.9% to 31.7% (sd 5.1%).

Evaluating the coercion. We evaluated the behavior of the coercion mechanism for all of the three traits in both p and R selection modes. For each trait (D, T, or A), we solved the traits-to-attributes problem with and without the capping

Table 5. Correlation gain between noCap and Cap conditions.

	P					R				
trait	noCap mean (sd)	Cap mean (sd)	gain	Fisher's p	noCap mean (sd)	Cap mean (sd)	gain	Fisher's p
D	0.619 (0.345)	0.992 (0.005)	**60.29%**	<0.001	0.276 (0.386)	0.964 (0.067)	**249.23%**	<0.001
T	0.776 (0.179)	0.820 (0.339)	5.68%	0.395	0.497 (0.385)	0.940 (0.085)	**88.95%**	<0.001
A	0.781 (0.176)	0.895 (0.186)	**14.60%**	<0.01	0.536 (0.356)	0.907 (0.181)	**69.29%**	<0.001

mechanism (Cap, noCap) by providing an input from 0.0 to 1.0 in 101 equidistant steps. In the Cap condition, the relaxation factor is automatically determined by trying to progressively solve the problem with relaxation starting from 0.0 and 0.1 step increments. When 1.0 is reached, the problem is by definition solved as in the noCap condition. In our tests, about 50% of the problems were solved with relaxation at 0.0. The remaining problems were solved with a relaxation value uniformly distributed between 0.1 and 1.0. We computed the correlations between the input trait value and every output attribute. Table 5 reports the average of the correlations among all attributes. The correlations systematically incremented in the Cap condition. The last column reports the significance of the difference between the two correlations using a Fisher r-to-z transformation. With the exception of trustworthiness in p mode, all the correlations increased significantly.

5   Examples and validation study

A prototype GUI (see Figure 1, left) allows artists an interactive exploration of the personality space through a set of sliders. The user can enable or disable each trait independently and can decide to minimize the number of attributes or maximize the perception of the traits. The system automatically selects the objective function which minimizes the error. Also, it tries to solve the problem with an initial relaxation factor of 0.0 and increments of 0.1. A text area previews the script that will be executed by MakeHuman. For the execution, we implemented a MakeHuman plugin which allows for the remote execution of scripts via TCP connections. Figure 4 shows several examples of generation using one to three attributes at the same time.

We ran three experiments to assess the quality of the generation model. In *Experiment 1*, following the same procedure described in Section 3, 36 participants (27 male, 9 female) of different nationalities (16 DE, 4 IN, 3 CH, 13 not listed) voted on 25 pairs randomly composed from 11 virtual characters. The characters were created by modulating *input* dominance from 0.0 to 1.0 with 0.1 increment steps. Similarly to the training experiment (Section 3), subjects had to answer "Which of the two characters looks more dominant?". An analysis of the paired comparison data determined a level of *perceived* dominance for each character. A linear regression between the *input* and the *perceived* dominance led to a correlation factor of 0.984.

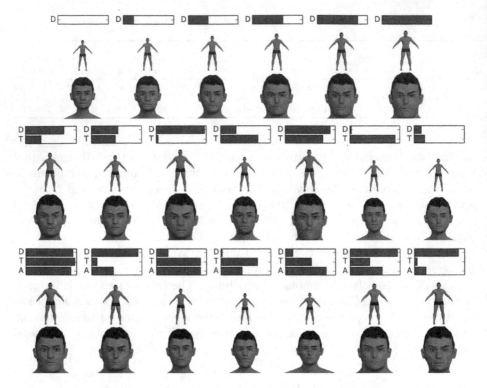

Fig. 4. Examples of generation in Maximize Perception mode (12 physical attributes). Top: progression of *dominance* from 0% to 100%. middle: generation with *dominance* and *trustworthiness*. bottom: including *agreeableness*.

In *Experiment 2*, 37 participants (28 male, 9 female) of different nationalities (16 DE, 4 IN, 3 CH, 14 not listed) voted on 25 pairs from 50 randomly generated virtual characters. The characters were created by randomly modulating both dominance and trustworthiness in the range 0.0 to 1.0. Subjects had to answer which of the two characters looked more dominant and which one more trustworthy. An analysis of the paired comparison data determined a level of *perceived* dominance and *perceived* trustworthiness for each character. A linear regression between the *input* and *perceived* dominance led to a correlation factor of 0.933, while the correlation between *input* and *perceived* trustworthiness is 0.716.

In *Experiment 3*, 40 participants (28 male, 12 female) of different nationalities (21 DE, 4 IN, 4 GR, 11 not listed) voted on 50 random pairs from 125 randomly generated virtual characters. The generation of the characters, the voting method, and the data analysis are the same as for Experiment 2, with the addition of agreeableness. The correlation between *input* and *perceived* trait is 0.903 for dominance, 0.733 for trustworthiness, and 0.717 for agreeableness.

We assessed the capability of the model to scale on multiple traits using a Fisher r-to-z transformation. The test measures the significance of the difference

Table 6. Results of the validation study. Left: The correlations between input and perceived trait values. Right: the significance of the variation of the correlations.

Exp	Traits	#participants	#characters	correlation D	T	A
1	D	36	11	0.984 -	-	
2	D, T	37	50	0.933 0.716	-	
3	D, T, A	40	125	0.903 0.735	0.717	

Trait	Experiments	Fisher's p
D	1 vs. 2	**0.067**
D	2 vs. 3	**0.259**
D	1 vs. 3	0.016
T	2 vs. 3	**0.810**

between two correlation factors, and we applied it on four pairs of correlations. In this case, the absence of significant difference is desirable, because it means that the correlation between the input and the perceived values of a trait is not affected by the introduction of more traits to the model. For *dominance*, there is no significant difference in the correlations between Experiments 1 and 2 (p=0.067), meaning that the insertion of trustworthiness did not degrade the perception of dominance. As well, there is not significant difference in the correlations between Experiments 2 and 3 (p=0.259), meaning that introducing agreeableness did not degrade the perception of dominance when dominance and trustworthiness are generated together. However, there is a significant difference between Experiments 1 and 3 (p=0.016), meaning that the capability to generate a dominant character significantly decrease when trustworthiness and agreeableness are added to the model. Yet, the significance is modest and the correlation for dominance is still above 0.9. For *trustworthiness*, there is no significant difference between experiments 2 and 3 (p=0.810), meaning that the capability of generating a trustworthy character in the dominance/trustworthiness model doesn't degrade when including agreeableness into the model.

Overall, the above described results (summarized in Table 6), suggest that the method scales relatively well when adding more traits to the generation process. Time and resource constraints prevented us from running studies with the three remaining combinations (trustworthiness and agreeableness, alone and paired), which is desired for future work.

6   Conclusions and future work

This paper introduced a method to draft virtual characters whose appearance suggests to observers a given personality. The method is composed of a training phase, based on reverse correlation experiments, and a real-time generation phase, exploiting linear programming. The method accounts for a *coercion* constraining mechanism which improves the linearity of the solutions. A subjective user study suggests that the system scales well when generating characters using both orthogonal and quasi-co-linear traits. In future experiments we will investigate how the method behaves with a higher number of traits, such as all of the Big Five [11] simultaneously. Although this work focuses on personality traits, the same method can be applied to any kind of subjective descriptor, such as beauty, scariness, appeal, empathy, and the like, paving the way for the generation of virtual characters based on textual input.

Acknowledgements

The authors would like to thank Nicolas Erbach for his precious help with the code development and in conducting the user studies.

References

1. Ames, D.R., Bianchi, E.C.: The agreeableness asymmetry in first impressions: Perceivers' impulse to (mis)judge agreeableness and how it is moderated by power. Personality and Social Psychology Bulletin 34(12), 1719–1736 (2008)
2. Bradley, R.A., Terry, M.E.: Rank analysis of incomplete block designs. Biometrika 39, 324–335 (1952)
3. Cassell, J.: Social practice: becoming enculturated in human-computer interaction. In: Universal Access in Human-Computer Interaction. Applications and Services, Lecture Notes in Computer Science, vol. 5616, pp. 303–313. Springer (2009)
4. Dotsch, R., Todorov, A.: Reverse correlating social face perception. Social Psychological and Personality Science 3(5), 562–571 (2012)
5. Durupinar, F., Kapadia, M., Deutsch, S., Neff, M., Badler, N.I.: PERFORM: Perceptual approach for adding OCEAN personality to human motion using laban movement analysis. ACM Transactions on Graphics 36(1), 1–16 (2016)
6. Hatzinger, R., Dittrich, R.: prefmod: an R package for modeling preferences based on paired comparisons, rankings, or ratings. Journal of Statistical Software 48(10), 1–31 (2012)
7. Loyall, A.B.: Believable agents: building interactive personalities. PhD dissertation, Carnegie Mellon University, Pittsburgh (1997)
8. Mangini, M.C., Biederman, I.: Making the ineffable explicit: estimating the information employed for face classifications. Cognitive Science 28(2), 209–226 (2004)
9. Mansour, S., El-Said, M., Rude-Parkins, C., Nandigam, J.: The interactive effect of avatar visual fidelity and behavioral fidelity in the collaborative virtual reality environment on the perception of social interaction. In: Proceedings of the 10th International Conference on Communications. pp. 387–395. WSEAS (2006)
10. Martinez, H., Yannakakis, G., Hallam, J.: Don't classify ratings of affect; rank them! Affective Computing, IEEE Transactions on 5(3), 314–326 (2014)
11. McCrae, R.R., John, O.P.: An introduction to the five-factor model and its applications. Journal of Personality 60(2), 175–215 (1992)
12. Oosterhof, N.N., Todorov, A.: The functional basis of face evaluation. Proceedings of the National Academy of Sciences 105(32), 11087–11092 (2008)
13. Streuber, S., Quiros-Ramirez, M.A., Hill, M.Q., Hahn, C.A., Zuffi, S., O'Toole, A., Black, M.J.: Body Talk: Crowdshaping realistic 3d avatars with words. ACM Trans. Graph. 35(4), 54:1–54:14 (2016)
14. Toscano, H., Schubert, T., Sell, A.N.: Judgments of dominance from the face track physical strength. Evolutionary Psychology 12(1), 1–18 (2014)
15. Vernon, R.J.W., Sutherland, C.A.M., Young, A.W., Hartley, T.: Modeling first impressions from highly variable facial images. Proceedings of the National Academy of Sciences 111(32), E3353–E3361 (2014)
16. Willis, J., Todorov, A.: First Impressions: Making Up Your Mind After a 100-Ms Exposure to a Face. Psychological Science 17(7), 592–598 (2006)
17. Windhager, S., Schaefer, K., Fink, B.: Geometric morphometrics of male facial shape in relation to physical strength and perceived attractiveness, dominance, and masculinity. American Journal of Human Biology 23(6), 805–814 (2011)

Effect of Visual Feedback Caused by Changing Mental States of the Avatar based on the Operator's Mental States using Physiological Indices

Yoshimasa Ohmoto ✉, Seiji Takeda, and Toyoaki Nishida

Kyoto University, Graduate school of Infomatics,
Yoshidahonmachi, Sakyo-ku, Kyoto-shi, Kyoto-hu, Japan
{ohmoto@,stakeda@ii.ist.,nishida@}i.kyoto-u.ac.jp

Abstract. Use of a virtual environment allows rehearsal or practice in specialized situations, extraordinary environments, or circumstances in which mistakes are not allowed. However, virtual experiences often do not translate to the real world. We propose to regard a virtual avatar as an agent which mediates between virtual experiences and the real ones. The aim of this study is to investigate how to enhance the effect of virtual experiences. To achieve this, we propose a method of providing feedback on human mental state by using affective avatar expressions based on physiological indices. We conduct experiments to evaluate the effect of the method. As a result, we find that feedback from avatar expressions can increase participants' physiological responses without reducing concentration on the task. We suggest that this feedback can enhance commitment to virtual-world experiences.

Keywords: physiological indices; mental state estimation; affective computing; mental feedback

1 Introduction

Virtual reality (VR) techniques and devices are developing rapidly. One application using virtual reality is a training game that is used in education, medical services, wellness, and fitness (e.g. [5]). In these applications, people acquire various techniques and abilities through game playing (e.g., [1]) or games used for physical rehabilitation (e.g., [8]).

However, there are significant differences between virtual experiences and real-world ones. Besides the fact that the physical feedback is different, social contexts that are provided in the virtual space are very different from ourselves in the real world. In many cases, we feel that the avatar in the virtual world is a different "person" from us. On the other hand, we expect that people often find themselves identifying strongly with the main character in a cinematic movie. This encourages us to think about making contents in a virtual world that could influence the behavior of people in the real world. Rosenberg et al. [9] showed

© Springer International Publishing AG 2017
J. Beskow et al. (Eds.): IVA 2017, LNAI 10498, pp. 315-324, 2017.
DOI 10.1007/978-3-319-67401-8_40

that playing prosocial video games could lead to greater subsequent prosocial behavior in the real world. They illustrated the potential of using VR technology to increase prosocial behavior in the physical world.

We propose regarding a virtual avatar as an agent which mediates between virtual experiences and real ones. In our preliminary experiment, we developed a semi-automated telepresence robot which modified behavior based on the operator's intentions. As a result, we confirmed that the telepresence robot could smoothly interact with interaction partners. By improving the architecture, we are developing a semi-automated mediation agent in the virtual world. The mediation agent reflects the intentions and the mental states of the operator based on the operator's physiological cues. As a first step towards making the mediation agent, we investigated that the effect of visual feedback caused by changing expressions of the avatar based on the operator's physiological cues.

On the other hand, it is difficult to estimate mental state from the observations of behavior. In previous work, we investigated continuous interaction in decision-making tasks (e.g., [6]) using physiological indices to estimate the participants' mental state in order to achieve a smooth and satisfactory human-agent interaction. We thus use the physiological indices to estimate the operator's mental states. In this study, "mental states" means relatively perceived change in emotions, such as happy, angry, and relaxed.

The long-term goal of our research is to develop a method for enhancing the degree to which a virtual experience in a video game corresponds to the equivalent experience in the real world. We think that it is helpful to regard a virtual avatar as an agent which mediates between virtual experiences and real ones. As a first step toward achieving this goal, the present study investigated an effect of providing feedback on the human operator's mental state based on physiological indices and the task context by an avatar's affective expressions. We focused on "commitment" to the virtual world experience, and the subjective feelings toward the avatar. In this study, the "commitment" means one of the mental states in which the operator is immersed to the virtual world.

2   Related works

There are diverse studies on estimating the states by measuring physiological indices, which are related to the sympathetic and the parasympathetic nervous system. Mandryk et al. [4] reported that the normalized physiological indices would correspond to subjective reported experience.

There are several studies that use physiological indices to estimate mental states of people in their virtual experineces. For example, Lin et al. [3] reported physiological data correlate with task performance data in a video game: with a decrease of the task performance level, the normalized Skin Conductance Responses (SCR) increases.

One of the studies which try to directly improve human's mental states using the physiological responses is biofeedback. Biofeedback is a process that enables an individual to learn how to change physiological activity for the purposes of improving health and performance. Brain activity measurements are also used in recent researches (e.g. [11]). The biofeedback techniques are often applied to medical care (e.g. [10]). In several researches, they are also applied to games [2].

Most previous works used the physiological indices for improving the task performance and regulating the task difficulties. The main aim of biofeedback studies is that the users control their mental state and improve performance. In human-human communication in virtual world, the operator's emotions are reflected using diverse ways, but the expressions are provided for communication partners. We used the avatar's expressions as visual feedback for matching the mental states in the real world and that in the virtual activities.

3   Biofeedback-driven avatar expressions

Using affective avatar expressions to reflect human mental state is a form of biofeedback. This is a process that enables an individual to learn how to change their physiological activity in order to improve health and performance. The feedback provided by the affective avatar expressions implicitly indicates the relationships between the virtual avatar and its human operator. In this study, we propose a feedback mechanism that is based on mental state estimation by physiological indices. We investigate the effects of the feedback on commitment to the virtual game task, and the subjective feelings toward the avatar.

3.1   The physiological indices for estimating mental states

Physiological indices are biological reactions caused by the autonomic nervous system, such as brain waves, potential differences in cardiography, variations in blood pressure, pulse waves, respiration, body temperature, muscle potential, and skin conductance. In continuous interaction, some of these are susceptible to noise from body motion. We used skin conductance responses (SCRs) and electrocardiograms (LF/HF values) because these are relatively resistant to noise.

Sweating is controlled by the sympathetic nervous system, and can be elicited by emotional stimuli, intellectual strain, or painful cutaneous stimulation. The underlying mechanisms of SCR are related more to anticipation, expectation, and attention concentration. We thus expected that the SCR could be used to tell when someone is dealing with an unexpected or thrilling situation. For electrocardiograms, the LF/HF value is calculated from the instantaneous heart rate. It shows heart-rate variability, which is controlled by the sympathetic and parasympathetic nervous systems and humoral factors. It is caused by sensory intake and sensory rejection. We thus expected that the LF/HF (heart-rate variability) would show reactive responses based on external stimuli.

3.2   Feedback mechanism in an interactive game environment

The multiple physiological indices mentioned above are possible clues to human mental states. We applied the method previously to an advice agent in an interactive exercise game and confirmed that the method was successful [7]. In this study, we used the estimation for providing mental feedback as the avatar's affective expressions in the same environment. The task is described below.

Task Participants performed a virtual exercise game that involved two rival playing characters. In addition, each participant was accompanied by an advice agent that supported the game play. The exercise game was an action video game in which three players (the human participant and two automated characters) competed for points in two different ways; carrying a teddy bear character to point-scoring area or hitting another player with a virtual ball. The human player was free to choose his strategy for maximizing his points. For example, he could hide in the game field after earning enough points to win the game. Alternatively, he could earn points by waiting near a point-scoring area for hitting other players. Each player had to consider his strategy based on that of the other players and his own states, such as game scores, motivations, and remaining time.

Affective avatar expression as mental feedback The avatar of the human player provided affective expressions when major events occurred in the task. The events and the corresponding affective expressions are listed below. a) Getting points: the avatar performs a "mopping the brow" motion when the operator earns points by carrying a bear. b) Hitting a player: the avatar performs a "fist pump" motion when the operator hits another player with a ball. c) Knock out: the avatar performs a "stamping the ground" motion when hit by a ball thrown by another player. These events occur approximately 15 times in a game played by an ordinary player. In other words, the player encounters an event every 30 s on average. The avatar provides the appropriate motion when the physiological indices of the operator show the following values. a) Getting points: LF/HF shows 20.0 or more and SCR shows 17.0 or more within 5 s after the event starts. b) Hitting a player: LF/HF shows 20.0 or more within 5 s after the event starts. c) Knock out: SCR shows 17.0 or more within 5 s after the event starts.

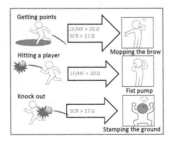

Fig. 1. Summary of the motions and thresholds.

The motions and thresholds are summarized in Fig. 1. The thresholds are determined by values in preliminary experiments. The conditions for providing feedback are different because the impressions based on the characteristics of each event are different. The conditions are determined by the experiences of the operator involved in the virtual world. For example, when "getting points" occurs, the operator feels happy (hence we expect the LF/HF value to be high) and anticipates getting more points (hence we expect the SCR value to be high). We thus set the conditions as presented above.

4   Experiment

The purpose of the experiments was to investigate whether the psychological feedback from the affective avatar expressions influenced the human player's unconscious mental state and/or their subjective feelings about the virtual experience. We conducted experiments using three types of avatar. First, there was a "feedback" avatar that provided psychological feedback using our proposed method (feedback group). Second, there was an "expression" avatar that randomly provided the same affective expressions as those of the feedback avatar irrespective of the participant's mental state with a constant probability (33% in this case) (expression group). Finally, there was a "no-response" avatar that did not provide any affective expressions (no-response group). The "expression" probability was based on the occurrence rate in a preliminary experiment using the feedback avatar. In the experiments, we measured physiological responses and issued a questionnaire that the participants answered afterward.

4.1   Experimental setting

The experimental setting is shown in Figure 2. We used a 360° octagonal immersive display that comprises eight portrait-orientated 65" LCD monitors and Unity[1] to construct the virtual environment and the two agents. In this environment, participants could easily look around in the virtual space with low cognitive load as in the real world. The player's virtual avatar could be controlled by their body motions using motion sensors placed on the participant's dominant arm, both feet, and waist. These sensors captured throwing and stepping motions and body orientation. The participant could control the virtual avatar intuitively using body motions with low physical constraints.

To estimate the mental state of the participant, an exercise quantity was estimated from the stepping motion. The SCR and the electrocardiogram (LF/HF) were recorded by a Polymate mini[2] to measure the physiological indices. These were sent to the game system in real time.

4.2   Procedure

Each participant was briefly instructed on the experimental procedures. Electrodes for measuring SCR and the LF/HF electrocardiogram value were then

---

[1] http://unity3d.com/
[2] http://www.miyuki-net.co.jp/en/

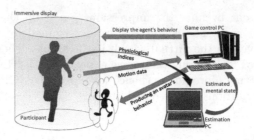

Fig. 2. The experimental setting.

attached to the participant's left hand and his chest. After a 2-min relaxation period, the experimenter started the video cameras and the recording of the physiological indices. The participant first performed a practice session, followed by four 8-min game sessions with a 1-min interval after each one. At the conclusion of the experiment, the participant completed a questionnaire.

The participants in the experiment were 30 male[3] undergraduate students between the ages of 19 and 22 (average of 20.8 years old). We separated the participants randomly into three groups: a feedback group (FB group), an expression group (EX group), and a no-response group (NR group).

4.3   Results

Based on the measured physiological indices, we calculated the number of peaks in LF/HF responses, and the number of peaks in SCR responses in each game session. Our analyses did not include data from the first game session in each experiment because the virtual-world experiences were still novel to the participants at that stage. The participants answered three questions on their subjective feelings about the experiences. The purpose of these questionnaires is to survey the subjective evaluation on the relationships between their mental states and the virtual world expressions intuitively. These were on a seven-point scale, presented as ticks on a black line without numbers.

LF/HF We counted the number of peaks in LF/HF responses over the thresholds in each game session. The thresholds were 5, 10, 15, 20, and 25. The results are shown in Fig. 3. The data were analyzed using Kruskal-Wallis H tests because a part of the data did not pass Bartlett test for homogeneity of variance. As a result, except at >10, there are significant differences or marginally significant differences (>5, $\chi^2=6.351$, p=0.041; >10, $\chi^2=2.883$, p=0.24; >15, $\chi^2=6.078$, p=0.047; >20, $\chi^2=5.665$, p=0.058; >25, $\chi^2=4.976$, p=0.082). After that, we performed Steel-Dwass multiple comparison tests. At >5, there is a

---

[3] To measure electrocardiograms, we had to put electrodes on the participant's chest, but no female experimenters belonged to our research group. Therefore, the participants were only males.

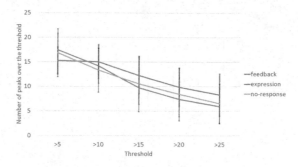

Fig. 3. The results of LF/HF response analysis.

significant difference between the expression group and the feedback group (expression group > feedback group: W=-3.704, p=0.022). However, after >15, the relationship is reversed (expression group ¡ feedback group: >15, W=3.557, p=0.030; >20, W=3.515, p=0.034; >25, W=3.095, p=0.076). The trend of each data after >15 is the same but the number of peaks in only the feedback group between >5 and >10 does not decrease. This means that the participants in the feedback group showed big responses to the external stimuli in the virtual world.

SCR We counted the number of peaks in SCR responses over the thresholds in each game session. The thresholds were 15.75, 16.0, 16.25, 16.5, 16.75, 17.0, 17.25, and 17.5. The results are shown in Fig. 4. The data were analyzed using Kruskal-Wallis H tests because a part of the data did not pass Bartlett test for homogeneity of variance. As a result, at >16.5, there are significant differences or a marginally significant difference (>15.75, χ^2=1.577, p=0.46; >16.0, χ^2=1.084, p=0.59; >16.25, χ^2=1.916, p=0.39; >16.5, χ^2=5.310, p=0.069; >16.75, χ^2=7.449, p=0.023; >17.0, χ^2=9.056, p=0.0098; >17.25, χ^2=11.69, p=0.0025; >17.5, χ^2=13.05, p=0.0011). After that, we performed Steel-Dwass multiple comparison tests. After >16.5, there are significant differences between them (no-response group < feedback group: >16.5, W=-3.528, p=0.033; >16.75, W=-4.303 p=0.0062; >17.0, W=-4.522, p=0.0028; >17.25, W=-5.039, p=0.00050; >17.5, W=-5.357, p=0.00030). However, there is no significant difference between the expression group and the feedback group as a whole. This means that the avatar's expression induced substantial emotional responses.

Questionnaires We post-coded the scores of questionnaires from 1 to 7. Fig.5 shows the results. We performed Kruskal-Wallis H tests on the questionnaire data. These show the subjective feelings of the participants toward the virtual-world experiences in the experiment.

For the Q1: "How deeply did you concentrate in each game session?", there is a marginally significant difference (χ^2=5.140, p=0.076). We performed a Steel-Dwass multiple comparison test, and there is a marginally significant difference

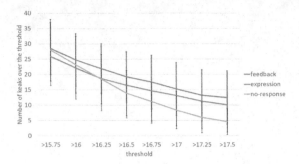

Fig. 4. The results of SCR analysis.

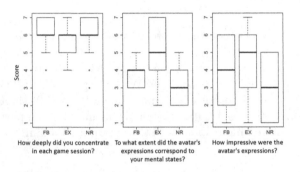

Fig. 5. The results of the questionnaires.

between the EX group and the NR group (W=3.006, p=0.077). We thus suggest that concentration on the game in the EX group was relatively low.

For the Q2: "To what extent did the avatar's expressions correspond to your mental states?", there is a significant difference (χ^2=5.907, p=0.048). We then performed a Steel-Dwass multiple comparison test. As a result, there is also a marginally significant difference between the EX group and the NR group (W=-3.044, p=0.074). The Fig.5 shows that the EX group may be a higher score than those of the NR and feedback groups. We thus suggest that the participants in the EX group felt a relatively high sense of unity with their avatar.

For the Q3: "How impressive were the avatar's expressions?", there is no significant difference (χ^2=2.769, p=0.26). Although we inquired as to the most impressive avatar expression after the experiments, many participants responded with an avatar motion that was not related to the difference between the groups. We think that the affective avatar expressions themselves were not impressive.

5   Discussion

There is a different trend between the results of the questionnaires and the results of physiological indices. The results of the questionnaires suggest that the feedback and no-response groups have similar characteristics. We thus consider that the affective expressions do not influence participant perception and mental state because the appropriate affective feedback does not disturb the participant's observation of the virtual-world activities. However, the results of the physiological indices show the feedback group > expression group = no-response group or feedback group > expression group > no-response group. From these results, we conclude that the affective expressions unconsciously influence the participant's mental states. The feedback group shows a low parasympathetic activity. This means that the participants in the feedback group were less relaxed than those in the other groups. In other words, the appropriate affective feedback that corresponds to the participant's mental states has an effect on increasing commitment to the virtual-world experiences.

The participants in the expression group were shown affective expressions irrespective of the participant's mental states at a certain probability. The result for the question Q2 show relatively high scores in the expression group. This may appear to increase commitment to the avatar. However, the concentration on the game in the expression group was relatively low and the physiological responses in the expression group were lower than those in the feedback group. From these results, we suggest that the expressions irrespective of the participant's mental states affect both positively and negatively because the expressions are easily noticed by the operator. Sometimes, the notification encourages a sense of unity, whereas at other times it prevents the operator from committing to the virtual-world experiences. In other words, creators of virtual content cannot control effects by affective expressions. Consistency is one of the most important points to enhance the reality of virtual experiences.

There are some limitations to our proposed method. The variance of the number of presentations of the affective expressions in the feedback group in game sessions is large. We set constant thresholds to determine whether the avatar provided motion. However, appropriate thresholds have to be determined depending on the contexts of the game, the individual differences, and the circumstances. The LF/HF values are used to estimate the mental states of the participants in the experiment. However, the LF/HF values were sometimes abnormal. We have to devise a method to estimate the mental states in real-time. In addition, we are considering using a brain measuring technique in future work.

6 Conclusion

The aim of this study is to investigate an effect of feedback on the human operator's mental state using an avatar's affective expressions. We conducted experiments to evaluate the effect of the feedback using three types of avatar: a "feedback" avatar that provided psychological feedback using our proposed method, an "expression" avatar that randomly provided the same affective expressions as those of the feedback avatar irrespective of the participant's mental state with a constant probability, and a "no-response" avatar that did not provide any affective expressions. As a result, we find that feedback from avatar expressions can increase participants' physiological responses without reducing concentration on the task. We suggest that this feedback can enhance commitment to virtual-world experiences. In future work, we will improve the analysis of the physiological indices to estimate mental states.

Acknowledgements

This research is supported by Grant-in-Aid for Young Scientists (B) (KAKENHI No. 16K21113), and Grant-in-Aid for Scientific Research on Innovative Areas (KAKENHI No. 26118002) from the Ministry of Education, Culture, Sports, Science and Technology of Japan.

References

1. Graafland, M., Schraagen, J., Schijven, M. Systematic review of serious games for medical education and surgical skills training. British Journal of Surgery, 99(10), 1322–1330 (2012).
2. Katmada, A., Mavridis, A., Apostolidis, H., Tsiatsos, T. Developing an adaptive serious game based on students bio-feedback. 6th international conference on Information, intelligence, systems and applications (iisa), 1–6 (2015).
3. Lin, T., Omata, M., Hu,W., Imamiya, A. Do physiological data relate to traditional usability indexes? In Proceedings of the 17th australia conference on computerhuman interaction: Citizens online: Considerations for today and the future, 110 (2005).
4. Mandryk, R. L., Inkpen, K. M. Physiological indicators for the evaluation of colocated collaborative play. In Proceedings of the 2004 acm conference on computer supported cooperative work, 102–111 (2004).
5. Mokka, S., Vtnen, A., Heinil, J., Vlkkynen, P. Fitness computer game with a bodily user interface. In Proceedings of the second international conference on Entertainment computing. Carnegie Mellon University, 1–3 (2003).
6. Ohmoto, Y., Kataoka, M., Nishida, T. The effect of convergent interaction using subjective opinions in the decision-making process. In Proc. the 36th annual conference of the cognitive science society, 2711–2716 (2014).
7. Ohmoto, Y., Takeda, S., Nishida, T. Distinction of intrinsic and extrinsic stress in an exercise game by combining multiple physiological indices. In 2015 7th international conference on games and virtual worlds for serious applications (vs-games), 1–4 (2015).
8. Rego, P., Moreira, P. M., Reis, L.P., Serious games for rehabilitation: A survey and a classification towards a taxonomy. In Information Systems and Technologies (CISTI), 5th Iberian Conference on. IEEE, 1–6 (2010).
9. Rosenberg, R. S., Baughman, S. L., Bailenson, J. N. Virtual superheroes: Using superpowers in virtual reality to encourage prosocial behavior. PloS one, 8(1), e55003, (2013).
10. Yucha, C., Montgomery, D. Evidence-based practice in biofeedback and neurofeedback. AAPB Wheat Ridge, CO. (2008).
11. Zotev, V., Phillips, R., Yuan, H., Misaki, M., Bodurka, J. Self-regulation of human brain activity using simultaneous real-time fmri and eeg neurofeedback. NeuroImage, 85, 985–995 (2014).

That's a Rap

Increasing Engagement with Rap Music Performance by Virtual Agents

Stefan Olafsson ✉, Everlyne Kimani, Reza Asadi, Timothy Bickmore

College of Computer and Information Science, Northeastern University, Boston, MA
{stefanolafs, kimani15, asadi, bickmore}@ccs.neu.edu

Abstract. Many applications of virtual agents, including those in healthcare and education, require engaging users in dozens or hundreds of interactions over long periods of time. In this effort, we are developing conversational agents to engage young adults in longitudinal lifestyle health behavior change interventions. Hip-hop and rap are one of the most popular genres of music among our stakeholders, and we are exploring rap as an engagement mechanism and communication channel in our agent-based interventions. We describe a method for integrating rap into a counseling dialog by a conversational agent, including the acoustic manipulation of synthetic speech and accompanying character dance animation. We demonstrate in a within-subjects study that the participants who like rap music preferred the rapping character significantly more than an equivalent agent that does not rap in its dialog, based on both self-report and behavioral measures. Participants also found the rapping agent significantly more engaging than the non-rapping one.

Keywords: relational agent, young adults, rap music, health counseling.

1 Introduction

Many applications of virtual agents, in areas such as health behavior change and education, require maintaining user engagement and retention over long periods of time and dozens or hundreds of interactions. Several approaches to maintaining engagement with virtual agents have been explored, including storytelling [1], automated camera motion [2], language variability, agent back-stories, and empathetic language use [3].

Music, including singing and dancing by a virtual agent, represents a relatively unexplored modality for user-agent interaction, but one that has the potential for significantly increasing user engagement. Most people find some form of music entertaining and this may add perceived value to interactions with an agent, thereby increasing the likelihood of user commitment to their relationship with the agent (according to the investment model of personal relationships [3]). "Entertainment education", using a variety of conventional media, has also been used as a successful health behavior

© Springer International Publishing AG 2017
J. Beskow et al. (Eds.): IVA 2017, LNAI 10498, pp. 325-334, 2017.
DOI 10.1007/978-3-319-67401-8_41

change modality [4], indicating that music may be an effective channel for health education.

Music has been used successfully in behavior change interventions [5] and could be used in a variety of ways in agent-based systems. For example, it can be a source of entertainment to further engage the user in conversations and for the agent to tell its backstory in an effort to build a relationship with the user. Through this medium, an agent can communicate health messages directly and succinctly. Lyrics provide the means to tell a story from multiple perspectives and for motivating behavior change, for example, through raising awareness of the importance of change and helping users reappraise the repercussions of inaction for other people and themselves.

We hypothesize that an agent that performs music in its interaction with users will increase user engagement and a higher likelihood of user retention in longitudinal interventions, at least for users who enjoy the particular genre of music being performed. In our current work, we are developing longitudinal health behavior change interventions for young adults. Since hip-hop and rap music are some of the most popular music genres among young adults (ages 18-25) in the world [6], there is reason to believe that this particular genre of music may be effective at boosting engagement for this demographic.

In this initial work we are exploring the use of rap music both to engage users and to establish backstory for the agent.

2   Related Work

Researchers have explored incorporating rap music into their (non-automated) health interventions, e.g., for substance use risk awareness [7]. In the fields of social work and psychotherapy, researchers have looked at engaging urban youth using rap music [8, 9]. DeCarlo and Hockman compared adolescents' perception of the usefulness of integrating rap music as a tool to support prosocial skills and traditional group therapy. The results showed that a large percentage of the participants were in favor of the rap therapy compared with the traditional therapy [10]. Additionally, Olson-McBride and Page showed that hip-hop and rap music promoted self-disclosure and self-expression in high-risk youths [11].

Several systems have been developed to automate some aspect of music composition or performance by a virtual agent, e.g., automating facial expression [12], conducting an orchestra [13], dancing [14], and lyric generation [15]. However, there is little empirical evidence that music performance increases engagement with virtual agents. To our knowledge, this is the first study that evaluates the use of music in an agent based interactions in the context of health education and counseling.

3   Design of a Rapping Health Counselor Agent

To explore the feasibility and acceptance of having a virtual agent health counselor perform rap music, we developed two virtual agents that counseled users on two different health topics, with or without a rap performance.

We designed three dialogues for the agents. The first two were brief health counseling dialogues motivating exercise and good nutrition. These dialogues also included greetings, extended social chat, and farewells. During the extended social chat, the agent performed the rap. The third dialogue was an extended social chat intended to test engagement in the evaluation study.

The agents in our study performed two short verses of rap from the popular 2009 rap and hip-hop song "Empire State of Mind" by the rapper Jay-Z, featuring Alicia Keys. This song was chosen because of its popularity [17] and used as part of the agents' backstory. Figure 1 shows the transcription of the first verse.

The agents are animated in a 3D game engine (Unity 3D), speak using synthetic speech (Windows 10 TTS), and use a range of conversational nonverbal behavior for their non-singing utterances, including hand gestures, posture shifts, head nods, and eyebrow raises. Interaction with the agents is driven using a hierarchical transition network-based dialogue engine, with user inputs to the conversation selected from a multiple-choice menu updated at each turn of the conversation (Figure 2). Agent nonverbal behavior for non-singing utterances is automatically generated using BEAT [16] and synchronized with the synthetic speech. The animation accompanying the music is manually created and consisted of the agent bobbing its head, facial expressions, and lip-sync.

To generate the agents' rap performance, the speech synthesizer was first used to record audio of the agent speaking the lyrics. We then manipulated the timing and duration of the words and the pitch contour of this speech sample.

To change the word durations, we needed to know the exact timings of the words in both original rap song and the synthesized sample. We used the "SPeech Phonetization Alignment and Syllabification" (SPPAS) toolkit [18] to align the song lyrics with voice samples. First, we performed Inter-Pausal Units (IPUs) segmentation to segment the audio signal into units of speech bounded with pauses of at least 300 milliseconds length. Each IPU was aligned with the corresponding segment of the lyrics. Then tokenization or "Text Normalization" was performed to remove punctuation, convert numbers and symbols to written forms, and segment text into words. Finally, words were converted into phonemes that were aligned with speech signal. SPPAS uses the Julius speech recognition engine [19] and HTK acoustic models trained from 16000 Hz audio samples to perform alignment. We aligned the song lyrics to both the original song and the synthesized voice.

We used Praat [20] to manipulate the synthesized sample word timings and pitch contour. The start and end times for each word in synthesized speech and original song were extracted from the SPPAS alignment outputs. The word timings in the synthesized sample were modified to match the corresponding times in the original song. We also extracted the pitch contour of the original song, which was used as the reference for manual modification of the pitch contour of the synthesized voice.

> *Yeah, I'm out that Brooklyn, now I'm down in Tribeca*
> *Right next to DeNiro, but I'll be hood forever*
> *I'm the new Sinatra and since I made it here*
> *I can make it anywhere, yeah, they love me everywhere*
> *I used to cop in Harlem*

Fig. 1. Transcript of the agent's first rap verse from 'Empire State of Mind'.

4 Evaluation Study

We conducted an empirical study to determine the impact of a health counseling agent performing rap in its dialog. The study was a randomized, counterbalanced, within-subjects experiment with two treatments: R, where an agent performs rap as a part of the conversation; and NoR, where no rap was performed. In addition to randomizing the order of the experimental treatments, we used two different agents (Figure 2) that discussed two health topics, either nutrition (N) or exercise (E). Thus, our conditions were RN, RE, NoRE, and NoRN. These were randomized such that the assignment of topic to experimental treatment was counterbalanced across subjects.

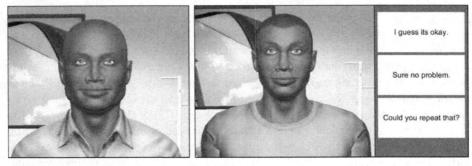

Fig. 2. The two conversational agents used in the study, with an example of user dialog options with the agent on the right.

4.1 Procedure

Participants were first asked to give informed consent, fill out a demographics questionnaire, and a questionnaire assessing their attitude towards rap music (see section 4.2). They were randomized using blocked randomization into either RE, RN, NoRE, or NoRN for their first conversation. The second conversation, therefore, consisted of the opposite configuration, e.g., if the first condition was RE, then the second would be NoRN. Following each of the first two conversations, participants were asked to fill out questionnaires regarding their experience of the agents (see section 4.2).

At this point participants were told that they would have a third conversation and that they could choose which agent they preferred to interact with. After selecting their preferred agent, the third conversation was launched. The content of this conversation was the same for all participants, consisting of 40 turns of social chat, with topics ranging from reading books to TV and movies, and users had the option to end the conversation at each turn after the 8th turn of dialog (with an option such as "Sorry, I have to go now").

Following the third conversation, we conducted a short semi-structured interview with participants about their experience with the agents.

4.2   Measures

At the start of the study, we collected socio-demographic information and assessed the degree to which participants liked rap music using the Rap Music and Attitude Perception (RAP) scale, a 25 5-Point scale item self-report questionnaire [21]. We also asked participants how often they listened to rap music and how much they liked the agent's rap, following their conversation with the rapping agent (Table 1).

We collected six measures of participant engagement. The first four were self-reported satisfaction, willingness to continue working with the agent, liking of the agent, and which agent participants felt was most engaging. The other two were behavioral measures: which agent the participant chose to have the third conversation with and the number of turns of talk the participant had with their chosen agent in the third conversation. Additionally, we collected a measure of trust in the agent.

The satisfaction, liking, and willingness to continue working with the agent were assessed with 7-Point scale items (Table 1). The trust questionnaire was a 15 item semantic-differential scale [22]. These assessments were obtained following each of the first two conversations.

The agent choice measure was collected after the second conversation by asking participants which agent they would prefer to interact with for a third and final conversation. The most engaging agent measure was collected by asking participants which agent they found most engaging, following all three conversations.

Participants reported on additional single 7-Point scale items touching on various aspects of their interaction with the agents (Table 1).

4.3   Participants

We recruited participants from a job listing website and by distributing flyers at various locations in Boston. Participants were required to be between 18-25 years old and be able to speak and read English. All participants were compensated $15 for their time. The study was approved by the University Institutional Review Board.

4.4   Evaluation Study Results

Participants. A total of 84 participants were enrolled, although one participant experienced a technical malfunction during the study session and had their data excluded. Participants were 60% male, aged 22.8 years (sd. 2.4), 79% Asian, 18% White, 2% Hispanic, and 1% Black, and 83% were students.

Table 1. Self-report single scale items (Wilcoxon Signed-Ranks tests, N=73).

Item (Anchor 1-7)	When assessed	R avg (sd)	NoR avg (sd)	p
How much did you like the agent's rap? (Not at all – Very much)	After Rap agent conversation	5.41 (1.6)	N/A	N/A
How satisfied are you with the agent? (Not at all – Very satisfied)	After each conversation	5.68 (1.2)	5.49 (1.3)	0.12
How much would you like to continue working with the agent? (Not at all – Very much)	After each conversation	5.52 (1.4)	5.32 (1.6)	0.19
How much do you like the agent? (Not at all – Very much)	After each conversation	5.63 (1.2)	5.47 (1.3)	0.16
How knowledgeable was the agent? (Not at all – Very knowledgeable)	After each conversation	5.71 (1.1)	5.95 (1.1)	0.08
How natural was your conversation with the agent? (Not at all – Very natural)	After each conversation	5.14 (1.6)	5.15 (1.7)	0.98
How would you characterize your relationship with the agent? (Complete stranger – Close friend)	After each conversation	4.14 (1.5)	3.7 (1.6)	0.001
How similar do you feel that you are to the agent? (Very different – Very similar)	After each conversation	4.36 (1.6)	4.26 (1.5)	0.43

Engagement. When all participants were included in the analysis, there were no significant differences between experimental treatments on engagement measures. We found that 13% of participants indicated they did not like rap music (scoring below 3 on the RAP scale). Thus, in the following analyses these participants are excluded.

Participants who like rap choose the agent in the R conditions significantly more often for the third conversation, (62% vs. 38%), $X^2(1)=3.96$, $p<.05$. When they were asked during the exit interview which agent was more engaging, they mentioned the R agent significantly more often than the NoR agent, (65% vs. 35%) $X^2(1)=6.21$, $p<.05$.

There were no significant differences in self-reported satisfaction between the two conditions (5.68 for R, 5.49 for NoR), Wilcoxon Signed-Ranks test W=284, n.s. However, trust in the NoR agent was rated significantly higher compared to the R agent, (6.64 for Rap, 6.81 for NoR), W=1501, $p<.05$. Desire to continue working with the agent was not significant between the two conditions, W=348.5, n.s.

Participants reported having a significantly closer relationship with the R agent compared to the NoR agent (scoring 4.1 vs. 3.7), W=184, $p<.001$. No significant differences were found between the groups on naturalness (W=565, n.s.), knowledgeability (W=556, n.s.), perceived similarity (W=606, n.s.), or liking of the agent (W=345, n.s.).

The number of dialogue turns in the third social conversation was not significantly different depending on the agent chosen, 22 for R, 25 for NoR, W=658.5, n.s.

Correlations. We conducted an exploratory bivariate correlational analysis of all quantitative measures, in order to understand how these factors influence one another. All were tested using Spearman's non-parametric rank order correlation.

There is a strong correlation between declaring that the R agent is most engaging and choosing the R agent for the third conversation (rho=.82, p<.001). There is a weak positive correlation between choosing the R agent and satisfaction with the R agent (rho=.22, p<.001), but a weak negative correlation between choosing the R agent and satisfaction with the NoR agent (rho=-.25, p<.05). Liking the agent's rap is weakly positively correlated with choosing the R agent (rho=.27, p<.05). Knowledge-ability is also positively correlated with agent trust ratings (rho=.48, p<.001).

Desire to continue working with the agent was strongly correlated with liking the agent (rho=.81, p<.001), agent satisfaction (rho=.82, p<.001), naturalness of the conversation (rho=.63, p<.001), and perceived relationship with the agent (rho=.6, p<.001).

Perceived similarity to an agent is positively correlated with the perceived relationship with the agent (rho=.64, p<.001), agent satisfaction (rho=.41, p<.001), and trust, (rho=.45, p<.001). Perceived similarity to the R agent is also weakly, positively correlated with liking the agent's rap (rho=.31, p<.001).

4.5 Qualitative Interview Analysis

We interviewed participants at the end of the session and asked for their thoughts on the experience of interacting with the agents. Specifically, they were asked about their impressions of each interaction, which agent they found most engaging, and why. The interviews were transcribed and analyzed to identify concepts, which were then used to form themes. Two main themes specific to the agent interactions emerged: *Relatability & Engagement* (RE) and *Information & Knowledge* (IK). Concepts within the RE theme came up more frequently when participants were describing the R agent. Conversely, descriptions related to the IK theme were more frequent in the context of the NoR agent (Table 2).

Table 2. Concepts extracted from the semi-structured interviews by condition, frequency of occurrance, and theme. RE="Relatability and Engagement", IK="Information and Knowledge". Concepts with a frequency < 5 are not included in the table.

Rap (R)	Frequency	Theme	No Rap (NoR)	Frequency	Theme
Relatable	14	RE	Informative	20	IK
Engaging	12	RE	Engaging	7	RE
Interesting	10	RE	Knowledgeable	5	IK
Informative	8	IK	Friendly	5	RE

There was a distinction in how participants spoke about the agents. A greater number spoke about the NoR agent as one they learned something from, while more used adjectives like 'fun' or 'entertaining' when talking about the R agent. Some participants spoke of engagement and relatability together, as if finding the agent engaging depended on how well they could relate to it.

Finding the agent relatable and interesting came up particularly often in the context of the R agent, specifically when describing various aspects of the interaction, such as the conversation flow. Participants often described the agent in the NoR condition as informative and knowledgeable. Their prior knowledge and interest in health topics seemed to factor into their descriptions. For some participants, even if the agents didn't provide them with any new information, they felt like the NoR condition had been more informative.

- *[I learned something from] the second one* [NoR condition] *because he talked a lot about the health and nutrition and the other one was a lot more fun* [R condition], *he had the music.* [#61 F 25]
- *The most engaging was the first one. It was more about, I could relate to him more that actually why I chose him for the third conversation and went with him.* [#17 M 19, R condition]
- *I could relate to it more like he was talking about music, rap music.* [#12 F 19, R condition]
- *It was more interesting flowing and it was like a friendly conversation.* [#10 M 23, R condition]
- *I learned some things so I would say the second was more informative.* [#13 F 19, NoR condition]
- *I didn't learn anything new from either about the nutrition or the health but I feel like maybe from the first one.* [#37 M 23, NoR condition]

5   Conclusion

In this pilot study we evaluated a virtual agent that performed rap music in conversations with users about nutrition and exercise. Our results indicate that users who enjoy this particular genre of music find the agent that raps more engaging than one that does not and they are more likely to want to interact with that agent again. This demonstrates that rap music could be used to boost retention and adherence in longitudinal treatments with young adults who enjoy this music genre.

Young adults in our study who like rap music are likely to want to have more than one interaction with an agent that performs rap, especially if they feel like they can relate to the agent. The conversation that included the musical performance was designed to give a backstory for the agent and bring about a sense of relatability. Our qualitative and quantitative results show that one's perceived similarity with the agent (relatability) was a particularly important determiner of ratings of trust in and satisfaction with the agent. This is in accordance with results from another study that found perceived similarity to be an important factor with respect to satisfaction with the agent [23].

Our results indicate that an agent that raps may have issues of credibility, given that the non-rapping agent was rated more trustworthy, described as more informative, and that trust and knowledgeability are significantly correlated. Desire to continue working with a particular agent was related to the perceived naturalness of the conversation, perceived relational closeness, liking, and satisfaction with the agent.

6 Future Work

This preliminary study is only a first step in our exploration of music in virtual agent interactions. There are numerous avenues for future investigations including, e.g., longitudinal applications. A variety of questions could also be studied as to the utility of embedding music within these applications, e.g., whether or not delivering health advice within rap lyrics increases knowledge retention.

Fully automated generation of singing and dancing behavior by a virtual agent is still an open problem, as is fully automated generation of rap lyrics to satisfy particular communicative and relational goals (beyond just coherence and entertainment goals, as targeted in [15]).

Ultimately, agents that dance and perform music must be evaluated in the context of longitudinal studies to determine, not only knowledge retention of content delivered through song, but the overall efficacy of health behavior change interventions incorporating these agents.

Acknowledgements. We thank Elise Masson, William Bond, Arsalan ul Haq, and Asimina Ino Nikolopoulou for their help designing the dialogue and conducting the pilot study.

References

1. Battaglino, C., Bickmore, T.: Increasing the Engagement of Conversational Agents through Co-Constructed Storytelling. In: Eighth Workshop on Intelligent Narrative Technologies (2015).
2. Ring, L., Utami, D., Olafsson, S., Bickmore, T.: Increasing Engagement with Virtual Agents Using Automatic Camera Motion. In: International Conference on Intelligent Virtual Agents (2016).
3. Bickmore, T., Schulman, D., Yin, L.: Maintaining Engagement in Long-Term Interventions With Relational Agents. Appl. Artif. Intell. 24, 648–666 (2010).
4. Hoffman, A.S., Lowenstein, L.M., Kamath, G.R., Housten, A.J., Leal, V.B., Linder, S.K., Jibaja-Weiss, M.L., Raju, G.S., Volk, R.J.: An entertainment-education colorectal cancer screening decision aid for African American patients: A randomized controlled trial. Cancer. 123, 1401–1408 (2017).
5. Lemieux, A.F., Fisher, J.D., Pratto, F.: A music-based HIV prevention intervention for urban adolescents. Heal. Psychol. 27, 349–357 (2008).
6. Hip-hop is the most listened to genre in the world | The Independent,

http://www.independent.co.uk/arts-entertainment/music/news/hip-hop-is-the-most-listened-to-genre-in-the-world-according-to-spotify-analysis-of-20-billion-10388091.html.   Date accessed: 4/23/17

7. Paukste, E., Harris, N.: Using rap music to promote adolescent health: pilot study of VoxBox. Heal. Promot. J. Aust. 26, 24 (2015).

8. Levy, I.: Hip hop and spoken word therapy with urban youth. J. Poet. Ther. 25, 219–224 (2012).

9. Elligan, D.: Rap therapy: a culturally sensitive approach to psychotherapy with young African American men. J. African Am. Men. 5, 27–37 (2000).

10. DeCarlo, A., Hockman, E.: RAP Therapy: A Group Work Intervention Method for Urban Adolescents. Soc. Work Groups. 26, 45–59 (2004).

11. Olson-McBride, L., Page, T.F.: Song to Self: Promoting a Therapeutic Dialogue with High-Risk Youths Through Poetry and Popular Music. Soc. Work Groups. 35, 124–137 (2012).

12. Mancini, M., Bresin, R., Pelachaud, C.: A virtual-agent head driven by musical performance. In: IEEE Transactions on Audio, Speech, and Language Processiong. pp. 1883–1841 (2007).

13. Reidsma, D., Nijholt, A., Bos, P.: Temporal interaction between an artificial orchestra conductor and human musicians. Comput. Entertain. 6, 1 (2008).

14. Reidsma, D., Nijholt, A., Poppe, R., Rienks, R., Hondorp, H.: Virtual rap dancer. In: CHI '06 extended abstracts on Human factors in computing systems - CHI '06. p. 263 (2006).

15. Malmi, E., Takala, P., Toivonen, H., Raiko, T., Gionis, A.: DopeLearning: A Computational Approach to Rap Lyrics Generation. In: Proceedings of the 22nd ACM SIGKDD International Conference on Knowledge Discovery and Data Mining - KDD '16. pp. 195–204 (2016).

16. Cassell, J., Vilhjálmsson, H.H., Bickmore, T.: BEAT: the Behavior Expression Animation Toolkit. In: Proceedings of the 28th annual conference on Computer graphics and interactive techniques - SIGGRAPH '01. pp. 477–486. ACM Press, New York, New York, USA (2001).

17. Jay-Z, Keys' "Empire" Tops Hot 100 For Fifth Week | Billboard, http://www.billboard.com/articles/news/266366/jay-z-keys-empire-tops-hot-100-for-fifth-week. Date accessed: 4/23/17

18. Bigi, B.: SPPAS: a tool for the phonetic segmentations of Speech. In: The eighth international conference on Language Resources and Evaluation. pp. 1748–1755 (2012).

19. Lee, A., Kawahara, T.: Recent Development of Open-Source Speech Recognition Engine Julius. In: APSIPA ASC 2009: Asia-Pacific Signal and Information Processing Association, 2009 Annual Summit and Conference. pp. 131–137 (2009).

20. Boersma, P.: Praat, a system for doing phonetics by computer. Glot Int. 5, 341–345 (2001).

21. Tyson, E.H.: Rap-music Attitude and Perception Scale: A Validation Study. Res. Soc. Work Pract. 16, 211–223 (2006).

22. Wheeless, L.R., Grotz, J.: The Measurement of Trust and Its Relationship to Self-Disclosure. Hum. Commun. Res. 3, 250–257 (1977).

23. Zhou, S., Bickmore, T., Paasche-Orlow, M., Jack, B.: Agent-User Concordance and Satisfaction with a Virtual Hospital Discharge Nurse. In: International Conference on Intelligent Virtual Agents (2014).

Design of an Emotion Elicitation Tool using VR for Human-Avatar Interaction Studies

P-H. Orefice[1] ✉, M. Ammi[2] M. Hafez[3], and A. Tapus[1]

[1] U2IS, ENSTA ParisTech, Univ. Paris-Saclay
[2] CNRS/LIMSI, University of Paris-Sud, Univ. Paris-Saclay
[3] CEA, List, Sensoriel and Ambient Interfaces Laboratory
pierre-henri.orefice@ensta-paristech.fr

Abstract. With the development of socially interacting machines, it is important to understand how people react depending on their emotional state. Research in this area require emotion elicitation devices. This paper presents such a tool using virtual reality (VR), that merges classical elicitation techniques to emphasize emotional response. The design choices are depicted for four emotions, and a performance analysis using questionnaires is achieved.

1 Introduction

Emotions are a fundamental component of human life. Indeed, they have an impact on human's psychology, physiology, and behavior, and they influence human social interactions. Several technology-based systems have been developed so as to socially interact with humans. However, they mostly lack of emotion embodiment in order to make interactions more realistic and natural. To address this issue, it is important to measure people's reaction caused by their emotional experience. That leads to design reliable tools that elicit a given emotion, in order to relate with the conducted measures. For instance, [6] explore the link between physiological data and the emotion elicited. Investigating how social interaction is altered by the emotional state of subjects has applications in human machine interaction in general. It would enable to detect the emotional state of a subject depending on its reaction during the social interaction. Our research project lays in this context and our approach is to compare social interactions before and after an emotion elicitation phase. This paper focuses on designing an emotion elicitation device that can generate an emotion long enough to remain during interaction phases.

Many methods enable to elicit emotions, using various modalities: through internal process or self-elicitation, by a passive reaction to discrete visual or audio stimuli displayed, or via an interactive tasks. In this study, we are interested in inserting discrete stimuli in a virtual reality (VR) scenario. Indeed, VR enables to use a succession of stimuli combining several modalities, to have the participant involved as he/she controls its mobility, and to increase emotional arousal while adjusting the sense of presence [1]. Several parameters can be balanced given the

© Springer International Publishing AG 2017
J. Beskow et al. (Eds.): IVA 2017, LNAI 10498, pp. 335-338, 2017.
DOI 10.1007/978-3-319-67401-8_42

emotion to be elicited, which gives higher control on elicitation [4]. [3] designed five environments to elicit joy, anger, anxiety, boredom, and sadness. Based on these examples and motivated by the idea that inserting in VR discrete stimuli from databases would magnify the emotional arousal and duration, the following describes an elicitation platform we designed and presents an evaluation study.

2   VR platform design

Elicitation design: The first steps we had to complete to create the system were to relevant emotions, the right stimuli, and the right timing and scenario. We selected 3 emotions, which are part of the 6 Ekman basic emotions and distant in the VAD space (**V**alence-**A**ctivation-**D**ominance), and a Neutral emotion. This makes 4 conditions. The hypothesis to answer are: *(a)* there is a significant difference in emotion felt depending on elicitation; *(b)* these emotions are close to the associated VAP values: Joy (high **V**, **A** and **D**), Fear (high **A**; low **V** and **D**), and Sadness (low **V**, **A**, and **D**). Neutral (medium **V** and **D**; low **A**). Elicitations of these emotions are respectively referred as **J**, **F**, **S**, and **N**.

The discrete stimuli were chosen from pre-evaluated databases including pictures, musics and video samples. Concerning images, the IAPS database [5] is well-known as it has been evaluated and tested by many studies, in VAD and qualitative [7] spaces. We extracted from this database 10 pictures per condition. For **J**, we picked all pictures noted with at least amusement, or contentment. We ordered them with highest scores for these dimensions, and selected the ones with high valence and arousal. We did the same for For **F** and For **S** with suitable categories and VAD. For **N**, we used the PAD space and selected pictures with valence just above the medium value and chose the ones with low arousal. Music brings a time dimension. The dataset we exploited [2] uses movies soundtracks. We decided to play, for each elicitation, two $1min$ musics and we selected the ones with high score for the given emotion, high arousal, and low level of confusion. Video content depicts more complex situations. We used a French database [8] and selected the samples with high arousal and high score for a given emotion. The VR scenario is as follow: the participant arrives in a corridor with pictures displayed on both sides. He/she has $1.5min$ to cross the corridor gazing at pictures with an average time of $6s$. During this step, a music is played. Then, the participant enters a theater room. A movie sample of $2min$ is displayed. When the video ends, the participant removes its VR helmet.

Elicitation evaluation tools: In order to evaluate our system measure the cognitive response of participants using questionnaires. This is done through two tools. The first one is the Self Assessment Manikin scale (SAM), which returns the emotional state on a 9 points three dimensional VAD scale. The second is composed of discrete adjectives to tick, several responses being accepted. The adjective list is from [8]. These questions are asked after each elicitation phase in VR. We also measure the variability of the emotion felt, and the modality to which the participant was the most attentive and receptive. After the experiment, participants had to watch again every stimulus separately on a screen, evaluate the emotion felt, and say if it was more intense than in the VR elicitation.

Experimental protocol: The experiment was carried out thanks to 16 participants with scientific background, aged between 22 and 30 years old, mainly used to play video-games. The first phase of the experiment is to let the subject train to use VR and the joystick, playing a basic game. When the participant is comfortable, the main phase begins. 4 emotional conditions are presented, and each occur in four steps. First, a relaxation step with the VR helmet on and a relaxing music of $2min$. Then, the VR environment is displayed, it last between 3 and $4min$. After that a quick questionnaire is answered, and a cognitive game of $2min$ (a Sudoku) enable the emotion to vanish. After the 4 conditions, the participant could provide some comments about the experiment. The total duration was one hour.

3   Results of the platform evaluation

In order to validate our work, we used one-way ANOVA and Tukey post-hoc test when significant. The p-value (**p**) used for significance is 0.05. The mean is noted μ and standard deviation sd.

Emotion elicitations The first step is to check significance in elicitation evaluation differences. Valence significantly depends on condition ($F(3; 58) = 14.2$, $\mathbf{p} < 10^{-6}$). **J** has more valence than all the others ($+2.7$ from **N**, $+3.5$ from **F**, and $+4.6$ from **S**). However, the Tukey test is not significant between **N**, **F**, and **S**. The arousal is discriminating ($F(3; 58) = 9.8$, $\mathbf{p} < 10^{-6}$) but just because **N** case has low arousal (-1.7 from **S**, -2.9 from **F**, and **J**). The Tukey test is not significant for other comparisons. The dominance component is not discriminant. In a second step, we check the correspondence with the expected VAD values. The **N** condition has neutral values: medium valence ($\mu : 4.9; sd : 2.5$) and low arousal ($\mu : 3.5; sd : 2.0$). **J** has high valence ($\mu : 7.6; sd : 1.6$), arousal ($\mu : 6.5; sd : 1.8$), and dominance ($\mu : 7.1; sd : 1.5$). **S** corresponds for valence which is low, but arousal and dominance remain medium. Finally, the **F** VAD responses lack of magnitude but go in the right tendency. If we count the number of good adjectives to describe the elicitation phases, **J** and **S** have good scores (79% and 77%) while the **N** case is noisy (56%) and the **F** case is often confused with "surprise" or "anger" (50%).

Comparison of modalities We also compare which modality is more efficient depending on the emotion elicited. We found that for **S**, subjects were more attentive and receptive to images. The same effect was seen for **F** with the video. In general, little attention was given to music. However, participants got the most receptive to this modality. Many people did not pay attention to a particular modality but they could choose an answer for receptivity. We finally compare the emotional intensity and category differences between viewing stimuli in the post-questionnaire (on a screen) and in VR. The images were not perceived significantly different from VR. However, videos were less intense during the post-questionnaire. Participant judged it more immersible in VR.

Music, however, was significantly perceived more intense in post-questionnaire, probably due to the higher attention level.

4   Discussion, conclusion, and perspectives

The experiment taught us a lot about how the stimuli we proposed are perceived and how VR alters this perception. Our system succeeded to elicit the right emotions, and more efficiently for **J**. The noise in **N** adjectives can be caused by the fact no adjective qualify precisely such an emotion. **S** had low valence, mainly thanks to images. However video and musics were evaluated as "calm" and mi-aroused in the post-questionnaire. Better stimuli may have strengthen the **S** condition. The **F** did not fit exactly the hypothesis. The individual stimuli evaluation are noisy, images have a lot of qualification errors and too low arousal, the video's valence is too random. The musics are better marked but subject payed less attention to this modality. This confirms that the attention given to a modality can change the emotion felt in the whole elicitation.

This paper proposed an example of emotion elicitation using virtual reality. Several benefits of VR, including the ability to merge several modalities, are shown. The proposed solution revealed that classical elicitation methods integrated in the VR setup improves immersion and emotional intensity. Future work will take advantage of the presented results in order to have a robust elicitation method, that will allow to do more complex evaluations, and study the link between tactile interaction with virtual agents or robots, and emotions.

References

1. Bouvier, P.: La présence en réalité virtuelle, une approche centrée utilisateur. Ph.D. thesis, Université Paris-Est (2009)
2. Eerola, T., Vuoskoski, J.: A comparison of the discrete and dimensional models of emotion in music. Psychology of Music (2010)
3. Felnhofer, A., Kothgassner, O., Schmidt, M., Heinzle, A.K., Beutl, L., Hlavacs, H., Kryspin-Exner, I.: Is virtual reality emotionally arousing? investigating five emotion inducing virtual park scenarios. International journal of human-computer studies 82, 48–56 (2015)
4. Geslin, E., Jégou, L., Beaudoin, D.: How color properties can be used to elicit emotions in video games. International Journal of Computer Games Technology 2016, 1 (2016)
5. Lang, P., Bradley, M., Cuthbert, B.: International affective picture system : Affective ratings of pictures and instruction manual. Technical report A-6 (2005)
6. Ménard, M., Richard, P., Hamdi, H., Dauce, B., Yamaguchi, T.: Emotion recognition based on heart rate and skin conductance. In: PhyCS. pp. 26–32 (2015)
7. Mikels, J., Fredrickson, B., Larkin, G., Lindberg, C., Maglio, S., Reuter-Lorenz, P.: Emotional category data on images from the international affective picture system. Behavior research methods 37(4), 626–630 (2005)
8. Schaefer, A., Nils, F., Sanchez, X., Philippot, P.: Assessing the effectiveness of a large database of emotion-eliciting films: A new tool for emotion researchers. Cognition and Emotion 24(7), 1153–1172 (2010)

Toward an Automatic Classification of Negotiation Styles using Natural Language Processing

Daniela Pacella[1]✉, Elena Dell'Aquila[1], Davide Marocco[2], Steven Furnell[1]

[1]Plymouth University, Centre for Robotics and Neural Systems, Plymouth, United Kingdom
{pacelladaniela,elena.dellaquila}@gmail.com,
s.furnell@plymouth.ac.uk
[2]University of Naples Federico II, Natural and Artificial Cognition Laboratory, Naples, Italy
davide.marocco@gmail.com

Abstract. We present a natural language processing model that allows automatic classification and prediction of the user's negotiation style during the interaction with virtual humans in a 3D game. We collected the sentences used in the interactions of the users with virtual artificial agents and their associated negotiation style as measured by ROCI-II test. We analyzed the documents containing the sentences for each style applying text mining techniques and found statistical differences among the styles in agreement with their theoretical definitions. Finally, we trained two machine learning classifiers on the two datasets using pre-trained Word2Vec embeddings.

Keywords: Natural Language, Classification, Virtual artificial agents, Negotiation.

1   Introduction

The effectiveness of intelligent assessment tools and tutoring systems on improving the learner's ability to retain information has been extensively proved in well-defined subjects, but also ill-defined ones, like negotiation [1] and communication skills [2]. Soft skills training, in particular negotiation, has shown to benefit the use of simulation games that include interactions with virtual humans [3]. In most game-based simulations, the user data is collected in the form of multiple choices or non-verbal information like facial expression [4]. While natural language processing (NLP) techniques have been used to generate human-like negotiations, via Wizard-of-Oz or machine learning algorithms (e.g. [3]), these have never been included in the user model. We aim at proposing the first step to fill this gap by presenting a NLP model that allows to map the features of the users' sentences to their predominant negotiation style. We asked participants to interact using natural language with virtual characters and then to complete the Rahim Organizational Conflict Inventory and we built documents of sentences for each style. We show the differences between the styles and then present the results obtained by training two machine learning classifiers on the dataset using Google's Word2vec pre-trained word embeddings.

© Springer International Publishing AG 2017
J. Beskow et al. (Eds.): IVA 2017, LNAI 10498, pp. 339-342, 2017.
DOI 10.1007/978-3-319-67401-8_43

2   Related Work

Several e-learning technologies have been developed to promote soft skill development. Among the others, Eutopia [5] constitutes an example of a multiplayer platform
that provides role-play simulations focused on the development of soft skills. An
adaptive tutoring system for communication skills has also been proposed [2]. None
of the platforms in literature, however, includes in its user model a NLP architecture
that evaluates the learner's soft skills from the user's natural speech.

3   Materials and Methods

The present work is based on Rahim and Bonoma's model [6], which defined five
negotiation styles: Integrating (high concern for self and others), Obliging (low concern for self and high concern for others), Dominating (high concern for self and low
concern for others), Avoiding (low concern for self and others) and Compromising
(intermediate in concern for self and others). This model is supported by the ROCI II
(Rahim Organizational Conflict Inventory-II). The virtual characters are taken from
Enact [7], a 3D game based on Rahim's model. The game is organized in 5 scenarios,
where users can negotiate in conflict situations between peers using verbal and non-
verbal cues. In the experiment, participants were asked to fill the consent form and
answer to 20 screenshots taken from Enact, 4 for each scenario (2 introductive screens
and 2 random interactive screens). Users were asked to answer with their own words
in a field under the interactive images using maximum 100 characters. Then, participants were asked to complete the ROCI-II (28 items on a 5–point Likert scale). 173
subjects (mean age = 23.12 ± 9.16) participated and 1730 sentences were collected.

4   Results and Discussion

The user sentences were tagged with the predominant style obtained in the ROCI-II.
A reliability test on the ROCI-II items' scores showed a consistent value (Cronbach's
alpha = .776, Standardized item's Cronbach's alpha = .797). Participants classified as
having two or more predominant styles were excluded from the sample. Five documents were built, each containing sentences belonging to one style. From this dataset
(the Full_Dataset), we extracted the sentences provided by users whose predominant
style score was at least .4 points above the others. This restricted dataset
(Rest_Dataset) consisted of five collections of sentences: 230 Avoiding (words count
= 1670, avg. sentence length = 16.40), 210 Compromising (words count = 1885, avg.
sentence length = 17.61), 220 Dominating (words count = 1665, avg. sentence length
= 16.33), 230 Integrating (words count = 1703, avg. sentence length = 17.42) and 240
Obliging (words count = 1994, avg. sentence length = 18.94). The vocabulary count
was of 462 words. We removed punctuation and stopwords, and tokenized using a
Porter stemmer. We calculated the similarity using WordNet's Leacock Chodorow
algorithm [8] and collected the most frequent pronouns and words (Tab 1).

Style	Words similar to "You"	Words similar to "I"	Most frequent pronouns	Most frequent words
Avoiding	Me, I, We	You, We, Give	You, it, I	Take, Don't
Compromising	I, We, Watch	You, We, It	You, I, it	Get, Take
Dominating	I, What, Us	You, Later, It	You, it, I	Let, Go
Integrating	I, We, It	You, We, Time	You, I, it	Take, Let
Obliging	It, Then, I	Go, When, Ok	You, it, I	Let, Take

Table 1. Words similar to the pronouns "I" and "You" for each style calculated with the Leacock Chodorow algorithm, most frequent words and pronouns for each style

Compromising and Integrating styles show a use of "We" comparably to that of "I" and "You" and showed "You" and "I" as the most frequent pronouns. This is in accordance with the styles' definition (interest for self and for other). Obliging style, whose self-concern is the lowest, used the pronoun "I" comparably to the word "Ok" showing a more condescending attitude. Then, we trained two classifiers, Multinomial Naive Bayes (MNB) [9] and Support Vector Machine (SVM) [10] on the datasets using Google Word2Vec word embeddings for the initialization [11] and compared the accuracy measured by F score using 10-fold cross validation for the train/test split. Rest_dataset was trained for 1000 iterations, Full_dataset for 3200 iterations (Fig 3).

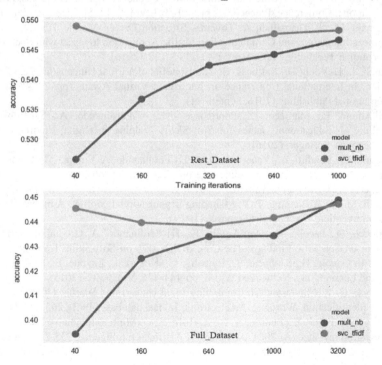

Fig. 1. Accuracy obtained by the two classifiers for the Rest_Dataset and the Full_Dataset.

Both the models reached an F score higher than 0.5, with MNB scoring slightly higher (0.552). The Rest_Dataset, even if smaller, gained a maximum accuracy 0.10 higher than the Full_Dataset. This measure proves that the score obtained with ROCI-II correlates with the accuracy with which the user's negotiation style can be predicted.

5   Conclusion

We presented a NLP model for the automatic categorization of the user negotiation style. We collected natural sentences used in the interactions with 3D virtual humans and associated their negotiation style using the ROCI-II test. We analyzed the corpus applying text mining techniques and found differences among the styles consistently with our theoretical framework. We trained machine learning classifiers (Multinomial Naive Bayes and Support Vector Machine) on the full dataset and on a dataset containing only the most representative sentences using Word2Vec embeddings, and reached a significantly higher accuracy in the case of the more representative dataset.

References

1. Pacella D., Di Ferdinando, A., Dell'Aquila, E., Marocco, D. Online Assessment of Negotiation Skills through 3D Role Play Simulation, in Conati, Cristina, et al., eds. AIED: 17th International Conference, Proceedings pp 921-923, Vol. 9112. Springer, 2015. (2015)
2. Khemaja, M., & Taamallah, A. Towards Situation Driven Mobile Tutoring System for Learning Languages and Communication Skills: Application to Users with Specific Needs. Educational Technology & Society, 19(1), 113-128. (2016).
3. Gratch, J., DeVault, D., & Lucas, G. The Benefits of Virtual Humans for Teaching Negotiation. In International Conference on Intelligent Virtual Agents (pp. 283-294). Springer International Publishing. (2016, September).
4. Dell'Aquila, E., Marocco, D., Ponticorvo, M., di Ferdinando, A., Schembri, M., & Miglino, O. Educational Games for Soft-Skills Training in Digital Environments: New Perspectives. Springer. (2016).
5. Miglino, O., Venditti, A., Veneri, A. D., & Di Ferdinando, A. Eutopia-Mt. teaching mediation skills using multiplayer on-line role-playing games. Procedia-Social and Behavioral Sciences, 2(2), 2469-2472. (2010).
6. Rahim, M. A., & Bonoma, T. V. Managing organizational conflict: A model for diagnosis and intervention. Psychological reports. (1979)
7. Marocco, D., Pacella, D., Dell'Aquila, E., Di Ferdinando, A. Grounding Serious Game Design on Scientific Findings: The Case of ENACT on Soft Skills Training and Assessment. In Conole, G., Klobučar, T., Rensing, C., Konert, J., Lavoué, É., Design for Teaching and Learning in a Networked World, pp 441-446, Vol. 9307. (2015)
8. Leacock, C., & Chodorow, M. Combining local context and WordNet similarity for word sense identification. WordNet: An electronic lexical database, 49(2), 265-283. (1998).
9. Kibriya, A., Frank, E., Pfahringer, B., & Holmes, G. Multinomial naive bayes for text categorization revisited. AI 2004: Advances in Artificial Intelligence, 235-252. (2005).
10. Joachims, T. Text categorization with support vector machines: Learning with many relevant features. Machine learning: ECML-98, 137-142. (1998).
11. Mikolov, T., Chen, K., Corrado, G., & Dean, J. Efficient estimation of word representations in vector space. arXiv preprint arXiv:1301.3781. (2013).

Interactive Narration with a Child: Avatar *versus* Human in Video-Conference

Alexandre Pauchet[1]✉, Ovidiu Şerban[1]✉, Mélodie Ruinet[2],

Adeline Richard[2], Émilie Chanoni[2]✉, and Mukesh Barange[1]✉

[1] Normandie Univ, INSA Rouen Normandie, LITIS, 76000 Rouen, France
`{surname.lastname}@insa-rouen.fr`
[2] Normandie Univ, UNIROUEN, PSY-NCA, 76000 Rouen, France
`{surname.lastname}@univ-rouen.fr`

Abstract. This article reviews a part of the data collected in a "Wizard-of-Oz" environment, where children interact with a virtual character in a narrative setup. The experiment compares children's engagement depending on the narrator type: either a piloted virtual character or a human in video-conference. The results show that engagement exists, but the modality of the interaction feedback varies in the two contexts.

1 Introduction

Designing a virtual environment, where the participants can interact without any difficulty, is very challenging. Particularly, introducing an autonomous dialogue-based virtual character (or Embodied Conversational Agent -ECA- [1]) increases the expectations of the human participants, up to the point where they can be disappointed by the agent's capabilities [4]. Among the various applications of ECAs, interactive storytelling is a growing scientific field since 2010 [2]. It includes situations from a reproduction of the familiar parent-child narration situation to a new form of user's experience with story generation. Nevertheless, interactive storytelling aims at improving the user's immersion, pleasure, feeling of control, believability of the virtual characters and interaction engagement [7].

A few experiments exist regarding interactive storytelling with children (e.g. [5–7]), but unfortunately they do not characterize standard data in child-agent interaction, such as the average response time (latency) of the child. This article proposes an interactive environment with a virtual character, centered around a familiar story telling activity so that the children feel comfortable. As the dialogue component of ECAs remains a technical difficulty [3], our environment is based on the Wizard of Oz (WoZ) paradigm, so that the collected data expresses what can be expected of "natural" interaction. We aim at answering the following research question: Is child-agent interaction different from child-adult interaction? This is studied from the interaction engagement perspective. We propose an experimental study to compare child ↔ avatar[3] interaction *versus* child ↔ human in video-conference.

---

[3]In the following, '*avatar*' refers to a virtual character driven during a WoZ experiment. A '*virtual character*' can be either an avatar or an ECA.

© Springer International Publishing AG 2017
J. Beskow et al. (Eds.): IVA 2017, LNAI 10498, pp. 343–346, 2017.
DOI 10.1007/978-3-319-67401-8_44

2 Experimental Study: Avatar *vs* Video-Conference

2.1 WoZ scenario for interactive narration with children

The chosen story is "The lost ball", illustrated by 15 images to support the narration. The narration is constructed as a sequential scenario. Several parallel branches are integrated to give the illusion of an open story, although all the children's answers generates the same comments or explanations. For example[4], *"Oh god, where will the ball fall? Do you know it?"* is used to induce an interaction that always lead at the end to the following statement: *"Booyah! Look at the ball! It's stuck on the roof!*. Moreover, as a dialogue is never completely predictable, a set of free-context utterances has been added. It consists in a series of statements not directly linked to the context of the story, such as: *"OK"*, *"You are right"*, *"Shall we continue?"*. They can be used to manage the dialogue and force the interaction to focus back on the story.

Six interactive errors were included to assess the children's attention ($A1$ and $A2$), emotional understanding ($E1$ and $E2$) and comprehension ($C1$ and $C2$). For example: 1) at $C1$, the narrator makes a semantic mistake by saying "the boy throws his *carrot* on the roof", instead of *boot*; 2) at $E2$, the narrator makes an emotional error: he says "oh, look at the teacher. Is he singing?", while he is currently shouting at the children; and 3) $A1$ presents a joint attention problem, with a black screen during 3s, while the narrator is describing the scene.

The story is split into two parts, narrated by two different actors, which enables the cross comparison of the interactions during the two conditions.

2.2 Participants and Procedure

20 children (6-8 years, average: 7.7) participated in this study and each session lasted approximately 20 minutes. 90% were familiar with animated virtual characters and 60% with occasional web-cam usage.

Various dependent variables were collected: the numbers of words, phrases and words per phrase; the mean disfluency rate for hundred words; the number of long pauses ($> 2s$); the response delay (latency) between avatar/adult's utterances and child's utterances; the number of out-of-context interactive phrases used by the narrator; the number of Emotional Mimics (EM - laughs, smiles, pouts,...) of the child, the number of Spontaneous Verbal Responses (SVR), as any verbal interaction initiated by the child and the number of Expected Response after a direct Verbal Question (ERVQ) from the narrator.

2.3 Results: child engagement and modality of interaction

Table 1 provides some quantitative measures of child engagement in interaction. Children use more words and longer sentences when interacting with the avatar than with the human in video-conference ($t_{words} = 0.883, p = 0.681 > 0.05$, *ns*

---

[4] All the presented utterances are translated from French.

Table 1. Children's engagement in interaction.

	Words	Phrases	Lengths	Ctx	Disf.	Pauses	Latency	EM	SVR	ERVQ
Video-conf	62.7	20.9	2.9	5.9	7.7	0.5	1955	11	8	19
Avatar	74.8	22.0	3.1	6.5	6.0	2.5	2182	4	17	14

Words: mean number of words; *Phrases*: mean number of phrases; *Lengths*: mean number of words by phrases; *Ctx*: the number of out-of-context interactive phrases used by the narrator; *Disf.*: mean disfluency rate for 100 words; *Pauses*: mean number of long pauses ($> 2s$); *Latency*: response delay (in ms) between avatar/adult's utterances and child's utterances. After an interactive error, *EM*: number of emotional mimics; *SRV*: number of spontaneous verbal responses; *ERVQ*: number of expected responses after a direct verbal question.

and $t_{phrases} = 0.846, p = 0.359 > 0.05$, *ns*). When interacting with the avatar, the average size of the child's sentences increases slightly ($t_{length} = 0.445, p = 0.881 > 0.05$, *ns*). Moreover, the number interactive phrases "triggered" by the narrator after an out-of-context utterance from the child enables to evaluate the children's spontaneous interaction. The results show that the avatar pronounces more additional sentences than the human in video-conference ($t_{out-of-context} = 0.653, p = 0.545 > 0.05$, *ns*).

Concerning the quality of the oral interactions, the disfluency rates shows that the children use more disfluencies and shorter pauses with human in video-conference than with the avatar ($t_{disfluencies} = 1.153, p = 0.277 < 0.05$, *ns* and $t_{pauses} = 1.775, p = 0.076 > 0.05$, *ns*). Concerning the high number of pauses with the avatar, we verified that this was not due to a lack of attention from the child in the post-experiment survey. All the participants have correctly answered when asked to describe some specific elements of the story. Finally, children have a longer latency when responding to the avatar compared to the human in video-conference ($t_{latency} = -0.741, p = 0.468 > 0.05$, *ns*). In each case, the latency is far higher than the known standard for children, even for complex questions. Therefore, the fact that the interaction is mediated seems to impact more the latency than using a virtual agent.

When focusing on the stimulated interactive situations, Table 1 also includes the children's reactions after an interactive error (EM, SVR and ERVQ). Our analysis shows that, after an interactive error, children communicate more with the human in video-conference than with the avatar ($EM + SVR + EVRQ$). However, they react more spontaneously with the avatar ($EM + SVR$), ($h^2 = 0.02$, $p = 0.362 > 0.05$, *ns*). Children also address the situation differently depending on the narrator: they prefer to communicate spontaneously with the avatar by verbal responses (SVR) rather than non verbal (EM) (significant, $p = 0.014 < 0.05$). Moreover, they also prefer to interact with the adult in video-conference using non verbal res¡ponses (significant, $p = 0.009 < 0.05$). These results are consistent with our previous results on verbal answers: the children use less words, less and shorter phrases with the video-conference than with the avatar.

2.4   Sum-up of the Results and Discussion

It seems that children are able to adapt to a virtual character and engage in the interaction: the number of children's interventions with the avatar does not statistically differ from that with the video-conference. However, communication with the avatar appears more spontaneous, more verbal and does not seem as natural as with the human, as they try to adapt their discourse to their inter-locutor. We have also noted a less hesitant, clearer and more assured speech from the children toward the avatar, confirmed by the disfluency rate measures.

The fact that the verbal modality is preferred with the avatar suggests that this modality is of particular importance for multi-modal interactive systems. Unfortunately, the transcription remains one of the biggest problems in ECAs, due to transcription time and errors.

3   Conclusion

In this article, we have presented a narrative WoZ experiment that compares child ↔ avatar interaction with child ↔ human in video-conference. The main re-sult is that children were engaged in narrative interaction with a virtual character in a different way but not less valuable than with a human in video-conference. In other words, any ECA dedicated to child-agent narrative interaction have to be designed so that the verbal understanding should be implemented with great care as the children seem to favor this modality.

As the children seem to have enjoyed their experience, using an avatar driven in a WoZ or in an ECA can be of great interest to psychologists. Dialogue or interaction models could be designed and tested to evaluate, for instance, chil-dren's language acquisition. Moreover, the particularities of a virtual narrator could also be exploited from a therapeutic point of view, such as children with communication difficulties, offering rehabilitation tools adapted to their difficul-ties of interaction.

Acknowledgements

This work was supported by the NARECA project (ANR-13-CORD-0015).

References

1. Cassell, J.: Nudge nudge wink wink: Elements of face-to-face conversation for em-bodied conversational agents. Embodied conversational agents pp. 1–27 (2000)
2. Crawford, C.: On Interactive Storytelling. New Riders Games (2013)
3. Kopp, S., van Welbergen, H., Yaghoubzadeh, R., Buschmeier, H.: An architecture for fluid real-time conversational agents: integrating incremental output generation and input processing. Journal on Multimodal User Interfaces 8(1), 97–108 (2014)
4. Mori, M.: The uncanny valley. Energy 7(4), 33–35 (1970)
5. Oviatt, S.: Talking to thimble jellies: Children's conversational speech with animated characters. In: Proceedings of ICSLP'00. pp. 67–70 (2000)
6. Ryokai, K., Vaucelle, C., Cassell, J.: Virtual peers as partners in storytelling and literacy learning. Journal of computer assisted learning 19(2), 195–208 (2003)
7. Theune, M., Linssen, J., Alofs, T.: Acting, playing, or talking about the story: An annotation scheme for communication during interactive digital storytelling. In: Proceedings of ICIDS'13. pp. 132–143 (2013)

Who, Me? How Virtual Agents Can Shape Conversational Footing in Virtual Reality

Tomislav Pejsa ✉, Michael Gleicher, and Bilge Mutlu

University of Wisconsin–Madison, USA
tpejsa@cs.wisc.edu

Abstract. The nonverbal behaviors of conversational partners reflect their conversational *footing*, signaling who in the group are the speakers, addressees, bystanders, and overhearers. Many applications of virtual reality (VR) will involve multiparty conversations with virtual agents and avatars of others where appropriate signaling of footing will be critical. In this paper, we introduce computational models of gaze and spatial orientation that a virtual agent can use to signal specific footing configurations. An evaluation of these models through a user study found that participants conformed to conversational roles signaled by the agent and contributed to the conversation more as addressees than as bystanders. We observed these effects in immersive VR, but not on a 2D display, suggesting an increased sensitivity to virtual agents' footing cues in VR-based interfaces.

Keywords: embodied conversational agents, virtual reality, gaze, orientation

1 Introduction

Many envisioned applications of virtual reality (VR) in games and social media involve multiparty conversations among avatar-mediated humans and virtual agents. In order to achieve natural and effective interactions, agents and avatars must produce humanlike nonverbal signals. In face-to-face social interactions, humans use nonverbal signals, such as spatial orientation and gaze, to regulate who is allowed to speak and to coordinate the production of speech utterances. Such signals help prevent misunderstandings, awkward silences, and people talking over one another. Conversational participants' nonverbal signals establish their roles—also known as *footing*— which determine their conversational behavior. Clear conversational roles are vital for smooth, effective multiparty interactions. However, there is a lack of computational models of footing-signaling behaviors for virtual agents as well as of studies that assess whether agents can use such behaviors to effectively shape the roles of human participants.

In this paper, we focus on two nonverbal signals of footing—spatial orientation and eye gaze—and introduce computational models of these behaviors. Building on prior work that has studied how humanlike robots can shape footing using their gaze [22], we develop a gaze model that generalizes to a wider variety of conversational scenarios and supplement it with a model that enables the agent to reconfigure the spatial configuration of the interaction. Our models are based upon the key insight that shifts in both spatial orientation and gaze can be realized as parametric variations of the same basic movement, allowing their integration in a single animation controller.

© Springer International Publishing AG 2017

J. Beskow et al. (Eds.): IVA 2017, LNAI 10498, pp. 347–359, 2017.

DOI 10.1007/978-3-319-67401-8_45

Fig. 1: (1–2) A virtual agent engaging in interaction with two participants (participant's view). The agent (1) puts participants on equal footing by distributing its gaze and body orientation evenly or (2) excludes a participant by looking and facing away from them. (3) Participants conform to their roles in virtual reality, but not on a 2D display.

We evaluate the effectiveness of the models in a study with human participants. Study results show that a virtual agent with appropriately designed gaze and spatial orientation cues can influence the footing of human participants, but only when using a VR display. We attribute this finding to wide field of view, stereo, and natural viewpoint control afforded by modern VR displays, which may enhance the effects of agent behaviors on the users of these systems.

2 Related Work

Our work focuses on two types of social signals in multiparty interaction: spatial orientation and gaze. Below, we summarize prior work on these signals from the social sciences and from research on virtual reality and embodied conversational agents (ECAs).

Human Communication — Conversational participants use nonverbal behaviors, particularly gaze and body orientation, to establish their conversational roles—what Goffman [13] has termed "footing." Participants use gaze to clarify who is being addressed [26], display attentiveness [15], and coordinate conversational turn-taking [18]. Speakers and addressees are the core participants, who make the majority of conversational contributions and spend most of the time gazing toward each other [22]. By contrast, bystanders make few conversational contributions and receive little gaze [22]. Spatial orientation is another footing cue; the core participants position and orient themselves in an "F-formation" [17], a spatial arrangement that creates a space between them to which they have equal, direct, and exclusive access and which excludes bystanders. When another participant joins the conversation, the core participants reorient themselves to include the newcomer in the F-formation.

Avatars in VR — A number of studies have investigated the effects of avatars' gaze and spatial positioning in VR. Avatars displaying gaze that matches their speech are attributed stronger presence and more positive traits [11]. When participants' eye gaze is accurately reproduced on their avatars, their gaze patterns match those observed in face-to-face conversations [27] and they also produce less speech [6], suggesting increased nonverbal communication. Studies [e.g., 7,29] have shown that participants in avatar-based communication tend to display compensatory interpersonal distance and gaze behaviors predicted by the Equilibrium Theory [4], even in a non-immersive setting [31]. Avatar spatial positioning produces similar effects; participants maintain greater distance from avatars who face them [8]. While these studies suggest that people are sensitive to gaze patterns and spatial orientation in VR, no prior work, to our knowledge, has assessed their ability to shape conversational footing in multiparty interactions.

Embodied Conversational Agents — Researchers have worked to endow virtual agents and robots with computational models of human conversational behaviors in order to increase their communicative capabilities. Well-designed gaze mechanisms on virtual agents have been shown to facilitate more efficient turn-taking [1,10,14], better management of engagement [9], and better recall of information [2]. Pedica et al. [23] have introduced a framework for automated generation of spatial positioning behaviors in virtual agents and found that interactions where agents employ such behaviors are viewed as more believable [24].

While no prior work has studied the ability of virtual agents to shape the footing of human participants, researchers have studied footing in the context of human-robot interaction. Mutlu et al. [22] have shown that participants conform to conversational roles signaled by a robot's gaze cues, while Kuzuoka et al. [19] have shown that a robot can reconfigure the conversational formation by reorienting its own body. These findings provide strong motivation for endowing virtual agents with equivalent capabilities.

3 Footing Behavior Models

Spatial orientation and eye gaze are key nonverbal cues that shape the footing of conversational participants. In this section, we describe the gaze controller used to synthesize gaze and body orientation shifts that comprise our footing behaviors. We then introduce the two models for synthesis of these behaviors. Finally, we give an overview of the models' prototype implementation in an embodied, multiparty dialog system.

3.1 Animating Gaze and Spatial Orientation Shifts

People shift their attention toward targets in their environment—objects, information, or other people—by performing coordinated movements of the eyes and head toward the target. In larger attention shifts, they may also shift their torso, while keeping their feet planted on the floor, or completely turn their body toward the target. Studies in

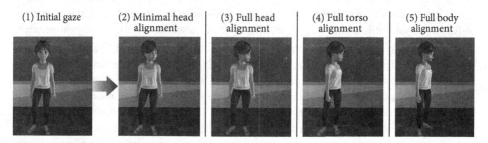

Fig. 2: Examples of synthesized gaze and body-orientation shifts: (1) eye contact with the observer, (2–5) gaze shifts with varying head, torso, and whole-body alignments.

neurophysiology [16,21,28] have found that eye, head, torso, and feet movements in attention shifts occur in tight coordination with one another and they display similar kinematic properties.

We have implemented a gaze animation controller for virtual agents that can synthesize coordinated movements of the eyes, head, torso, and whole body based on earlier work by Pejsa et al. [25]. In this model, the controller synthesizes a gaze movement toward a target in the environment by employing a set of kinematic laws derived from neurophysiological measurements of human gaze. A high-level model of conversational behavior provides the following parameters of each gaze shift to the controller: target position, $\mathbf{p}_T$, and head and torso alignment parameters, α_H and α_T. The alignment parameters control how much the head and torso participate in the gaze shift (Figure 2). For example, by setting $\alpha_H = 0$ and $\alpha_T = 0$, we can control the agent to gaze at the target out of the corner of its eye (Figure 2.2).

In this work, we extend the model proposed by Pejsa et al. [25] by adding support for whole-body orientation shifts that are required to change the agent's spatial orientation. We introduce a new parameter, α_B, which specifies how much the agent's lower body should turn toward the target. Setting $\alpha_B = 1$ results in the agent turning its whole body toward the target (Figure 2.5). We integrate the gaze controller with a custom turning controller, which replants the feet over the course of the gaze shift, resulting in a new spatial orientation of the agent. This extended model enables us to control the eye-gaze and body-orientation shifts of the virtual agent in a coordinated way and to signal the conversational footing of the agent.

3.2   Spatial-Reorientation Model

When two people interact, they typically face each other directly, creating a "vis-à-vis" arrangement, or stand at a 90° angle, forming an "L-shape" configuration [17]. Conversation between more than two participants generally occurs in a circular formation. Kendon [17] has coined the term "F-formation" to refer to these spatial arrangements of interacting participants. In order to correctly establish conversational footing, a virtual agent must maintain an F-formation with other participants. Specifically, when a new addressee approaches, the agent must turn toward the newcomer to reconfigure the F-formation. When a participant leaves, it may need to reorient itself toward the remaining participants. Below, we describe a model of body orientation, which achieves correct F-formation and utilizes our gaze controller to synthesize the required body movements.

When the first participant approaches, the agent performs a gaze shift toward the participant with the head, torso, and whole-body alignment parameters all set to 1 ($\alpha_H = \alpha_T = \alpha_B = 1$), facing the participant head-on. If the interaction already involves other participants, the agent must evenly distribute its body orientation among all the participants. To do so, we set $\alpha_H = 1$ and $\alpha_B = 1$ as before, whereas α_T is set such that the agent is oriented toward the midpoint between the leftmost and rightmost participant. To compute α_T, we project all direction vectors defined in Figure 3 onto the ground plane. The agent must realign its body such that its torso facing direction is $\mathbf{v}_T = slerp(\mathbf{v}_L, \mathbf{v}_R, 0.5)$ where $slerp$ denotes spherical linear interpolation between two

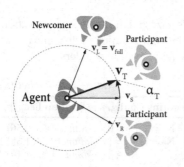

$\mathbf{v}_S$	Current torso direction
$\mathbf{v}_T$	Target torso direction
$\mathbf{v}_{\text{full}}$	Torso direction for full alignment with newcomer
$\mathbf{v}_L$	Direction vector to the leftmost participant
$\mathbf{v}_R$	Direction vector to the rightmost participant
α_T	Realignment needed to accommodate newcomer

Fig. 3: Computing the torso alignment parameter α_T needed for the agent to reconfigure the F-formation when a new participant has joined the interaction.

direction vectors. The torso alignment α_T needed to achieve the facing direction $\mathbf{v}_T$ is:

$$\alpha_T = \frac{\angle(\mathbf{v}_S, \mathbf{v}_T)}{\angle(\mathbf{v}_S, \mathbf{v}_{\text{full}})} \qquad (1)$$

This mechanism can be used to reestablish the F-formation when the leftmost or rightmost participant has departed or moved. In that case, using an updated α_T, the agent shifts its body orientation toward the participant at the opposite end of the formation.

3.3   Eye-Gaze Model

Conversational footing is also reflected in participants' gaze behavior. Speakers use gaze to indicate the addressees of the utterance or to release the floor to them, while the addressees gaze toward the speaker to display attentiveness. As a result, speakers and addressees gaze toward each other most of the time and only infrequently toward bystanders. Mutlu et al. [22] have calculated the gaze distributions of human speakers engaging in interactions involving addressees and bystanders. According to their data, speakers spend 26% of the time looking at each addressee's face (making eye contact) and avert their gaze toward the addressees' torsos and the environment other times in order to regulate intimacy [3]. When a second addressee is present, the amount of gaze toward each addressee's face remains around 26%, likely because switching gaze among the addressees now also achieves the purpose of intimacy regulation.

We build our footing gaze model based on the distributions reported by Mutlu et al. [22]. Our model defines a discrete probability distribution over the set of potential gaze targets, which includes the faces and torsos of all the addressees and bystanders as well as the environment. The distribution is characterized by the probability mass function, $p_T = p(T, N_A, N_B)$ (Table 1). The function p_T specifies the probability of looking toward the candidate target T given the current footing configuration, defined by the number of addressees, N_A, and the number of bystanders, N_B. In addition to the spatial distribution of the agent's gaze, our model specifies temporal durations of gaze fixations, shown in Table 1, defined as *gamma* distributions by prior work [22]. While the exponential distribution is commonly used to model events such as gaze shifts that occur at a constant average rate, we find the gamma distribution to more accurately

Table 1: Spatial probability distribution of the speaker's gaze and the agent's gaze fixation lengths (in seconds) toward possible targets in the given configuration of conversational roles. N_A is the number of addressees, while N_B is the number of bystanders.

	Spatial probability distributions		*Gaze fixation lengths*	
Gaze Target	**Footing Config.**	**Gaze Prob.**	**Footing Config.**	**Fixation Length**
Addressee face	$N_A = 1$	26%	$N_A = 1, N_B = 0$	*Gamma*(1.65, 0.56)
	$N_A \geq 2$	54%/N_A	$N_A = 1, N_B = 1$	*Gamma*(0.74, 1.55)
			$N_A \geq 2$	*Gamma*(1.48, 1.10)
Addressee torso	$N_A = 1$	48%	$N_A = 1, N_B = 0$	*Gamma*(1.92, 0.84)
	$N_A \geq 2$	16%/N_A	$N_A = 1, N_B = 1$	*Gamma*(1.72, 1.20)
			$N_A \geq 2$	*Gamma*(1.92, 0.52)
Bystander face	$N_B = 1$	5%	$N_B \geq 1$	*Gamma*(2.19, 0.44)
	$N_B \geq 2$	8%/N_B		
Bystander torso	$N_B = 1$	3%	$N_B \geq 1$	*Gamma*(1.76, 0.57)
	$N_B \geq 2$	5%/N_B		
Environment	$N_A = 1, N_B = 0$	26%	$N_A = 1, N_B = 0$	*Gamma*(0.90, 1.14)
	$N_A = 1, N_B = 1$	18%	$N_A = 1, N_B = 1$	*Gamma*(1.84, 0.59)
	$N_A = 1, N_B \geq 2$	13%	$N_A \geq 2$	*Gamma*(2.23, 0.41)
	$N_A \geq 2, N_B = 0$	30%		
	$N_A \geq 2, N_B = 1$	24%		
	$N_A \geq 2, N_B \geq 2$	17%		

represent human gaze, as it assigns a low probability to short fixations that are unlikely due to human motor limitations.

To illustrate the operation of our model, let us consider a scenario where the agent is speaking with two addressees ($N_A = 2$) named Alice and Bob, with two bystanders present ($N_B = 2$). To shift the agent's gaze, we draw from the spatial probability distributions to determine the target of the next gaze shift. According to Table 1, the probability of looking toward Alice's face is 54%/2 = 27% (Row 2). If Alice's face is the desired target, we supply the target to the gaze controller, which performs a gaze shift toward it. We hold the agent' gaze there for a duration determined by drawing from the distribution *Gamma*($k = 1.48, \Phi = 1.10$) (Table 1, Row 3). Alternatively, if the environment is the desired target, resulting in a gaze aversion, the direction of this shift can be computed using a supplemental model of conversational gaze aversion [e.g., 1,20].

Because our goal was to support a wide range of footing configurations, we extrapolated the data provided by Mutlu et al. [22] to derive probability distributions for configurations of three or more addressees and two or more bystanders.

3.4   System Design & Implementation

We implemented the footing behavior models within a high-level *behavior controller*, which controls the agent's gaze behavior and spatial orientation based on current dialog state. When an addressee joins or leaves the interaction, the behavior controller triggers a body orientation shift to reconfigure the conversational formation using the mechanism described in Section 3.2. While the agent is speaking or releasing the floor to addressees, the controller triggers gaze shifts based on the probabilistic model introduced in Section 3.3. Gaze shifts and body orientation shifts are synthesized by our gaze animation controller (Section 3.1) and rendered on the virtual embodiment.

Our prototype system is implemented in the Unity game engine. System components such as the behavior controller and gaze controller are implemented as Unity C# scripts. The system uses Microsoft Speech SDK to detect and recognize users' speech utterances and to synthesize the agent's speech. The visemes generated by the Speech SDK are used to animate the agent's lip movements.

4   Evaluation

To evaluate the models introduced above, we conducted a study with human participants aimed at answering two research questions: "Can a virtual agent use our models to shape the footing of participants in multiparty interactions in virtual reality?" and "Does the display type (e.g., VR or on-screen) influence these effects?" In the study, human participants engaged in a short conversation with a virtual agent and a simulated, avatar-embodied confederate that lasted 10 minutes. The virtual agent displayed gaze behaviors and spatial-orientation shifts that either included the participant as an addressee or excluded them as a bystander. We measured whether or not participants conformed to the conversational role signaled by our behavior models, for example, when assigned the role of bystander, by conversing less with the agent.

While our models are independent of input and display type, we expected their effects to be more salient in a virtual-reality setting. A VR application using a head-mounted display provides different affordances than a desktop display, such as a wide field of view and natural control of viewpoint using head tracking, which may strengthen the perception of social cues. Therefore, we expected people to be more sensitive to footing-signaling behaviors displayed by agents within an immersive VR environment. To test this prediction, our study also manipulated *display type*, comparing a VR headset (Oculus Rift CV1) and a desktop display.

4.1   Hypotheses

Based on prior work, we developed and tested the following hypotheses:

H.1 Participants will demonstrate conversational behavior that conforms to the footing signaled by the agent. Specifically, participants in addressee roles will speak more.
H.2 Participants in addressee roles will feel more groupness and closeness with the agent, as well as evaluate the agent more positively than those in bystander roles.
H.3 The agent's footing cues will have a stronger effect on the participants' conversational behavior (H.1) in VR than when using a 2D display.
H.4 The agent's footing cues will have a stronger effect on perceptions of the agent and feelings of closeness and groupness (H.2) in VR than in a 2D display.

H.1 is consistent with findings that conversing partners orient themselves in an F-formation [17] and that people look toward the addressees of their utterances [18]. H.2 is based on findings that people report negative feelings about a group and its members when being ignored or excluded [12].

H.3–4 are based on the premise that the improved affordances of a modern VR display will heighten awareness of the agent's nonverbal signals. Immersive VR blocks out external visual stimuli and creates a better sense of space due to stereoptic vision. Moreover, the Rift's high field of view (110°) affords a better view of the agent, confederate, and environment than the low-FOV camera settings typically utilized on 2D displays. Finally, the head tracking capabilities allow more intuitive control over the viewpoint than the traditional mouse-look interface, making it more intuitive and quicker for participants to reorient their viewpoint toward the agent during the interaction.

4.2 Study Design

The study followed a mixed, 2×2 factorial design, manipulating *agent behavior* (between-participants) and *task setting* (within-participants). Agent behavior was either *exclusive* or *inclusive*. In the exclusive condition, the agent displayed nonverbal behaviors that excluded the participant from the interaction, treating the participant as a bystander. It oriented its body toward the confederate and gazed toward the confederate much more. In the inclusive condition, the agent displayed nonverbal behaviors that included the participant in the interaction as an addressee. It distributed its body orientation evenly between the participant and the confederate and gazed toward them equally. Figure 4 illustrates these agent behaviors.

The conditions of the other independent variable, task setting, were either *2D display* or *VR*. Both conditions were designed to approximate the expected usage of interactive, virtual agent systems. In the 2D display condition, the participant experienced the interaction on a 27" Dell monitor, at 2560×1440 resolution and a field of view of $50°$, and used the mouse to control the viewpoint. In the VR condition, the participant wore a VR headset (Oculus Rift CV1). The participant saw the scene at the resolution of 1080×1200 per eye and a $110°$ field of view. Built-in head-orientation tracking and the external positional tracker allowed the participant to control the viewpoint by moving the head.

Because the study had a within-participants factor (*task setting*), we implemented two versions of the task, described in the next section, to reduce transfer effects. The

Fig. 4: Conditions of the *agent behavior* independent variable. Graphs show the conversational formations, and screenshots show the participant's view of the scene.

participants were assigned to conditions in a stratified order, counterbalanced with respect to task setting (*2D display* or *VR*) and task version (*Task 1* or *Task 2*).

4.3 Task & Procedure

The study task was a three-party, casual conversation between a virtual agent, the participant, and a "simulated confederate," which was a human-voiced agent producing prerecorded utterances in a virtual room. The participants were told that the confederate was a real human in another room. The task started with the participant standing at the entrance of the room with a view of the agent and confederate facing each other in a vis-à-vis formation. The participant was prompted to approach them by clicking a button. Depending on the agent behavior condition, the agent then either continued facing the confederate (*exclusive*) or reoriented herself toward the participant (*inclusive*). The agent then asked the participant and confederate casual, interview-style questions about themselves, such as "Where are you from?" or "What is your favorite movie about?" Most questions were implicitly addressed at both parties, giving them the choice to answer them. We expected participants to speak more if the agent used inclusive cues.

Implementation — The task was implemented in Unity, and the task logic and measurements were implemented as C# scripts. The confederate's lip movements were animated using Oculus Lip Sync. The character models for the agent and the confederate were imported from DAZ.[1] Both models had a looping, idle body motion applied to enhance the naturalness of their behavior.

Procedure — Following informed consent, participants were seated at a table with a PC in the study room. They received verbal task instructions and printed instructions to serve as a reminder. Participants then put on an audio headset (*2D display*) or Oculus Rift (*VR*). The experimenter launched the task application and left the room. Upon task completion, participants filled out a questionnaire. Next, participants performed a second trial of the task and filled out another questionnaire. Finally, participants received $5 USD as compensation. The procedure took approximately 30 minutes.

Participants — We recruited 32 participants (17 female and 15 male) through an online student job website and through in-person solicitation from the University of Wisconsin–Madison campus. All participants were students, and 27 of them were native English speakers.

4.4 Measures

The experiment involved two behavioral and several subjective measures. The behavioral measures were designed to capture the level of participation by the participant in the interaction to test H.1 and included the *number of speaking turns* taken over the course of the interaction and *total speaking time* in seconds. To alleviate acclimation effects, we excluded responses to the first five questions (out of twenty-five total).

The subjective measures were collected using a questionnaire consisting of seven-point scale items. To measure the agent's likeability, we asked participants to rate the agent on nine traits such as likeability, cuteness, and friendliness. From this data,

---

[1] DAZ Productions: http://www.daz3d.com/

we constructed a scale consisting of two factors: *likeability* (two items, Cronbach's $\alpha = 0.824$) and *attractiveness* (three items, Cronbach's $\alpha = 0.929$). Feelings of *closeness* were measured using a four-item scale (Cronbach's $\alpha = 0.823$) adapted from Aron et al. [5], who asked participants to indicate their agreement with statements such as "The agent paid attention to me." *Groupness* was measured using a seven-item scale adapted from Williams et al. [30] (Cronbach's $\alpha = 0.827$), which included statements such as "I felt ignored or excluded by the group." The questionnaire also included a check for the agent-behavior manipulation, implemented as a two-item scale, including "The agent faced me during the interaction" and "The agent faced the other participant."

4.5   Results

Our analysis began with averaging the two manipulation-check items and performing a one-way analysis of variance (ANOVA). We found a significant effect of agent behavior on the check, $F(1,61) = 5.743, p = .0196$.

Next, we analyzed our behavioral measures with a two-way, mixed-design ANOVA. We found a marginal effect of agent behavior on the *number of speaking turns* ($F(1,30) = 3.757, p = .062$) and no effect on the *total speaking time* ($F(1,30) = 1.159, p = .290$), providing partial support for H.1.

We found no interaction between agent behavior and task setting on the *number of speaking turns* ($F(1,30) = 2.217, p = .147$). However, we did find a marginal interaction between agent behavior and task setting on the *total speaking time* ($F(1,30) = 3.637, p = .066$). In the *VR* setting, participants took a significantly higher number of turns in the *inclusive* condition than in the *exclusive* condition ($M = 5.7$ versus $M = 8.4$), $F(1,55) = 5.970, p = .0178$). No such effect of agent behavior was found in the *2D display* setting, $F(1,55) = 0.465, p = .498$. An equivalent set of comparisons for speaking time found a marginal effect of agent behavior in the *VR* setting ($F(1,59) = 3.472, p = .0387$). No such effect of agent behavior was found in the *2D display* setting ($F(1,59) = 0.287, p = .594$). All the pairwise comparisons used a Bonferroni-corrected alpha level of .025. These findings provide support for H.3.

To analyze the subjective measures, we performed a two-way, mixed-design ANOVA. We found no effects of agent behavior on any of our subjective measures: *likeability*

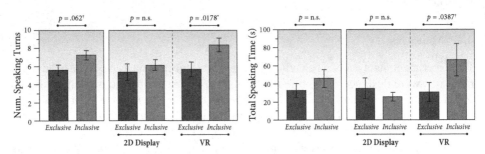

Fig. 5: Results from behavioral measures. Number of speaking turns (left) and total speaking time (right) by agent behavior (*exclusive* vs. *inclusive*) and task setting (*2D display* vs. *VR*). (∗) and (†) denote significant and marginal effects, respectively.

$(F(1,30) = 0.363, p = .551)$, *attractiveness* $(F(1,30) = 1.719, p = .200)$, *closeness* $(F(1,30) = 0.606, p = .443)$, or *groupness* $(F(1,30) = 0.140, p = .711)$. We also found no significant interactions between agent behavior and task setting on any of the subjective measures: *likeability* $(F(1,30) = 1.233, p = .276)$, *attractiveness* $(F(1,30) = 0.417, p = .243)$, *closeness* $(F(1,30) = 0.092, p = .764)$, *groupness* $(F(1,30) = 0.086, p = .771)$. H.2 and H.4 were not supported by these results.

4.6 Discussion

The study results suggest that our models enable virtual agents to use gaze and spatial orientation to shape the conversational roles of human users, but only in an immersive VR setting. We found no evidence that these cues improve user experience. Some of the effects of our manipulations were not as strong as expected, possibly due to limitations of the dialog system and the agent's behaviors, reducing the overall realism and fluency of the interaction. Speech recognition lag, coupled with some participants' tendency to pause between utterances, occasionally caused our system to interpret speech gaps as floor releases and to cut participants off. This behavior of the system might have discouraged participants from speaking, limiting speaking to minimally sufficient responses and reducing the variability in the speaking-time measurement. Furthermore, the effects of the agent's footing signals might have been confounded by the minimal body animation of the agent and the confederate.

5 Limitations and Future Work

The behavior models introduced in this work, while effective at influencing conversational behavior in VR, are still rudimentary compared to behaviors observed in real-world multiparty interactions. These interactions are characterized by much greater variation in spatial arrangement of participants. Supporting such variation in virtual agents will require more sophisticated behavior models for spatial positioning and orienting. Moreover, gaze behaviors in human interactions demonstrate complex contingencies that are not adequately described by first-order statistical models. Variables such as interpersonal distance, discourse structure, personality, sex, and many others influence human gaze. Supporting such complexity will require more advanced models.

While our study suggests that a virtual agent's footing cues are only effective in immersive VR, it is unclear which aspects of VR support their effectiveness. We speculate that the high field of view, stereopsis, and head tracking all contribute, but further research is needed to understand the individual effects of these features and whether or not they affect social signals more generally. Future work may show that immersive, head-worn VR is not required to achieve believable multiparty interactions; for example, high FOV can be achieved with an ultra-wide curved display, while head tracking can be performed with an encumbrance-free device such as TrackIR.[2]

---

[2] TrackIR, http://www.naturalpoint.com/trackir/

6   Conclusion

In this paper, we have introduced computational models of gaze and spatial reorientation for virtual agents that enable them to signal conversational footing in multiparty interactions. An experimental evaluation has shown that participants interacting with the virtual agent conform to the conversational role signaled by the agent using our mechanisms, making more conversational contributions if they are treated as addressees than if they are treated as bystanders. However, this effect was observed only when participants interacted with the agent in a modern VR display and not a conventional 2D display. We speculate that this effect results from the immersion and more natural inputs that VR technology affords.

Designers can use the proposed models to give agents the ability to more effectively manage multiparty interactions. This work also provides impetus for further research on behavioral mechanisms that allow such interactions to proceed smoothly and effectively. As the new generation of VR devices becomes more widely adopted, more nuanced multiparty interactions could become an integral part of social experiences from online games to virtual worlds. The current work represents a stepping stone toward understanding and implementing such interactions.

Acknowledgements

This research was supported by the National Science Foundation awards 1017952 and 1208632. We thank Faye Golden for her help in conducting the experiment.

References

1. Andrist, S., Mutlu, B., Gleicher, M.: Conversational gaze aversion for virtual agents. In: Proc. IVA'13, vol. 8108, pp. 249–262 (2013)
2. Andrist, S., Pejsa, T., Mutlu, B., Gleicher, M.: Designing effective gaze mechanisms for virtual agents. In: Proc. CHI'12. pp. 705–714 (2012)
3. Argyle, M., Cook, M.: Gaze and mutual gaze. Cambridge University Press (1976)
4. Argyle, M., Dean, J.: Eye-contact, distance and affiliation. Sociometry 28, 289–304 (1965)
5. Aron, A., Aron, E.N., Smollan, D.: Inclusion of other in the self scale and the structure of interpersonal closeness. Journal of Personality and Social Psychology 63(4), 596 (1992)
6. Bailenson, J.N., Beall, A.C., Blascovich, J.: Gaze and task performance in shared virtual environments. The Journal of Visualization and Computer Animation 13(5), 313–320 (2002)
7. Bailenson, J.N., Blascovich, J., Beall, A.C., Loomis, J.M.: Equilibrium theory revisited: Mutual gaze and personal space in virtual environments. Presence 10(6), 583–598 (2001)
8. Bailenson, J.N., Blascovich, J., Beall, A.C., Loomis, J.M.: Interpersonal distance in immersive virtual environments. Personality and Social Psychology Bulletin 29(7), 819–833 (2003)
9. Bohus, D., Horvitz, E.: Models for multiparty engagement in open-world dialog. In: Proc. SIGDIAL'09. pp. 225–234 (2009)
10. Bohus, D., Horvitz, E.: Multiparty turn taking in situated dialog: Study, lessons, and directions. In: Proc. SIGDIAL'11. pp. 98–109 (2011)
11. Garau, M., Slater, M., Vinayagamoorthy, V., Brogni, A., Steed, A., Sasse, M.A.: The impact of avatar realism and eye gaze control on perceived quality of communication in a shared immersive virtual environment. In: Proc. CHI'03. pp. 529–536 (2003)
12. Geller, D.M., Goodstein, L., Silver, M., Sternberg, W.C.: On being ignored: The effects of the violation of implicit rules of social interaction. Sociometry pp. 541–556 (1974)

13. Goffman, E.: Footing. Semiotica 25(1–2), 1–30 (1979)
14. Heylen, D., Van Es, I., Van Dijk, E., Nijholt, A., Van Dijk, B.: Experimenting with the gaze of a conversational agent. In: Proc. CLASS'05. pp. 93–100 (2002)
15. Heylen, D.K.J.: Head gestures, gaze and the principles of conversational structure. International Journal of Humanoid Robotics 3(3), 241–267 (2006)
16. Hollands, M.A., Ziavra, N.V., Bronstein, A.M.: A new paradigm to investigate the roles of head and eye movements in the coordination of whole-body movements. Experimental Brain Research 154(2), 261–266 (2004)
17. Kendon, A.: Conducting interaction: Patterns of behavior in focused encounters. Cambridge University Press (1990)
18. Kendon, A.: Some functions of gaze-direction in social interaction. Acta psychologica 26, 22–63 (1967)
19. Kuzuoka, H., Suzuki, Y., Yamashita, J., Yamazaki, K.: Reconfiguring spatial formation arrangement by robot body orientation. In: Proc. HRI'10. pp. 285–292 (2010)
20. Lee, S.P., Badler, J.B., Badler, N.I.: Eyes alive. ACM ToG 21, 637–644 (2002)
21. McCluskey, M.K., Cullen, K.E.: Eye, head, and body coordination during large gaze shifts in rhesus monkeys: Movement kinematics and the influence of posture. Journal of Neurophysiology 97(4), 2976–2991 (2007)
22. Mutlu, B., Kanda, T., Forlizzi, J., Hodgins, J., Ishiguro, H.: Conversational gaze mechanisms for humanlike robots. ACM TiiS 1(2), 12:1–12:33 (2012)
23. Pedica, C., Vilhjálmsson, H.H.: Spontaneous avatar behavior for human territoriality. Applied Artificial Intelligence 24(6), 575–593 (2010)
24. Pedica, C., Vilhjálmsson, H.H., Lárusdóttir, M.K.: Avatars in conversation: The importance of simulating territorial behavior. In: Proc. IVA'10. pp. 336–342 (2010)
25. Pejsa, T., Andrist, S., Gleicher, M., Mutlu, B.: Gaze and attention management for embodied conversational agents. ACM TiiS 5(1), 3:1–3:34 (2015)
26. Schegloff, E.A.: Sequencing in conversational openings. American anthropologist 70(6), 1075–1095 (1968)
27. Steptoe, W., Wolff, R., Murgia, A., Guimaraes, E., Rae, J., Sharkey, P., Roberts, D., Steed, A.: Eye-tracking for avatar eye-gaze and interactional analysis in immersive collaborative virtual environments. In: Proc. CSCW'08. pp. 197–200 (2008)
28. Uemura, T., Arai, Y., Shimazaki, C.: Eye-head coordination during lateral gaze in normal subjects. Acta Oto-Laryngologica 90(3–4), 191–198 (1980)
29. Wieser, M.J., Pauli, P., Grosseibl, M., Molzow, I., Mühlberger, A.: Virtual social interactions in social anxiety-the impact of sex, gaze, and interpersonal distance. Cyberpsychology, Behavior, and Social Networking 13(5), 547–554 (2010)
30. Williams, K.D., Cheung, C.K.T., Choi, W.: Cyberostracism: effects of being ignored over the internet. Journal of Personality and Social Psychology 79(5), 748 (2000)
31. Yee, N., Bailenson, J.N., Urbanek, M., Chang, F., Merget, D.: The unbearable likeness of being digital: The persistence of nonverbal social norms in online virtual environments. CyberPsychology & Behavior 10(1), 115–121 (2007)

Cubus: Autonomous Embodied Characters to Stimulate Creative Idea Generation in Groups of Children

André Pires[1,2] ✉, Patrícia Alves-Oliveira[1,3] ✉, Patrícia Arriaga[3] ✉
and Carlos Martinho[1,2] ✉

[1] INESC-ID, Av. Professor Cavaco Silva, 2744-016 Porto Salvo, Portugal
patricia.alves.oliveira@inesc-id.pt
[2] Instituto Superior Técnico, University of Lisbon, Av. Professor Cavaco Silva,
2744-016 Porto Salvo, Portugal
{andre.b.pires,carlos.martinho}@tecnico.ulisboa.pt
[3] Instituto Universitário de Lisboa (ISCTE-IUL), CIS-IUL, Av. das Forças Armadas,
1649-026 Lisboa, Portugal
patricia.arriaga@iscte.pt

Abstract. Creativity is an ability that is crucial in nowadays societies. It is, therefore, important to develop activities that stimulate creativity at a very young age. It seems, however, that there is a lack of tools to support these activities. In this paper, we introduce Cubus, a tool that uses autonomous synthetic characters to stimulate idea generation in groups of children during a storytelling activity. With Cubus, children can invent a story and use the stop-motion technique to record a movie depicting it. In this paper, we explain Cubus' system design and architecture and present the evaluation of Cubus' impact in a creative task. This evaluation investigated idea generation in groups of children during their creative process of storytelling. Results showed that the autonomous behaviors of Cubus' virtual agents contributed to the generation of more ideas in children, a key dimension of creativity.

Keywords: autonomous virtual agents, child-agent interaction, creativity support tool, group creativity with children, creative storytelling

1 Introduction

The role of creativity is paramount in our current day societies. Creativity contributes in a major way to both our professional and personal growth. It is, therefore, important to encourage the growth of this ability from a very young age [17]. Although many schools already feature storytelling activities which help promote the children's creative thinking [6], these activities are cumbersome for teachers to prepare and manage, with scarce tools existing to support these activities [4].

With this work, we propose to enhance children's creativity, by focusing on the stimulation of idea generation during their creative process. As identified by

© Springer International Publishing AG 2017
J. Beskow et al. (Eds.): IVA 2017, LNAI 10498, pp. 360–373, 2017.
DOI 10.1007/978-3-319-67401-8_46

Torrance [27], idea generation (also denominated by *fluency*) is one of the primary aspects of the creative process. Inspired in literature regarding this aspect of creativity we designed a system and activity that explored techniques to improve idea generation using agents' autonomous behaviors. Our system, Cubus, emerges as a virtual environment that allows groups of children to engage in creative storytelling while interacting with autonomous synthetic characters that are part of Cubus. As a design guideline we adopted the *Concrete Stimuli* technique (which suggests using physical things to provide stimuli during creative sessions) [23]. In our particular application, we expect to use our agents' behaviors to produce these stimuli. Additionally, we believe that it is important to conduct our study in a social setting as most of our interactions and problem solving have a social component. This focus should help children learn how to better express and represent their knowledge and ideas. To this end, while designing our activity we intended to leverage the *Group Interaction* technique, in which ideas verbalized by one member of a group can prompt other members to suggest more ideas [23].

Three dimensions were taken into account for the evaluation of how Cubus enhances creativity: *creative process*, *creative product*, and impact on the participants' creative idea generation (fluency). This paper focuses on the analysis of the *creative process*. Our evaluation study was planned to test the hypothesis that the inclusion of the characters' *autonomous behaviors* would increase idea generation in groups of children during the creative process of storytelling.

1.1 Creativity

Creativity is a concept that has no consensual definition, but there is an overall agreement that creativity can be defined as the "interaction among aptitude, process, and environment by which an individual or group produces a perceptible product that is both novel and useful as defined within a social context" [18]. This work is framed within the research area of computational creativity. Before starting the development of the Cubus system it was crucial to study and understand the different ways that tend to contribute to a creative process. Torrance [27], cites four fundamental creative abilities in the creative process: fluency, flexibility, originality and elaboration. With this work, we focus only on stimulating *fluency*, the number of ideas generated during a creative process. Not only we want to stimulate fluency during the creative process, as we are interested in improving this creative ability within a group and as a result in a social context. Henceforth, creativity deviates from emerging from an *individual* creative process, to become an ability that is stimulated in a *distributed way within a group* [21,9]. During the unscripted collaborative efforts that emerge during the creative process, improvisation is key as it involves creating different ideas as well as adapting to concepts introduced by others and building upon them [24]. In our study, we used Cubus to stimulate fluency in groups of children during storytelling.

Creativity Support Tools: Our work contributes towards the enhancement of creativity with the aid of computers, defined as the field of Creativity Support Tools (CSTs) [22]. We took inspiration from works such as *Dr. Inventor* [7] and a work that uses a physical agent to aid children in creative storytelling [20].

1.2   Human-Agent Interaction

Cubus system includes synthetic characters and their design inspiration includes previous work in the area of Human-Agent Interaction (HAI). Given that our characters are non-humanoid, we faced several challenges in designing their emotional expressive behaviors. To address emotional expression when designing characters with a restrictive appearance, we followed an extensive survey carried out by Bethel and Murphy [3] in which different means of expression are suggested, such as movement [28, 2], color [2, 25], sound and proxemics [10]. We incorporated several of these means and guidelines while designing how our synthetic characters should interact with the user and with each other to increase their chances of expressing themselves successfully.

Cubus offers a similarly structured environment as presented in the Oz Project, designed for the creation and presentation of dramas in a virtual setting [15]. Cubus uses non-humanoid characters to allow children's imagination to direct the characters' narratives freely. The use of simple shapes as been shown to allow the creation of rich narratives in similar contexts [11].

In the study of creativity, *motivation* is one of the foundations for a successful creative experience [1], as such we will use agents to motivate users in their task [14]. Additionally, the use of a synthetic character does not hinder communication and is able to enhance discussion in a collaborative task with pairs of children [19], reinforcing our motivation to include synthetic characters in our scenario. These prior findings were taken into account when planning our study.

2   Cubus System

Our work features a virtual environment which contains a small set of world building tools and synthetic characters (Figure 1). The system was tailored to fit the target audience of children between the ages of 7 and 9 years old. Our main concern during the development of Cubus was to keep it accessible for children and open-ended to leave space for creation, allowing the creative storytelling process to unfold. Cubus can be divided into two primary components:

- **Synthetic characters:** Our characters will be featured in the children's story as their *actors*;
- **Virtual environment:** The environment is responsible for supporting the world building features and recording the story that children create.

The development of this work was carried out with the Unity^{TM} game engine (version 5.3.5f1) and our testing environment consists in a Samsung^{TM} Galaxy Tab Pro 10.1 tablet through the use of its touch interface (Android^{TM} 5.1.1).

Fig. 1. Virtual environment.

2.1 Synthetic Characters

The *synthetic characters* were designed to be non-humanoid and rely on the emergent interaction between them for emotional expression. Using this interaction among the characters toward stimulating creativity is the most innovative part of this work. For brevity, "synthetic characters" will be addressed as "agents" for the remainder of this paper.

Agents' Implementation: Each agent corresponds to one of five specific emotions (anger, happiness, fear, sadness, disgust), displaying behaviors autonomously that are consistent with that emotion [28]. There is no limit to how many agents of a given emotion can be present in our environment at a given time. To add more depth to the agents' emotional displays, two types of behaviors were created for each emotion: a *standard behavior* and an *intense behavior*, the latter being perceived as a stronger display of the given emotion.

Additionally, each agent has two drives: one that triggers *standard behavior* and another that triggers *intense behavior*. These drives vary between 0 and 90. The **standard drive** starts at a random value between 0 and 35 and increases with the passing of time (1-second intervals). When this drive reaches 90, it triggers the standard behavior and resets its value to 0. Additionally, this timed increase "step" is affected by a multiplier, within the range of 1 to 1.5 for the standard drive and 1 to 1.3 for the intense drive. These multipliers are set randomly within these ranges at the moment of the agent's creation. Both elements of randomness introduce diversity to the different agents' behaviors, reducing their predictability and making their interaction appear more natural. The same drive also increases when other agents display any behavior within a certain radius of the agent. The **intense drive** starts at 0 and only increases with time until 65, after this point only increases when stimuli from other agents' behaviors (which share the same emotion) are received. When this drive reaches 90 the corresponding behavior is triggered and both drives are reset. It should be noted that while a behavior is occurring, no stimulus is received from other agents.

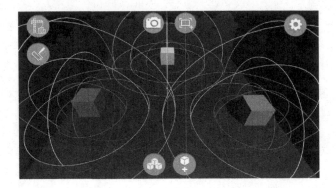

Fig. 2. Proxemic distances that weight agents' interaction.

These agents' interact with each other by broadcasting stimuli to the surrounding agents when they display a behavior. The intensity of these stimuli differs taking into account the distance at which the other agents are (closer agents provide stronger stimuli). These distances are fixed for every agent and divided into three intervals as evidenced in Figure 2. The contributions from the stimuli vary from 25 to 45 when contributing toward the standard drive and between 35 and 60 for the intense drive. With the combination of these mechanisms, we empowered children to create unique scenes in their story that emerged from the actors they choose, as well as how they place them.

Appearance: We have chosen a neutral appearance for the agents' design to provide the possibility for children to project any desired character. To this end, the geometric shape of *a cube* was selected, inspired by LEGO^{TM} bricks. Since emotions seem to enhance creativity in video games [13] it was important to establish which emotions we were attempting to represent. We considered Ekman's [8] model of six emotions to be appropriate for our context, omitting surprise emotion given that there is no consensus regarding its inclusion as an emotion.

Expression: We focused on two primary means of communication for the agents: color and body movements/posturing. To combine these features appropriately and make them be perceived as natural during the agents' animations, we studied Disney^{TM}'s twelve principles of animation [26]. These principles address the human need for more pronounced cues in order to correctly perceive actions or displays of affection by synthetic characters. The most relevant principles in our design were: squash and stretch, anticipation, follow-through, and staging.

Color: In order to create an identity for our emotions, some emotion-color associations were selected, the inspiration for these was drawn from Disney^{TM}'s movie *Inside Out*. Ekman was one of the scientific consultants for this movie and the emotions present in the movie feature one predominant color. As such, we considered that the unique colors associated with each emotion would create

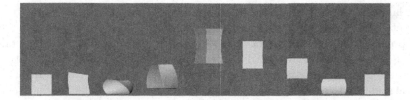

Fig. 3. Happiness emotion's spinning jump (key frames).

distinguishable agents. Additionally, in an effort to direct the users' attention to the agents' behaviors we added a blinking effect triggered in the beginning of the agents' behaviors. This blinking remains within the hue of each agent's base color and depending on the valence of its emotion the blink varies, being brighter when the valence is positive (*e.g.*, happiness) or darker for a negative valence (*e.g.*, anger). This blinking effect also varies according to the arousal of each emotion, *e.g.*, happy and angry emotions have a high arousal. Thus, the blinking will have a higher frequency than, for instance, when sadness is being displayed. These blinking frequencies were tuned to ensure they were distinguishable and represented the different arousals levels.

Body Movement and Posture: In addition to detailed animation principles, we explored character deformation in our animations to create simple but organic movements for the agents. This step toward deformable characters enabled a more appropriate representation of simple actions (*i.e.*, jumps, nods, squats, etc). Some of the aforementioned animation principles, such as squash and stretch or follow-through, helped convey the physical impact actions have on a character's body as seen in Figure 3. To convey our particular set of emotions through animation, we considered Wallbott's [28] work, which summarizes some of Darwin's observations regarding movement and posture in emotional expression. These observations provided insight to create the desired set of emotions for our agents, as well as for their arousal state. For example, stretching the body and mimicking an inflated chest while leaning forward conveys anger, while squashing and tilting down while staying motionless conveys sadness. When combined and properly timed, these cues produced the final version of our animations for the agent's expression. In an effort to increase our agents' expressiveness, two animations were designed for each emotion. Each agent exhibits two different intensity levels for every emotion: standard and intense. This allows the agent to express the heightened emotional intensity of agents interacting with the same emotion.

2.2   Interactive Virtual Environment

The virtual environment sustains both the interaction between children and our agents, as well as the children's storytelling process (Figure 1). This environment allows the recording of the children's story, managing and directing the agents and customizing virtual scenarios. For the design of the system, we followed a modular approach with four major components: screen recorder, world building tool set, agents, and user interface (UI) manager. The screen recorder module is responsible for the capture of objects within the scene that are 3D, while excluding any screen overlays or UI elements. The world building tools control and carry out children's inputs when managing their scenes. This ranges from changing the scenario to creating and deleting agents. An UI manager module serves as the interface between the children's inputs and both the agents and the tool set.

Stop-motion: To allow the recording of the stop-motion story, children can perform screen captures when creating scenes to feature in their movie. These screen captures omit the application's UI elements and record only the actors and scenario. The images resulting from the screen captures are stored within the device and, at a later stage, imported into an application that supports the creation of a stop-motion movie. Two features were added to help children understand how to use the system: an effect mimicking a camera flash each time a screen capture is performed, helping reaffirm the action; and an overlay with small opacity covering the entire screen of the previous screen capture (visible in Figure 1). This last feature was useful, as some children showed difficulties recalling their last recorded moment in the story when they *e.g.*, changed the story scene. It is also possible to create intertitle screens (as seen in silent movies). These allow children to record a screen with a written message, enabling them to explore and explain more drastic changes within their story.

World: The virtual environment gives children enough degrees of customization to personalize the story. Several scenarios are available in our environment, these are very distinguishable from each other and allow for different uses. Their topologies are quite different (*e.g.*, curvilinear, rectilinear or with sharp angles), while still being very much open to interpretation. To point out an example, our "spiky" scenario was seen as pine trees, mountains or traps by children. To provide children more creative freedom, a color selection screen was added, enabling children to select a color for the scenario and another for the skybox that envelops it.

Interacting with the actors: The building tools allow children to create and manage their actors. To this end, children are able to select which type of agent (or actor) they wish to feature in their story. Additionally, children can access a list of all their actors, through which they can hide or reveal actors or delete them. The ability to toggle an actor's visibility is useful for actors that aren't in every scene of the story, allowing children the creative freedom to experiment with more complex storytelling narratives. To control the actors, children can perform dragging (press on the agent with their finger and drag it from one point to another) and rotation movements (press on the agent with one finger to select it and use another finger to slide up or down, to rotate forward or backward) of their actors. These movements allow children to represent characters walking around or facing an important object or character in any given scene.

3 Evaluation study

This section presents the evaluation study performed to investigate Cubus' potential to stimulate idea generation. Two other studies were carried out during the development of Cubus: a co-design study, to guide and validate our design, and a usability test, to validate the functionalities and workflow offered by Cubus. Both studies are covered elsewhere. For the creativity evaluation and prior to children's participation, parents signed an informed consent which stated their willingness in letting their child perform the study, and each child provided, verbally, their assent to participate. This study was performed in a school setting to investigate whether Cubus with the inclusion of autonomous behavior in the characters' can stimulate fluency of ideas in children while performing a storytelling task. To study this, we have analyzed the fluency of ideas (number of ideas generated) by comparing two experimental conditions:

- **Autonomous condition:** in which children interacted with the autonomous version of the agents;
- **Non autonomous condition:** in which children interacted with the same agents whose behavior they control directly. Additionally, children can select one of three sizes for each agent (small, medium or large).

We hypothesize that children will have higher fluency in the autonomous condition when compared to the non-autonomous one.

Sample: 20 children participated in the evaluation of Cubus, with ages ranging from 7-9 years old ($M = 8.10$, $SD = 0.72$, 14 female). Our sample was split evenly between conditions with 10 children featured in each condition. Children performed the task in pairs, henceforth, each session consisted of two children interacting with Cubus with a total number of 10 sessions. The pairs of children were organized by their school teacher who selected children that were friends and that played well together. Each session lasted approximately 1h and was lead by two researchers: one researcher with a computer science background and with knowledge on the specifics of Cubus, and a psychologist.

Procedure: Pairs of children entered the designated classroom in which the study would be performed. The flow of the study can be divided into four stages:

1. *Saying hello.* The initial phase consisted of the presentation of each child and of each researcher in order to get to know each other. During this phase, the leading researcher explained that the goal of the activity was to create a stop-motion movie using Cubus. As most children were not familiarized with stop-motion animation, this notion was explained to them. To do this, the researcher used Cubus to provide a basic example of an agent walking from one side to the other in the virtual environment while performing screen captures of each frame, and then showed the end product of the movie. As children got engaged with the notion of stop-motion, they were motivated to

Fig. 4. Children interacting with Cubus system.

try it by themselves using Cubus. This enabled the explanation of the basic features of Cubus and at the end of this stage, children were familiar with the system and ready to start their own movie;

2. *Hands on Cubus.* The researcher explained to the pair of children that their movie had to follow a theme (*i.e.*, their story needed to start with someone dreaming and to end with someone waking up). For all sessions, Cubus was set to the following mode: a clear Cubus world with a white color as a metaphor for a white paper sheet. Children started to create their story collaboratively (actors, actions, scenarios, and plot) (see Figure 4) and the role of the researchers was to support their questions regarding any dynamics with respect to using Cubus, or to keep the storytelling flow and rhythm going by asking questions such as, "what's your actor going to do now?" or "what happens next?". Children had no knowledge about the behavior and color associations of the agents' emotions. This stage continued until the pair of children finished their story using the stop-motion technique;

3. *Narration.* After having completed their stop-motion movie, children performed the voice narration for their story. The voice narration of the movie consisted of children speaking (either as narrators, actors, or even making a soundtrack) to a voice recorder while watching their movie play. As children did not have a written script, they were able to train the narration several times until they felt comfortable. It is important to note that although each narration was grounded on the main story plot defined by children, each narration was different and tied with the improvisation between children about what was happening in the movie. This stage ended when the stop-motion movie had a narration;

4. *Saying goodbye.* The last stage of this study consisted of watching together with children their movie and congratulating them on their accomplishment.

Data analysis: To study if the presence of autonomous agents during a storytelling task increased the fluency of ideas (*i.e.*, number of ideas generated) by children, we performed behavior video analysis of the recorded sessions (10 sessions in total). The video analysis was focused only on the *Hands on Cubus* phase, described in the Procedure. Therefore, the behavior analysis concerned only the *process* of the stop-motion movie creation. The main goal of the behavioral analysis was to analyze the *fluency of ideas of children during the creative process of creating the stop-motion movie while interacting with Cubus in each experimental condition*. To this end, a coding scheme for fluency of ideas was generated in order to perform the behavioral analysis, and is described below:

- **Idea** - The first step was to define what an actual *idea* was in the context of the storytelling activity, to differentiate it from the rest of the interaction. Therefore, *an idea was defined as a verbal interaction between children that has the potential to add a detail to the story that is being created. Ideas can appear in duplicate and are still considered ideas even if children decide not to use them in the final story.* In this context, an idea can be a verbal detail related to the actors, actions, scenario, or other, if related to the story that is being created. An interaction that concerns technical details of how to manage Cubus was not considered an idea, *e.g.*, when a participant asked "how can I add another actor?".

The next step was to differentiate between the *types of ideas* that were generated. This type of coding is dependent on the content of the ideas and can be divided into two different types of ideas, described below:

- **Idea-agents** - An idea that derives from the interaction with the agents needs to be *related with the agents' characteristics, such as color, size, and/or behavior*. For example, if a participant states that an agent "became bigger", it does not count as an idea. Whereas if a participant says that "[the agent] has become bigger to scare someone", is considered an idea derived from the interaction with the agent;
- **Idea-children** - In this category belongs *any idea that derives from the imagination of the participants and that connects with the story* (and that is not related to the agents). Examples can be the choice of a shape for a given scenario (*e.g.*, a spikier world) or the colors of the scenario.

Video analysis was performed using ELAN software [29] and conducted by two researchers. One researcher coded 100% of the data and the second researcher coded 40% (selected randomly) [12]. Since one of the variables was a constant, the Percent Agreement Method [16] was used to calculate the inter-judges agreement for the coding of "Ideas", revealing an agreement of 87%. Cohen's Kappa [5] was used to calculate the inter-judges agreement for "Ideas-agents" and "Ideas-children", revealing an agreement of $K = 0.947$ and $K = 0.932$, respectively.

Results: The results of this study include the analysis of the number of *ideas-agents* (ideas generated by children resulting from the interaction with the

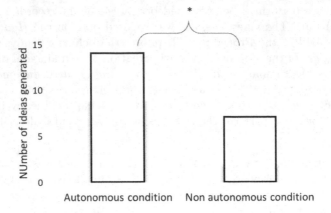

Fig. 5. Mean ranks of the ideas generated (fluency) by children, resulting from the interaction with the agents. (*) denotes $p<0.01$.

agents) and *ideas-children* (ideas generated by children connected only with the story and not dependent on the interaction with the agents). Given the small size of the sample, non-parametric tests were used to analyze the data. Therefore, to analyze the **ideas-agents**, a Mann-Whitney U test was used revealing that the number of ideas that emerged from the interaction between the participants and the agents differed statistically across conditions, $U = 15$, $p = .007$, $r = 0.60$. By analyzing the mean ranks it can be seen that the number of ideas generated was higher when participants interacted with autonomous agents (*Mean rank* $= 14.00$) compared to the non autonomous agents (*Mean rank* $= 7.00$) (see Figure 5). Additionally, we have calculated the difference for the number of **ideas-children** between conditions. A Mann-Whitney U test showed that the number of ideas generated by children that are connected with the story and that were not dependent upon the interaction with the agents does not statistically differ across conditions, $U = 38$, $p = 0.364$, $r = 0.20$. Despite the non-significant result, the number of ideas generated was higher in the autonomous condition (*Mean rank* $= 11.70$) in comparison with the non-autonomous condition (*Mean rank* $= 9.30$). Overall, results suggest that the number of ideas generated by participants differs statistically between conditions when looking at the number of ideas generated by children when interacting with the agents. This result corroborates our study hypothesis, showing that children are able to generate more ideas when interacting with an autonomous agents compared to a non autonomous one.

4   Conclusion

In this paper, we present Cubus, a system designed to stimulate children's idea generation during storytelling. Cubus is comprised of a virtual environment and autonomous agents that children interact with through a touch interface on an Android^{TM} tablet. The innovative component of Cubus concerns the autonomous agents whose behaviors were designed to stimulate children's creativity, and in particular the creative process of idea generation in children while interacting with Cubus. The results suggest that children are able to generate a significantly higher number of ideas when interacting with the autonomous agents compared to the control condition in which the agents were not autonomous.

The main contribution of this work to the area of intelligent virtual agents is to demonstrate that the inclusion of synthetic characters with autonomous behaviors can have a strong impact on creativity based tasks with children. The evaluation of Cubus as a tool to stimulate idea generation in children comprises additional evaluation aspects that are still ongoing. One of these aspects is related with the evaluation of the *creative products*, *i.e.*, the movies children created. These will be evaluated by a panel of judges with expert knowledge in animation. Additionally, children's *creative skills* will be analyzed by applying validated tests that quantify individuals' creative potential. For future work we also aim to extend the study with Cubus to a larger sample size, since the number of participants included in this study was relatively small.

Acknowledgements

This work was supported by national funds through Fundação para a Ciência e a Tecnologia (FCT) with reference UID/CEC/50021/2013 and through project AMIGOS (PTDC/EEISII/7174/2014). P. Alves-Oliveira acknowledges a FCT grant with reference SFRH/BD/110223/2015. We would also like to thank the school São Francisco de Assis for their support.

References

1. Amabile, T.M., Hennessey, B.A.: The motivation for creativity in children. Achievement and motivation: A social-developmental perspective pp. 54–74 (1992)
2. Argyle, M.: The Syntaxes of Bodily Communication. Linguistics 11(112), 71 (1973)
3. Bethel, C., Murphy, R.: Survey of Non-facial/Non-verbal Affective Expressions for Appearance-Constrained Robots. IEEE Transactions on Systems, Man, and Cybernetics, Part C (Applications and Reviews) 38(1), 83–92 (jan 2008)
4. Chan, S., Yuen, M.: Personal and environmental factors affecting teachers' creativity-fostering practices in Hong Kong. Thinking Skills and Creativity 12(1), 69–77 (jun 2014)
5. Cohen, J.: Weighted kappa: Nominal scale agreement provision for scaled disagreement or partial credit. Psychological bulletin 70(4), 213 (1968)
6. Di Blas, N., Paolini, P., Sabiescu, A.G.: Collective digital storytelling at school: a whole-class interaction. International Journal of Arts and Technology 5(2-4), 271–292 (2012)
7. Donoghue, D.P.O., Saggion, H., Dong, F., Hurley, D., Abgaz, Y., Zheng, X., Corcho, O., Zhang, J.J., Careil, J.M., Mahdian, B., Zhao, X.: Towards Dr Inventor: A Tool for Promoting Scientific Creativity. Proc. 5th International Conference on Computational Creativity (ICCC) (October), 268–271 (2014)
8. Ekman, P., V. Friesen, W., Ellsworth, P.: Emotion in the Human Face. Pergamon Press Inc., Fairview Park, Elmsford, New York, 1st edn. (1972)

9. Fischer, G.: Meta-design and Social Creativity: Making All Voices Heard. Human-Computer Interaction – INTERACT 2007 pp. 692–693 (2007)
10. Friedman, D., Steed, A., Slater, M.: Spatial Social Behavior in Second Life. Intelligent Virtual Agents 4722, 252–263 (2007)
11. Gordon, A.S., Roemmele, M.: An Authoring Tool for Movies in the Style of Heider and Simmel. The Seventh International Conference on Interactive Digital Storytelling (ICIDS 2014) pp. 1–12 (2014), http://link.springer.com/10.1007/978-3-319-12337-0_5
12. Heyman, R.E., Lorber, M.F., Eddy, J.M., West, T.V.: Behavioral Observation and Coding. In: Reis, H.T., Judd, C.M. (eds.) Handbook of Research Methods in Social and Personality Psychology, pp. 345–372. Cambridge University Press, New York, 2nd edn. (2014)
13. Hutton, E., Sundar, S.S.: Can video games enhance creativity? effects of emotion generated by dance dance revolution. Creativity Research Journal 22(3), 294–303 (2010)
14. Kahn, P.H., Kanda, T., Ishiguro, H., Gill, B.T., Shen, S., Ruckert, J.H., Gary, H.E.: Human creativity can be facilitated through interacting with a social robot. In: 2016 11th ACM/IEEE International Conference on Human-Robot Interaction (HRI). pp. 173–180. IEEE, Christchurch, New Zealand (mar 2016)
15. Kelso, M.M., Weyhrauch, P., Bates, J.: Dramatic presence. Presence: The Journal of Teleoperators and Virtual 2(1), 1–15 (1993), http://citeseerx.ist.psu.edu/viewdoc/download?doi=10.1.1.105.2349&rep=rep1&type=pdf
16. McHugh, M.L.: Interrater reliability: the kappa statistic. Biochemia medica 22(3), 276–282 (2012)
17. Mellou, E.: Can Creativity be Nurtured in Young Children? Early Child Development and Care 119(1), 119–130 (1996)
18. Plucker, J.A., Beghetto, R.A., Dow, G.T.: Why Isn't Creativity More Important to Educational Psychologists? Potentials, Pitfalls, and Future Directions in Creativity Research. Educational Psychologist 39(2), 83–96 (jun 2004)
19. Ryokai, K., Vaucelle, C., Cassell, J.: Virtual peers as partners in storytelling and literacy learning. Journal of Computer Assisted Learning 19(January), 195–208 (2003)
20. Ryokai, K., Lee, M.: Children's storytelling and programming with robotic characters. C&C '09 Proceedings of the seventh ACM conference on Creativity and cognition pp. 19–28 (2009)
21. Sawyer, R.K., DeZutter, S.: Distributed creativity: How collective creations emerge from collaboration. Psychology of Aesthetics, Creativity, and the Arts 3(2), 81–92 (2009)
22. Shneiderman, B.: Creativity support tools: accelerating discovery and innovation. Communications of the ACM 50(12), 20–32 (dec 2007)
23. Smith, G.F.: Idea-Generation Techniques: A Formulary of Active Ingredients. The Journal of Creative Behavior 32(2), 107–134 (jun 1998), http://doi.wiley.com/10.1002/j.2162-6057.1998.tb00810.x
24. Sowden, P.T., Clements, L., Redlich, C., Lewis, C.: Improvisation Facilitates Divergent Thinking and Creativity: Realizing a Benefit of Primary School Arts Education. Psychology of Aesthetics, Creativity, and the Arts 9(2), 128–138 (2015)
25. Terada, K., Yamauchi, A., Ito, A.: Artificial emotion expression for a robot by dynamic color change. In: 2012 IEEE RO-MAN: The 21st IEEE International Symposium on Robot and Human Interactive Communication. pp. 314–321. IEEE, Paris, France (sep 2012)

26. Thomas, F., Johnston, O., Thomas, F.: The illusion of life: Disney animation. Hyperion Books, New York, United States, revised edn. (1995)
27. Torrance, E.P.: The Search for Satori and Creativity. Creative Education Foundation, Buffalo, New York, 1st edn. (1979)
28. Wallbott, H.G.: Bodily Expression of Emotion. European Journal of Social Psychology 28(6), 879–896 (1998)
29. Wittenburg, P., Brugman, H., Russel, A., Klassmann, A., Sloetjes, H.: Elan: a professional framework for multimodality research. In: Proceedings of LREC. vol. 2006, p. 5th (2006)

Interacting with a semantic affective ECA

Joaquín Pérez[1]✉, Yanet Sánchez[1], Francisco J. Serón[1], and Eva Cerezo[1]

Aragón Institute of Engineering Research (I3A)
Department of Computer Science and Systems Engineering (DIIS)
University of Zaragoza, Spain
{jpmarco,ysanchezl,fjseron,ecerezo}@unizar.es

Abstract. This paper presents an affective enhanced semantic ECA named E-VOX. The core of E-VOX is a cognitive-affective architecture based on Soar and extended with an affective model inspired by ALMA, that takes into account emotions, mood, and personality. E-VOX works as an assistant to provide useful information from Wikipedia, supporting real-feel human-computer interaction. User interaction with the ECA is explained and first tests with users are shown. These tests have revealed that the ECA is perceived as useful, easy to use and entertaining. Thanks to the cognitive-affective architecture, the agent's behavior is modulated its personality, influencing agent-user interaction and the perception of the agent by the user. The agent's emotional behavior has been perceived by users as realistic though not always sufficiently expressive.

Keywords: embodied conversational agent, cognitive architecture, emotional models

1 Introduction

The concepts of affect and emotion are often used interchangeably, but affect can be seen as a superordinate category that includes emotion, mood and also, personality. At the same time, affect and cognition have demonstrated to be closely related: affective aspects play an essential role in cognitive process such as decision making, learning, and planning. Therefore, nowadays there is a consensus about the need of considering affective aspects (emotions, mood, and personality) to obtain human-like behavior in ECAs (embodied conversational agents). An ECA is a virtual embodied agent with conversational and learning skills, realistic body, expression, and the ability to perceive the environment, to reason about it and act accordingly. An approach to support all these aspects in ECAs is the use of cognitive architectures. A cognitive architecture can be defined as a scheme or pattern for structuring the functional elements that make an intelligent agent as a whole, so it simplifies the design of an integrated system in which all desired features can be included. Cognitive architectures seem appropriate to provide ECAs with capabilities for cognitive processing such as learning, decision making, planning, and perception. Nevertheless, in spite of the great advances achieved in the last years in the development of ECAs, there is a lack of architectures that effectively combine cognitive and affective aspects so

J. Beskow et al. (Eds.): IVA 2017, LNAI 10498, pp. 374-384, 2017.
DOI 10.1007/978-3-319-67401-8_47

that they can be used to model ECAs that support real-feel human-computer interactions.

On the other hand, in the last years, a huge amount of information has become available thanks to the Web. Computers are good at processing huge amounts of data, but most contents in the Web have been (and still are) mainly human-oriented, i.e. users have to interpret the meaning of the information that is exposed to them. Therefore, it was proposed to move into the Semantic Web [?], a Web where the semantics of the different resources are made explicit, thus allowing computers to process automatically that structured information. This has raised new opportunities to develop intelligent agents that help users find what they are looking for, as users are often overloaded with vast amounts of information, most of which is inaccurate, misleading or unsolicited. Among the Semantic Web applications, DBpedia is one of the most representative and active of them [?]. It provides a semantic entry point to the Wikipedia that is able to perform intelligent searches and return only results relevant to a particular knowledge domain.

In this paper, we present a first evaluation of E-VOX, an affective semantic ECA designed to work as a virtual assistant, providing the user information available through DBpedia. An important aspect of this agent is that it uses extensively an advanced cognitive-affective architecture based on Soar. This architecture allows the ECA to take into account features needed for social interaction such as learning and affective management.

The paper is structured as follows. In Section 2, related work is presented. Section 3 describes the architecture of the E-VOX system. Section4 describes system-user in-teraction and the first test carried out with users. Finally, concluding remarks and future work are discussed in Section 5.

2   Related Work

ECAs have been used in diverse application domains, as medical scope [4], mobile applications [17], e-Learning [14] and games [2,12]. In some applications, special effort has been made to endowed the agent with affective capabilities. When trying to do so, emotions are the most modeled affective aspect. Several emotional theories have been used, being the OCC model [25] the most widely used one. Other affective aspects usually modeled in ECAs are mood and personality. The most used model to represent mood in ECAs is the PAD model [23] and, for personality, the OCEAN model [22]. Most of the affective models of ECAs combine severals of these affective aspects (Soar-Emote [20] and ALMA[11]), and include other features such as learning (FLAME [9]), empathy (FAtiMA [8]), and coping (EMA [21]) to build believable and complex affective agents. Among the numerous works and ECAs applications that have focused in those affective aspects, we highlight:

- The **VirtualHuman** System [27], a 3D interactive application, includes the affective model ALMA to provide it with affective processed information useful to improve its conversational abilities.

- **EMO**, a virtual therapist that helps with different kind of problems of the user using *solution focused training* is shown in [1]. It uses the OCEAN and PAD models to work with the mood and the personality of the agent.
- The **Mission Rehearsal Exercise** project [13], a virtual-based training program intended to teach soldiers how they should act in stressful situations, includes EMA to influence the decision-making of computational agents.
- **EMMA** (*Empathic MultiModal Agent*) [6] as a third interaction partner in a conversational agent scenario in which the virtual human MAX acts as a museum guide [18]. They use PAD model to work with emotions and other theories to model empathic behavior.
- **Greta**, is an interactive ECA platform endowed with socio-emotional and communicative behaviors [3, ?]. The Greta's affective behavior combines emotions, based on OCC emotional model, and personality traits.
- **Tinker**, is a museum guide that establishes social empathic bonds with users, and encourages continued interaction and repeated visits [5].
- An **affective avatar**, aimed at engaging the user in a social interaction with the purpose of assisting in communication therapies [16].
- **HWYD**, a companion ECA that is able to provide advice and support to the user, taking into account emotions expressed through dialogue [7].
- **DiscoRT**, a real-time architecture for ECAs with both virtual and robotic embodiments, to provide social support for isolated older adults [24].

3   E-VOX

E-VOX is an affective enhanced semantic ECA that helps users find useful information. Figure 1 shows the architecture of the system. In the next subsections, the different modules of the system and the interaction possibilities with E-VOX are briefly explained.

3.1   Cognitive-Affective Architecture

The core of E-VOX is a cognitive-affective architecture based on Soar [19] and extended with an affective model inspired by ALMA. Soar is a cognitive architecture designed to model the intelligent behavior of an agent that integrates knowledge, planning, reaction to events, and learning in a simple and homogeneous architecture. Soar includes a wide set of mechanisms such as semantic memory, epi-sodic memory, reinforcement learning, and spatial and visual information system. ALMA is an emotional model based on three layers: emotion (short-term, based on the OCC model), mood (medium-term, based on the PAD model), and personality (based on the OCEAN model). The combination of Soar and ALMA allows E-VOX to include and take advantage of features such as reinforcement learning, episodic memory, and emotion management. More details can be found in [26].

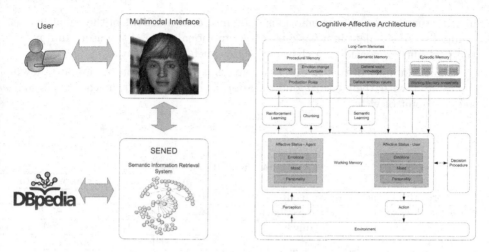

Fig. 1: E-VOX: General architecture

3.2 Multimodal Interface and SENED module

The multimodal interface is based on a 3D ECA. It is responsible for capturing all the inputs (sensing and perceiving the different input channels) and sending the information to the cognitive-affective architecture. Moreover, this module is also in charge of generating the animations of the 3D virtual agent. On the other hand, the SENED module provides access to the semantic knowledge stored in DBpedia, processing the semantic keyword based queries that are received from the multimodal interface during the interaction with the user. More details can be found in [28].

4 Interacting with E-VOX

4.1 Agent-user interaction

In the interaction process, for each event, every possible action is proposed, and de-pending of the available information, including the emotional state of the agent and the user, one action is chosen. This action is sent to the multimodal interface, repre-senting the reaction of the system to that event. The system manages the emotional state of the agent and the user, and the emotional impact of the events during the interaction (user inactivity, too many search results, asking for a new search, no search results...) for them. The relationship between events and specific generated emotions is not an one-to-one relationship, as an agent could react emotionally to the same event in different ways depending on its previous actions and current emotional state. Based on [10] we selected two sets of emotions: one of the agent (*boredom, anger, fear, remorse, pride, hate* and *relief*) and one for the user (*joy, anger, hope, love/like* and *hate*). The consideration of two sets of emotions managed independently allows the architecture to manage the emotions and emotional reactions of the agent, while being able to simulate in a basic way the emotional state of the user, and opens the posibility of considering characterisctics such as empathy.

Some examples of typical events during the user-agent interaction are shown in Table 1 with their corresponding appraisal tag, both from the user's and agent's point of view.

Table 1: Events and appraisal tags

Event	Agent appraisal tags	User appraisal tags
User provides explicit positive feedback	good_ event	–
User provides explicit negative feedback	bad_ event	–
A new information search is launched	–	good_likely ; future_event
User likes the information found	good_act_self	good_act_other
User does not like the information found	bad_act_self	bad_act_other
User has been too long without interacting with the agent	bad_event	–
Agent cannot find results for the specified topic	bad_act_self	bad_act_other
Agent finds an appropriate result for the specified topic	good_act_self	good_act_other
Agent cannot find a different information other than the one already provided	bad_act_ self	bad_act_ other
Agent decides to ignore a user search request	good_act_ self	good_act_ other

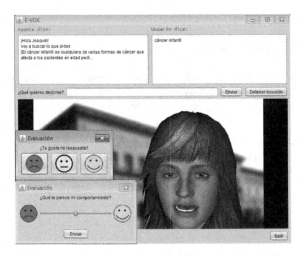

Fig. 2: E-VOX user interface and feedback controls

The first time the user interacts with the system, a brief personality test is conducted. The concept of user session has been added to the system. After logging in, the agent is able to remember his or her search history, personality and last emotional state when the previous session ended (if applicable). Figure 2 shows a screenshot of the application interface. It shows the main window with the animated 3D ECA, areas to display information from agent (left panel) and user (right panel), and additional controls to provide explicit feedback to the system about how satisfied is the user with the current behavior of the agent and how appropriate are the search results provided by the agent. This allows the agent to modify its behavior if it seems inappropriate, or reinforce it if it seems correct. The user can provide feedback to the system at any time. This allows the system to adjust the interaction and responses of the agent to fit more adequately to the expectations of the user. Some examples of interaction are shown below:

- *Search attempt*: The user requests the agent to search some information. Depending of its emotional state and personality, the agent will choose to perform the task or will refuse it, ignoring the user.
- *Inactivity*: The user stops interacting with the system for a long time. The agent may get angry (*Come back immediately!*), get bored (*Are you here? I'm bored...*) or worry about it (*Are you OK? Has something awful happened to you?*) depending on the current emotional state and previous interactions with the user.
- *No results*: The agent cannot find any results for the provided search terms from the user. It may feel very sorry for the userabout its own inability, or even blame the user for providing bad input, depending on its personality and current mood.
- *The user repeats the same request*: Given that the ECA ranks and stores all retrieved results and chooses which one to provide to the user (usually the best ranked one), it can choose to provide a different result for the same request, usually in a closely related subject (*As I already told you about Ferrari, I will tell you something about Lamborghini*). It uses the integrated episodic memory mechanism to remember which search results it has already provided.

4.2   First tests

The goal of these first tests has been to study the general usability of E-VOX system, the suitability and realism of the ECA and the impact of the agents behavior on users interaction and perception. Although the limited scope of the tests, special emphasis has been made in trying to assess the impact of the emotional components. In particular, we were interested in getting information about the following questions:

- 1) Has the personality defined for the agent an impact on the user-agent interaction?

– 2) Is the emotional behavior of the agent perceived by the user?
– 3) Does the user perceive the emotional behavior of the agent as realistic?

These first tests have been carried out with a fairly small number of participants, but interesting issues are emerging.

Methodology

A total of 22 persons (11 male, 11 female), aged between 17 and 62 years, have participated so far in the evaluation sessions. In each testing session, it has been carried out a pre-test with questions about age, sex, education and experience with ECAs, and a short OCEAN personality test (`http://psychcentral.com/quizzes/personality.htm/`) that allows to adjust the emotional model of the user and adapt subsequent interaction with the agent.

After the personality test, the user performs a search task, each comprising two searches of information: a predefined search (*childhood cancer*) and a free search for any topic chosen by the user. The tasks are repeated using an agent with a positive personality (happy, extrovert), a negative personality (angry, quarrelsome) and no personality at all (disabling the affective mechanisms of the system), so the user can notice the distinct behavior of the agent in each situation. The order in which the different personalities appear is randomized, to avoid bias. The user is not informed about which personality has the agent. This allows to evaluate the performance of emotional system and the influence of personality and emotions in the acceptance of ECA by the user. After each task, the user fills a short post-task questions as shown in Table 2. For each question, the user chooses in a five-point scale between 1 (disagree completely) and 5 (agree completely). At the end of the test, the user fills the post-test questions presented in the table 3. The scale used was the same as in the post-task questions.

Table 2: Post-task questions

T1	The behavior of the agent is appropriate for the task
T2	The emotional behavior of the agent is realistic
T3	The physical appearance of the agent is realistic

Results

The post-test questionnaire statistical results for each question are presented in Figure 3, and the post-task average values, for each different task (positive, negative, disabled affective module), are shown in Figure 4. Although the sample size is fairly small for the moment, some interesting conclusions can be drawn from the evaluation.

Regarding the usability of the system, it was generally perceived as reasonably fast (Q1), easy to use (Q3), useful (Q5) and entertaining (Q6). Most users did not need to change their way of expressing themselves, since the system performs an intelligent keyword filtering and the SENED module is somehow robust

Table 3: Post-test questions

Q1	The answers have been quick
Q2	The answers have been correct and relevant
Q3	The system has been easy to use
Q4	It has not been necessary to change how to express myself
Q5	The system has been useful
Q6	It has been entertaining to work with the system
Q7	I would like to use the system at home
Q8	I feel that the system has potential in the future

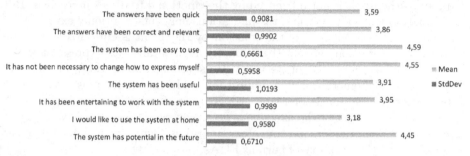

Fig. 3: Post-test questionnaire results

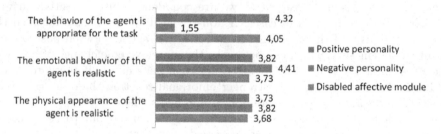

Fig. 4: Post-task questionnaire results

to bad input (Q4). The majority of the users were genuinely curious about the agent itself and its possibilities (most of them had little to none experience in the use of ECAs) and thought that it had great potential (Q8).

However, some mean values are lower than expected and have high variance. The use of ECAs as assistants is not always accepted by users, so some of them were not convinced that they needed it (Q7). Besides, during the evaluation there were some problems with the DBpedia semantic entry point, particularly regarding response speed and relevance of the results, which affected only some of the users (Q1, Q2).

The users perceived the physical appearance of the agent almost equally realistic for every task (T3). There is little difference between the results with positive personality and disabled emotion module, probably due to the small change both in facial expression and characteristics of the voice. In an application where the ECA is used as a search assistant, extreme and unrealistic joy or happiness facial expressions are not used, which further reduces the difference between those situations.

Regarding the first research question (*Has the personality defined for the agent an impact on the user-agent interaction?*) the answer is definitely yes, as it can be seen in the impact of personality in T1. All users rated the ECA with negative personality as not appropriate for the task, compared to the not affective agent and the positive personality.

The answer to the second research question (*Is the emotional behavior of the agent perceived by the user?*) is not so positive. Little difference is found between the positive personality and the non-emotional system (T1). One reason could be that an ECA with no emotional capabilities still helps the user with their requests, although it is not influenced by the emotional feedback it receives. But we think that the main reason is the limitations in agents emotional expressivity. The physical representation of the emotion by the agent is currently limited to small facial expression changes (basic happy, neutral and sad expressions), and the tone, pitch and speed of its voice. It is widely known that the physical expression of the emotion is very important, and difficult for most complex or subtle emotions like pride or regret, which is another open issue in the field. This way, the richness of the affective aspects covered by the cognitive-affective architectures (emotion, mood and personality) is somehow lost by the basic expressivity of the majority of current ECAs.

In regard to the third research question (*Does the user perceive the emotional behavior of the agent as realistic?*), we are confident about a positive answer, as shown in (T2) in all three cases. A non-trivial difference exists between the perceived realism of the emotional behavior of the agent between positive and negative person-ality, which can be due to the more extreme change of behavior the ECA shows. When the ECA has a negative personality, it tends to ignore or blame the user, and gives a stronger emotional reaction than an agent with positive personality that is generally nice and helps them.

Nevertheless, a complete evaluation should be carried out to get a better comprehension of all these interesting issues.

5 Conclusions and Future Work

In this paper, we have presented E-VOX, an affective enhanced semantic ECA working as an assistant to provide useful information from Wikipedia, supporting real-feel human-computer interaction. It is based on a powerful cognitive-affective architecture that allows to combine all features of the cognitive architecture Soar and the three-layered model of affect proposed in ALMA. Although still a prototype, it is a completely functional one that shows the feasibility of our approach. First tests with users have been conducted to study the impact of the agent affective behavior in the user-ECA interaction, and we strongly think that they have provided valuable information to improve the ECA in the future. However, we are aware that there is still plenty of work to be done. We are now considering to extend E-VOX with a number of features:

- To expand the emotional expression possibilities of the agent. We plan to add more different facial expressions, and work on the voice characteristics associated with each personality. This would allow us to support the next more complete evaluation.

- To incorporate to the system emotional-sensing capabilities that allow to the ECA to have direct access to the emotional state of the user during interaction. To do so, we plan to incorporate previously developed real-time facial recognition techniques [15].This will complement the evaluation coming from the affective module.
- To carry out a complete evaluation with users to assess the impact of the cognitive-affective architecture.

Acknowledgements

This work was supported by the Spanish "Dirección General de Investigación", contract number TIN2011-24660 and TIN2015-67149-C3-1R. We want to thank Carlos Bobed and Eduardo Mena for the design and development of the SENED module.

References

1. Allison, M., Kendrick, L.M.: Towards an expressive embodied conversational agent utilizing multi-ethnicity to augment solution focused therapy. In: FLAIRS Conference (2013)
2. Becker-Asano, C., Meneses, E., Riesterer, N., Hu, J., Dornhege, C., Nebel, B.: The hybrid agent marco: A multimodal autonomous robotic chess opponent. In: Proc. of the 2nd Intl. Conf. on Human-Agent Interaction (2014)
3. Bevacqua, E., Prepin, K., Niewiadomski, R., de Sevin, E., Pelachaud, C.: Greta: Towards an interactive conversational virtual companion. In: Artificial Companions in Society: perspectives on the Present and Future. pp. 143–156 (2010)
4. Bickmore, T.W., Utami, D., Matsuyama, R., Paasche-Orlow, M.K.: Improving access to online health information with conversational agents: A randomized controlled experiment. Journal of medical Internet research 18 (2016)
5. Bickmore, T.W., Vardoulakis, L.M.P., Schulman, D.: Tinker: a relational agent museum guide. Autonomous Agents and Multi-Agent Systems 27(2), 254–276 (sep 2013)
6. Bizer, C., Lehmann, J., Kobilarov, G., Auer, S., Becker, C., Cyganiak, R., and Hellmann, S.(2009). DBpedia - A crystallization point for the Web of Data. Web Semantics: Science, Services and Agents on the World Wide Web, 7(3):154–165.
7. Boukricha, H., Wachsmuth, I.: Empathy-Based Emotional Alignment for a Virtual Human: A Three-Step Approach. KI - Künstliche Intelligenz 25, 195–204 (2011)
8. Cavazza, M., De La Camara, R.S., Turunen, M.: How was your day?: a companion eca. In: Proceedings of the 9th International Conference on Autonomous Agents and Multiagent Systems: volume 1-Volume 1. pp. 1629–1630. International Foundation for Autonomous Agents and Multiagent Systems (2010)
9. Dias, J., Mascarenhas, S., Paiva, A.: Fatima modular: Towards an agent architecture with a generic appraisal framework. In: Emotion Modeling, pp. 44–56. Springer (2014)
10. El-Nasr, M.S., Yen, J., Ioerger, T.R.: Flame: Fuzzy logic adaptive model of emotions. Autonomous Agents and Multi-Agent Systems 3(3), 219–257 (Sep 2000)
11. Flavián-Blanco, C., Gurrea-Sarasa, R., Orús-Sanclemente, C.: Analyzing the emotional outcomes of the online search behavior with search engines. Comput. Hum. Behav. 27(1), 540–551 (Jan 2011)

12. Gebhard, P.: A layered model of affect. In: 4th International Joint Conference of Autonomous Agents & Multi-Agent Systems (AAMAS'05). pp. 29–36. ACM Press (2005)
13. Helgadóttir, H.E., Jónsdóttir, S., Sigurdsson, A.M., Schiffel, S., Vilhjálmsson, H.H.: Virtual General Game Playing Agent, pp. 464–469. Springer International Publishing, Cham (2016)
14. Hill, R.W., Gratch, J., Marsella, S.C., Swartout, W., Traum, D.: Virtual Humans in the Mission Rehearsal Exercise System. In: Kunstliche Intelligenzi (KI) (special issue on Embodied Conversational Agents) (Jun 2003)
15. Huang, H.H., Ida, Y., Yamaguchi, K., Kawagoe, K.: Development of a Virtual Classroom for High School Teacher Training, pp. 489–493. Springer International Publishing, Cham (2016)
16. Hupont, I., Baldassarri, S., Cerezo, E.: Facial emotional classification: from a discrete perspective to a continuous emotional space. Pattern Analysis and Applications 16(1), 41–54 (2013)
17. Johnson, E., Hervás, R., Gutiérrez López de la Franca, C., Mondéjar, T., Ochoa, S.F., Favela, J.: Assessing empathy and managing emotions through interactions with an affective avatar. Health Informatics Journal p. 1460458216661864 (2016)
18. Klaassen, R., Hendrix, J., Reidsma, D., op den Akker, H.J.A.: Elckerlyc goes mobile enabling technology for ecas in mobile applications. UBICOMM (2012)
19. Kopp, S., Gesellensetter, L., Krämer, N.C., Wachsmuth, I.: A Conversational Agent as Museum Guide Design and Evaluation of a Real-World Application. In: In International Workshop on Intelligent Virtual Agents. pp. 329–343. Springer Berlin Heidelberg (2005)
20. Laird, J.E.: The Soar Cognitive Architecture. The MIT Press (2012)
21. Marinier, R., Laird, J.: Computational Modeling of Mood and Feeling from Emotion. Proceedings of the Cognitive Science 29(29) (2007)
22. Marsella, S.C., Gratch, J.: EMA: A process model of appraisal dynamics. Journal of Cognitive Systems Research 10(1), 70–90 (Mar 2009)
23. McCrae, R.R., John, O.P.: An introduction to the five-factor model and its applications. Journal of Personality 60(2), 175–215 (1992)
24. Mehrabian, A.: Pleasure-arousal-dominance: A general framework for describing and measuring individual differences in temperament. Current Psychology 14(4), 261–292 (1996)
25. Nooraei, B., Rich, C., Sidner, C.L.: A real-time architecture for embodied conversational agents: Beyond turn-taking. ACHI 14, 381–388 (2014)
26. Ortony, A., Collins, A., Clore, G.L.: The cognitive structure of emotions. Cambridge University Press Cambridge [England] ; New York, pbk. ed. edn. (1988)
27. Pelachaud, C. (2015). Greta: an interactive expressive embodied conversational agent. In Proceedings of the 2015 International Conference on Autonomous Agents and Multiagent Systems, pages 5–55. International Foundation for Autonomous Agents and Multiagent Systems.
28. Pérez, J., Cerezo, E., Serón, F.J., Rodríguez, L.F.: A cognitive-affective architecture for ECAs. Biologically Inspired Cognitive Architectures 18, 33 – 40 (2016)
29. Reithinger, N., Gebhard, P., Löckelt, M., Ndiaye, A., Pfleger, N., Klesen, M.: Virtualhuman: dialogic and affective interaction with virtual characters. In: ICMI '06: Proceedings of the 8th international conference on Multimodal interfaces. pp. 51–58. New York, NY, USA (2006)
30. Serón, F.J., Bobed, C.: Vox system: a semantic embodied conversational agent exploiting linked data. Multimedia Tools and Applications 75(1), 381–404 (2016)

Towards Believable Interactions between Synthetic Characters

Ricardo Rodrigues[1]✉ and Carlos Martinho[1]✉

Instituto Superior Técnico, University of Lisbon and INESC-ID,
Taguspark Campus, Av. Prof. Dr. Cavaco Silva,
2744-016 Porto Salvo, Portugal.
ricardo.proenca.rodrigues@tecnico.ulisboa.pt
carlos.martinho@tecnico.ulisboa.pt

Abstract. Believable interactions between synthetic characters are an important factor defining the success of a virtual environment relying on human participants being able to create emotional bonds with artificial characters. As important as the characters being themselves believable is that the interaction with or between such characters is believable. In this work, we bridge affective computing and traditional animation principles to create *3Motion*, a model for synthetic character interaction based on anticipation and emotion that allows for precise affective communication of intention-based behaviors. We present an exploratory study with 52 participants supporting that our approach is able to increase overall interaction believability.

Keywords: Virtual Agents, Synthetic Characters, Believable Interactions, Anticipation, Emotion, Traditional Animation

1 Introduction

In movies, when characters perform an action, intentions are generally clear to the viewer and supported through eye or body movement. This flow creates anticipation and a sense of presence in the audience, leading to the suspension of disbelief, the notion that the implausibility of something can be suspended for the sake of enjoyment. While videogames strive to achieve such level of engagement with their player audience, we are still far from been able to achieve, in real-time, such believable interactions.

To mitigate this problem, we propose an anticipatory and affective behavior model for synthetic characters that bridges traditional animation principles[2] with modern affective and anticipatory modeling. Our main hypothesis is that by explicitly modeling the traditional three-stage split of an action animation into anticipation, action, and follow-through stages, we will be able to communicate the intentions of a character in a clearer way and give a richer emotional context for all the characters involved in the scene, consequently improving the overall believability of the interaction.

© Springer International Publishing AG 2017
J. Beskow et al. (Eds.): IVA 2017, LNAI 10498, pp. 385-388, 2017.
DOI 10.1007/978-3-319-67401-8_48

2 3Motion

Our approach to the creation of a believable interaction is to give structure to the way a virtual agent's behavior is modeled and change the way an action is executed in the context of all that is happening in a scene at that moment.

2.1 Behavior Cycle

Our agent's behavior is a 4-step *anticipation-based* cycle: (1) the agent *perceives* changes in the world based on its *expectations*, (2) *reacts* to them emotionally based on what was *anticipated*, (3) *decides* what to do next and *anticipates* what will happen, (4) and *performs part* of an on-going action, then repeats. This cycle occurs multiple times in the course of an action allowing the virtual agents to perceive events and express different emotions, among other things, while performing a same action that gives context to that expression.

Our main contribution with *3Motion* is how our approach deconstructs the traditional atomic action generally used when implementing synthetic character behavior, into three explicit and distinct stages: *anticipation*, *action*, and *follow-through*. Each stage may take a certain time to play out, and interaction at different points in the sequence will have a different meaning for the other agents participating in the scene, as well as for the viewer passively watching or actively interacting with the scene, allowing for the creation of a richer interaction.

2.2 Sample Execution Flow

To better showcase the expressive potential of our approach, we present an example of its execution flow (depicted in Figure 1). In our example, three agents take part in the action: Bob, Hanna and Steve. We join the action as Bob, currently in a happy mood, decides to throw a ball (decide step). In the perform step, the action is initiated: raising his arm in preparation for the throw, Bob enters the first stage of the expression of an action, *anticipation*.

The *anticipation* stage serves the purpose of communicating the intent so every other agent understands it and can expressively prepare for it. In this stage, an agent broadcasts its intent and associated emotion, and receives feedback in the form of emotions from the other agents that are aware of the expression: Bob is happy and wants to throw the ball, Hanna responds she is happy for Bob, while Steve is afraid Bob will miss his mark. This allows Bob to interpret the emotional reactions in the context of his intentions and modulate his behavior accordingly.

Anticipation is further subdivided into two substages: an *interruptible* stage in which the agent is still able to cancel the initiated action, and an *uninterruptible* stage in which the action reached a point where it cannot be stopped. While Bob has the ball in his hand, he is able to cancel the throw. While Steve is fearful, Hanna is happy for him, so Bob decides to proceed with the throw. He releases the ball and enters the uninterruptible stage, in which the action is still not finished and the agent creates an expectation about its outcome, which is broadcast as an emotion and provoke an affective response from the other

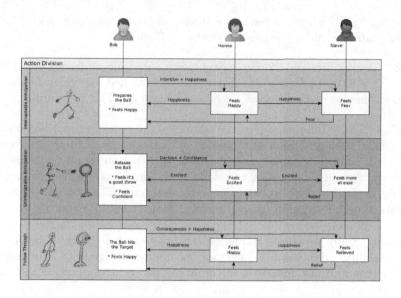

Fig. 1. Example of *3Motion* execution flow in action

agents: Bob is confident about his throw, which gets Hanna excited and Steve more at ease. The precise timing of the expression and affective responses is crucial in this stage, otherwise, the audience may not be able to understand how decision-making took place in this shared affective context.

The *action stage* is instantaneous and only exists conceptually. This stage represents the moment the action is resolved and the state of the virtual world changes. In the example, this would occur when the ball hits or misses the target.

The *follow-through stage* is entered after the action is resolved and broadcasts the result of the action, which will meet or challenge the expectations of the agents. As in the anticipation stage, the agent sends its affective appraisal to others along with the result, allowing them to feel happy, sorry, etc. and receives their affective feedback to perform a final appraisal of the action: Bob hits the target and is very happy! Hanna rejoices sharing on the happiness; Steve is now relieved because all went well.

Since we focus on non-verbal communication, emotions play a very important role on the communication of the actions progression. With the use of emotions, we hope to improve the believability of the interaction without compromising other forms of communication.

3   User Study

To understand the expressive power of *3Motion*, an exploratory study was conducted where users were asked to watch one of three different videos depicting interacting agents implemented using three different approaches and fill a same questionnaire measuring various dimensions of believability.

Sample: Testing involved 52 participants with ages ranging from 18 to 55 ($M = 25.10$, $SD = 6.06$, 14 female). Each participant watched one video before filling the questionnaire and each session had a duration of 15 to 20 minutes.

Procedure: Three different videos were shown to the participants: (*classic*) agents implemented without action subdivision, emulating a classic approach to behavior control; (*3Motion*) agents implemented with action subdivision and using correct timing when expressing emotions, and; (*misguided*) agents implemented with our model but with incorrect expression timing. The last video controlled if having more information (even if not well timed) would make the interaction perceived as more believable. The questionnaire was based on the work from [1] and essentially measured the following dimensions: awareness, behavior understandability, predictability, behavior coherency, change with experience and social metrics, but also measures the ability of an agent to perceive and interact with other agents.

Results: Participants rated the interaction supported by *3Motion* as more believable in almost every statement of the questionnaire when compared to both the *classic* and *misguided* video, between which no statistically significant differences were found on the dimensions of believability explored by the questionnaire.

4 Conclusions

In this paper, we presented *3Motion*, an approach to synthetic character interaction explicitly modelling the three-stage split of an action animation from an anticipatory and affective perspective. We also described an exploratory study with 52 participants supporting that *3Motion* was able to create interactions perceived as more believable than more traditional approaches. Encouraged by these results, we are now looking at how this model could help with real-time interaction with both users and synthetic characters simultaneously.

Acknowledgements
This work was partially supported by national funds through Fundação para a Ciência e a Tecnologia (FCT) with ref. UID/CEC/50021/2013, and FCT grant from project Tutoria Virtual with ref. TDC/IVC-PEC/3963/2014.

References

1. Gomes, P., Paiva, A., Martinho, C., Jhala, A.: Metrics for Character Believability in Interactive Narrative BT - Interactive Storytelling. In: Interactive Storytelling, pp. 223–228. Springer International Publishing (2013)
2. Thomas, F., Johnston, O., Rawls, W.: Disney animation: The illusion of life, vol. 4. Disney Editions; Rev Sub edition (1981)

Joint Learning of Speech-Driven Facial Motion with Bidirectional Long-Short Term Memory

Najmeh Sadoughi ✉ and Carlos Busso

Multimodal Signal Processing (MSP) Laboratory,
Department of Electrical and Computer Engineering,
The University of Texas at Dallas

{nxs137130 and busso}@utdallas.edu

Abstract. The face conveys a blend of verbal and nonverbal information playing an important role in daily interaction. While speech articulation mostly affects the orofacial areas, emotional behaviors are externalized across the entire face. Considering the relation between verbal and non-verbal behaviors is important to create naturalistic facial movements for *conversational agents* (CAs). Furthermore, facial muscles connect areas across the face, creating principled relationships and dependencies between the movements that have to be taken into account. These relationships are ignored when facial movements across the face are separately generated. This paper proposes to create speech-driven models that jointly capture the relationship not only between speech and facial movements, but also across facial movements. The input to the models are features extracted from speech that convey the verbal and emotional states of the speakers. We build our models with *bidirectional long-short term memory* (BLSTM) units which are shown to be very successful in modeling dependencies for sequential data. The objective and subjective evaluations of the results demonstrate the benefits of joint modeling of facial regions using this framework.

1 Introduction

While spoken language is the primary way of communication, nonverbal information provides important information that enriches speech during face-to-face interaction. Nonverbal information not only complements speech, but also conveys extra information [26]. Humans unconsciously use different channels to express and externalize their thoughts, emotions and intentions. These channels are integrated in a non-trivial manner. However, listeners can easily decode the message, inferring each of these communicative goals. The models should consider these relationships, if we want to design better *conversational agents* (CAs) that express realistic expressive human-like behaviors.

The face is one of the primary channels to express different communicative goals. Different facial muscles contribute in creating speech articulation and facial expression. Previous studies have shown the temporal and spatial interplay

J. Beskow et al. (Eds.): IVA 2017, LNAI 10498, pp. 389–402, 2017.
DOI 10.1007/978-3-319-67401-8_49

between speech and emotion in the face [8, 24]. In general, the activity in the orofacial area is dominated by speech articulation, and the activity in the upper face area is dominated by emotions. However, the interplay is not trivial. Since humans can easily decode these communication goals, an effective CA should capture this interplay. Likewise, emotional traits associated with an emotion may involve multiple facial movements (e.g., surprise externalized as opening of mouth and raising of eyebrows). Even a single facial muscle may activate different facial regions. For example, the Zygomaticus major, which affects the cheek area, allows us to smile. The activation of the Levator labii superioris affects the lips and the upper facial region. The aforementioned relations not only between speech and facial expression, but also across facial regions suggest that generating realistic behaviors for CAs require careful consideration of these underlying dependencies. In fact, previous studies have demonstrated that joint models for eyebrow and head motion produced more realistic sequences than the ones created with separate models [13, 23].

Speech carries verbal and nonverbal cues, including the externalizations of the affective state of the speaker. Given the strong correlation between speech and facial expressions [6], speech-driven models offer appealing solutions to generate human-like behaviors that preserve the timing relation between modalities. This study proposes to create joint speech-driven models for facial expressions using the latest advances in deep learning. The framework relies on *bidirectional long-short term memory* (LSTM) units to capture (1) the relation between speech and facial expressions, (2) the relation across facial features. We use deep structures that help learning the interplay between the facial movements in different regions of the face in a systematic and principled manner. We achieve this goal by using multitask learning, where predictions for lower, middle and upper facial regions are jointly estimated. Our results demonstrate the benefit of learning the facial regions jointly rather than separately. While other studies used generative models to jointly model facial behaviors [13, 23, 28], this is the first study that solves this problem using multitask learning with deep learning.

2   Related Works

The conventional approach for facial animations is the use of rule-based system. For example, predefined shapes based on the target articulatory unit can be concatenated to generate facial movements [12, 32]. Defining facial trajectories that are tightly coupled with speech is a challenge, especially in the presence of emotion (rhythm, emphasis). Although some studies have considered continuous emotional descriptors (e.g. Albrecht et al. [1]), the most common approach to model emotion is to consider specific models created for prototypical emotional categories [25, 27]. However, defining the facial expressions per emotion reduces the subtle differences that exist between slightly different facial expressions, and makes the animation seem repetitive. As an appealing alternative, data-driven methods are usually better at handling these fine changes, by learning the variations shown in real recordings [2, 10, 21]. This study focuses on data-driven solutions.

There are several data-driven studies to predict facial movements from speech. Brand [4] proposed to use HMMs to learn the mapping between speech and facial features using entropy minimization. Gutierrez et al. [18] designed a system to synthesize facial movements from speech features. Their system used 12 *perceptual critical band features* (PCBFs), fundamental frequency and energy. The approach predicts lip movements by identifying the 12 *nearest neighbors* (NNs) in the speech feature space The selected segments are concatenated and smoothed by a moving average window. Taylor et al. [30] proposed to use *deep neural network* (DNNs) composed of densely connected *rectified linear units* (RELUs) to predict lip movements from speech. They used 25 *mel frequency cepstral coefficients* (MFCCs) as speech features. They concatenated the acoustic features extracted for each frame over a window, predicting the lip movements, which are smoothed by averaging the estimations over a target window. Subjective and objective evaluations demonstrated better performance over an *HMM inversion* (HMMI) method proposed by Choi et al. [11]. Fan et al. [16] explored different *deep bidirectional LSTMs* (DBLSTMs) for mapping speech or speech plus text into lips movements. When using speech as input, they extracted 13 MFCCs, and their first and second order derivatives (i.e. 39D) as the input. When the text is provided, they concatenate the input with tri-phonemes. Their objective and subjective evaluations showed better results for the DBLSTMs compared with HMMs. All these studies did not directly consider emotional information.

There are also studies that have generated expressive facial movements using data driven models, when the input is text. Cao et al. [10] conducted one of the early data-driven works on generating expressive facial movements. Their approach relied on defining expressive units of articulations. They segmented and stored their recordings into anime nodes indexed by the corresponding phoneme, emotion, prosodic features, and motion capture features. For synthesis, suitable anime nodes are selected, time warped, concatenated and smoothed as dictated by the target requirement. Mana and Pianesi [22] trained different left-to-right HMMs for pairs of visemes and emotions. Anderson et al. [2] proposed a visual text-to-speech system that synthesizes expressive audiovisual speech with a set of continuous weights for emotional categories. They used *cluster adaptive training* (CAT) which is built upon *hidden Markov models* (HMMs) for text-to-speech. The HMM states are modeled by decision trees, and the model learns the appropriate weight vector for each emotion, which is used to find the linear combination of states. They evaluated the synthesized results in terms of the precision of the perceived target emotion. All these studies used text as input.

To the best of our knowledge, there is only one study on expressive facial movement synthesis, using emotional audio features and the target emotion as the input. Li et al. [21] proposed several structures using DBLSTMs to synthesize emotional facial movements based on limited emotional data. They used a neutral corpus with 321 utterances, and an emotional corpus of 44 subjects reading sentences in six different emotional categories. They evaluated their proposed structures in terms of the perceived naturalness and expressiveness of the videos. Their best structure is composed of two models. The first one is trained with neutral data, and is used to predict the movements for emotional inputs. These predictions are concatenated with the input audio features and used as the input to another model which is trained with emotional data to predict the emotional movements. Our study also generates expressive facial behaviors from speech. However, (1) our approach does not require the target emotion of the input speech to be known, rather it captures the relationship between facial movements and emotional features extracted from speech, (2) we rely on a bigger database, and (3) we investigate joint versus separate modeling of facial features from the speech signal using powerful deep learning structures with BLSTMs under multitask framework.

3   Resources

3.1   IEMOCAP Corpus

This paper uses the *interactive emotional dyadic motion capture* (IEMOCAP) database [9]. This database is multimodal, comprising audio, video, and motion capture recordings from 10 actors during spontaneous and script-based dyadic interactions. We use the data from all the actors in our experiments. From the motion capture data, we use the position of the facial markers grouped into three regions; upper face region, middle face area, and lower face area (Fig. 1(a)). Note that the three regions here are chosen inspired by the study conducted by Busso et al. [7]. In the extreme case, we can consider each marker as a region. Busso et al. [9] provides more details about this corpus.

3.2   Multimodal Features

From the motion capture recordings, we use 19 markers for the upper facial region ($19 \times 3D$), 12 markers for the middle facial region ($12 \times 3D$), and 15 markers for the lower facial region ($15 \times 3D$). The motion capture data is recorded at 120 *frame per second* (fps). From the speech signal, we extract 25 MFCCs, fundamental frequency, and energy with Praat over $25\,ms$ windows every $8.3\,ms$. Eyben et al. [14] proposed the *extended Geneva minimalistic acoustic parameter set* (E-GeMAPS), which is a compact set of features that were carefully selected for paralinguistic tasks. The set has 23 *low level descriptors* (LLDs), where six of them are already included in the features extracted by Praat. Therefore, we add the rest of these features (17 D). These features are extracted over $20\,ms$ or $60\,ms$ every $10\,ms$. We up-sample the speech features using linear interpolation to get 120 fps, matching the sampling rate of the motion capture data. We use Z-normalization per subject for the speech and visual features.

3.3   Rendering the Animations with Xface

For rendering the animations, we use Xface [3]. Xface uses the MPEG4 standard to define *facial points* (FPs). To animate the face, Xface uses *facial action*

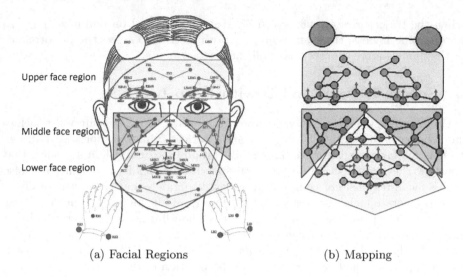

(a) Facial Regions   (b) Mapping

Fig. 1. Layout and groups of facial markers (a) markers belonging to upper, middle and lower face regions, (b) markers mapped to FAPs in Xface (highlighted with arrows).

parameters (FAPs) which change the position of the FPs. Most of the markers used in the IEMOCAP database were placed following the FPs defined by the MPEG4 standard, facilitating the mapping between markers and FAPs. We follow the same mapping proposed by Mariooryad and Busso [23]. Figure 1(b) highlights the markers that are mapped into FAPs in Xface. We use the idle position of the markers for the actors as the neutral pose, and extract the range of movements for each actor. The neutral pose is mapped to the neutral pose of the face in Xface defined by FAPs, and the changes in the position of the markers are scaled to the changes of FAPs allowed by Xface. While there are other more realistic talking heads, the direct map between markers and FAPs facilitate the evaluation of this study.

3.4 Objective Metrics

The models in this paper learn how to derive facial movements. Therefore, the outputs of the models are continuous variables, where previous studies have either minimized the *mean squared error* (MSE) [15,30], or maximized the *concordance correlation* (ρ_c) [31]. If x and y are the target and predicted values, Equation 1 defines ρ_c, where ρ is the Pearson correlation between x and y, and μ_x and μ_y, and σ_x and σ_y are the means and variances of x and y, respectively.

$$\rho_c = \frac{2\rho\sigma_x\sigma_y}{\sigma_x^2 + \sigma_y^2 + (\mu_x - \mu_y)^2} \tag{1}$$

Our preliminary experiments showed that using ρ_c as the optimizing criterion generates higher range of movements for the target variable, which looks better when the trajectories are visualized. Therefore, we relied on minimizing $1 - \rho_c$ for our experiments. However, we report both metrics to assess the performance of the models after concatenating all the test segments.

4 Speech-Driven Models with Deep Learning

Deep learning structures are very powerful to learn complex temporal relationships between modalities, hence, they are a perfect framework for speech-driven models for facial expressions. This study proposes to build joints models that consider the relation not only between speech and facial movements, but also across facial regions. For comparison, we assess models that either separately or jointly generate facial movements for the lower, middle and upper facial regions.

We build our models by stacking multiple non-linear layers where the input corresponds to the 44D speech feature set (Sec. 3.2). The models have densely connected layers with *rectified linear units* (RELUs), BLSTMs, and a linear layer at the top, since the task is to generate the position of the markers.

4.1 Bidirectional Long-Short Term Memory (BLSTM)

We rely on *recurrent neural networks* (RNNs) to capture the temporal dependencies for continuous signals. RNNs use temporal connections between consecutive hidden units at each layer to model the dependencies between time frames. However, as the length of the input signal increases, RNNs are susceptible to the problem of exploding or vanishing gradients [19]. LSTMs are an extension of RNNs, which were introduced to handle this problem [19].

LSTM utilizes a cell to keep track of the useful past content given the input, and previous hidden state. LSTM uses gating mechanisms to capture the long and short term dependencies in the temporal signals. It uses three gates for this goal: input, forget, and output gates. The input gate controls the amount of the current input to be stored in the cell unit. The forget gate controls the amount of the previous cell content being retained in the cell. The output gate modulates the amount of the cell content being used as the output of the hidden state at time t. We use the implementation of LSTM in Keras.

An extension of LSTM is its bidirectional version, BLSTM, which utilizes the previous and future frames to predict the outputs at each time (Fig. 2). The implementation of BLSTM consists of training forward and backward LSTMs, and concatenating their hidden units. The key benefit of BLSTMs is that they generate more smooth movements. Although BLSTMs can be used in real time by using a post-buffer, this study estimates the facial movements off-line using the whole turn sequence. We run BLSTMs on each turn, predicting a sequence of the same length as the output (speech features are up-sampled to 120fps).

4.2 Separate Models

Our baseline models consists of structures that separately generate facial behaviors for the lower, middle and upper face regions. These models independently

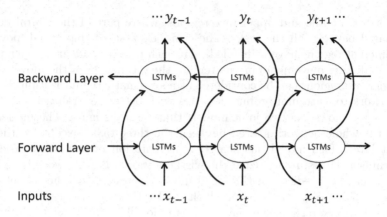

Fig. 2. Illustration of BLSTM composed of forward and backward paths.

create the facial markers trajectories for each region. While local relationships within regions are preserved, the intrinsic relationship across regions are neglected. The underlying assumptions is that these relationships across the three regions are not important. Figure 3 shows two alternative frameworks. *Separate-1* uses one BLSTM layer, whereas *Separate-2* uses two BLSTM layers. We consider these model as baseline for our joint models.

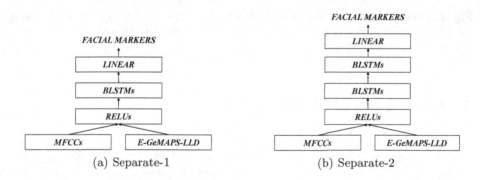

Fig. 3. Baseline speech-driven models, where the facial movements for the lower, middle and upper face regions are separately generated.

4.3   Joint Models

We create the proposed joint models using multitask learning. Multitask learning aims to jointly solve related problems using shared layer representation. In our formulation, we have three related tasks consisting of predicting the movements of the lower, middle and upper face regions, where part of the neural networks are shared between all the tasks. These models assume that facial movements over different regions have principled relationships. From a learning perspective, when predicting movements in one region, the estimation of the movements for the other two regions can be considered as a systematic regularization that helps the network to learn more robust features with better generalization.

Figure 4 shows the two joint models that we investigate. The model *Joint-1* has the whole network shared between the three tasks except for the linear output layer. This model has shared representation of the three tasks in all the nonlinear layers, regularizing the whole network. This network is equivalent to a model that predicts all the facial movements at once. The model *Joint-2* shares the first two layers between all the tasks. However, the last two layers are task-specific. The task specific layers capture localized facial relationship within regions, while the shared layers preserve relationship across regions.

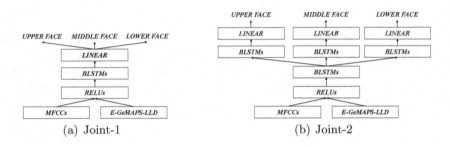

(a) Joint-1   (b) Joint-2

Fig. 4. Proposed joint speech-driven models for facial movements. The *Joint-1* model has shared layers. The *Joint-2* model has shared and task-specific layers.

5 Experiment & Results

The proposed models are implemented and evaluated using the IEMOCAP corpus, where we used 60% of the data for training, 20% for validation, and 20% for testing. We use Keras with Theano as backend to implement and train the models. We rely on *adaptive moment estimation* (ADAM) [20] for the optimization of the parameters. ADAM keeps track of estimates of first and second moments of gradient during training, and utilizes the ratio between the bias-corrected first moment and the bias-corrected second moment of the gradient to update the parameters. This process helps scaling the update, according to the uncertainty (second moment), and making the step size invariant to the magnitude of the gradient. We use different learning rates ($\backsim \{0.1, 0.01, 0.001, 0.0001\}$), and evaluated the model on the validation set. The results demonstrated that a learning rate of 0.0001 works better. Furthermore, all the layers use dropout of 0.2 to counter overfitting [29]. Our training examples have various lengths. We set a

Table 1. Objective metrics for facial movements generated with joint and separate models for the lower, middle and upper face region.

Model	# nodes per layer	# params	Upper face		Middle face		Lower face	
			ρ_c	MSE	ρ_c	MSE	ρ_c	MSE
Separate-1	512	12.8M	0.140	1.47	0.268	1.36	0.401	1.12
Joint-1	512	4.4M	0.150	1.32	0.274	1.30	0.390	1.26
Separate-1	1024	50,8M	0.149	1.41	0.277	1.16	0.411	1.05
Joint-1	1024	17,1M	0.160	1.40	0.297	1.24	0.413	1.14
Separate-2	512	31.7M	0.135	1.44	0.260	1.24	0.392	1.04
Joint-2	512	23.2M	0.160	1.37	0.307	1.14	0.411	1.06

batch size of 4,096, making sure that the total number of frames used in one batch does not exceed this number. As a result, we have different number of sequences in different batches. All the weights are initialized with the approach proposed by Glorot et al. [17]. We train all the models with 50 epochs.

5.1 Objective Evaluation

We train the models with different number of nodes and layers for the joint and separate models. Table 1 summarizes the results. When we compare *Joint-1* and *Separate-1* with 512 nodes, the results show improvements in the joint model for the middle and upper face regions. When we increase the number of nodes to 1,024, we observe improved performance for all the regions, where the joint model achieves higher ρ_c and smaller MSE. The table also compares the *Separate-2* and *Joint-2* models which have the same number of layers. Changing the structure to the *Joint-2* and *Separate-2* models tend to improve the MSE for all the facial regions, compared to the *Joint-1* and *Separate-1* models. Furthermore, the *Joint-2* model achieves better concordance correlation than the *Separate-2* model. Note that the *Separate-1* model requires approximately three times more parameters than the *Joint-1* model. Likewise, the *Separate-2* model has 36.31% more parameters than the *Joint-2* model. The proposed joint structure not only provides better performance, but also requires less parameters which is an advantage due to memory requirements.

Emotional Analysis We compare the performance of *Separate-2* and *joint-2* models for different emotional categories. The IEMOCAP corpus is emotionally annotated at the speaking turn level by three annotators in term of nine emotional categories (neutral, anger, happiness, sadness, fear, frustration, surprise, disgust, and other). We derive a consensus label using the majority vote rule, where turns without consensus are excluded from this analysis. In the test set, we have the following distribution: 113 (neutral), 161 (anger), 86 (happiness), 131 (sadness), 3 (fear), 247 (frustration), 12 (surprise), 0 (disgust), and 2 (other). We only consider emotional classes with more than 50 speaking turns. We concatenate all the speaking turns belonging to a given emotion, estimating ρ_c and MSE.

Figure 5 shows the average ρ_c and MSE for the three facial regions per emotional category. For the upper face area, the *Joint-2* model shows better results across the emotions, except for ρ_c for neutral. Furthermore, for the middle face region, the results show improvements for all the emotions. For the lower face region, ρ_c shows improvements for neutral speech, happiness, and sadness, while MSE is improved only for happiness.

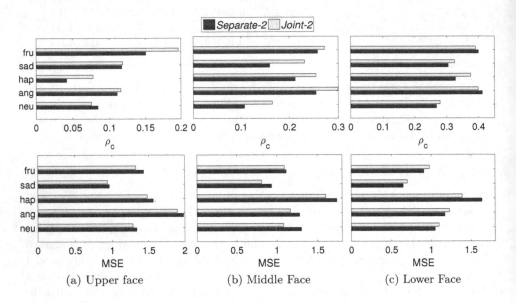

Fig. 5. Comparison of the results achieved for ρ_c and MSE per emotional category using the *Separate-2* and *Joint-2* models.

5.2 Subjective Evaluation

Subjective evaluations provide convincing evidences about the performances of the models. Table 1 shows that the *Joint-1* and *Separate-1* models provide better results with 1,024 nodes per layer than with 512 nodes per layer. Therefore, we only include the *Joint-1* and *Separate-1* models trained with 512 nodes per layer. The *Joint-2*, and *Separate-2* models are trained with 512 nodes. The evaluation also includes the animations generated with the *original* motion capture data. Therefore, we have five conditions per speaking turn. We randomly selected 10 turns from the test set, and generated their animations for all of these five conditions using Xface (50 videos). We do not include head motion, so our raters can focus on facial movements. We use the original eyelid and nose markers positions across all the videos.

The evaluation is conducted using crowdsourcing with *Amazon mechanical turk* (AMT). We limit our pool of evaluators to workers who have performed well in our previous crowdsourcing tasks [5]. We ask each evaluator to rate the *naturalness* of the 50 videos in a likert-like scale from 1 (low naturalness) to 10 (high naturalness). The task requires to annotate the perceived naturalness for the overall animation. In addition, we ask the raters to annotate the naturalness of the eyebrow and lips movements (i.e., three questions per video). Since we have only animated one of the markers in the cheek area (see Fig. 1(b)), we do not ask the annotators for separate ratings for the middle face region. We show one video at a time to the annotators, displaying the questionnaire only after the video is fully played. This approach reduces the chance of annotators providing random answers without even looking at the video. We randomize the order of the videos per evaluator. We recruited 20 subjects for this evaluation.

Figure 6 shows the average scores for the five conditions. The Cronbach's alpha between the annotators is $\alpha = 0.6720$. *One way analysis of variance* (ANOVA) shows statistically different values between the five cases for all three questions ($p < 0.001$). Pairwise comparisons of the results between the five conditions only show that the animations generated with the *original* sequences are significantly better than the animations automatically generated from speech, which is expected. This result reveals that the differences between the animations generated with the joint and separate models were subtle. From the objective metrics, we observe that the middle face region shows the highest improvements when the joint models are used (Sec. 5.1). However, these differences may not be visually perceived due to limitations in Xface. We hypothesize that the difference in facial movements will be more clear if we use a more expressive talking head, which is the focus of our future work. Even with the these results, it is important to highlight that using joint models allows the network to achieve similar performances than separate models using fewer parameters.

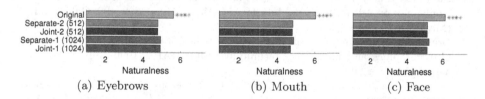

(a) Eyebrows   (b) Mouth   (c) Face

Fig. 6. Perceived naturalness of the animations. The color-coded asterisks indicate that the bar is significantly higher than the bars identified by the asterisks' colors ($p < 0.01$).

6 Conclusions

This paper explored multitask learning architectures to train speech-driven models for facial movements. The framework relied on BLSTMs to capture temporal information, using speech features as the input to predict facial movements. The models jointly learn the relationship not only between speech and facial expressions, but also across facial regions, capturing intrinsic dependencies. We compared the results with models that separately estimate movements for the lower, middle and upper part of the face, ignoring relations between regions. Objective evaluation of the results showed improvements for the joint models in different facial regions as measured by ρ_c and MSE. The improvement are higher for the *Joint-2* model, which has shared layers and task specific layers. Interesting, by sharing the layers the proposed solutions reduced the number of parameters, which is another advantage of our approach. While subjective evaluations did not reveal any significant difference between the joint and separate models, we believe that this result is due to the lack of expressiveness of Xface to create animations with subtle behaviors. We will explore more sophisticate toolkits to present our results, including photo realistic videos [30]. We will also evaluate generating head motion driven by speech as an extra task in the multi-task learning framework. We expect that the behaviors will be better synthesized with the rest of the facial movements, providing better speech driven solutions.

Acknowledgements

This work was funded by NSF grants (IIS: 1352950 and IIS: 1718944).

References

1. Albrecht, I., Schröder, M., Haber, J., Seidel, H.P.: Mixed feelings: expression of non-basic emotions in a muscle-based talking head. Virtual Reality 8(4), 201–212 (September 2005)
2. Anderson, R., Stenger, B., Wan, V., Cipolla, R.: Expressive visual text-to-speech using active appearance models. In: IEEE Conference on Computer Vision and Pattern Recognition (CVPR 2013). pp. 3382–3389. Portland, OR, USA (June 2013)
3. Balci, K.: Xface: MPEG-4 based open source toolkit for 3D facial animation. In: Conference on Advanced Visual Interfaces (AVI 2004). pp. 399–402. Gallipoli, Italy (May 2004)
4. Brand, M.: Voice puppetry. In: Proceedings of the 26th annual conference on Computer graphics and interactive techniques (SIGGRAPH 1999). pp. 21–28. New York, NY, USA (1999)
5. Burmania, A., Parthasarathy, S., Busso, C.: Increasing the reliability of crowd-sourcing evaluations using online quality assessment. IEEE Transactions on Affective Computing 7(4), 374–388 (October-December 2016)
6. Busso, C., Deng, Z., Grimm, M., Neumann, U., Narayanan, S.: Rigid head motion in expressive speech animation: Analysis and synthesis. IEEE Transactions on Audio, Speech and Language Processing 15(3), 1075–1086 (March 2007)
7. Busso, C., Narayanan, S.: Interrelation between speech and facial gestures in emotional utterances: a single subject study. IEEE Transactions on Audio, Speech and Language Processing 15(8), 2331–2347 (November 2007)
8. Busso, C., Narayanan, S.: Interplay between linguistic and affective goals in facial expression during emotional utterances. In: 7th International Seminar on Speech Production (ISSP 2006). pp. 549–556. Ubatuba-SP, Brazil (December 2006)
9. Busso, C., Narayanan, S.: Scripted dialogs versus improvisation: Lessons learned about emotional elicitation techniques from the IEMOCAP database. In: Interspeech 2008 - Eurospeech. pp. 1670–1673. Brisbane, Australia (September 2008)

10. Cao, Y., Tien, W., Faloutsos, P., Pighin, F.: Expressive speech-driven facial animation. ACM Transactions on Graphics 24(4), 1283–1302 (October 2005)
11. Choi, K., Luo, Y., Hwang, J.: Hidden Markov model inversion for audio-to-visual conversion in an MPEG-4 facial animation system. The Journal of VLSI Signal Processing 29(1-2), 51–61 (August 2001)
12. Cohen, M.M., Massaro, D.W.: Modeling coarticulation in synthetic visual speech. In: Magnenat-Thalmann N., Thalmann D. (Editors), Models and Techniques in Computer Animation, Springer Verlag. pp. 139–156. Tokyo, Japan (1993)
13. Ding, Y., Pelachaud, C., Artieres, T.: Modeling multimodal behaviors from speech prosody. In: Aylett, R., Krenn, B., Pelachaud, C., Shimodaira, H. (eds.) International Conference on Intelligent Virtual Agents (IVA 2013), Lecture Notes in Computer Science, vol. 8108, pp. 198–207. Springer Berlin Heidelberg, Edinburgh, UK (August 2013)
14. Eyben, F., Scherer, K., Schuller, B., Sundberg, J., André, E., Busso, C., Devillers, L., Epps, J., Laukka, P., Narayanan, S., Truong, K.: The Geneva minimalistic acoustic parameter set (GeMAPS) for voice research and affective computing. IEEE Transactions on Affective Computing 7(2), 190–202 (April-June 2016)
15. Fan, B., Wang, L., Soong, F.K., Xie, L.: Photo-real talking head with deep bidirectional LSTM. In: International Conference on Acoustics, Speech, and Signal Processing (ICASSP 2015). pp. 4884–4888. Brisbane, Australia (April 2015)
16. Fan, B., Xie, L., Yang, S., Wang, L., Soong, F.K.: A deep bidirectional LSTM approach for video-realistic talking head. Multimedia Tools and Applications 75(9), 5287–5309 (May 2016)
17. Glorot, X., Bengio, Y.: Understanding the difficulty of training deep feedforward neural networks. In: International Conference on Artificial Intelligence and Statistics (AISTATS 2010). pp. 249–256. Sardinia, Italy (May 2010)
18. Gutierrez-Osuna, R., Kakumanu, P., Esposito, A., Garcia, O., Bojorquez, A., Castillo, J., Rudomin, I.: Speech-driven facial animation with realistic dynamics. IEEE Transactions on Multimedia 7(1), 33–42 (February 2005)
19. Hochreiter, S., Schmidhuber, J.: Long short-term memory. Neural Computation 9(8), 1735–1780 (November 1997)
20. Kingma, D., Ba, J.: Adam: A method for stochastic optimization. In: International Conference on Learning Representations. pp. 1–13. San Diego, CA, USA (May 2015)
21. Li, X., Wu, Z., Meng, H., Jia, J., Lou, X., Cai, L.: Expressive speech driven talking avatar synthesis with DBLSTM using limited amount of emotional bimodal data. In: Interspeech 2016. pp. 1477–1481. San Francisco, CA, USA (September 2016)
22. Mana, N., Pianesi, F.: HMM-based synthesis of emotional facial expressions during speech in synthetic talking heads. In: International Conference on Multimodal Interfaces (ICMI 2006). pp. 380–387. Banff, AB, Canada (November 2006)
23. Mariooryad, S., Busso, C.: Generating human-like behaviors using joint, speech-driven models for conversational agents. IEEE Transactions on Audio, Speech and Language Processing 20(8), 2329–2340 (October 2012)
24. Mariooryad, S., Busso, C.: Feature and model level compensation of lexical content for facial emotion recognition. In: IEEE International Conference on Automatic Face and Gesture Recognition (FG 2013). pp. 1–6. Shanghai, China (April 2013)
25. Marsella, S., Xu, Y., Lhommet, M., Feng, A., Scherer, S., Shapiro, A.: Virtual character performance from speech. In: ACM SIGGRAPH/Eurographics Symposium on Computer Animation (SCA 2013). pp. 25–35. Anaheim, CA, USA (July 2013)

26. Mehrabian, A.: Communication without words. In: Mortensen, C. (ed.) Communication Theory, pp. 193–200. Transaction Publishers, New Brunswick, NJ, USA (December 2007)
27. Pelachaud, C., Badler, N., Steedman, M.: Generating facial expressions for speech. Cognitive Science 20(1), 1–46 (January 1996)
28. Sadoughi, N., Liu, Y., Busso, C.: Speech-driven animation constrained by appropriate discourse functions. In: International conference on multimodal interaction (ICMI 2014). pp. 148–155. Istanbul, Turkey (November 2014)
29. Srivastava, N., Hinton, G.E., Krizhevsky, A., Sutskever, I., Salakhutdinov, R.: Dropout: a simple way to prevent neural networks from overfitting. Journal of Machine Learning Research 15, 1929–1958 (June 2014)
30. Taylor, S., Kato, A., Matthews, I., Milner, B.: Audio-to-visual speech conversion using deep neural networks. In: Interspeech 2016. pp. 1482–1486. San Francisco, CA, USA (September 2016)
31. Trigeorgis, G., Ringeval, F., Brueckner, R., Marchi, E., Nicolaou, M., Schuller, B., Zafeiriou, S.: Adieu features? end-to-end speech emotion recognition using a deep convolutional recurrent network. In: IEEE International Conference on Acoustics, Speech and Signal Processing (ICASSP 2016). pp. 5200–5204. Shanghai, China (March 2016)
32. Xu, Y., Feng, A.W., Marsella, S., Shapiro, A.: A practical and configurable lip sync method for games. In: Motion in Games (MIG 2013). pp. 131–140. Dublin, Ireland (November 2013)

Integration of Multi-modal Cues in Synthetic Attention Processes to Drive Virtual Agent Behavior

Sven Seele[1] ✉, Tobias Haubrich[1], Tim Metzler[1], Jonas Schild[1,2],
Rainer Herpers[1,3,4], and Marcin Grzegorzek[5]

[1] Institute of Visual Computing, Bonn-Rhein-Sieg University of Applied Sciences,
Grantham-Allee 20, 53757 Sankt Augustin, Germany,
sven.seele@h-brs.de
[2] Hochschule Hannover – University of Applied Sciences and Arts
[3] University of New Brunswick
[4] York University, Toronto
[5] Research Group for Pattern Recognition, University of Siegen

Abstract. Simulations and serious games require realistic behavior of multiple intelligent agents in real-time. One particular issue is how attention and multi-modal sensory memory can be modeled in a natural but effective way, such that agents controllably react to salient objects or are distracted by other multi-modal cues from their current intention. We propose a conceptual framework that provides a solution with adherence to three main design goals: natural behavior, real-time performance, and controllability. As a proof of concept, we implement three major components and showcase effectiveness in a real-time game engine scenario. Within the exemplified scenario, a visual sensor is combined with static saliency probes and auditory cues. The attention model weighs bottom-up attention against intention-related top-down processing, controllable by a designer using memory and attention inhibitor parameters. We demonstrate our case and discuss future extensions.

Keywords: intelligent virtual agents, synthetic perception, virtual attention

1 Introduction

Virtual environments created for simulations, virtual training, or (serious) games carry the potential of providing immersive and believable experiences to users. Tapping into this potential can, e.g., improve learning effects. Visual fidelity is often regarded as the most important aspect of improving immersion and presence. However, another critical aspect is the generation of plausible behavior for simulated entities (agents). Populating virtual worlds with intelligent virtual agents (IVAs) can drastically improve a user's sense of presence by making the world feel alive. Often this requires simulating plausible behavior for multiple agents in real-time. Additionally, designers typically need to control agent behavior in order to support the specific purpose of the application.

© Springer International Publishing AG 2017
J. Beskow et al. (Eds.): IVA 2017, LNAI 10498, pp. 403-412, 2017.
DOI 10.1007/978-3-319-67401-8_50

The most obvious area to improve agent behavior is decision making or action selection. However, we agree with other researchers that the selection of plausible action sequences, which directly affects the perceived realism of an agent's behavior, starts with the agent forming a plausible model of its environment (e.g., [3, 26]). Consequently, modeling an agent-centric perception approach that mimics the limitations of an agent's real-world counterpart has become a standard approach (cf. [18, 25]). We argue that this approach is required to facilitate more human-like agent behavior.

An all purpose perception framework must support a variety of sensor modalities. These should ideally include all five human senses and possibly even more to perceive application specific stimuli (e.g., semantic information). Although we will focus on the processing of visual information in the synthetic perception process, we will discuss how to integrate other modalities, specifically audio. Additionally, we will describe a model of attention; an important component of human perception. A virtual attention process allows agents to identify objects of importance regarding both reactive behavior and cognitive processes. Furthermore, synthetic attention can improve computational efficiency by reducing the amount of sensory data that is processed by an agent.

The underlying intention of our efforts is to model the abilities and limitations of human perception for IVAs. The main goal of the work presented here is to demonstrate how a typical human behavior with regard to attention can be re-created using our proposed approach. Imagine yourself leaving your apartment, house, or office. Since you want to lock the door after leaving, you try to remember whether you noticed your keys on your way to the door. In one case you noticed them, in another you were distracted by an auditory cue and did not perceive the keys. Your current mental model of the world is the foundation for your following behavior. The same should be true for an IVA.

To realize a proof of concept, we propose a framework that adheres to three main design goals: natural behavior, real-time performance, and controllability. We implement a unified sensor interface in combination with an attention process and showcase effectiveness in a real-time game engine scenario.

2   Related Work

In virtual reality and agent community, virtual perception and attention models are an important part of the research [25]. Although, agents generally do not need to differentiate between the virtual environment and their model of the environment, perception capabilities of simulated entities are often limited to mimic their real-life counterparts to generate believable behavior [18]. However, since solutions within the area of virtual human research must fulfill real-time requirements to allow for interactive experiences, applied approaches are often limited in complexity (e.g., [16]). Most research in this area focuses on simulating eye gaze (cf. [1, 23]). However, similar to human perception, virtual attention models can also be used to reduce the complexity of a scene saving computational and memory resources. At the same time such an approach can create the impression of an overlooking or unobservant agent [2], creating a more realistic representation. Typically, solutions generate *saliency maps* to identify regions or objects that attract an agent's attention [12]. Many of such approaches are inspired by computational attention methods developed in computer vision research, e.g., [5, 11]. In virtual environment applications, these techniques require rendering the view of every agent, although in reduced resolution (e.g., [6]). While mimicking neurobiological models of visual attention, their complexity often prohibits usage in real time or even multi-agent applications. Several approaches address attention processes within larger agent frameworks, e.g., as filters [4] or subscriptions [20]. While presenting a versatile middleware approach, the actual implementation of specific attention algorithms or strategies is typically not addressed, but left to an application designer. Our approach provides an integrated attention process that is instead configurable by a designer to address application specifics.

The idea of limiting sensor capabilities of agents to simulate perception is a more common approach than considering actual attention models. In game development it is mostly concerned with detecting and reacting to players [17]. However, while game AI programmers try to create plausible behavior, the most important aspect is always providing a fun game experience. Consequently, agent behavior must always be obvious to players. In our model, attention parameters can be changed to influence the simulated outcome.

Virtual human researchers are not constrained by considerations present in game development and are able to explore more realistic perception models within their work. In general, IVAs are equipped with a set of virtual sensors often representing actual sensory organs of humans. Due to the importance of the visual channel in human perception processes, simulating visual sensation is the most frequent approach to generate more authentic behavior for simulated entities. However, a few examples exist that deal with the perception of stimuli using several sensor modalities. For example, Kuiper and Wenkstern proposed the DIVAs framework, which includes a perceptual combination module to integrate multiple senses [15]. The approach is specifically geared towards the use in multi-agent, real-time systems, but their sense combination relies on a set of pre-defined entries in an event knowledge base. Balint and Allbeck demonstrate an approach of modeling perceptual attention using a set of heuristics based on a linear sense combination [2]. While specifically considering semantic information and multi-modal sensors, they did not explore the connection between different sensor types and attention. Furthermore, top-down and bottom-up attention only depends on the type of interaction (object-object or object-agent). Finally, Kim et al. focused on creating a model of perception that mediates between top-down and bottom-up attention and at the same time determines the benefit of shifting attention [13]. However, their implementation only considers a single sensor that pre-combines all sensor modalities.

The simulation of the visual sense is most commonly implemented in one of two approaches: geometric algorithms or synthetic vision [25]. Geometric approaches utilize techniques such as ray-casts to test objects for visibility. Synthetic vision approaches render a low resolution image of the environment from

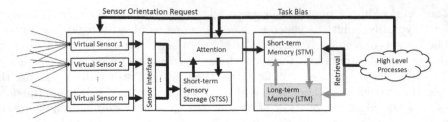

Fig. 1: Virtual sensors gather stimuli from an environment in a STSS. Objects of interest are selected by an attention process. Attended objects become percepts residing in STM. From there percepts can be retrieved by high level processes, e.g., decision making. The attention mechanism can request orientation of sensors and high level processes can bias attention for top-down perception. LTM is not considered here.

each agent's point of view to determine which object is visible to an agent. The challenge is extracting information from the rendered scene view. Noser et al. [19] simplified the image analysis by rendering objects with a unique color; neglecting textures and lighting. As a result of this *false coloring*, an object is visible if at least one pixel of the rendered image contains the object's unique color. Other researchers extended this approach to encode more information or improve performance, e.g., [7, 22]. We adapt such an approach and demonstrate how to integrate it into our perception framework including attention.

Furthermore, we build upon the ideas of a sensor interface to provide a unified entry point for data provided by different sensors and how to represent the sensed objects in a hierarchical memory structure (cf. [7, 15, 24]). To improve efficiency we rely on the common approach of attaching semantics to virtual objects. Thus, agents do not have to interpret sensor data to gain relevant knowledge such as object affordances. For an overview of semantic modeling see, e.g., [21].

3   Synthetic Perception for Intelligent Virtual Agents

In this section we will describe our approach of a generic perception framework based on previous work [9, 10]. The framework combines several existing approaches, but specifically considers real-time constraints and provides controllability (to an application designer). To generate plausible behavior in a complex virtual environment additional high level concepts are required, such as decision making, planning, and navigation. The presented framework is part of a larger agent architecture concept, which includes examples of these high level processes (see [14, 27]). The main focus of this work is on perception modeling; specifically sensing and attention. The adopted memory model is in large part based on a hierarchical model popularized by Peters and O'Sullivan [24]. Its main components are a short-term sensory storage (STSS), a short-term memory (STM) and a long-term memory (LTM). Details can be found in the original publication or in [9, 10]. An overview of our framework's structure is depicted in Figure 1.

3.1 Sensing

For an agent to sense information from it's virtual environment, a multitude of different approaches are possible. Instead of focusing on a specific set of sensors, we decided to implement an open solution by providing a unified sensor interface similar to [7] and [15]. Since all sensors have to provide collected stimuli through the interface, implemented sensors can produce redundant or complementary information depending on application specific requirements. At the same time sensors can be tailored towards an intended use case by being implemented as simple or complex as necessary. Ideally, a sensor implementation provides sufficient parameterization to allow a designer or the application to balance performance against accuracy. Additionally, due to the interface structure, sensors are able to represent any perception modality, such as hearing. In the following we discuss examples of possible sensor realizations.

GPU-based Vision Sensor. Currently, the main source of visual information in our realization of the framework is a GPU-based vision sensor. The sensor is based on the false coloring approach described by Noser et al. [19], but optimized towards performance by processing result textures using graphics hardware. This approach has two advantages: First, occlusion will automatically be handled correctly by the render pipeline. Second, as soon as a pixel with a unique color is found in the resulting texture, it is clear that the associated object is visible in the agent's field of view. All additional information can be retrieved from the object itself or from associated semantics. The main disadvantage of the approach is having to render separate views for each individual agent.

Pre-computed Visual Importance. In order to improve scalability of the GPU-based sensor, we adapted ideas from real time rendering of global illumination in game engines, mainly the use of precomputed radiance transfers or image based lighting (IBL). IBL allows light transport in a virtual scene to be pre-computed off-line. The results of the process are stored in light probes, which are distributed across the scene and sampled for lighting information during runtime.[6] We use a similar approach to pre-compute *saliency probes* that store visibility information and saliency values of static objects within a virtual scene in the form of cubemaps. For this purpose a saliency map is calculated alongside a false colored texture for a specific point in the scene. At runtime the closest probe(s) are sampled to determine the most salient object visible from that particular location. The advantage of the approach is that saliency calculations can be very complex and highly accurate without affecting run-time performance.

Integration of Auditive Cues. For demonstration purposes, we decided to implement a straightforward solution of a second modality. A hearing sensor is attached to the agent and senses all perceivable audio objects in a scene. Physical filters and pre-selectors are used to parameterize sensor capabilities. A simple pre-selector selects only objects that exceed a certain volume threshold. Additionally, filters can be used to exclude all objects beyond a certain distance

---

[6] e.g., Global Illumination in Unity with Enlighten, `https://developer.arm.com/docs/100140/latest/global-illumination-in-unity-with-enlighten`, accessed 2017-07-17

to the agent. Currently, no further selection mechanism is applied; all audio emitting objects that are not excluded by the pre-selector or filters are converted into auditive stimuli. A stimulus encodes a saliency and the volume of the object.

The perception of stimuli from several multi-modal sensor modalities is implemented as a simple weighted sum, following the approach presented in [2]. The heuristic used here is based on pre-assigned saliency values. All perceived stimuli are normalized such that $\sum_{s \in stimuli} saliency(s) = 1.0$. The final score of the objects is calculated similar to the approach presented in [2]. We also use a configuration in which the agent gives more weight to visual stimuli ($w_{visual} = 0.7$, $w_{auditive} = 0.3$). These parameters could be adjusted to generate different behavior patterns. The attention target for the agent is chosen across all senses according to our attention model.

3.2   Attention

In order to generate believable behavior, a suitable attention process needs to consider bottom-up as well as top-down attention [13, 25, 20]). The former facilitates reactive behavior as it will direct attention towards *salient* objects, which is typically not consciously controllable [8, 25]. Top-down attention describes the ability to direct attention based on current tasks or knowledge in order to reach a certain goal, e.g., finding a specific object among other objects [8].

Our approach is mainly based on two well-known theories of attention: *Feature Integration Theory* and the *Guided Search Model* (for a definition see, e.g., [8]). During acquisition, stimuli will be gathered in parallel and associated with a saliency value. In contrast, information about a stimulus' source object can only be retrieved sequentially by focusing attention on one object at a time. The general procedure within our framework is as follows.

A filter process will select the current object of interest from the agent's STSS based on saliency values across all sensor modalities. The values are set using object semantics or determined by either a sensor or the agent itself (see top-down attention). The most salient object as determined by the selection mechanism is set as the object of interest and a request is sent to the actuators to orient the visual sensor towards the object.

To simulate the process of object classification or information retrieval, agents will dwell on an object of interest. Once the agent has spent a certain dwell time looking at the object, the stimulus has been attended to. Using only this process an agent would continuously focus on the most salient object in its surroundings. To avoid this behavior, the currently attended object may be inhibited during the next cycle. Scenario designers can determine when, how and how many objects are inhibited. These parameters can be adjusted to achieve different search behaviors or to represent certain cognitive capabilities and states.

Top-down attention is expressed by adding an agent-central bias to an object's global saliency. The amount of bias can be pre-determined by a designer or generated from within the agent itself, possibly based on object ontologies (cf. [21]). This ensures that goal related stimuli are prioritized, but can still be suppressed by objects with high bottom-up saliency.

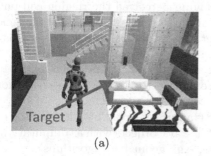 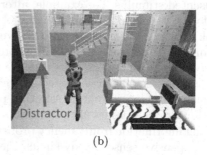

(a)   (b)

Fig. 2: In (a) the agent traverses the scene, focuses and perceives the target object. In (b) the scene is identical, except an auditory distraction prevents the agent from perceiving the target object.

4 Proof of Concept Scenario and Discussion

In the introduction we described a typical scenario that we wanted to recreate using the proposed perception framework. Both the evaluation scenario and the framework were implemented using the Unity game engine[7]. Within the scenario we are using an auditive cue to distract an agent from an otherwise interesting object. The agent walks towards the door of an appartment. On its way to the exit, two interesting objects are present on opposite sides of the path: an object of interest ("target") and a distractor object, in this case a cell phone.

The scenario is run under two conditions: (1) The only object with a high saliency value is the target object and (2) a highly salient auditory stimulus will be activated at a specific point in time. In this case, the cell phone will ring. Figure 2 shows the results of running the application under both conditions.

In condition (1), at the depicted point in time, the agent is focused on the target object, indicated by its gaze direction. While the distractor object would be clearly visible to the agent, it chose to focus on the target instead, because of the top-down attention bias. In condition (2) the agent is looking at the distractor object. Figure 2 (b) shows approximately the same point in time that is shown in (a). Since the agent's visual sensor is oriented towards the distractor, it will not be able to sense and perceive the target object. Thus, after arriving at the door, the agent will not "remember" having seen the target. By providing sample implementations for certain aspects of our synthetic perception framework we were able to demonstrate agent behavior that was described in the introduction. An agent can be distracted from a specific object by integrating an additional auditive cue into the synthetic perception process. We are confident that the same result can be achieved in other similar scenarios. However, extensive evaluations are still required.

Although satisfied with the results, we are aware that the current design is not without limitations. An obvious shortcoming is the agent not reacting to the

---

[7] Unity Technologies, www.unity3d.com

presented stimulus. For example, after having perceived the ringing cell phone, it does not change its current action of walking towards the door to take a closer look at the phone or to answer it. However, the actual action selection is separate from the perception and attention processes as they were described here. Our current work focuses on these aspects of agent behavior generation as the basis for the subsequent action selection process. Due to this focus we chose not to implement a specific action selection procedure for this scenario.

Performance issues of the false coloring approach could be mitigated by combining information from saliency probes for static objects with a computationally less expensive sensor for dynamic objects, e.g., geometric algorithms.

Obviously, as soon as a scene changes all information stored within a saliency probe will be invalidated. However, a set of probes could be provided for predetermined scene variations. Also, depending on scene complexity and the saliency map generation process, probes could also be updated during runtime, comparable to reflection probes in modern game engines. A strength of generating saliency cubemaps is that they could be used to identify salient areas on the surface of a single object. Since our framework implements object-based perception, this information is not utilized at the moment. This becomes especially obvious when agents look at large objects.

5   Conclusions

In this contribution we discussed how synthetic perception can be used to improve the behavioral realism of intelligent agents in real-time virtual environments. For this purpose we proposed a generic framework consisting of a virtual sensor interface, a hierarchic memory module, and an attention model. Further, we discussed how to integrate multi-modal cues into the process, using sight and hearing as examples. The framework enables both the simulation of human-like sensors and approaches that are focused on real-time capability and controllability. The memory module stores both stimuli and, after they have been attended to, percepts. Although it has not been specifically addressed in this work, the module also acts as interface from and to subsequent high level processes, such as decision making. The included attention model combines bottom-up reactive attention and top-down task-oriented processing. Parameters like dwell time or the number of inhibited objects can be set by a designer to fit an applications specific needs. In an example scenario we demonstrated several functionalities of the framework and provided a set of implementation examples for sensors. Furthermore, we showed that the framework can be used to distract an agent from an otherwise salient target object within a reasonably complex environment. However, to truly evaluate the presented approach, several user studies need to be conducted following this basic proof of concept.

A logical next step is to integrate high level processes into the framework. Decision processes should be involved more closely in perception, e.g., deciding when an object has been attended to. Other considerations are: How does perceiving an object influence an agent's current goal? How long will the agent be

able to remember having seen an object? How does the type of object or interaction influence an agent's ability to recall an object in the future? These are
just a few interesting questions we would like to address.

Furthermore, the presented approach – just as many others – does not consider an agent's current state of mind (i.e., emotions, personality, etc.) as part
of the perception process. However, such factors influence human attention processes and therefore should be integrated into synthetic perception for agents. In
previous work we already modeled the influence of personality and emotion on
decision processes [14], which we intend to transfer to the perception framework.

In summary, we believe that the proposed framework offers a flexible and
customizable solution for modeling multi-modal virtual perception where focus
can either be on neurobiological accuracy or computational performance.

Acknowledgements
The authors gratefully acknowledge financial support by the Harrison McCain Foundation as part of the McCain Visiting Professorship Award Program.

References

1. Andrist, S., Pejsa, T., Mutlu, B., Gleicher, M.: Designing effective gaze mechanisms
   for virtual agents. In: Proc. of the SIGCHI Conf. on Human Factors in Computing
   Systems. pp. 705–714. CHI '12, ACM, New York, NY, USA (2012)
2. Balint, T., Allbeck, J.M.: What's going on? Multi-sense attention for virtual agents.
   In: Aylett, R., Krenn, B., Pelachaud, C., Shimodaira, H. (eds.) Intelligent Virtual Agents. IVA 2013. pp. 349–357. LNCS, vol 8108, Springer, Berlin, Heidelberg
   (2013)
3. Blumberg, B.M.: Old Tricks, New Dogs: Ethology and Interactive Creatures. Ph.D.
   thesis, Massachusetts Institute of Technology, Cambridge, MA, USA (1997)
4. Bordeux, C., Boulic, R., Thalmann, D.: An efficient and flexible perception
   pipeline for autonomous agents. Computer Graphics Forum 18, 23–30 (1999),
   http://dx.doi.org/10.1111/1467-8659.00324
5. Bruce, N.D.B., Tsotsos, J.K.: Saliency, attention, and visual search: An information
   theoretic approach. Journal of Vision 9(3), 1–24 (March 2009)
6. Brunnhuber, M., Schrom-Feiertag, H., Luksch, C., Matyus, T., Hesina, G.: Bridging
   the gap between visual exploration and agent-based pedestrian simulation in a
   virtual environment. In: Proc. of the 18th ACM Symposium on Virtual Reality
   Software and Technology. pp. 9–16. VRST '12, ACM, New York, NY, USA (2012),
   http://doi.acm.org/10.1145/2407336.2407339
7. Conde, T., Thalmann, D.: An integrated perception for autonomous virtual agents:
   Active and predictive perception. Computer Animation and Virtual Worlds 17,
   457–468 (2006), http://dx.doi.org/10.1002/cav.148
8. Frintrop, S.: Computational Visual Attention. Sprinter (2011)
9. Haubrich, T., Seele, S., Herpers, R., Bauckhage, C., Becker, P.: Synthetic perception for intelligent virtual agents. In: Proc. of the 1st ACM SIGCHI Annual
   Symposium on Computer-Human Interaction in Play (CHI PLAY) (2014)
10. Haubrich, T., Seele, S., Herpers, R., Bauckhage, C., Becker, P.: Modeling sensation
   for an intelligent virtual agent's perception process. In: Brinkman, W.P., Broekens,
   J., Heylen, D. (eds.) Intelligent Virtual Agents. IVA 2015. pp. 87–97. LNCS, vol
   9238, Springer, Cham (2015)

11. Herpers, R., Kattner, H., Rodax, H., Sommer, G.: Gaze: An attentive process-
    ing strategy to detect and analyze the prominent facial regions. In: Workshop on
    Automatic Face and Gesture Recognition. Zurich, Switzerland (1995)
12. Itti, L., Dhavale, N., Pighin, F.: Realistic avatar eye and head animation using a
    neurobiological model of visual attention. In: Bosacchi, B., Fogel, D.B., Bezdek,
    J.C. (eds.) Proc. SPIE 48th Annual Int. Symposium on Optical Science and Tech-
    nology. vol. 5200, pp. 64–78. SPIE Press, Bellingham, WA (Aug 2003)
13. Kim, Y., van Velsen, M., Hill, R.W.: Modeling dynamic perceptual attention in
    complex virtual environments. In: Panayiotopoulos, T., Gratch, J., Aylett, R.,
    Ballin, D., Olivier, P., Rist, T. (eds.) Intelligent Virtual Agents. IVA 2005. pp.
    266–277. LNCS, vol 3661, Springer, Berlin, Heidelberg (2005)
14. Krueger, F., Seele, S., Herpers, R., Becker, P., Bauckhage, C.: Adaptive decision
    making in microsimulations of urban traffic in virtual environments. In: Pisan, Y.,
    Sgouros, N.M., Marsh, T. (eds.) Entertainment Computing. pp. 220–222. LNCS,
    vol 8770 (2014)
15. Kuiper, D.M., Wenkstern, R.Z.: Virtual agent perception combination in
    multi agent based systems. In: Proc. of the 2013 Int. Conf. on Autonomous
    Agents and Multi-agent Systems (2013), http://dl.acm.org/citation.cfm?id=
    2484920.2485017
16. Kuiper, D.M., Wenkstern, R.Z.: Agent vision in multi-agent based simulation sys-
    tems. Autonomous Agents and Multi-Agent Systems 29(2), 161–191 (2015)
17. Leonard, T.: Building an AI sensory system. http://www.gamasutra.com/view/
    feature/131297 (2003), accessed: 2017-07-16
18. Luck, M., Aylett, R.: Applying artificial intelligence to virtual reality: Intelligent
    virtual environments. Applied Artificial Intelligence 14, 3–32 (2000)
19. Noser, H., Renault, O., Thalmann, D., Magnenat-Thalmann, N.: Navigation for
    digital actors based on synthetic vision, memory, and learning. Computers &
    Graphics 19, 7–19 (1995)
20. van Oijen, J., Dignum, F.: Scalable perception for bdi-agents embodied in virtual
    environments. In: Proc. of the 2011 IEEE/WIC/ACM Int. Conf. on Web Intelli-
    gence and Intelligent Agent Technology - Volume 02 (2011)
21. van Oijen, J., Vanhee, L., Dignum, F.: CIGA: A middleware for intelligent agents
    in virtual environments. In: M., B., Brom C., D.F., VW., S. (eds.) Agents for Ed-
    ucational Games and Simulations. AEGS 2011. LNCS, vol 7471, Springer, Berlin,
    Heidelberg (2011)
22. Ondřej, J., Pettré, J., Olivier, A.H., Donikian, S.: A synthetic-vision based steering
    approach for crowd simulation. ACM TOG 29(4), 123:1–123:9 (2010), http://
    doi.acm.org/10.1145/1778765.1778860
23. Pejsa, T., Andrist, S., Gleicher, M., Mutlu, B.: Gaze and attention management for
    embodied conversational agents. ACM Trans. Interact. Intell. Syst. 5(1), 3:1–3:34
    (2015)
24. Peters, C., O'Sullivan, C.: Synthetic vision and memory for autonomous virtual
    humans. Computer Graphics Forum 21, 743–752 (2002)
25. Peters, C., Castellano, G., Rehm, M., André, E., Raouzaiou, A., Rapantzikos,
    K., Karpouzis, K., Volpe, G., Camurri, A., Vasalou, A.: Fundamentals of Agent
    Perception and Attention Modelling, pp. 293–319. Springer, Berlin, Heidelberg
    (2011)
26. Reynolds, C.W.: Flocks, herds and schools: A distributed behavioral model. SIG-
    GRAPH Computer Graphics 21(4), 25–34 (1987)
27. Seele, S., Herpers, R., Bauckhage, C.: Cognitive agents for microscopic traffic sim-
    ulations in virtual environments. In: Entertainment Computing, ICEC 2012

A categorization of virtual agent appearances and a qualitative study on age-related user preferences

Carolin Straßmann ✉ & Nicole C. Krämer

University Duisburg-Essen, Social Psychology: Media and Communication, 47057 Duisburg, Germany
carolin.strassmann@uni-due.de,
nicole.kraemer@uni-due.de

Abstract. Various variables influence the perception of appearance, which are difficult to examine holistically in a quantitative approach. To give a holistic overview of appearance variables, a systematic categorization of different dimensions was developed. This is also of special importance with a view to the application field of companions for seniors whose preferences regarding appearance are under-researched. Therefore, based on the categorization, 11 interviews with two different target groups (six students, five elderly) were conducted. Results indicate that seniors tend to prefer a realistic humanoid agent, while students mostly rejected this appearance and instead favored zoomorphic or machinelike agents in comic stylization. In sum, the current research gives a first hint that there are age-related differences with regard to appearance.

Keywords: visual appearance, categorization, daily-life support, age differences

1 Introduction

One primary factor that influences human-agent interaction is the visual appearance of the virtual agent. It was shown that appearance has an effect on various variables such as motivation [1], buying intent [2], learning outcomes [3], persuasive effects [4] and the agent's overall evaluation [5]. Although numerous studies (e.g. [6–9]) are focusing on the visual design of virtual agents, there is a lack of systematic research. Multiple variables can be changed and varied in order to design the virtual agent's appearance. In this context, most prior studies compare alternate types of agents differing in a variety of features concerning their appearance; thus using an unsystematic approach in regards to agent appearance. In order to explore the effects of specific appearance variables in a structured way, the relevant variables have to be categorized first. Therefore, the current approach presents a categorization of appearance variables that has been constructed based on prior research. In order to create virtual agents that are engaging, it is necessary to take the users' needs into account, and thus, it is important to know the preferences of the agent's target group. Since current developments aim to maintain the elderly's autonomy by using virtual agents [10], it is of particular interest to explore the preferences of this target group. Until now, little is

J. Beskow et al. (Eds.): IVA 2017, LNAI 10498, pp. 413-422, 2017.
DOI 10.1007/978-3-319-67401-8_51

known about age-related differences with regard to appearance preferences, but since assistive technologies like virtual agents can be extremely beneficial for seniors, knowledge about their preferences is necessary.

In sum, the current approach provides two main contributions: (1) to give a more systematic overview about the agent's appearance and therefore present a categorization of different appearance variables, and (2) to explore the users' preferences regarding age-related differences. Therefore, a qualitative interview study was constructed in the context of daily life support with six students and five seniors.

2   Categorization of appearance variables

Numerous studies have investigated effects of appearance e.g. [6–9] but most studies compared agents that vary in various features. In order to explore those effects more systematically, theses have to be categorized first based on prior research.

(0) **Embodiment vs. no embodiment.** When it comes to the design of a virtual agent's appearance, the first decision needs to be, whether the agent should have an embodied appearance or not. Recent speech-based systems (e.g. Apple's Siri) mostly do not have an embodiment. However, prior research demonstrates that an embodied character can enhance the interaction. An overall meta-analysis [11] demonstrated that an embodied character evokes a more positive social interaction than a non-embodied one. Therefore, having an embodiment seems to be beneficial for the human-agent interaction. When an embodied character is used, multiple factors can be manipulated. Based on prior research, a categorization is constructed that results in four main categories: (1) species, (2) realism, (3) 2D vs. 3D, and (4) feature specifications. These categories are not distinct ones, and they influence each other.

(1) **Species.** Most of the used agents are humanoid [16], while they could easily take various other forms. Koda and Maes [6] for instance compared in their study a human face, a dog, and a smiley. In line with these different forms, Gulz and Haake [13] called this differentiation humanness and stated that agents could be designed as human, animal or another creature, nonliving object and as combinations of the former. Figuring out different degrees of realism, Sträfling et al. [3] distinguished between zoomorphic and anthropomorphic agents and therefore compared a rabbit to a female human in their experimental study. Beside humans, animals and objects machinelike agents like robots are also considered (e.g. [2, 8]). Ring et al. [5] sum those differentiations up using the term species and list humanoid, animal and robot as examples for that category. Sticking to this term, the described category "species" is defined as different classes of individuals that have common attributes and are identified by a common name. There are at least five different types of species: human, animal, robots, objects, and mystical creatures.

(2) Realism. Numerous studies examined the realism of the agents' appearance (e.g. [2, 3, 5, 6, 9]). Realism can be described "in a simple binary manner; things are more real, the more they look exactly like a real object" [9, p. 109-110]. However this definition is quite vague, and since there is no universal understanding of realism, various studies focus on different dimensions of realism. Koda and Maes [6] investigated the effect of realism by comparing a realistic and caricature male and a smiley face. However the authors' understanding of realism is not defined. In some way the stylization of the character is seen as part of realism, while the species or human-likeness is also taken into account. In line with these gradations, Sträfling et al. [3] defined three realism dimensions. The first named degree was naturalness vs. cartoon-likeness, which fits to the comparison of realistic and caricature humans by Koda and Maes [6]. As already mentioned above, the species of the agents is also seen as one part of realism [3]. The third dimension by Sträfling et al. [3] is the resolution, which is described by the poles low resolution and hyperrealistic. However, it should be mentioned that those dimension are not described in more detail. The dimension naturalness vs. cartoon-likeness [3] is also called naturalism vs. stylization and can be seen as a sub-dimension of graphical style, which is characterized by the artistic quality [13]. Gulz and Haake [13] describe this dimension as complex since there are various expressions of this appearance dimension and no simple linear relation in this design space. As second sub-dimension of graphical style the degree of detailedness vs. simplification was listed [13]. The degree of details might also influence the stylization, while a naturalistic design could also have more or fewer details [13]. Further on, the degree of stylization may be characterized by the two sub-categories: shading style and proportions [5]. In sum, there is no universal definition of realism, but it can be characterized by three sub-categories: stylization, resolution and detailedness.

(3) 2D vs. 3D. While most of the modern embodied agents are 3D models [e.g. 5], it would also be possible to design a 2D character. Besides the presentation of 2D or 3D models within a 2D-simulation (e.g. a computer screen), due to the rise of modern technologies (e.g. Oculus Rift) there is also the possibility to present these characters in a 3D environment. Since this approach is focusing on visual appearance only the former two dimensions (2D vs. 3D agent in a 2D-simulation) are of interest.

(4) Feature specification. Especially, for humanoid characters, there are various features that can be specialized in more detail. For instance, Ring et al. [5] name demographic parameters, selection of clothing and accessories as well as hairstyle as further design decisions. There are studies [e.g. 19] focusing on socio-demographic parameters like gender and ethnicity. Gulz and Haake [7] stated based on the theory of physical personality [15] that features such as sex, race, hair, clothing make up etc. create an impression of personality. Therefore, even this detail decisions might have a big influence on the overall perception of the virtual agent. Within those specific features, there are two sub categories: socio-demographic parameters and styling. Although most of these features belong to humanoid characters, those decisions are also of interest about other species (e.g. the race of an animal, as well as fur patterns).

3 Derivation of hypotheses and research questions

The current approach aims to give a more holistic and systematic overview of a virtual agent's appearance. Regarding the design of a virtual agent, first, it must be decided whether it should be embodied or not. Although users are familiar with disembodied agents (e.g. Siri or Cortana), embodied virtual agents were found to enhance social interactions in a positive way [11]. Therefore, the following hypothesis is assumed:

Users will prefer an embodied character as their personal assistant over interacting with a solely speech-based system (H1).

Still, visual appearance contains many different factors which may be manipulated and, in turn affect the outcome. The categorization is needed to explore the effect of the mentioned factors more systematically, e.g. in experimental studies. Since it is not possible to investigate every variable in quantitative studies, the current approach explores the categorization for the first time and can give initial hints to (a) the users' preferences regarding the categories and (b) what categories seems to be more important and should, therefore, be investigated more.

A growing amount of research focuses on the implementation of virtual agents in assistive technologies for seniors, aiming to maintain their autonomy. Prior research demonstrates that such agents can enhance the mental and physical state of seniors [16]. However, it is still unknown how a virtual daily life assistant for elderly should look like and whether there are any age-related differences regarding its preferred visual appearance. Therefore this study addresses the following research question:

Does age influence the users' preferences concerning the agents' appearance in the context of daily life support (RQ1)?

4 Method

In order to explore the meaning of virtual agents' appearance in more depth, elven qualitative interviews in the context of daily-life support were conducted. This method captures the thoughts and attitudes of individuals more deeply and is less strict than standardized questionnaires. In these semi-structured interviews the conducted categorization of the appearance variables are explored for the first time.

Sample. Overall, eleven interviews were conducted with to different target groups. The small sample size is acceptable for a qualitative research, which aims to explore the research questions more in depth instead of providing statements of incidence or prevalence [17]. Therefore, it is not required to ensure a high sample size to determine statistical significance [17]. Since the influence of the users' age should be investigated, two different age groups were interviewed. Six students, aged between 20 and 39 years (M = 24.17, SD = 7.44), participated, and five seniors with an age between 61 and 74 were interviewed (M = 67.00, SD = 6.12). Gender was equally distributed (45.45 % women) and all interviewees were German. Most of the interviewees had no prior experiences with virtual agents (7 of 11), while four had interacted with a virtual agent before.

Interview guidelines and Analyses. Based on the categorization of the agent's appearance categories a guide for the semi-structured was constructed. Interview questions about different categories of the agents' appearance were asked in order to derive the interviewees' preferences. First of all, some general questions about visual appearance and the importance of virtual embodiment were asked. Afterwards the questions became more precise and focused on the described categories. Interviewees should state what kind of species they would prefer ("Please imagine all possible species your virtual agent could have. Which species would you like your virtual assistant to be?"). Further on, the interviewer tried to figure out what level of realism (e.g. realistic vs. line drawing, comic-like, unrealistic body characteristics like a blue skin or unrealistic big eyes etc.) the interviewees liked the most (e.g. "Within the continuum of photorealistic and line drawing, how should your virtual assistant look like?"). Interviewees also stated their preferences concerning dimensions (2D vs. 3D). For all questions the interviewer tried to evoke highly detailed answers and therefore asked after each statement for the interviewees' reasons and explanations. Additionally, further questions were asked and interviewees had the chance to design their own virtual agent that are not contributing to the current research questions and therefore are not presented here. In the end, socio-demographic data were obtained. To analyze the data, all captured videos were transcribed into plain text and the data was evaluated deductively and inductively [18] with reference to the research questions. Based on the interview guideline, a first version of the coding scheme was defined. This version was modified with regard to the interviewees' statements and some codes were excluded, since they became irrelevant for the current research questions [19]. The final coding system of the interview questions contains 8 main codes and 34 sub-codes (c.f. supplementary material). To guarantee the internal consistency of the constructed coding scheme, one interview of each target group has been cross-coded by a second coder. Results show substantial inter-rater reliabilities [20]. The cross-coding of the student interview reached a Cohen's Kappa of 0.69 (69.70% of agreement), while the scores of the elderly interview were even better with Cohen's Kappa = 0.78 (79.45 % of agreement).

5   Results

To get a better overview of the age-related differences, results of the sub-samples are presented separately. Statements are marked with the interviewees' number and age.

Student sample. Surprisingly only one student stated to prefer an embodied agent as personal assistant, while four students preferred a speech-based system. Additionally, one student had no preference. Interviewees who preferred a disembodied character justified it referring to a potential distraction "I don't know, in that case [of a disembodied character] there might be more space for the information" (6, 24Y) or uncanniness. Furthermore, interviewees liked the idea of not being restricted to one certain device "If I would know the system is around me and I can use it [without any device], I would like that" (5, 39Y). Two students further argued that the virtual assistant is not human and therefore should not simulate to be one "I know that it is not a real human and this embodiment simulates one." (2, 20Y). Additionally, students see the potential value of a virtual embodied character to be perceived as interlocutor, who can be addressed: "When I am talking to someone, it is nice to have an image of this person." (1, 20Y). With regard to species, most of the students rejected a humanoid agent (1 interviewee) and preferred non-humanoid creatures (animals (2 interviewees), objects (1 interviewee) or machinelike agents (2 interviewees)). Reasons for liking a humanoid agent were the natural interaction ("I think it would be most naturally." (6, 24Y)), and the familiarity ("Since it is a habit to talk to other humans, to communicate with them, to negotiate appointments... and therefore I would take a human", 6, 24Y). Additionally, it was mentioned that a humanoid character would be the most serious one. People who disliked a humanoid appearance justified it with missing variety ("There are enough humans around me. I don't feel the need to interact with a human in this way in addition.", 5, 39Y), they disliked the simulation of a human ("that is no person anyways", 3, 20Y), and assumed that the humanoid character would trigger specific expectations: "I would like to interact normal with a humanoid character and do chit-chatting or something like that. And I cannot do that with a virtual agent, since he has no personality" (2, 20Y). While humans were described as serious, objects and animals were chosen because of their funny appearance: "Simple because it is funny" (4, 22Y). Some interviewees wished for something neutral and task-related: "Yes, I like an object, because it is neutral (...) on the other hand it is related to the topic" (3, 20Y). Animals were preferred since there are pet-like ("You have dogs and cats around you in your life and they are your pets... and it is not unnaturally, if there are with you in your home", 6, 24Y) and will be perceived as likable: "I think an animal is likable ... a little helper" (3, 20Y). In regard to realism, only one student preferred a realistic appearance of his virtual agent: "I think that would be nice... realistic... I would appreciate it, if the appearance would be natural and not completely absurd" (6, 24Y). Most of the other students rejected a realistic appearance: "I don't have to see any hair and pore of it, like it gets popular in recent graphical developments. That doesn't need to be. Depending on how the character is designed that could be deterrent to me." (5, 39Y). Moreover, most of the interviewees stated that they did not like the fact that realistic-looking humans reminded them of humans from their real world: "I think one would link it to already existing people and therefore I like the cartoon version more." (1, 20Y) or "it is no realistic human, because it is no real human" (6, 24Y) or "In my opinion, I interact with a virtual person... so the distance between my computer and me will be still maintained. Because I have a fictional character I am still aware of it" (5, 39Y). The majority of the student sample prefers a 3D agent (5 interviewees), while only one person enjoyed the 2D version more, because it appeared to be more simple and less distracting. The other interviewees liked the possibility to make movements and turns within the virtual space of a 3D agent. Further on, they appreciate the modern look of it: "I would create it with 3 dimensions, so that it is more modern-looking" (1, 20Y) and "it looks better done" (3, 20Y). Contradicting to the prior findings in regard to species and realism, interviewees stated that they liked the more realistic look of a 3D agent: "I think 3D is more realistic" (6, 24Y) and "I think, it looks more likable, if it is more real" (3, 20Y).

Elderly sample. In contrast to the student sample, most of the elderly interviewees preferred to have an embodied character (4 interviewees), while only one elderly person stated that a speech-based system would be sufficient: "It is no human being. It is a computer voice in my opinion, and I don't need an embodied character."(5, 65Y). In line with some statements of the student interviewees, the elderly subjects explained that they would like to have a contact person who they can address during the interaction, and therefore prefer an embodied agent: "There has to be some kind of reference point in the wider sense." (1, 62Y) or "I like to look in the people's eyes while I am talking to them. And I don't like it when there is only a voice present." (2, 73Y). Another person stated to be more interested in a conversation with an embodied agent: "I think it is interesting if I look at it and the character talks to me." (3, 74Y) and the character seemed to attract attention in the interviewee's opinion: "In the moment, when there is any kind of reference – figure, image whatever- for me there is another degree of attention." (1, 62Y). Additionally, the opportunity to display non-verbal behavior was perceived as beneficial. One person went on to attribute more trust to an embodied agent: "I think, in that case you show more trust to it. I like that." (2, 73Y), another described a simple speech-based system as "something impersonal, something foreign, something mechanical" (1, 62Y). Contradicting the statements of the student sample, almost all elderly persons tend to prefer a human as their personal assistant (4 interviewees), while one person picked an animal (category 1). The one person, who preferred an animal, could not accept a humanoid agent: "Because it is a computer, I can not accept it as a human." (5, 65Y). One elderly stated that she would feel more related to a humanoid agent: "you might have a relation to it or a better relation" (4, 61Y). Furthermore, a humanoid agent seemed to trigger a more familiar interaction compared to an animal: "... she talks to me... great I can talk to her... and if I see an animal.. well, yes I can talk to it too, but it does not respond. Therefore, I would choose a human." (3, 74Y). For some people it even felt absurd to interact with an animal ("I imagine a better interaction (with a human) instead of such kind of puppet", 2, 73Y) or object ("in regard to the object I feel somehow stultified", 4, 61Y). A realistic appearance was preferred by most of the elderly (3 interviewees), while only 2 of them indicated they would like to have an agent "which is clearly recognizable as fictional character" (1, 62Y) and like "the comic-style... since it is no real human on the computer, I don't need a realistic image" (5, 65Y). In contrast the other three elderly, who preferred a realistic appearance, liked the fact that it came pretty close to a real human: "yes when I see this natural image... this is a human, but this figures are not (...) here I had the feeling of talking to a real human" (2, 73Y) and "A normal looking human, really normal." (3, 74Y). They stated that they could trust a realistic-looking human: "I can trust him, if I talk to him" (2, 73Y) and could even imagine some bonding to the agent: "That would be the best! In that case you could even build some kind of relation, if you interact with it longer" (4, 61Y). Furthermore, they describe a more unrealistic look as "kid's stuff" and "abnormal" (3, 74Y). The seniors did not have a major preference in regard to dimensionality (category 3). One interviewee evaluated the dimensionality as "irrelevant in the end" (1, 62Y). While two interviewees preferred the 2D agents, the other two would choose 3D.

6   Discussion

The main goals of the presented approach were (a) to explore the constructed categorization of different appearance variables for the first time as a basis for further investigations and (b) to gather first insights into age-related users' preferences of a virtual assistant's appearance. Therefore, a qualitative interview study with five seniors and six students was conducted and interviewees expressed their preferences in regard to the constructed categories of the agent's appearance. In hypothesis H1 it was proposed that users would prefer an embodied character instead of a merely speech-based system. Results indicated that this is true for elderly, while students perceived more advantages in a solely speech-based system. The elderly favored having an interlocutor to talk to and look at. Students looked at the system in a more technical way and stated that they would like the opportunity to use it without being restricted to any device (such as a computer display or smart TV). This might be due to the current developments of personal assistants on smartphones. Most of the students might be used to the mobile usage of those systems. On the other side, the elderly, who are less experienced with technical devices, might wish for an embodied character as a reference. Although most of the students did not prefer having an embodied character, this does not necessarily mean, that an embodied character would not be beneficial to them; as prior research demonstrates the potential positive effects of an embodied agent [11].In regard to research question RQ1 different virtual appearances were preferred. Most of the currently used virtual agents are humanoid agents. It became evident, that this is appropriate for seniors, since they prefer to interact with a realistic-looking human; but students mostly rejected this kind of appearance. In line with prior findings [6], students stated that they prefer a more cartoon-like appearance in order to avoid distractions from important information. While students consider the social effects of a realistic humanoid appearance as negative, the elderly do see advantages. Students are aware of the social expectations of a realistic humanoid appearance, while the elderly prefer to interact naturally with it. Thus, for elderly a more realistic looking humanoid agent seems to be the most suitable. This may either be caused by the novelty of seniors to talk with fictional, technical entities or might be due to the students' higher ability to immerse in those kinds of realities. The overall preferences of students and elderly differed in most categories. These results indicate age-related differences in the preferred visual appearance of a virtual agent. While interviewees had quite precise imaginations with regard to specie and realism of the agent, the dimensional degree (2D vs. 3D) seems to have no importance.

7   Conclusion & Future Research

Due to the qualitative method, the sample size is very small and therefore the generalizability of the results is limited. But since the interviewees' statements are highly consistent, the presented research gives interesting first insights into the preferences of potential users of a virtual daily-life assistant. Those results should be investigated in more detail in the future using quantitative methods in order to enhance generalizability. It should be investigated how interviewees would respond to different appearances and whether these responses fit to the current results of this qualitative analysis. Those quantitative experiments would compare the evaluation of the presented appearance categories systematically by producing different stimuli combinations of the various categories. These stimuli further should be evaluated from different target groups, to explore the current findings more deeply in a quantitative study with a larger sample size. Most of the examined appearance variables were investigated based solely on imaginations and without designing the virtual agent in real time. Therefore, it might be hard for the interviewees to imagine all possibilities within the different categories. Moreover, it might be one thing to imagine the perfect assistant and another to interact with it. When interviewees had to interact with virtual agents, their preferences and evaluations might have been quite different.

This approach presents a categorization of different appearance variables, to explore different appearance features more systematically than it has been done before. Qualitative interviews revealed that the species as well as the realism (especially stylization) seem to be the categories of most interest. Thus, further research should focus on these variables. Moreover, the presented findings indicate that it is highly important to study the aimed target group, since various differences between students and seniors were found. For seniors, the social and familiar point in a virtual agent's appearance is the most important feature. They like to stick as close to a real human as possible, since they desire the most natural and social interaction with this kind of appearances. In contrast, students reject those kinds of appearances, since they clearly want to distinguish between real and virtual humans. The agent should not pretend to be a real human, and students would like to be aware that it is solely a computer system which should not simulate being more social than it is. To conclude, there are first hints that age-related differences in user preferences of a virtual agent's appearance exists.

References

1. Baylor, A.L.: Promoting motivation with virtual agents and avatars: role of visual presence and appearance. Philos. Trans. R. Soc. Lond. B. Biol. Sci. 364, 3559–65 (2009). doi:10.1098/rstb.2009.0148

2. Terada, K., Jing, L., Seiji Yamada: Effects of Agent Appearance on Customer Buying Motivations on Online Shopping Sites. CHI' 15 Ext. Abstr. Apr 18-23,. 929–934 (2015)

3. Sträfling, N., Fleischer, I., Polzer, C., Leutner, D., Krämer, N.C.: Teaching learning strategies with a pedagogical agent: The effects of a virtual tutor and its appearance on learning and motivation. J. Media Psychol. 22, 73–83 (2010). doi:10.1027/1864-1105/a000010

4. Hanus, M.D., Fox, J.: Assessing the effects of gamification in the classroom: A longitudinal study on intrinsic motivation, social comparison, satisfaction, effort, and academic performance. Comput. Educ. 80, 152–161 (2015). doi:10.1016/j.compedu.2014.08.019

5. Ring, L., Utami, D., Bickmore, T.: The Right Agent for the Job ? The Effects of Agent

Visual Appearance on Task Domain. In: Intelligent Virtual Agents. pp. 374–384 (2014)

6. Koda, T., Maes, P.: Agents with faces: the effect of personification. Proc. 5th IEEE Int. Work. Robot Hum. Commun. RO-MAN'96 TSUKUBA. 189–194 (1996). doi:10.1109/ROMAN.1996.568812

7. Gulz, A., Haake, M.: Design of animated pedagogical agents - A look at their look. Int. J. Hum. Comput. Stud. 64, 322–339 (2006). doi:10.1016/j.ijhcs.2005.08.006

8. Bergmann, K., Eyssel, F., Kopp, S.: A second chance to make a first impression? how appearance and nonverbal behavior affect perceived warmth and competence of virtual agents over time. In: Intelligent Virtual Agents. pp. 126–138 (2012)

9. James, T.W., Potter, R.F., Lee, S., Kim, S., Stevenson, R.A., Lang, A.: How Realistic Should Avatars Be? J. Media Psychol. 27, 109–117 (2015). doi:10.1027/1864-1105/a000156

10. Yaghoubzadeh, R., Kramer, M., Pitsch, K., Kopp, S.: Virtual Agents as Daily Assistants for Elderly or Cognitively Impaired People. Proc. 13th Int. Conf. Intell. Virtual Agents. 8108, 91 (2013). doi:10.1007/978-3-642-40415-3_7

11. Yee, N., Bailenson, J.N., Rickertsen, K.: A meta-analysis of the impact of the inclusion and realism of human-like faces on user experiences in interfaces. Proc. SIGCHI Conf. Hum. factors Comput. Syst. - CHI '07. 1 (2007). doi:10.1145/1240624.1240626

12. Chattaraman, V., Kwon, W.-S., Gilbert, J.E., Shim, S.I.: Virtual agents in e-commerce: representational characteristics for seniors. J. Res. Interact. Mark. 5, 276–297 (2011). doi:10.1108/17505931111191492

13. Gulz, A.: Visual Design of Virtual Pedagogical Agents : Naturalism versus Stylization in Static Appearance. 6th Int. Conf. Intell. Virtual Agents, IVA 2006. 2006, 1–9 (2006). doi:10.1007/11821830_44

14. Baylor, A., Kim, Y.: Pedagogical agent design: The impact of agent realism, gender, ethnicity, and instructional role. Intell. Tutoring Syst. 592–603 (2004). doi:10.1007/978-3-540-30139-4_56

15. Brahnam, S.: Creating Physical Personalities For Agents with Faces: Modeling Trait Impressions of the Face. Proc. UM2001 Work. Attitudes, Personal. Emot. User-Adapted Interact.

16. Bickmore, T.W., Caruso, L., Clough-Gorr, K., Heeren, T.: "It"s just like you talk to a friend' relational agents for older adults. Interact. Comput. 17, 711–735 (2005). doi:10.1016/j.intcom.2005.09.002

17. Ritchie, Jane & Lewis, J.: Qualitative Reasearch Practice A Guide for Social Science Students and Reasearchers. Sage Publications, London (2003)

18. Schreier, M.: Qualitative content analysis in practice. Sage Publications (2012)

19. Mayring, P.: Qualitative Inhaltsanalyse. In: Handbuch Qualitative Forschung in der Psychologie. pp. 601–613 (2010)

20. Landis, J.R., Koch, G.G.: The Measurement of Observer Agreement for Categorical Data. Int. Biometric Soc. 33, 159–174 (2008). doi:10.2307/2529310

Towards Reasoned Modality Selection
in an Embodied Conversation Agent

Carla Ten-Ventura[1]✉, Roberto Carlini[1],
Stamatia Dasiopoulou[1], Gerard Llorach Tó[1], and Leo Wanner[1,2]✉

[1]Universitat Pompeu Fabra, [2]ICREA
Barcelona, Spain
email: first_name.last_name@upf.edu

Abstract. We present work in progress on (verbal, facial, and gestural) modality selection in an embodied multilingual and multicultural conversation agent. In contrast to most of the recent proposals, which consider non-verbal behavior as being superimposed on and/or derived from the verbal modality, we argue for a holistic model that assigns modalities to individual content elements in accordance with semantic and contextual constraints as well as with cultural and personal characteristics of the addressee. Our model is thus in line with the SAIBA framework, although methodological differences become apparent at a more fine-grained level of realization.

1 Introduction

In order to appear natural and thus be accepted by human interlocutors, embodied conversation agents are expected to appropriately use language, facial expressions and gestures. A considerable number of works addresses the two aspects of the problem: (i) when to select what modality, and (ii) how to synchronize the different modalities such that the overall (verbal and non-verbal) behavior of the agent appears coherent and natural. In the recent past, the problem has often been restricted to planning of the non-verbal behavior of an agent [7, 19]. In this case, the verbal mode is assumed to be already given, either as speech (i.e., acoustic stream) [1, 12] or in terms of written statements [20]. To plan the facial expressions and gestures, the speech respectively written statements are then analyzed and, depending on the identified linguistic and/or content features [18, 4, 5], specific facial expressions and gestures are assigned to acoustic / linguistic (word sequence) segments. While this strategy seems appropriate when an off-the-shelf verbal communication generator is used or when the agent is supposed to follow a predefined already spelled-out script, it is counter-intuitive from a holistic perspective on dynamic communication: facial expressions and gestures are not simply an add-on to language. Rather, as argued in theoretical studies [10, 13, 14, 9] and as already assumed in the early days of the research on conversation agents [3], all modalities play together in order to produce a natural communication move of the agent. For instance, in an affirmative act, the agent may nod, smile and say *Yes, that's correct!* or simply nod; to indicate

J. Beskow et al. (Eds.): IVA 2017, LNAI 10498, pp. 423-432, 2017.
DOI 10.1007/978-3-319-67401-8_52

a location, it may say *Over there* and/or produce a deictic gesture; to express an intense rejection, it may say *I don't like it* and signal via a facial expression the intensity, or choose the verbal mode to communicate the intensity as well (*I don't like it at all!*); and so on. Such a holistic view on the planning of a move is required, for instance, in the context of a flexible embodied multilingual and multicultural conversation (i.e., dialogue) agent as targeted in the KRISTINA Project. This agent (henceforth referred to as "KRISTINA") is expected to be able to flexibly act in different contexts as a basic care assistant, health care adviser or social companion of humans; see [23] for an overview.

In multimodal dialogue and virtual agent research, several proposals have been made towards a holistic *fission* model. Cf., e.g., [6, 22] for proposals on the dialogue side, which tend to assign a specific modality or a combination thereof to moves or to move elements in predefined dialogue scripts. The problem with these proposals is that when broader conversation topics are to be covered and the agent needs to count with spontaneous interventions of the human (as is our case), predefined dialogue scripts are not adequate. In the context of virtual agent research, the most influential proposal has been the SAIBA-framework[1]. SAIBA foresees three stages of behavior realization (see, e.g., [21]): Intent Planning, Behavior Planning, and Behavior Realization. Modality selection is foreseen to take place in the Behavior Planning (BP) module. However, BP has to span between abstract *Functional Markup Language* communicative intention representations as output by the Intent Planning (see [2] for examples) to a very detailed synchronization alignment between specific modality realizations. We believe that it is necessary to separate modality assignment from synchronization of the specific modality realizations since both tasks are situated at very different levels of abstraction and require different types of information.

In what follows, we present work in progress on a holistic versatile modality selection model that is embedded into the multimodal dialogue architecture of the KRISTINA agent. Section 2 situates modality selection in this architecture. In Section 3 then our approach to modality selection and realization is discussed. Section 4, finally, draws some conclusions and discusses our ongoing and future work on modality selection.

2   Modality Selection in KRISTINA

Figure 1 displays the part of the KRISTINA architecture into which our modality selection model (marked in the figure by a box) is embedded. KRISTINA is a knowledge-based agent. The semantic structures produced by the multimodal communication analysis modules (not shown in Figure 1) are projected onto genuine ontological (OWL) structures, fused and integrated by the knowledge integration (KI) service into the knowledge base (KB). Furthermore, a dedicated search engine feeds into the KI service background multimodal information from the web and relevant curated information sources in order to ensure that the

---

[1] http://www.mindmakers.org/projects/saiba/wiki

agent is knowledgeable about the topics raised by the human counterpart and to facilitate the realization of flexible reasoning-based dialogue strategies.

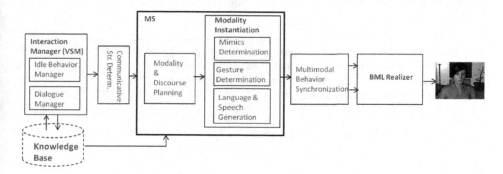

Fig. 1. Situating modality selection in the KRISTINA architecture

Modality Selection (MS) receives input from two sources: the modules controlled by the Interaction Manager and the addressee (or human conversation counterpart) profile, which is stored in the KB. The Interaction Manager is embedded in the *Visual Scene Maker* (VSM) framework [8]. While the original purpose of VSM has been to support the definition of the interactive behavior of virtual characters, we use it, on the one hand, as a communication shell between the dialogue management module and the modules it interacts with, and, on the other hand, for modeling the idle behavior of the agent. The dialogue manager (DM) chooses the best system reaction (in terms of ontological structures), in accordance with the analyzed user move, the user's emotion and culture and the recent dialogue history. For this purpose, it solicits first from the KI module possible reactions that are reasoned over the KB. In other words, in contrast to most of the state-of-the-art DM models, the determination of the turn of the system is distributed between a high level control DM and a reasoning KB module; see [15] for details. On its way to the MS module, the DM output is enriched by *communicative* labels. The communicative labels mark which parts of the content are considered to be the core of the trasmitted message, which are to be highlighted, which are to be backgrounded, etc. Their distribution depends on the communicative intention of the agent. So far, we mark only the core of the message and the "topic" on which this core elaborates. Note that in linguistic terms, the core of a message is referred to as *rheme* (the content that the speaker aims to transmit, i.e., the essential part) and the topic of the core as *theme* (to what the transmitted content refers). For instance, in the statement *You look worried today*, the theme is *You* (the statement is about 'you') and rheme is *look worried today*. Theme and rheme are reflected by prosody and body gestures of a speaker. Several works on behavior modeling thus analyze the given verbal part of an agent move to detect theme and rheme in order to introduce, e.g., gestures or pitch accents to mark the rheme; see, e.g., [18, 20, 4]. Consider, for illustration, an example of the APML codification of rheme, in this case, in the early Greta agent in Figure 2: it is assigned to the string *Good morning Mr. Smith*, which is further enriched by prosodic markers.

```
<turnallocation type="take"> <performative type="greet">
<rheme>Good<emphasis x-pitchaccent="Hstar">morning
</emphasis> Mr Smith.<boundary type="LL"/></rheme>
</performative></turnallocation>
```

Fig. 2. Codification of a sentence in APML (example taken from [4])

This retrospective analysis is obsolete in our design. Furthermore, the assignment of communicative labels to content elements (instead of linguistic constructions) has the advantage that they can be used and realized by each individual modality independently, by means that are available to this modality. For instance, in the case of the verbal modality, the theme/rheme tags are used to shape and later linearize the syntactic structure and to derive prosodic markers. In the case of gestures, they are used, e.g., to determine beat gestures.

Figure 3 shows a sample input structure provided to MS, i.e., the DM output structure after it has been enriched by the thematicity tags.[2]

:sa1 a la:SystemAction ;	:stmt1 la:context (:like1 a onto:Like) ;
dialogue:contains :da1 .	la:agent (:Alp a onto:CareRecipient).
:da1 a dialogue:Declare ;	:Alp thematicity:theme true.
dialogue:arousal 0.5 ;	:stmt2 la:context :like1 ;
dialogue:valence 1.0 .	la:theme (:ins1 a onto:Baklawa) .
dialogue:semContent :sit1, :sit2.	:ins1 thematicity:rheme true.
:sit1 a la:Situation ;	:stmt3 la:context :like1
la:contains :stmt1, :stmt2 .	la:manner (:ins2 a onto:Always);
:sit2 a la:Situation ;	:ins2 thematicity:rheme true.
la:contains :stmt2, :stmt3 .	:like1 thematicity:rheme true.

Fig. 3. Input structure to Modality Selection

The structure contains the following types of information: 1. name of the dialogue act (`Declare`), 2. the content that is to be communicated by the agent (under 'dialogue:semContent'), 3. valence (of the agent), 4. arousal (of the agent), and 5. thematicity (theme/rheme) labels. It encodes the facts that a care recip-

---

[2] Note that we use the Turtle notation (`https://www.w3.org/TR/turtle/`), such that, e.g., ":da1 a dialogue:Declare" means that ':da1' is an instance of the dialogue act class 'Declare').

ient Alp likes Baklawa, and that he always used to like it. Alp is thus the theme and the other content elements constitute the rheme.

From the addressee (or user) profile, MS uses a series of features: culture to which the addressee belongs (Central European, South European, Northern, ...), age, gender, personality (extroverted or introverted), proximity to the agent (close, familiar, or distant), etc. This allows us to adapt the communication of the agent to its conversation counterpart, e.g., in terms of the quantity, distribution and type of gestures and mimics.

Modality Selection (MS) is performed in KRISTINA in two stages. In the first stage, the modalities are first assigned to the content elements in the received input structure (note that a structure can consist of one single element, and that to a given element more than one modality can be assigned) and then related in terms of a discourse structure.[3] In the second stage, the modalities are instantiated, i.e., for each modality it is determined how it will be realized (smile, head turn, specific verbalization, etc.). The first stage is processed by the *Modality & Discourse Planning* module; the second stage by the *Modality Instantiation* module.

The output of the Modality Instantiation module is fed into the *Behavior Synchronization* module, which is the lean version of the *Behavior Planner* in the sense of the SAIBA-framework (it focuses only on the synchronization of the modalities) and, which, in its turn, passes its output to the BML realizer (again, in the sense of SAIBA). Let us focus now, however, on the two stages of modality selection.

3 Getting the Multimodal Message Across

Prior to the choice of a specific realization of a modality to express some content, as, for instance, *Hello!* (rather than *Good evening, Sir!*) for the verbal modality of greeting, or head shaking for the gesture modality of negation (either to emphasize the verbal *No* or as a sole act), we must first choose the appropriate modalit(y/ies) for each content element provided by the DM. The nature of both types of choices is rather different, as far as cognitive and communicative criteria are concerned. Furthermore, it is desirable from the theoretical[4] and methodological viewpoints to treat language, gesture and mimics generation analogously. Thus, in language generation, a content structure is projected (preferrably in a cascade of transitions) onto one of its possible linguistic realizations in accordance with linguistic means that are not known by the modality selection. In the same way, a content structure should be projected, e.g., onto a concrete facial expression respectively gesture by separate modules, without that modality selection has to know how rich the facial expression/gesture repertoire of the facial

---

[3] While the dialogue manager plans the structure of the discourse between dialogue acts, it does not intervene in the definition of the internal discourse structure of a dialogue act/move because this would require a "look-ahead" for the acquisition of information on the realization of the move.

[4] Cf. the references to the theoretical studies in the Introduction

expression/gesture realizer (in our case, the virtual character) is. Therefore, we deal with modality selection and modality determination separately in different submodules. On the other hand, when we decide, for instance, that a greeting is to be expressed by a verbal statement and a gesture, we need to already relate both expressions to each other (whether one is to be considered as an emphasis of the other, as an "elaboration", etc.). In other words, we need to establish the internal discourse structure of the move of the agent. As a consequence, we deal with the modality assignment and internal discourse structure determination in one module.

3.1 Modality and discourse planning

The output of the *Modality & Discourse Planning* module looks as shown in Figure 4

:sa1 a la:SystemAction ;	:stmt1 la:context (:like1 a onto:Like) ;
dialogue:contains :da1, **fe1** ; .	la:agent (:Alp a onto:CareRecipient).
ms:verbal :da1 .	:Alp thematicity:theme true.
ms:facialExpression :fe1 .	:stmt2 la:context :like1 ;
:da1 a dialogue:Declare ;	la:rheme (:ins1 a onto:Baklawa) .
dialogue:arousal 0.5 ;	:ins1 thematicity:rheme true.
dialogue:valence 1.0 .	:stmt3 la:context :like1
dialogue:semContent :sit1, :sit2.	la:manner (:ins2 a onto:Always);
:sit1 a la:Situation ;	:ins2 thematicity:rheme true.
la:contains :stmt1, :stmt2 .	:like1 thematicity:rheme true.
:sit2 a la:Situation ;	**:fe1 a ms:JoyfulExpression ;**
la:contains :stmt2, :stmt3 ;	**ms:hasIntensity "high" ;**
rst:restatement :sit1 .	**rst:parallel :da1 .**

Fig. 4. Output structure of Modality Selection

As we can observe, the modalities have already been assigned to the content elements (cf. 'ms:verbal :da1' and 'ms:facialExpression :fe1'). In what follows, we outline how this is achieved.

Modality planning. The assignment of the modalities to the individual content chunks is currently rule-based. Consider, for instance, a fragment of a rule, formulated for transparencey in pseudo-code XML format in Figure 5. This rule assigns to the whole dialogue act an intense joyful facial expression (which will be mapped during the determination of the facial expression onto a broad smile; see below) if, for instance, KRISTINA tells a care giver that the elderly Turkish person in question, who is from the region of Ankara, likes Baklawa. Note that in order to deduce the required information, the agent needs to reason.

```
<conditions>
    <da>Declare<id>'id1'</id> </da>
    <topic>eating_habits</topic>
    <CareRecipient><age>elderly></CareRecipient>
    <theme> type(theme) == 'food' ∧ type(food) == 'traditional' ∧
        region(food) == origin(CareRecipient)</theme>
</conditions>
<modality> <id>'id1'</id>
    <fe> JoyfulExpression <intensity>high</intensity></fe>
    <valence> valence(id1)</valence><arousal>arousal(id1)</arousal></fe>
</modality>
```

Fig. 5. Fragment of a mode selection rule

Intra-move multimodal discourse structure planning. Given that in KRI-STINA there is no "ground" modality (as, e.g., language in many of the previous works) to which then the other modalities are assigned (and thus synchronized), but, rather, all three modalities are used as equal and assigned to content elements in the same dialogue act quasi independently from each other, they need to be related in order to form a coherent discourse. This is especially of relevance if a dialogue act contains several statements (see also Footnote 1 on the competence of the dialogue manager). Then, apart from the discourse alignment between the modalities, a discourse structure between the verbal elements must be defined. For this purpose, we explore a discourse structuring technique that originates from text generation [17]. The technique is based on the *Rhetorical Structure Theory* (RST) [11]. Apart from the conventional set of RST relations (such as ELABORATION, CAUSE, JUSTIFICATION, etc.), the relation SIMULTANE-ITY is to be used. The relations hold between *elementary discourse units* (EDU) (usually, individual facts) to which one or several modalities are assigned. In the output structure above, the discourse relation tag is introduced as 'rst:parallel'.

3.2 Modality Instantiation

As described above, modality selection determines the modality of each content element or EDU, but it does not determine the specific implementation of the modality, i.e., it does not instantiate it. For instance, in the rule example above, it is determined that the facial expression has to be a intense and joyful, but not that it is a broad smile. Each modality is instantiated separately and then passed to the *Multimodal Behavior Synchronization* module, where the instantiations in different modalities are synchronized in terms of the *Behavior Markup Language* (BML) [21], drawing upon the temporal conditions imposed by the relations of the RST discourse structure. The output is a BML description that is passed to the BML Realizer, where the instantiated gestures and facial expressions are generated, in synchrony with the language uttered by the agent.

The realization of the verbal modality is carried out by a full-fledged multilingual text generator [16]. The facial expressions and gestures that can be handled by the character are specified in the so-called *mimicon* respectively *gesticon*, where to each facial expression / gesture its high level description features as provided by the MS are assigned. Consider, for illustration, a sample entry in the *mimicon* Figure 6.

```
<description>
    <fe>JoyfulExpression<intensity>high</intensity></fe>
    <valence>1.0</valence><arousal>0.5</arousal></description>
<mimics> broad_smile</mimics>
```

Fig. 6. Sample entry of the *mimicon*

4 Conclusions and Future Work

We have presented work in progress on dynamic modality selection in embodied conversational agents. Being dynamic, i.e., guided by contextual, content and addressee profile features, it is different from most of the approaches to modality handling in multimodal dialogue systems, which tend to assign modalities *a priori* to predefined dialogue scripts. At the first glance, it is similar to the design of the *Plan Enricher* in the MagiCster project [4] in that it receives its input structure from the dialogue manager and draws upon a knowledge base. However, unlike the Plan Enricher, which provides an APML structure in which, e.g., the verbal statements are already predefined, and the mimicry fully spelled out and synchronized, we delegate language generation to a dedicated language generator and the mimicry and gestures realization to the BML Realizer. We also separate modality selection from intra-move multimodal discourse structure planning and modality instantiation. This has the advantage that the model is more generic. Our model can be considered as a proposal for an alternative realization of the Behavior Planner in the SAIBA-framework. Instead of dealing with the problem of the projection of very abstract communicative intention representations onto specific behavior realizations, we propose to divide the problem into a series of subproblems, each of which is dealt with in a separate submodule: (i) modality selection, (ii) discourse planning, (iii) modality instantiation, and (iv) modality synchronization.

Our illustrations draw upon the current rule-based prototypical implementation of the module. This implementation takes so far only a limited number of contextualized conditions into account and makes only limited use of the reasoning and inference potential of KRISTINA's reasoning engine. Also, it ignores the fact that several rules that target the selection of the same modality may overlap in their conditions and thus lead to a conflict during modality realization. This is excluded within the current simplified model, but cannot be ruled out in a more complex model. In the future, we plan to complete the development of the proposed model, including a mechanism for rule conflict resolution, and also to learn modality selection using supervised learning techniques. For this purpose, we are in the process of annotating a corpus of multimodal spoken conversation recordings with modality and valence/arousal information. Furthermore, a quantitative and qualitative evaluation is about to be carried out in order to assess the performance of our modality selection strategy compared to the state of the art.

Acknowledgements

The presented work is funded by the European Commission as part of the H2020 Programme, under the contract number 645012–RIA. Many thanks to the three reviewers for their very helpful comments and suggestions.

References

1. Albrecht, I., Haber, J., Seidel, H.P., Earnshaw, R.: Automatic generation of non-verbal facial expressions from speech. In: Proceedings of the International Computer Graphics Conference. pp. 283–293 (2002)
2. Cafaro, A., Vilhjalmsson, H., Bickmore, T., Heylen, D., Pelachaud, C.: Representing Communicative Functions in SAIBA with a Unified Function Markup Language. In: Intelligent Virtual Agents. pp. 81–94. Springer Verlag, Heidelberg (26 Aug 2014)
3. Cassell, J., Bickmore, T., Billinghurst, M., Campbell, L., Chang, K., Vilhjámsson, H., Yan, H.: Embodiment in conversational interfaces: Rea. In: Proceedings of CHI '99. pp. 520–527. ACM (1999)
4. De Carolis, B., Pelachaud, C., Poggi, I., Steedman., M.: APML, a mark-up language for believable behavior generation. In: Prendinger, H., Ishizuka, M. (eds.) Lifelike Characters. Tools, Affective Functions and Applications. Springer Verlag (2004)
5. Endrass, B., Rehm, M., André, E.: Planning Small Talk behavior with cultural influences for multiagent systems. Computer Speech and Language 25, pp. 158-174 (2011)
6. Foster, M.: Interleaved preparation and output in the comic fission module. In: Proceedings of the ACL Workshop on Software. Ann Arbor (2005)
7. Freigang, F., Kopp, S.: This is whats important – using speech and gesture to create focus in multimodal utterance. In: Lecture Notes in Computer Science, pp. 96–109 (2016)
8. Gebhard, P., Mehlmann, G.U., Kipp, M.: Visual SceneMaker: A Tool for Authoring Interactive Virtual Characters. Journal of Multimodal User Interfaces: Interacting with Embodied Conversational Agents, Springer-Verlag 6(1-2),pp. 3–11 (2012)
9. Kendon, A.: Gesture. Visible action as utterance. Cambridge University Press, Cambridge (2004)
10. Lock, A. (ed.): Action, gesture, and symbol: The emergence of language. Academic Press, London & New York (1978)
11. Mann, W.C., Thompson, S.A.: Rhetorical structure theory: Toward a functional theory of text organization. Text - Interdisciplinary Journal for the Study of Discourse 8(3),pp. 243–281 (November 2009)
12. Marsella, S., Xu, Y., Lhommet, M., Feng, A., Scherer, S., Shapirok, A.: Virtual character performance from speech. In: SCA '13 Proceedings of the 12th ACM SIGGRAPH/Eurographics Symposium on Computer Animation. pp. 25–35 (2013)

13. McNeill, D.: Hand and mind: What gestures reveal about thought. University of Chicago Press, Chicago (1992)
14. McNeill, D. (ed.): Language and gesture. Cambridge University Press, Cambridge (2000)
15. Meditskos, G., Dasiopoulou, S., Pragst, L., Ultes, S., Vrochidis, S., Kompatsiaris, I., Wanner, L.: Towards an Ontology-Driven Adaptive Dialogue Framework. In: Proceedings of the 1st International Workshop on Multimedia Analysis and Retrieval for Multimodal Interaction (MARMI). pp. 15–20. ACM, New York (2016)
16. Mille, S., Burga, A., Carlini, R., Wanner, L.: FORGe at SemEval-2017 Task 9: Deep sentence generation based on a sequence of graph transducers. In: Proceedings of SemEval '17. Association for Computational Linguistics, Vancouver (2017)
17. Moore, J., Paris, C.: Planning Text for Advisory Dialogues. Capturing Intentional and Rhetorical Information. Computational Linguistics 19(4), pp. 1–46 (1993)
18. Pelachaud, C., Badler, N.I., Steedman, M.: Generating facial expressions for speech. Cognitive Science 20, pp. 1–46 (1996)
19. Quintas, J., Menezes, P., Dias, J.: Auto-Adaptive interactive systems for active and assisted living applications. In: IFIP Advances in Information and Communication Technology, pp. 161–168 (2016)
20. de Rosis, F., Pelachaud, C., Poggi, I., Carofiglio, V., De Carolis, N.: From Greta's Mind to her Face: Modeling the Dynamics of Affective States in a Conversational Embodied Agent. International Journal of Human-Computer Studies 59(1–2), pp. 81–118 (2003)
21. Vilhjalmsson, H., Cantelmo, N., Cassell, J., Chafai, N.E., Kipp, M., Kopp, S., Mancini, M., Marsella, S., Marshall, A., Pelachaud, C., Ruttkay, Z., Thórisson, K., van Welbergen, H., van der Werf, R.: The behavior markup language: Recent developments and challenges. In: Intelligent Virtual Agents. pp. 99–111. Springer Verlag, Heidelberg (17 Sep 2007)
22. Walker, M., Whittaker, S., Stent, A., Maloor, P., Moore, J., Johnston, M., Vasireddy, G.: Generation and evaluation of user tailored responses in multimodal dialogue. Cognitive Science 28(5), pp. 811–840 (2004)
23. Wanner, L., André, E., Blat, J., Dasiopoulou, S., Farrùs, M., Fraga, T., Kamateri, E., Lingenfelser, F., Llorach, G., Martínez, O., Meditskos, G., Mille, S., Minker, W., Pragst, L., Schiller, D., Stam, A., Stellingwerff, L., Sukno, F., Vieru, B., Vrochidis, S.: KRISTINA: A Knowledge-Based Virtual Conversation Agent. In: Demazeau, Y., Davidsson, P., Vale, Z., Bajo, J. (eds.) Advances in Cyber-Physical Multi-Agent Systems. The PAAMS Collection – 15th International Conference, PAAMS 2017. Springer, Heidelberg (2017)

Lay Causal Explanations of Human vs. Humanoid Behavior

Sam Thellman ✉, Annika Silvervarg & Tom Ziemke

Department of Computer and Information Science, Linköping University, Linköping
{sam.thellman, annika.silvervarg, tom.ziemke}@liu.se

Abstract. The present study used a questionnaire-based method for investigating people's interpretations of behavior exhibited by a person and a humanoid robot, respectively. Participants were given images and verbal descriptions of different behaviors and were asked to judge the plausibility of seven causal explanation types. Results indicate that human and robot behavior are explained similarly, but with some significant differences, and with less agreement in the robot case.

Keywords: Human-robot interaction, attribution, behavior explanation

1   Introduction

There is ample evidence that people interpret and explain the behavior of robots and other artificial agents using common-sense folk-psychological concepts such as beliefs, desires, intentions, and emotions [1, 2, 3]. Consider a robot bumping into a person. Such behavior could be explained as caused by a *goal* to bump into people, by a *temporary state* of sensory confusion, by a *behavioral disposition* from bad design, or by an *event* outside the robot's control (e.g. a slippery floor). Mental state attributions fundamentally shape people's interaction with others in that they set the course for how people perceive and respond to behavior. So far, however, there has been very little comparative research on how people actually interpret the behavior of different types of artificial agents, and how this compares to human-human social interaction. This study is intended to make a small contribution towards closing that gap by investigating people's lay causal explanations of human vs. humanoid behavior.

Fritz Heider, the founder of attribution theory, suggested that people have internalized and mastered a causal network of formal connections between concepts which underlies their social understanding of the world [4]. Böhm and Pfister recently proposed and empirically validated a model of people's lay causal explanations of human behavior, the *causal explanation network* (CEN) model (cf. Fig. 1), which suggests that people's explanations follow a specific inference pattern [5]. The model is based on previous attribution research and specifies seven cognitive categories that are assumed to be used for both behavior encoding and explanation: *goals, intentional actions, action outcomes, temporary states, dispositions, uncontrollable events,* and *stimulus attributes.* The categories are related to each other through "inference rules"

© Springer International Publishing AG 2017

J. Beskow et al. (Eds.): IVA 2017, LNAI 10498, pp. 433-436, 2017.

DOI 10.1007/978-3-319-67401-8_53

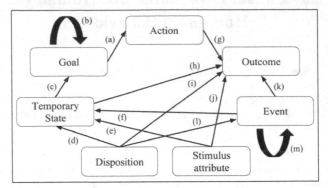

Fig. 1. Behavior and explanation types (boxes) and inference rules (arrows) in the Causal Explanation Network (CEN) model. Adapted from Böhm & Pfister [5].

which are assumed to reflect relations between behaviors and causal explanations (see arrows in Fig. 1).

2   Method

Sixty university students (mean age = 23, SD = 3.5 yrs., 80% women) individually completed a survey concerning how people interpret and explain behaviors. Participants in one experimental condition were presented with images of human behavior while participants in a second condition were presented with images of humanoid robot behavior (cf. Fig 2). The selection of behaviors used as experimental stimuli was based on the CEN model which distinguishes between four behavior types: *actions*, *outcomes*, *states*, and *events* [5]. To deal with positivity bias, i.e., the tendency to make different attributions for positive and negative events [6], one desirable and one undesirable behavior were presented for each behavior type. This resulted in eight individual behavior stimuli: positive action (A+): "Ellis mops the floor", negative action (A−): "Ellis lies about having cooked the dinner", positive outcome (O+): "Ellis makes a fantastic cake", negative outcome (O−): "Ellis burns the cake", positive event (E+): "Ellis gets tipped by the dinner guests", negative event (E−): "Ellis breaks a glass", positive state (S+): "Ellis is happy to be in the kitchen", negative state (S−): "Ellis is frustrated over cooking".

Fig. 2. Stimuli for the negative outcome, "Ellis burns the cake", in human and robot conditions.

Participants were asked to judge the plausibility of seven causes as explanations for the eight behaviors on a 7-degree ordinal scale ranging from "not at all" to "completely". The seven causal explanation types were derived from the CEN model and were given in the form *"Rate how plausible it is that the cause of Ellis' behavior is X"*, where X could be a *conscious goal*, an *action*, an *outcome*, an *uncontrollable event*, a *temporary state* (psychological or physical), a *disposition, or* an *attribute of someone or something in Ellis' environment*. The experimental conditions did not statistically significantly differ with regard to participant age, gender or self-assessed technical competence. Each participant gave written informed consent prior to participation.

3   Results

Participants' plausibility-ratings of behavior explanations statistically significantly differed between conditions in 8 out of 58 cases, as shown in **Table 1**. We note that *disposition* was rated as a more plausible cause for human behavior than humanoid behavior in 5 out of 8 cases, and that there were no statistically significant differences between participants' ratings of the positive event and negative action when enacted by the human versus the robot. Kendall's W was run to assess inter-rater reliability of participants' judgements in human and robot conditions. Agreement was higher in the human condition, $W = .391, p < .0005$, than in the robot condition, $W = .294, p < .0005$.

Table 1. Judged plausibility of causal explanation types (rows) for human (left value in cell) and robot (right value in cell) behaviors (columns) with statistically significant differences at $p < .05$ marked in inverted colors.

	A+	O+	E+	S+	A−	O−	E−	S−
Goal	5.9/6.0	6.6/5.8	5.3/5.4	5.1/4.8	5.9/5.4	1.5/2.3	1.5/2.4	2.4/3.3
Action	6.2/5.9	6.0/5.7	4.7/5.3	5.0/4.6	5.6/5.5	4.7/4.3	4.7/4.9	4.8/4.0
Outcome	5.5/5.3	6.1/5.7	6.0/5.8	5.3/5.0	5.8/5.5	5.9/5.6	5.8/5.3	5.9/5.7
Event	2.7/2.3	2.3/2.1	3.4/3.0	2.6/3.3	2.3/2.9	4.1/3.7	4.7/3.7	4.6/3.7
Temp. state	2.9/3.0	2.7/3.3	3.1/3.1	4.8/4.3	3.9/3.9	3.1/3.8	3.8/3.5	5.1/4.6
Disposition	3.6/3.3	4.5/3.1	4.2/4.0	5.2/4.0	5.1/4.8	3.5/2.4	4.0/2.7	4.2/3.3
Stimulus attr.	3.4/4.9	4.0/4.0	5.2/5.1	3.8/4.6	3.7/4.5	3.3/4.0	3.5/3.7	3.7/4.5

4   Conclusion & Discussion

The seven causal explanation types were judged to be similarly plausible for human and robot behaviors in 50 out of 58 cases. This indicates that people perceive the causes of human and humanoid robot behavior similarly, at least given the particular participant demographic, scenario, human actor and robot featured in the study presented here. This can be taken to suggest that people rely on a common-sense conceptual framework of mind in judgments of robot behavior similar to those that has been studied and modeled in the human case [e.g., 4, 5, 7].

There were, however, a few notable differences between the two conditions. Firstly, we observed a trend in the data indicating that participants judged *dispositions* as generally more likely to be causes of human behavior. Robots were, for example, considered less likely to have dispositions that would cause them to be happy to be in the kitchen, to make fantastic cake, to burn a cake, or to break glasses. This raises the question whether people think of robots as less likely to have dispositions in the human sense, or as having less stable dispositions as humans, or whether people see robot dispositions as less efficacious in causing behavior than human dispositions. Secondly, we observed lower agreement among the participants judging causes of robot behaviors compared to judgements of human behavior. This might be taken to suggest that the influence of a shared folk-psychological framework is weaker in people's judgements of artificial behavior as compared to human behavior. While the present study does not provide answers as to why this effect occurred we suggest this as a future research topic.

We hope that the relatively simple methodology used in this initial study of human versus humanoid behavior can be applied and developed further to contribute to addressing the broader and more fundamental question of how people's social interactions with different types of both natural and artificial autonomous agents – such as robots, virtual agents, or automated cars – are effected by folk-psychological causal explanations of observed behavior, and to what degree the underlying mechanisms overlap or differ for different types of natural and artificial agents.

References

1. Sciutti, A., Ansuini, C., Becchio, C., & Sandini, G.: Investigating the ability to read others' intentions using humanoid robots. *Frontiers in psychology, 6*, 1362 (2015)
2. Wykowska, A., Chaminade, T., & Cheng, G.: Embodied artificial agents for understanding human social cognition. *Phil. Trans. R. Soc. B, 371*(1693), 20150375 (2016)
3. Dennett, D. C.: Intentional systems. *The Journal of Philosophy, 68*(4), 87-106 (1971)
4. Heider, F.: The Psychology of Interpersonal Relations. Mansfield Center, CT, Martino Publishing (1958)
5. Böhm, G., & Pfister, H. R.: How people explain their own and others' behavior: a theory of lay causal explanations. *Frontiers in psychology, 6*, 139 (2015)
6. Mezulis, A. H., Abramson, L. Y., Hyde, J. S., & Hankin, B. L.: Is there a universal positivity bias in attributions? A meta-analytic review of individual, developmental, and cultural differences in the self-serving attributional bias. *Psychological bulletin, 130*(5), 711 (2004)
7. Malle, B. F., & Knobe, J.: The folk concept of intentionality. *Journal of Experimental Social Psychology, 33*(2), 101-121 (1997)

Generating Situation-Based Motivational Feedback in a PTSD E-health System

Myrthe Tielman[1]✉, Mark Neerincx[1],[2], and Willem-Paul Brinkman[1]

[1] Delft University of Technology, Netherlands,
`m.l.tielman@tudelft.nl`
[2] TNO Perceptual and Cognitive Systems, Netherlands

Abstract. Motivating users is an important task for virtual agents in behaviour chance support systems. In this study we present a system which generates motivational statements based on situation type, aimed at a virtual agent for Post-Traumatic Stress Disorder therapy. Using input from experts (n=13), we built a database containing what categories of motivation to use based on therapy progress and current user trust. A statistical analysis confirmed that we can significantly predict the category of statements to use. Using the database, we present a system that generates motivational statements. Because this system is based on expert data, it has the advantage of not needing large amounts of patient data. We envision that by basing the content directly on expert knowledge, the virtual agent can motivate users as a human expert would.

Keywords: e-health, virtual agent, PTSD, motivation, behavior change

1 Introduction

Virtual agents are often included in behaviour change support systems (BCSS) [3], and motivating users is on of their important functions. But given the diversity of situations it is not always exactly clear what this motivation should entail. However, human experts work in many domains of behaviour change, and they harbour a wealth of knowledge and experience in motivating people. In this paper we present a feedback system for a virtual agent operating in a Post-Traumatic Stress Disorder (PTSD) e-health system. This feedback system can generate motivational comments based on patient situation. It does this with the use of a database containing motivational statements with corresponding likelihood rates, which was developed using human expert knowledge.

Many e-health systems can be classified as BCSS, aiming to promote healthy behaviour and discourage habits detrimental to health. Systems exist for physical health[4], but many are also aimed at mental health disorders [3]. Motivation is important in such systems, but difficult to understand both in terms of construct and the question of how to improve it. Self-determination theory (SDT) separates the concepts intrinsic and extrinsic motivation, the former being more effective [1]. A sub-theory of SDT states that external motivation can be internalized though. For this the concept of *relatedness* is important, if a person feels related to the one offering the external motivation, it is more likely to be internalized.

The concept of relatedness might explain why a virtual agent can be more successful in changing behaviour than a purely text-based interface [8]. This

© Springer International Publishing AG 2017

J. Beskow et al. (Eds.): IVA 2017, LNAI 10498, pp. 437-440, 2017.

DOI 10.1007/978-3-319-67401-8_54

implies that virtual agents successfully motivate people even by being present. However, they might be able to improve motivation even more. Interviews with therapists reveal that motivational statements are important for a virtual agent to use during therapy [5]. Although theoretical models exist on how to improve motivation [2], short motivational statements are commonly not included. One study into statements was done by studying human-human interactions and translating these into a motivating system [4]. However, a virtual agent does not always operate in the same real-life situation as a human, and will usually have more limited input from the user. Moreover, this method of studying real life interactions is very data-intensive. In this paper we therefore present a method wherein human therapists are presented with the same information a virtual agent would have. Using their input as a base, we developed a system that generates personalized motivational feedback based on situation.

2 Feedback system

The vision of our motivational feedback system is that it offers the right type of feedback depending on the situation of the patient at that point in time. The situation is described firstly by symptom progression, which can be indicated by the trend (up,stable,down) of scores on the PTSD-check-list (PCL), a short questionnaire measuring PTSD symptoms [7]. The second factor in a patients situation is their current trust in the outcome of therapy. We envision that in different situations, different motivational statement will be appropriate. To decide which statements will be used, the system uses the likelihood ratios of statement categories. The number of statements also depends on the situation, and the exact wording of the statement can be chosen from the database containing the different sentences used by experts. This full process is shown in Fig. 1.

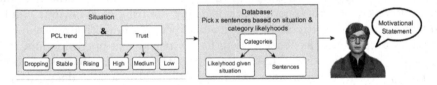

Fig. 1. Vision of the system, generationg motivational feedback based on situation.

Data collection

A survey was held among psychotherapists (n=13, 5 male, 8 female) from six different clinics to study what motivational feedback a virtual agent should give in what situation. They were presented with 18 situations describing the trust the patient had in the therapy at that point in text and a graph depicting PCL scores. Six different graphs were shown, either showing dropping scores, a stable score, or rising scores. The therapists were asked to write down what they would say to the patient in this situation to increase their trust in the therapy and their motivation to continue.

Results

For categorization all answers were split into different statements, divided based on subject. This resulted in between 1 and 8 statements per feedback answer, 844 in total. All statements were categorized based on topic using categories that arose during this process. A random subset of 32 statements was coded by a second coder, interrater reliability was substantial ($\kappa=0.73$, $p<.001$). After categorization, all categories with less than 10 instances were removed and statements were either only analysed with their super-category, or left out entirely. This resulted in 97% of statements being included when taking the resulting 12 super-categories, and 91% when taking the total of 20 categories.

The data was analysed with R version 3.3. For every given answer in each situation, it was marked whether a category type was used in one of the statements or not. A multi-level analysis was done with participant as random intercept, and the variables of PCL, trust and category type, as well as their interaction effects as fixed effects. This analysis showed that category type ($F(49,11238)=101.43$, $p<.001$), as well as the interaction between this factor and both trust ($F(98,11238)=3.68$, $p<.001$), and PCL ($F(98,11238)=16.03$, $p<.001$) were significant predictors for whether a category was used or not. This confirms that the situation type as defined by trust and PCL is relevant for predicting category type. A second multi-level logistic regression was done per category, using participant as random intercept and the two-way interaction between PCL graph trend and trust as fixed effect. This resulted in the odds of a category occurring given the situation, which were then transformed into probabilities. These numbers, the mean number of statements per answer, and a further description of the categories, can be found in [6].

Motivational System

With the results from the expert survey, we can design a system which generates motivational feedback. This system is described in Figure 2. It picks categories up to the required amount for that situation (three or four), based on the probability of a category occurring, keeping in mind the sub-super category relationships. An example of feedback generated by this system for the situation with rising PCL scores and high trust in therapy outcome would be the following motivational statement. (translated from the original Dutch).

I see your scores have been rising. (note rising PCL) *It is normal if at first your scores do not go down, many people experience that.* (give perspective) *Your trust in the therapy is still high.* (note high trust) *Good job!* (compliment)

3   Discussion & Conclusion

In this paper we present a system which can generate motivational feedback during PTSD therapy based on the patients current situation, usable by a virtual agent. We show that the motivational statements given by experts can be categorized with a good fit, covering 97% of the utterances. Moreover, we can predict how likely it is that category of statement will occur in a situation, resulting in a system generating personalized motivational feedback.

One of the main strengths of the method used in this paper is that no patient dataset is necessary to train a virtual agent to make motivational statements. Especially with mental health disorders, such data can be confidential and difficult

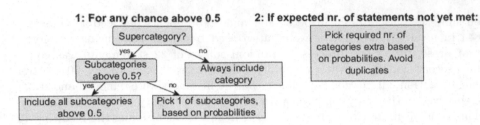

Fig. 2. Outline of the system generating motivational feedback.

to gather. Although the dataset presented in this paper is focused on motivation for during PTSD treatment, a similar type of system could applied to other domains as motivation is relevant for many health interventions. To appreciate the contribution of the system presented in this paper it is, however, also necessary to consider its limitations. The main limitation of this system is that it only considers two parameters for describing a situation. To study whether all important parameters are taken into account it would be necessary to study therapists in a more natural session with a patient, noting what factors they base their choice for statements on.

Despite these limitations, our system can be a valuable addition to a virtual agent as it enables the agent to give personalized situational motivation. Moreover, this method is extendable to more complex situations or different domains as it does not require large amounts of patient or observational detail. Given the importance of motivations in all areas of BCSS, this can be a valuable addition.

Acknowledgements

This work is part of the programme VESP, which is financed by the Netherlands Organization for Scientific Research (pr. nr. 314-99-104).

References

1. Deci, E.L., Ryan, R.M.: Intrinsic motivation and self-determination in human behaviour. Plenum (1985)
2. Prochaska, J., DiClemente, C.: The transtheoretical approach. Handbook of psychotherapy integration pp. 147–171 (2005)
3. Provoost, S., Lau, H., Ruwaard, J., Riper, H.: Embodied conversational agents in clinical psychology: A scoping review. JMIR 19, e151 (2017)
4. Süssenbach, L., Riether, N., Schneider, S., Berger, I., Kummert, F., Lütkebohle, I., Pitsch, K.: A robot as fitness companion: towards an interactive action-based motivation model. In: Symp. on RHIC (2014)
5. Tielman, M., Brinkman, W., Neerincx, M.: Design guidelines for a virtual coach for post-traumatic stress disorder patients. In: Intelligent virtual agents (2014)
6. Tielman, M., Neerincx, M., Brinkman, W.: Dataset. categories & probabilities of statementsformotivatingptsdpatients.(2017), http://10.4121/uuid:97c0c9c1-00ab-45da-8bffc4e5dd6328d1
7. Weathers, F., Litz, B., Keane, T., Palmieri, P., Marx, B., Schnurr, P.: The PTSD Checklist for DSM-5 (PCL-5) (2013)
8. Yee, N., Bailenson, J.N., Rickertsen, K.: A meta-analysis of the impact of the inclusion and realism of human-like faces on user experiences in interfaces. In: CHI (2007)

Talk About Death: End of Life Planning with a Virtual Agent

Dina Utami,[1] Timothy Bickmore,[1] ✉ Asimina Nikolopoulou,[1] Michael Paasche-Orlow[2]

[1] Northeastern University, Boston, MA 02115, USA
[2]Boston Medical Center, Boston, MA 02118, USA
bickmore@ccs.neu.edu

Abstract. For those nearing the end of life, "wellness" must encompass reduction in suffering as well as the promotion of behaviors that mitigate stress and help people prepare for death. We discuss the design of a virtual conversational palliative care coach that works with individuals during their last year of life to help them manage symptoms, reduce stress, identify and address unmet spiritual needs, and support advance care planning. We present the results of an experiment that features the reactions of older adults in discussing these topics with a virtual agent, and note the importance of discussing spiritual needs in the context of end-of-life conversations. We find that all participants are comfortable discussing these topics with an agent, and that their discussion leads to reductions in state and death anxiety, as well as significant increase in intent to create a last will and testament.

Keywords: conversational agent, relational agent, spirituality, palliative care.

1 Introduction

Palliative care is a medical specialty that helps people with serious, typically life-limiting illnesses, and focuses on the alleviation of suffering, rather than on curing an underlying medical condition. Areas of care include the alleviation of pain, and other physical symptoms such as nausea, as well as the treatment of mental health conditions such as stress, anxiety, and depression. In the US, palliative care is distinct from hospice care, with the latter being explicitly concerned with end of life relief measures, although palliative services are offered during hospice care as well.

While palliative care has the potential to greatly improve quality of life in terminally-ill patients, in the US it is typically provided only during the last few days or weeks of a patient's life, even when patients could have benefitted from these services months earlier. Indeed, many patients have inadequate control of their symptoms and one third of hospice patients die within a week of initiating hospice services. Accordingly, identifying mechanisms to initiate palliative and hospice care earlier in a person's disease trajectory has become a strategic priority for quality improvement efforts [1].

© Springer International Publishing AG 2017
J. Beskow et al. (Eds.): IVA 2017, LNAI 10498, pp. 441-450, 2017.
DOI 10.1007/978-3-319-67401-8_55

To help address this need, we have been developing a virtual agent that plays the role of a palliative care coach, supporting patients directly and identifying opportunities for referral to human palliative care specialists or other resources. Our goal is to offer this agent to terminally-ill patients while they are in their last year of life, so that they can benefit from the alleviation of suffering that the agent may be able to provide.

One important aspect of palliative care that is frequently overlooked by medical professionals is a patient's spiritual needs. Spirituality is a complex construct, but is broadly recognized as a core dimension of palliative care [2]. For many patients, religion and spirituality can empower them by promoting broader perspectives on illness and mortality. This can help patients transcend anxiety relating to their immediate physical condition and provide support for coping with their advanced illness. One fundamental question in developing a virtual palliative care agent is whether patients would even accept spiritual counseling from an agent and, if they did, how should the agent relate to patients' religion, spiritual beliefs, and practices.

In this work we report the preliminary design of a virtual palliative care agent and results from an empirical study investigating how accepting older adults are of the concept. To specifically test acceptance of spiritual counseling by the agent, we created three versions of it with varying degrees of spiritual involvement, so as to determine whether there is a limit to how engaged older adults would want an agent to be in their religious and spiritual life.

2 Related Work

A number of virtual agents and robots have now been developed to counsel patients on health problems in general, and mental well-being in particular [3, 4]. Many researchers have also explored agents and robots as a social companion for older adults to address loneliness and isolation [5]. However, only one study to date describes a robotic companion that supports spiritual activities, including reading the bible [6]. For many people, religion and spirituality are private matters, and thus studies investigating self-disclosure with virtual agents are of relevance [7].

Although agent-based spiritual applications are rare, there are a very large number of commercial applications available that do not use agents, in addition to several research projects. Sterling and Zimmerman studied a Zen Buddhist community and noted that engagement in communal meditative sessions and other related practices via technology applications boosted users' sense of religiosity and their connectedness with their community [8]. Similarly, Hlubinka et al. developed AltarNation, an interactive environment using telepresence for meditation purposes, and noted positive outcomes in enhancing community engagement by minimizing physical distance [9]. Buie and Blythe studied meditation videos online and found that they are positively reviewed by users, in spite of the distraction of abrasive commentary and advertising [10]. Wyche et al. discussed the use of Podcasts, Powerpoint, email and other networked technologies in "spiritual formation," a deliberate process of spiritual life transformation via prayer, study and discussion with one's community in a Christian church, and noted varied efficacy of such technologies depending on the audience [11]. In another study, Buie and Blythe outlined the most prevalent instances of applications based on Bell's definition of "technospiritual practices," including Sonic Cradle by Vidyarthi, Riecke and Gromala, which aims to create a sense of immersion and mindfulness in meditative settings [12]. Finally, Wyche et al. discussed application design for faith-related purposes, and emphasized the importance of imagery integration in "Sun Dial," a prayer reminder tool that increased users' sense of connectivity with their communities of practice [13].

3 Design of a Virtual Palliative Care Agent

We have designed a touchscreen tablet-based virtual agent that counsels terminally-ill patients on topics related to palliative care (Figure 1). The agent is animated in a 3D game engine and speaks using synthetic speech driven by a hierarchical transition network-based dialogue engine. Conversational nonverbal behavior is generated using BEAT [14], animated in synchrony with speech, and includes hand gestures, posture shifts, head nods, and facial displays. User contributions to the conversation are made via a multiple-choice menu of utterances updated at each turn of the conversation.

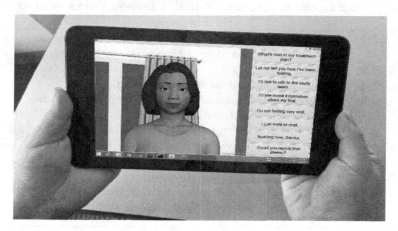

Fig. 1. A Mobile Embodied Conversational Agent

To test the acceptability of our palliative care agent, we designed the initial system to discuss three death-related topics with users: last will and testament, healthcare proxy, and funeral preparations. A will or testament is a legal document in which someone describes their wishes regarding how their property is to be distributed after they die. A healthcare proxy designates another person who can make healthcare decisions for them if they are unable to make or communicate those decisions. In each topic, the agent describes the content, explains why it was important for anyone to address the topic, and then provides details and answers to frequently asked questions. These topics are related to end-of-life decision-making, and are relevant to everyone even if they are not terminally ill.

3.1 Spiritual Counseling

We also designed a spiritual counseling dialogue for initial evaluation and acceptance testing. The dialogue asks users about their spiritual orientation, specific religious beliefs, family religious background, religious practices, and beliefs regarding the meaning of death. The dialogue accounts for six major religions (Christianity, Judaism, Islam, Hinduism, Buddhism and Sikhism), as well as for atheism, spiritual humanism, and secular humanism.

AGENT:	*So, I am really interested in the relationship between religion and spirituality. Do you consider yourself spiritual, religious, both, or neither?*
USER:	*I would rather call myself religious, which I think is different from spiritual.*
AGENT:	
USER:	*That's an interesting distinction to make. How would you identify your religion?*
AGENT:	
USER:	*I'm Jewish.*
AGENT:	*I wish I knew more about Jewish traditions. Were you raised religiously?* *Yes, I was.*

Fig. 2. Excerpts from the PRO-SPIRITUAL Dialogue with a Jewish User

AGENT:	*So, I am really interested in the relationship between religion and spirituality. Do you consider yourself spiritual, religious, both, or*
USER:	*neither?*
AGENT:	*I would say I'm spiritual, but not religious.*
USER:	*OK, great. Would you call yourself a Spiritual Humanist?*
AGENT:	*I don't know. What does that mean?*
	A Spiritual Humanist believes in some kind of spiritual life without subscribing to the beliefs or practices of a religious system, and above
USER:	*all, he or she believes in the innate value and dignity of human life.*
AGENT:	*I would say I'm a Spiritual Humanist.*
USER:	*OK, so were your family religious when you were growing up?* *No, they were spiritual, but not conventionally religious.*

Fig. 3. Excerpts from the PRO-SPIRITUAL Dialogue with a Spiritual Humanist User

In order to support testing of our research question concerning the degree of religious involvement the agent should demonstrate, we created two versions of this dialogue. In the NEUTRAL version, the agent simply takes note of the user's responses, and adapts dialog as necessary to reflect utilitarian/functional use of the information in subsequent dialog, but otherwise no interest or follow-up. In the PRO-SPIRITUAL version the agent takes active interest in the user's spirituality, tailors dialog to the user's religious orientation, demonstrates knowledge of the user's religious beliefs and orientation, and acts supportive.

Design decisions on the spiritual module have taken into consideration ethical concerns about the agent's engagement with spirituality and religion. We were specifically concerned with discussions that could be construed as blasphemous, deceitful, or indicative of misplaced trust. We also ensured adequate representation of all beliefs and provided pluralistic options for user responses in order to minimize any feelings of coercion, discomfort or unrest. The project team included representatives from six religious and spiritual backgrounds, who worked collaboratively throughout the length of the study to ensure that the dialogue was appropriate. In addition, the PRO-SPIRITUAL dialogue was reviewed by two different hospital chaplains to ensure that the content was thorough and respectful. Figures 2 and 3 shows excerpts of the PRO-SPIRITUAL dialogue.

4 Acceptance Study

We conducted an exploratory study to determine the reaction of older adults to discussing end-of-life topics with a virtual agent, and to examine the importance of spirituality within the context of this conversation. We recruited older adults (55 and up) for the study, since we felt that end-of-life planning would be more relevant to them than to a younger population. The study was conducted in a single session in a usability laboratory and was approved by our University Institutional Review Board.

All participants discussed the three end-of-life topics with the agent. To evaluate different levels of religious involvement by the agent, the study was conducted as a between-subjects randomized experiment with three arms:
1. CONTROL. The agent does not discuss spiritual needs at all.
2. NEUTRAL. The agent includes the NEUTRAL spiritual dialogue in the end-of-life discussion at the end of the interaction.
3. PRO-SPIRITUAL. The agent includes the PRO-SPIRITUAL dialogue in the end-of-life discussion at the end of the interaction.

4.1 Measures

In addition to sociodemographic measures, participants were asked to fill out the following self-report measures:

1. Death anxiety: Assessed at intake and after interacting with the agent using the Death Anxiety Scale (DAS) questionnaire. Representative questions include "I am very much afraid to die", and "I am often distressed by the way time flies so very rapidly" [15]. We used the version of DAS with 7-point Likert-scale, which has been shown to have higher internal consistency and discriminability [16].
2. State Anxiety: Assessed at intake and after interacting with agent using the State-Trait Anxiety Inventory (STAI) [17]. STAI has 20 items for assessing state anxiety. State anxiety items include: "I am tense; I am worried" and "I feel calm; I feel secure." All items are rated on a 4-point scale (e.g., from "Almost Never" to "Almost Always").

3. Death preparation stages of change: Assessed before and after interacting with the agent. We first asked participants whether they have already made a funeral plan, written their last will and testament, and filled out a health care proxy form. For each item, if a participant indicated that they had not, we asked them how likely they would be to complete these preparations in the following year.
4. Working Alliance: Working alliance is the trust that a patient has in working with a counselor or healthcare provider to achieve particular therapeutic goals. This was assessed after interacting with the agent using the bond items from the Working Alliance Inventory (WAI) [18].
5. Participant attitude towards agent: Assessed after interacting with agent using 12 single-item questions on a 7-point scale (Table 1).

4.2   Participants.

We recruited 44 older adults (24 males, 20 females, ages 55-82, mean 61.5) via an online advertisement, with 16 randomized to CONTROL, 11 to NEUTRAL, and 17 to PRO-SPIRITUAL. Of these 44 participants, 45% reported that they have at least one chronic health condition, 93% had spent time with someone who was dying, and 64% had some knowledge of advance directives (legal instructions on what medical care they should receive if they are incapacitated). Our participants had varying degrees of computer experience and educational backgrounds, ranging from not graduating high school to having an advanced degree. When the agent asked whether the participants were secular, spiritual, or religious, 22 answered religious, 15 answered spiritual, and 7 answered secular. Of the religious participants who volunteered their religious affiliations to the agent, 4 self-identified as Catholic, 3 as Christian, and 2 Jewish.

4.3   Quantitative Results

State Anxiety. There was a significant decrease in state anxiety during the interaction with the agent (PRE: 29.7 (8.7), POST: 27.8 (8.9), Wilcoxon signed rank, $p<.05$).

Death Anxiety. There was a trending decrease on death anxiety during the interaction with the agent (PRE: 3.82(1.04), POST: 3.71 (0.98), paired t, $p=0.096$).

Death Preparation Stages of Change. Of the 44 participants, 32 reported that they did not have a last will and testament, 33 had not shared their funeral plans with their family, and 20 had not filled out a health care proxy form. There was a significant increase in participants' intention to complete a last will and testament after talking to the agent (PRE:3.83(2.26), POST:4.27(2.43), Wilcoxon signed rank, $p=0.05$). We found no significant differences between pre and post intentions to write and share funeral plans or health care proxy forms.

Agent Rating. In general, participants were satisfied with the agent, wanted to continue working with the agent, and found it easy to talk to the agent. Participants also felt that the agent was honest, trustworthy, and likable. We found significant differences between study arms in the agent's rating of repetitiveness, ease of use, and interestingness, with the PRO-SPIRITUAL agent rated the most interesting (Table 1).

Table 1. Agent's Rating by Study Group (Kruskal-Wallace H-tests)

Question (Anchors 1-7)	CONTROL Mean (SD)	NEUTRAL Mean (SD)	PRO-SPIRITUAL Mean (SD)	p-value
How close do you feel to the agent? (Not at all – Very close)	2.94 (1.95)	3.45 (1.69)	4.06 (2.33)	.39
How satisfied are you with the agent? (Not at all – Very satisfied)	4.88 (1.89)	5.82 (1.17)	4.82 (1.94)	.35
How much would you like to continue working with the agent? (Not at all – Very much)	4.56 (2.03)	5.91 (0.94)	4.71 (2.14)	.21
How much do you trust the agent? (Not at all – Very much)	4.81 (2.01)	6.09 (1.04)	5.53 (1.37)	.21
How much do you like the agent? (Not at all – Very much)	4.75 (1.81)	5.27 (1.74)	5.12 (1.76)	.76
Was the agent repetitive? (Not at all – Very repetitive)	4.56 (2.03)	2.94 (2.3)	1.73 (0.9)	.01
How easy was talking to the agent? (Easy – Difficult)	3.13 (2.00)	1.45 (1.51)	2.59 (2.06)	.02
How interesting was the agent? (Boring – Interesting)	3.56 (1.93)	4.55 (1.51)	5.12 (1.65)	.04
How would you characterize your relationship with the agent? (Complete stranger – Close friend)	3.44 (2.13)	3.00 (2.19)	3.41 (2.24)	.80
How much do you feel that the agent cares about you? (Not at all – Very much)	3.87 (2.33)	4.18 (2.32)	3.71 (2.44)	.82
How much do you feel that you and the agent understand each other? (Not at all – Very much)	4.73 (2.05)	5.36 (1.91)	4.47 (2.21)	.56
How much do you feel that the agent was honest about her feelings towards you? (Not honest – Very honest)	4.33 (2.41)	5.2 (1.87)	5.29 (1.69)	.56

Working Alliance. We found no significant differences between study groups on working alliance scores (all: 4.53 (1.24), CONTROL: 4.39 (1.39), NEUTRAL: 4.42 (1.12), PRO-SPIRITUAL: 4.73 (1.23)).

4.4 Qualitative Results

In general, we found that participants had positive impressions of the experience. The agent was positively evaluated as, "*very easy to work with*" [p4: 56 M Catholic], "*self-explanatory*" [p5: 57 M Spiritual Humanist], "*thorough, thoughtful and pleasant*" [p16: 56, F, Religious Unspecified], "*open, honest and able to speak with a great deal of clarity*" [p6: 58 F Protestant]. Reflecting on the topic of the conversation, participants noted that, "*it was thought-provoking*" [p5: 57 M Spiritual Humanist] and "*it gave one an opportunity to think about these matters*" [p6: 58 F Protestant].

The agent managed to evoke conversations that the participants have had with human interlocutors in the past and to instigate new ones, thus informing a more holistic mindset towards death and death preparation. Most participants indicated that the conversation was a reminder of something that was "*in the back of [their] mind*" [p15: 56 M Religious/ Unspecified]. A participant also stated: "*I already knew about health proxy but the two other things, I've never thought about those things. The funeral and the will I haven't thought about those because I'm all about living my life, I didn't think about those arrangements.*" [p13: 63 M Spiritual Humanist]

Participants noted the benefits of including spirituality in end of life discussions, especially on the preparation front: "*Well it's important especially when you have to take into context the funerals, arrangements that must be made, different religions have different aspects you know. Jewish religion has to be buried right away while Catholics can wait you know with the funerals homes and everything and um, it all has to be taken into account.*"[p43: 61 F Catholic]; "*Yes. Because you are given a certain level of peace of mind.* [p6: 58 F Protestant]; "*Oh yes, I know God has more plans for me and I'll never be shy about talking about that. He ain't done with me yet.*" [p20: 62 F Christian];"*Huge yeah, whatever that spirituality means for the person.*" [p36: 55 M Catholic]

The reactions to the spirituality discussion with the agent were mixed. Some participants said that they didn't mind discussing spirituality with an agent but thought that it might be intrusive or too personal for other people. Some participants said that the level of detail was just enough for it not to be intrusive, while others suggested that we add more depth to it. This finding brings to light the importance of tailoring the inclusion and/or the depth of the spirituality discussion to users' specific need. One user suggested that we add the options "*can we change the topic?*" or "*I don't even want to talk about that subject.*" for users who find spirituality to be a very personal subject [p6: 58 F Religious].

When we asked whether they would rather talk about spirituality with a person than an agent, twelve participants indicated that they would prefer to talk to a person: "*Like I said it was nice talking to Tanya about it, but as for specifics in the end I need someone who [is] like the person who's going to be doing this for me. I guess what I liked best was what she made me think about spirituality and religion*" [p29: 55 M Secular humanist]. Eight participants said they have no preference: "*Doesn't matter. She was very friendly though and I liked talking to her a lot, I could trust her like she was a real person sitting in front of me*" [p20: 62 F Christian]. And, seven participants said they would prefer talking to an agent: "*[...] easier to talk to a computer agent about it. People tend to be pretty opinionated about that stuff, especially when they get to be around my age*" [p40: 57 M Spiritual].

5   Discussion

This study demonstrates that older adults react positively to an agent talking about end of life preparation. Older adults are comfortable discussing these topics with an agent and the discussion leads to significant reduction in state anxiety and a significant increase in intent to create a last will and testament. We also found that, regardless of their religious or spiritual background, participants thought that an agent discussing their spiritual orientation and demonstrating knowledge of and interest in their spirituality was significantly more interesting, less repetitive, and easier to talk to than an equivalent agent that did not discuss their spirituality at all.

5.1   Future Work

There are many interesting areas of research related to palliative care and spiritual counseling delivered by virtual agents. Rather than feeling uncomfortable with more religious involvement by the agent, our users indicated they wanted even more spiritual involvement in these conversations. Whether users will actually want significantly more involvement—in activities such as prayer with or by the agent—remains to be seen.

   We have expanded the palliative care agent into a longitudinal palliative care support system encompassing the following topics: (1) physical activity promotion, (2) symptom tracking and medication promotion (3) stress reduction, (4) spiritual needs assessment and counseling, and (5) advanced care planning. The system tracks user progress on behaviors of interest (e.g., exercise) and also tracks user symptoms and quality of life ratings to provide comparative feedback and recommendations (e.g., "Sorry to hear your pain is worse. Do you have medication for that?"). The spiritual counseling module supports a range of religious activities, such as praying, fasting, studying sacred verse/ scripture, and reflecting on past holidays. The system is designed to interact with patients at home for six months, as well as to provide communication channels to a nurse monitoring the system and a family caregiver. A clinical trial is underway.

Acknowledgments

This work was supported by the US National Institutes of Health grant R01NR016131. We thank Elise Masson, William Bond, and Arsalan ul Haq for their help designing the system and conducting the pilot study.

References

1. Cassel, C.K., Field, M.J.: Approaching death: improving care at the end of life. National Academies Press (1997)
2. Puchalski, C.M.: Spirituality and the Care of Patients at the End-of-Life: An Essential Component of Care. OMEGA - Journal of Death and Dying 56, 33-46 (2008)

3. Ring, L., Bickmore, T., Pedrelli, P.: An Affectively Aware Virtual Therapist for Depression Counseling. ACM SIGCHI Conference on Human Factors in Computing Systems (CHI) workshop on Computing and Mental Health, (2016)
4. DeVault, D., et al: SimSensei kiosk: a virtual human interviewer for healthcare decision support. AAMAS, (2014)
5. Sidner, C., Bickmore, T., Rich, C., Barry, B., Ring, L., Behrooz, M., Shayganfar, M.: Demonstration of an Always-On Companion for Isolated Older Adults. 14th Annual SIGdial Meeting on Discourse and Dialogue (SIGDIAL) (2013)
6. Yan-You, C., Jhing-Fa, W., Po-Chuan, L., Po-Yi, S., Hsin-Chun, T., Da-Yu, K.: Human-robot interaction based on cloud computing infrastructure for senior companion. In: TENCON 2011 - 2011 IEEE Region 10 Conference, pp. 1431-1434. (Year)
7. Lucas, G.M., Gratch, J., King, A., Morency, L.-P.: It's only a computer: Virtual humans increase willingness to disclose. Computers in Human Behavior 37, 94-100 (2014)
8. Sterling, R., Zimmerman, J.: Shared moments: opportunities for mobile phones in religious participation. Proceedings of the 2007 conference on Designing for User eXperiences, pp. 2-7. ACM, Chicago, Illinois (2007)
9. Hlubinka, M., Beaudin, J., Tapia, E.M., An, J.S.: AltarNation: interface design for meditative communities. CHI '02 Extended Abstracts on Human Factors in Computing Systems, pp. 612-613. ACM, Minneapolis, Minnesota, USA (2002)
10. Buie, E., Blythe, M.: Meditations on YouTube. Proceedings of the 6th International Conference on Designing Pleasurable Products and Interfaces, pp. 41-50. ACM, Newcastle upon Tyne, United Kingdom (2013)
11. Wyche, S.P., Hayes, G.R., Harvel, L.D., Grinter, R.E.: Technology in spiritual formation: an exploratory study of computer mediated religious communications. Proceedings of the 2006 20th anniversary conference on Computer supported cooperative work, pp. 199-208. ACM, Banff, Alberta, Canada (2006)
12. Buie, E., Blythe, M.: Spirituality: there's an app for that! (but not a lot of research). CHI '13 Extended Abstracts on Human Factors in Computing Systems, pp. 2315-2324. ACM, Paris, France (2013)
13. Wyche, S.P., Caine, K.E., Davison, B.K., Patel, S.N., Arteaga, M., Grinter, R.E.: Sacred imagery in techno-spiritual design. Proceedings of the SIGCHI Conference on Human Factors in Computing Systems, pp. 55-58. ACM, Boston, MA, USA (2009)
14. Cassell, J., Vilhjálmsson, H.H., Bickmore, T.: BEAT: the Behavior Expression Animation Toolkit. In: Prendinger, H., Ishizuka, M. (eds.) Life-Like Characters: Tools, Affective Functions, and Applications, pp. 163-185. Springer Berlin Heidelberg, Berlin, Heidelberg (2004)
15. Templer, D.I.: The Construction and Validation of a Death Anxiety Scale. The Journal of General Psychology 82, 165-177 (1970)
16. McMordie, W.R.: Improving Measurement of Death Anxiety. Psychological Reports 44, 975-980 (1979)
17. Spielberger, C.D.: State- Trait anxiety inventory. Wiley Online Library (2010)
18. Tracey, T.J., Kokotovic, A.M.: Factor structure of the Working Alliance Inventory. Psychological Assessment: A Journal of Consulting and Clinical Psychology 1, 207-210 (1989)

Social Gaze Model for an Interactive Virtual Character

Bram van den Brink, Christyowidiasmoro and Zerrin Yumak ✉

Utrecht University, Princetonplein 5,
de Uithof, Netherlands
a.c.vandenbrink@uu.nl
c.christyowidiasmoro@uu.nl
z.yumak@uu.nl

Abstract. This paper describes a live demo of our autonomous social gaze model for an interactive virtual character situated in the real world. We are interested in estimating which user has an intention to interact, in other words which user is engaged with the virtual character. The model takes into account behavioral cues such as proximity, velocity, posture and sound, estimates an engagement score and drives the gaze behavior of the virtual character. Initially, we assign equal weights to these features. Using data collected in a real setting, we analyze which features have higher importance. We found that the model with weighted features correlates better with the ground-truth data.

Keywords: Gaze model, Engagement, Situated interaction

1 Introduction

Gaze movement is important for modeling realistic social interactions with virtual humans. While gaze animation based on low-level kinematics is well-studied, autonomous generation of gaze at the high-level during social interactions and in real settings still remains as a challenge [1]. One of the open problems is how to drive the gaze behavior of an interactive virtual character situated in a real environment, i.e. a virtual receptionist. It requires understanding which user has an intention to interact with the virtual character, in other words which user is more engaged. The users might be approaching the virtual character alone, in groups or they might just be passing by.

Recognition of goals, intentions and emotions of other people is important for a fluent communication. If one has to give human-like capabilities to artificial characters, they should also be able to predict the intentions of others. In this paper, we focus on the engagement detection problem as a prerequisite to initiating a conversation with a user and propose a model to autonomously drive the gaze behavior of the virtual character. Fig. 1 shows our Virtual Character Sara interacting with a group of users.

J. Beskow et al. (Eds.): IVA 2017, LNAI 10498, pp. 451–454, 2017.
DOI 10.1007/978-3-319-67401-8_56

Fig. 1. Virtual Receptionist Sara interacting with users

Previous work modeled engagement based on heuristic rules [2][3]. It has been shown that machine learning approaches [4][5] outperform the basic heuristics. Both approaches have advantages and disadvantages. While the former does not involve extensive validations of their model, the latter depends on huge data collection and analysis efforts. An overview of multi-party interactions and a discussion on open research challenges can be found in our previous work [6]. In this research, our contribution is two-fold: (1) We present a practical and general engagement model combining multiple behavioral cues to drive the gaze of an interactive virtual character. (2) We find the importance of these behavioral cues based on data collected in a real environment.

We collected 31 mins of data from 18 subjects. The data was labelled and engaged/non-engaged and we run a logistic regression in order to find the weights of the features in the model. Our findings show that distance, velocity, body orientation, horizontal head rotation and mouth movement have significant effects on the model. Sound, vertical head orientation and field of view parameters didn't behave as we initially expected. There were also limitations of our work. In order to improve the reliability of the annotations, multiple annotators can be employed by looking at the correlations among the annotators. Instead of using binary engagement labels, annotations can also be done over a range. It will also be interesting to apply and compare other machine learning models. Finally, further data collection and analysis can be done to capture various combinations of user behaviors. Although our results provide useful insights in terms of the importance of feature weights, a validation experiment should be run in order to see whether the new model is more socially adept. This paper is a first attempt to collect and analyze real-life data for engagement detection in a truly open space.

The model is published in the Computer Animation and Virtual Worlds journal and was presented in CASA 2017 [7]. More details about the model and the experiment results can be found in the paper.

2   Description of the Demo

Fig. 2 shows the overall architecture of our system. The Virtual Human Controller receives the information about where to look at from the Engagement Detection component and controls the gaze behavior of the character. The dialogue of the character is based on AIML Pandorabots[1]. For speech recognition, we use Google Speech Recognition.

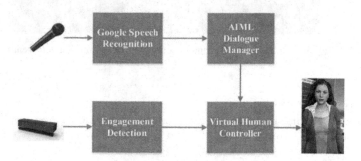

Fig. 2. Overall Architecture

We developed the virtual character in Unity 3D game engine. The 3D model is created in Daz3D[2]. The character has the capability of speaking, gazing, displaying facial expressions, conversational gestures and idle animations. Lip-synch and the low-level gaze movement are based on third-party assets from the Unity Asset Store[3][4]. Gestures are recorded with a Vicon Motion Capture system and applied to our character. Facial expression and visemes are exported as blend shapes from Daz3D. The synchronization between speech, gaze, facial expressions and gestures is realized using the Behavior Mark-up Language [8]. For this, we developed a BML Realizer for Unity[5].

A video of the demo can be found at https://youtu.be/M57kkeoz7zQ. For more information we refer to https://www.staff.science.uu.nl/~yumak001/UUVHC/index.html. Our demo uses two screens. While one screen shows the virtual character, the other one shows the Kinect stream with individual features and overall engagement score in real-time. That enables the visitors to see how the engagement score and the gaze behavior of the character changes based on the underlying model. Fig. 3 shows an example screenshot of the Kinect stream with feature and engagement scores for two people.

---

[1] http://www.pandorabots.com
[2] http://www.daz3d.com
[3] http://lipsync.rogodigital.com
[4] http://tore-knabe/unity-asset-realistic-eye-movements
[5] https://github.com/christyowidiasmoro/BMLNet

Fig. 3. Features and engagement scores shown on the Kinect stream

Acknowledgements

This work is supported by the Horizon 2020 RAGE - Realizing an Applied Gaming Eco-system project (Grant no. 644187) and Utrecht University Game Research Seed Money.

References

1. Ruhland, K., Peters, C. E., Andrist, S., Badler, J. B., Badler, N. I., Gleicher, M., Mutlu, B., McDonnell, R.: A review of eye gaze in virtual agents, social robotics and HCI: Behavior generation, user interaction and perception. Computer Graphics Forum, 34(6):299–326, (2015).
2. Sidner, C. L., Lee, C., Kidd, C.D., Lesh, N., Rich, C.: Explorations in engagement for humans and robots. Artificial Intelligence, 166(1- 2):140–164, (2005).
3. Michalowski, M.P., Sabanovic, S., Simmons, R.: A spatial model of engagement for a social robot. In: 9th IEEE International Workshop on Advanced Motion Control, pp. 762–767. IEEE, (2006).
4. Bohus D., Horvitz, E.: Learning to predict engagement with a spoken dialog system in open-world settings. In: Proceedings of the SIGDIAL 2009 Conference, The 10th Annual Meeting of the Special Interest Group on Discourse and Dialogue, pp. 244–252, Stroudsburg, PA, USA, (2009).
5. Foster, M.E., Gaschler, A., Giuliani, M.: How can I help you? Comparing engagement classification strategies for a robot bartender. In: Proceedings of the 15th International Con- ference on Multimodal Interaction (ICMI 2013), Sydney, Australia, (2013).
6. Yumak, Z., Magnenat-Thalmann, N: Multimodal and multi-party social interactions. In: Magnenat-Thalmann, N., Yuan, J., Thalmann, D., You, B. (eds), Context Aware Human-Robot and Human-Agent Interaction, pp. 275–298, Springer International Publishing, (2016)
7. Yumak, Z., van den Brink, B., Egges, A.: Autonomous Social Gaze Model for an Interactive Virtual Character in Real-Life Settings, Computer Animation and Virtual Worlds, (2017).
8. Kopp, S., Krenn, B., Marsella, S., Marshall, A. N., Pelachaud, C., Pirker, H., Thorisson, K.R., Vilhjalmsson, H.: Towards a common framework for multi-modal generation: The behavior markup language. In: Proceedings of the 6th International Conference on Intelligent Virtual Agents, IVA'06, pp. 205–217, Springer-Verlag, Berlin, Heidelberg, (2006).

Studying Gender Bias and Social Backlash via Simulated Negotiations with Virtual Agents

L.M van der Lubbe and T. Bosse ✉

VU Amsterdam, De Boelelaan 1105, 1081 HV Amsterdam, the Netherlands,
lauravanderlubbe@hotmail.com, t.bosse@vu.nl

Abstract. This research investigates whether (female and male) virtual negotiators experience a social backlash during negotiations with an economical outcome when they are using a negotiation style that is congruent with the opposite gender. An interactive turn-based negotiation using a virtual agent as employee is used in an experiment with 93 participants. Results show that the effect of gender on negotiation outcome and social backlash was less pronounced in this experiment than expected based on existing literature. Nevertheless, the results found provide several interesting pointers for follow-up research.

Keywords: virtual agents, salary negotiations, social backlash, gender bias, gender pay gap.

1 Introduction

The gender pay gap refers to the phenomenon that women on average have lower salaries than men for the same type of job, even when adjusting for external factors like working time. One of the possible explanations of this phenomenon is the fact that men often achieve better negotiation outcomes than women [4], which may be caused by the fact that behaviors that are congruent with the female gender role are typically not seen as efficient for negotiations [1]. Women overall demonstrate a slightly less competitive negotiation style, compared to men [8]. The female negotiation style can be seen as a more cooperative or altruistic style [2], it is also described as an accommodating style, which leads to lower outcomes than the competitive negotiation style of men [8]. Female negotiators ask for less and make more generous offers compared to male negotiators [2]. Moreover, male negotiators often start with a high demand, which is shown to result in higher outcomes [6]. Female negotiators are more likely to agree on an offer earlier compared to males, which is an ineffective strategy [2].

Unfortunately, adjusting the negotiation style in such a way that it is no longer congruent with the gender role can lead to a social backlash (e.g., being perceived as less friendly) [1]. Female negotiators suffer more from social backlash than male negotiators [3], both regarding the economic outcome of the negotiation and the evaluation of the negotiator [7].

This research investigates whether this effect of gender on negotiation outcome and social backlash is also present when people negotiate with virtual

© Springer International Publishing AG 2017
J. Beskow et al. (Eds.): IVA 2017, LNAI 10498, pp. 455-458, 2017.
DOI 10.1007/978-3-319-67401-8_57

agents. By using a virtual agent in the role of either a male of female employee, and a human participant in the role of manager, it is possible to manipulate only the variables of interest and keep other variables constant among different conditions. Research has shown that the effects of emotions on the outcomes of human-machine negotiations are comparable to human-human negotiations [5]. Therefore for this research it is expected that the negotiation outcomes in the experiment are comparable to human-human negotiation outcomes. If this is the case, virtual agents may be used in the future to develop interventions to make people aware of their gender bias during negotiations.

Two negotiation styles, one congruent with the male gender role and one congruent with the female gender role, have been implemented in a female and male virtual agent in the role of employee. It is investigated whether females and males negotiating with a negotiation style opposite to the style of their gender role are punished for this, meaning their outcome benefits less from the other negotiation style compared to the opposite gender.

2   Research Method

Our main research goal is to study how the gender of a virtual agent influence its negotiation outcome and social backlash during salary negotiations with a human negotiation partner. In particular, the following hypothesis is tested: *Both female and male virtual agents experience a social backlash when negotiating using a negotiation style that is not congruent with their gender role.*

A total of 93 people (55 male, 38 female) participated in this study. All participants were at least 18 years old and had an adequate level of English to understand the negotiation. Only 15% of the participants had professional negotiation experience. None of the participants knew the goal of the research.

Within the experiment four conditions are used, corresponding to four virtual negotiation partners: a female employee with an assertive negotiation style (21 participants; 38% female), a female employee with a non-assertive negotiation style (25 participants; 44% female), a male employee with an assertive negotiation style (24 participants; 42% female), and a male employee with a non-assertive negotiation style (23 participants; 39% female).

For the experiment a between-subjects design was chosen, to prevent results from being affected by negotiations conducted earlier. Each participant was randomly assigned to one of the conditions. The type of virtual employee and the gender of the participant were independent variables, whereas (monetary) negotiation outcome and social backlash were dependent variables.

To start the experiment, participants could download a compressed folder via a website which randomly assigned the participant to a condition. The compressed folder contains an application that can be run without installation, to conduct the virtual negotiation followed by an online questionnaire[1]. The virtual negotiation consists of a background sketch[2] and a turn-based dialogue[3].

3 Results

The hypothesis focuses at the social backlash experienced by both genders, measured in terms of subjective evaluation. The main results are shown in Figure 1. This figure contains five characteristics: two of these (friendly and sensitive) are assumed to be typically female properties, whereas two others (arrogant and independent) are typically male properties [1]. The fifth characteristic concerns whether the employee used appropriate language.

As shown in the figure, the differences between the male and female negotiators are small. For each characteristic, we tested, both for the female and for the male employees, whether there was a significant difference between the rating of the assertive and the non-assertive employee. This was done using independent t-tests with a Bonferroni correction to reduce the chance of a Type-I error.

For the female employees, significant differences were found for the characteristics Friendly ($p < 0.001$), Arrogant ($p < 0.001$), and Language ($p < 0.005$). For the male employees, significant differences were found for the characteristics Friendly ($p < 0.001$), Arrogant ($p < 0.001$), Language ($p < 0.001$), and, interestingly, Sensitive ($p < 0.005$). Furthermore, also the difference in appropriate language between assertive males and assertive females was significant ($p < 0.05$).

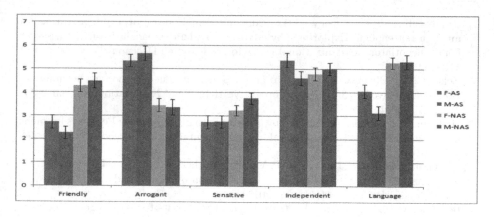

Fig. 1. Subjective evaluations

These results partly confirm our hypothesis that both genders would experience a social backlash when using a negotiation style that is not congruent with their gender role. Since the stereotypical female style is non-assertive, we can

---

[1] The questions of the questionnaire can be found at https://goo.gl/i2PWKb
[2] The used background sketch can be found at https://goo.gl/Fbybyo
[3] The dialogue can be found at https://goo.gl/CPwums

conclude that our female agents suffered from a backlash on some points: when adopting an assertive style, they were considered less friendly, more arrogant, and using less appropriate language. Instead, such negative effects cannot be observed when male agents switch from their stereotypical style (i.e., assertive) to a non-assertive style. On the contrary, in this case they are considered more friendly and sensitive, less arrogant and using more appropriate language.

Moreover, interesting differences between the genders were found for sensitivity (non-assertive male agents were considered more sensitive than non-assertive female agents) and for appropriate language (assertive female agents were considered to use more appropriate language than assertive male agents).

Besides the subjective measures also the monetary outcomes of the negotiation were analyzed. For the non-assertive employees, the salary raises that were reached be women and men are very similar. Testing whether there were significant differences in the outcomes reached by both genders, again using a t-test with Bonferroni correction, pointed out that there were no significant differences.

When considering the assertive employees only, the female employees on average achieved slightly higher raises than the male employees. This difference was not found to be significant. However, when leaving out the negotiations in which no deal was reached, the difference actually is significant ($p<0.05$). This is a surprising insight because most of the existing literature claims that it does not pay off for women to negotiate using an assertive style.

References

1. Amanatullah, E.T., Tinsley, C.H.: Punishing female negotiators for asserting too much or not enough: Exploring why advocacy moderates backlash against assertive female negotiators. Organizational Behavior and Human Decision Processes 120(1), 110–122 (2013)
2. Eckel, C., De Oliveira, A., Grossman, P.J.: Gender and negotiation in the small: are women (perceived to be) more cooperative than men? Negotiation Journal 24(4), 429–445 (2008)
3. Heilman, M.E., Wallen, A.S.: Wimpy and undeserving of respect: Penalties for men's gender-inconsistent success. Journal of Experimental Social Psychology 46(4), 664–667 (2010)
4. Mazei, J., Hüffmeier, J., Freund, P.A., Stuhlmacher, A.F., Bilke, L., Hertel, G.: A meta-analysis on gender differences in negotiation outcomes and their moderators. Psychological Bulletin 141(1), 85 (2015)
5. de Melo, C.M., Carnevale, P., Gratch, J.: The effect of virtual agents' emotion displays and appraisals on people's decision making in negotiation. In: International Conference on Intelligent Virtual Agents. pp. 53–66. Springer (2012)
6. Miles, E.W.: Gender differences in distributive negotiation: When in the negotiation process do the differences occur? European Journal of Social Psychology 40(7), 1200–1211 (2010)
7. Tinsley, C.H., Cheldelin, S.I., Schneider, A.K., Amanatullah, E.T.: Women at the bargaining table: Pitfalls and prospects. Negotiation Journal 25(2), 233–248 (2009)
8. Walters, A.E., Stuhlmacher, A.F., Meyer, L.L.: Gender and negotiator competitiveness: A meta-analysis. Organizational behavior and human decision processes 76(1), 1–29 (1998)

The Dynamics of Human-Agent Trust with POMDP-Generated Explanations

Ning Wang[1] ✉, David V. Pynadath[1], Susan G. Hill[2], and Chirag Merchant[1]

[1] University of Southern California Institute for Creative Technologies
[2] U.S. Army Research Laboratory
{nwang,pynadath,merchant}@ict.usc.edu, susan.g.hill.civ@mail.mil

1 Introduction

Partially Observable Markov Decision Processes (POMDPs) enable optimized decision making by robots, agents, and other autonomous systems. This quantitative optimization can also be a limitation in human-agent interaction, as the resulting autonomous behavior, while possibly optimal, is often impenetrable to human teammates, leading to improper trust and, subsequently, disuse or misuse of such systems [1]. Automatically generated explanations of POMDP-based decisions have shown promise in calibrating human-agent trust [3]. However, these "one-size-fits-all" static explanation policies are insufficient to accommodate different communication preferences across people. In this work, we analyze human behavior in a human-robot interaction (HRI) scenario, to find behavioral indicators of trust in the agent's ability. We evaluate four hypothesized behavioral measures that an agent could potentially use to dynamically infer its teammate's current trust level. The conclusions drawn can potentially inform the design of intelligent agents that can automatically adapt their explanation policies as they observe the behavioral responses of their human teammates.

2 Hypotheses

Prior work measured the impact of agent explanations on overall team performance [3]. Here, we instead focus on *dynamic* trust. For an agent to reason about trust, it must consider how its actions (and its explanations) cause trust to change.

Hypothesis I: *The human teammate's action immediately following a self report of trust is indicative of the level of self-reported trust in the agent's ability.*

One obvious question is whether there is any correspondence between people's observable behavior and their self-reported trust. In particular, any decision people make immediately following a self report should reflect their reported level. If this hypothesis is true, then this would also validate that the self-reported trust levels correspond to a "true" trust level, one that has an impact on domain-level behavior. For example, if people who report trusting an agent always ignore its recommendations, then an effort to increase that feeling of trust would be a waste of the agent's effort.

Hypothesis II: *The human teammate's actions before and after a mistake by an agent are indicative of the self-reported trust in the agent's ability.*

© Springer International Publishing AG 2017
J. Beskow et al. (Eds.): IVA 2017, LNAI 10498, pp. 459–462, 2017.
DOI 10.1007/978-3-319-67401-8_58

In an uncertain domain, even an optimal decision can be incorrect in hindsight. People's responses to errors can provide an agent with information about their trust. An untrusting person might view an error as confirmation to remain skeptical about the agent. More trusting teammates might resume trusting the agent at once.

Hypothesis III: *The number of times an agent's recommendations are followed/ignored by human teammates is indicative of their self-reported trust in the agent's ability.*

Testing Hypothesis I is limited by how often people can be asked about their trust. Testing Hypothesis II is limited by how often the agent makes mistakes. In domains where mistakes are infrequent, the agent needs to glean information from responses to its correct decisions as well. Someone who distrusts the agent should both report a low level of trust in it and ignore more of its recommendations.

Hypothesis IV: *The number of times the human teammate makes a correct decision is indicative of the self-reported trust in the agent's ability.*

Trust in an agent is only a means of achieving good human-machine teamwork, not a goal in and of itself. People who blindly follow a system's recommendations (i.e., misuse) may not trust it as much as those who sometimes *ignore* it but do so because they understand its strengths and weaknesses. Therefore, while compliance may be indicative of trust, we also expect that people who end up making the right decision, *regardless of compliance*, will trust the robot more than people who do not.

3 Evaluation

We evaluate our hypotheses in a POMDP-based HRI scenario where a human teammate works with an intelligent virtual robot to search buildings [2]. The robot has a nuclear/biological/chemical (NBC) weapon sensor, a camera that can detect armed gunmen, and a microphone that can identify suspicious conversations. The human must choose between entering with or without protective gear. If there is danger inside the building, the human will be fatally injured if not wearing the protective gear (and have to restart the mission from scratch). However, it takes time to put on and take off protective gear. To induce trust failures, we introduce an error into our otherwise optimal simulated robot, namely a faulty camera that cannot detect armed gunmen. As a result, it will occasionally give an incorrect "safe" assessment.

We studied four levels of *explanation* [3]: no explanation, explanation of two sensor readings, explanation of three sensor readings, and a confidence-level explanation:

- **NoExp** The robot informs its teammate of only its decisions, e.g., *"I have finished surveying the Cafe. I think the place is safe."*
- **Exp2Sensor** The robot adds observations from its NBC sensor and camera: *"... My sensors have detected traces of dangerous chemicals. From the image captured by my camera, I have not detected any armed gunmen in the Cafe. ...."*
- **Exp3Sensor** The robot adds observations from all three sensors—NBC sensor, camera, and microphone: *"... My sensors have not detected any NBC weapons in here. From the image captured by my camera, I have not detected any armed gunmen in the cafe. My microphone picked up a suspicious conversation."*

– **ExpConf** The robots adds uncertainty: *"I am 78% confident about this assessment."*

We gathered data from a total of 105 Amazon Mechanical Turk participants (30 NoExp, 31 Exp2Sensor, 21 Exp3Sensor, and 23 ExpConf). After each of three missions, participants filled out a survey containing measures of the participants' trust and understanding of the robot's decision-making process.

3.1 Immediate Behavior

Hypothesis I states that the first action following the self-report is indicative of the self-reported trust in an agent's ability. Participants reported on their trust in the robot's ability at the end of each mission. One-way ANOVA indicates that when the participants followed the robot's recommendation at the beginning of mission 2, they also reported significantly higher levels of trust at the end of mission 1 ($F(1) = 14.8576, p = .0002$). This is replicated in the self-reported trust data at the end of mission 2 and the first action taken at the beginning of mission 3 ($F(1) = 11.3057, p = .0011$). It is clear that people who follow (ignore) the robot's recommendation trust (distrust) its ability more. While this result is as expected, it is a useful validation that the virtual domain is stimulating feelings of trust that are reflected in human behavior.

3.2 Error Response

Hypothesis II states that when an agent makes a mistake, the actions taken before and afterward are indicative of trust in the agent's ability. We conducted a one-way ANOVA on self-reported trust at the end of missions 2 and 3 with the four possible behaviors (follow/ignore right before the mistake, follow/ignore right after) as a between-subjects factor. Results show that there is a significant effect of the behavior sequences on the self-reported trust ($F(1,3) = 21.5595, p < .0001$ for mission 2; $F(1,3) = 33.6151, p < .0001$ for mission 3). Participants who correctly ignored a robot's incorrect recommendation, then followed its subsequent correct one (ignore-follow), reported significantly higher levels of trust ($p < .0001$ compared to follow-ignore, $p < .0001$ compared to follow-follow, and $p = .0075$ compared to ignore-ignore).

This result indicates one informative case for an agent to pay attention to when it makes a mistake. In particular, the people feeling the most trust in its ability are those who correctly identify the robot's mistake (and ignore its recommendation) and then immediately resume following its recommendations. While the lack of compliance in the first step would suggest distrust (according to Hypothesis I), this special case of an erroneous decision by the robot overrides that finding. In other words, a teammate who optimally responds to a mistake by the robot can be inferred to have a high level of trust in its ability. In fact, the level of trust felt by the people in this case is higher than those who comply in Hypothesis I.

On the other hand, there was no significant difference in trust between participants exhibiting other patterns of behavior. The rough equivalence among them suggests that, when people cannot correctly account for the agent's mistakes, they will distrust it equally, regardless of whether that distrust manifests itself in misuse or disuse. Despite the finding of Hypothesis I, participants who complied with the agent's mistaken recommendation did not end up feeling a high level of trust.

3.3 Compliant Behavior

Hypothesis III states that the number of times the agent's recommendations are followed is indicative of the self-reported trust in the agent's ability. Pearson correlation tests indicate that the more often the participants followed the robot's recommendation, the higher the self-reported trust in the robot right afterward. This correlation is of weak strength in data from mission 2 ($r(104) = .244, p = .0125$) and from mission 3 ($r(104) = .275, p = 0.0048$). This correlation is not statistically significant in data from mission 1 ($r(104) = -.008, p = .933$). The weakness of these correlations limits the value of compliance behavior in providing information about the trust relationship.

3.4 Correct Behavior

Hypothesis IV states that the number of *correct* decisions made is indicative of the self-reported trust in an agent's ability. Pearson correlation tests indicate that the more often the participants made correct decisions, the higher the self-reported trust in the robot right afterward. This correlation is of weak strength in mission 1 ($r(104) = .256$, $p = .0086$), of moderate strength in data from mission 2 ($r(104) = .345, p = .0003$), and of strong strength in mission 3 ($r(104) = .538, p < .0001$). Steiger's Z-tests confirm that the correlation between the self-reported trust and percentage correctness is stronger than that of the percentage compliance in mission 1 ($Z = -5.683, p < .0001$), 2 ($Z = -2.74, p = .006$), and 3 ($Z = -4.322, p < .0001$).

This finding is strong evidence that a robot can better estimate its teammates' trust from the correctness of their decisions, rather than from whether they follow the robot's recommendations. In other words, a person's trust in the robot's ability depends more on the human-robot team's combined decision-making, rather than on the robot's decision-making in isolation. While somewhat surprising, this result indicates that trust may be less about a person's confidence in the robot's correctness and more about a person's understanding of when the robot is right or wrong. As a result, explanations that best achieve this transparency are most conducive to human-robot trust.

Acknowledgements

This work was sponsored by the U.S. Army Research, Development, and Engineering Command (RDECOM) and the U.S. Army Research Laboratory.

References

1. Parasuraman, R., Riley, V.: Humans and automation: Use, misuse, disuse, abuse. Human Factors 39(2), 230–253 (1997)
2. Wang, N., Pynadath, D.V.: Building trust in a human-robot team. In: Proceedings of the Inteservice/Industry Training, Simulation and Education Conference (2015)
3. Wang, N., Pynadath, D.V., Hill, S.G.: The impact of POMDP-generated explanations on trust and performance in human-robot teams. In: Proceedings of the International Joint Conference on Autonomous Agents and MultiAgent Systems (2016)

Virtual Role-Play with Rapid Avatars

Ning Wang[1]✉, Ari Shapiro[1], David Schwartz[2], Gabrielle Lewine[2], Andrew Wei-Wen Feng[1]

[1] Institute for Creative Technologies, University of Southern California, Playa Vista, CA, USA
[2] Department of Psychology, University of Southern California, Los Angeles, CA, USA
nwang@ict.usc.edu

Abstract. Digital doppelgangers possess great potential to serve as powerful models for behavioral change. An emerging technology, the Rapid Avatar Capture and Simulation (RACAS), enables low-cost and high-speed scanning of a human user and creation of a digital doppelganger that is a fully animatable virtual 3D model of the user. We designed a virtual role-playing game, DELTA, with digital doppelgangers to influence a human user's attitude to-wards sexism on college campuses. In this demonstration, we will showcase the RACAS system and the DELTA game.

Keywords: Persuasive technology, Digital doppelganger, Virtual role-playing game, Rapid avatar.

1 Digital Doppelgangers

Digital doppelgangers are virtual humans that highly resemble the real self but behave independently [1]. Because digital doppelgangers possess a strong resemblance to the physical self – as they are actually a digital copy of the physical body – they have great potential to serve as powerful models [2][3]. Human reactions to doppelgangers have been observed to induce behavior changes in many areas, including promoting healthy lifestyles, e.g. routine exercise and better eating habits [3], be-coming more future-oriented, e.g. increasing retirement savings [4], altering consumer behavior [5], and alleviating public speaking anxiety [6], among others. The efficacy of doppelgangers in behavioral change can be explained using Social Cognitive Theory [7][8]. Bandura's theory states that people do not need to experience rewards or punishments themselves in order to learn behaviors, but rather they can learn behaviors through the observation of models. Moreover, according to the theory, greater similarity and identification with a model leads to more imitation of modeled behaviors. Similarity may be based on physical traits, personality variables, or shared beliefs and attitudes [9].

2 RACAS: Rapid Avatar Capture and Simulation

Traditionally, such "digital doubles" required complicated and expensive capture systems, as well as many man-months of effort from experts in various aspects of 3D

© Springer International Publishing AG 2017
J. Beskow et al. (Eds.): IVA 2017, LNAI 10498, pp. 463–466, 2017.
DOI 10.1007/978-3-319-67401-8_59

technology. An emerging technology, called Rapid Avatar Capture and Simulation (RACAS), makes the digital doppelganger a more accessible reality [10]. The RACAS takes scans of a user from the front, back, left, and right sides using an RGB-D sensor, then "stitches" the four images together to construct a 3D model. The 3D model is enhanced by inferring a skeletal and muscular structure, as well as generating a model for the deformation of the skin and clothes (see Fig. 2). SmartBody, a character animation system, drives the animation of the 3D virtual character [11]. Using RACAS, we can easily create a digital doppelganger that serves as an ideal model for maximizing feel-ings of similarity, enabling the demonstration of a wide range of rewards and punishments, and customizing the virtual self's behavior to portray an optimal performance that the physical self cannot yet achieve.

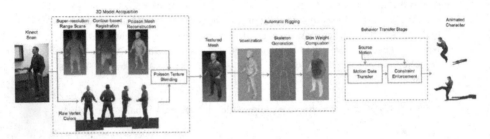

Fig. 1. Screenshot of one of the virtual encounters of sexist behavior in DELTA game.

3   The DELTA Game

We designed a virtual role-playing game – DELTA – integrated with digital doppelgangers, to influence a human user's attitude toward sexism on college campuses (Fig. 2). Human users guide digital doppelgangers of themselves created by RACAS to navigate through various scenarios where their doppelgangers encounter sexist attitudes on a virtual college campus. In each scenario, the virtual doppelganger witnesses the use of sexist comments and is asked to use his/her own words to counter such comments. The virtual role-playing game is designed following a well-studied behavioral alteration paradigm called induced-hypocrisy [12]. The induced-hypocrisy paradigm involves a specific sequence of events. First, individuals are asked to advocate for a desirable behavioral state (e.g., being an active bystander). Next, they are reminded of their own opposing tendencies (e.g., a history of being a passive bystander) and encouraged to engage in a state of mindful reflection. The inconsistency between their advocated stances and their actual behavior, is then presumed to produce negative emotions, called cognitive dissonance [13], that the individual is motivated to decrease. As a result, he or she effects a behavioral change in a desired direction. Induced hypocrisy interventions have been used to address a wide variety of problematic behaviors over the last two decades including unsafe sex [14], speeding [15], racial prejudice [16], smoking [17], eating disorders [18], excessive UV expo-sure [19], etc.

Fig. 2. Screenshot of one of the virtual encounters of sexist behavior in DELTA game.

We hypothesize that interacting with one's digital doppelganger in the virtual role-playing game can facilitate the reduction of the human user's own sexist attitude. Evaluations are currently under way to assess the efficacy of the DELTA game. In the demonstration, we will showcase the capture and creation of the Rapid Avatar and the DELTA role-playing game.

References

1. Bailenson, J. N.: Doppelgangers-a new form of self?. Psychologist , 25(1), 36-38 (2012).
2. Bailenson, J.N., & Segovia, K.Y. (2010). Virtual doppelgangers: Psychological effects of avatars who ignore their owners. In W. S. Bainbridge (Ed.), Online worlds: Conver-gence of the real and the virtual (175-186). Springer: New York. Bandura, A. (1977). Social learning theory. Englewood Cliffs, NJ:Prentice-Hall.
3. Fox, J., & Bailenson, J.N. (2010). The use of doppelgängers to promote health behav-ior change. CyberTherapy & Rehabilitation, 3(2), 16-17.
4. Hershfield, H. E., Goldstein, D. G., Sharpe, W. F., Fox, J., Yeykelis, L., Carstensen, L. L., & Bailenson, J. N. (2011). Increasing saving behavior through age-progressed render-ings of the future self. Journal of Marketing Research, 48, S23-S37.
5. Ahn, S.J., & Bailenson, J.N. (2011). Self-endorsing versus other-endorsing in virtual envi-ronments: The effect on brand attitude and purchase intention. Journal of Adver-tising, 40 (2), 93-106.
6. Aymerich-Franch, L. & Bailenson, J.N. (2014). The use of doppelgangers in virtual re-ality to treat public speaking anxiety: a gender comparison. Proceedings of the Inter-national Society for Presence Research Annual Conference. March, 17-19, Vienna, Aus-tria.
7. Bandura, A. (1977). Social learning theory. Englewood Cliffs, NJ: Prentice Hall.
8. Bandura, A. (2001). Social cognitive theory of mass communication. Media Psychol-ogy, 3, 265–299.

9. Stotland, E. (1969). Exploratory investigations of empathy. In L. Berkowitz (Ed.), Advances in experimental social psychology (Vol. 4, pp. 274–314). New York: Academic Press.
10. Shapiro, A., Feng, A., Wang, R., Li, H., Bolas, M., Medioni, G., & Suma, E.: Rapid avatar capture and simulation using commodity depth sensors. Computer Animation and Virtual Worlds, 25(3-4), 201-211, (2014).
11. Shapiro, A.: Building a character animation system. Motion in Games. pp. 98-109. (2011).
12. Aronson, E. (1999). Dissonance, hypocrisy, and the self-concept. Readings about the social animal, 219-236.
13. Festinger, L. (1957). A Theory of Cognitive Dissonance. California: Stanford Univer-sity Press.
14. Eithel, P., & Friend, R. (1999). Reducing denial and sexual behviours in college stu-dents. Annals of Behavioural Medicine, 21, 12–19.
15. Fointiat, V. (2004). "I know what I have to do, but…" When hypocrisy leads to behavioral change. Social Behavior and Personality, 32(8), 741–746.
16. Son Hing, L. S., Li, W., & Zanna, M. P. (2002). Inducing hypocrisy to reduce prejudi-cial responses among aversive racists. Journal of Experimental Social Psychology, 38, 71–78.
17. Simmons, V. N., Webb, M. S., & Brandon, T. H. (2004). College-student smoking: An initial test of an experiential dissonance-enhancing intervention. Addictive Behav-iors, 29, 1129–1136.
18. Stice, E., Rohde, P., Butryn, M., Menke, K. S., & Marti, C. N. (2015). Randomized Controlled Pilot Trial of a Novel Dissonance-Based Group Treatment for Eating Disorders. Behaviour research and therapy, 65, 67-75.
19. Chait, S. R., Thompson, J. K., & Jacobsen, P. B. (2015). Preliminary development and evaluation of an appearance-based dissonance induction intervention for reducing UV exposure. Body image, 12, 68-72.

Motion Capture Synthesis with Adversarial Learning*

Qi Wang[1,2] ✉ and Thierry Artières[1,2]

[1] Ecole Centrale Marseille, France
[2] LIF, Université d'Aix Marseille and CNRS, France

Abstract. We propose a new statistical modeling approach that we call Sequential Adversarial Auto-encoder (SAAE) for learning a synthesis model for motion sequences. This model exploits the adversarial idea that has been popularized in the machine learning field for learning accurate generative models. We further propose a conditional variant of this model that takes as input an additional information such as the activity which is performed in a sequence, or the emotion with which it is performed, and which allows to perform synthesis in context.

1 Introduction

Synthesizing realistic motion capture data is a key issue in the animation domain. A number of statistical models have been proposed for designing such synthesis systems with the expectation of producing highly realistic animation by learning these statistical models from large corpora of motion capture data [2,6]. These works rely on markovian models such as Hidden Markov models (HMMs) or Conditional Random Fields (CRFs). Such models rely on an assumption on the shape of the probability distribution of the data, which is usually strong and may lead to bad performance. We propose a new generative framework that we call Sequential Adversarial Auto-encoder (SAAE). It builds on recent advances in adversarial learning and on sequence autoencoders [9,4]. One may interest of adversarial learning is that it does not make any assumption on the distribution of the data. We propose here a specifi model for dealing with sequences and with motion capture data.

Moreover in the animation area, one needs to capture multiple variant styles of motions for controlling each animation character, a key feature is the high level control a designer may have on a synthesized animation. Few motion editing techniques have been proposed, such as inverse kinematics, style transfering, etc [7,5,8]. With this goal in mind we propose a variant of our framework enabling taking into account in the learning stage as well as during the synthesis stage such side information (e.g. activity, emotion, age, gender etc.)

---

* We are very grateful to Catherine Pélachaud for fruitful discussion and for access to and help with the Emilya dataset

J. Beskow et al. (Eds.): IVA 2017, LNAI 10498, pp. 467-470, 2017.
DOI 10.1007/978-3-319-67401-8_60

2 Sequential Adversarial AutoEncoders (SAAE)

SAAE is built on the basis of two advanced ideas: seq2seq models[10], adversarial autoencoder [9]. Seq2seq has been proposed for machine translation tasks [10] and it is well adapted when there are complex and eventually long term dependencies or forward references in the sequence data. It consists of an encoder and a decoder and both of them are built on RNN. Given a sequence $\mathbf{x} = x_1, ..., x_T$, the encoder encodes $\mathbf{x}$ into a latent vector: $z = Enc(\mathbf{x})$ which is a fixed dimensional vector (usually low dimensional). Then, the decoder aims to reconstruct the input sequence from the latent vector z. It is expressed as $\hat{\mathbf{x}} = Dec(Enc(\mathbf{x}))$. The model is trained by minimising the reconstruction error on the training set, $\mathbf{E}_{x \sim p_{data}} [\Delta(\mathbf{x}, Dec(Enc(\mathbf{x})))]$ where Δ is a distance between a sequence $\mathbf{x}$ and its reconstruction by the autoencoder $\hat{\mathbf{x}} = Dec(Enc(\mathbf{x}))$.

In the generation process, we wish we can generate a new motion sequence from a given latent vector z which includes all the information of the motion to be generated. For achieving this, we need to know the distribution of the latent vector z. Therefore, we exploit adversarial learning to enforce the distribution of the latent codes z to satisfying a prior distribution $p(z)$. Then in the generation stage, a z can be sampled from the prior distribution $p(z)$ and fed into the decoder to obtain a new motion sequence. The adversarial learning part introduces a discriminator, D, into the modeling whose training samples come from two sources: On the one hand, the outputs of the encoder $Enc(\mathbf{x})$, for real data $\mathbf{x}$. On the other hand, noise vectors sampled from a prior distribution $p(z)$. The discriminator is trained to distinguish which source an input comes from while the encoder aims at increasing the probability that the discriminator makes a mistake, i.e. fooling the discriminator. It is a two player game. The whole training process of SAAE can be expressed as follows (1) and its structure is illustrated in Fig.1.

$$\min_{Enc,Dec} \max_{D} \left\{ \mathbf{E}_{x \sim p_{data}} [\Delta(\mathbf{x}, Dec(Enc(\mathbf{x})))] + \mathbf{E}_{x \sim p_{data}} [log(D(Enc(x)))] \right.$$
$$\left. + \mathbf{E}_{z \sim p(z)} [log(1 - d(z))] \right\} \tag{1}$$

where the $D(\cdot)$ represent the output of the discriminator.

In order to exploit the contextual information (e.g. activity, emotion...), one may add contextual information as input to both the encoder and the decoder in the training process. This implicitly induces the model to learn the dependency between the motion and the contextual information. In any case after learning a SAAE, the decoder may be used to generate a sequence as explained above.

3 Experiments

We performed experiments with the Emilya Dataset [3]. It includes motion capture sequences performed by 12 actors corresponding to 8 activities performed

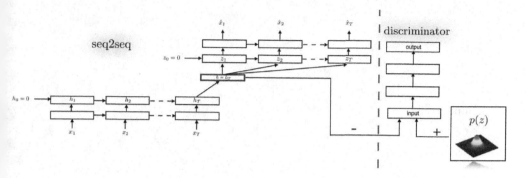

Fig. 1: Illustration of the Sequential Adversarial AutoEncoder (unfolded in time)

under 8 emotions. Each actor recorded each of 8 activity under each of the 8 emotions. All data are captured by 120Hz rate. Data are segmented, i.e. one sequence corresponds to a single activity performed by an actor under one emotion.

We first compare the standard seq2seq and SAAE with respect to their performance as a generative model. We follow [4,1] and use Gaussian Parzen Estimator. For each of these two models, we use its generated sequences to fit a Gaussian Parzen estimator which is the estimated PDF represented by this model. Then we randomly select 10 000 test sequences and we compute the mean log-likelihood of these under each of these two estimators. Note that to get a generative model from the standard seq2seq model we first estimate the distribution of latent vectors assuming a Gaussian distribution. The results are reported in Table 1 and show that SAAE outperforms Seq2Seq as a generative model on the test set.

Models	EmilyaDataset
Seq2Seq	1704.85 ± 5.117
SAAE	1722.53 ± 3.344

Table 1: Likelihood of the training data by a generative model gained from traditional (Seq2Seq) and from an adversarial (SAAE) learning.

Figure 2 shows examples of generated motion sequences from these two conditional SAAE. These qualitative results show that conditional SAAE can learn the variations corresponding to the contextual label and generate plausible motions matching the specified activity or emotion. More animation examples are available at https://drive.google.com/drive/folders/0B8-1q1MI01iJalhPcmxvZmpiMFk.

4 Conclusion

We proposed to mix two recent ideas, adversarial learning and sequence to sequence models for proposing new models for the synthesis of motion capture

"Lift"

"Simple Walk"

"Sadness"

"Pride"

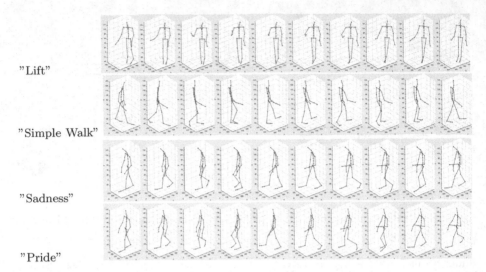

Fig. 2: Examples of generated motion from activity-conditioned ("Lift","Simple Walk") and from emotion-conditioned SAAE ("Sadness","Pride")

animations, with a conditional variant enabling synthesizing new sequences with a high level of monitoring.

References

1. Denton, E., Chintala, S., Szlam, A., Fergus, R.: Deep Generative Image Models using a Laplacian Pyramid of Adversarial Networks. Arxiv pp. 1–10 (2015)
2. Ding, Y., Prepin, K., Huang, J., Pelachaud, C., Artières, T.: Laughter animation synthesis. In: AAMAS, 2014
3. Fourati, N., Pelachaud, C.: Emilya: Emotional body expression in daily actions database. In: LREC. pp. 3486–3493 (2014)
4. Goodfellow, I., Pouget-Abadie, J., Mirza, M., Xu, B., Warde-Farley, D., Ozair, S., Courville, A., Bengio, Y.: Generative Adversarial Nets. Advances in Neural Information Processing Systems 27 pp. 2672–2680 (2014)
5. Grochow, K., Martin, S.L., Hertzmann, A., Popovic, Z.: Style-based inverse kinematics. Acm Transactions on Graphics 23(3), 522–531 (2004)
6. Hofer, G., Shimodaira, H.: Automatic head motion prediction from speech data. In: INTERSPEECH. pp. 722–725 (2007)
7. Holden, D., Saito, J., Komura, T.: A deep learning framework for character motion synthesis and editing. ACM Transactions on Graphics 35(4), 1–11 (2016)
8. Huang, J., Wang, Q., Fratarcangeli, M., Yan, K., Pelachaud, C.: Multi-variate gaussian-based inverse kinematics. In: Computer Graphics Forum (2017)
9. Makhzani, A., Shlens, J., Jaitly, N., Goodfellow, I.: Adversarial Autoencoders. arXiv pp. 1–10 (2015), http://arxiv.org/abs/1511.05644
10. Sutskever, I., Vinyals, O., Le, Q.V.: Sequence to Sequence Learning with Neural Networks. Nips pp. 3104–3112 (2014)

Author Index

J. Beskow et al. (Eds.): IVA 2017, LNAI 10498, pp. 471–473, 2017.
DOI 10.1007/978-3-319-67401-8

Printed in the United States
By Bookmasters